VINTAGE

THE IDEA OF ANCIENT INDIA

Upinder Singh is professor in the Department of History, Ashoka University, Sonepat. After studying in St Stephen's College and the University of Delhi, she obtained her PhD from McGill University, Montreal. She taught in St Stephen's College from 1981 to 2004 and in the Department of History, University of Delhi, from 2004 to 2018. She has been a recipient of the Netherlands Government Reciprocal Fellowship (1985–1986), Ancient India and Iran Trust/Wallace India Visiting Fellowship (2009), Daniel Ingalls Fellowship at the Harvard-Yenching Institute (2005), and Erasmus Mundus Fellowship at the University of Leuven (2010). In 2009, she was awarded the Infosys Prize in Social Sciences–History by the Infosys Science Foundation.

She is the author of *Kings, Brāhmaṇas, and Temples in Orissa: An Epigraphic Study (AD 300–1147)* (1994); *Ancient Delhi* (1999); *The Discovery of Ancient India: Early Archaeologists and the Beginnings of Archaeology* (2004); *A History of Ancient and Early Medieval India: From the Stone Age to the Twelfth Century* (2008; 2nd edn. 2023); *Political Violence in Ancient India* (2017), and *Ancient India: Culture of Contradictions* (2021). She has edited *Delhi: Ancient History* (2006), *Rethinking Early Medieval India* (2011), and *The World of India's First Archaeologist: Letters from Alexander Cunningham to J.D.M. Beglar* (2021); and co-edited *Ancient India: New Research* (2009), *Asian Encounters: Exploring Connected Histories* (2014), and *Buddhism in Asia: Revival and Reinvention* (2016).

Singh's current research interests include ancient Indian political ideas and the interactions between ancient India and the wider world.

35 INDIA

Celebrating 35 Years of
Penguin Random House India

The IDEA *of* ANCIENT INDIA

Essays on Religion, Politics & Archaeology

UPINDER SINGH

VINTAGE
An imprint of Penguin Random House

VINTAGE

USA | Canada | UK | Ireland | Australia
New Zealand | India | South Africa | China | Singapore

Vintage is part of the Penguin Random House group of companies
whose addresses can be found at global.penguinrandomhouse.com

Published by Penguin Random House India Pvt. Ltd
4th Floor, Capital Tower 1, MG Road,
Gurugram 122 002, Haryana, India

Penguin
Random House
India

First published by SAGE Publications India Pvt. Ltd 2016
Published in Vintage by Penguin Random House India 2023

10 9 8 7 6 5 4 3 2 1

ISBN 9780143461531

Typeset in 10/12.5 pt Minion by Zaza Eunice, Hosur, Tamil Nadu, India.
Printed at Replika Press Pvt. Ltd, India

www.penguin.co.in

For my parents
Manmohan Singh and Gursharan Kaur

Contents

List of Tables

List of Figures

Preface to the Second Edition

The first edition of this book was published about seven years ago, in 2016. This second edition includes all the essays in that work, along with two new ones (chapters 10 and 13). The new essays flow from the broad themes in the earlier edition but also reflect the directions in which my thinking as a historian has moved over the past few years. In that sense, this book takes off from where the first edition left off.

Throughout my academic career, I have had a special interest in analysing epigraphic sources, be they the inscriptions of Aśoka, Sanchi, Mathura or Nagarjunakonda. From my earliest work on the inscriptions of Odisha, I have also been especially interested in the intersection of politics and religion. The first new essay in this book, 'Inscribing Power on the Realm: Royal Ideology and Religious Policy in India, c. 200 BCE–300 CE (Chapter 10) engages with inscriptions, politics and religion. But it also moves beyond my earlier writings in terms of method, in that it combines an empirical approach with an analysis of epigraphic intertextuality.

Several essays in this book deal with the momentous five centuries sandwiched between the Maurya and Gupta empires—c. 200 BCE and 300 CE—which were marked by agrarian expansion, urban growth, social change, and important developments in the religious and cultural spheres. The proliferation of states and a series of invasions from the north-west were accompanied by new expressions of political power and ideology through coinage, inscriptions, images, and monuments. While regions form an important frame for unfolding political processes, the 'circle of kings' in ancient India often cut across regions. The epigraphic process did not only include conceptualization and execution but also reception and reaction. The epigraphic universe was dynamic and interactive, and it was not constrained by dynastic or regional boundaries. It is therefore necessary to look at political ideas and practise within a dialogic frame. An intertextual analysis of inscriptions indicates that information about the form, content, and larger material context of inscriptions flowed across kingdoms and regions. This helps understand continuities and innovations in epigraphic practice, and the eventual emergence of pan-Indian patterns which accommodated elements of regional political and cultural traditions. Chapter 10 discusses the dialogic and circulatory aspects of the epigraphic process and tries to reconstruct conversations between certain specific inscriptions, reflecting not only on what they say but also on their silences.

The first major set of royal inscriptions in the Indian subcontinent are those of the Maurya emperor Aśoka, whose political philosophy is discussed in detail in Chapter 9. Within the Indian epigraphic corpus, Aśoka's inscriptions are unique in several respects, including in the use of the first person and their containing reflections of the political philosophy and dhammic obsession of the emperor. Aśoka appears as a unique king with impossible dreams, passionate about inculcating morality, non-violence and inter-religious concord within and beyond his empire. But what about Aśoka's epigraphic legacy? The epigraphic *praśasti* (panegyric) which appeared at the turn of the millennium is usually seen as qualitatively different in style and content from the Aśokan corpus and is understood in relationship to the birth of *kāvya* (literature). As I pointed out in my book, *Political Violence in Ancient India* (2017), the *praśasti* can be understood not only through what it expressed but also through what it sought to conceal, invisibilize, and transform into something else, namely political violence. It presented an idealized description of the king and his rule rooted in larger political and cultural traditions and became an essential prerequisite for claims to legitimate political authority.

The 2nd-century CE Junagadh inscription of the Kārdamaka Kṣatrapa ruler Rudradāman and the 4th-century Allahabad pillar inscription of the Gupta king Samudragupta are usually identified as important milestones in the evolution of the epigraphic *praśasti*. Rudradāman's is the first long inscription that expressed political ideology in fine Sanskrit prose; it presents a model of a warrior-king who possesses many benevolent, pacific virtues. The Allahabad inscription of Samudragupta uses verse and prose to combine claims to political paramountcy with territorial specificity; it contains an even more elaborate and impressive advertisement of martial prowess balanced with benevolent peace-time accomplishments.

In Chapter 10, I focus on three themes: religion, ideology, and historical memory in the Hathigumpha inscription of Khāravela; the foundation of a new Purāṇic Brahmanical kingship in Sātavāhana and Western Kṣatrapa inscriptions at Naneghat and Nashik; and royal religious policy and persecution in early historic India. I argue that the fundamental template of ancient Indian political ideology and religious policy was established during c. 200 BCE–300 CE through a continuous dialogic process. The ways in which kings inscribed their power in words and proclaimed it visually and monumentally were important parts of the cut and thrust of political interactions. I discern the impact of Aśoka on later kings and try to reconstruct some of the epigraphic dialogues in post-Maurya India. I suggest that the earliest expressions of what is sometimes referred to as the 'classical' ancient Indian model of kingship occur before the time of Rudradāman and Samudragupta, and these expressions were not in Sanskrit but in Middle Indic. They are represented by the Hathigumpha inscription of Khāravela and the inscriptions of the Sātavāhanas and western Kṣatrapas. I think that a close intertextual reading of inscriptions in their archaeological and monumental contexts is an approach that can be fruitfully extended to the study of other inscriptions of ancient and early medieval India.

My interest in the intersection between political ideas and practice, with special reference to the problem of violence, is reflected in my essays on Aśoka, the *Raghuvaṁśa* and *Nītisāra* (chapters 9, 11, and 12) in this book. This interest developed into a detailed, chronological treatment of the subject in my book *Political Violence in Ancient India.* In that work, I used a variety of textual, archaeological, epigraphic, numismatic, and visual sources to analyse the intersection between the theory and practise of political violence in India between c. 600 BCE and 600 CE, with special reference to the state's punitive role, war, and interactions with the forest. I divided this period into three overlapping phases—c. 600–200 BCE, c. 200 BCE–300 CE and c. 300–600 CE—representing respectively the foundation, transition, and maturity of monarchical states and political ideology in north India. The book documents the connection between the growth and systemization of state violence and the increasingly sophisticated attempts to mask, invisibilize, justify, and aestheticize that violence. It argues that political theorists, poets, and religious thinkers played important roles in crafting and disseminating ideologies that transformed political violence into something essential for the well-being of subjects and the maintenance of the social order. Jainism and Buddhism—religious traditions that raised non-violence to a cardinal ethical element—also acknowledged that a certain amount of violence was necessary for kings. At the same time, political discourse distinguished force that was necessary, proportionate and legitimate from force that was unnecessary, excessive and illegitimate. This left open a window for questioning the state's coercive power. In the new essay included in this book, 'The State, Violence, and Resistance, c. 600 BCE–600 CE (Chapter 13), I extend my exploration of the problem of violence by discussing three issues: the specific ways in which violence was inherent in the early Indian state; the relationship between kingship and sexual violence; and resistance and rebellion against the state.

Political processes and ideas can be distinguished for analytical purposes, but it is just as important to recognize that the two are inextricably intertwined. The influence of the 'normative' varied a great deal, but it potentially formed a model or at least a reference point for praxis. Further, if normative texts are read against the grain, their contents can offer glimmers of insight into political realities which are not so evident in the minutiae of the supposedly factual details contained in dynastic accounts. In fact, there is no disinterested, value-neutral political narrative in ancient texts. All political accounts found in these texts were representations of events, moulded and worked into a narrative that was in consonance with the composers' perspective, keeping in mind their purpose and audience.

Understanding the intertwined theory and practice of political violence involves identifying the ways in which violence was folded into the structures of state and society and identifying the multiple, changing discourses around its forms and manifestations. Chapter 13 spells out some of the things implicit in *Political Violence in Ancient India*, including the social underpinnings of political violence. In my earlier writings, my interest in gender as an important aspect of social history was reflected in highlighting women as religious patrons at sites such as Sanchi and Nagarjunakonda. Here, I look at a very different aspect—textual perspectives on sexual violence against women in the political sphere. Further, a discussion of the violence of the state also needs to address the issue of responses to it. Chapter 13 takes up this issue by identifying the anxieties about rebellion and resistance in texts such as the *Arthashastra*. A focus on the structures, ideologies, and impact of political violence not only forms an important part of political history but also allows us to think about political continuities, transitions, and disjunctures in a different way.

My most recent work is reflected in my two recently published books. The first is an edited volume titled *The World of India's First Archaeologist: Letters from Alexander Cunningham to J.D.M. Beglar* (2021). This carries forward from the essays in Section II of this book ('Archaeologists and the Modern Histories of Ancient Sites') and from my earlier book *The Discovery of Ancient India: Early Archaeologists and the Beginnings of Archaeology* (2004). The letters edited and discussed in *The World of India's First Archaeologist* present an exciting new source which shows Cunningham and the history of 19th-century Indian archaeology in a new light. The second recent book, *Ancient India: Culture of Contradictions* (2021) does not fit easily into the themes of this present volume. It emerged directly from my teaching a course at Ashoka University on Indian civilizations. Written for general readers rather than a specialist audience, it addresses some popular misconceptions about ancient India, focusing on certain key contradictions that can be seen in ancient Indian history and thought—between social inequality and religions that promised salvation to all; desire and detachment; goddess worship and misogyny; violence and non-violence; and philosophical and religious dialogue and conflict. Further ways in which my ideas have evolved since the publication of the first edition of *The Idea of Ancient India* are reflected in the forthcoming second, revised edition of my *History of Ancient and Early Medieval India* (2023). Thinking and writing about history is always work in progress!

The issues that currently preoccupy me can be seen as an extension of the ones raised in the chapters in this book but cast on a larger geographical canvas. The Introduction to the first edition of *The Idea of Ancient India* and the essays in the last section ('Looking beyond India to Asia') touch on the importance of examining links with Sri Lanka and Southeast Asia, but I now recognize the need to also explore the links with other parts of the ancient world, especially Central Asia, Iran, and China. The many ways in which the history of the subcontinent has been connected with other parts of Asia, Europe, and Africa are, of course, addressed in histories of trade. However, there are great possibilities in examining interactions beyond trade, to take a fresh look at the movement of people and ideas as parts of rapidly expanding and evolving religious and intellectual networks. Situating the history of ancient India within the frame of global history, without sacrificing the regional, sub-regional, and the local specificities is a tall order, but it needs to be done.

Towards the end of the Introduction to the first edition of this book, I talked about the relationship between the past and the present. Apart from researching and writing about new or under-studied areas and bringing in new perspectives, it is extremely important for historians to reach out to a larger audience to try to explain how historians construct history. It is also important to communicate to this audience the excitement involved in uncovering the early Indian past, the open-endedness of debates, and the difference between rigorous historical analysis and superficial, uninformed opinion. I hope that the essays in this new edition of *The Idea of Ancient India* will convey some of these things to readers.

Introduction

Among historians, debates on the idea of antiquity and periodization have led to a sharp decline in the use of the adjective 'ancient' in favour of 'early'. I prefer to talk about 'ancient' rather than 'early' India, mainly for aesthetic reasons. The adjective 'early' is bland, dull, nondescript; 'ancient,' on the other hand, has depth, mystery, resonance. Similarly, I use the singular 'idea' rather than 'ideas' in the title of this book because it seems to me to possess far greater weight. Moreover, it does not exclude plurality, which is an intrinsic aspect of the past as well as of all historical interpretation. 'The idea of ancient India' can, therefore, encompass infinite ways of understanding the ancient past of India, or rather, South Asia. This book reflects the ways in which my own thoughts on the subject have evolved and changed over the past two decades.

My initial writing belongs to the long period of time I taught at St Stephen's College. Although I wrote three books over those years, the combined pressure of undergraduate teaching and family responsibilities meant that time for research and writing was scarce; it had to be created with considerable difficulty and struggle. Moving to the History Department of the University of Delhi in 2004 was an exhilarating experience—for the first time, I had enough time to read, think, and write and also the opportunity to incorporate my research into teaching. Most of the chapters in this book were written after I joined the University Department.[1]

Although these chapters cover many of my interests, some were left out, and at least two of them are important. The first is the village-to-village survey that I conducted in 1994–1995 along with my friend and colleague Nayanjot Lahiri (Tarika Oberoi joined us subsequently) in Faridabad district in Haryana. This project sensitized me to the importance of the materiality of India's ancient past and how it lives on, incorporated but transformed in meaning, in contemporary villages.[2] The second aspect missing here is my work on Delhi's ancient history, published as a book titled *Ancient Delhi*.[3] Writing that book presented two challenges—to construct a continuous narrative of Delhi's ancient past on the basis of very meagre sources, and to write in a style accessible to the general reader. The second was much more difficult than the first. My work on Delhi was accompanied by a conviction that exposing students to local history was one of the best ways of generating an interest in the discipline of history in their minds. This led to the idea of introducing a series of courses on Delhi's history in the undergraduate programme of the University of Delhi.

Religion and Region

The chapters in the first section of this book reflect my enduring interest in analyzing epigraphic data and situating inscriptions within their larger contexts. The approach is strongly empirical, not only because the minutiae of details have always attracted me but also because I think that historical hypotheses must be very thoroughly grounded in the empirical data and very carefully calibrated with regard to chronology.[4] Many of the inscriptions I studied were associated with religious sites. My interest in religion was in large measure an instinctive one, but was also influenced by dissatisfaction with the manner in which Indian historians of the 1970s and early 1980s tended either to sideline this important aspect of history or to reduce it to legitimation strategy.

'Sanchi: The History of the Patronage of an Ancient Buddhist Establishment' (Chapter 1) was the first paper I wrote after completing my PhD. I visualized it as part of a larger project on the inscriptions of early Buddhist sites in India. The chapter offers a diachronic view of the patronage of Sanchi, bringing out the elements of continuity and change over five phases, beginning with Aśoka in the 3rd century BCE and ending in the 12th century. The epigraphic data from this site was very amenable to statistical analysis, but I also thought it could be fruitfully juxtaposed with textual, sculptural, and archaeological evidence.

Between the 2nd century BCE and the 1st century CE, there was a massive upsurge of popular support for Buddhism all over the subcontinent, of a kind never seen before or since. At Sanchi, this period saw busy construction activity, especially the building of *stūpa*s, and the engraving of over 800 donative inscriptions.[5] The chapter discusses how the people who financed the Sanchi establishment identified themselves—for instance, through their names, kinship relations, occupations, native place, and their status as members of the monastic order or laity. Of course, we have to remember that these do not necessarily include all the bases of social identity prevalent at the time, but rather the elements that were considered most important for the purpose of pious donation, given the limited space that was available for inscribing the records. The notable aspects of the donations include the large number of gifts made by members of the monastic community, the prominence of women donors, and collective gifts made by the laity, monks, or nuns of certain villages and towns. The gifts by groups of nuns point towards the existence of nunneries. This is precious evidence, given the fact that after its inception, the history of the *bhikkhunī saṅgha* in India is shrouded in mystery. Apart from what the inscriptions say, equally important are their silences, especially the absence of references to *varṇa* or *jāti*. Clearly, the early history of these social institutions is much more complex than is often assumed.[6]

The chapter begins with a cautious disclaimer, stating that it does not aim at adding to knowledge about the theoretical aspects of patronage. But in retrospect, I think that it does. It situates donative inscriptions and their empirical content within their larger archaeological and artistic contexts. It compares textual precepts with monastic and lay practice.[7] It shows that the testimony of texts and inscriptions can be marked by similarity, asymmetry, as well as stark difference. It treats gender as part of a larger matrix of social participation in religious patronage. The chapter also argues that the relationship between royalty and the growth of religious establishments needs to be interrogated. Finally, I engage with the hypothesis of urban decline, pointing out that the abundant evidence of inscriptions and structural remains belonging to the Gupta and post-Gupta periods at Sanchi contradicts the hypothesis of urban decline in what is known, for the sake of convenience, as the early medieval period.[8]

The second chapter in this section, 'Nagarjunakonda: Buddhism in the "City of Victory"' (Chapter 2) transports us from central India to Andhra. I visualized it as part of a long-term continuous history of the site, from prehistory to the 21st century. The larger idea was that of biographies of sites and monuments that traced their lives across the centuries, unconstrained by the standard chronological divides of the ancient, medieval and modern. Nagarjunakonda is an incredibly complex and disconcerting site. For one thing, it no longer exists. It was drowned in the waters of the Krishna river when the Nagarjunasagar dam became functional. What is visible on the island in the middle of the river is a surreal recreation of some of its parts via a re-assemblage of a few selected structures, models, and replicas. Further, the various excavation reports do not easily dove-tail into one another. Nagarjunakonda is a puzzle whose pieces had not only got horribly jumbled up, but many of them were also irretrievably lost. All this made it a challenging subject for research.

The chapter on Nagarjunakonda, written over a decade after the one on Sanchi, marks a methodological advance. It interrogates the goals of archaeological investigation and the perspectives of archaeological reports. By now, I was also much more conscious of the need to understand the inscriptional discourse more carefully, to be attentive to its purpose, audience, and reception, and to look closely at the idiom of religious piety. As pointed out by Gregory Schopen, an analysis of such donative inscriptions has to begin with the question: Why were these inscriptions inscribed? Schopen's answer to this question is that a magical efficacy was attached to the writing of names, and that the inscriptions gave the donors a permanent place in the shadow of the relics.[9] I add to this the observation that the *degree* of proximity to the relics was also a factor, and that donors did not only seek proximity to the relics, but also to the monastic community. Schopen has also drawn attention to the great importance of the idea of the transfer of religious merit in Buddhist donative inscriptions. The chapter extends this by talking about the *sharing* of merit, and argues that the 'circle of merit' revealed in the epigraphs can be seen as an important part of religious practice in a society that was already stratified to some extent on the basis of class, but in which kinship still played a pivotal role. I also think that it is extremely important to underline the fact that the idea of the sharing of merit was not confined to Buddhism or to the subcontinent.

The chapter focuses on the early historic phase and the approach, once again, involves integrating evidence from different sources in order to address issues related to Buddhist monasticism and its lay patrons. Women patrons—royal and non-royal—are prominent, and this reflects their importance in the political and social structures of the time. The chapter highlights the archaeological evidence of the everyday lives of monks, ranging from pots to sickles to remains of board games. The contrast between monastic theory and practice is clear from the thriving relic cult at Nagarjunakonda. It emerges even more starkly in the evidence of animal sacrifice from one of the *stūpa*s, which, I argue, shows the permeation of local practices into Buddhist funerary rituals. Buddhism cannot be seen as insulated from the larger social context; local custom impinged on monastic practice, sometimes with startling results.

It was clear to me that any discussion of religious sites had to give due importance to their artistic elements. In approaching the domain of art history, I benefitted greatly from the writings of art historians. Vidya Dehejia's discussion of early Buddhist narrative art opened up an exciting range of issues related to the language of the visual sources and showed how these should not be seen simplistically as visual translations of textual material.[10] Monika Zin's writings directed my attention to the problems involved in reading the sculptural narratives, and to the fact that some of the routinely accepted interpretations were, in fact, flawed.[11] The need to continually interrogate 'standard' interpretations can also be seen in the case of the *āyaka* pillars which often mark Andhra *stūpas*—which I now realize do not necessarily (as is frequently suggested), represent five scenes from the Buddha's life.

While early historic Buddhist sites have some things in common, their communities of patrons and donors could also be markedly different. Monks, nuns, and whole villages appear as donors at Sanchi and Bharhut, but not at Nagarjunakonda. Sanchi owed its inception to a king (Aśoka), but was relatively independent of royal patronage thereafter. At Nagarjunakonda, on the other hand, ruling elites—not kings, but women of the royal household—played a crucial role. It is, therefore, important to construct profiles of individual sites before talking in general terms about 'Indian Buddhism'. It is also necessary to work out the relationship between the Indian sites and monastic communities in other Asian lands, especially Sri Lanka, in order to understand the role of pan-Asian networks of Buddhist pilgrimage, patronage, and monastic interaction, which had an important role to play in the efflorescence, decline, and revival of Buddhism in the subcontinent. Further, the study of Indian Buddhism has to be integrated into the larger political, religious, and cultural landscape. The chapter on Nagarjunakonda acknowledges this fact towards the end, by drawing attention to Vijayapurī as a political centre and by referring to its Hindu and Jaina temples.

While much of my work has focused on Buddhist sites, I have also been interested in other religious traditions. 'Cults and Shrines in Early Historical Mathura (c. 200 BC to AD 200)' (Chapter 3) was written for a special issue on the archaeology of Hinduism, edited by Nayanjot Lahiri and Elizabeth Bacus.[12] Notwithstanding its internal diversity and the absence of a canon or priesthood, I think that one can and should use the term 'Hinduism'. Mathura, an extremely important ancient Indian site with an extraordinarily rich and diverse cultural and religious landscape, offered great potential for the exploration of early Hinduism. To my surprise, I discovered that apart from the site of Sonkh (for which there is a full archaeological report), the archaeological documentation of Mathura is very patchy.

This chapter discusses the religious landscape of Mathura before it developed its strong associations with Kṛṣṇa. Here again, I discuss the trajectories of religious developments on the basis of the archaeological, sculptural, and epigraphic material. The chapter points out that much of the textual evidence used to construct ancient Indian religious history is not only difficult to date but also masks the popular, regional, and local. Of course, the archaeological data is by no means inherently superior; it too has its limitations. My analysis of the epigraphic and sculptural data from Mathura shows that the worship of *yakṣa*s and *yakṣī*s, *nāga*s and *nāgī*s, and anonymous goddesses (often incorrectly given the label of a generic 'Mother Goddess') was a prominent feature of the religious landscape of early historic Mathura. The analysis supports the hypothesis put forward by Ananda K. Coomaraswamy about the importance of these cults as sources of the *bhakti* tradition.[13] I also draw attention to certain aspects of popular religious practice, represented by ordinary, unremarkable artefacts that do not find their way into the texts of the Great Tradition—the so-called 'votive' tanks and shrines, which are more accurately described as miniature tanks and shrines. Clearly, there is a need to examine ancient religious thought and practice by carefully interrogating the categories of urban and rural, popular and elite, classical and folk, domestic and public. And this cannot be done by looking at texts alone.

At the turn of the millennium, the old cults receded into the shadows in the face of an efflorescence of Hindu pantheons and cultic practices (along with the continuing importance of sacrificial ritual) associated with the worship of deities such as Vāsudeva-Kṛṣṇa, Sūrya, Viṣṇu, Śiva, Durgā and Lakṣmī. In fact, considering that the sculptural evidence precedes the Purāṇas by several centuries, we see a much more elaborate and well-developed Hindu sectarian landscape than we might expect. This is because textual references represent a relatively late stage in the history of religious ideas and practices, after they had been accepted by religious elites. There is also the political angle to consider. While there is some ambiguous evidence of the worship of deified kings at the Kuṣāṇa site of Mat, it is significant that the patronage of Brāhmaṇas was important for dynasties whose roots lay outside India. Further, the religious patronage of political elites was usually pluralistic. This has usually been seen as a reflection of a laudable Indian attitude of 'religious toleration', but is better understood as a deliberate royal religious policy, rooted in the absence of a strong monotheistic tradition, the monolatrous nature of Hinduism, and the presence of several competing religious traditions, none of which were able to successfully capture the state.

The chapters in this book have been arranged according to historical theme and chronology, but in terms of the chronology of my own work, the subject matter of 'Early Medieval Orissa: The Data and the Debate' (Chapter 4) comes before everything else. The chapter is based on my doctoral work, the full results of which were published in the book *Kings, Brāhmaṇas and Temples in Orissa: An Epigraphic Study* (AD *300–1147*).[14] My interest in Orissa was based on many months of desultory reading of inscriptions in the library of the Kern Institute, Leiden, in 1984–1985. As I read inscriptions of different periods and regions, I found those of Orissa and its adjoining areas had a unique character and were extremely lively compared to the sedate inscriptions of Bengal that I had studied for my MPhil thesis. Professor J. G. de Casparis urged me to focus on Orissa and Professor J. C. Heesterman encouraged me to look at the intersection of *śrauta* sacrifice and theistic sectarianism reflected in the epigraphs. This is how I came to work on Orissan inscriptions for my doctoral research. My interest in exploring the religious aspects of the inscriptions was sharpened in the course of my interactions with Professor Katherine Young, my PhD supervisor at McGill University.

Working on land grants was quite the rage in the 1970s and early 1980s, largely in order to construct the economic and social history of the subcontinent. My work, therefore, fitted in with both the contemporary debates on the early medieval period as well as the increasing focus on the regional profiles of historical processes. However, the chapter (and my book) goes beyond standard economic and political history. My analysis of over 300 Sanskrit inscriptions ranging from the 4th to the mid-12th century gave me the opportunity to establish elements of continuity and change in the theory and practice of kingship and the relationship between Brahmanism and tribal religious traditions. Towards this end, I attached great importance to the phraseology of the *praśasti*, carefully examining royal epithets and imagery. I also examine the manner in which Brāhmaṇas are described in the inscriptions and emphasize that they cannot be treated as a homogenous social category.[15] The triumvirate of kings, Brāhmaṇas and temples represents important nodes in historical developments, but this relationship changed significantly over time. For instance, the king is advertised as a temple builder only after the 10th century, especially from the reign of the imperial Gaṅgas, when we see changes in royal patronage and royal policy, and a swing towards royally endowed temples.

All these issues are discussed before I get to the nitty-gritty of the technical vocabulary of the land grants. The fiscal exemptions and privileges help identify the nature of the land transfers recorded in the land grant inscriptions, the donors' position being between that of landlord and landowner. I argue that the impact of these grants must have varied depending on a variety of factors, and that regional and sub-regional specificities have to be factored in while talking about pan-Indian processes.[16] When framed within the debate on the feudalism versus integration model, the evidence from Orissa fits in better with the latter. But the chapter also goes on to raise questions about the integration model, especially its obsession with legitimation, its overwhelming focus on the region, and its comparative lack of interest in issues related to the rural economy. I now think that it is possible to combine some of the insights of both the feudalism and integrative frameworks, but that it is also necessary to move beyond them. The chapter ends on a note of ennui, pointing to the ways in which the feudalism debate has stifled investigations into various aspects of the period c. 600–1300. This is expressed more frankly and forcefully in the Introduction of my book *Rethinking Early Medieval India*.[17]

Looking at the range of issues raised in the first section of this book, I can identify several that tie in with my later work. But when I now approach inscriptions, I begin by discussing the epigraphic process which includes looking at their composers, intent, audience, and reception. If I were to re-write the chapters printed here, my conclusions would not change substantially, but I would nuance them more carefully, foregrounding this epigraphic process. And I would extend my geographical frame of reference beyond the subcontinent, southwards to Sri Lanka and eastwards to Southeast Asia.

Archaeology and the Modern Histories of Ancient Sites

As mentioned earlier, I envisaged my essay on Sanchi as part of a larger research project that would weave together the histories of early historic Buddhist sites. But I abandoned this plan when one day in 1998, while going through the site reports of early historic cities in the Archaeological Survey of India library, I put in a requisition for James Fergusson's *Archaeology of India with Especial Reference to the Works of Babu Rajendralala Mitra*, to which I had recently noted a reference.[18] When the book arrived, I got a shock because it was profusely annotated in pencil, with comments scrawled all over the top and margin of several pages. The comments were excited, enraged ones and talked of people like Cunningham, Fergusson and Burgess and sites such as Bodhgayā. I had clearly stumbled on an angry book owner. I excitedly turned over the pages, wondering who he was, and eventually found the name 'JDM Beglar' stamped on several pages. I vaguely recollected that Beglar was a 19th century archaeologist, one of the assistants of the more famous Alexander Cunningham.

My encounter with that book created a fever that could only be assuaged by finding out more about the story I had stumbled on by accident. This meant delving into the National Archives and piecing together the history of 19th century archaeology. The problem was: Was moving from the 2nd century BCE to the 19th century CE not a rather risky venture? I eventually overcame my initial misgivings—largely because of the archival sources which were so excitingly different from the ancient texts and inscriptions that I was used to dealing with. It helped that, through an interesting coincidence, Nayanjot Lahiri, a constant companion in my explorations of ancient India, was also examining the archival material at that very time, in order to reconstruct a later part of the history of archaeology—the discovery of the Indus civilization.[19] My friends Tanika and Sumit Sarkar convinced me that an ancient historian could step into more recent times with ease. The full results of the research I embarked on were eventually published in my book, *The Discovery of Ancient India: Early Archaeologists and the Beginnings of Archaeology*.[20] Chapters 5 and 6 in this book represent part of that work.

Some of the important initiatives in exploring the construction of archaeological and historical knowledge have been taken by anthropologists and historians of modern India. Many of them share a common interest in analyzing Orientalist constructions of knowledge. Because of my background and training as a historian of ancient India with a special interest in archaeology, my approach was somewhat different. There is no doubt that the history of the 19th century archaeology was embedded in a colonial context, that archaeological research and initiatives for the conservation of historical monuments and artefacts developed within very real political and institutional constraints. But my own study was to reveal a much more untidy and complex picture than was often presumed or presented. Although I was interested in how archaeological knowledge was constructed in its colonial context, I was also interested in the *content* of that knowledge; in interpretations, methods, and techniques; and in the contributions and limitations of these from the perspective of the long-term history of archaeological research. I was also interested in the lives of the men who constructed this knowledge. And, I also wanted to piece together the stories of what was actually happening to ancient artefacts and sites during those decades, and the impact of these events on the archaeological and historical enterprise.

Because of the nature of my entry into the subject, I was keen to weave together the personal, professional, institutional, and political. The chapter 'Archaeologists and Architectural Scholars in 19th Century India' (Chapter 5) has as its starting point the conflict that took place in the early history of the Archaeological Survey of India between James Fergusson and James Burgess on the one hand and Alexander Cunningham and his associates on the other. We know that academic discourse is never cocooned from politics, but James Fergusson's book, written against the background of the Ilbert bill controversy of 1883–1884, reveals this with extraordinary candour. It leaves no doubt that the fact that India was a British colony had important bearing on academic debates about the origins of stone architecture and the arch.

The chapter goes beyond the analysis offered in my *Discovery of Ancient India*, insofar as it looks more closely at Cunningham, not as a field archaeologist—the role in which he is best known—but as an art historian. Cunningham shared with many western scholars a fascination and idealization of Buddhism. But his archaeological discoveries and publications marked a significant departure from text-based studies of Indian Buddhism, and his writings on the material remains of Buddhism included a discussion of architecture and sculpture. One of the debates that was going on in official circles in the 1870s and 1880s related to whether the Archaeological Survey of India should focus on field archaeology or on art historical studies. Fergusson and Burgess saw these as alternative paths. Cunningham, with his much wider understanding of what was included in archaeology, could see the possibility, even the urgent necessity, of combining various approaches towards the Indian past—the archaeological, epigraphic, art historical and even textual, in spite of his having talked dismissively at one time of 'the rubbish contained in the 18 Puranas'.[21]

Although Fergusson and Burgess were not impressed by his credentials, Cunningham's contribution to the study of Buddhist art and architecture was, in fact, substantial. The chapter describes how his understanding of early Buddhist art evolved over time, from *Bhilsa Topes* (1854) to *The Stûpa of Bharhut* (1879) and *Mahâbodhi* (1892). I also discuss the debate on the age of the arches of the Mahābodhi temple and the bitter war of words between the field archaeologists and art historians over the restoration work at the site. We should remember that Cunningham had a significant personal connection with the sites and monuments he described in these three books. He was the one who discovered the Bharhut *stūpa* in 1873. He was the one, who along with Lieutenant Maisey, spent the winter of 1851 roaming around central India, opening up and hunting for relics in the *stūpa*s of Sanchi, Sonari, Satdhara, Bhojpur, and Andher. And he and Beglar had a great deal to do with the restoration work at Bodhgayā. For all these reasons, although we can situate Cunningham's work within the context of the growing western interest in and understanding of early Indian Buddhism, we should also recognize the fact that his was a unique perspective born out of a close contact with the materiality of Buddhism.

As mentioned earlier, my interest in the early history of Indian archaeology was accompanied by an interest in the modern history of ancient monuments. 'Amaravati: The Dismembering of the *Mahācaitya* (1796–1886)' (Chapter 6) tells the 19th century history of an important ancient Buddhist site in Andhra Pradesh.[22] Much has been written about Amaravati, largely because of the eventual dispersal of its fabulous sculptures, which were frequently referred to in the 19th century as the 'Amaravati marbles', even though they were made of limestone. The Amaravati story has sometimes been compared with that of the 'Elgin marbles' in the context of the debate on the repatriation of cultural treasures. My chapter uses archival sources to tell the story of what was happening at the site and to the site from the time of its discovery by Colin Mackenzie in 1797 till the removal of a large number of sculptures in 1886. This forms part of the larger history of archaeology and conservation in colonial India. The chapter begins at the time of the dilettante surveyors and collectors and goes up to the point of time when the colonial state was forced to formulate policies with regard to ancient antiquities. At Amaravati too, we see the familiar conflict between the field archaeologists and architectural scholars. But the specific issue that became the focus of intense debate was the conflict between *in situ* preservation and the museumization of antiquities. The chapter describes how documentation and destruction went hand in hand and how in 1886, after Cunningham's final nod, a large consignment of Amaravati sculptures was removed from the site and despatched to the Madras Museum.

Apart from Cunningham, Burgess, and Fergusson, who have already been mentioned, we encounter the irascible H. H. Cole, who was Curator of Ancient Monuments during 1881–1883. Cole was an outspoken critic of the vandalism of the archaeologists and a passionate spokesperson for the *in situ* preservation of antiquities in India, for India. It is interesting to note that this man was the son of Sir Henry Cole, a leading figure in the movement for the reform of industrial design in Britain and the first Director of the South Kensington Museum, which later came to be known as the Victoria and Albert Museum. The chapter shows that what happened at a site was the result of a conjunction of various factors and individuals, and that the emergence of 'official policy' was a chaotic, rather messy affair.

Comparisons are instructive. Today, the Amaravati *stūpa* is marked by a low, nondescript mound and the three major collections of its sculptures are distributed between the Government Museum in Chennai, the British Museum in London, and the Site Museum at Amaravati. Most of the sculptures from the Bharhut *stūpa* were moved to the Indian Museum in Calcutta, where some of the architectural elements were assembled in a special gallery. Sanchi was the subject of a large-scale on-site restoration project. But there were other trajectories as well. For instance, the restored (or, according to Fergusson, renovated) Mahābodhi temple, received a fresh lease of life not only as a historical monument but as a living shrine within an increasingly internationalized Buddhist world; it also became a contested shrine over which Śaivas and Buddhists claimed custody. Each site tells a different story.

The history of ancient archaeological sites in the colonial period includes the elements of destruction, documentation, and conservation. But we need to reflect on the extent to which the situation changed in post-colonial times. 'Buddhism, Archaeology, and the Nation: Nagarjunakonda, 1926–2006' (Chapter 7) does precisely this. Highlighting the interpretative aspects of archaeological exploration and analysis, it points to continuity in the privileging of Nagarjunakonda's Buddhist associations in the colonial and post-colonial periods. The chapter also shows how, from the early 20th century, conservation policy in India came to be increasingly influenced by public opinion. The focus is on two important moments in the history of Nagarjunakonda—the earliest excavations in the 1920s and the decision to build the dam which destroyed the site in the 1950s. The discussion is based largely on hitherto unknown archival material.

In 1927, the Archaeological Survey was still very much an institution dominated by British officers. It is, therefore, not surprising that A. H. Longhurst, Superintending Archaeologist of the Southern Circle, tried to steal the thunder of his junior Indian officer M. H. Kuraishi when it came to publishing the preliminary report of the important discoveries at Nagarjunakonda. A few years earlier, John Marshall had made the announcement of the sensational discovery of the Indus civilization in the *Illustrated London News*. Now, it was not considered appropriate to announce the discovery of the Nagarjunakonda remains in a British newspaper. And yet, when the news—highlighting the discovery of Buddhist relics—was published in two Indian newspapers in 1930, the names of the Indians who had discovered the site (A. R. Saraswati) and conducted the first excavations (M. H. Kuraishi) were not mentioned. As is the case with Amaravati, at Nagarjunakonda too, there was discussion of how and where the ancient remains should be preserved and displayed. But this was the 20th century, not the 19th, and packing the excavated material off to England was not considered an option. Further, Buddhist relics and relic caskets, for long an object of fascination for British archaeologists, dilettantes, and treasure-hunters, were by now recognized as a special class of antiquities. Buddhist, regional, and national sentiments were involved and invoked.

The second important juncture in the history of Nagarjunakonda that I examine in the chapter is located in the 1950s and involved a very different issue—the conflict between economic development and the preservation of cultural heritage. The project to build the Nagarjunasagar dam across the River Krishna was part of the nation-building priorities of the time. The problem was that the dam would result in the complete submergence and destruction of a site whose historical importance was by that time well known. The matter was not taken lightly—it was discussed in Parliament and Prime Minister Jawaharlal Nehru took a keen personal interest. The tension and conflict between development and cultural heritage has enormous, even greater, relevance today. Now, as then, economic development usually trumps the preservation of cultural heritage, although with much less national-level discussion and debate.

The issues raised in Chapter 7 are carried forward in 'Exile and Return: The Reinvention of Buddhism and Buddhist Sites in Modern India' (Chapter 8). The chapter begins by looking at the decline of Buddhism in India in the early medieval period. It points to the pockets of resilience, especially the long, continuous Buddhist tradition in Ladakh, Lahaul, and Spiti, areas that had enduring religious and cultural ties with Tibet. Moving to more recent times, I note how Buddhism has had considerable symbolic significance in India, of a kind that is at complete variance with the fact that Buddhists form a very small religious minority in the country. I also point out that the sites associated with the life of the Buddha and the places where famous ancient monasteries were located have, in recent years, become important nodes of activity. Extinct sites offer spaces that are sought to be appropriated by various religious and secular groups for a variety of reasons. Among the processes that have led to the revival and reinvention of ancient Indian Buddhist sites, it is the exile and internationalization of Tibetan Buddhism that has attracted the greatest scholarly attention. I argue that this has to be viewed in conjunction with several other processes, namely the neo-Buddhist movement initiated by B. R. Ambedkar, the increasing interest of the Indian state in promoting 'spiritual tourism' at ancient Buddhist sites, and international (especially Japanese) investment in the conservation and development activity at these places. We see a convergence of neo-Buddhists, Tibetan Buddhists, and international pilgrim-tourists at these sacred sites. However, given the enormous cultural and social differences between the proponents of these very different 'Buddhisms', although pilgrimage brings them to the same places, it does not necessarily bring them together.

I also discuss how the production of archaeological knowledge, state policies, global (especially East Asian) pilgrim flows, and new ceremonials and rituals have coalesced to create new material, monumental and iconographic additions to the landscape of ancient sites, altering them in significant ways. At Nagarjunakonda, recent years have seen intensification in the privileging of the site's Buddhist associations reflected in a considerable amount of new imagery. While an 'iconography of convergence' is occasionally visible, by and large it is Buddhism that is writ large—whether in the *caitya* arches of the site museum and its emphasis on a Buddhist display or in the Buddhist imagery that surfaces frequently in the town, including at the dam site and electricity station. Perhaps telling a simple story about this site, any site, is easier than advertising its more complex history.

The chapters in this section reflect my conviction that there is absolutely no reason for scholars working on ancient India to restrict themselves to ancient times. Not only is the transgressing of customary boundaries of periodization desirable, it is also essential if the most interesting questions are to be posed. I think that a grounding in ancient Indian history gives an important perspective to investigations into the history of archaeology, sites, and museums. The most important aspect of this is the recognition that although all histories and archaeologies of ancient India are discourses whose political contexts must be recognized and whose underpinnings, presuppositions, and prejudices must be revealed, some of these discourses do, to a greater or lesser extent, contribute to a body of growing knowledge about that past. After all, the past did once exist.

The Intersection of Political Ideas and Practice

The third and fourth sections of this book deal with my current research interests. The third reflects my journey from the material world to the world of ideas. My interest in intellectual history was sparked off when, a few years ago, I reached out for a book that had been lying on my shelves, unread, for many decades. It was the text and translation of Kāmandaka's political treatise, the *Nītisāra*. Sometimes a source speaks. As I read the *Nītisāra*, it spoke to me about ancient ideas of kingship, governance, and warfare. This was also the time when I realized that in all the years that I had taught and researched on ancient Indian history, I had missed an important point, namely the fact that the entire political history of ancient India was marked by pervasive violence and that this needed to be investigated. This realization and my encounter with the *Nītisāra* led me to sharply change my track from the study of Buddhist sites to an exploration of political violence in ancient India.

In ancient Indian historiography, political history in the traditional sense became passé in the late 1960s, and the focus shifted to the study of economic and social history. This was an important breakthrough, which especially affected the way in which the transition to the early historic and the early medieval (a term that I do not like but use just for the sake of convenience) were understood. One of the casualties of this historiographical shift was that cultural and intellectual history became low priorities. However, recent years have seen a revival of interest in these spheres, and among the scholars who have contributed to the field of political ideas, three deserve special mention. The first is Sheldon Pollock. Pollock's *The Language of the Gods in the World of Men*[23] is significant for drawing attention to several issues—the importance of the 'political imagination'; the histories and travels of languages and texts; the connections between language, literature, and power; and the relationship between *kāvya* and *praśasti*. Also significant is Pollock's eloquent discussion of literary cultures[24] and his strong (though overstated) critique of legitimation theory. Another scholar who has provided valuable primary source material as well as much food for thought on the subject of ancient Indian political ideas is Patrick Olivelle. This remarkably prolific scholar has produced critical editions and translations of the *Arthaśāstra* and *Mānavadharmaśāstra*, translations of the *Buddhacarita*, the early Upaniṣads, and Dharmasūtras, as well as extremely thought-provoking essays on a wide range of issues including kingship, *dharma*, the *āśramas*, and renunciation.[25] A third scholar whose work is very germane to the historical investigation of political ideas and practice is Daud Ali. Ali's writings mark a significant departure from the conventional historiography of early medieval India, creatively analyzing a variety of sources in order to reconstruct the ideas and practices of courtly culture in first-millennium India.[26]

While drawing on the insights of these and other scholars, my own perspective is defined in certain ways. Given the nature of my training as a historian, my approach towards the world of ideas is naturally very historically grounded and I am especially interested in the relationship between political ideas and practice. Further, while it is important to analyze the political discourse represented in texts and inscriptions, I believe that the investigation should be very carefully calibrated with respect to chronology and spatial context and the genre and nature of the source. The sources provide different windows, different perspectives into the world of ideas. Therefore, we cannot talk about *the* representation of kingship, war, *dharma*, the city, love, or any other issue in first-millennium India. There were *several* representations, *several* perspectives; discovering the multiplicity of representations and perspectives is, in fact, what makes the investigation so interesting. The chapters in Section III of this book historicize three different kinds of sources through a thorough, careful reading, disentangling the strands of political thought and practice. They look at ideas of kingship, empire, violence, war, justice, and punishment, underlining the role of the royal household and the importance of emotions in the political sphere. They also discuss the relationship between the state and the forest, especially comparing attitudes towards the royal hunt.

Although my interest in ancient Indian political ideas began with the *Nītisāra*, the chapter on Aśoka is placed first in this section. My earlier essay on Aśoka is not included here.[27] Written many years ago, that essay argued that Aśokan pillars should be considered as epigraphic monuments, that the text of an Aśokan inscription must be viewed in conjunction with the surface on which it is engraved and the sculptural motifs which accompany it; and that a discussion of Aśoka's *dhamma* must pay due attention to the modes of transmission and reception of the *dhamma* message. It also argued that Aśoka's epigraphic monuments have an interesting post-Maurya history which deserves investigation—whether it is the pillars' association with epic heroes, their long-distance travels in the time of Firuz Shah Tughluq, or their absorption into a variety of cultic practices in modern times.

The chapter included in this book 'Governing the State and the Self: Political Philosophy and Practice in the Edicts of Aśoka' (Chapter 9) complements the earlier one, but is very different. Here, I argue that the obsession with connecting the ideas in the edicts with various religious and textual traditions, the tendency to reduce these ideas to legitimization strategy, and the setting up of false dichotomies between the personal–political and the political–religious domains have prevented a careful reading of the edicts on their own terms. The edicts seem disarmingly simple. Behind the deceptive simplicity lies complex subtlety. Every reading reveals a new thread, a new nuance.

As the first self-representations of imperial power in ancient South Asia, the inscriptions of Aśoka provide a unique, first-person account of an ancient Indian king's vision of empire and governance. Understanding this vision requires reconstructing the internal logic of the ideas expressed in the edicts, including both what they say and what they imply. Politics, ethics, and metaphysics are closely interlinked in ancient Indian political discourse, and Aśoka's ideas are no exception. I argue that the edicts talk about two kinds of overlapping empire—political and moral. The geographical extent of the latter was much greater than the king's political realm, and the goal here was the inculcation of happiness among all beings, including humans and animals. The king's ruminations reveal a political philosophy consisting of a set of interconnected ideas and arguments on fundamental issues such as the relationship between political power, violence, happiness, and the good. These ideas were rooted in the contemporary cultural and religious milieu, which included, but was not restricted to, Buddhism. The ideas of *karma*, merit, and the attainment of heaven were important links in the attempt to persuade his subjects to follow *dhamma* as well as in Aśoka's understanding of his own *dhamma* as king. This ruler was especially concerned about violence and strife, whether directed against humans or animals, a concern that was, no doubt, rooted in his Buddhist persuasions. But his was not simply a desire for the *absence* of violence; this desire was accompanied by a positive attitude of care, expressed in his initiatives for the welfare of men and animals, and in his insistence that the relationship between people of different sects should be one of mutual respect, understanding, and concord. This was an emperor with strong opinions, so it is not surprising that he also made some sharp idiosyncratic interventions. The most significant of these is in his thirteenth major rock edict, where he presents a reasoned critique of war and announces that he will never wage one again.

Aśoka was no arm-chair political theoretician. His impassioned pleas for morality were tempered with pragmatism and we also see him grappling with issues connected with practical governance. This was a state with fiscal needs, which struggled to ensure that its officials discharged their duties efficiently, which was concerned that the administration of justice should be fair, and which faced hurdles in the process of political consolidation. But while announcing that all men were like his children, Aśoka had no qualms about dealing aggressively with aggressive forest tribes. While talking incessantly about non-violence, he did not abolish the death penalty, only announcing a three-day respite for those condemned to die. This indicates that he accepted the impossibility of absolute non-violence and recognized a certain amount of force as necessary and legitimate in the political sphere.

'Politics, Violence, and War in Kāmandaka's *Nītisāra*' (Chapter 11) represents my first foray into the area of political ideas; this is why the textual analysis is preceded by a discussion of several more general issues. These include my impatience with the dominant concerns of the historiography of the period c. 600–1300 CE, which is usually called the 'early medieval' period in Indian history. I argue that the debate over whether the polities of this period were feudal or segmentary, or should be seen through the prism of an integrative perspective, has run its course, and that the time is ripe for shifting the focus to other questions. I dwell on the neglect of intellectual history and the importance of historicizing and incorporating the ideas of political theorists into political history. The early part of the chapter also talks about authority, debate, authorial perspective, and interdisciplinarity in the ancient Indian intellectual tradition.

The chapter historicizes the *Nītisāra* through a close reading of the text and a comparison with the older, more famous political treatise, the *Arthaśāstra* of Kauṭilya. Admittedly, one of the problems in such an enterprise is the dating of both these texts. I have considered the *Arthaśāstra* as a complex text whose history may go back to the Maurya period but extends into the early century CE; the *Nītisāra* can be located in the middle of the first millennium. Both works share a common conceptual vocabulary. Their morphology of the state, court, and household recognizes the intersection between the personal and the political. The court protocols including detailed guidelines to the courtier on how to conduct himself in order to be successful are broadly similar. We encounter in both texts a strong insistence that the king exercises control over his senses, an idea that must have been rooted in a philosophical perspective as well as pragmatism. In a monarchical state, where there were no institutional constraints to the king's power, it made sense to try to convince him that it was in his own interest to control himself.

The chapter also foregrounds the need to investigate the problem of violence in ancient India. The political theorists were aware of the necessity as well as the limits of force in the political sphere, and they make a distinction between necessary force and violence. But Kauṭilya and Kāmandaka have a different understanding of precisely how this distinction was to be made; this is apparent in their attitudes towards war, capital punishment, and the royal hunt. Kauṭilya presents a brilliant model of an arrogant omnipotent state. Kāmandaka offers a later, more sober reflection on political power, one with a distinct philosophical bent that veers towards non-violence. Clearly, the routine description of the *Nītisāra* as an unoriginal verse summary of the *Arthaśāstra* is incorrect.

Having examined political treatises and Aśoka's inscriptions, I was keen to see how political ideas were expressed in poetry. I therefore extended my inquiry to Kālidāsa's *Raghuvaṁśa*, a work of exquisite poetic beauty and enormous political importance. 'The Power of a Poet: Kingship, Empire, and War in Kālidāsa's *Raghuvaṁśa*' (Chapter 12) reads this text as a literary political manifesto, taking care to keep the genre demands of *kāvya* conventions in mind. Kālidāsa was not only a brilliant poet, but also a keen political theorist and synthesizer with considerable political acumen. His narrative of the reigns of the kings of Raghu's line, which knits together the locales of city, palace, forest, and *tapovana* into an interacting and interdependent whole, created a composite idea of normative kingship, one that was rooted in the cultural and political milieu of the time. His description of Raghu's *digvijaya* captures with elegance and specificity the subcontinental geo-political canvas of the *vijigīṣu* and presents an idea of empire based on victory rather than conquest.

But as is the case with the earlier two chapters, I also explore how the *Raghuvaṁśa* addressed very real problems related to monarchical power politics and offered certain solutions. As the poet narrates the story of Raghu's lineage, he touches on succession problems, harem intrigues, and royal vices. If Kālidāsa showcases exemplary kings such as Raghu and Rāma, he also describes not-so-exemplary kings such as Aja who loves his queen too much, or Agnivarṇa, who is a debauch. I emphasize that notwithstanding the constraints presented by some of the better-known stories (especially that of Rāma) and the fact that the poet wove his words within *kāvya* conventions, Kālidāsa succeeded in expressing in brilliant Sanskrit poetry a wide range of ideas about both ideal kingship as well as flawed kingship. This, I argue, is the reason for the fame and influence achieved by the *Raghuvaṁśa* in India and Southeast Asia.

A more general issue raised in the chapter is that of comparing the political discourses of poetry, inscriptions, political treatises, and epics. We see conversations, a shared political vocabulary, and many similar ideas, but there are also differences, major as well as minor. Kālidāsa and Vālmīki both tell the story of Rāma, but their tellings are by no means identical. The description of Raghu's *digvijaya* bears some affinity with Hariṣena's description of Samudragupta's campaigns in the Allahabad *praśasti*, but there is also divergence. All of these works contributed towards the creation of normative political traditions, but although consensus was achieved on some issues, there were differences in perspective, sometimes amounting to radical disagreement. For instance, not all ideologues of kingship would have agreed with Kālidāsa that renunciation should be part of an ideal king's life. Kauṭilya would certainly not have.

Looking beyond India to Asia

One of my major dissatisfactions with ancient Indian history writing—perhaps greatest one—is the fact that most of it is incredibly India-centric and ignores the rest of Asia. India–Southeast Asia relations were of great interest to historians who wrote under the influence of nationalism, but they looked at these relations from the perspectives of 'Greater India' and 'Indianization'. Scholars such as R. C. Majumdar and K. A. N. Sastri talked of Hindu political and cultural colonization of the lands of Southeast Asia, although they differed to some extent in the details, for instance on whether the significant Indian influences emanated from Bengal or South India. Of course, the Indianization model was not only favoured by Indian historians; the French scholar Georges Cœdès, in his *l'Inde extérieure* talked about 'Further India' and also visualized the lands of Southeast Asia as primitive cultural colonies.[28]

The Indianization hypothesis was not universally accepted, and powerful critiques followed in its wake. For instance, O. W. Wolters argued that while foreign influence was undeniable, the history of Southeast Asia also included an important 'something else'. In his memorable words, 'Indian materials tended to be fractured and restated and therefore drained of their original significance', through the process he termed 'localization'.[29] It is unfortunate that Indian historians, who had a place in Southeast Asian historiography during the hey-day of the Indianization hypothesis, were nowhere in the picture when the critical turn in Southeast Asian historiography took place in the 1960s. They had missed the boat. The 'Greater India' model was critiqued and replaced by an indifference towards Southeast Asia, except in the context of trade. This can be seen as part of the 'inward turn' in ancient Indian historiography—pan-Indian histories were to a large extent replaced by a great interest in bringing out the different textures and trajectories of history in the various regions of the subcontinent. Connections with other parts of the world came to be largely ignored.

My own first exposure to research on Southeast Asia was in 1984, when I was in the Kern Institute in Leiden. Professor J. G. de Casparis, who urged me to work on Orissa, was a renowned scholar of Southeast Asian inscriptions and history, and many researchers in the Kern Institute were working on Indonesia. However, so deeply ingrained was my India-centric focus that none of this made any impact on me. My realization of the insular and parochial nature of much of ancient India historiography is very recent. It has been accompanied and intensified by a series of travels, in the course of which I have visited some of the important historical sites of Southeast Asia—Cambodia, Indonesia, Myanmar, and subsequently, Sri Lanka.

Moving into Southeast Asia was daunting. Luckily, I had a friend and colleague—art historian Parul Pandya Dhar—who was thinking along these very lines. There were two important turning points. One was our decision in 2011 to teach a master's-level course on cultural interactions between South and Southeast Asia. At that time, we had next to no primary or secondary material at hand for ourselves or for our students. But generous help, advice, and PDFs poured in from scholars located in different parts of the world. For the first time, I felt that I was part of a larger academic community that went out of its way to help its members, and did so with great generosity. Arlo Griffiths of the École française d'Extrême-Orient was especially helpful in the venture. Veena Sachdev opened the doors of the library collection of my former teacher, the late Professor Devahuti, which turned out to be a gold mine containing many of the classics of Southeast Asian history. The MA course means that the history of pre-modern Southeast Asia is once again on the radar of students of the University of Delhi, and I am sure that eventually, some of them will go on to conduct research on the subject. The second turning point was a conference on Asian Encounters in pre-modern times, the brainchild of Dr Kapila Vatsyayan, who brought us together on a platform along with the Archaeological Survey of India, the Indira Gandhi National Centre for the Arts and the India International Centre-Asia project. The outcome of the conference was a book co-edited by myself and Parul Pandya Dhar—*Asian Encounters: Exploring Connected Histories*.[30] The aim is to keep the momentum going.

Chapter 14 ('Gifts from Other Lands: Southeast Asian Religious Endowments in India') is based on the paper I presented at the Asian Encounters conference. Instead of plunging into completely unknown terrain, I thought it best to begin my own research encounter with Southeast Asia by dealing with something about which I knew at least the Indian part. I decided to examine inscriptions recording religious endowments made by Southeast Asian rulers in India—the Śailendra gift at Nālandā; the Burmese/Myanmarese endowments at Bodhgayā, and the Śrīvijayan gifts at Nāgapaṭṭinam. The aim was to assess the historical significance of these transactions by carefully analyzing their epigraphic representations.

The chapter cautions us against viewing these gifts simply as a part of 'religious diplomacy'. It is interesting to note that the only land grant known to have been made to the celebrated monastery of Nālandā was a generous gift of five villages made in the 9th century by the Pāla king Devapāla at the request of Bālaputra, the Śailendra ruler of Yavabhūmi. The Burma–Bodhgayā connections were more prolonged and intense. They took the form of pilgrimage, gifts, and 'repairs' to the temple at the behest of Burmese kings. The chapter examines the epigraphic evidence of these interactions from the 11th/12th to the 19th centuries. The larger and smaller Leiden plates record gifts made over a long period of time by the Śrīvijaya rulers to a Buddhist monastery at Nāgapaṭṭinam. The chapter raises questions about the interplay between war, diplomacy, and religious gifts in the relationship between South and Southeast Asian elites. There is also the issue of the impact of trans-regional patronage and pilgrimage. It can be argued that Buddhist internationalism played an important role in sustaining Buddhism during the period of its decline in the subcontinent.

The chapter concludes by raising an issue that is not related to religious endowments but to the expanse of water that separates the Indian subcontinent from maritime Southeast Asia. In spite of its long coastline of a little over 7,516 km, why does the ocean figure in the fantasy of power in ancient India as a general boundary rather than as something specific and to be traversed? What accounts for the generally land-locked nature of ancient Indian military expansionism and ideas of empire? Why did Indian armies cross the seas so rarely? Of course there are some exceptions such as the Cōḻa conflicts with Sri Lanka and Śrīvijaya, but they are, nevertheless, exceptions.

The Burmese/Myanmarese connections with Bodhgayā feature in Chapter 14 and Chapter 15 ('Politics, Piety, and Patronage: The Burmese Engagement with Bodhgayā'). When I wrote *Discovery of Ancient India*, I was very struck by the incident of certain Burmese gentlemen landing up at Bodhgayā in 1877 and proceeding to 'repair' the Mahābodhi shrine. I did not know then that this was but a relatively late episode in a long-standing relationship. By the time I wrote the essay on religious endowments, I had realized that it was not possible to fully comprehend what the Burmese were doing at Bodhgayā without understanding the relationship between the state and Buddhism in Myanmar. By the time I wrote 'Politics, Piety and Patronage...' my interest in India–Burma interactions, fuelled by a visit to Pagan and some of the other important historical sites of Myanmar, had grown considerably. Although there is some overlap between the two chapters, Chapter 15 is more detailed, introduces new evidence and presents a new argument.

In this last chapter, I discuss the symbolic significance of Mahābodhi in the Burmese Buddhist world, reflected in the building of so-called Mahābodhi 'replicas' and the various other ways in which this pre-eminent shrine came to be represented. The principal new evidence and argument relates to certain Buddhapādas (Buddha footprints) found at Bodhgayā. My interest in these was sparked by a photograph of one such Buddhapāda that formed part of Naman Ahuja's 'Representing the Body' exhibition in Brussels (2014). The image may not have made much impression on me were it not for the fact that I had just returned from Myanmar, and a shrine engraved on the Buddhapāda in the photograph seemed rather Burmese. This hunch led to an exciting chase, which culminated in the discovery of some more Buddha footprints with a Burmese signature. The hypothesis I put forward in the chapter is that the Burmese pilgrims and repair missions that came to Bodhgayā from time to time may have been responsible for the promotion, perhaps even the introduction, of footprint worship—important in Burma at least from the early Pagan period onwards—at Mahābodhi, by turning miniature *stūpas* into Buddhapādas, creating a unique hybrid cultural artefact in the process. Looking at the very wide prevalence of Buddhapādas in India, Sri Lanka and Myanmar (as also in other parts of the world), I am convinced that tracking down the history of these small, seemingly insignificant artefacts, usually ignored by both historians and art historians, is an exciting project. This is especially so when we consider the rather ubiquitous prevalence of footprint worship in many religious traditions. But beyond footprint worship, there is a need to work out the many aspects of the long-term relationship and interactions between eastern India and Burma/Myanmar.

Although my interest in India's connections with Asia began with Southeast Asia, it is very clear to me now that the important key to understanding Asian interactions must begin closer home, in the island of Sri Lanka. This is not only because of the great importance of Sri Lanka in the Indian Ocean trade networks but also the pivotal role played by Sri Lanka in Asian Buddhist networks, a fact alluded to in my discussion of Nagarjunakonda and also in the context of Myanmar–Sri Lanka monastic links. The contrast with Sri Lankan Buddhism can, in fact, help us understand the decline of Buddhism in the subcontinent. Much as our democratic impulses may militate against such a conclusion, it is clear to me that one of the most important reasons for this decline was the failure of Buddhism to capture the state.

Reconstructing Asian interactions is both exciting and disconcerting. It means moving into unfamiliar terrain. Given the enormous geographical range that has to be covered and the very varied nature of the source material, the project requires genuine international and cross-disciplinary collaboration. But from the perspective of Indian historians, the writing is on the wall: we can no longer be content to confine ourselves to regional or subcontinental frames.

These days, thinking about Asian interactions seems once again to be becoming important, even fashionable, in India. The question is: in this second round of engagement, through what perspectives are Indian scholars going to view these interactions? There are dangers when a revival of interest in India's Asian connections takes place within a context of hypernationalism and cultural chauvinism, where obscurantist interpretations of ancient India are given the kind of platform and respectability that they do not deserve. What is required is a sober, rigorous historical analysis of the various types of networks of interaction cutting across Asia, Africa, and Europe. This will involve looking at trade, religion, politics, ideas, and art in conjunction with each other. Conflict and war are also part of the story, not only within the macro-regions of South and Southeast Asia but also across them. The latter are reflected, for instance, in the Chinese conflicts with the Đại Việt and the Cōḻa campaigns in Sri Lanka and Śrīvijaya. The project will involve identifying the historical contexts and networks through which Asian interactions evolved. It will require acknowledging that the travels of languages, texts, ideas, institutions, and practices often resulted in the creation of completely new cultural forms and syntheses. It is my hope that the interest in the connections between ancient India and the rest of the world expands exponentially in our universities and research institutes and leads to the production of serious, high-quality research.

The Academic and the Political

While the chapters in this book focus on a variety of issues, I think it should be apparent that there are also many connecting links. Looking back at my work, I used to think there was randomness to what struck my fancy at different points of time, as well as a feeling of regret that I had not started working earlier on the kinds of things that interest me today. However, perhaps there is some kind of logic to the trajectory—I would not have got to the point where I am if I had not sorted out various other things first.

My book *A History of Ancient and Early Medieval India*, published in 2008, marked a watershed in my career as a historian.[31] It emerged from over 20 years' experience of teaching undergraduate students and incorporated some of the results of my research over those years. It was my way of clearing my desk. By this time, I had certain very definite ideas about what I wanted to achieve—some methodological, some pedagogic. These ideas were very specifically grounded in the realities of the nature of Indian academia and university education and stemmed from a strong dissatisfaction with existing approaches towards the writing of ancient Indian history and with the manner in which the subject was taught in our universities. I thought it necessary to integrate archaeology into the historical narrative; to be frank about the frequent dissonance between textual and archaeological testimony; to incorporate women and other marginalized groups into social history; and to give adequate space to the cultural domain, especially art and architecture. At the level of pedagogy, I felt that undergraduate students needed to be exposed to the primary sources on which history is based. I was tired of the fact that they were expected to unquestioningly imbibe the conclusions of the so-called 'dominant historiography' and reproduce them in the examinations. Surely, there was an urgent need to encourage students to dare to ask questions. And there was the equally, if not more, important need to make them realize that learning about ancient India could be an incredibly exciting voyage of discovery.

The book was also shaped by my exasperation with an academic atmosphere marked by the tyranny of ideologies, where academic critique was a risky business and was not tolerated beyond a point. Some years earlier, I had expressed the view that the writing and teaching of history in India appeared to suffer from a peculiar form of bipolar disorder—one which tried to force individuals to choose between a rightist and a leftist history, as though no other histories existed or were possible. *A History of Ancient and Early Medieval India* reflects my strong conviction of the need for a 'non-aligned' history-writing, one that self-consciously distances itself from the agendas and factionalism of the left and the right. The book's subversive intent did not escape notice. The fact that it encouraged a reasoned critique of all, including certain well-entrenched, historiographical positions is, in my opinion, the main reason why it attracted exceptionally sharp criticism from some established scholars.

If I were to write another book on the history of ancient India, I would still want to do all the things I had tried to do earlier, but I would want to do more. I would underline the need to move beyond a simplistic correlation of historical sources towards more reflective intertextual readings. I would be more attentive to the interface between political ideas and practice. I would pay far greater attention to the cultural, to the literary, to the aesthetic, to the world of ideas and emotions. I would more extensively explore the web of connections that bind India with Asia and the rest of the world. And I would even more strongly emphasize the need to expand the space for a history that is not subservient to political ideology.

Notes

1. The chapters published in this book have been edited for typographical errors, stylistic consistency, and sequential organization in order to make them suitable for inclusion in this book.
2. See Nayanjot Lahiri, Upinder Singh and Tarika Oberoi, 'Preliminary Field Report on the Archaeology of Faridabad: The Ballabgarh Tehsil,' *Man and Environment* 21 (1), 1996, pp. 32–57.
3. Upinder Singh, *Ancient Delhi* 2nd edition, with a new Preface and Introduction (New Delhi: Oxford University Press, [1999] 2006). I also have an edited volume on Delhi's ancient history: *Delhi: Ancient History* (New Delhi: Social Science Press, 2006). The Hindi version of this book was published as *Dilli: Prachin Itihas* (New Delhi: Orient Blackswan, 2009).
4. These points should be taken for granted, but I have found that this is often not the case.
5. When I wrote my essay, I uncritically referred to these as 'votive inscriptions'. I am now aware that there is no reason to presume that the donative inscriptions were votive in nature.

6. See my essay, 'Varṇa and Jāti in Ancient India: Some Questions,' in Kesavan Veluthat and Donald R. Davis Jr., eds, *Irreverent History: Essays for M. G. S. Narayanan* (New Delhi: Primus, 2014).
7. This is an issue that Gregory Schopen has written eloquently on from the 1980s, but I was not aware of his writings at the time I wrote my essay on Sanchi.
8. For a detailed critique of the term 'early medieval' and a discussion of the limitations of existing debates about this period, see Upinder Singh, ed., *Rethinking Early Medieval India* (New Delhi: Oxford University Press, 2011), Introduction.
9. Gregory Schopen, 'What's in a Name: The Religious Function of the Early Donative Inscriptions', in Gregory Schopen, ed., *Buddhist Monks and Business Matters: Still More Papers on Monastic Buddhism in India* (Honolulu: University of Hawai'i Press, 2004), pp. 390–392.
10. Vidya Dehejia's *Discourse in Early Buddhist Art: Visual Narratives of India* (New Delhi: Munshiram Manoharlal, [1997] 2005). I have greatly benefitted from Dehejia's prolific writings throughout my research career, especially from her work on the temples of Orissa and the cave temples of western India.
11. See, for instance, Monika Zin, 'When Stones Are All That Survived: The Case of Buddhism in Andhra', in Agata Bareja-Starzyńska and Marek Major, eds, *Rocznik Orientalistyczny: Oriental Studies, Past and Present*, Proceedings of the International Conference of Oriental Studies (Warszawa, 2012), pp. 236–245.
12. Nayanjot Lahiri and Elizabeth Bacus, eds, 'The Archaeology of Hinduism', *World Archaeology* 36 (3), 2006.
13. Ananda K. Coomaraswamy, *Yakshas,* 2nd edition (New Delhi: Munshiram Manoharlal, 1980), p. 36.
14. Upinder Singh, *Kings, Brāhmaṇas and Temples in Orissa: An Epigraphic Study* (*AD 300–1147*) (New Delhi: Munshiram Manoharlal, 1994).
15. On this issue, also see Upinder Singh, 'Brāhmaṇa Settlements in Ancient and Early Medieval India', in B. D. Chattopadhyaya, ed., *A Social History of Early India*, Project of History of Indian Science, Philosophy and Culture, Vol. II, Part 5 (New Delhi: Pearson Longman, 2009), pp. 157–175.
16. This point is also made and elaborated in Singh, 'Brāhmaṇa Settlements in Ancient India'.
17. Upinder Singh, ed., *Rethinking Early Medieval India: A Reader* (New Delhi: Oxford University Press, 2011).
18. James Fergusson, *Archaeology of India with Especial Reference to the Works of Babu Rajendralala Mitra* (London: Trübner, 1884).
19. See Nayanjot Lahiri, *Finding Forgotten Cities: How the Indus Civilization Was Discovered* (New Delhi: Permanent Black, 2005).
20. Upinder Singh, *The Discovery of Ancient India: Early Archaeologists and the Beginnings of Archaeology* (New Delhi: Permanent Black, 2004).
21. Alexander Cunningham, 'Proposed Archaeological Investigation', *Journal of the Asiatic Society of Bengal* 17 (1848), p. 535.

22. My *Discovery of Ancient India* reconstructs the 19th century histories of other sites as well, such as Sanchi, Bharhut and Chandravati.
23. Sheldon Pollock, *The Language of the Gods in the World of Men: Sanskrit, Culture and Power in Premodern India* (Berkeley: University of California Press, 2006).
24. Sheldon Pollock, ed. *Literary Cultures in History: Reconstructions from South Asia* (Berkeley: University of California Press, 2003), Introduction.
25. See, for instance, the collection of essays in Patrick Olivelle, *Ascetics and Brahmins: Studies in Ideologies and Institutions* (London: Anthem Press, [2011] 2012) and his *Language, Texts and Society: Explorations in Ancient Indian Culture and Religion* (London: Anthem Press, [2011] 2012).
26. See, for instance, Daud Ali, *Courtly Culture and Political Life in Early Medieval India* (Cambridge: Cambridge University Press, 2004).
27. Upinder Singh, 'Texts on Stone: Understanding Aśoka's Epigraph-Monuments and Their Changing Contexts', *Indian Historical Review* 24 (1–2), 1998, pp. 1–19.
28. See R. C. Majumdar, *Ancient Indian Colonization in South-East Asia* (Baroda: The Majaraja Sayajirao University of Baroda Press [1955] 1971); and G. Cœdès, *The Indianized States of Southeast Asia* (Honolulu: University of Hawaii Press, 1968).
29. O. W. Wolters, *History, Culture, and Region in Southeast Asian Perspectives* (Singapore: Institute of Southeast Asian Studies, 1982), p. 52.
30. Upinder Singh and Parul Pandya Dhar, eds, *Asian Encounters: Exploring Connected Histories* (New Delhi: Oxford University Press, 2014).
31. Upinder Singh, *A History of Ancient and Early Medieval India: From the Stone Age to the 12th Century* (New Delhi: Pearson Longman, 2008).

SECTION I

Religion and Region

1

Sanchi: The History of the Patronage of an Ancient Buddhist Establishment

The object of this chapter is to examine the details and patterns of patronage of the Buddhist establishment of Sanchi (Raisen district, Madhya Pradesh), known variously in the ancient period as Kākaṇāva, Kākaṇāya, Kākanāda-boṭa, and Boṭa-Srīparvvata.[1] The epigraphic data from Sanchi can be placed and understood within a variety of different frameworks: those of the political history of the Indian subcontinent, the history of the Malwa region and its interactions with other areas, the history of trade and urban settlements, and most importantly, the history of Buddhism. The inscriptions also give us valuable information regarding the role of royal patronage in the establishment and growth of early Indian religious establishments. The importance of this role has more often been assumed than demonstrated.

This chapter does not attempt to offer any new theoretical insights into the nature of patronage.[2] It is an empirical exercise aimed at a thorough, detailed examination of the epigraphic data from Sanchi. Such an exercise is necessary because a less rigorous analysis of this data has often lent itself to conclusions that are more impressionistic than accurate.[3] The brevity of the text of most of the Sanchi inscriptions is

This chapter was previously published in *The Indian Economic and Social History Review* 33 (1), 1996, pp. 1–35.

offset by the very large *number* of inscriptions available (over 800) and the long period of time that they cover (about twelve centuries). This makes them a valuable source for the computation and comparison of data. The majority of the Sanchi inscriptions belong to the period between the 2nd century BC and 1st century AD. The Pali canon of the Buddhists, the *Tipiṭaka,* contains material that may go back to the 6th century BC and was put down in writing in the 1st century BC. Thus, there is some degree of overlap between the earliest sacred texts of the Buddhists and one of the earliest and most substantial sets of donative inscriptions at Sanchi. Hence, apart from analyzing the inscriptional data, this chapter also tries to locate correspondences and divergences between literary and epigraphic evidence, keeping in mind the problems of dating the textual tradition precisely and also the differences in the *nature* of the two sources being juxtaposed—one canonical and prescriptive, the other a record of the faith and monetary endowments of hundreds of individuals who financed the building of the Sanchi monuments.

The Beginnings of the Stūpa Cult and the Sanchi Stūpa Complex

> And as they treat the remains of a king of kings, so, Ānanda, should they treat the remains of the Tathāgata. At the four crossroads a *thūpa* should be erected to the Tathāgata. And whosoever shall place there garlands, perfumes or paint, or make salutation there, or become in its presence calm in heart—that shall long be to them a source of profit and joy.[4]

While the Pāli texts suggest that the tradition of raising *stūpa*s over the mortal remains of kings predates Buddhism, the oldest surviving Buddhist *stūpa*s belong to the 3rd century BC.[5] Dominating the hilltop with its size and the richness of the carvings of its gateways, Stūpa 1 (also known as the Great Stūpa) is the most impressive of the structural remains at Sanchi. Concealed beneath its stone encasing lies the brick core of one of the oldest surviving Buddhist *stūpa*s in the world. The Mauryan emperor Aśoka is described in the Avadāna literature as having distributed portions of the Buddha's relics to every important town in the country, ordering the erection *of stūpa*s over the relics. We are told that he erected 84,000 *stūpas.*[6] Xuanzang refers to Buddhist *stūpa*s and monasteries built by Aśoka in various parts of the country. The fragmentary Nigali-Sagar pillar inscription records Aśoka's enlargement of the *stūpa* of Buddha Konākamana when he had been consecrated fourteen years and his subsequent visit to the site. Marshall gives good reasons to prove that the core of Stūpa 1 belongs to Aśoka's reign, and suggests that Aśoka played an important role in popularizing the building and veneration of *stūpas*.[7] There is a panel on the western pillar of the southern gateway of Stūpa 1 and another on the bottom lintel of the Eastern Gateway which, Foucher suggests, represent Aśoka's visit to the bodhi tree.[8] M. Hamid ascribes a *vihāra* lying to the east of Stūpa 2 (unearthed in the course of excavations carried out in 1936) to the Mauryan period on the basis of the size of the bricks used in the structure.[9] Thus, the beginnings of the history of Sanchi have a royal connection, and not an insignificant one. The beginnings of structural activity at Sanchi coincide with the first large Indian empire.[10]

While the beginning of the *stūpa* building activity at Sanchi can be placed in the 3rd century BC, additions to the core structure of Stūpa 1—the stone encasing, the ground, stairway, berm and balustrades, pavement of the procession path and the main terraces—were made between the 2nd century BC and 1st century AD. This was also the period during which the various parts of Stūpas 2 and 3 were built. Numerous smaller *stūpa*s appeared on the summit and the sides of the hill during these and succeeding centuries.[11] Marshall tells us that many of the small *stūpa*s clustering around Stūpa 1 were destroyed in 1881–1883 in the process of clearing the area around the ground balustrade of the Great Stūpa.[12] While Stūpa 1 did not yield any relics, the relic box found in Stūpa 2 contained four caskets containing fragments of bone. The inscriptions on the caskets and the relic box identify the relics as belonging to the following ten monks: Kāsapagota, Majhima, Hāritiputa, Mahavanāya, Āpagira, Koḍiniputa, Kosikiputa, Gotiputa, Mogaliputa, and Vāchi-Suvijayita.[13] Stūpa 3 contained relics (bone fragments, beads) of the famous Buddhist *thera*s Mahāmogalāna and Sāriputa.[14]

Besides *stūpa*s, the remains at Sanchi include pillars, shrines, living quarters for monks, and sculptures—ranging from the 3rd century BC to the 12th century AD. Coomaraswamy refers to early Buddhist art as 'the art of the people, used for the glorification of religion, telling the story of Buddhism in the clearest and simplest possible ways . . . .'[15] The monuments, sculptures, and inscriptions of Sanchi give us a history of Buddhism in stone, a history that spans fifteen centuries.

Why Sanchi?

Neither Sanchi nor the city of Vidiśā (on the outskirts of which the Sanchi establishment is located) have any known Buddhist religious significance. Neither are associated with the life of the Buddha. Vidiśā is mentioned in the *Sutta Nipāta,* but just as one of the various places that the pupils of Bāvarī set out towards in search of the Buddha.[16] John Marshall begins his account of the monuments of Sanchi with references from Buddhist texts describing the ideal location of a *saṅghārāma* (monastery) to be outside, but in close proximity, to the city. He points out that several of the important early Buddhist monasteries were situated on the outskirts of an important city—the structures at the Mṛgadāva outside Kāśī; the numerous Buddhist structures including the great Dharmarājikā *stūpa* and monastery outside Taxila; and our site of Sanchi outside Vidiśā.[17]

In ancient times, the eastern part of Malwa was known as Ākara (or sometimes Daśārṇa) and had Vidiśā, located at the confluence of the Bes and Betwa (ancient Vetravatī) rivers, as its capital. The western part of Malwa was known as Avanti and had its capital at Ujjayinī on the banks of the Sipra river. Around the end of the 5th century BC, parts of the Malwa region came to be absorbed into the Magadhan empire, but in the succeeding centuries, we hear more of Ujjayinī than Vidiśā in the literary sources. During the Mauryan period, Ujjayinī seems to have been a provincial headquarters and may have been the political centre of the western part of the Mauryan empire during the rule of the later Mauryas.[18] Vidiśā seems to have been an important political centre in the Śuṅga period. In Kālidāsa's *Mālavikāgnimitra,* Agnimitra rules at Vidiśā as viceroy of his father Pusyamitra Śuṅga. According to D. C. Sircar, it is possible that the later Śuṅgas shifted their capital to Vidiśā.[19]

Apart from its importance as a political and administrative centre at certain points of time, Vidiśā was also an important city on the trade routes of ancient India.[20] Both Ujjayinī and Vidiśā were important nodes on the trade routes that connected the towns of the northern and north-western part of the subcontinent with ports such as Bharukaccha and Suppāraka on the Western coast as also with cities of the Deccan and the far south.[21]

We also need to note the links between Aśoka and the city of Vidiśā. It is well-known that the *Dīpavaṁśa* and *Mahāvaṁśa* (5th/6th century AD) speak of Aśoka's romance with Devī, daughter of a merchant of Vidiśā. They also refer to Aśoka's son Mahinda visiting a place named Vedisagiri prior to his departure for Sri Lanka. These texts suggest that a monastic establishment existed in the vicinity of Vedisa at this time; there seems little reason to doubt that this is a reference to the monastic establishment at Sanchi. Later Buddhist tradition explicitly attributes the construction of the great *vihāra* near Vidiśā to Devī.[22] These stories give us a more specific explanation of why a *vihāra* complex came up at this particular place. Once it had been established, the fame of Sanchi as a Buddhist site and place of pilgrimage no doubt came to rest to a great extent on the eminence of the monks whose remains were enshrined in the caskets buried within the body of the *stūpa*s here. There seems to have been an early period of intense building activity at Sanchi between the 2nd century BC and 2nd century AD. With the one possible exception cited by M. Hamid, the monasteries and shrines that survive belong to a later period.

The ruins of the ancient city of Vidiśā are to be found at Besnagar, 3 km away from modern Vidisha city. An early account of excavations conducted at this site refers, among other things, to an irrigation canal, various brick structures identified as sacrificial pits, and a large number of coins found here.[23] Subsequent excavations at Besnagar revealed an archaeological sequence ranging from the mesolithic to the modern period, with some breaks in occupation.[24] M. D. Khare reports that the cutting at BSN-1 revealed six periods of habitation; that the site seems to have been deserted after Period V (ascribed to the Gupta period), and reoccupied (Period VI) after a gap of a few centuries. Period II (chalcolithic) seems to have come to an end due to a fire. The cutting at BSN-2 revealed a shorter five-phase archaeological sequence, with no evidence of post-Gupta remains. BSN-3, in the vicinity of the famous Heliodorus pillar, revealed the remains of a temple of about the 2nd century BC, and a long break in occupation thereafter; occupation was resumed in the 19th century and continued till recent times.[25] Two trial trenches at BSN-4, among other things, confirmed the occurrence of a massive fire which had already been suggested by the earlier excavations at BSN-1.[26] In the absence of horizontal excavation at this site, in view of the disparities in the sequences revealed at BSN 1–4 and the meagreness of the published details, it is difficult to reconstruct a coherent, detailed archaeological profile of the history of ancient Vidiśā.

The Sanchi Inscriptions

Over 800 donative inscriptions (often inaccurately described as 'votive' inscriptions) have been found at Sanchi. These inscriptions, which form the principal focus of this chapter, have been divided for the purposes of this investigation, into five broad chronological phases[27]:

1. the Aśokan inscription (3rd century BC)
2. inscriptions of the 2nd century BC to the 1st century BC/1st century AD[28]
3. inscriptions of the Kuṣāṇa period (2nd century AD)
4. inscriptions of the Gupta period (5th–6th century AD)
5. inscriptions of the early medieval period (6th–9th century AD)

The Aśokan Edict

The Aśokan edict at Sanchi is a variant of the schism edict, of which other versions are found on the Allahabad-Kosam and Sarnath pillars, the Sanchi version being closer to the Allahabad-Kosam version, the Sarnath version being a little longer and containing additional material.[29] The inscription (in the Prakrit language and the Brahmi script) is damaged in parts and refers to the *saṅgha* of monks and nuns having been united and Aśoka's decree that any monk or nun causing *saṅgha-bheda* (schism in the Order) would be made to put on white robes and to reside outside the *āvāsa* (monastery). The inscription concludes with Aśoka expressing his desire that the *saṅgha* endure long as a united body. It suggests the appearance of serious divisions within the Order in Aśoka's time, divisions which merited the king's intervention and his supplementing the punishment prescribed in the *Vinaya Piṭaka* for the serious offence of *saṅ gha-bheda.* The schism edict is evidence of Aśoka's position of authority vis-à-vis the *saṅgha.* The contents of this edict also suggest that the places where it has been found were important Buddhist monastic centres in Aśoka's time. Kausambi and Sarnath we know of from other sources; Sanchi we do not.

The Inscriptions of the 2nd Century BC to the 1st Century BC/1st Century AD

The second group of Sanchi inscriptions (in the Prakrit language and Brahmi script) are the largest in number (846) and form the main focus of this chapter.[30] Two of these are imprecatory, the rest are donative in nature. The inscriptions of this group include 206 that are fragmentary in varying degrees. While a few epigraphs (nos. 805, 741, 427) do not give any information about the donors, the majority of them do identify them in one or more ways.

The various bases of identification of the donors are: name, kinship relations, occupation, native place, ethnic stock (in the case of the few Yavana donors), as members of either the monastic order (*bhikkhu*s or *bhikkunī*s) or the laity (*upāsaka*s or *upāsikā*s).[31] It may be noted that references to *varṇa* or *jāti* do not occur. Of course, the basis of identification of donors must be considered within the context of the purpose of the inscriptions. For instance, *jāti* (caste) may have been an important basis of identification of an individual in the society of the time, but may not have been considered a detail that merited mention in the donative inscriptions. Then there is also the practical limitation placed on details by constraints of space. Or perhaps the briefest inscriptions are reflective of a not-so-lavish endowment. In spite of these factors, the details that donors chose to have engraved about themselves at Sanchi remain of interest and significance.

Donors, Named and Unnamed

In this second group of Sanchi inscriptions, thirty-six donors are unnamed. Out of the cases where the gender of these unnamed donors can be identified, four are individual males, 23 are individual females, and four are groups of female donors. The number of unnamed women is considerably greater than that of unnamed men. At the other end of the spectrum are inscriptions (117) that identify the donors by their name alone. These donors include 59 individual males, 51 individual females, five groups of males, and two groups of females.

Apart from these statistics, is there anything of significance that we can wrest out of the donors' names? Bühler and Majumdar have already made some observations about personal names in the Sanchi inscriptions. Bühler drew attention to the large number of Buddhist names (Araha, Arahaguta, Arahadāsī, Dhamarakhita, Budhapālita, Saṁgharakhita, etc.), which is an aspect that should be taken into consideration in discussions of Buddhist identity during this period. He also pointed to the large number of names derived from names of *nakṣatra*s (Asāḍa, Phaguna, Rohiṇī, Pusinī, etc.) and others (Bahadata, Mhiada, Mitā, etc.) derived from the name of Vedic gods. Names like Vinhukā, Upidata, Balaka, Nadiguta, Sivanadi give evidence of the existence of the worship of the gods Viṣṇu and Śiva while others (Nāgā, Nāgila, Nāgadatta) are suggestive of the prevalence of *nāga* worship.[32] N. G. Majumdar refers to names (Yakhadāsī, Yakhadina, Yakhī, Yakhila) which are indicative of the existence of Yakṣa cults, and names (Gandhāra, Kāmboja, Kekaṭeyaka, Cirātī, Patiṭhana) derived from geographical names.[33]

Gender and Patronage

While the total number of donations made by men, singly or in groups (367 + 13 = 380), is greater than those made by women, singly or in groups (336 + 8 = 344), the high degree of 'visibility' of women as donors is a striking aspect of the Sanchi inscriptions. This visibility is in remarkable contrast to the majority of ancient Indian inscriptions, where women appear rarely, shadowy figures who usually merited mention only if they happened to be queens or goddesses. Women appear in the Sanchi inscriptions in large numbers both as lay worshippers and as *bhikkhunī*s. They also appear in significant numbers compared to men among donors who made multiple donations to the *stūpa* complex in this period. It may also be mentioned that one of the gateway inscriptions (no. 391) records a gift made by a woman. This visibility raises certain questions ranging from the relationship of women to early Buddhism to women's control over economic resources. Against what sort of background can we view the epigraphic evidence? We can look at the references to women as donors in the textual tradition and also for reflections of the textual and inscriptional evidence in the depiction of women as donors in Sanchi sculpture. See Tables 1.1 and 1.2.

In the Pali canon, women appear most frequently as givers of food, clothes, and medicines. Certain women make more lavish gifts. Ambapālī gifts an *ārāma* (grove) to the *saṅgha.*[34] Visākhā, mother of Migāra, desires to build a *pāsāda* with a verandah, supported on pillars with capitals of elephants for the *saṅgha,* and the Buddha gives his permission for such gifts.[35] Elsewhere, Visākhā brings small jars, brooms, and earthenware foot-scrubbers to the Buddha. The first two items are accepted while the third is returned.[36]

Women appear in a variety of different situations in Sanchi sculpture, not only as ornamental figures, but in many cases as an important part of the narrative of the reliefs. There are the mandatory *yakṣī*s, *śālabhañjikā*s, celestial women, but there is more. There is the depiction of Māyā in scenes of the birth of the Buddha. There are what may be royal couples.[37] There are townswomen looking down with interest from buildings at a passing royal procession.[38] But we are here concerned with women as donors. In this context, we should note the sculptural depictions of the scenes of Sujātā's offering to the meditating Gotama.[39] But apart from this particular scene from the life of the Buddha, we see in the Sanchi sculptures countless images of women prostrating themselves or making offerings on trays or in containers before trees associated with the various Buddhas, *bodhi* trees, and *stūpa*s.[40] The classic representation of the *saṁbodhi* scene has a circle of males and females performing obeisance, the females bearing ewers. Some of the scenes have groups of men

Table 1.1
Gender break-up of donors (where identifiable)

Gender of Donors	*Number of Records*
Individual males	367
Individual females	336
More than one male	13
More than one female	8
Corporate groups that included men and women	4 (gifts made by *gāmas*)
Corporate groups that may have included men and women	5 (gifts made by *goṭhis*)
Kin groups that may have included men and women	10

Table 1.2
Gender break-up of givers of multiple donations

Gender	*Number of Records*
Men	28
Women	17
Kin groups (that may have included men and women)	1

and women, while others have women alone. Another interesting aspect is the possible depictions of the Sanchi donors themselves in the panels where couples appear, sometimes accompanied by children.[41]

The unequivocal evidence of the Sanchi inscriptions, supplemented by the more subtle evidence of the Sanchi sculpture, indicates that during the period between the 2nd century BC and the 2nd century AD a strong element of monetary support for the building activity at Sanchi came from women. This amounts to an endorsement of the frequent appearance of women donors in the early Buddhist textual tradition. On the other hand, with regard to the *volume* of female vis-à-vis male donations, in this case, the epigraphic evidence is indicative of a much *greater* degree of female participation than a reading of the Pali canon might lead us to expect.

Gender and Kinship

Kinship is a basis of identification in the case of 101 donors of this group of inscriptions, but does not feature in a majority of the inscriptions. Kinship relations are significantly much more often specified in the case of female (69 individuals and four groups) than male donors (17 individuals and six groups). The number of women for whom kinship is the sole basis of identification (28 individuals and four groups) is considerably higher than the number of men (six individuals and three groups) for whom this is so. It may be added that there are three inscriptions which record gifts made by groups including men *and* women in which the donors are identified solely on the basis of kinship.

Six inscriptions (nos. 387, 434, 435, 603, 626, 797) record gifts made by a *kula* (lineage group). One inscription (no. 102) records a gift made by all the *ñāti*s (the extended kin group) of a monk named Nāgila. To these references to gifts made by extended kin groups we may add the references to gifts made by the Dhamakas of Ujenī (no. 40), Tāpasiyas of Ujenī (no. 87; also mentioned in no. 285), Magalakaṭiyas of Kakaḍaka in Ujenī (no. 103), and the Vakiliyas of Ujenī (no. 115).[42] These may have been kin groups. It may be noted that all of these groups belonged to Ujenī. Another inscription (no. 264; fragmentary) refers to the gift of the Kācāniputas (Kātyāyanī-putras) from Vāghumata. This gives us a total of 11 inscriptions recording gifts made by extended kin groups. See Table 1.3.

It may be noted that six monks are identified in kinship terms, and for four of them, kinship is the only basis of identification. Two nuns are identified in kinship terms, both as mothers. It may also be noted that two inscriptions record gifts by relations of monks (one by a mother, the other by all the *ñāti*s of the monk concerned), while one records a gift made by a relative (mother) of a nun.

Women donors are most frequently identified as mothers (*mātā*)—much more often of sons rather than daughters—and next as wives (*pajāvatī, bhāyā, jāyā*).[43] A few are identified as sisters (*bhagini*), daughters-in-law (*husā, nusā, hnusā*), and daughters (*duhitā*) of their fathers more often than their mothers. One is identified as her uncle's niece (no. 565). For men, where kinship relations are specified, it is as fathers (*pitā*), sons (*putra*), brothers (*bhātā*), or as member of a kin group. Inscription no. 464 records the gift of one Varadata and his nephew (*bhāgineya*), apparently his sister's son. A lone male (inscription no. 30) is identified as a son-in-law. It may be noted that seven male donors are identified in terms of their relationship with their mother. This is indicated by the use of matronyms. Inscription no. 175 records the gift of the *rāja-lipikara* (royal scribe) Subāhita Gotiputa (son of Goti, i.e., Gauptī). Inscription no. 264, which is fragmentary, records the gift of the Kācāniputas (sons of Kācānī, i.e., Kātyāyanī) of Vāghumata. Inscription no. 290 records the gift of the monk [Go]tiputa Bhaṁḍuka. Inscription no. 307 records the gift of the monk Gotiputa Bhaḍuka (who seems to be the same donor as of no. 290). Inscription

Table 1.3
Gender and types of kinship identification

Kinship Relationship Specified	*Number of Records*
Father (of son)	2
Son (of father)	6
Son (of mother)	5
Brother	4
Mother (of son)	22
Mother (of daughter)	9
Mother, the sex of whose progeny is not clear	2
Daughter (of father)	3
Daughter (of mother)	1
Nephew	1
Niece	1
Wife	20
Daughter-in-law	4
Sister (of brother)	2
Son-in-law	1
Member of a kin group	13

no. 398 records the gift of Vāsiṭhiputra Anaṁda, *āvesani* (foreman of the artisans) of the rājan Sirī Sātakaṇi. Inscription no. 809 records the gift of the monk Vāchiputa (son of Vātsī) Isika, while no. 824 records the gift of Vāsiṭhiputa Kusumaka.

Certain inscriptions record joint gifts made by husbands and wives, fathers and sons, mothers and sons/daughters, sisters, brothers and sisters, etc. Donations by various members of a family or an entire kin group making a gift (mentioned earlier) fit in well with the impression given by the textual sources. In the Pali texts, the Buddha's convincing a particular person of the origins of *dukkha* (suffering) and the path to its extinction is frequently followed by his enjoying the hospitality of that person in his home and giving a discourse to members of his family. The impression conveyed is that once a person was convinced of Gotama's Truth, that conviction tended to become a family affair.[44]

Occupational Background of Donors

While the social background of the lay supporters of early Buddhism was diverse, the texts refer frequently to *gahapati*s and *seṭṭhi*s among the important *upāsaka*s. Going by Uma Chakravarti's analysis, the *gahapati* in the Buddhist canonical texts (which were composed roughly between the 5th and 1st centuries BC) indicates an individual of high social status and political influence associated particularly with landed property and wealth.[45] The term *seṭṭhi* indicates a wealthy urban-based, again politically influential, individual associated particularly with money-lending.[46] The *Cullavagga* credits a *seṭṭhi* of Rājagaha with the idea of building dwellings for the *saṅgha.*[47] The story of the benefactions made to the *saṅgha* by Anāthapiṇḍika, the *gahapati* of Sāvatthi, is well known.[48] The overlap between the two categories of *gahapati* and *seṭṭhi* is indicated by the use of the compound term *seṭṭhi-gahapati* for certain individuals. It was a *seṭṭhi-gahapati* who was the first person to become an *upāsaka* by the three-fold formula (seeking refuge in the Buddha, the *dhamma,* and the *saṅgha*). The first female lay disciples also came from the family of this *seṭṭhi-gahapati.*[49] Lay support for early Buddhism also came from the trader (*vaṇija*). Tapussa and Bhallika, two merchants travelling on the road from Ukkala (Utkala), were the first persons to become lay disciples of the Buddha by the formula of the dyad (taking refuge in the Buddha and the *dhamma*).[50] To what extent is this impression of strong support from the land-owning, banking, and trading classes corroborated by the inscriptional evidence from Sanchi? What was the occupational background of the Sanchi donors?

Occupation is specified in the case of 35 individual men (for 12 of whom it is the sole means of identification, other than name) and two groups of men (out of which one group is identified apart from their names, on this basis alone). Only one inscription refers to the occupation of a female donor. This is inscription no. 160, which describes the donor Sijhā of Virahakaṭa as a *ghariṇī* (housewife?).

On the whole, the occupation of donors is specified in comparatively few cases in the Sanchi inscriptions. The handful of references to donors with an artisanal background may be noted. The reference to a *rājuka* is also noteworthy. This term seems to have referred to an important category of rural officers, originally concerned with revenue administration. During the time of the Maurya king Aśoka, their powers were enlarged to include judicial duties as also the propagation of *dhamma.*[51]

As shown in Table 1.4, among the occupational groups, references to *seṭṭhi* donors (12) outnumber the others, followed by *vaṇija*s (six) and *gahapati*s (four). It may be added that two inscriptions record gifts made by relatives of *gahapati*s (in one case a sister-in-law, and in another a daughter-in-law), while six inscriptions record gifts made by relatives of *seṭṭhis* (two of mothers, three of wives, and one by a brother of a *seṭṭhi*). However, considering the total *volume* of inscriptions that belong to this group (846), the number of references to *seṭṭhi*s (12), *vaṇija*s (six), and

Table 1.4
Occupations of male donors (where specified)

Occupation of Donors	*Number of Records*
Gahapati	4
Seṭṭhi	12
Lekhaka (scribe)	4
Vaṇija (trader)	6
Kaṁmika/kamika (artisan)	2
Āvesani (foreman of artisans)	1
Daṁtakārehi (ivory workers)	1
Vaḍhaki (mason)	2
Pāvārika (cloak seller)	1
Sotika (weaver)	1
Rajuka	1

*gahapati*s (four) is rather small compared to the importance that is given to these groups in the textual tradition as lay supporters of the *saṅgha.*[52] It is a matter of concern that secondary literature on the subject has misrepresented the evidence on this important point. Thus, Romila Thapar's statements that the *seṭṭhi-gahapati* groups are the most frequently mentioned ones in the inscriptions at early Buddhist sites and that women donors tended to come from *seṭṭhi-gahapati* and artisanal families are simply not borne out by evidence of the Sanchi inscriptions.[53] Similarly unsubstantiated is Vidya Dehejia's claim that the largest single group of lay donations at Sanchi came from the *gahapati* and the *ghariṇī*.[54]

Monks and Nuns as Donors

The donors of this group of inscriptions include 252 records of gifts made by members of the *saṅgha.* These donors comprise 123 individual monks, six groups of monks, 118 individual nuns, and five groups of nuns. Monks and nuns can be identified in the inscriptions in various ways. In most cases, they are explicitly described as *bhikkhu*s or *bhikkhunī*s. In some cases, they can be identified as monks by honorific epithets or titles—*aya, bhādata, thera.* Others can be identified by reference to their being pupils—*atevāsin,*[55] *atevasini, sejha* (no. 633), *sādhivihārin* (no. 338),[56] or novices—*sāmanera, sāmanerī*. Apart from such frequently occurring terms, a few others are of interest. For instance, two inscriptions (nos. 529, 691) refer to the donors as *bhāṇaka*s (preachers, reciters of texts). Another inscription (no. 288) refers to the donor Bharaḍiya as a *sapurisa* (sat-puruṣa, good man, saint).[57] There is an inscription (no. 631) which records the gift of Budharakhiṭa, the *sutātika* (versed in the *suttantas*) from Arapāna. Budharakhita's female counterpart is Avasinā from Maḍalāchikata, who is described (no. 304) as a *sutātikini.* Two inscriptions (nos. 399, 402) record the gift of Balamitra, pupil of Aya Cuḍa, the *dhamakathika* (preacher of the *dhamma*). An important reference occurs in inscription no. 242, which describes the donor as a *pacanekayika.* Bühler points out that this is a mis-spelt form of *pācanekāyika* or *pañcanekāyika* meaning 'one who knows the five Nikāyas', indicating that the five Nikāyas of the *Sutta Piṭaka* were in existence at this time.[58]

One inscription (no. 113) records the gift of a male ascetic (*tāpasa*). It may be noted that 18 inscriptions record gifts made by monks identified as students of a particular teacher. Six inscriptions record gifts made by nuns who are identified as pupils of a particular teacher. A fragmentary inscription (no. 645) seems to record a gift made by two students of a teacher named Koramikā. Koramikā was also the teacher of Sagharakhitā, donor of inscription no. 85. One record (no. 242) talks of a gift made jointly by a male teacher along with his student. It may be noted that teachers and their students belonged to the same sex. The only possible exception is inscription no. 704, where the female pupil Ava[m]u is described as the pupil of Aya Paḍaniya. Apart from the consideration of grammatical construction, this does seem to be a male teacher, because of his epithet *aya.* Unlike their male counterparts, none of the female teachers mentioned in the Sanchi inscriptions are given any honorific titles or epithets. Another point that emerges is that there are a number of gifts made by pupils of the same teacher. To the example of Koramikā cited above we may add the names of certain monks—Bhaṁḍuka/Bhaduka, Bhaḍika, Cuḍa—who are mentioned in more than one place as teachers of donors.[59]

The large number of donations (29.79 per cent of the total number of recorded gifts of this period) at Sanchi by members of the *saṅgha* has been noted by scholars. Monks (15.24 per cent of the total number of gifts) and nuns (14.54 per cent of the total number of gifts) appear in almost equal strength as donors. Another point that may be noted is that monks and nuns sometimes appear at Sanchi as donors of multiple gifts.[60] How could monks and nuns appear in such large numbers as donors at Sanchi? Bühler suggested that monks and nuns obtained the resources to make gifts at sites such as Sanchi through begging.[61] According to Marshall, gifts made by members of the Order are not surprising. There was the possibility of monks and nuns going back to their worldly, social existence and resuming control over their erstwhile property. There is also the possibility of their having made gifts to the *saṅgha* without breaking the prohibition against the actual handling of money. While Buddhist texts do refer to individuals leaving the *saṅgha* and returning to the world, a gift made by such an individual on his or her return to the world would scarcely qualify as a gift made by a *bhikkhu* or a *bhikkhunī*—which is what we are interested in.

In the *Vinaya Piṭaka,* the receipt, storing, or handling even through an intermediary, of gold and silver, as also buying and selling, are Pācitteya offences (i.e., those requiring repentence).[62] The ten precepts for novices include a prohibition against accepting gold or silver.[63] The *Mahāvagga* refers to *upāsaka*s investing gold with a *kappiya-kāraka* in order to provide for the needs of the *bhikkhus*. The Buddha here says that he allows the *bhikkhu*s to accept what is allowable. 'But I do not say by that, O Bhikkhus, that you may, on any pretext whatsoever, accept or seek for gold.'[64]

Extreme frugality of possessions was enjoined on the members of the Order. Nevertheless, they did not sever all links with their erstwhile property as is suggested by the reference in the *Cullavagga* to much property in brass, wood, and earthenware coming into the possession of the *saṅgha* when Kassapa of Uruvela went forth from the world (i.e., joined the *saṅgha*).[65] The *Mahāvagga* also makes provisions for any large amount of property belonging to a deceased *bhikkhu* to be transferred to the *saṅgha* of the four directions.[66]

Marshall points out that in spite of the strict injunctions against handling money, ancient Buddhist monasteries have often yielded coins, sometimes large quantities—under monastic cells and in other hiding places.[67] More specific and unequivocal is M. Hamid's account of the 1936 excavation of the *vihāra* lying to the east of Stūpa 2 at Sanchi:

> After digging about a foot deep, 8 Western Kshatrapa silver coins, ancient copper coins of different periods, a strainer of light green jade (minus the handle) with 8 holes in the middle, an uncut sapphire and several interesting iron objects among which an iron trident (one arm lost) were found in a cell. From the other cells were recovered a gold medallion embossed with the head of a Greek king, but with no inscription, one roughly cut squareshaped [*sic*] diamond with a hole in the middle, two fairly big, oval-shaped carnelian balls or beads, several beads of agate, cat's eye and other semi-precious stones, fragments of emerald and ruby, fragments of bangles of ivory and crystal, copper and brass finger and toe rings, ankle and toe ornaments, and other interesting antiquities.[68]

Thus, whatever hints the textual tradition gives regarding the economic resources of members of the *saṅgha*, the evidence from excavations at Sanchi and the epigraphic evidence of monks and nuns making a large number of gifts at this site from the 2nd century BC onwards is unambiguous in this regard.

The Three Yavana Donors

Yavanas occur as donors in three Sanchi inscriptions: The reading of inscription no. 89 is not absolutely certain. It seems to read: '[Sv]etapathasa (Yona?)sa dānaṁ' ('The gift of Yona? of Svetapatha'). Inscription no. 433 (engraved on two adjacent pavement slabs), reads: 'Cudayo[vana]kasa bo silayo' ('Two slabs of Cuda, the Yovanaka'). Inscription no. 475 reads: 'Setapathiyasa Yonasa dānaṁ' ('The gift of Yona of Setapatha').

The term Yavana may originally have referred to Greeks, but very soon was being used in a more general way to refer to foreigners from various parts of West Asia or the eastern Mediterranean region.[69] Svetapatha and Setapatha sound like the same place. The Purāṇas refer to the Śveta mountain range lying to the north of Meru mountain.[70] They also mention Śvetadvīpa as a place associated with Viṣṇu and visited by Nārada.[71] This place appears in the *Śānti Parva* of the *Mahābhārata* as well, as an island lying to the north of Meru mountain, at the northern border of the ocean of milk, where Mahāviṣṇu performed austerities in order to obtain *brahma-vidyā*. The text adds that the people of Śvetadvīpa are worshippers of Śiva and are rich in knowledge. They have certain peculiar physical traits—they do not have sense-organs, do not have to eat food in order to live; their bodies and bones are very hard, their heads very broad and flat; they have four arms and sixty teeth, and have very loud voices.[72] This Śvetadvīpa of the great epic and the Purāṇas seems to be a mythological place, and is of little help in identifying the place where our Sanchi Yavanas came from. One is tempted to suggest an identification of Śvetapatha with the Śvetapāda of the Kalyan plates of Yasovarman;[73] a place which corresponds with the area around Nasik, and where one could visualise Yavanas visiting or residing in this period for trade purposes. But the inscription in question is very late (11th century), and the time-gap between the Sanchi references and this inscription is too great for the identification to be pressed.

Gifts Made by Goṭhis

Inscriptions no. 96, 97 and 98 record the gifts of crossbars by the Bodhagoṭhi of the inhabitants of Dhamavaḍhana. No. 178 records the gift of the *goṭhi* of the Barulamisas of Vedisa. No. 793 records the gift of two pillars by the *goṭhi* of the Barāyasikhas of Aboda (Arbuda). According to Bühler, a *goṭhi* or a *goṣṭhi* is 'a committee of trustees in charge of a temple or a charitable foundation'.[74] That such *goṭhis* existed in this period is of significance. What the terms Barulamisas and Barāyasikhas refer to, we do not know.

Native Place

Native place is specified in 366 records of this group, making it the single most often specified detail of the donors at Sanchi (apart from personal names).[75] In the case of individual male donors, native place is specified in 157 instances (in 101 of which it is the only basis of identification apart from name), and in the case of groups of male donors in six instances (out of which in three it is the sole basis of identification apart from name). In the case of female donors, it is specified for 178 individual donors (the sole detail apart from name for 58) and eight groups (out of which it is the sole basis of identification for one). There are two records where the native place of groups of joint male and female donors is specified, in one case being the only detail specified, apart from the name of the donors. Mention should also be made of 16 inscriptions which record the native place of groups which could have had a mixed gender composition—five *goṭhi*s and 11 kin groups. For the latter, native place is the only supplementary detail mentioned in two inscriptions.

For women donors, kinship is more often specified than native place, while the reverse is true for male donors. On the other hand, place specification for nuns (74 records, out of which in 71 cases it is the only basis of identification apart from name) is much more frequent than in the case of monks (34 records, out of which in 27 it is the sole basis of identification apart from name). Three *gahapati*s, ten *seṭṭhi*s and three *vaṇija*s are among the members of occupational groups whose native place is specified. Two inscriptions record the native place of *upāsaka*s (out of which this is the only basis of identification apart from name in one) and ten that of *upāsikā*s (in all cases the only basis of identification).

We may note the relatively high incidence of specification of native place in the case of *seṭṭhi*s, *gahapati*s, and *vaṇija*s. The native places of ten of a total number of 12 *seṭṭhi* donors, three out of a total number of four *gahapati* donors, and three out of the total number of six *vaṇ ija* donors is specified. This coincides with the very frequent association in the Pali texts of *seṭṭhi*s and *seṭṭhi-gahapati*s with particular places, and the occasional occurrence of place specification even in the absence of the specification of the name of the person concerned.[76]

The total number of places that monks came from is 23, while the total number of places nuns came from is 15 (Tables 1.5 and 1.6). Can this be read as suggestive of a wider circuit of monk participation in the Sanchi establishment or of a greater degree of spatial mobility of monks vis-à-vis nuns? The evidence is not conclusive unless the places mentioned can be identified. What does seem clear is that the monks come from a variety of places, out of which no particular place or places stand out. The situation is different in the case of the nuns: a large number of nuns came from the following places—Nadinagara, Kurara, and Ujenī. Also significant is the fact that there are records of collective gifts made by the nuns of a particular place: Vāḍivahana (no. 22), Maḍalāchikaḍa (no. 341), and Ujenī (no. 780). These references suggest the existence of *bhikkhunī-saṅgha*s at these places.[77] Interestingly, corporate gifts of this kind do not occur among monk donors.

Equally noteworthy are collective gifts made by the laity of a particular place—the gift of the *upāsaka*s of Kaṁṭakañuya (no. 776) and those of the *upāsikā*s of Ejāvatī (no. v) and Navagāma (no. 70). Such instances do not occur very frequently in the epigraphic record of India. While it is possible that males and females were encompassed in the first inscription cited (no. 776), the latter two cases clearly indicate an interesting phenomenon of collective gifts made along gender lines. The two instances of gifts by the *upāsikā*s of a particular place can be correlated with the instances of gifts made collectively by the nuns of particular places referred to earlier.

Certain inscriptions of this group record gifts made by another sort of corporate entity—the village. There are records of gifts made by the following villages: Vejaja (no. 308), Asavatī (no. 345), Morajābhikaṭa in Ujenī āhāra (no. 359), Pāḍukulikā (no. 635), Cuḍamoragiri (no. 642).[78] Inscription no. 393 (a gateway inscription) possibly records a gift of the people of Vidiśā, but the reading is not certain. Bühler points out that though these records do not prove the Buddhist affiliations of all the inhabitants of these places, they do indicate that the most influential persons in that place owed allegiance to the Bauddha *dhamma,* and that Buddhism had in this period a hold among the agriculturists of the Malwa region.[79] See Table 1.7.

Identification of Place Names

The maximum number of donors whose native places are specified came from Koraghara/Kuraghara/Korara/Kurara (68). N. G. Majumdar points out that this place is mentioned in the Jātakas, and that it can be identified with the Kuraghara which is mentioned in the *Vinaya Piṭaka*

Table 1.5
Places where monks and nuns came from

	Number of Records	
Places	*Monks*	*Nuns*
Achavaṭa	1	–
Anaṁmita	2	–
Arapāna	1	–
Āṭhakanagara	1	–
Cahaṭha	1	–
Ejāvata	2	–
Goṇada	2	–
Kacupatha	1	1
Kāpāsī	–	2
Kaṭakañuya/Kaṁṭakañuya	1	–
Koraghara/Kuraghara	3	5
Korara/Kurara	1	15
Koḍijila	1	–
Maḍalāchikaṭa/ Maḍalāchikaḍa	–	5; + 1 gift made collectively by all the nuns of this place
Madhuvana	1	3
Morajāhikaṭa	1	–
Nadinagara/Naṁdinagara	2	17
Pāḍāna	–	2
Pemuta	–	1
Perikupa	1	–
Pokhara	3	–
Sasāda/Sāsāda	2	–
Tubavana	–	1
Ujenī	2	7; + 1 gift made collectively by all the nuns of this place
Vaḍivahana/Vāḍivahana	1	3; + 1 gift made collectively by all the nuns of this place
Vālīvahana	–	1
Vāghumata	–	1
Vedisa	–	8
Veja	1	–
Yugapaja (place-name?)	1	–

Table 1.6
Native place of various occupational groups

Places	*Number of Records*
Gahapatis:	
Tubavana	3
Seṭṭhis:	
Abā	2
Achāvaḍa	1
Seṭṭhi at Achāvaḍa from Kurara	2
Kaṁdaḍigāma	1
Koraghara	2
Paḍukulikā	1
Rohaṇipada	1
Vaṇijas:	
Asvavati	1
Ujenī	1
Verohakaṭa	1

as being situated in Avanti (western Malwa) and as a place where *thera* Mahākaccāna resided for some time.[80] Its exact position is not known. Bühler suggests a possible identification with Kurawar (23° 38′ N.; 77° 5′ E.).[81] Next in the frequency of references comes Ujenī (59 references), which appears in the Sanchi inscriptions as the name of a place and also that of an *āhāra* (an administrative unit). Navagāma (eight references) and Morajābhikaṭa (six references) are described as being situated in Ujenī āhāra (inscriptions nos., 165, 359). Ujenī is modern Ujjain. Nadinagara/Naṁdinagara occurs in 32 inscriptions. Bühler identified it with Nandner near Tonk (23° 4′ N.; 76° 6′ E.), though he had an important word of caution as regards the identification of this and other such common-place place names.[82] Vedisa (16 references) is modern Besnagar, outside modern Vidisha city. Tubavana (seven references), from literary and epigraphic references, appears to have been located in the vicinity of Eran, Sagar district. Erakinā (one reference) can be identified with modern Eran.[83]

Ancient Māhiśmatī has been identified by some with Maheshwar (22° 11′ N., 75° 36′ E.) on the northern bank of the Narmada, at the junction of the Narbada and the Maheshvari rivers, about 50 miles south of Indore.[84] Other scholars have identified it with Oṁkār Māndhātā (22° 14′ N., 76° E.), an island in the Narmada, situated about 38 miles

Table 1.7
Number of references to various place names

Aboda 1	Koḍijila 1	Puruviḍa 1
Abā 2	Koraghara/Kuraghara/	Rohaṇi/Rohāṇipada 4
Achāvaṭa/Achāvaḍa 7	Kosaghara 1	Sagarī 1
Adhapura 1	Kothukapada 2	Sānukagāma 1
Ājanāva 2	Kuthupada 1	Sāsāda 2
Amata? 1	Maḍalāchikaṭa 8	Sedakaḍa/Sidakaḍa 5
Anaṁmita 2	Madhuvana 6	Setapatha 1
Arapāna/Arapana 7	Mahāmoragiri 1	Sonada 1
Asvavatī/Asāvatī 2	Mahisatī 10	Subhagapatha 1
Āṭhakanagara 1	Morajāhikaṭa/kaḍa/	Svetapatha 1
Avāḍhī 1	Morajābhikaṭa/	Tākārāpada/
Bedakaḍa 2	Morayahikaṭa	Tākāripāda/Tākāripada 4
Bhadanakaṭa/kaḍa 2	(in Ujjenī āhāra) 6	Taṁbalamaḍa 1
Bhogavaḍhana 6	Nadinagara 28	Tiriḍapada 2
Cahaṭa 1	Naṁdinagara 4	Tubavana 7
Cuḍa-Moragiri 3	Navagama/gāma 8	Udubharaghara 5
Dakhiṇāji 1	Osena 2	Ugirā 1
Dhamavaḍhana 3	Pāḍāna 2	Ujenī 59
Ejāvata/vatī 7	Pāḍukulikā 2	Vaḍivahana/Vāḷivahana/
Erakinā 1	Paripana 1	Vāḍivahani 6
Goṇada 2	Pāthūpakasa 1	Vāghumata 2
Ijavatī/Ijāvatī 1	Patiṭhāna 1	Vedisa 16
Kacupatha 2	Peḍita? 1	Veja/Vejaja 2
Kakaḍaka?	Pemata/Pemuta? 3	Vepa 1
(nagara? in Ujenī) 1	Perikupa 1	Verohakaṭa 1
Kaṁdaḍigāma 5	Phujakapada 1	Virahakaṭa 1
Kapāsi/Kaspasi/Kāpāsī/	Poḍavida 3	Vitirinahā/Vitiriñahā 2
Kāpāsigāma 13	Pokhara 11	Yugapaja (?) 1
Kaṭkañuya/	Pulapha 1	
Kaṁṭakañuya 8	Puñyavaḍhana 1	

away from Maheshwar. Cunningham suggested that it should be identified with Mandla, situated on the right bank of the Narmada. Sankalia, Subbarao, and Deo, give sound reasons to support the identification of Māhiśmatī with Maheshwar.[85]

Bühler suggests, very tentatively, the identification of Kāpāsigāma (13 references) with Kapasi (23° 28′ N.; 77° 54′ E.), Sonada (one reference) with Sonari near Sanchi, and Pāḍāna (two references) with Pāḍāna (23° 36′ N.; 76° 38′ E.).[86]

According to N. G. Majumdar, the place names in the Sanchi inscriptions suggest that it was the people of Malwa that played a major role in financing the adjuncts to the *stūpas*.[87] He suggests that although most of the place names referred to in the inscriptions remain unidentified, it is likely that many of them were situated in Malwa or adjoining areas.

N. G. Majumdar also points out the occurrence in the Sanchi inscriptions of the places mentioned in the *Suttanipāta* in connection with the route followed by the pupils of Bāvarin from the banks of the Godāvarī in Aśmaka country to Vesālī in Magadha—Patiṭṭhāna, Mahissati, Ujenī, Gonaddha, Vedisā, and Vanasahvaya or Tumbavana. Patiṭṭhāna is modern Paithan in Aurangabad district. Gonaddha can be identified with the Goṇada of the Sanchi inscriptions (two references), and the *Suttanipāta* describes this place as being situated between Ujenī and Vedisā (a similar location of this place is suggested in the *Mahāmāyūrī*).[88]

References to Places Outside Central India

There are a few places mentioned in this group of Sanchi inscriptions that can be identified as situated outside central India. Aboda (one reference) may be Mount Abu (Arbuda) in the old Sirohi State of Rajasthan.[89] Pokhara (11 references) is Pushkara near Ajmer.

Bhogavadhana (six references) can be identified with modern Bhokardan, headquarters of a taluk in the Aurangabad district of Maharashtra. It was an important place on the trade route from Ujjayinī to Pratiṣṭhāna. Excavations at this site have revealed that the settlement was rather insignificant before the 3rd/2nd century BC (Period Ia). During Period Ib (1st century BC—2nd/3rd century AD), the Sātavāhana-Kṣatrapa period, it became a flourishing place. Coins of the Kṣaharātas and the Sātavāhanas occur in Period Ib as do abundant black and red ware, red polished ware, amphorae, sealings, bullae, rotary querns, and beads. Buddhist remains have been found in plenty at this site.[90] As for the evidence of its Buddhist affiliations, apart from the fact that donors from Bhogavardhana appear in several inscriptions at Sanchi and Bharhut, reference may be made to the Buddhist symbols on amulets and pottery found at Bhokardan.[91] This was a period of the most intensive structural activity at the site. In this period (Ib), the site also seems to have become a centre of bead, shell and ivory working. Decline set in during the post-Sātavāhana period (from the 3rd century onwards), though the site continued to be inhabited till the early medieval period.

'Dakhinājiya', which occurs as an adjective describing a donor in one inscription (no. 467) may perhaps be equated with Avanti-Dakṣiṇāpatha, the southern division of the Avanti country mentioned in the *Vinaya*.[92] On the other hand, perhaps it just indicates a place situated somewhere in southern India.

The occurrence of Takārī (four references) among the place names is interesting. Ṭakārī (Tarkārī, Tarkārikā, Tarkāra, Ṭakkāikā, etc.) occurs in inscriptions from various parts of the country, especially in the early medieval period, as the native place of learned Brāhmaṇa recipients of royal land grants. There is some amount of confusion and disagreement about its location; some scholars place it around the border of Gonda and Bahraich districts of U.P., while others locate it in the Bogra district of north Bengal. As pointed out by D. C. Sircar, the reason for the confusion seems to be that Brāhmaṇa migrants from the U.P. area sometimes named their new settlements in Bengal after their native villages.[93]

Connected with the problem of identification of the place names is the problem of determining the nature of the settlements. While in some cases literary and/or archaeological evidence gives information on the latter score, in most cases, we just do not know whether the place being referred to was an urban or rural settlement. Can the suffixes of place names help us out? The suffixes that occur in the Sanchi inscriptions are: *vaṭa/vaḍa, pura, nagara, kaṭa/kaḍa, giri, vaḍhanapatha, pada, vana, maḍa, ghara.* Do they help us place these names within a regional context? Do they indicate the urban/rural nature of the settlement? It seems that the answers to these questions is, unfortunately, no. On their own, suffixes such as *gāma* do not necessarily indicate a rural settlement; one can visualise an expanding settlement coming to outgrow this suffix without its name being changed. In the absence of corroborative literary and/or archaeological evidence, one would hesitate to make statements about the nature of the settlements mentioned in the inscriptions on the basis of the place names alone. It may be added that most of the suffixes seem to be too generally prevalent to be placed within any specific regional context.

Court Connections

Kings appear often in the Pali texts as soliciting instruction from Gotama and as givers of gifts to the *saṅgha.* Some, like Bimbisāra, are credited with having intervened and raised points which were incorporated by the Buddha as part of the rules for the Order. The Buddha's diplomatic attitude towards royalty is reflected in his response to Bhikkhus who conveyed to him *seniya* Bimbisāra's wish that the *vassa* period be postponed to the next full-moon day. 'I prescribe, O Bhikkhus, that you obey kings.'[94]

What do the early inscriptions and monuments at Sanchi suggest regarding royal involvement? While royal involvement marked the beginnings of the history of the Sanchi establishment (Aśoka), there is little evidence of the royal hand in building activity of the subsequent period. As for royal donors, we may mention rāño Suhaḍadata of Kosaghara (no. 825), who we do not know from other sources; and Vākalā devī, mother of Ahimita, who may have been a queen (no. 364).[95] It may also be noted that only four donors in this group of inscriptions had some sort of connection with royal courts. Subāhita, son of Gotī, was a royal scribe (rājalipikara) (no. 175); Ānaṁda, son of Vāsiṭhī, was foreman of the artisans (āvesanin) of (Sātavāhana) king Siri-Sātakaṇi (no. 398).[96]

Multiple Gifts

As for the background of the makers of multiple gifts at Sanchi, in the case of female donors, reference may be made to inscriptions no. 171(?), 172, and 175, which record the benefactions of the wife of a royal scribe and some sets of inscriptions which record multiple gifts made by nuns (nos. 304, 305; 560, 561). Male donors of multiple gifts include a cloak seller (nos. 615 and 617), a *lekhaka* (nos. 46, 47, 48), monks (nos. 54, 55; 147–149; 182, 221; 291–293; 399, 402; 572, 573; 615, 617), a *baudha-goṭhi* (nos. 96–98), the *goṭhi* of the Barulamisas of Vedisa (no. 178, 179?), a *vaṇija* (nos. 200–202), a *seṭṭhi* (nos. 211–212), and a *kula* (nos. 603–626).

Donors of the Gateway Inscriptions (nos. 389–404)

The above discussion includes data from the 16 gateway inscriptions of Sanchi, yet there seems to be good reason to look at them more closely, separately. Surely, one may not be wrong in assuming that the endowments of sections of the richly sculpted gateways would have involved greater expense and prestige than the others?

It may be noted in Table 1.8 that in this group of gateway inscriptions, there is only one female donor, the rest being males, except for the possibility that the donors of no. 393 may have included both men and women. The gateway donations include three gifts by monks (the same monk being the donor of nos. 399 and 403). If the reading of no. 393 can be accepted as referring to a gift made by the people of Vedisa, this is of considerable interest. Inscription no. 399 suggests the existence of some sort of corporate functioning/organisation among artisans and no. 400 indicates that the dexterity of the ivory workers who executed the carving of the panel in question extended to stone carving as well. Artisans, thus, make an appearance as donors in two of these gateway inscriptions. The appearance of a *seṭṭhi* among the gateway donors is of significance. It may be noted that

Table 1.8
Donors of the gateway inscriptions

Inscription No.	*Donor*
389 (North Gateway)	?; fragmentary, imprecatory inscription
390 (North Gateway)	Dhamagiri, a monk
391 (North Gateway)	Balamitā
392 (North Gateway)	Asamita
393 (North Gateway)	the Vedisikas (?) (reading not certain)
394 (North Gateway)	?; fragmentary inscription
395 (East Gateway)	Jiva
396 (East Gateway)	?; imprecatory inscription
397 (East Gateway)	Nāgapiya of Kurara, a/the seṭṭhi at Achāvaḍa[97]
398 (South Gateway)	Ānaṁda, son of Vāsiṭhī, foreman of the artisans of rāño Siri-Sātakaṇi
399 (South Gateway)	Balamitra, a pupil of Aya-Cuḍa, the dhamakathika
400 (South Gateway)	the ivory-workers of Vedisa (they did the carving)
401 (South Gateway)	?; fragmentary inscription
402 (West Gateway)	Balamitra, pupil of Aya-Cuḍa, the dhamakathika
403 (West Gateway)	Nāgapiya of Kurara, a/the seṭṭhi at Achāvaḍa, and his son Sagha
404 (West Gateway)	?; imprecatory inscription

none of the gateway inscriptions include a royal donation, and only one refers to a donor who had something to do with a royal court.

Inscriptions of the Kuṣāna Period, 2nd Century AD

The beginnings of the worship of the image of the Buddha and the *bodhisattvas* is well-documented at Sanchi from the evidence pertaining to the post-1st century AD period. Several of these inscriptions are inscribed on images. What is striking, however, is the very few number of inscriptions belonging to this and later chronological groups. Only three inscriptions seem to belong to the Kuṣāṇa period.

Inscription no. 828 is inscribed on the pedestal of a *bodhisattva* image and belongs to the reign of *rājātirāja devaputra śāhi* Vāsaṣka. It records the setting up of an image of the Bhagavat in the Dharmadeva-vihāra by Maḍhurikā, daughter of Vera. The regnal year mentioned in the inscription has been variously read as 78, 68, and 28. The last date is the most acceptable one and Vāsaṣka of the Sanchi inscription can be identified with the Kuṣāṇa king Vāsiṣka, a co-ruler and subsequently successor of Kaṇiṣka I.[98]

Inscription no. 829 is inscribed on an image of the Buddha. It speaks of the setting up of an image of the Śākyamuni during year 22 of the reign of a king whose name has been read as Vasṇuṣāṇa by Chanda and Vaskuṣāṇa by N. G. Majumdar. The donor was a woman named Vidyāmati, who is described as having made the gift for the welfare and happiness of her parents and all creatures (the complete sense cannot be restored because the inscription is fragmentary). The Vaskuṣāṇa of this inscription can be identified with the Kuṣāṇa king Vāsiṣka.[99]

The third inscription belonging to the Kuṣāṇa period is no. 830. This is inscribed on an image of the *bodhisattva* Maitreya. Some of the letters are lost, but what can be made out is that the donor was a woman, described as a *kuṭubinī,* that is, the wife of a householder. The woman's name is lost (as is that of her husband), but she is described as the daughter of a person named Viṣakula. The object of the gift is the welfare and happiness of all beings.

Two of these three inscriptions refer to the regnal year of a king, but nothing in the inscriptions suggests that the donors had any royal connection. All three are inscribed on images of the Buddha or a *bodhisattva,* indicating the beginnings and prevalence of the worship of such images in this period. The donors in all three cases are women, in the first case identified by means of her paternal parentage, and in the third case as a daughter and wife. It may be noted that while significant information about inscription no. 829 may be lost because of the fragmentary nature of the inscription, there is a reference to the donor's parents at the end of the inscription.

Inscriptions of the Gupta Period, 4th–6th Centuries AD

Eight Sanchi inscriptions belong to the Gupta period.[100] The details are given in Table 1.9.

Of these eight inscriptions, the details of three merit special attention. Inscription no. 833 is an 11-line prose epigraph inscribed on the outer side of the East Gateway of Stūpa 1. The inscription is damaged in places and there are disagreements among scholars regarding its reading and interpretation. It is dated in year 93 of the Gupta era (i.e., AD 412–413) and belongs to the reign of *mahārājādhirāja* Candragupta, referred to in line 7 of the inscription as Devarāja. The text begins with a salutation to and eulogy of the *saṅgha* of the *mahāvihāra* of Kākanādaboṭa. It goes on to introduce Āmrakārddava, son of Undāna, a subordinate, and from his description apparently a military commander of *mahārājādhirāja* Candragupta (II). The donor came from a place in the Sukuli country, the

Table 1.9
Donors of the inscriptions of the Gupta period

Inscription No.	*Donor*	*Nature of Gift*
832 (fragmentary)	a person belonging to the Śūra kula	Image
833	Āmrakārddava, son of Undāna, a subordinate of Candragupta II; Candragupta II himself	purchased land or whole village and an investment of 25 dīnāras
834	Harisvāminī, wife of upāsaka Sanasiddha	an investment of 16 dīnāras
835	Rudras(iṁha?), son of the vihāra-svāmī gośura Siṁhabala	pillars, a pavillion attached to a monastery, a gateway
836 (very damaged)	?	?
837	the venerable [R]ekh-agupta (monk)	an image
838 (very damaged)	?	?
840	śrī Kulāditya	a Buddha image

location of which has not been identified. The inscription records the gift of: (*a*) a piece of land, perhaps a village, named Iśvaravāsaka, and (*b*) 25 *dīnāras*. The gift was made in perpetuity.[101] Half of the endowment (this seems to refer to the income from the land) was to support in perpetuity the feeding of five monks and the maintenance of a lamp in the *ratnagṛha* (literally 'Jewel House', apparently referring to a shrine), on behalf of the *mahārājādhirāja* Candragupta. The other half of the income (this seems to refer to the interest on the monetary endowment) was to support the perpetual feeding of five monks and the maintenance of a lamp in the *ratnagṛ ha* on behalf of Āmrakārddava himself. Certain parts of this inscription have been read and interpreted in different ways. Line 6 of the inscription contains the phrase 'pañca-maṇḍalyā praṇipatya'. Fleet amended 'maṇḍalyā' to 'maṇḍalyā[m*]' and saw in this section of the inscription a reference to Āmrakārddava as having prostrated himself before the village *pancāyat* before making the gift.[102] N. G. Majumdar retains 'pañca-maṇḍalyā praṇipatya', translates it as 'having prostrated himself together with the group of five', adding in a note that he is not clear about the purport of this phrase.[103] According to Bhandarkar and Gai, Fleet's amended reading and interpretation of this line make little sense because if the *pañca-maṇḍalī* was indeed a village body, one would expect this word to appear in the accusative and not the locative case. They suggest that the phrase in question refers to Āmrakārddava prostrating himself (prior to making the gift) so that his forehead, elbows, waist, knees, and feet rested on the ground.[104] The second disagreement concerns the interpretation of lines 5 and 6. According to N. G. Majumdar, these lines indicate that the land in question was bought from members of the royal household or family (*rājakula*) named Maja, Śarabhaṅga, and Āmrarāta.[105] Fleet thought likewise. On the other hand, according to Chhabra and Gai, *rājakula* here means palace and Maja, Śarabhaṅga, and Ārarāta are the names of palaces occupied by Candragupta II during his sojourn in Vidiśā in the course of his military expeditions. According to this interpretation, Īśvaravāsaka was bought from the proceeds of the sale of these palaces.[106] D. C. Sircar accepts the standard meaning of *rājakula* as member of a royal family, but adds that it seems as though one half of the money and the price of the *vāsaka* (which he tentatively translates as 'house-site') was paid by Āmrakārddava and the other by his friends.[107]

What is to be made of these controversies? The interpretation of 'pañca-maṇḍalī' as referring to a *pancāyat*-type village body consisting of five individuals seems more plausible than the other suggestions and the reference to Āmrakārddava prostrating himself before or saluting this body before making this gift fits in well with the details of several other land grant inscriptions of the Gupta period which mention the role played by local-level administrative functionaries or departments in the land transactions leading to the making of the endowment. Likewise, the reference to the land being bought—either from or by certain members of a royal family—prior to being gifted is also in tune with several land grant charters of this period. Thirdly, it may be noted that this inscription perhaps associates the emperor Candragupta with the grant of land and Āmrakārddava with the monetary gift, though this is far from certain. Whether Candragupta displayed some direct initiative in making this gift or whether this inscription merely reflects the devotion of Āmrakārddava to his master and his desire that the latter share in the religious merit that would accrue from this pious gift—who can say? But it should be noted that this is the only known record of a grant of land made in favour of the Sanchi establishment. Chhabra and Gai suggest that as the income from the land and interest on the money were to support identical activities, the value of the two gifts must have been the same.[108]

The details of inscription no. 834 also should be noted. This is inscribed on the outer face of a cross-bar on the south side of the East Gateway. It is dated in year 131 of the Gupta era (i.e., AD 450–451). The donor is a woman named Harisvāminī, wife of the *upāsaka* Sanasiddha. She made a permanent monetary gift of 16 *dīnāra*s to the *saṅgha* of the four quarters at the *mahāvihāra* of Kākanādaboṭa. The interest on 12 of these *dīnāras* was for the feeding of one monk of the monastery every day (perhaps a different monk every day?); the interest on three coins was for the maintenance of three lamps in the *ratna-gṛha,* and the proceeds from one coin were for maintenance of the place where the images of the four Buddhas were seated. The inalienability of the gift is indicated by the occurrence of the technical term *akṣaya-nīvī* in line 8 of the inscription, while the phrase *ā-candr-ārkka* (to last as long as the moon and the sun) in line 9 testifies to its perpetual nature.

Inscription no. 835 is inscribed on a pillar. It does not bear a date, but has been assigned on palaeographic grounds to the 5th century AD. It records the gift of a Vajrapāṇi-stambha (a pillar surmounted by an image of Vajrapāṇi), two pillars supporting an arch (*toraṇa-stambha-dvaya*), a pavilion attached to a monastery (*vihāra-maṇḍapa*), and a gateway (*pratolī*). The donor was Rudras(iṁha?), son of the *vihāra-svāmī,* the A(raka?) (= *āryaka?*) *gośura* Siṁhabala. While the term *vihāra-svāmī* suggests that the donor's father had something to do with monastic establishment, in all likelihood the one at Sanchi, the meaning of *gośura* is not clear.

Looking at the Sanchi inscriptions of the Gupta period as a group, several points emerge. As far as the gender break-up of the donors is concerned, there is one lone female donor versus five (or possibly six) male donors. One of the inscriptions (no. 833) indicates benefactions made by an imperial Gupta king and his military commander. It may be noted that two of the donors (nos. 835, 837) are associated with the monastic order, one of them probably with the *vihāra* at Sanchi itself. The nature of the gifts in this period is also interesting. While these include structures and parts of structures, inscription no. 835 refers specifically to gifts supporting the building of parts of the *vihāra* (unlike in the first two periods of our chronological scheme where it was the *stūpa* complexes that were the focus of endowments). Gifts of images, which are documented for the Kuṣāṇa period, continue in the Gupta period. Two new items, however, make their appearance now. These are monetary investments and land. The purport also of some of the gifts has expanded to refer specifically to the support of the *vihāra* establishment. This fits in well with the structural evidence: while the foundations of some of the structures in the Eastern and Southern Areas of the Sanchi complex—halls, shrines, and monasteries—do overlie the remains of structures that go back to an earlier period (in the case of the Pillared Hall no. 40, perhaps to the pre-Śuṅga period),[109] the uppermost plinths and structures of the shrines and monasteries belong to the post-4th-century period, many of them ranging between the 7th and 11th centuries. Marshall has spoken of the gradual evolution of *vihāras*, pointing out that large, permanent, self-contained *vihāra* complexes made their appearance in the north-west only in the Kuṣāṇa period, and in northern and central India not till the early Gupta period.[110] The structural remains, as also the epigraphic evidence, suggest a significant expansion of the *vihāra* component of the Sanchi establishment in the Gupta and post-Gupta periods.

Inscriptions of the Early Medieval Period (6th–9th Centuries AD)

Only two Sanchi inscriptions have been assigned to the post-Gupta period. Inscription no. 841 is inscribed on the back slab of a Buddha image, now lost. The script belongs to about the 9th century. It speaks of the momentous revelations of the Tathāgata.

Inscription no. 842 was found in Monastery 43 and was engraved on a slab of sandstone which was found in several pieces. It is in Sanskrit verse, and the script belongs to about the 7th century. It is damaged in many places, and this makes it difficult to understand its precise purport. Opening with a eulogy of the *boddhisattvas* Lokanātha and Vajrapāṇi, it seems to refer to the building of a *vihāra* with cells (*layana*) by someone at Boṭa-Śrīparvvata (i.e., Sanchi). Persons who are mentioned in the inscription include the lord of Mahāmālava; a ruler named Vappakadeva and his son *mahārāja* Śarvva; a person named Rudra; and a person named Tuṅ ga. Part of the text seems to record the genealogy of the donor/donors.

Building activity in the shrines and monastic quarters continued in the post-Gupta period till about the 11th century, soon after which the Sanchi establishment wound up. Inscription no. 842 speaks of this building activity, but its fragmentary nature makes it difficult to identify the individuals connected with the endowment. The titles of these persons as well as the fragments of a genealogy in the inscription suggest that some of them may have been minor rulers.

Conclusion

The period from the 3rd century BC to the early centuries of the Christian era was a very important one in the history of Buddhist sites in different parts of the Indian subcontinent. We have already seen testimony of this in the structural remains and hundreds of inscriptions found at Sanchi. Building activity at the site of Bharhut (Satna district, Madhya Pradesh) commenced from the Śuṅga period. The beginnings of the *mahācaitya* at

Amaravati (Guntur district, Andhra Pradesh) apparently go back to the Mauryan period,[111] reaching a peak during the late Sātavāhana and Ikṣvāku periods (2nd to 4th century AD). The nucleus of the Buddhist establishment at Nagarjunakonda (also in Guntur district) may have existed in Sātavāhana times, but maximum activity took place during the Ikṣvāku period.[112] At Sarnath (Varanasi district, Uttar Pradesh), the site of the Buddha's *dharmacakrapravartana*, there is the Aśokan pillar, and the Dharmarājikā and Dhamekh *stūpa*s that seem to have originated in the Mauryan period.[113] At Rajgir (Patna district, Bihar), Mauryan-type bricks were found in the western part of the mound marking the site of a *stūpa*.[114]

The beginnings of the Dharmarājikā *stūpa* at Taxila also may go back to the Mauryan period, and building activity continued through the succeeding centuries.[115] With regard to the cave sites of western India, Dehejia describes the period 120 BC–AD 200 as the early formative phase of rock architecture in this region.[116] She also points out that the beginnings of rock-cut *caitya* architecture go back to the Aśokan period (the Sudāmā and Lomaṣa Ṛṣi caves in the Barabar hills).[117]

We can juxtapose the early history of these Buddhist establishments with the chronology and history of urban growth in the Indian subcontinent. The beginnings of structural activity at Buddhist sites in India coincides precisely with that period which witnessed significant expansion of urban centres in the Indian subcontinent. Dilip K. Chakrabarti has delineated three phases in the history of early (post-Harappan) urban growth in the Indian subcontinent—Phase I: 6th/5th century BC; Phase II: 3rd/2nd century BC; Phase III: the early centuries AD.[118] The site of Sanchi was humming with activity during the second and third phases. The evidence further indicates an expansion of the establishment during the Gupta and post-Gupta periods. The inscriptions document continued patronage till around the 9th century and the structural remains reveal the demise of the Sanchi complex a few centuries later, in the 12th century.

The rather dim archaeological profile of the site of Besnagar (ancient Vidiśā) does not lend itself easily to correlation with the history of the Sanchi establishment. Marshall refers to Vidiśā falling to ruins during the Gupta period and making way for Bhilsā.[119] D. R. Bhandarkar refers to sites in old Beś being pilfered and material from here being used to build Bhilsā around the 8th century AD.[120] However, contrary to R. S. Sharma's statement that the Sanchi monastic establishment was deserted after the 4th century AD,[121] the evidence of the structures and inscriptions clearly indicates that the establishment continued to grow during the Gupta and post-Gupta phase. This is the very period which, according to Sharma, saw the decline of Indian urban centres, including Vidiśā.[122]

The question that arises is: if from its inception the Sanchi establishment was so closely linked with the city of Vidiśā, how did it survive for so many centuries the sharp decline in fortune that Sharma suggests the city experienced during and after the Gupta period?

One aspect of this discussion has been the effort to try to ascertain the extent and importance of royal patronage in the development of the Sanchi establishment. Such patronage was definitely important during the time of Aśoka, but during the succeeding period the number of records suggesting patronage from kings and courtiers is unsubstantial and the number of private endowments overwhelming.

This raises a more general question regarding the relationship between political history, political patronage, and religious establishments in ancient India. Once the relative autonomy of many ancient religious establishments from royal patronage is recognised, the value of several arguments made on the basis of the religious predilections of kings in the ancient past become somewhat dubious. The fact that at Sanchi the 2nd century BC to the 1st century AD was a period of intensive activity is not proof of Puṣyamitra Śuṅga not being anti-Buddhist.[123] Puṣyamitra may well have earned the reputation accorded to him in Buddhist literature of being violently anti-Buddhist; he may well have been the one who, as suggested by Marshall, ordered the inflicting of deliberate damage on the Aśokan Stūpa.[124] And at the same time, Sanchi was growing. It was growing not as a result of royal favour and patronage; it could have grown despite royal disfavour. Because, apart from its inception, the growth of this important Buddhist complex had little to do with kings and courts.

Acknowledgements

I would like to thank the participants of the Seminar on Government and Society, organised by the Department of History, University of Delhi, 5–7 April 1994. A nascent version of this chapter was read out at this Seminar and the discussion that followed helped a great deal in its elaboration.

Notes

1. In early Brāhmī inscriptions, it is Kākaṇāva and Kākaṇāya; in two inscriptions of the time of Candragupta II, it is Kākaṇāda-boṭa; in an inscription of the

7th century, it is Boṭa-Śrīparvvata. John Marshall, Alfred Foucher, and N. G. Majumdar, *The Monuments of Sanchi,* 3 Vols. (Kolkata: Swati Publications, [1940] 1983), p. 12. The numbering of the inscriptions in this chapter follows that in Vol. 3. It may be added that inscription no. 828 (of the 2nd century AD), refers to the establishment as Dharmadeva vihāra.

2. For a discussion on the various aspects of patronage in ancient India, see Barbara Stoler Miller, ed., *The Powers of Art: Patronage in Indian Culture* (Delhi: Oxford University Press, 1992); specially Romila Thapar, 'Patronage and Community', pp. 19–34, and Vidya Dehejia, 'The Collective and Popular Bases of Early Buddhist Patronage: Sacred Monuments, 100 BC–AD 250', pp. 35–45. Both Thapar and Dehejia draw on the Sanchi inscriptions in the course of their discussion.
3. The only piece of writing in recent times which, in my opinion, has undertaken a thorough analysis of data from the Sanchi inscriptions is Kumkum Roy's 'Women and Men Donors at Sanchi: A Study of the Inscriptional Evidence,' in L.K. Tripathi, ed., *Position and Status of Women in Ancient India* (Varanasi: Banaras Hindu University, 1988), pp. 209–223. Some of the epigraphic data from Sanchi and other sites has also been catalogued by Uma Chakravarti, *The Social Dimensions of Early Buddhism* (Delhi: Oxford University Press, 1987). A most perplexing piece of writing which speaks of the epigraphic data from early Buddhist sites is by Janice D. Willis, 'Female Patronage in Indian Buddhism', in Miller, ed., *The Powers of Art,* (Delhi: Oxford University Press, 1992), pp. 46–53. Apart from certain inaccurate statements regarding the chronology of the inscriptions, it is not clear why, out of the hundreds of female donors at Sanchi, Bharhut, and Amaravati, Willis chooses to tell us about only five.
4. *Mahāparinibbāna-sutta* V. 26; adapted from T. W. Rhys Davids, trans., *Buddhist Suttas* (Oxford: Clarendon Press, 1881) [1989, Reprint edition, Delhi]; Max Muller, gen. ed., *The Sacred Books of the East,* Vol. 11, pp. 91–93. 'Thūpa' is the Pāli form of '*stūpa*'.
5. V. S. Agrawala traces the antiquity of the *stūpa* cult to the *Ṛg Veda,* wherein there is a reference (he does not specify exactly where) to the *hiraṇya-stūpa,* the golden *stūpa* of Agni, out of which the cosmos is produced. *Studies in Indian Art,* Varanasi, 1965, p. 77. Although the terms *stūpa* and *hiraṇya-stūpa* occur in Vedic literature, the references are rather insubstantial in number, and do not correspond in meaning to what the term *stūpa* meant (initially at least) in the Buddhist tradition—a funerary or reliquary mound. A question that arises is: if the practice of erecting *stūpa*s, according to the testimony of the Buddhist texts, pre-dates Buddhism, and there is little or no evidence of this practice in the Brahmanical textual tradition, then who were the kings whom the *Mahāparinibbāna-sutta* alludes to ('And as they treat the remains of a king of kings...'), and within which cultural tradition can we place them? Certainly not the Vedic.
6. For instance in *Divyāvadāna* XXVI and *Mahāvaṁśa* V, 209.
7. Marshall, Foucher, and Majumdar, *The Monuments of Sanchi,* Vol. 1, pp. 20–22.

8. Marshall, Foucher, and Majumdar, *The Monuments of Sanchi,* Vol. 2; pp. 18, a2; 18, b2; 40, 3.
9. *Annual Report of the Archaeological Survey of India,* 1936–1937, pp. 85–87.
10. Of course, it is possible that some sort of structure or structures of Buddhist significance existed at Sanchi before Aśoka's time. In 1975, M. R. Raghava Varier and M. G. S. Narayanan found a fragmentary label inscription at the site of Temple 40. They read it as follows: 'Vim-du-sā-ra-du-tarā....' If their conclusions regarding the palaeography of this inscription are to be accepted, then this would push back the beginnings of structural activity at Sanchi to the time of Aśoka's father Bindusāra, and perhaps even to the pre-Mauryan period. M. R. Raghava Varier and M. G. S. Narayanan, 'Bindusara, Sāñci and Aśoka', *Journal of Indian History* 54, 1976, pp. 53–71.
11. On the chronology of the Sanchi monuments, see Marshall's Table on p. 18 of Marshall, Foucher, and Majumdar, *The Monuments of Sanchi,* Vol. 1.
12. Marshall, Foucher, and Majumdar, *The Monuments of Sanchi,* Vol. 1, p. 47.
13. Marshall points out that some of these names also occur on relic caskets found at Sonari and Andher. Marshall, Foucher, and Majumdar, *The Monuments of Sanchi,* Vol. 1, p. 291.
14. Marshall—Marshall, Foucher, and Majumdar, *The Monuments of Sanchi,* Vol. 1, p. 296—points out that Faxian (4th century AD) refers to *stūpas* in honour of these *theras* at Mathura, and that their names appear on relic boxes at Satdhara near Sanchi.
15. Ananda K. Coomaraswamy, *Introduction to Indian Art,* 2nd edition. (Munshiram Manoharlal: Delhi, 1969), p. 30.
16. Max Muller, ed., *The Sacred Books of the East,* Vol. 10, p. 188.
17. Marshall, Foucher, and Majumdar, The *Monuments of Sanchi,* Vol. 1, p. 1.
18. *Pariśiṣṭaparvan* X, XI; cited in Romila Thapar, *Aśoka and the Decline of the Mauryas* (Delhi: Oxford University Press, 1963) [2nd edition, 1973], p. 195.
19. D. C. Sircar, *Ancient Malwa and the Vikramāditya Tradition* (Delhi: Munshiram Manoharlal Publishers, 1969), pp. 59–60. He cites the following evidence: the Besnagar pillar inscription of Heliodorus; an inscription showing that the ninth Śuṅga king Bhāgavata built a temple of Viṣṇu at Vidiśā; the evidence that a local ruler of the Bharhut region acknowledged the supremacy of the later Śuṅgas; the fact that the Purāṇas seem to connect the end of Śuṅga rule with Vidiśā.
20. The relationship between the location of Buddhist cave sites and ancient trade routes has been noted by many scholars. See, for instance, D. D. Kosambi, 'At the Cross-roads: A Study of Mother-Goddess Cult Sites', *Myth and Reality: Studies in the Formation of Indian Culture* (Mumbai: Popular Prakashan, 1962), pp. 93–96, 100; Himanshu P. Ray, *Monastery and Guild: Commerce under the Sātavāhanas* (Delhi: Oxford University Press, 1986), pp. 207–208; Vidya Dehejia, *Early Buddhist Rock Temples: A Chronological Study* (London: Cambridge University Press), 1972, pp. 17–18, 30. I think, however, that there is good reason to ascertain the *volume* of evidence, especially epigraphic, regarding the relationship between monasteries and guilds.
21. Moti Chandra, *Trade and Trade Routes in Ancient India* (New Delhi: Abhinav Publications, 1977), p. 23.

22. According to Radhakumud Mookerji, the *Dīpavaṁśa* and *Mahāvaṁśa* credit Devī with building the *mahā-vihāra* at Vedisagiri: *Asoka* (London: Macmillan, 1928), p. 8. This is not so. The relevant passage in the *Dīpavaṁśa*, XII, pp. 14–15 reads as follows: 'Gradually moving about they (i.e., Mahinda and his five companions) went to Vedisagiri and dwelt in the Vedisagiri monastery as long as they liked. Instructing his mother in the refuges, precepts, and uposatha ceremonies, he established the dwellers of the island in the true law and religion': B. C. Law, ed. and trans., 'The Dipavamsa', *The Ceylon Historical Journal,* 7, 1957–1958. *Mahāvaṁśa,* XIII, p. 6 likewise speaks of prince Mahinda's visit to Vedisagiri prior to his departure for Sri Lanka. 'When he came in time to Vedisagiri, the city of his mother Devī, he visited his mother and when Devī saw her dear son, she made him welcome and his companions likewise, with foods prepared by herself, and she led the *thera* up to the lovely vihāra Vedisagiri': Wilhelm Geiger, trans., *The Mahāvaṁsa or The Great Chronicle of Ceylon* (London: Luzac and Co., 1934), p. 88. However, the 12th century Pali *Thūpavaṁśa* explicitly connects the building of this monastery with this queen. It refers to Mahinda reaching Vedisa, where his mother lived. 'And when the queen mother of the Elder saw that the Elder had arrived, she bowed her head at his feet, and offered him food, and dedicated to the Elder Vedisa Hill monastery, built by herself': B. C. Law, trans., *The Legend of the Topes* (*Thūpavaṁsa*), reprint edition (Kolkata: Asiatic Society, 1993), p. 42. M. Hamid suggests that the *vihāra* he excavated in 1936 at Sanchi represents the abode of the royal nun Devī (*Annual Report of the Archaeological Survey of India,* 1936–1937, p. 87).
23. D. R. Bhandarkar in *Annual Report of the Archaeological Survey of India,* 1914–1915, pp. 66–89.
24. A. Ghosh, ed., *An Encyclopaedia of Indian Archaeology,* Vol. 2 (New Delhi: Munshiram Manoharlal Publishers, 1989), p. 62.
25. Ghosh, *An Encyclopaedia of Indian Archaeology: A Review,* 1963–1964, pp. 16–17.
26. Ghosh, ed., *An Encyclopaedia of Indian Archaeology: A Review,* 1964–1965, pp. 19–20.
27. This division is based on N. G. Majumdar's palaeographic analysis: Marshall, Foucher, and Majumdar, *The Monuments of Sanchi.* Vol. 1, p. 264. Majumdar, however, has divided the inscriptions into six chronological groups. I have collapsed his second and third phases into one because the inscriptions of these groups are close enough in time to justify this. Taken together, these two phases represent the period of maximum private endowments. Apart from the fact that a more detailed chronological stratification than Majumdar's on the basis of palaeography or on a correlation of the inscriptions with the relief sculptures would be very tenuous, it is not necessary for the purposes of identifying the broad trends that this chapter tries to establish. For more details on the language and palaeography of the inscriptions, see N. G. Majumdar, in Marshall, Foucher, and Majumdar, *The Monuments of Sanchi,* Vol. 1, pp. 264–278.
28. The estimate of the chronology of this phase depends to some extent on the identity of the 'Sirī Sātakaṇī' mentioned in inscription no. 398 (on the south gateway) and the debate on Sātavāhana chronology.

29. The schism edict is supposed to belong to the later part of Aśoka's reign. Thapar, *Aśoka and the Decline,* p. 44.
30. Some of this data from these inscriptions has already been considered by Roy, 'Women and Men Donors at Sanchi'. The computations given in this article are, however, my own.
31. Donors are identified as *upāsaka*s in seven records and *upāsikā*s in 17. Of course, all other donors not specifically identified as monks and nuns would also fall within these categories.
32. G. Bühler, 'Votive Inscriptions from the Sānchi Stūpas', *Epigraphia Indica,* 2, 1894, p. 95. According to Bühler, a study of the personal names of the donors indicates the prevalence of Paurāṇic worship of the deities Viṣṇu and Śiva, and evidence that the recommendation of some *Gṛhya Sūtras* of giving the name according to the *nakṣatra* was actually followed.
33. Majumdar in Marshall, Foucher, and Majumdar, *The Monuments of Sanchi,* Vol. 1, p. 299.
34. *Mahāvagga* VI, 30, 5, cited in T. W. Rhys Davids and Hermann Oldenberg, trans., *Vinaya Texts,* Part II, p. 108, in Max Muller, ed., *Sacred Books of the East,* Vol. 17.
35. *Cullavagga* VI, 14; Rhys Davids and Oldenberg, trans., *Vinaya Texts,* Vol. 3, pp. 208–209.
36. *Cullavagga,* V, 22, 1; *Vinaya Texts,* Vol. 3, p. 130. The *Mahāvagga* also refers to a possible range of gifts (some appropriate, some not) that are associated with a group of people that includes women (harlots, adult girls, eunuchs, relations, kings). The context is situations in which a monk may interrupt his *vassa* (retreat). If any of the above categories of individuals offers a monk who has entered upon *vassa* gold, bullion, a field, a site (for a house or a garden), an ox, a cow, a slave, a female slave, a daughter for a wife, herself (in the case of a female) as a wife, or another woman as a wife, if the monk fears that the purity of his life is threatened, he should leave that place and is not guilty of interruption of *vassa.* It seems to be the negative nature of the intention of the persons making the offer as well as the inappropriate nature of what is being offered that leads the Buddha to give the *bhikkhu* the advice to leave the place. *Mahāvagga* III, 11, 3–4; *Vinaya Texts,* Vol. 1, pp. 315–316.
37. See for instance Marshall, Foucher, and Majumdar, *The Monuments of Sanchi,* Vol. 3, pp. 103, b.
38. Marshall, Foucher, and Majumdar, *The Monuments of Sanchi,* Vol. 2, pp. 35, al; 35, b2.
39. Marshall, Foucher, and Majumdar, *The Monuments of Sanchi,* Vols. 2 and 3, pp. 19, d1?; 19, d3?; 101, 4?; 29, 2.
40. For scenes where women appear (in all-female groups or along with men) making offerings at *bodhi* trees, which are in some cases surrounded by an enclosure, see Marshall, Foucher, and Majumdar, *The Monuments of Sanchi,* pp. 12, 4; 13, 4; 16, 5; 17, 5; 22, 1; 22, 2; 31, 4; etc. For scenes of women kneeling before a *stūpa,* with offerings, see pp. 32, 3 and 22, 1. There are also depictions of the first sermon represented by the wheel surrounded by men and women bearing offerings: pp. 43, 2.

41. *Monuments of Sanchi,* Vols. 2 and 3, pp. 26, 1; 33, 4; 34, a2; 34, a3; 103, e.
42. Bühler, 'Votive Inscriptions', p. 93 suggests that there could be a connection between the Vākaliyas and Vākalā devī mentioned in inscription no. 364. If so, the Vākaliyas belonged to a royal family or lineage. Vākiliya, he goes on to add, stands for Vākaliya and corresponds to the Sanskrit 'Vārkalīya' and Vākalā to Sanskrit 'Vārkalā', both possibly being irregular patronymics from Vṛkala, a name that occurs in the mythological lists in the Purāṇas.
43. The term *pajāvatī* is used most often in the inscriptions for wife.
44. One such instance is the story of Yasa, son of a *seṭṭhi-gahapati* of Benaras. His father became the first *upāsaka* by the formula of the triad (the declaration of taking refuge in the Buddha, the *dhamma,* and the *saṅgha*) and his mother and former wife became the first female lay disciples by this formula: *Vinaya Texts,* Vol. 1; *Mahāvagga* 7-8; pp. 102–110. The matter did not end here. For we are told that four, and then 50 friends of Yasa, all of a similar social background, followed their friend's example and joined the *saṅgha: Mahāvagga* 9–10; *Vinaya Texts,* Vol. 1, p. 110–112.
45. Chakravarti, *The Social Dimensions of Early Buddhism,* pp. 77, 79–88.
46. Chakravarti, *The Social Dimensions of Early Buddhism,* pp. 73–79. Chakravarti points out that in the Pali texts, the terms *seṭṭhi, seṭṭhi-gahapati,* and *gahapati* are fairly distinct categories and are not used loosely as they are in later works such as the commentaries on the canonical texts. She also points out that in the Pali canon, the terms *seṭṭhi* and *seṭṭhi-gahapati* occur most frequently in the *Vinaya Piṭaka,* and do not appear at all in some of the earliest texts such as the *Sutta Nipāta* or the *Dīgha Nikāya.*
47. *Cullavagga* VI; *Vinaya Texts,* part 3, pp. 157–160.
48. See, for example, *Cullavagga* VI. 4; *Vinaya Texts,* pt. 3, pp. 179–189.
49. *Mahāvagga* I, 7; *Vinaya Texts,* pt. 1, pp. 102–110.
50. *Mahāvagga* I. 4; *Vinaya Texts,* pt. 1, pp. 81–84.
51. See Thapar, *Aśoka and the Decline,* pp. 105–108.
52. On the meaning of these terms and the importance of the *gahapati*s and *seṭṭhi*s in the Pāli canon, see Uma Chakravarti, *The Social Dimensions of Early Buddhism,* pp. 65–100.
53. 'Patronage and Community', pp. 25–28.
54. 'Early Buddhist Patronage', p. 37.
55. Thapar refers to a few inscriptions where this word occurs and suggests that it may refer to apprenticeship of a different kind, one associated with the building of the monuments. She argues that if a purely religious pupilage was intended to be indicated, it would be more likely to find the use of the word *śiṣya,* 'Patronage and Community', p. 30. This argument is not convincing. At Sanchi, the term *atevāsin,* and its feminine counterpart *atevasini* appear to be used very frequently in the conventional sense of a pupil within the monastic context. The term *śiṣya* does not occur at all.
56. Majumdar translates this term as companion or co-resident, adding that the reading might be *sādhavihārin:* Marshall, Foucher, and Majumdar, *The Monuments of Sanchi,* Vol. 1, p. 334. The term, however, appears to be close enough to *saddhivihārika,* which is used frequently in the texts for a pupil. See *Mahāvagga* I, 25, 7; in *Vinaya Texts,* pt. 1, p. 154ff.

57. The word 'Yugapajakasa' also occurs in this inscription. Majumdar interprets it as a place name (Yugapaja), while Bühler translates it as 'the path-[finder] *of* the age: Marshall, Foucher, and Majumdar, *The Monuments of Sanchi,'* Vol. 1, p. 328, and n. 5.
58. Bühler, 'Votive Inscriptions', p. 93.
59. Bhaṁḍuka/Bhaḍuka—nos. 265, 267, 269, ii; Bhaḍika—348, 349; Cuḍa—399, 402.
60. Inscription nos. 572, 573, 615, 617 record multiple gifts by monks; the following inscriptions record multiple gifts by nuns—304, 305, 560, 561.
61. Bühler, 'Votive Inscriptions…', p. 93. Bühler also refers to Jaina votive inscriptions at places such as Mathura, which indicate that Jaina ascetics exhorted lay persons to make gifts and saw to it that this fact was mentioned in the inscriptions.
62. Pātimokkha; Nisaggiyā Pācittiyā dhammā 18–20; *Vinaya Texts,* Vol. 1, pp. 26–27.
63. *Mahāvagga* 1. 56; *Vinaya Texts,* Vol. 1, p. 211.
64. *Mahāvagga* VI, 34, 21; *Vinaya Texts,* Vol. 2, p. 128–129. According to Rhys Davids and Oldenberg, 'A kappiya-kāraka is one who by offering a thing to a Bhikkhu makes that thing kappiya, allowable, to the Bhikkhu.' (p. 59, n. 2).
65. *Cullavagga* V, 37; *Vinaya Texts,* Vol. 3, p. 155.
66. *Mahāvagga* VIII, 27, 5; *Vinaya Texts,* Vol. 2, p. 245.
67. Marshall in Marshall, Foucher, and Majumdar, *The Monuments of Sanchi,* Vol. 1, p. 34, and n. 2.
68. H. Hamid, in *Annual Report of the Archaeological Survey of India,* 1936–1937, pp. 85–86. It was on the basis of these opulent finds that Hamid suggested that this *vihāra* was the abode of Aśoka's consort Devī.
69. On *yavana,* see Aloka Parasher, *Mlecchas in Early India* (New Delhi, 1991), pp. 224–228.
70. See S. M. Ali, *The Geography of the Puranas* 2nd edition (People's Publishing House: New Delhi, 1966, 1973), pp. 52, 53, 201, n. 4.
71. V. R. Ramachandra Dikshitar, gen. ed., *The Purana Index,* Vol. 3 (Chennai: University of Madras, 1951–1952), p. 495. The text cited is *Bhāgavata Purāṇa* VIII.4. 18; X.6. 24; X.87.10; XI.15.18.
72. *Śānti Parva,* Dakṣiṇātya Pāṭha, Chapter 335, cited in Vettam Mani, *Purāṇic Encyclopaedia: A Comprehensive Dictionary with Special Reference to the Epic and Purānic Literature* (Delhi: Motilal Banarsidass, [1975] 1989, p. 780.
73. R. D. Banerji, 'The Kalyan Plates of Yasovarman', *Epigraphia Indica,* 19, 1927–1928): 72, 1.25. This reference to Śvetapāda was noted by Sashi Bhusan Chaudhuri, *Ethnic Settlements in Ancient India: A Study on the Puranic Lists and Peoples of Bharatavarsa* (Kolkata: General Printers & Publishers, 1955), p. 150.
74. Bühler, 'Votive Inscriptions', p. 92. Among the relevant translations of the Sanskrit *goṣṭhī* are: an assembly, meeting-place, society, association, family connections, partnership, fellowship: M. Monier-Williams, *Sanskrit-English Dictionary,* 1988 reprint, p. 367.
75. According to Dehejia, 'While the occupations of donors frequently remain unspecified, the home town is always stated': 'Early Buddhist patronage', p. 37. This is incorrect.

76. Chakravarti, *The Social Dimensions of Early Buddhism*, p. 78.
77. This was pointed out by Amarjiva Lochan.
78. Dehejia seems to suggest that these are gifts *of* villages, whereas it is fairly clear from the inscriptions that these are gifts made *by* villages. The village was the donor, not the item gifted: 'Early Buddhist Patronage', pp. 38–39.
79. Bühler, 'Votive inscriptions', p. 92.
80. Marshall, Foucher, and Majumdar, *The Monuments of Sanchi,* Vol. 1, p. 299.
81. Bühler, 'Votive Inscriptions', p. 96.
82. Bühler, 'Votive Inscriptions', p. 96.
83. Bühler, 'Votive Inscriptions', p. 96.
84. Sankalia, Subbarao, and Deo, *The Excavations at Maheshwar and Navdatoli* 1952–1953, Poona, Baroda, 1958, p. 1.
85. *The Excavations at Maheshwar and Navdatoli,* p. 15.
86. Bühler, 'Votive Inscriptions', p. 96.
87. Marshall, Foucher, and Majumdar, *The Monuments of Sanchi,* Vol. 1, p. 299.
88. Marshall, Foucher, and Majumdar, *The Monuments of Sanchi,* Vol. 1, p. 300.
89. Marshall, Foucher, and Majumdar, *The Monuments of Sanchi,* Vol. 1, p. 300.
90. S. B. Deo, ed., *Excavations at Bhokardan* (*Bhogavardhan*), Nagpur, 1974, pp. 18, 210–212.
91. Deo, *Excavations at Bhokardan,* p. 211.
92. N. G. Majumdar in Marshall, Foucher, and Majumdar, *The Monuments of Sanchi,* p. 300.
93. D. C. Sircar, *Studies in the Geography of Ancient and Medieval India,* second revised edition (Delhi, 1971), p. 297. S. C. Mishra has suggested (personal communication) that the references in these inscriptions are more likely to be to Tagara identified with Ter in Osmanabad district on the bank of the river Terna, an important place on the trade routes of the early historical period. This possibility cannot be ruled out.
94. *Mahāvagga* III, 4, 3; *Vinaya Texts,* Vol. 1, p. 301.
95. See n. 42.
96. Which particular Sātavāhana king is this a reference to and whether he and this inscription belong to the second or the 1st century BC is a matter of debate? It may be mentioned that one coin bearing the legend: 'rano Siri Sātakanisa' and several others with the legend: 'raño Siri-Sātasa' have been found at Vidisa: K. D. Bajpai, 'Some Rare Early Coins from Central India and Andhra Pradesh', *Journal of the Numismatic Society of India* 41 (1979), p. 39. The palaeography of the legend on the first mentioned coin seems to match that of the Sanchi inscription. Bajpai places the coin and inscription in the 2nd century BC: 'Numis matic evidence on the extension of Sātavāhana rule in central India', *Journal of the Numismatic Society of India* 43 (1981), p. 65.
97. Nāgapiya also appears as a donor in no. 660.
98. B. N. Mukherjee, *Studies in Kushāna Genealogy and Chronology,* Vol. 1: *The Kushāna Genealogy* (Kolkata: Sanskrit College, 1967), pp. 107, n. 192.
99. Marshall, Foucher, and Majumdar, *The Monuments of Sanchi,* Vol. 1, pp. 65, 74, 108, n. 193.
100. Inscription no. 839 is dated in the year 241, probably of the Śaka era (= AD 319). The stone on which this inscription is inscribed was found built into a

well at Kanakhera, a village near Sanchi. It is badly damaged in many places. The purport is to record the construction of a well by the *mahādaṇḍanāyaka* Śaka Śrīdharavarmman, son of Śaka Nanda in the thirteenth year of the former's reign. I have not included this inscription in the table because it was found at a place near Sanchi, not at Sanchi itself.

101. '... yāvac-candr-ādityau tāvat ...' (1. 8); i.e., to last as long as the moon and the sun. B. Chhabra and G. S. Gai, ed., *Corpus Inscriptionum Indicarum,* Vol. 3 (New Delhi: Gaurav Publishing House, 1981).
102. Chhabra and Gai, *Corpus Inscriptionum Indicarum,* p. 251, n. 2.
103. Marshall, Foucher, and Majumdar, *The Monuments of Sanchi,* p. 389, 1. 6; p. 388 and n. 7.
104. Chhabra and Gai, *Corpus Inscriptionum Indicarum,* Vol. 3, p. 251, and n. 2.
105. Chhabra and Gai, *Corpus Inscriptionum Indicarum,* Vol. 3, p. 389.
106. Chhabra and Gai, *Corpus Inscriptionum Indicarum,* Vol. 3, p. 251, and n. 4.
107. D. C. Sircar, *Select Inscriptions,* Vol. 1, p. 272, n. 7.
108. Chhabra and Gai, *Corpus Inscriptionum Indicarum,* Vol. 3, p. 251, n. 6.
109. Marshall, Foucher, and Majumdar, *The Monuments of Sanchi,* Vol. 1, pp. 64–65. For the earlier remains at the site of Temple and Monastery 45, see pp. 71–72. See also the table showing the dates of monuments at Sanchi on p. 18.
110. Marshall, Foucher, and Majumdar, *The Monuments of Sanchi,* pp. 63–64. There is, of course, the *vihāra* excavated by Hamid, which he thinks, belongs to the Mauryan period.
111. The fragment of an inscribed Aśokan pillar made of local quartzite was found at Amaravati. N. Ramesan, *Amaravati: The Art and History of the Stupa and the Temple,* (New Delhi, 1975), p. 7.
112. H. Sarkar and B. N. Misra, *Nagarjunakonda,* 2nd edition (New Delhi: Munshiram Manoharlal, 1972), p. 13.
113. V. S. Agrawala, *Sārnāth* (New Delhi: Prestige Books, 1992), p. 7.
114. Mohammad Hamid Kuraishi, *Rajgir,* revised by A. Ghosh (New Delhi: Archaeological Survey of India, 1987), p. 11.
115. John Marshall, *A Guide to Taxila,* 3rd edition (New Delhi: Gyan Books, 1936).
116. Dehejia, *Early Buddhist Rock Temples,* p. 9. Dehejia further divides this period into two phases: the first being 100 BC–20 BC and the second from about AD 50–AD 200 with a seventy year or so lull in between, p. 148.
117. Dehejia, *Early Buddhist Rock Temples,* p. 71.
118. Dilip K. Chakravarti, 'Iron and Urbanization: An Examination of the Indian Context', *Puratattva,* 15, pp. 68–74.
119. Marshall, Foucher, and Majumdar, *The Monuments of Sanchi,* Vol. 1, p. 7.
120. *Annual Report of the Archaeological Survey of India,* 1914–1915, p. 67.
121. R. S. Sharma, *Urban Decay in India (c. 300–c. 1000)* (New Delhi: Munshiram Manoharlal, 1987), p. 66.
122. Sharma, *Urban Decay in India,* p. 67.
123. The argument contested here is made by Thapar, *Aśoka and the Decline,* p. 200.
124. Marshall in Marshall, Foucher, and Majumdar, *The Monuments of Sanchi,* Vol. 1, pp. 23–24.

2

Nagarjunakonda: Buddhism in the 'City of Victory'

Nagarjunakonda (in Guntur district, Andhra Pradesh, India) is a site with a dramatic history. Situated on the banks of the river Krishna and surrounded on three sides by offshoots of the Nallamalai hills, the 15 sq km site was rich in remains ranging from the prehistoric to the medieval periods. It is best known, however, for the remains of Vijayapurī—the 'City of Victory'—capital of the Ikhāku (Ikṣvāku) dynasty, that ruled in this part of South India during the 3rd and 4th centuries CE.[1]

Nagarjunakonda forms an exceptionally rich subject for a 'continuous history'. By this, I mean a biography of a site which moves beyond concentrating on a single episode in its history to trace its long-term trajectories. Such a history of Nagarjunakonda would stretch from the prehistoric period to the early 21st century. This chapter, part of this kind of longer study, focuses on the Buddhist remains of the early historical period. The four specific issues I have dealt with are: royal and non-royal patrons; relic interment and consecration rituals; the material remains of monastic life; and the narrative relief sculptures. These issues have been addressed through a contextual and interrelated analysis of the archaeological evidence, including structural remains, inscriptions, sculptures, and other artefacts.

From the methodological point of view, I would especially like to emphasize three things: The first is the need to read the inscriptions as carefully as we read textual sources, asking fundamental questions about their purpose, audience, reception, and the idiom in which religious piety was expressed. Second, I would like to emphasize the need to treat sculptural evidence (and 'art remains' in general) as an important source for history, not only for art history. Third, a meaningful interpretation of the Buddhist remains of this or any other site requires a contextualization of these remains within the broader political and social contexts and also within the larger religious landscape.

Archaeological reports are often treated as though they embody a set of self-evident facts. It is actually necessary to interrogate them in the way in which any historical source would be interrogated. The history of the exploration, excavation, documentation, and interpretation of the remains at Nagarjunakonda reveals several distinct phases. Discovered in 1926 by A. R. Saraswati, Nagarjunakonda was excavated early in the next year by Muhammad Hamid Kuraishi and subsequently by A. H. Longhurst.[2] Longhurst's report represents the first stage in the interpretation of Nagarjunakonda, one in which it was seen essentially as a Buddhist site.[3] The second series of excavations were conducted by T. N. Ramachandran in 1938. The results, published many years later in 1953, for the first time drew attention to the many Hindu temples in the early historic city.[4] This report situated Nagarjunakonda within a framework dominated by regional history and the sentiment of regional pride.

During the 1950s, plans for building a massive irrigation dam across the Krishna were drawn up, and Nagarjunakonda's impending submergence led the Archaeological Survey of India to undertake a massive project of exploration, excavation, and documentation. About 136 new structures and structural complexes were unearthed. And before the valley was turned into a gigantic lake, nine of the most important structures were transplanted and rebuilt on top of the Nagarjunakonda hill and on the banks of the reservoir; smaller-scale replicas of 14 other structures were made.

The first part of the report of the 1954–1960 excavations, published in 1975, focused on the site's prehistoric and megalithic remains.[5] The second part, published as recently as 2006, was suffused with the sentiment of national pride, with frequent, rather florid eulogies of the site and of the Ikṣvāku dynasty.[6] The report offers a consolidated view of the early historic remains, artefacts, and inscriptions of this ancient 'City of Victory'.

The Emergence of a Cosmopolitan Buddhist Centre

The Andhra region was dotted with many Buddhist monasteries well before Vijayapurī emerged as a premier Buddhist centre.[7] The Amaravati *stūpa*, located 125 km downstream on the Krishna, was one of the most renowned, and had the designation of a *mahācaitya* (Prakrit *mahācetiya*), a term which seems to have been reserved for the most sacred of *stūpas*, those containing the Buddha's relics. Some sort of settlement and at least one Buddhist monastery existed at Nagarjunakonda before the Ikṣvāku period.[8] However, the just-over-one-century of Ikṣvāku rule—comprising the reigns of Vasiṭhiputa Siri Cāṁtamūla (c. 210–250 CE), Māṭharīputa Siri Vīrapurisadatta (250–275 CE), Vaseṭhiputa Ehuvala Cāṁtamūla (275–297/300 CE), and Siri Rudrapurisadatta (300–325 CE)—saw a major mushrooming of monasteries. This activity seems to represent a concerted attempt, to a significant extent sponsored by the royal family, to create and patronize an exceptionally magnificent and prestigious centre of Buddhism.

The foremost basis of Vijayapurī's prestige was the *mahācaitya* (Figure 2.1), which contained a bone relic of the Buddha.[9] However, the site's prestige must have also rested on the sheer presence of a very large number of Buddhist monasteries, affiliated to different sects. The Aparamahāvinaseliya sect (Site 1) has been tentatively identified with the Aparaselikas, one of the two divisions of the Mahāsaṁghikas.[10] The Bahuśrutīyas (Site 5) were a sub-sect of the Gokulika sect which belonged to the Mahāsaṁghika school. The Vibhajyavādins (Site 38), on the other hand, were associated with the Sthaviravādins. It may be added that an inscription found to the north of Nagarjunakonda has a reference to the Mahiśāsakas, a sub-sect of the Sarvāstivādins.[11]

Another basis of Vijayapurī's fame was its self-proclaimed cosmopolitan nature. Inscriptions suggest that some of its monasteries housed high-profile monks of great renown who hailed from many lands and had engaged in proselytizing activities far and wide. An inscription on the floor of the apsidal temple to the east of the *mahācaitya* refers to the great community of Buddhist monks (*mahābhikhu-saṁgha*) who had renounced the world and who had assembled from various countries (*nānā-desa-samanāgata*). Inscriptions found at the *maṇḍapa* (pillared hall) associated with the *mahācaitya* refer to the *mahāvihāra* and the *mahābhikhu-saṁgha* who had assembled from various lands. A stone carving of a pair of the Buddha's feet (*bhagavato-pāda-saṁghāḍā*) from

Figure 2.1
The mahācaitya

Source: Author

another monastery (Site 38) refers to the residents of the *mahāvihāra* as *ācāryas* and *theriyas* of the Vibhajyavāda school, who had gladdened the hearts of the people of Kasmira, Gaṁdhāra, Yavaṇa, Vanavāsa, and Taṁbapaṁnidipa.[12] The strongest statement comes from the apsidal temple associated with the Cula-Dhammagiri Vihāra (Site 43), endowed by an *upāsikā* named Bodhisiri. This shrine is described as having been constructed for the benefit of the *ācāryas* from Taṁbapaṁna (Sri Lanka), who had gladdened (through their teaching) the lands of Kasmira, Gaṁdhāra, Cīna, Cilāta, Tosali, Avaraṁta, Vaṅga, Vanavāsi, Yavana (?), Damila (?), Palura (?), and the island of Tambapaṁni.[13]

Nagarjunakonda is also unique in the great variety of form in its religious architecture. The *stūpas* include those made of heaped-up brick or rubble, those with a spoked wheel plan (the innermost spokes numbered 4, 6, 8, or 10), and those with a *svastika* plan (Figure 2.2).[14] There is marked variety in the plans of the *caityas* and *vihāras* as well (Figures 2.3–2.5). This diversity can only partly be explained by sectarian affiliations. Considering that all this happened within a time-frame of about

Figure 2.2
Stūpa with svastika inset

Source: Author

a hundred years, we seem to be looking at a concerted policy to create a spectacular centre of Buddhism, one marked by deliberate architectural experimentation and variety.

Epigraphic evidence is the key to identifying the people who were responsible for all this. The inscriptions are variously in Prakrit, Sanskrit and mixed Prakrit-Sanskrit, and are written in the Brahmi script. Of the 31 Buddhist *stūpa*/monastery complexes identified at Nagarjunakonda, 13 have yielded inscriptions; out of these, in 7 cases we have an idea of the donors. In addition, there are at least four inscriptions whose structural affiliations are not known, but which contain some information about the donors.

The purpose of the inscriptions has to be kept in mind when reading and interpreting them. Pious gifts represent a blend of many different ideas, aspirations, and sentiments. The Nagarjunakonda inscriptions do not record the names of all donors who may have contributed to the

Figure 2.3
Apsidal temple enshrining Buddha image (Site 4)

Source: Author

Figure 2.4
Apsidal temple enshrining stone stūpa

Source: Author

Figure 2.5
Ruins of a monastery (Site 43)

Source: Author

monastic establishments in different ways. It is the names of those who contributed to the building and embellishment of the structures that are recorded. There is scarce mention of people who may have contributed in cash or kind towards the maintenance of the monasteries.

Gregory Schopen has suggested that donative inscriptions were inscribed to give the donors a permanent place in the shadow of the sacred relics.[15] It may be added that the degree of proximity was connected with degrees of honour and prestige as well. Physical proximity to the relics must have made it exceptionally prestigious to gift an *āyaka* pillar and to have one's name inscribed on it.[16] However, donors also sought proximity to the monastic community (and prestige through such association) when they gifted entire *caitya-gṛha*s, monastic cells, pillared *maṇḍapa*s (halls), *maṇḍapa* pillars, tanks, sculpted slabs, Buddha images, and *patipadā*s (footprint slabs). Monetary gifts are rare—the *āyaka* pillar inscription of *mahādevī* Rudradharabhaṭārikā refers to a contribution of 170 *dīnāra-māsakas.* And as we shall see further on, the donative inscriptions also had the important function of specifying the nature and distribution of the *puṇya* (merit) that was expected to accrue from the pious gift.

Whatever else they may or may not have conveyed, the most important functions of the donative inscriptions were to assert the donors' identity, the nature of the gift, and the beneficiaries of the merit in a manner that was both public and enduring. How many people could actually read the donative inscriptions is an important question, the answer to which is linked to questions of literacy and language.[17] But readability does not seem to have been crucial in this enterprise. Prestigious activity required expression in a prestigious language, not in some local vernacular.

Power and Patronage: The Dominance of Royal Women

Studies of ancient Indian political structures have tended to focus primarily on the king and have not taken adequate cognizance of the importance of the royal household, including royal women.[18] Considering the close relationship between power and patronage, it is significant that while inscriptions herald their performance of great *śrauta* sacrifices, the Ikṣvāku kings do not appear to have been very actively involved in making donations to religious establishments, Hindu or Buddhist.[19] The leading roles in extending such patronage were played by women of the royal family, high-ranking military commanders and affluent non-royal people.

There were three stages in the evolution of the *mahācaitya* complex (Site 1), associated with the Aparamahāvinaseliya sect. The *stūpa* was built in the 6th regnal year of Vīrapurisadatta. In spite of the existence of other *stūpa*s, in terms of size, with its diameter of about 91 ft, the *mahācaitya* remained the largest in the city. Its *maṇḍapa* and *vihāra* cells were built in the 15th year of the same king's reign. The *stūpa-caitya* (temple enshrining a 'votive' *stūpa*) was added in the king's 18th regnal year. The location of the complex suggests that it was accessible not only to the royal family but to the city as a whole.

In the early Ikṣvāku period, the *mahācaitya* seems to have been a major—if not the central—royal ceremonial centre in the city of Vijayapurī. The *āyaka* pillars at the *mahācaitya* identify seven women donors, all connected to the royal family. The most prominent was Cāṁtisiri, sister of the deceased first king, aunt and mother-in-law of the reigning second king, and wife of a man who bore titles of high rank—*mahāsenāpati* as well as *mahātalavara*. Cāṁtisiri's name appears in nine redactions of inscriptions distributed over the four cardinal directions.[20]

These inscriptions, with their elaborate eulogy of the Buddha, the deceased king Cāṁtamāla and his sister Cāṁtisiri, speak in tones of authority. They suggest a woman who exercised power during the reign of her brother as well as during that of her nephew (who also became her son-in-law at some point). Cāṁtisiri was also associated with building the monastery and the apsidal temple at the site, and her connection is hammered home through repetition at the *stūpa* and the *maṇḍapa* and on the floor slab of the *caitya*. At least five other *stūpa*-monastery complexes (Sites 5, 7–8, 9, 24, 106) at Vijayapurī reflect the patronage of royalty, and here again, it is royal women who dominate.

Royal women are also conspicuous in a remarkable *chāyā-stambha* (memorial pillar) which records the names of 29 mourning women relatives of Cāṁtamūla (mothers, sisters, queens), along with two non-royal women, set up in year 20 of Vīrapurisadatta's reign.[21] Together with the donative inscriptions, it suggests several things: a strong sense of corporate identity among women of the royal family, and their importance in religious patronage as well as in the articulation and exercise of power. The Ikṣvāku kings had matronyms and practised cross-cousin marriage. Royal women were married to high-ranking officials (or their husbands were elevated to such rank). References to natal families in women's donative inscriptions (both among royal and non-royal women) are common, as are statements that the merit of their pious gifts should accrue to both sides of their family. The prominence of royal women as donors and merit-recipients at Vijayapurī was evidently rooted in the kinship system of the Ikṣvākus, which was, in turn, an extension of the kinship system prevalent at the time in this part of Andhra. It suggests a significant degree of power and authority vested in the women of the royal family, in spite of the fact that succession to the throne remained firmly patrilineal.

Non-royal Patrons: The Upāsikā Bodhisiri

Making pious gifts was an activity that created a community of patrons, identifying persons of consequence among the laity.[22] Although royal women stand out as donors at the *mahācaitya* complex, there was at least one non-royal donor there: a slab and coping stone were the gift (*deyadhamma*) of Cadakapavatica and his housewife (*gharinī*) Padumavānī, together with their sons Hagasiri and Nagatara and the latter's wife and daughters. The donors at another monastic site (Site 106) were a *sreṣṭhin* (banker/businessman) named Kumāranandin, his wife (the *sreṣṭhinī*), son and other relatives. A foot-print slab, the find-spot of which is unknown, mentions the donor as a woman named Budhi, sister of a Śaka named Moda. An inscription found on Polugubodu mound seems to record a donation made by a non-royal family consisting of the principal donor/s, his/their sons, daughters, sons-in-law, grandsons, and grand-daughters, along with other relatives, friends, and kinsmen. Yet another inscription on a carved slab mentions the name of the donor simply as Dhama.

However, the most prominent non-royal patron at Vijayapurī was Bodhisiri, whose benefactions are recorded in an inscription on the floor of the apsidal temple built at her behest, dated in the 14th regnal year of the second Ikṣvāku king Vīrapurisadatta.[23] The whole complex, consisting of a *stūpa*, *vihāra*, and *stūpa-caitya*, was located towards the eastern side of the valley, not far from the main entrance into the city. From the honorific 'siri' suffix in her name, Bodhisiri might be mistaken for a royal woman. However, she is the only person in her family with this suffix, and further, she is described as the wife of a man named Budhaṁnika, son of a *gahapati* named Revata. The family does, however, seem to have had some court connections, going by the mention of the *koṭhākārika* (treasurer) Bhada, who was evidently related to Bodhisiri in some way.

Apart from building this temple, the inscription indicates that Bodhisiri had made gifts of various kinds in many *vihāra*s in the area—a *caitya-gṛha* at the Kulaha *vihāra*, a shrine for the bodhi-tree at the Sīhala *vihāra*, a cell at the Mahādhammagiri *vihāra*, a *maṇḍapa* pillar at the *mahāvihāra*, a hall for religious practice at Devagiri; a tank, verandah, and *maṇḍapa* at Puvasela; a stone *maṇḍapa* at the eastern gate of the *mahācaitya* at Kaṇṭakasela, three cells at Hirumuṭhuva, seven cells at Papilā, a stone *maṇḍapa* at Puphagiri, and a stone *maṇḍapa* at another *vihāra.*

While Cāṁtisiri was the preeminent patron at the *mahācaitya*, Bodhisiri stands out as a non-royal donor whose benefactions were extensively spread over many monastic establishments at Vijayapurī and beyond. Taken together, the epigraphic evidence points to a dominant role played by royal and non-royal women in the emergence of Vijayapurī as a premier Buddhist centre.

The Circle of Merit

Apart from identifying the donors of pious gifts, donative inscriptions also performed the very important function of expressing the nature of the expected results of the gift and indicating to whom they were to accrue.[24] Historians tend to understand religious donations as attempts of social or political groups to assert or legitimize their status. This is no doubt an important aspect, but the language and expression of religious piety in donative inscriptions tells us something significant about people's religious beliefs as well as social structure. It has been pointed out that inscriptions from Buddhist sites indicate the widespread prevalence of a belief in the transfer of merit, that is, the idea that an individual could make a pious gift and that the merit of the gift could accrue to another person or persons, a belief that is not alluded to in Buddhist texts.[25] This is actually an idea that is not confined to Buddhism. It should also be noted that at Nagarjunakonda, what is as striking as the transfer of merit is the sharing of merit, a sentiment that fits in well with a social fabric in which, as mentioned earlier, kinship ties were exceptionally strong.

Inscriptions refer to several kinds of anticipated results of the pious gift, including the longevity and victory of the king. More frequent are expressions of a desire for the happiness and welfare of the donor in both the worlds and/or her attainment of *nirvāṇa.* These are frequently extended to the relatives of the donor, to all sentient beings, and to the whole world. The most elaborate 'merit list' occurs in Bodhisiri's inscription, which lists 30 of her relatives by name and relationship including her husband and his father, mother, brothers, sister, brother's sons, sister's sons; her own father, mother, brother, sisters, grandfather, grandmother, maternal uncle(/s?), maternal grandmother, daughter, sons, and daughters-in-law. Apart from these individually named merit-beneficiaries, the inscription also states that the gift was dedicated to the endless welfare and happiness of the assembly of good people (*sādhūs*) and of the whole world.

While generosity and gift-giving are considered meritorious acts in Buddhist texts, such activities are not considered capable of enabling a person to attain *nirvāṇa.* The inscriptions, however, reflect precisely such a belief. Further, specifying the 'merit list' was important. It created a circle, a community who shared in the merit—and also the prestige—of the gift.

Relics and Rituals

The interment of relics at Nagarjunakonda reveals various facets related to the relic cult and the funerary practices of Buddhist monks. Unlike at Sanchi, there are no inscriptions on the relic caskets. But just whose relics were embedded in a *stūpa* would have been known to the monks who lived here and the laity and pilgrims who visited, and would have become part of collective memory. This is probably why (apart from the fact that inscriptions on the relic caskets would not have been seen by anyone anyway), unlike the names of donors and the recipients of merit, it was not considered necessary to inscribe the names of the monks whose relics, and by extension presence, were embedded in the *stūpas*.

There is clear evidence of a royal connection of four out of a total of nine relic *stūpa*s at Nagarjunakonda. However, patronage towards the building of such *stūpas* was not exclusively a royal prerogative. There are two broad types of relic interment at this site—in earthenware pots (Stūpas 4, 5) and the 'nestling' of reliquaries (Stūpas 1, 2, 3, 4, 6, 8, 8A, 9). The latter procedure is described in Pali texts and highlights the sanctity of the relics.[26] It is likely that the relics of local monks may have been interred in earthenware pots, while the 'nestling technique' was used for famous monks whose relics had been acquired from elsewhere. The proliferation of relic *stūpa*s in fact presupposes an ancient transactional network in relics, the details of which deserve to be worked out.[27]

An instance of nestled reliquaries was found in the north-western section of the *mahācaitya*. Here, a bone fragment was placed in a small round gold reliquary, ¾ inches in diameter. This was placed inside a silver casket shaped like a miniature *stūpa*, 2½ inches high, together with a few gold flowers, pearls, garnets, and crystals. The silver casket was, in turn, placed inside an earthenware pot (found in a crushed state), along with three large crystal beads and a round ear ornament. In other *stūpa*s, the caskets included those in *stūpa*-shapes as well as in other forms. The items found therein included bone fragments (always in the inner-most reliquary), beads (coral, pearl, and semi-precious stones), gold and silver leaf flowers, crystal objects, and gold medallions. Stūpa 4 gave evidence of nestled reliquaries as well as 12 water pots covered by inverted bowls. This suggests the practice of interring the relics of principle disciples with those of highly venerated monks. Some *vihāra*s gave evidence of the storage of monks' bone and tooth relics, indicating that when certain monks died, their corporeal relics were stored carefully until enough had been collected to warrant the construction of a *stūpa*.

Relics are to be expected in *stūpa*s (although they do not occur in all *stūpas*). More unusual is the discovery of animal bones. Within Stūpa 9 (Figure 2.6), apart from two red earthenware water-pots and two food-bowls (apparently devoid of ashes or relics), there were also some calcified animal bones. These included deer and hare bones and what appeared to be the frontal skull bones (with horn-bearers but no horns) of a cow or bull.[28] The *mahācaitya* yielded a heap of burnt bones of peafowl.[29] We seem to be looking at consecration rituals involving animal

Figure 2.6
View of Stūpa 9 during excavations

Courtesy: Archaeological Survey of India

sacrifice. These rituals can perhaps be seen as reflecting the encounter and mingling of the Buddhist relic cult with local funerary practices. This is suggested by the occurrence of animal remains in some of the megalithic graves at Nagarjunakonda.[30]

The Material Remains of Monastic Life

Monastic complexes at Nagarjunakonda included various combinations and arrangements of *stūpas*, *caityas*, *vihāras*, and *maṇḍapas*. Within *vihāras*, variations in size, ornamentation, location, and accessibility of cells suggest hierarchies within the monastic communities. Similarly, on the basis of the location and plan of the monasteries, inferences can be made about the level of engagement or disengagement of monastic communities with the laity. Within the monastic complexes, the *stūpa* areas may have been accessible to the laity. Certain detached *stūpas* seem to have been associated with less monastic control. As it is not possible to describe and discuss all the monasteries at the site, the focus here will be on Sites 3 and 32a, which actually consist of three complexes that together form the largest monastic cluster at ancient Vijayapurī.[31]

In this cluster, the layout of the monastery lying to the south suggests that worship at shrines was an integral part of monastic routine. The fact that there was both a Buddha-*caitya* as well as a *stūpa-caitya* indicates that monks had the option of worshipping at either or both. The Buddha-*caitya* contained a colossal Buddha image (found headless and in four pieces), which must have stood about 8 ft high. The *padmāsana* of this statue contained a gold tube which had in it 95 pearls and possibly bone ash. The discoveries in the *vihāra* area included a toilet and bathing area, a workshop devoted to the making of stone images, and what may have been a store room for ritualistic paraphernalia. One of the cells in the *vihāra* had a limestone *pūrṇa-ghaṭa* in which were found two small teeth. The artefacts found in the *vihāra* included a rusty iron axehead, a corroded iron measure containing a lead coin, a coin with the Ujjain symbol, a round stucco bead and two pieces of ivory bangles. The *stūpa*, which stood to the west of the *vihāra* complex, could have been accessed by monks directly from the *vihāra*. It could also have been accessed by the laity by skirting the living quarters of the monks, from either side.

Two other complexes were located to the north and north-east of the monastic unit described earlier. The arrangement of cells within a high-walled enclosure in the latter was taken by some scholars as indicating that it was meant for *bhikkhunīs*.[32] However, this is purely speculative, as the arrangement for privacy could equally have been for the sake of monks of high rank. A fragmentary Sanskrit inscription ('A') found at site 32a records certain details pertaining to a *maṇḍapa* and a monastery wing.[33] The donor is described as *vipul-ārtha-kākṣin* (one who desires the welfare of others). The inscription refers, among other things, to the *mukhya-pācaka* (principal cooks), a *vihāra-mukhya* (chief or head of the monastery). The feature that has attracted most attention in this inscription is the phrase *vigata-jvar-ālaya*, interpreted by some scholars as 'a place for those recovering from fever', that is, a hospital. This is not a particularly far-fetched interpretation, and corroborates the suggested connection between Buddhist monasteries and healing traditions.[34] Whether this 'hospital' was exclusively for members of the monastic community or otherwise, remains an open question. If the whole or part of the complex in the north-western part of Site 3 and 32a is the hospital in question, then it can be noted that its approaches were not from the adjacent monasteries but from independent entrances in the western and eastern walls of the enclosure.

Utilitarian objects found in monastic contexts direct our attention to the daily life of monks. These include pottery, including some with religious symbols such as the *triratna* and *svastika*.[35] There is the occasional graffiti on potsherds. In most cases, this gives names of monks; in one case, there is the name of a monastery—Nakatara *vihāra*. Interestingly, one potsherd has an incised sketch of the plan of a monastery.

Stone artefacts found in monastic contexts include items used in food-processing—fragments of 3-legged querns, an intact rotary quern, a cylindrical red sandstone muller, a complete granite rotary quern, and a large grindstone. There are iron objects such as an iron hook, iron needle with eye, spoon (?) with broken handle, arrowhead, wedge, awls/points. Two iron sickles (Figure 2.7) and a hoe point to the involvement of monks in agricultural activities.

Figure 2.7
Iron implements, including sickles

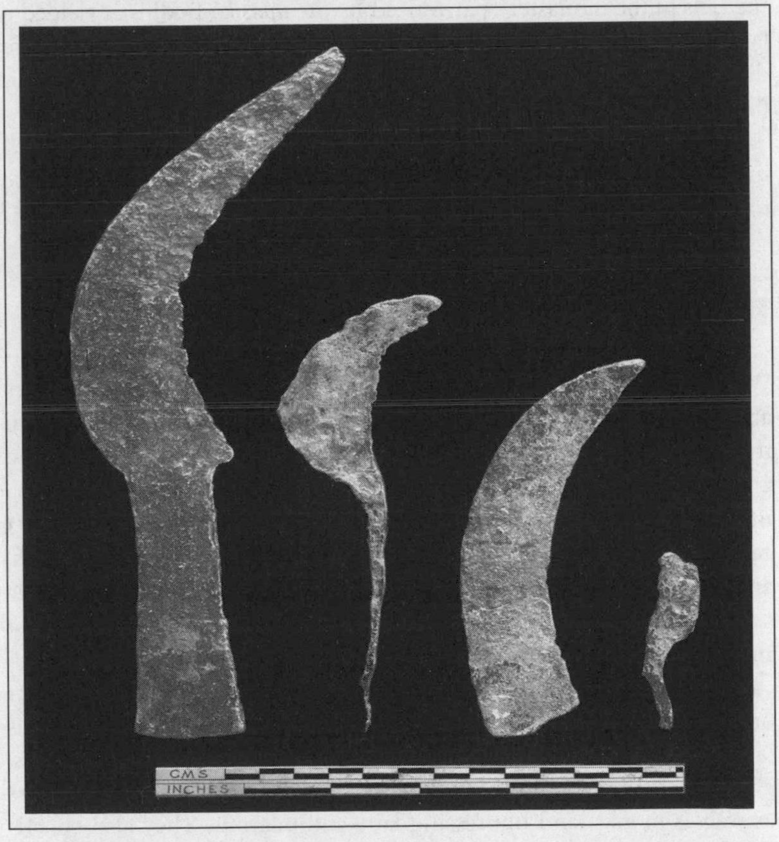

Courtesy: Archaeological Survey of India

Metal objects (copper, bronze, lead) include finger rings, toe-rings, and antimony rods. A bronze object with a double *makara* design and a prong in the centre and two perforations on the shaft may have been part of some ritual paraphernalia. Terracotta objects included pendants and fragments of miniature shrines (referred to in the report as 'votive shrines', Site 38), which seem to have been used in rituals. Shell bangles and armlets have also been found in moderate quantities in all monasteries. Beads of various materials reported at *stūpa*/monastery sites include those in various shapes made of green jasper, red jasper, carnelian, banded agate, terracotta, and glass. These could have been ornaments, talismans, or prayer beads.

Textual and inscriptional evidence from many sites indicates that the supposed antipathy of monks towards money is part of an idealized image of the Buddhist monk based largely on the *Tipiṭaka*. One of the cells in the monastery patronized by the *upāsikā* Bodhisiri yielded a large number of small lead coins, a lump of lead ore and an earthenware die—evidence of a coin-minting apparatus.[36] Unfortunately, there is no description of these coins.

That monks also had fun is indicated by the remains of a game board inscribed on the floor of one of the monasteries (Site 38) and ivory dice found at two monastic sites (Sites 85 and 106).

The Themes of the Narrative Reliefs

While the inscriptions and structural remains allow us to make inferences about the activities of monks, laity, and patrons, the sculptures take us to the realm of images that animated their world. Nagarjunakonda yielded a great deal of stone sculpture including three-dimensional Buddha images, *patipadās* (Buddha footprints), and relief carvings. The relief carvings are found on drum slabs, *āyaka* slabs and their cornices, pillars, and moonstones located at entrances, especially of shrines. The *āyaka* sculptures are of special importance as the devout would have stopped at these points to pray and place offerings.

The large repertoire of visual narratives formed an important part of the universe of lived, experienced Buddhism, for monks as well as laity. These sculptures gave meaningful ornamentation to the structures, endowing them with beauty and grandeur, conferring prestige on donors as well as monks, and impressing laity and pilgrims. They also constituted visual teachings for monks and laity alike, embodying, conveying, and emphasizing people, events, and virtues that were valorized in the

Buddhist tradition. The artists used different kinds of narrative techniques to tell the stories.[37] The viewers' degree and quality of engagement with the sculptures and their familiarity with the narratives must have varied.[38] But the didactic potential of the relief images must have been considerable, especially for the laity, who may not have had much access to written sources of the Buddhist tradition.

A major problem in reconstructing the sculptural programme of Nagarjunakonda is the fragmentary nature of the surviving evidence and the fact that there is no complete list of sculptures indicating where exactly they were found. Therefore, it is not possible to ascertain the frequency of particular scenes and their precise placement within the larger architectural programme. Many scholars have referred to the apparent randomness and repetition of themes in the sculptural representations at early Buddhist sites. However, the choice of themes must have been the result of a dialogue between several people, chief among whom were the patrons and the *navakaṁmika*, the monk who supervised the construction of the edifice. Architects, master-craftsmen, masons, and sculptors, may also have offered their technical advice.

The relief sculptures can be divided into six broad categories.[39] The first consists of representations of the Buddha's presence or the totality of his life in an abstract way. The second includes the most important events in his hagiography. The third comprises scenes illustrating other incidents associated with the Buddha's life, especially his great feats. The fourth consists of representations of the Jātaka stories. The fifth is a residual category comprising miscellaneous events and images with a wide-ranging cast of characters. And the sixth comprises ornamental and auspicious symbols. In all cases, the images were not part of an ordinary narrative; they were endowed with layers of meaning and significance that the devout monk or layperson who moved in their midst could imbibe and absorb, if he or she desired.

The most abstract representations of the totality of the Buddha's life are the *āyaka* pillars, which are generally understood as representing the Buddha's birth, his departure from Kapilavastu, enlightenment, first sermon, and death. (This interpretation can, however, be questioned.) Further, representations of ornamented *stūpa*s have been found in large numbers at Nagarjunakonda, many of them part of *stūpa* drum slabs (Figure 2.8). These *stūpa*s provide a central frame for the Buddha sitting or standing in different formal attitudes—standing with his hands raised in the *abhaya mudrā*, sitting on the coils of the *nāga* Mucalinda, or represented by a stack of symbols. The *stūpa* has often been interpreted as representing the *parinirvāṇa*. However, what we seem to have here

Figure 2.8
Stūpa relief

Source: Author

is a graphic expression of a more abstract idea—the Buddha's presence within the *stūpa*.

Among the relief sculptures, great importance was attached to certain events that were evidently considered central to the Buddha's hagiography—the birth (Figure 2.9), the renunciation, Māra's assault on the meditating Siddhārtha, the first sermon in the deer park at Sārnath

Figure 2.9
The birth of Siddhārtha

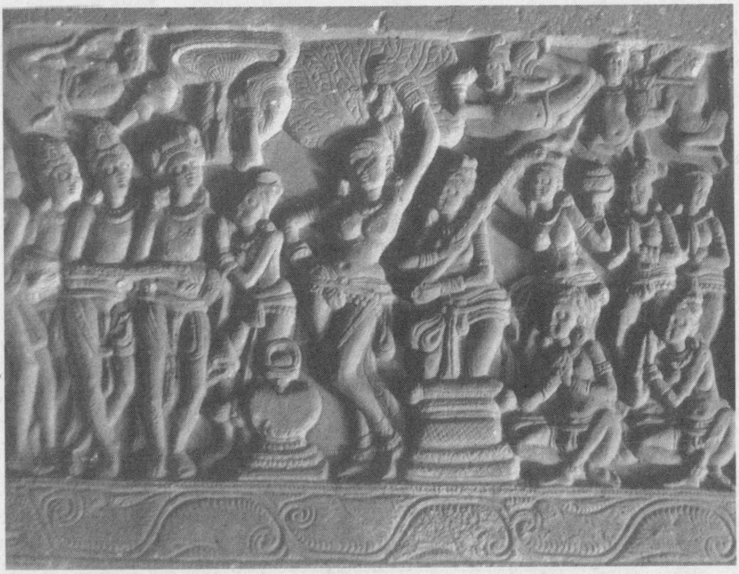

Courtesy: Archaeological Survey of India

(Figure 2.10), and the *parinirvāṇa.* These events were often represented in sequence, including on *āyaka* platforms or cornices. However, many other episodes from the Buddha's life were also singled out for sculptural representation, and this shows an awareness of a more detailed biography. These include several scenes based in Kapilavastu—the conception, the casting of the horoscope (Figure 2.11), the seer Asita's visit to the palace, the presentation of the child at the Śākya temple, and the grown prince Siddhārtha in his palace or his pleasure garden. There is one representation of Siddhārtha seeing a corpse, one of the famous 'four sights' of the hagiography, and apart from representations of the 'Great Departure', there is a beautifully executed relief depicting the father Śuddhodana's grief on hearing the news of that event from the groom Chandaka (Figure 2.12).

Another set of relief sculptures draws us into events at Gayā, leading up to and following the enlightenment. These include Māra's assault, Sujātā's food offering, the Buddha protected by the *nāga* Mucalinda, the gods celebrating the enlightenment and exhorting the Buddha to

Figure 2.10
The first sermon

Courtesy: Archaeological Survey of India

proclaim his doctrine to the world, and the food offerings made to the enlightened one by the merchants Tapussa and Bhallika. The sculptors also carved scenes which showed the Buddha using his extraordinary powers to defeat or transform skeptical or inimical beings. These include the 'conversion' of Nanda, the miracle of Śrāvastī, the visit of Sakka (Indra) to the Buddha in the Indraśaila cave, the subjugation of the elephant Nalagiri, and the conversion of king Kapinna.[40] The vanquishing of *nāgas* and *yakṣas* (who were initially the focus of popular cults in their own right) is represented in scenes such as the 'conversion' of the *yakṣa* Alavaka or the Buddha defeating the *nāga* king Apalāla.[41]

Unlike at Bharhut in central India, the Jātaka scenes at Nagarjunakonda do not have labels. This suggests that they were either known and understood well, or that the laity may have required and taken the help of monks to understand them. Just which of the hundreds of Jātaka stories were chosen for visual representation is also significant. At Nagarjunakonda, scholars have variously identified representations of the Māndhātu, Mahāpaduma, Vessantara, Śibi, Sasa, Dīghītikosala, Dasaratha, Unmagga, and Campeyya Jātakas. Again, it

Figure 2.11
The casting of Siddhārtha's horoscope

Courtesy: Archaeological Survey of India

must be mentioned that some of the identifications are problematic.[42] However, the point being emphasized here is that individually and collectively, these visual narratives emphasize the qualities of a *bodhisattva* that were worthy of emulation by monks and laity alike—compassion and restraint in injuring another in the face of grave provocation, even when having the power to do so; the eventual triumph of good over jealousy and villainy; supreme self-sacrifice for the sake of others; the merits of renunciation; and extraordinary generosity. The Māndhātu Jātaka is depicted most frequently. The story of Māndhātā, the *cakravartin* with an insatiable desire for power, drives home the destructive nature of such propensities and the mortality of all men.

A correlation of the details of the narrative scenes with texts suggests a variety of possible textual sources. But the visual narratives did not necessarily follow the details of such sources closely, probably due to the fact that their composition may equally have been guided by oral traditions, or because the artists felt free to take liberties while translating the textual/oral into the visual/sculptural, in order to maximize dramatic effect or to grapple with the constraints of space.

Figure 2.12
Śuddhodana hearing of Siddhārtha's departure

Courtesy: Archaeological Survey of India

The men and women who flank the Buddha, throne, or *stūpa* are an important part of the compositions, connecting and drawing the viewing laity into the narrative, conveying the sense of a community of worshippers, which endured over time. In addition, certain scenes depict exemplary laypersons, emphasizing the importance of giving. The most interesting among these are representations of gifts of food made to the Buddha (Figure 2.13) including, possibly, offerings by Sujātā and by the first lay disciples, the merchants Tapussa and Bhallika.

Equally significant are the numerous representations—specific and general—of royalty.[43] These include a scene which seems to show the gift of earth to the Buddha by Aśoka while the latter was a child (Figure 2.14).[44] There are also several representations of kings or kingship in the form of the *cakravartin* flanked by his seven treasures. These (*ratanas*) are the *cakka* (wheel), *hatthi* (elephant), *assa* (horse), *maṇi* (jewel), *itthī* (woman/queen), *gahapati* (land-owning householder), *pariṇāyaka*

Figure 2.13
Devotees offering food to the Buddha

Source: Author

Figure 2.14
The gift of earth to the Buddha by Jaya (the emperor Aśoka in a previous life)(?)

Source: Author

Figure 2.15
Mithuna couple

Source: Author

(prince/advisor/general).[45] The *cakravartin* and his treasures occur in a relief that was associated with Stūpa 9.[46] There is another representation of the *cakravartin* and his jewels in Longhurst's report (Plate 32 c); the find-spot of this sculpture is not known. The sculptures found at Site 5 included a fragmentary sculpture with the *cakravartin* standing with two of his 'jewels'—the queen and wheel.[47]

The visual narratives at *stūpa*s and monasteries created a space within which the Buddha's presence, life, and teaching were encoded and expressed in stone. And yet, a great deal of the outer world entered into the inner world of the *stūpa.* The sculptural programme at Nagarjunakonda does not reflect a cold, austere, ascetic didacticism. The arresting 'glue' that holds the visual narratives together (and this is a feature of all early Buddhist narrative relief art) throngs with people, gods, trees, animals, ornaments, and auspicious symbols, all integral to the scenes. Amorous couples (*mithuna* figures) (Figure 2.15), langorous *śālabhañjikā*s, nymphs, and dwarf garland-bearers serve as dividers, framers, or end-markers in narrative sequences. The narrative reliefs represent the meeting of many worlds—those of Buddhist piety, popular belief and practice, nature, and of ordinary, everyday life.

Conclusions

Nagarjunakonda is in many respects a very atypical early historical Indian Buddhist site, differing in several ways from sites such as Sanchi and Bharhut.[48] We see a strong royal stamp, especially the stamp of royal women. Monks, nuns, inhabitants of entire villages do not appear as donors here. Clearly, patronage created communities of donors, monks, and merit-recipients and knitted these communities together. But membership of these communities varied from one site and region to another.

It is important to remember that while Vijayapurī was a major Buddhist centre in early historical India, it was more than this. The Buddhist monasteries were integrated into a larger, complex sociopolitical and religious landscape. Vijayapurī was the political centre of the Ikṣvāku dynasty. It was also a city in which the Hindu cults were represented in the form of many fine temples dedicated to Kārttikeya, Aṣṭabhujasvāmin (Viṣṇu) and Śiva as Sarvadeva and Puṣpabhadrasvāmin. There is evidence of a Hārīti temple and several medieval Jaina shrines.

The Buddhist monasteries of Vijayapurī may have rivaled, even eclipsed nearby Amaravati, but their fortunes were crucially linked to the patronage of political elites. This explains why this important Buddhist centre, created in a brief but intense burst of activity during about a century of Ikṣvāku rule, faded away with the decline of that dynasty. Hindu traditions, on the other hand, had a much longer legacy in the Nagarjunakonda valley. Any history of Nagarjunakonda has to take into account its long-term history and its many varied, religious strands.

Acknowledgements

I would like to thank the organizers of the Conference on 'Buddhism Across Asia: Networks of Material, Intellectual and Cultural Exchange', 16–18 February 2009, Institute of Southeast Asian Studies, Singapore, in which I presented an earlier version of this chapter. I would also like to acknowledge a research grant given by the University of Delhi, which facilitated this research.

Notes

1. Prakrit has been retained for proper names and for quotations from Prakrit inscriptions. All other words have been given in their more familiar Sanskritized form (e.g., *caitya, maṇḍapa*, etc.).
2. 'Nagarjunakonda' literally means Nagarjuna's hill (*koṇḍa* is Telugu for hill). An inscription (J. Ph. Vogel, 'Prakrit Inscriptions from a Buddhist site at Nagarjunikonda', *Epigraphia Indica* 20, 1929–1930, pp. 1–36; 'F') refers to a monastery called Cula-Dhammagiri on Siriparvata on the eastern side of Vijayapurī. This suggests that the early historical city was known as Vijayapurī. A Tibetan tradition refers to the famous Buddhist philosopher Nāgārjuna spending the later part of his life in a monastery at Śrīparvata. This is the basis of the supposed connection of this site with Nāgārjuna. It may be noted that several early writings spell the name of the site as Nagarjunikonda.
3. A. H. Longhurst, *The Buddhist Antiquities of Nagarjunakonda, Madras Presidency*. Memoirs of the Archaeological Survey of India, No. 54. Reprint edition (New Delhi: Archaeological Survey of India, [1938] 1999).
4. T. N. Ramachandran, *Nagarjunakonda 1938*. Memoirs of the Archaeological Survey of India, No. 71 (New Delhi: Archaeological Survey of India, [1953] 1999).
5. R. Subrahmanyam et al., *Nagarjunakonda (1954–1960): Volume I,* Memoirs of the Archaeological Survey of India, No. 75 (New Delhi: Archaeological Survey of India, 1975).
6. K. V. Soundararajan, ed., *Nagarjunakonda (1954–1960): Volume II (The Historical Period),* Memoirs of the Archaeological Survey of India, No. 75 (New Delhi: Archaeological Survey of India, 2006).
7. The early sites include Bhattiprolu, Gudivada, Alluru, Ghantasala, Gummadidurru, Chandavaram, Sankaram, Bavikonda, Salihundam, and Dhulikatta.
8. Inscriptional and numismatic evidence indicates a 'Sātavāhana' phase at the site, and the 2006 Report also touches on 'pre-Ikṣvāku' deposits and 'Ikṣvāku' remains. Fifty-four copper coins issued by Sātavāhana kings were found at the site. An inscription on a limestone pillar belonging to the sixth regnal year of Gautamīputra Vijaya Sātakarṇi was found close to Site 126. The inscription has the invocation: *[Na]mo bhagavato Agapogalasa* ('Adoration to the Lord, the best among men'). It was probably part of a Buddhist *maṇḍapa* (hall).
9. Several inscriptions (C1, C2, C3, B4, B5) at the *mahācaitya* begin with a salutation to the Buddha in a string of epithets ending with *saṁna-saṁbudhasa dhātuvara-parigahitasa*, followed by the word *mahācetiye.* Going by the suggestion made to him by L. de la Vallee Poussin, Vogel read *mahacetiye* as part of the next sentence and translated *saṁna-saṁbudhasa dhātuvara-parigahitasa* as 'the perfectly enlightened one who is absorbed by the best of elements, that is, by *nirvāṇa*' (J. Ph. Vogel, 'Prakrit Inscriptions from a Buddhist Site at Nagarjunikonda', p. 17). But *dhātuvara* can more readily be

translated as 'the most excellent relic'. The problem is how to translate *parigahita* and to decide whether this phrase qualifies the Buddha or the *mahācetiya*. Hirananda Sastri (editorial note p. 29, fn 1) suggested that the relevant portion perhaps meant to say that the *mahācaitya* was 'protected by the corporeal remains of the Buddha', and that the genitive case may have been used to differentiate this *stūpa* from others which were not similarly consecrated. Gregory Schopen, *Bones, Stones, and Buddhist Monks: Collected Papers on the Archaeology, Epigraphy, and Texts of Monastic Buddhism in India* (Honolulu: University of Hawaii Press, 1997), p. 158, sees *dhātuvara-parigahita* as qualifying the Buddha, and translates the sense as 'one who is enclosed within the most excellent relics', or 'one who is enclosed in the relic chamber'. He points out that the former is more likely and that in either case, we have an indication of an important aspect of the understanding of 'relics' in the Buddhist tradition. These were not understood as the remains of a dead being but as a part of his living presence residing in his shrine (the *stūpa*). Presently, the bone relic in question is enshrined in the Mūlagandhakuṭi vihāra at Sarnath.

10. It can be noted that Dhānyakaṭaka (Amaravati) was also an important centre of the Mahāsaṁghikas.
11. J. Ph. Vogel, 'Prakrit Inscriptions from a Buddhist Site at Nagarjunikonda', p. 24; 'H'.
12. Kasmira can be identified with the Kashmir valley, Gandhāra with the Rawalpindi-Peshawar area, Yavaṇa perhaps with the Kabul valley, Vanavāsa with the area around Banavasa in Karnataka, and Tāmraparṇi with Sri Lanka.
13. Cīna can be identified with China, Cilāta could be a reference to the Kirātas, Tosali was in Orissa, Avaraṁta can perhaps be identified with Aparānta in western India, Vaṅga was in Bengal. The readings of the words Yavana, Damila, and Palura are very uncertain. Damila could refer to the Tamil country, and Palura to Dantapura in Orissa (J. Ph. Vogel, 'Prakrit Inscriptions from a Buddhist Site at Nagarjunikonda', pp. 7–8).
14. H. Sarkar, *Studies in Early Buddhist Architecture of India* (New Delhi: Munshiram Manoharlal, [1966] 1993) has tried to correlate differences in monastic plans with sectarian affiliation.
15. Gregory Schopen, *Buddhist Monks and Business Matters: Still More Papers on Monastic Buddhism in India* (Honolulu: University of Hawaii Press, 2004), p. 390.
16. The *āyaka stambhas*—a notable feature of many Andhra *stūpas*—were five pillars that stood together on platforms located at the four cardinal points. They are believed to represent the Buddha's birth, his departure from Kapilavastu, enlightenment, first sermon, and death. However, this interpretation is very conjectural.
17. It may be noted that except for a few of the Aśokan inscriptions using Greek and Aramaic in the northwest and the early Tamil inscriptions of South India, Prakrit was the dominant epigraphic language of early historic India. In the Deccan and South India, Prakrit and Sanskrit co-existed as epigraphic languages in the 3rd and early 4th centuries. Between the 4th and 6th centuries, Prakrit was dethroned by Sanskrit all over the

subcontinent. The Nagarjunakonda inscriptions reflect a transitional stage in this process. Their careless orthography suggests that the composers and/or scribes were dealing with a language that they were not fully comfortable with. Further, the orthography and some of the proper names reflect a vernacular substratum that was probably a proto-Kannada dialect (Sten Konow's post-script to Vogel, 'Prakrit Inscriptions from a Buddhist site at Nagarjunikonda', p. 26).

18. For recent work highlighting the historical importance and variety of households, see Kumkum Roy, ed., *Essays in Honour of Nandita Prasad Sahai: Looking Within, Looking Without—Exploring households in the subcontinent through time* (Delhi: Primus, 2015).
19. An exception is Ehuvala Cāṁtamūla, whose Patagandigudem copper plates record the building of a four-hall compound and the grant of land in favour of a Buddhist monastery which seems to have been close to Amaravati (see Harry Falk, 'The Pātagaṇḍigūḍem Copper-plate Grant of the Ikṣvāku King Ehavala Cāntamūla', *Silk Road Art and Archaeology* 6, 1999–2000, pp. 275–283. The first king Cāṁtamūla is described in inscriptions as having performed the *aśvamedha, agniṣṭoma,* and *vājapeya* sacrifices. Ehuvala Cāṁtamūla, third in the line, is described as having performed the *aśvamedha*. Princes also occasionally appear as donors—for instance, prince Vīrapurisadatta made a grant along with his mother in favour of the Puṣpabhadrasvāmin temple (Sircar, D. C. and Krishnan, K. G. 'Two Inscriptions from Nagarjunikonda', *Epigraphia Indica* 34, 1961–1962, pp. 17–22.).
20. The others royal women are: Aḍavi-Cātasiri (daughter of the first king), Cula-Cāṁtisirinikā (sister of the first king), *mahādevī* Rudrabhaṭārikā (perhaps wife of the reigning king), *mahādevī* Bapisirinikā (wife of the reigning king), *mahādevī* Chaṭhisiri (wife of the reigning king), and the wife of a person named Mahākaṁdasiri. All except two (Rudrabhaṭārikā and perhaps the wife of Mahākaṁdasiri) of the women donors belonged to the Ikṣvāku blood-line. There is one non-royal gift recorded at the *mahācaitya* site; this will be discussed further on.
21. D. C. Sircar, 'More Inscriptions from Nagarjunikonda', *Epigraphia Indica* 35, 1963–1964, pp. 1–36. The pillar was found near Site 9. Sircar thinks that year 20 refers not to a regnal year but to the Jupiter cycle.
22. This is with reference to Nagarjunakonda. However, at sites such as Sanchi, members of the monastic community also appear as donors in large numbers.
23. J. Ph. Vogel, 'Prakrit Inscriptions from a Buddhist Site at Nagarjunikonda', pp. 22–23.
24. There is a need for a closer study of the typology of gifts and gift-giving in ancient and early medieval India. Terms such as 'gift' and *dāna* are used too often, without reflecting on important differences in their context and nature.
25. Schopen, *Bones, Stones, and Buddhist Monks,* pp. 36–55.
26. Michael Willis, *Buddhist Reliquaries from Ancient India* (London: British Museum Press, 2000), p. 20.
27. Such a study of the movement of relics can fruitfully be extended to more recent times as well.

28. Longhurst, *The Buddhist Antiquities of Nagarjunakonda, Madras Presidency*, p. 23.
29. It may be noted that one of the cells in Monastery II revealed an earthenware pot filled with bones of hares and field rats (Longhurst, *The Buddhist Antiquities of Nagarjunakonda, Madras Presidency*, p. 23).
30. Animal bones were found in Megaliths IV, VI, and XIV. Megalith XII yielded a complete bovine skeleton with cut marks and another small animal (Subrahmanyam et al., *Nagarjunakonda (1954–1960)*, pp. 169, 171, 177, 180). Although the reports treat them as separate from and earlier than the early historic remains, the two must have been at least partly contemporaneous.
31. This includes Longhurst's Stūpa 3 and Ramachandran's Site 6.
32. Soundararajan, *Nagarjunakonda (1954–1960)*, p. 170
33. Sircar, 'More inscriptions from Nagarjunikonda', pp. 17–18.
34. Kenneth G. Zysk, *Asceticism and Healing in Ancient India: Medicine in the Buddhist Monastery* (New York and Mumbai: Oxford University Press, 1991).
35. Soundararajan, *Nagarjunakonda (1954–1960)*, pp. 357–475.
36. Longhurst, *The Buddhist Antiquities of Nagarjunakonda, Madras Presidency*, p. 10.
37. See Vidya Dehejia. *Discourse in Early Buddhist Art: Visual Narratives of India* (New Delhi: Munshiram Manoharlal, [1997] 2005), pp. 3–35.
38. For two very different views of the devotee's engagement with Buddhist narrative reliefs, see Dehejia, *Discourse in Early Buddhist Art;* and Robert L. Brown, 'Narrative as Icon: The *Jātaka* Stories in Ancient Indian and Southeast Asian Architecture', in Juliane Schober, ed., *Sacred Biography in the Buddhist Traditions of South and Southeast Asia* (Honolulu: University of Hawaii Press, 1993).
39. The sources of the following discussion are the descriptions and Plates in Longhurst, *The Buddhist Antiquities of Nagarjunakonda, Madras Presidency;* Ramachandran, *Nagarjunakonda 1938;* and Elizabeth Rosen Stone, *The Buddhist Art of Nāgārjunakoṇḍa* (New Delhi: Motialal Banarasidass, 1994). I have only referred to those scenes where the identification appears to be secure.
40. I have used the word 'conversion' as a convenient short-hand for a person embracing the Buddha's doctrine. But I have placed it in inverted commas because I think that there are problems in using such words in the context of ancient Indian religious traditions.
41. It must be acknowledged that there is a strong element of subjectivity in the interpretation of some of these scenes. For instance, *nāgas* are easy to recognize in the reliefs, but precisely which story featuring which *nāga* is being told, is often difficult to ascertain.
42. For instance, Monika Zin (personal communication) has pointed out that the scenes identified by Longhurst as the Dīghītikosala and Dasaratha Jātakas (Plates 47a and 45a) belong to the same slab and it is difficult to interpret the scene in question.

43. Kings appear variously attired in *laṅgoṭī* (loin cloth), *pravaraṇa* (upper garment), very often with a *kamarabandha* tied around their waists; pyjama or *dhotī*-like lower garments are rare. They usually wear distinctive head-dresses and they can often be identified by means of insignia such as throne, *chattra* (umbrella), attendants bearing *cāmaras* (fly-whisks), or *dhvajas* (standards, banners) (K. Krishna Murthy, *Nagarjunakonda: A Cultural Study* [Delhi: Concept Publishing Company, 1977], pp. 38, 126–127, 232–238).
44. This scene appears often at Amaravati and Jaggayyapeta.
45. The seven jewels are enumerated, for instance, in the *Mahā-Sudassana Suttānta.*
46. Longhurst, *The Buddhist Antiquities of Nagarjunakonda, Madras Presidency*, p. 31, Plate 30b.
47. T. N. Ramachandran, *Nagarjunakonda 1938*, Plate XXXIII-C.
48. For Sanchi, see Upinder Singh, 'Sanchi: The History of the Patronage of an Ancient Buddhist Establishment', *The Indian Economic and Social History Review* 33, 1996 and for Bharhut, see H. Luders, ed., *Bharhut Inscriptions.* Revised by E. Waldschmidt and M. A. Mehendale. *Corpus Inscriptionum Indicarum* Vol. 2, Part 2 (Ootacamund: Government Epigraphist for India, 1963).

3

Cults and Shrines in Early Historical Mathura (c. 200 BC–AD 200)

The history of Hinduism has generally been constructed on the basis of frameworks provided by religious texts, which are not always accurately reflective of popular practice. Apart from their elite authorship and the notorious problems of dating, brahmanical texts reflect a phase when the practices they mention have been accorded brahmanical sanction, and hence conceal their much earlier origin. Further, traditions seeking to attain or having attained the position of cultural dominance try to marginalize other traditions that may have been very important at the time and in the process give us a distorted impression of prevailing religious practice. Regional or local variations are not always clearly reflected in early texts, and there are some widely pervasive practices that find no mention whatsoever.

This chapter argues that archaeology can be fruitfully used to identify the roots and early history of popular Hinduism. This includes the evidence of either polytheistic or monolatrous worship, deities that came to be assigned places of prominence or subordination in the Hindu pantheons, the devotional worship of images of deities in religious shrines, and cults which had more than a local significance. Of course the limitation of the archaeological perspective is that although it gives us ample information regarding the tangible forms, objects and material contexts

---

This chapter was previously published in *World Archaeology* 36 (3), 2004, pp. 378–398.

of worship, it is less forthcoming when it comes to the experiential, spiritual, emotional and theological aspects of religious practice, and, like many texts, it tends to have an urban bias.

The focus of this chapter is on the Mathura district of the Indian state of Uttar Pradesh, especially on the city of Mathura and the sites of Sonkh and Mat (25 km south-west and 14.5 km north of Mathura, respectively), between c. 200 BC and c. AD 200. In the 6th century BC, Mathura was the capital of the Śūrasena kingdom. Absorbed into the Mauryan empire in the 3rd century BC, Mathura's cultural efflorescence is particularly marked during the centuries when it came under the successive control of local rulers—the Mitras and Dattas (the late 3rd century BC to the late 1st century BC), the Kṣatrapas (late 1st century BC to the first quarter of the 1st century AD) and then the Kuṣāṇas (the 1st century AD to the late second/early 3rd century AD). Strategically poised at the entrance to the fertile Gangetic plains, Mathura burst forth as a major cultural crossroad, a locus of the activity of political elites, a flourishing city noted for specialized craft production (especially its fine cotton textiles), a junction of major trans-regional trade routes, a centre of diverse religious establishments, and a trend-setter of sophisticated sculptural styles.

The Archaeological Profile of Sites in the Mathura Area

The Yamuna divides Mathura district into an eastern and western part; most of the archaeological sites are located to the west of the river. The first somewhat systematic archaeological explorations, documentation and excavations (in Chaubara and Kankali Tila mounds) of the Mathura area (Figure 3.1) were conducted by Alexander Cunningham between 1861 and 1882.[1] While other 19th century archaeological accounts of Mathura[2] focused on the Buddhist remains, Vogel's reports[3] brought out other key aspects of the early religious history of the area, such as the worship of images of *nāgas*, *yakṣas* and brahmanical deities.

In the post-independence decades, the Archaeological Survey of India carried out excavations in different parts of Mathura city in 1954–1955 and between 1973 and 1977, but no full report has been so far published.[4] A summary of the cultural sequence revealed by these excavations is given in Table 3.1.

Figure 3.1
Important sites in the Mathura area

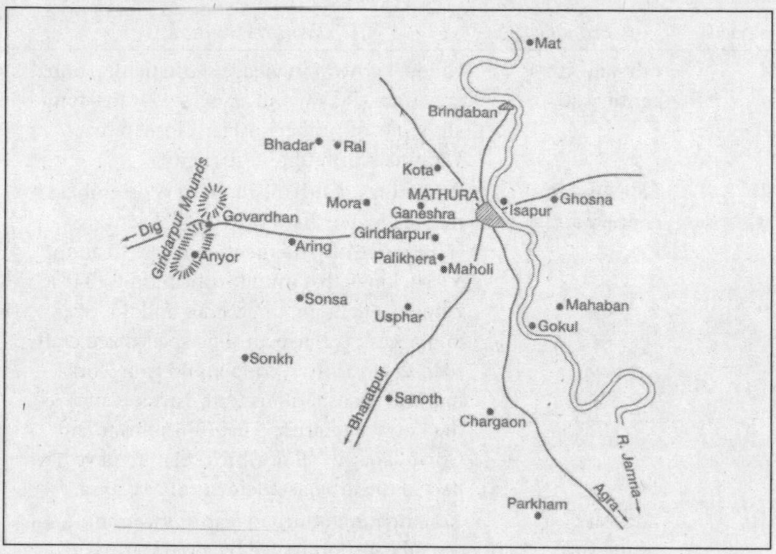

Source: Härtel, 1993, p. 12

Between 1966 and 1974, more intensive and extensive excavations were carried out at Sonkh (25 km south west of Mathura) by the Indian Art and Archaeology Research Team of the Museum fur Indische Kunst, Berlin, under the direction of Herbert Härtel.[5] Eight periods of occupation, divided into forty habitation levels, were identified. A summary of the cultural sequence revealed by the excavations is given in Table 3.2.[6]

The Mathura region is most strongly associated with the legend and worship of Krishna, but between c. 200 BC and AD 200, its religious landscape was extremely diverse. The details of sculptural and inscriptional discoveries in 19th and early 20th century accounts enable us to identify the location of some of the shrines, even though structural remains are absent or near-absent. To give a few examples, the Katra was the site of a Buddhist *vihāra* from the early 2nd century AD; the Jamalpur/Jail Mound was the site of a Buddhist establishment and a shrine of the *nāga* deity Dadhikarṇa; a Jaina establishment stood on the Kankali Tila from the 2nd century BC. There are other mounds (e.g., Kota mound, a small village about 4.8 km north of Mathura) where the evidence of sculptures and inscriptions is ambiguous and suggests the existence of ancient shrines of uncertain denomination.

Table 3.1
The Mathura cultural sequence

Period	*Chronology*	*Features, remarks*
I	6th–late 4th century BC	Gradual growth in village settlement; painted grey ware (PGW) and associated wares found at the site of Ambarish Tila, close to the Yamuna, north of Mathura city.
II	Late 4th–2nd century BC	Beginnings of urbanism; pottery assemblage marked by northern black polished ware (NBP); size of settlement increases to about 3.9 sq. km with a mud fortification wall (the Dhulkot) flanking three sides and the river on the east; coinage, prolific specialized crafts such as terracottas, copper and iron working, and beads; NBP is found at sites such as the Katra, Saptarishi Tila, Bhuteshwar and Govindanagar, all of which seem to have been part of the urban settlement of Mathura.
III	2nd–late 1st century BC	Accentuation of urban features; ceramic assemblage dominated by a red ware, with some grey ware as well; beginning and gradual increase in the number of burnt brick structures; inscribed coins, seals and sealings; increased stylistic sophistication in terracottas and other craft items; fortification wall falls into disuse.
IV	1st–3rd century AD	Urban efflorescence; red wares, including pots with painted and stamped designs, a more limited quantity of fine red polished ware including sprinklers; great variety and technical finesse in artefacts; fortification wall strengthened, enlarged and supplemented with an inner fortification.
V	4th–6th century AD	No regular archaeological sequence identified or established for these or subsequent centuries.

Table 3.2
The Sonkh cultural sequence

Period	*Levels*	*Description of Period*	*Chronology*
Period I	40–37	PGW and BRW	c. 800–400 BC
Period II	36–29	Pre-and early Maurya, Maurya and 'Śuṅga Cultural Phase'	c. 400–late 2nd century BC
Period III	28–25	Mitras of Mathura	Late 2nd-late 1st century BC
Period IV	24–23	Kṣatrapas and Rāmadatta	End of 1st century BC–early 1st century AD
Period V	22–16	Kuṣāṇas	1st–3rd century AD
Period VI	15–12	Guptas to early medieval	4th–10th century
Period VII	11–18	Medieval levels	10th–16th centuries
Period VIII	7–1	Mughals to Jats, late fortress levels	16th–18th centuries

Goddesses, Miniature Tanks and Shrines

The abundance of stone and terracotta images of early historical Mathura indicates goddesses, *yakṣa*s, *yakṣī*s, *nāga*s and *nāgī*s formed important features of the religious landscape. The 'mother goddess' or 'goddess' label shelters a number of distinct and different goddesses, most of whom may always remain anonymous to us. These terms are used here only as a convenient abbreviation for female figurines whose attributes suggest some sort of cultic or ritualistic significance—as objects of worship, votive offerings, or as part of the paraphernalia of domestic rituals—with the additional caveat that the discernment of such a significance is often subjective.

The importance of the worship of images of goddesses in early historical Mathura is represented in an abundance of carved ring stones and disc stones, terracotta images and plaques. A number of 'mother goddess' figurines have been reported in stratified contexts in the course of Mathura excavations.[7] They form the earliest objects of cultic significance, and make their appearance in the later part of Period II. The 'goddess' figurines of succeeding centuries display greater stylistic refinement, technical innovations and increase in number and variety. They usually have prominent breasts and broad hips, and wear ornaments such as appliqué necklaces, bracelets, ear-rings and girdles. Some are crowned by a profusion of rosettes, while others have more elaborate head-dresses consisting of a mass of conical sprouts or grass blades encircled by a cluster of cactus-like plants (Figure 3.2).

At Sonkh, the first female figurines, some of which may have had a cultic significance, appear in Period II. The cultic significance is more discernible in Period III, whose finds include some terracottas depicting a female figure holding a fish and a female figure with an attendant in adoration. A plaque found in Period IV levels could represent the earliest depiction of Durgā Mahiṣāsuramardinī (the goddess Durgā killing the buffalo demon Mahiṣa) at the site. *Yakṣas* and *nāgas*, 'mother goddesses', and Durgā are represented at subsequent levels.[8]

The 'goddesses' are sometimes associated with terracotta artefacts that are usually referred to in archaeological literature as 'votive tanks' and 'votive shrines' but should be more appropriately described as miniature tanks and shrines. The Sonkh excavations yielded 266 fragments of such objects.[9] The bulk of them belong to Period III, and Härtel describes the 1st century BC as the most inventive phase for miniature tanks. These artefacts vary in shape and size and are associated with one or more of the following features: lamp-cups and/or birds and lamps on their rim; houses built around a courtyard structure or a structure (probably a shrine) raised on a platform supported with pillars and approached by a staircase or ladder; a lotus plant standing upright in the tank; figures of snake, frog or fish at the base of the tank; 'mother goddesses' seated along the wall, carrying a child in their arms and a bowl in their lap. Most of the varieties were clearly supposed to be filled with water. The miniature shrines can be seen as representations of popular shrines, apparently connected with the worship of goddesses and *nāgas*.

Miniature tanks and shrines have been found at many other sites in the subcontinent, from Taxila in the north-west to Chirand in the east to Kolhapur in the south, in contexts ranging from the 3rd century BC to the 3rd century AD.[10] At Sonkh, on the other hand, they were discovered from the 3rd century BC to medieval levels, showing that such objects were a part of the paraphernalia of domestic rituals or worship for over thousand years.[11]

The Worship of *Yakṣas* and *Yakṣīs*

The *yakṣas* were deities connected with water, fertility, trees, the forest and the wilderness. The evidence of literature and sculpture graphically illustrates the metamorphosis of the *yakṣa* from a benevolent, powerful

Figure 3.2
A Mathura 'mother goddess' found at NBP levels in the 1974–1975 excavations

Courtesy: Archaeological Survey of India

deity who was the focus of exclusive worship to a terrifying, demonic creature, reduced to the position of a subsidiary, attendant figure associated more with fertility than wealth.[12] *Yakṣīs* or *yakṣinīs*, the feminine counterparts, were originally benign deities connected with fertility. Many of the *śālabhañjikās*—a generic term for sensuous sculptural representations of women grasping the branches of a tree—of various ancient religious establishments were also *yakṣīs*. The literary image of the *yakṣī* in the texts of the brahmanical, Buddhist and Jaina traditions, on the other hand, is generally demonic and frightening.[13] In spite of their eventual absorption, marginalization and demonization in the dominant religious traditions, the sheer pervasiveness of the presence of *yakṣas* and *yakṣīs* in these texts illustrates just how important and widespread their worship once was.

Although the worship of *yakṣas* and *yakṣīs* probably goes back to an older rural milieu, between the 3rd century BC and 2nd century AD, they occur in the urban landscape, and cannot be described or dismissed (as they often are) as the focus of minor, exclusively rural, 'folk' cults. The imposing stone images from the Mathura area and elsewhere were the products of urban ateliers, financed by affluent urban patrons. They reflect the existence of iconographic conventions and artisanal skills, and imply community worship in shrines. The money-bag that the *yakṣa* sometimes holds in his left hand (in the images found at Besnagar and Pawaya in central India) connects him with wealth. The *yakṣa* himself increasingly takes on an urbane look, and it is difficult to distinguish between some of the *yakṣa* figures and portraits of sophisticated and wealthy mortal men of substance.

The most celebrated of the Mathura *yakṣas* is the colossal grey sandstone figure (2.59 m high) discovered at Parkham village, south of Mathura city (Figure 3.3). Generally assigned on stylistic grounds to the 2nd/1st century BC, the palaeography of the inscription on its pedestal, however, suggests a 3rd century BC date. The inscription[14] states that this image, made by Gomitaka, pupil of Kunika, was set up by eight brothers, members of the Maṇibhadra *puga* (congregation). It also indicates that it represents the *yakṣa* Maṇibhadra, who, according to a variety of textual and epigraphic references, was a tutelary deity of merchants and travellers, and was especially worshipped in important trading centres. It may be added that the torso of a figure of Kubera (king of the *yakṣas*) was found in Parkham village, and a relief figure of the same deity was obtained from somewhere in the same district.[15]

Two fragments of a colossal *yakṣa* image were found at Baroda, not far from Parkham which, when intact, must have been a towering figure,

Figure 3.3
The Parkham yakṣa

Courtesy: Author

about 3.65 m or so in height. Stylistically similar to the Parkham *yakṣa*, it seems to belong to the same period or maybe a little earlier. Yakṣa figures have also been discovered in a stratigraphic context in the course of excavations at Mathura.[16]

The worship of female deities associated with fertility and childbirth, protectresses of children who had the power of warding off disease, is an important aspect of popular Hinduism all over India today. In the early historical period, these functions were associated with a number of *yakṣīs*. A colossal 1.57 m × 1.06 m red sandstone image in the Mathura Museum represents the *yakṣī* Lavāyā seated on a wicker stool. The image was found at Jhinga-ka-nagla and can be assigned on stylistic grounds to the 2nd/1st century BC. Of the same period is the fragment of a colossal *yakṣī* standing under an Aśoka tree that was obtained from Vrindaban.[17] The synopsis of the 1974–1975 Mathura excavations refers to two *yakṣī* figures found in Period III levels (c. 1st–3rd century AD).[18] *Yakṣīs* are also very well represented in smaller stone and terracotta statuettes of the Mathura area.

The colossal stone *yakṣas* and the profusion of smaller stone and terracotta *yakṣas* and *yakṣīs* indicate the importance of the *yakṣa* cult both in the public and in the domestic domain. Although the earliest stone images of these deities can be dated to the 3rd/2nd centuries BC, they seem to represent cults whose antiquity goes back to an earlier time, difficult to estimate. Colossal images of *yakṣas* and *yakṣīs* disappear around the turn of the millennium, but small statuettes continue to be found in large numbers thereafter. Their worship had not died out but had been pushed from the public into the domestic sphere.

The Worship of *Nāgas* and *Nāgīs*

Another major aspect of iconic worship in the Mathura area was the worship of serpent deities—*nāgas* and *nāgīs* (or *nāginīs*)—who, like the *yakṣas*, were associated with water and fertility. Such images were found from different parts of the district such as Chhargaon, Khamni, Itauli and Baldev, and all belong stylistically to the early centuries AD.[19] Vogel noted that ancient *nāga* images in the Mathura district were being worshipped as Dauji or the god Baladeva/Balarāma and that modern images of Balarāma which were being manufactured in large numbers at Mathura and Brindaban were, in fact, imitations of ancient *nāga* images. He suggested that the plough-wielding, snake-canopied god Baladeva may have been a *nāga* deity who came to be absorbed into the Kṛṣṇa cult.

The imposing nature of some of the *nāga* images belonging to the early centuries AD and the technical finesse of their carving make it apparent that they represent more than a simple folk cult. The impressive seven-hooded Chhargaon *nāga* image (dated in year 40 of the Kaniṣka era, i.e., AD 118, in king Huviṣka's reign) was a majestic 2.33 m in height (Figure 3.4). It bears an inscription recording its installation near a tank by Senahastin and Bhoṇuka.

The Jamalpur mound yielded a profusion of Buddhist remains and was the site of a major *vihāra* (monastery) established by the Kuṣāṇa king Huviṣka in AD 125. An inscription on a stone slab discovered here refers to its installation in the place sacred to Dadhikarṇa, lord of the *nāgas*, by the Cāndaka brothers, chief among whom was Nandibala, the sons of the *śailālakas* (translated variously as actors, dancers or stone masons) of Mathurā. The date on the inscription, tentatively read as the year 26 of the Kaniṣka era (AD 104), suggests that a *nāga* shrine existed at this place *before* the setting up of the Buddhist *vihāra*. An inscription on a pillar base, presumed to have belonged to the Buddhist *vihāra*, records that this was the gift of Devila, a servant of the shrine of Dadhikarṇa. The fact that the donative inscription of the Dadhikarṇa shrine and Buddhist donative records here and elsewhere describe their aim in similar terms—the promotion of the welfare and happiness of all sentient beings—indicates an element of shared religious vocabulary and sentiment.

Many other images and inscriptions indicate that the *nāga* cult enjoyed considerable patronage in the Mathura region in the early centuries AD.[20] The inscribed base of a statuette of a standing *nāga* figure was reportedly found on the Bhuteshwar mound. The pedestal of a headless *nāga* statuette, inscribed with the name 'Dadhikarṇa' was recovered from the Yamuna. An epigraph on the pedestal of a *nāga* image accompanied by two *nāgīs* from the mound of Ral Bhandar (c. 13 km north-west of Mathura) refers to a tank and a garden having been made for the revered Bhumināga. The inscribed pedestal of a slab depicting a *nāgī* and a male figure with a spear in his left hand and the right raised in the protection-granting *abhayamudrā* from Girdharpur Tila may record the gift of a cloak-maker. An inscription on a sculpted stone slab in the British Museum, originally from Mathura, possibly representing a *nāga* and *nāgī*, records the construction of a small temple (*hārmya*) in a village.

Like the *yakṣas* and *yakṣīs*, the *nāgas* and *nāgīs* were the focus of an ancient cult that was prevalent in many parts of the subcontinent, and which attracted the patronage of urban elites. The *nāgas* and *nāgīs* too were gradually dethroned (in about the 3rd century AD, a little later than the *yakṣas*) in urban centres from their position as major foci of exclusive

Figure 3.4
The Chhargaon Nāga

Courtesy: Author

worship in the public realm to become attendants of other deities and objects of worship in the domestic sphere. In the story of Kṛṣṇa subduing the Kāliya *naga* we can perhaps see an allegorical reference to the ultimate victory of Vaiṣṇavism over the once very popular *nāga* cult.

Pantheons Old and New

The turn of the millennium was a momentous time from the point of view of the religious history of ancient India. Coomaraswamy[21] argued persuasively that the worship of the *yakṣas* and *yakṣīs* implied temples, *pūjā* (devotional worship with offerings) and a cult, and that the worship of *yakṣas* and *yakṣīs*, *nāgas* and *nāgīs* and goddesses was the natural source of the *bhakti* (devotional) elements that became so pervasive in Indian religions during the ensuing centuries. The period between c. 200 BC and AD 200 was a time of equipoise, when the older cults of the *yakṣas*, *nāgas* and goddesses jostled with the cults of newer brahmanical deities and pantheons, and held their ground. But, during the succeeding centuries, they were eventually displaced as major foci of worship in the urban public domain by the deities associated with Puranic Hinduism.

A rough method of assessing the relative importance of various brahmanical and non-brahmanical foci of worship in the Mathura area is to collate the details of acquisition of stone sculptures in the catalogues of the Mathura Museum.[22] These catalogues arrange the images according to type and dynastic periods; the entries under the 'Śuṅga' and 'Kuṣāṇa' period headings are relevant here, roughly corresponding to c. 200 BC and AD 200 (see Table 3.3).

It may be noted that the stone images are dominated by *yakṣas*, *yakṣīs*, *nāgas* and representations of Kubera (king of the *yakṣas*), Hārīti (a yakṣī, consort of Kubera), the Matṛkās (the Mothers) and Vasudharā (a goddess associated with wealth and prosperity, usually represented in association with a vase or a fish). These were clearly very popular during the period up to the 2nd century AD, but there is a marked decline in representations of all of these in stone sculptures of subsequent centuries. Agrawala[23] has pointed out that the iconographic conventions of images of many brahmanical deities were settled by the 1st century AD. The most numerous images from the Mathura area are those of Śiva, Viṣṇu, Sūrya (the sun god) and the goddesses Durgā and Lakṣmī.

The Śaiva images include representations of the deity in the anthropomorphic or liṅga (phallic) forms and in a combination of the two (the

Table 3.3
Number of stone images and reliefs

Yakṣas (including Kubera, sometimes with goddesses/*yakṣīs*, including Hārīti)	57
Nāgas and *nāgīs*	46
Śiva (in anthropomorphic and liṅga forms)	30
Viṣṇu	28
Mātṛkās	26
The *yakṣī* Hārīti	22
Durgā (including Durgā-Mahiṣāsuramardinī)	18
Sūrya	16
Lakṣmī (including Gaja-Lakṣmī)	15
Vasudharā	10
Brahmā	4
Balarāma	4
Gaṇeṣa	3
Agni	3
Garuḍa	5
Navagrahas	2
Kārttikeya	2
Indra	2
River goddesses	2
Sarasvatī (?)	1
Kinship triads depicting Vāsudeva-Kṛṣṇa, Ekānaṁśā and Balarāma	1
Kṛṣṇa līlā	1

mukha-liṅgas and vigraha liṅgas). One of the earliest representations is an architectural fragment found at Bhuteshwar (c. 2nd century BC) showing the worship of a liṅga on a platform under a pipal tree encircled by railing, by two-winged figures[24] (Figure 3.5). Śiva images of the 1st and 2nd centuries AD indicate an already diverse (albeit formative) iconographic base. The early Mathura images depict Śiva alone or with the bull, Śiva with his consort Pārvatī, and in various forms including Caturvyūha Śiva (Śiva with his three emanations), Ardhanārīśvara (the god who is half woman) and Harihara (Śiva with Viṣṇu).

The Vāsudeva-Kṛṣṇa cult was an important connecting link between Mathura and the brahmanical tradition. That Mathura was an important centre of the worship of the Vṛṣṇi heroes in the early centuries AD is reflected in kinship triads depicting Vāsudeva-Kṛṣṇa, his brother

Figure 3.5
Architectural fragment with relief carving of winged creatures worshipping a Śiva liṅga

Source: Author

Baladeva or Balarāma and their sister Ekanaṁśā. Their relative size and position indicate that initially Balarāma was more important than Kṛṣṇa. An inscription found in the terrace of a well at Mora[25] refers to the installation of images of the five *vīras* (heroes) by a woman named Toṣā during the reign of king Ṣoḍāsa (i.e., in the late 1st century BC–early 1st century AD). Fragmentary sculptures of two male and one female figures were also found at Mora. The male figures may represent two of the Vṛṣṇi heroes. The inscription on the pedestal of the female statue, dated in the reign of the Kuṣāṇa king Kaniṣka, suggests that it may have been commissioned and installed at the place by one of Toṣā's descendants about a century later, suggesting a custom of the installation of donor images at religious shrines. Toṣā is described as the wife of a *kālavaḍa* of Mathurā. The meaning of the term *kālavaḍa* is unclear. Luders[26] translates it as a high-ranking official, while Sircar[27] suggests a possible connection with the Sanskrit *kalyapāla*, a vintner.

Another inscription (possibly originally from Mora), inscribed on a door-jamb, belonging to the reign of the ruler Ṣoḍāsa, refers to a *toraṇa* (gateway) and *vedikā* (railing) which formed part of a *mahāsthāna* (a large temple) of Vāsudeva. Pandit Radha Krishna's excavations at Mora resulted in the discovery of several fragments of very large inscribed bricks of the 3rd/2nd century BC.[28] The legend on one of the bricks reads: 'Made by order of Yasamatā, daughter of Bṛhasvātimita, the king's consort and the mother of living sons.' Archaeological evidence indicates that Mora was an important religious centre in early historical Mathura, and that the shrine or shrines here attracted the patronage of urban social and political elites such as Toṣā and Yaśāmatā over several centuries.

The Kuṣāṇa period marks an explosion in the number and varieties of Vaiṣṇava images produced in Mathura, and the city becomes the premier centre of the creation and dissemination of Vaiṣṇava plastic art.[29] Most frequent are the depictions of Vāsudeva-Kṛṣṇa, but there are also a large number of small stone statuettes of the god Viṣṇu (usually four-armed), Viṣṇu on *garuḍa* (the mythical bird who is his vehicle) and in anthropomorphic *varāha* (boar) form. The *avatāra* (incarnation) concept is in its infancy, and the *caturvyūha* (the four emanations of Viṣṇu) concept becomes visible in the late Kuṣāṇa period. Reference may also be made to a colossal Nārāyaṇa image found at Mathura.[30]

Among the goddesses at Mathura, apart from the anonymous 'mother goddesses', Matṛkās and *yakṣīs*, the benevolent Lakṣmī and the militant Durgā stand out. Lakṣmī is also depicted on the coins of local kings of Mathura, and appears in her Gaja-Lakṣmī form (flanked by two elephants) on coins of Rajuvula, Śoḍāsa and Toraṇadāsa.[31] At Sonkh, a relief carving of Lakṣmī on an architectural fragment was found at pre-Kuṣāṇa levels, and seems to be the oldest stone sculptural piece found at the site[32] (Figure 3.6). That the worship of this goddess associated with good fortune and prosperity was not a local phenomenon is indicated by the discovery of a terracotta Gaja-Lakṣmī plaque in the context of an apsidal temple in a late NBP level (Phase IV D, dated c. 200–250 BC) at the site of Atranjikhera, in Uttar Pradesh.

Special note may be taken of representations in which deities who formed the focus of independent worship are associated with each other, for instance a slab showing Lakṣmī along with Hārīti and child, and a stele with representations of Kubera, Lakṣmī and Hārīti.[33] A relief sculpture, 7½" in height and 10" in length, assigned to the 1st century AD, depicts four figures standing with their hands in *abhayamudrā*—Śiva-Ardhanārīśvara, Viṣṇu, Gaja-Lakṣmī and Kubera.[34] We can see in such sculptures the earliest signs of pantheon formation.

While iconic worship dominated religious practice in early historical Mathura, there are some indications of the remains of sacrificial activity as well, in the form of pits containing ash, animal bones and pottery discovered in residential structures.[35] The more dramatic and unequivocal evidence of the performance of brahmanical sacrifices comes from the stone *yūpa*s (sacrificial posts) discovered at Isapur, on the left bank of the Yamuna, opposite the Vishrant Ghat. A girdle rope with a noose at

Figure 3.6
Lakṣmī (?) standing on lotus

Courtesy: National Museum, New Delhi

the end, representing the rope to which the sacrificial animal was tied, is clearly carved on both pillars. An inscription on one of the pillars—dated in year 24 in the Kuṣāṇa king Vasiṣka's reign and in pure Sanskrit—states that the pillar was set up by a Brāhmaṇa named Droṇala while performing a *sattra* (sacrifice) of twelve nights.[36] The stone *yūpa*s of Isapur were evidently stone copies of the wooden posts actually used in the sacrifice; they are suggestive of a grand sacrifice and a *yajamāna* who had considerable resources.

That Isapur had diverse religious associations is indicated by the discovery of three fragmentary donative inscriptions, one on a Jaina image.[37] The variety of stone images found at sites such as Isapur from the early centuries AD to the early medieval period illustrates the diverse foci of popular worship in the Mathura area.

Sonkh

The discoveries at the site of Sonkh include the remains of two ancient temples. Located in the south-western section of the excavated area, Apsidal Temple No. 1 was the central focus of the residential structures and streets around it. The temple, oriented roughly in an east–west direction, was a small structure, renovated and enlarged over time.[38] Roughly nine structural phases, belonging to the 1st and 2nd centuries AD were identified. The temple began as a small squarish structure, about 3.05 × 3.30 m. It developed into an apsidal structure, about 9.70 × 8.85 m, standing on a raised platform, enclosed by a thick wall on its northern, western and southern sides, with a room-like structure in the entrance area on the eastern side. On the floor of the apse was a 60 cm-high plinth covered with a slab, probably used as an altar for an image. A Matṛkā plaque (19 × 13.6 × 3.7 cm) carved on mottled red sandstone was found on the floor at its base, and may have been the central cult image which was probably re-installed in the various structural phases.[39] A large number of plaques depicting Durgā as Mahiṣāsuramardinī were found in or around the temple. In its last structural phase, just before it fell into disuse, the apsidal shrine seems to have reverted to its squarish shape, measuring about 3.80 × 3.80 m.

Remains of the much more elaborate Apsidal Temple No. 2 were discovered 400 m north of the main excavated area at Sonkh. The structural phases of the temple ranged from the beginning of the 1st century BC to the 2nd century AD and clearly reflect a stage when brick was supplemented by stone in early temple architecture. In its most developed form,[40] the brick temple can be visualized standing high above the surrounding buildings on a 15 × 11.50 m brick platform, with a pond to its east. The apsidal cella had a vaulted roof, and a slanting wooden roof probably ran around the temple and covered the space between the cella and the surrounding row of brick pillars (Figure 3.7). Härtel suggests that the vault carried pinnacles, probably green-glazed. The entrance was furnished with an arch-shaped carved stone tympanum above the doorway. To the north of the temple was a row of cells arranged on three sides of a courtyard. The entire temple complex was enclosed by a stone railing, for the most part carved on both sides. The beautifully carved remains of a stone gateway, consisting of two pillars supporting a superstructure of three architraves with voluted ends, were found on the southern side of the

Figure 3.7
A reconstruction of what the Apsidal Nāga Temple at Sonkh might have looked like

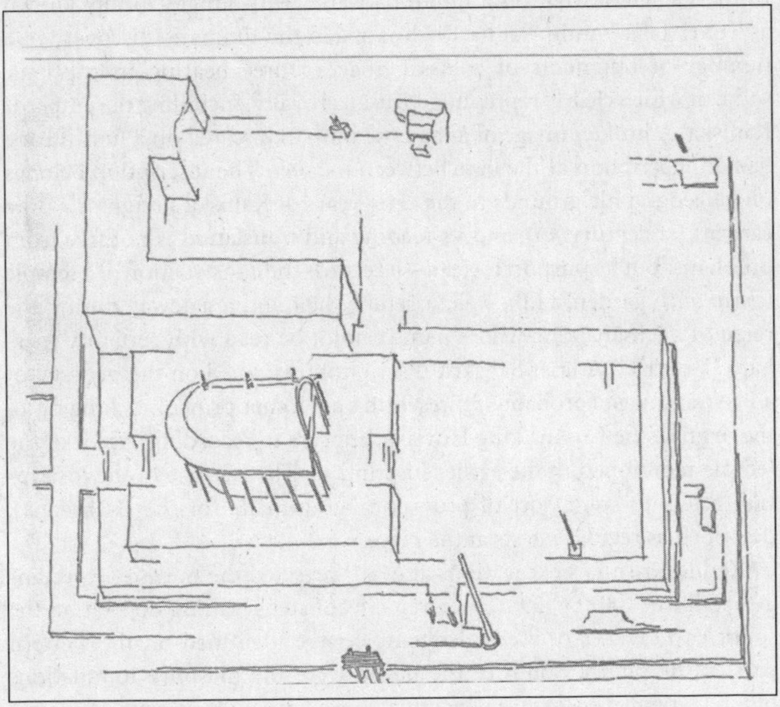

Source: Härtel, 1993, p. 422

railing. An architectural fragment belonging to the bottom lintel of the gateway bears a relief carving of a *nāga* and *nāgī* seated on thrones, surrounded by attendants and people with hands folded in obeisance. This and the other depictions of *nāga*s in stone sculptures and reliefs, terracotta *nāga* figurines and moulds, inscriptions found in the temple area and the discovery of the top half of a four-sided, seven-hooded stone *nāga* image (143 cm in height up to the stumps of the thighs) leave no doubt that Apsidal Temple No. 2 was a magnificent *nāga* temple.

Sonkh thus provides evidence of an early historical multi-temple urban complex and reveals the architectural form of the shrines. It also proves that *nāga* and Matṛkā images were worshipped in structural temples, and we can infer that many of the images found in and around Mathura were similarly enshrined and worshipped.

The Devakula at Mat

In the village of Mat, on a mound covered with jungle, locally known as Tokri Tila, Pandit Radha Krishna made the dramatic discovery of a number of fragments of colossal images, three bearing inscriptions, some of which clearly represented Kuṣāṇa royalty, including the emperor Kaniṣka. A broken image of a majestic monarch seated on a lion-throne had an inscription at the base between the feet. The inscription belongs on palaeographic grounds to the early years of Kaniṣka's reign or a little earlier (1st century AD), and its reading and translation is not free from problems. But its purport is clear—it records the construction of a temple (*devakula*), garden, tank, well, assembly hall and a gateway during the reign of a Kuṣāṇa king whose name cannot be read with certainty (perhaps 'Vema').[41] A later Sanskrit inscription inscribed on the pedestal of a broken image (probably representing a Kuṣāṇa prince), belonging to the reign of the Kuṣāṇa king Huviṣka, appears to record the repair of the temple mentioned in the earlier inscription. The last line of the inscription refers to some sort of provision being made for the Brāhmaṇas, described as regular guests at the place.[42]

Radha Krishna's excavations at Mat[43] revealed the traces of a rectangular plinth, 100 ft × 59 ft, with remains of steps leading up to it on the south east. Traces of a circular temple were identified on the western part of the plinth. South of the plinth were the masonry foundations of a rectangular enclosure which may have contained a series of rooms, and to the west were the remains of a tank, constructed of large bricks of the same dimensions as the temple, within which some *nāga* and other images were found.

Was the *devakula* a shrine where deified kings were worshipped (of the kind mentioned in Bhāsa's drama, the *Pratimānāṭaka*) or was it a royal temple dedicated to some other deity or deities, also housing images of Kuṣāṇa royalty? Vogel was quite definite on the point that the royal images were found *outside* the shrine proper. Further, there was the discovery of the almost life-size lower half of a dhoti-clad standing image (1.12 m height), accompanied by a dwarf behind which is a lion, which, according to V. S. Agrawala, could possibly represent the god Shiva. Agrawala[44] also suggested that another fragmentary image found at Mat, depicting the lower half of a female figure standing against a lion couchant, could perhaps be identified as Durgā. These two images would suggest that the Mat shrine was a Śaiva shrine, perhaps built during the time of Vima Kadphises, who is known from his coins to have been a devotee of Shiva. The Śaiva affiliations of the shrine are further supported by the reference to Śarva and Candīśvara (i.e., Śiva) in the preamble to an inscription (No. 99) found at Mat.

The evidence from Mat has to be seen in conjunction with that from two sites in Afghanistan—Rabatak and Surkh Kotal. The former has yielded an important inscription in the Bactrian language and script, reflecting the claims of Kuṣāṇa kings to divine status.[45] There is a striking similarity between the *devakula* at Mat and the *bago lango* at Surkh Kotal.[46] At Surkh Kotal, the statues of the Kuṣāṇa kings were found *in situ*, not in the cella, but in the south-eastern corner of the courtyard. While two of the temples at Surkh Kotal seem to have been fire temples, there is uncertainty about the cultic affiliations of Temple A. The fact that an (admittedly small in size) image depicting Śiva, Pārvatī and Nandi has been found at the site together with the evidence of *triśūla*s (tridents) engraved in a later period on the stone steps of the shrine's staircase is strongly suggestive that the main cult image in Temple 'A' was Śaiva. This would tie in with Agrawala's interpretation of the sculptural fragments at Mat with Śiva and Pārvatī, although the interpretation is not free from problems and there are other possibilities.[47] Whether the tantalizing but inconclusive evidence from Mat and Surkh Kotal reflects a Kuṣāṇa tradition of royally endowed monumental temples where deified kings, or gods, or both, may have been worshipped, we are looking at a striking innovation in the theory and practice of kingship.

Political Elites and the Patronage of Brahmāṇas

The phenomenon of the Kuṣāṇa kings spreading their munificence in different directions and the reputation of Kaniṣka as a patron of Buddhism have distracted attention from certain other facts, which anchor the kings of this dynasty to the brahmanical tradition. Although there are a handful of early Sanskrit inscriptions belonging to the 1st century BC, the use of Sanskrit, or a dialect very close to Sanskrit, as the language of epigraphs really took off in the 1st century AD, during the time of the Kṣatrapas (cf. the inscriptions of the time of the Kṣatrapa Ṣoḍāsa) and the early Kuṣāṇas. Mathura seems to have been an important epicentre of this phenomenon. During the Kuṣāṇa period, the use of Sanskrit gradually spread to Buddhist donative records as well.[48]

The circuit between political elites, urban elites and Brāhmaṇas is well revealed by a stone inscription found in a field opposite the Chaurasi Jaina Temple in Mathura in a well called Lal Kuan.[49] The inscription, in mixed Prakrit and Sanskrit, refers to the eastern hall of merit (*puṇya-śālā-pracinī*) being given as a permanent endowment under the custom of *akṣaya-nīvi* (an investment, the capital of which could not be touched) by a person described as the Kanasarukamāṇa, lord of Kharāsalera, and a Vakanapati. The donation was a monetary one—500 coins called purāṇas were invested with a guild whose name is not clear and 550 purāṇas with a guild of *samitakaras* (perhaps flour-makers). From the interest of this endowment, 100 Brāhmaṇas were to be served food in the open hall and a specified number of food items were to be provided to destitute, hungry and thirsty people. The fact that the inscription is dated in a Macedonian month of Gorpiaios in the year 28 suggests that the donor was a foreigner from the northwest. Judging from the fact that the merit accruing from the gift was to accrue to the Kuṣāṇa emperor Huviṣka, the donor seems to have been a subordinate of this Kuṣāṇa king.

The depiction of a great variety of deities on Kuṣāṇa coins is conventionally interpreted as a reflection of their religious eclecticism, catholicism, or as indicative of an attitude of 'toleration'.[50] Such an interpretation is premised on a misperception of ancient Indian cults as mutually exclusive, aggressively antagonistic religious denominations. It also displays a lack of reflection on the religious dimensions of royal policy and the political dimension of royal religious patronage. The dispersed patronage and the impressive variety of religious symbols that the Kuṣāṇas sought to identify themselves with can best be interpreted as a version of Hocart's[51] idea of 'incorporative kingship' associated with polities that were not highly centralized, in which the king incorporated the divinities worshipped not only by his subordinates but also his subjects. Seen in this way, Kuṣāṇa policy was just an exaggerated version of the royal policies pursued by many other dynasties of ancient India. In later centuries, even in the case of dynasties that adopted consistent sectarian symbols on their coins and seals, royal patronage was not generally restricted by narrow sectarian boundaries.

Conclusions

The archaeological evidence from the Mathura area between c. 200 BC and AD 200 clearly indicates the importance of goddesses, *yakṣa*s, *nāga*s and deities associated with Puranic Hinduism, in both temple and domestic contexts. The images display a certain level of iconographic standardization, and it is clear that certain cults had a trans-regional importance. While the earliest structural temples at Sonkh indicate they were an integral part of the urban settlement, at Mat there is striking evidence of a royal shrine, situated distant and aloof from the main settlement.

The post-3rd-century period saw the displacement of these old cults and the eventual triumph of the brahmanical tradition. The historical processes that lay behind the multiple religious accommodations, incorporations, displacements and marginalizations are not easy to identify. At a general level, the features that gave brahmanism its position of dominance were the social dominance and prestige of the Brāhmaṇas within the caste hierarchy and their links with political power. Royal patronage did play an important role in defining dominant cults, not as much by direct patronage of religious establishments, but indirectly through the patronage of Brāhmaṇas. The fact that dynasties with as varied origins and backgrounds as the Kuṣāṇas in the north and the Sātavāhanas in the Deccan extended patronage towards Brāhmaṇas points to an underlying thread that helps explain some of the patterns in the religious history of ancient and early medieval India.

In spite of the many changes in the religious landscape of Mathura over the centuries, what is equally striking are certain elements of continuity. A large, 18th century Śiva temple marks the spot of the 2nd century BC Śaiva shrine at Bhuteshwar. Even more striking is the evidence that while the older cults and their images were jostled out of the urban milieu ('ruralized') by the gods and goddesses of Puranic Hinduism, they were not exterminated. Sometimes, the old images were reinterpreted. The

Figure 3.8
The modern Parkham yakṣa

Source: Author

Nāgarāja once enshrined in Apsidal Temple No. 2 at Sonkh is still being worshipped in the village, but as the goddess Cāmuṇḍā. Old *nāga* images are today worshipped as Balarāma. The *nāga*s and the goddesses associated with fertility, children and the warding off of diseases have held their ground in villages across India. But the most amazing reflection of the continuity and resilience of the older cults in popular Hinduism comes from the village of Parkham. The imposing colossal image of the *yakṣa*, which once stood next to the village tank, was removed from the village to the Mathura Museum many years ago. But, in the month of Magh (January), a 'Jakhaiya Mela' (i.e., *yakṣa* fair) is held in the village, and hundreds of people from surrounding villages converge at Parkham to worship the Jakhaiya. On this occasion, a small *yakṣa* image—a poor substitute for the original—is brought out, placed in a makeshift enclosure next to the tank, and worshipped (Figure 3.8). The broken right hand of the colossal Parkham *yakṣa* was probably raised in the protection-granting *abhayamudrā*. His diminutive modern incarnation raises his left hand in what looks like a cheerful wave. Nevertheless, on three consecutive Sundays in January in Parkham, the *yakṣa* regains some of the importance he once enjoyed in the Mathura area over two thousand years ago.

Notes

1. See A. Cunningham, *Four Reports Made during the Years 1862–1863–1864–1865. Reports of the Archaeological Survey of India*, 1 (Shimla: ASI, 1871); *Report for the Year 1871–1872. Reports of the Archaeological Survey of India*, 3 (Kolkata: ASI, 1873); *Report of a Tour in the Central Provinces and Lower Gangetic Doab in 1881–1882. Reports of the Archaeological Survey of India*, 17 (Kolkata: ASI, 1884); *Report of a Tour in Eastern Rajputana. Reports of the Archaeological Survey of India*, 20 (Kolkata: ASI, 1885).
2. See, for instance, F. S. Growse, *Mathura—A District Memoir* (New Delhi: Asian Educational Services [1979] 1882).
3. J. P. Vogel, 'Nāga Worship in Ancient Mathurā'. *Annual Report of the Archaeological Survey of India* (1908–1909), pp. 159–163; 'The Mathurā School of Sculpture'. *Annual Report of the Archaeological Survey of India* (1909–1910), pp. 63–79; *Catalogue of the Archaeological Museum at Mathura.* (Allahabad: Government Press, United Provinces, 1910); 'The Sacrificial Posts of Isapur'. *Annual Report of the Archaeological Survey of India* (1910–1911), pp. 40–48; 'Explorations at Mathurā'. *Annual Report of the Archaeological Survey of India* (1911–1912), pp. 120–133.
4. *Indian Archaeology—A Review (IAR)*, 1976–1977, pp. 88–89; M. C. Joshi, 'Mathurā as an Ancient Settlement', in D. M. Srinivasan, ed., *Mathurā: The Cultural Heritage* (New Delhi: Manohar, 1989), pp. 165–170.
5. H. Härtel, *Excavations at Sonkh: 2500 Years of a Town in Mathura District* (Berlin: Dietrich Reimer Verlag, 1993), p. 12.
6. The Sonkh sequence is largely based on dynastic/political phases, which, according to the excavators, could in many cases be identified on the basis of numismatic finds and which, according to them, provided clear dividing lines between the various archaeological levels. The term 'Śuṅga cultural phase' is used instead of 'Śuṅga phase'. This is because of the possible objection that the rule of the Śuṅgas did not extend to Mathura. The use of this term is the reason why there is a discrepancy between the chronology given in this table and the chronology of political history.
7. M. C. Joshi and C. Margabandhu, 'Some Terracottas from Excavation at Mathurā: A Study'. *Journal of the Indian Society of Oriental Art, New Series*, 8, 1976–1977, pp. 16–32.

8. Härtel, *Excavations at Sonkh,* p. 88ff.
9. Härtel, *Excavations at Sonkh,* p. 195ff.
10. A. Ghosh, ed., *An Encyclopaedia of Indian Archaeology*, Vol. 1 (New Delhi: Munshiram Manoharlal, 1989), p. 277.
11. The making and use of such artefacts for household rituals continued till fairly recent times in Bengal (Dilip K. Chakrabarti, personal communication).
12. A. K. Coomaraswamy, *Yakṣas*, 2nd edition (New Delhi: Munshiram Manoharlal, 1980); G. V. Mitterwallner, '*Yakṣas* of Ancient Mathurā', in D. M. Srinivasan, ed., *Mathurā: The Cultural Heritage* (New Delhi: Manohar, 1989), pp. 368–382.
13. G. H. Sutherland, *Yakṣa in Hinduism and Buddhism: The Disguises of the Demon* (New Delhi: Manohar, 1992), p. 137ff.
14. H. Lüders, *Mathurā Inscriptions*, unpublished papers, ed. K. L. Janert (Gottingen: Vandenhoeck and Ruprecht, 1961), pp. 177–178.
15. Lüders, *Mathurā Inscriptions,* p. 179.
16. *IAR* 1976–1977, pp. 55.
17. V. N. Srivastava and S. Misra, 'Inventory of Mathura Museum Sculptures since 1939 up to date', *Journal of the U.P. Historical Society, Sangrahalaya Puratattva Patrika* 11–12, 1973, pp. 42–121.
18. *Indian Archaeology—A Survey (IAR)*, 1974–1975, pp. 50.
19. Vogel, 'Nāga Worship in Ancient Mathurā'.
20. Lüders, *Mathurā Inscriptions,* p. 38, No. 12; 126–127, No. 95; 148–149, No. 102; 164, No. 124; 208–209, No. 182.
21. Coomaraswamy, *Yakṣas*, p. 36.
22. A. K. Srivastava, *Catalogue of Śaiva Sculptures in Government Museum* (Mathura: Government Museum, 1999). Srivastava and Misra, *Inventory of Mathura Museum Sculptures since 1939 up to date*; Vogel, *Catalogue of the Archaeological Museum at Mathura*; updated by V. S. Agrawala, 'A Catalogue of the Images of Brahmā, Viṣṇu and Śiva in Mathurā Art', *Journal of the U.P. Historical Society* 22 (1949): 102–210.
23. V. S. Agrawala, *Masterpieces of Mathurā Sculpture* (Varanasi: Prithivi Prakashan, [1965] 1985).
24. Srivastava, *Catalogue of Śaiva Sculptures in Government Museum,* p. 47, GMM 52.3625.
25. H. Luders, 'Seven Brahmi Inscriptions from Mathurā and its Vicinity', *Epigraphia Indica* 24, 1937–1938 pp. 194–210.
26. Lüders, 'Seven Brahmi Inscriptions from Mathurā and its Vicinity', p. 202.
27. D. C. Sircar, *Indian Epigraphical Glossary* (Delhi: Motilal Banarsidass, 1966), p. 139.
28. Vogel, 'Explorations at Mathura', p. 127.
29. D. M. Srinivasan, 'Vaiṣṇava Art and Iconography at Mathurā', in D. M. Srinivasan, ed., *Mathurā: The Cultural Heritage*, pp. 383–392.
30. Srinivasan, 'Vaiṣṇava Art and Iconography at Mathurā', pp. 389.
31. J. P. Singh, 'Study of Local Coin Types of Mathurā with Particular Reference to Religious Motifs', in D. M. Srinivasan, ed., *Mathurā: The Cultural Heritage*, pp. 146–152.

32. Härtel, *Excavations at Sonkh*, p. 247.
33. Srivastava and Misra, 'Inventory of Mathura Museum Sculptures since 1939 up to date', p. 70, Nos. 57.4349, 61.5371.
34. Agrawala, 'A Catalogue of the Images of Brahmā, Viṣṇu and Śiva in Mathurā Art', pp. 142, GMM. No. 2520.
35. *IAR*, 1974–1975, p. 49.
36. Lüders, *Mathurā Inscriptions*, pp. 125–126; Vogel, 'The Sacrificial Posts of Isapur', pp. 40–48.
37. Lüders, *Mathurā Inscriptions*, pp. 124–125, Nos. 91–93.
38. Härtel, *Excavations at Sonkh*, pp. 64–67.
39. Härtel, *Excavations at Sonkh*, p. 245.
40. Härtel, *Excavations at Sonkh*, pp. 413–417.
41. Lüders, *Mathurā Inscriptions*, pp. 131–132, No. 98.
42. Lüders, *Mathurā Inscriptions*, pp. 139–140, No. 99.
43. These are described in Vogel, 'Explorations at Mathurā', pp. 120–122.
44. Agrawala, 'A Catalogue of the Images of Brahmā, Viṣṇu and Śiva in Mathurā Art', pp. 126–127, 152.
45. B. N. Mukherjee, 'The Great Kushana Testament', Indian Museum Bulletin 30 (Kolkata: Indian Museum, 1995).
46. G. Fussman, 'The Māṭ Devakula: A New Approach to its Understanding', in D. M. Srinivasan, ed., *Mathurā: The Cultural Heritage*, (New Delhi: Manohar, 1989), pp. 193–199.
47. M. Rosenfield, *The Dynastic Arts of the Kushans* (New Delhi: Munshiram Manoharlal, 1993), pp. 150–151.
48. Salomon, *Indian Epigraphy: A Guide to the Study of Inscriptions in Sanskrit, Prakrit, and the Other Indo-Aryan Languages* (New Delhi: Munshiram Manoharlal, 1998), pp. 87–88.
49. S. Konow, 'Mathurā Brahmi Inscription of the Year 28', *Epigraphica Indica* 21 (1931–1932): 55–61.
50. B. N. Mukherjee. *The Rise and Fall of the Kushana Empire.* (Kolkata: Firma KLM, 1988).
51. A. M. Hocart, *Kings and Councillors: An Essay in the Comparative Anatomy of Human Society* (Chicago and London: University of Chicago Press, 1970 [1936]), p. 89.

4

Early Medieval Orissa: The Data and the Debate

The current debate on the nature of the society, polity, and economy of early medieval India has acquired a vintage quality, spanning as it does almost half a century.[1] Historians have come a long way in recognizing that this period was one of profound historical change. However, when it comes to the *nature* of these changes, we are faced with a number of hypotheses that contradict each other in crucial respects. On the one hand, we have the hypothesis of Indian feudalism, which presents early medieval India as a period of fragmentation, an age which saw the transformation of peasants into serfs, the feudalization of power relations and administrative organization, and a decline in urban life and the use of money. The feudalism hypothesis has been applied to both north and south India. For south India, we have another interpretative framework—the segmentary state model, which presents the kings of this period as shadowy ritual figures devoid of the two important props of real power—an organized revenue infrastructure and a standing army. The third major interpretative framework for early medieval India suggests that in many parts of the subcontinent, this was not an age of political fragmentation and break-down, but of the emergence and development of state societies and polities. It identifies and emphasizes the forces that made for integration rather than disintegration. We can

This chapter was previously published in Martin Brandtner and Shishir Kumar Panda, eds, *Interrogating History: Essays for Hermann Kulke* (New Delhi: Manohar, 2006).

further connect this interpretation with the marshalling of evidence that the early medieval period was a period of change in urban patterns, but not of urban decay, and that there was a decline in the number of coin types but not of coinage.[2]

This chapter has two interwoven aspects, one specific, the other general. The specific focus is on certain features of the history of early medieval Orissa as reflected in the details in the royal land-grant inscriptions about donors, donees, and the gifted land. This discussion is based on an analysis of a little over 300 Sanskrit inscriptions from Orissa and adjacent areas of Madhya Pradesh and Andhra Pradesh, ranging in time from the fourth to the mid-12th century AD.[3] The second, general, focus is on the extent to which explanatory models currently used for early medieval India are helpful in furthering our understanding of this period. The overall perspective informing the discussion of these issues is that there are several questions that can be posed regarding both the somewhat euphemistically labelled 'dominant' and 'alternative' interpretative frameworks.[4]

In order to discuss the epigraphic evidence from Orissa, the data can be divided into three overlapping phases, Period I (the 4th to the 7th century), Period II (the 7th to the 10th century), and Period III (the 10th to the 12th century).[5] Taking a long time-frame divided in this manner makes it possible to identify patterns of historical change. The brevity of inscriptions is offset by their sheer number, and also by the fact that notwithstanding differences of opinion about the initial year of certain eras, they can at least be dated approximately.

Royal Donors and the Nature of Polities

The political history of ancient and early medieval Orissa is fairly complex, and includes the rise and fall of many dynasties. One of the problems in reconstructing a continuous narrative of the political history of this region is the uncertainty that surrounds the initial year of some of the eras used in the inscriptions, such as the Bhauma era and the Gaṅga era.[6] These hurdles are not, however, insurmountable, and it is possible to plot out a broad political narrative of dynastic histories and their geographic contexts.

The thirteenth major rock edict of the Mauryan emperor Aśoka speaks of his successful military campaign against the Kaliṅgas.[7] The administrative centres of Mauryan rule in Orissa were located in or around Dhauli (in Puri district) and Jaugada (in Ganjam district), and the Mauryan administrative infrastructure seems to have been extended in some form to these areas. In about the 1st century BC, the nuclear area of the Cedi kingdom of Khāravela was located in and around the Mahanadi delta. The outlines of the succeeding centuries remain rather faint. Although there is some numismatic evidence of contact with the Kuṣāṇa empire, the available inscriptional material is scanty. In the 4th century, certain parts of southern Orissa and adjacent areas came to be included in the Gupta empire, as is suggested by lines 19–20 of the Allahabad *praśasti* of Samudragupta, which refer to certain kings who were captured and then released.[8] Presumably these kings continued to rule over their principalities with the proviso that they accept Gupta suzerainty. The evidence of the Aśokan edicts and the Hathigumpha inscription, the archaeological remains from Sisupalgarh (which range from the 3rd century BC to the 4th century AD) and the Udayagiri and Khandagiri caves, and the references to a number of political units in the area in the Allahabad *praśasti* are suggestive of a certain level of political and social complexity in some parts of Orissa in early historic times. More archaeological evidence from ancient settlements of this period and a better understanding of the structure of the imperial polities would make possible a more meaningful discussion of these centuries, which otherwise tend to get reduced to an unnuanced story of conquest and encapsulation, as if nothing much else was going on in the area.

From the 4th century onwards, there is evidence of a number of lineages who carved out principalities in different parts of Orissa and contiguous areas, establishing control over a resource base that was in some cases rich enough to permit them to fan out and expand their power through conquests and alliances. Not surprisingly, most of these principalities were located in areas of rich agricultural potential—the river valleys and deltas of the Mahanadi, Brahmani, Vaitarani, Rishikulya, Vamsadhara, and Nagavali. Between the 7th and 10th centuries, we see the Śailodbhavas and Bhauma-Karas carving out fairly large kingdoms. Inscriptions from the highlands of interior Orissa indicate the establishment of principalities in these areas from the 9th and 10th centuries. In Period III, smaller kingdoms continued to exist on their peripheries, but the Somavaṁśīs and the Imperial Gaṅgas succeeded in uniting large parts of Orissa through conquest.

When we move to the question of the nature and structure of the polities of early medieval India, we are on more tentative ground. Part of the problem is one of definition (what exactly do we mean by a state? How do we distinguish between a pre-state and state society?). Another part of it lies in interpreting the evidence from the rather reticent sources to assess the nature of the political system they reflect. These problems are particularly acute when we are looking at the period of transition from chiefdoms to states and also at early, as opposed to mature, states. At a very general level, when we talk of the transition to statehood, we are talking of political elites that had effectively established certain formal mechanisms of power, control, and authority, backed by force, over the resources of certain areas, particularly over land. The political success stories, the large kingdoms, reflect effective extraction and control over a resource base that was rich enough to permit further military expansion.

It is possible to identify certain more specific features of early medieval polities. Compared to earlier centuries, we see higher levels of militarization and many more foci of military power in different parts of the subcontinent. The political narrative of incessant warfare suggests large armies maintained by the great kings of the time. Apart from a central hired core, these armies would have included mercenaries. A large number of Pāla land grant inscriptions (from Bihar and Bengal) address, among others, the Gauḍas; Mālavas, Khaśas, Kulikas, Hūṇas, Karṇāṭas, and Lāṭas. These seem to be references to military contingents recruited from amongst these people into the Pāla armies. The *Rājataraṅgiṇī* of Kalhaṇa also indicates the recruitment by kings of Kashmir of mercenaries from other areas.[9] The core and mercenary troops were supplemented when the need arose by the military capacity of allied and subordinate rulers. The effective mustering and deployment of the mechanism of force led to an unparalleled phenomenon of political and military expansion and the high levels of spatial mobility of a number of political elites virtually all over India. The titles and designations used in the land grants are suggestive of different tiers, ranks, and functionaries in the administrative infrastructure in some of the kingdoms, although it is not always possible to identify the precise meaning of some of the terms.[10] But we see states whose horizontal and vertical linkages are more visible than ever before, and we can connect the emergent political elites with landed groups, some of them created and buttressed by royal land grants.

There is one aspect of the description of the polity of early medieval India in the writings of the feudalism school that is acceptable: the relationship between paramount kings and subordinate kings, between kings and *sāmantas*. However, the other aspects of the thesis, including the idea of political fragmentation and the interpretation of the relationship between kings and the beneficiaries of royal grants is not convincing.[11]

The interpretations of early medieval India that highlight the expansion of state society and state formation are better grounded in the empirical evidence from the different regions. Viewing royal land grants within a framework of 'integration' rather than 'disintegration' suits areas such as Orissa well. But certain points can be raised with regard to the integrationist interpretations as well. While state *formation* is often presented as a major theme of this period, once the socio-politics of statehood had made their appearance in an area, the period seems better described as one that saw a *proliferation* of state polities. Second, the definition of what exactly constitutes the regional level remains problematic and is sometimes assumed rather than defined or demonstrated. And third, although the 'alternative framework' talks about developments at the sub-regional, regional, and supra-regional level, it tends to privilege the regional. It can also be asked whether the configurations of regional culture, whether defined in terms of political units, language or other cultural sign-posts, do not crystallize or fructify only towards the end or even after the end of the early medieval period.

The contours of the kingdoms of early medieval India were fluid and difficult to define. These kingdoms are, in fact, more easily identifiable by their nuclear areas and political centres than by their boundaries. At the same time, a glance at the narrative of the political history of early medieval India reveals some large empires such as those of the Rāṣṭrakūṭas, Pālas, and Pratihāras, and many more numerous short-lived dynasties with much more modest levels of territorial control, who did not make such a grand splash on the political scene. This makes us pause and consider whether through most of the early medieval period the sub-regional and trans-regional were not perhaps as, if not more, prominent aspects of political formations as the 'regional,' however the region may be defined.[12]

Royal inscriptions represent, among other things, an articulation of royal power. The *praśasti*s of the inscriptions give us important clues regarding the antecedents of various lineages, the political geography of kingdoms, and political centres. Most of this period was marked by swiftly changing political configurations—the result of incessant contests for power among various lineages. The continuing process of the redefinition of power equations was reflected in the *praśasti*s in an idiom of ranking of power relations, in terms of paramountcy and subordination. In Orissa, some of the royal titles assumed by kings embodied territorial claims (e.g., *Kaliṅgādhipati* and *sakala-Kaliṅgādhipati*). From the Gupta period onwards, claimants to paramountcy usually assumed the triple title of *mahārājādhirāja, parama-bhaṭṭāraka,* and *parameśvara.* Subordinate kings had to be content with *mahārāja, mahāsāmanta,* and *rāṇaka,* and were frequently given the epithet *samadhigata-pañca-mahāśabda* (one who has obtained the five great sounds).[13]

The names and scarcely-brahmanized origin myths of some Orissan lineages (such as the Śailodbhavas, Śulkīs, and Kulikas) betray their local tribal roots and suggest their recent emergence from the stage of tribal chiefdoms to early statehood.[14] On the other hand, there is evidence of certain lineages being migrants into Orissa—the Pāṇḍuvaṁśīs came from Mekala (the area around Amarakantaka), the Bhauma-Karas possibly from Assam, the Tuṅgas from Rohitagiri in Bihar, the Somavaṁśīs from South Kosala (the Raipur, Bilaspur, Sambalpur area), and the Gaṅgas of Śvetaka and Kaliṅganagara from Karnataka. The Gaṅga inscriptions further indicate the fanning out of collateral lineages, while the many groups of Bhañja kings may represent different lineages sharing a common clan affiliation.

The origin myths in the *praśasti*s can be seen as an expression of staking and intensifying claims to political power. In Orissa, the elaboration of such myths seems to have particularly come to the fore from about the 7th century onwards. Some of these myths show a complex interweaving of puranic and tribal elements. In the case of the Bhañjas, for instance, it is possible to discern the process of brahmanization. The early Bhañjas of Khiñjalimaṇḍala describe themselves as *aṇḍaja-vaṁśa-prabhava* (the egg-born lineage) but also introduce the *ṛṣi* Vasiṣṭha and the epic hero Rāma into the story.[15] We can see a similar process at work in the Śailodbhava origin myth which traces the origins of the dynasty to the worship of the god Svayambhū by a man named Pulindasena.[16]

None of this sort of thing (miraculous birth from an egg or a rock) for the two major dynasties who came to the fore in Orissa in about the 10th century. Both the Somavaṁśīs and Imperial Gaṅgas anchored themselves quite firmly to the pan-Indian epic-puranic tradition. The Somavaṁśīs claimed to belong to the lunar dynasty. The genealogy of the Imperial Gaṅgas became more and more elaborate and grandiose over time, with the kings of this dynasty ultimately tracing their ancestry to Viṣṇu. This more or less coincides with a shift from Śaiva to Vaiṣṇava affiliations during the time of Anantavarman Coḍagaṅga, which can be seen as an attempt to promote a new sectarian symbol for the expanding empire.

The *praśasti* of the royal grants contains poetic embellishment, conventional rhetoric, and downright flattery. But if examined carefully, the *praśasti,* and the seals and invocations of the grants allow us to reconstruct certain elements that comprised both the ideals and the practice of kingship. The ideal king of the inscriptions of Orissa appears, as he does in literature, in a variety of roles—as victorious warrior, protector of his subjects, maintainer of the social order, giver of gifts, and as one who wards off the evils of the Kali age. Only one dynasty highlights the king as performer of *śrauta* sacrifices. Inscriptions of the Śailodbhavas (who may be placed between the late 6th and 9th century) mention the performance of the Aśvamedha and the Vājapeya sacrifices by Mādhavavarman.[17] Mādhavavarman's inscriptions tell us that he had caused satisfaction to the gods by his performance of the Aśvamedha and other sacrifices, the very mention of which had fallen into abeyance due to the impiety of the kings of the Kali age.[18] However, such boasts are not found in the inscriptions of any other dynasty of early medieval Orissa. This silence indicates that the performance of *śrauta* sacrifices was not an important component of the ideology or practice of kingship in ancient and early medieval Orissa.

Kings of early medieval Orissa established and proclaimed their connection with the religious domain in other ways. The sectarian epithets of kings reflect more than their personal religious predilections, and can also be viewed from the perspective of royal policy. Seen from this point of view, consistencies in and changes in sectarian affiliations assume political importance. The earliest assumption of specific Vaiṣṇava or Śaiva sectarian epithets by kings of Orissa dates to about the 5th century, and becomes quite common thereafter. While *parama-māheśvara* is the usual Śaiva epithet, the Vaiṣṇava epithet *parama-bhāgavata* is replaced early on by *parama-vaiṣṇava*. On the other hand, there are references to certain kings being worshippers of what seem to be tribal goddesses or brahmanized tribal goddesses such as Stambheśvarī.[19] This goddess is mentioned in the Terasingha plates of Tuṣṭikāra, and in some of the grants of the early Bhañjas of Khiñjalimaṇḍala and the Śulkīs. The Śulkī inscriptions (the Dhenkanal and Hindol plates of Kulastambha) describe Stambheśvarī as the *kula-devatā* of these kings. Although the specific term *kula-devatā* does not occur in Gaṅga inscriptions, the phraseology of the text suggests that Śiva-Gokarṇa occupied much this sort of position for them.

As far as the exclusive association of a dynasty with a particular deity is concerned, the dynasties that display a consistency in sectarian affiliations (the Śailodbhavas, Ādi-Bhañjas, Śulkīs, Tuṅgas, Somavaṁśīs, the Gaṅgas of Śvetaka and the early Gaṅgas of Kaliṅganagara) were all Śaiva. This is not surprising, as it is well-known that, notwithstanding the proliferation of a large variety of religious cults, until the construction of the Jagannātha temple in the mid-12th century, it was Śaivism that prevailed in a big way in Orissa. At the same time, it is interesting to note that although the *praśasti* of kings of early medieval Orissa routinely gives them sectarian epithets, it rarely highlights the king in his role as a builder of temples. This is intriguing in an age which saw the proliferation of temples.

The Donees: Brāhmaṇas, Temples, and Others

As elsewhere in the subcontinent, the early medieval period in Orissa saw a systematic and sustained royal patronage of brāhmaṇas and the king–brāhmaṇa relationship was an important aspect of the polities of this period. In spite of evidence of a great variety in vocations pursued by brāhmaṇas from the earliest times, many scholars tend to treat them as a homogeneous social group and persist in routinely translating the word brāhmaṇa as 'priest.' The literary and epigraphic sources of early medieval India present the brāhmaṇas in a variety of roles. As panegyrists and genealogists, they were experts in crafting claims to royal legitimacy, an important skill in times of political turbulence. As ritual advisors to kings, some of them were closely associated with the court circle. As occupants of various official posts, some of them played an important role in the administration of kingdoms. And as the prime beneficiaries of royal grants of land, they emerged as an important landed class and as influential mediators of social and religious values at the village level.

The inscriptions help us break up the category of the brāhmaṇa into its parts by indicating the various bases of differentiation within the community. They also indicate how brāhmaṇa identity was defined over time. *Gotra* appears as the single most consistently specified basis of brāhmaṇa identification in the Orissan inscriptions from the 4th to the mid-12th century. From about the 7th century, reference to the *pravara* and *anupravara* of the brāhmaṇas becomes frequent as well.[20]

The Vedic school to which the brāhmaṇa donees were affiliated was another important basis of identity; the terms *caraṇa* (Vedic school) and *śākhā* (recension of a Veda) were often used interchangeably in the inscriptions. A tabulation of the number of representatives of the various Vedic schools among the brāhmaṇa beneficiaries of royal land grants in Orissa indicates that throughout the period under review, brāhmaṇas of the *Yajur Veda*, particularly those associated with the Vājasaneya school, were especially favoured. Brāhmaṇas of the *Atharva Veda*, on the other hand, are almost totally absent among the beneficiaries of royal grants. During the whole period under review, only one inscription—the Neulpur plate of the Bhauma-Kara king Śubhākara—records a grant in favour of *Atharva Veda* brāhmaṇas.[21] The preponderance of *Yajur Veda* brāhmaṇas may have had to do with their ritual expertise, but invoking such an explanation requires further investigation into the precise role and importance of such expertise in the context of what we know about the religion of this period (which was no longer centred on sacrifice but on the temple) and the lack of advertisement of kings as sacrificers in the royal inscriptions.

The routine specification of the ancestry of the donees becomes a regular feature in Orissan inscriptions from about the 10th century, as does the specification of their native place and place of residence. This can be related to the fact that this period saw the influx into Orissa of brāhmaṇas from other parts of India. There was a flow of brāhmaṇas into Orissa from renowned centres of brahmanical learning in Madhyadeśa such as Ṭākarī, Śrāvastī, Kolāñca, and Hastipada. A few came in from other places in the modern state boundaries of Gujarat, Madhya Pradesh, and Karnataka. Political turmoil and pressures on land have been cited as factors responsible for this spatial mobility, especially from the heartland of the Gaṅgā valley to the peripheral areas of the subcontinent. Brahmanical migrations into various parts of India had been going on for many centuries, and the major impetus must have been a search for a better livelihood. There were two things that were new in the early medieval period. One was the intensification of this process and the second was the conjunction of this migration with the proliferation of kingdoms in various parts of the subcontinent.

The brāhmaṇa of the Orissan inscriptions conforms in some ways to his counterpart in the normative texts. There is an emphasis on his Vedic learning. There is also frequent reference to his being a performer of the six acts enjoined on brāhmaṇas in the Dharmaśāstras—sacrificing and conducting sacrifices for others, studying and teaching, offering gifts and receiving gifts (*yajana, yājana, adhyayana, adhyāpana, dāna, pratigraha*). References to sacrificial expertise occur in a few inscriptions, and epithets such as *dīkṣita, agnihotrin* and the less common *upāsanin* also signify this sort of expertise.[22]

The brahmadeyas are sometimes seen as important hubs in the diffusion of temple-based sectarian religion and the *śāsana* brāhmaṇas are associated with the management of temple establishments and estates. The close connection between the brahmadeyas and temples comes out clearly in regions such as Kerala. If we look at the inscriptions of Orissa, a number of things can be noted. There is a virtual absence of references to the sectarian affiliations of the brāhmaṇa donees. The only instances are the Adhabhara plates of the Pāṇḍuvaṁśī king Mahā-Nannarāja, where the donee is described as a *bhāgavata*; the Sirpur inscription of the Pāṇḍuvaṁśī queen Vāsaṭā, where the term *bhāgavata* is used for the two donees; and the Dhenkanal plate of the Śulkī king Kulastambha, where the donee is described as *parama-vaiṣṇava.* The inscriptions associate very few of the donees with temple establishments or *maṭhas.*[23] Either the *śāsana* brāhmaṇas were only marginally involved in the spread of sectarian religion, or the inscriptions are deliberately silent on their association with temples, as this sort of association was not considered particularly prestigious. The *śāsana* brāhmaṇa is consistently presented in his traditionally prestigious role as Vedic scholar.

Howsoever the text of the inscriptions may specifically describe the donees, their contents highlight the brāhmaṇa in the role of the receiver of royal favours and as a land-holder. The brahmanical sources have different opinions on this issue. On the one hand, receiving gifts is one of the six acts considered appropriate for brāhmaṇas and generosity to brāhmaṇas is prescribed as a meritorious act for ordinary folk and kings alike. On the other hand, there are statements to the effect that the acceptance of gifts from kings should be avoided as it diminished the stature of the brāhmaṇas.[24] This sort of tension is not surprising in a tradition that often incorporated and sometimes tried to reconcile divergent points of view. Although the texts reflect different stances on the appropriateness of gift-acceptance, inscriptions from all over the country clearly show that in the early medieval period, certain brāhmaṇa families carved out large landed estates for themselves, benefiting from a series of royal grants of land. The exhortations to avoid such gifts had little impact on this upwardly mobile section of the community.

In Orissa and adjoining areas, throughout the early medieval period, the majority of royal grants were made in favour of brāhmaṇas, but some were made to religious establishments. Literary and archaeological evidence tells us about the prevalence of various Buddhist and Jaina sects in this area. Ratnagiri was a major Buddhist monastic establishment flourishing from about the 5th to the 12th centuries. The Udayagiri and Khandagiri caves were retreats of both Buddhist and Jaina monks. The earliest extant temples in Orissa belong to the 6th century (the Lakṣmaṇeśvara, Bharateśvara, and Śatrughneśvara temples at Bhubaneswar). Orissa seems to have been a stronghold of the Śaiva Pāśupata sect in this period. The 8th and 9th centuries saw an upsurge in the building of temples, most of which display an amalgam of Śaiva, Śākta, and Tāntric elements. The Liṅgarāja temple at Bhubaneswar was built by the Somavaṁśī kings in the 11th century. Until the middle of the 12th century, Orissa was a land of Śaiva temples, and Vaiṣṇava shrines were few and far between. A major shift of gravity from Śaivism to Vaiṣṇavism started during the reign of the Imperial Gaṅga king Anantavarman Coḍagaṅga, who began the construction of the Puruṣottama (later known as Jagannātha) temple at Puri.

Much remains to be understood about the mechanisms, institutions, and patrons that lay behind the early stages in the spread of sectarian religion. The association between kings and temples in India has usually been assumed rather than demonstrated. The sectarian titles claimed by the kings of various dynasties of ancient and early medieval Orissa are not matched by much evidence of their building or patronage of temple establishments until around the 10th century. In comparison with the large number of grants made by the kings of Orissa in favour of brāhmaṇas during most of the period under review, the number of grants to temples is comparatively few. The majority of royal grants to temples benefited Śaiva establishments. There are a few references to the royal patronage of *maṭha*s. Royal grants to Buddhist and Jaina establishments are very few. The inscriptions suggest that during most of the period royal patronage was *not* crucial to the building or maintenance of temples in Orissa. And the patronage of temples did *not* have an important place in royal policy during most of this period. Apart from kings, members of the royal family, and subordinate rulers, there were a variety of other social groups—local land-holders, administrative functionaries, and wealthy private individuals—who extended patronage to temple establishments.

There seems to have been a change as far as all this was concerned in the 10th century. During the reigns of the Imperial Gaṅga kings, there was an increase in the direct initiative of the king in making grants to temples, an increase in the number of secular grants in favour of *nāyaka*s or military chiefs, and also a large volume of inscriptions recording temple grants made by members of the royal family. This indicates an important shift in royal policy. With the building of the Jagannātha temple at Puri by the Imperial Gaṅga king Anantavarman Coḍagaṅga in the middle of the 12th century, the royally-endowed temple emerged as an important component in the practice of kingship.

The Gifted Land

An important part of the land grant charters is the information they give regarding the nature of brahmadeya settlements. One of the limitations of the inscriptional sources is that they tell us little about what was going on in non-brahmadeya villages, which would have outnumbered the brahmadeyas greatly (it is difficult to say what the precise ratio of the two might have been). Details of the extent and location of the holdings, the nature of the land granted, the description of the boundaries (where this occurs), and the terms and conditions of the grants are crucial in order to understand agrarian structure and agrarian change in early medieval Orissa. The specifications of village boundaries suggest in some cases the clustering of brahmadeya settlements. The evidence from Orissa is significant as it indicates that while *most* of the grants do stipulate that the gift in question was free of the obligation to render taxes to the state (and therefore involved a permanent loss of actual or potential income to the state), *some* royal endowments were not tax free. The latter are known as *kara-śāsana*s, and 13 of them have been found in Orissa.[25] They generally specify the annual rent that the donee was to pay.

An analysis of the inscriptions indicates that the brahmadeyas in Orissa were, in most cases, made free from any kind of state intervention. The privileges granted to the beneficiaries were not restricted to revenue matters. They included comprehensive rights over the natural resources of the area. Some—but not all or even most of the inscriptions (those of the Pāṇḍuvaṁśīs and Somavaṁśīs) may suggest the grant of certain judicial rights as well: The relevant term is *sa-daś-āparadha.* But this term can be interpreted in two ways, either as giving the right to punish those guilty of the ten offences or the right to realize fines from those guilty of the ten offences. From the 9th or 10th century, epigraphic evidence indicates an increase in some areas of the control of the brāhmaṇa beneficiaries over sources of revenue other than land. Grants of the Bhauma-Karas, Udayavarāha, the Śulkīs, and Tuṅgas give the donees control over outposts situated in the village, landing or bathing places, and ferries (*sa-kheṭa-ghaṭṭa-nadi-tara-sthān-ādi-gulmaka*). From the 9th or 10th century, some of the inscriptions of the Bhauma-Karas, Ādi-Bhañjas, Śulkīs, and Tuṅgas contain the term *sa-tantravāya-gokuṭa-śauṇḍik-ādi-prakṛtika* (along with the weavers, cowherds, brewers, and other inhabitants). But this is not a universal phenomenon. It may be noted, for instance, that the grants of the Imperial Gaṅgas do not contain any terms that can be interpreted as transferring judicial rights or rights over the inhabitants of villages to the donees. The grant of a large number of privileges was offset by what seems to have been the only restriction imposed by the state—that the gifted land was inalienable. This was indicated by terms such as *akṣaya-nīvī dharma* and *a-lekhanī-praveśatayā*. The evidence regarding the nature of the rights bestowed on the brahmadeyas suggests that while these varied to some extent from dynasty to dynasty, the position they created for the donee was one that fell somewhere between that of a landlord and landowner—more than a landlord, and just short of an owner of land in the modern sense of the term. The insertion of a brāhmaṇa landed elite into the countryside initiated a churning process that led to changes in agrarian relations and that had far-reaching impact on many aspects of rural society.

There seems little doubt that the creation of brahmadeya settlements and the terms of the land grants created a class that enjoyed superior rights and control over the inhabitants and the resources of the village. The technical terms of the grants clearly indicate that in economic terms, the relationship between the brāhmaṇa donee and other rural groups was one of exploitation. Whether the substitution of state exploitation and control by the more close-at-hand brāhmaṇa exploitation and control meant increased levels of subjection of the average cultivator is however a more tricky question. One point that can be made, however, is that the degrees of social and economic stratification, dominance and subordination that resulted from royal land grants depended on a number of variables that could differ from region to region and even within regions. These factors included ecology, the availability of arable land, and the existence or absence of competing groups or institutions. In Assam, where cultivable land was not in short supply, and where non-brāhmaṇa groups also held land, the extent of social and economic stratification was not as rigid as in other regions.[26] Levels of social stratification varied greatly between upland Andhra and wet zone lowlands.[27] Corporate organizations of brāhmaṇas such as the *sabhā* furthered the authority of the *śāsana* brāhmaṇas in the Tamil region. In Kerala, the influence of such corporate organizations was enhanced by the absence of competition from corporate organizations of other social groups such as the *nāḍu* or *nāṭṭār*.[28]

The Interpretation of Royal Patronage

A major point of disagreement among historians has to do with how precisely the act of royal grants to brāhmaṇas and temples is to be interpreted and understood. Part of the problem in the feudalism hypothesis is its understanding of power relationships in overwhelmingly competitive terms. One can question the assumption that an increase in the power and wealth of certain classes (brāhmaṇas) and institutions (temples) necessarily had to be at the *expense* of royal power. If our understanding of the politics of early medieval India gives adequate importance to collaboration and alliances, we can think in terms of the *parallel* increase in power of kings, brāhmaṇas, and temples. Strategies of control, alliances, and collaboration with political competitors and prestigious social groups were crucial facets of the politics of the time.

Another fundamental problem with the feudalism hypothesis is that it rests on a misunderstanding of the politics and economics of patronage. In the post-Gupta period, two different kinds of contexts of land grants can be identified.[29] In certain situations (in fledgling, unstable monarchies) it was part of a quest for power or staking a claim to it. In others (established, more stable states), it was a proclamation and advertisement of power. *Dāna*—ritual giving—has to be understood within the context of religious practice, social custom, and political precept. It cannot be understood in the way we would interpret a mundane economic transaction in which he who gives without material recompense is the loser. Evidence from many parts of South Asia can be invoked to demonstrate that more and larger gifts were signifiers of more, not less, power. In Orissa, for instance, the maximum number of grants were made by the most powerful dynasties, the Bhauma-Karas, Somavaṁśīs, and Imperial Gaṅgas. If we look for evidence of lavish gifts of land to *hundreds* of brāhmaṇas, we find these are absent in Period I, and virtually absent in Period II.[30] There is an increase in the number of such generous grants in Period III and again, we find that it is kings of the most powerful dynasty—the Imperial Gaṅgas—who were making grants to hundreds of brāhmaṇas at a time. Examples of this include the Madras Museum plates of Vajrahasta (in favour of 500 brāhmaṇas), the Galavalli plates of Rājarāja I (300 brāhmaṇas), and the two sets of Korni plates of Anantavarman Coḍagaṅga (300 brāhmaṇas). Such grants, made at the peak of power of a dynasty, cannot be interpreted as a symptom or a cause of political disempowerment.[31]

The increase of royal grants of land indicates the more systematic and extensive deployment and redistribution of resources by kings. These sorts of equations are recognized for the earlier periods of Indian history. For example, references to kings distributing cows, gold, horses, villages, etc., in the *dāna-stutis* in later Vedic literature are generally seen as an indication of (or at least within a context of) increasing, not decreasing royal power. However, the interpretation is reversed for the early medieval period, where grants are seen as a sort of 'selling out' or disinvestment strategy undertaken by a state that was in the grip of a crisis. In early medieval India (as in the modern world) the more powerful gave to the less powerful, and generous hand-outs did not as a matter of course led to an erosion of the power of the giver. They arose out of the king's superior control over resources, and also marked a special but unequal power relation between the giver and the recipient.

The importance of land grants in the legitimation of political power has been highlighted by many historians. Political power is mercurial, something that waxes and wanes, that has to be grasped, cemented, claimed, and proclaimed. Legitimation is therefore a constant need, an on-going process involving repeated reiteration and display. However, there are a number of issues related to legitimation that need to be considered carefully. These concern the precise working of the mechanisms of legitimation, the different audiences that the various strategies of legitimation targeted, and the kind of responses they may have elicited.[32] It is also necessary to highlight the connection between legitimation strategies and socio-political alliances, to which they were inextricably linked. Another aspect that can be considered is the reciprocal element of legitimation strategies, enhancing as they did not only the prestige and position of the legitimized but also of the legitimizers.

In the emphasis that is placed on the importance of legitimation strategies, we should not lose sight of the fact that they were a part of political processes in which force was ultimately the most important ingredient. There is also a need to spell out just how the patronage of a socio-religious elite group can be envisaged as an effective strategy in such a situation, which means reflecting more closely on the relationship between power, status, and authority in ancient India.[33] Another question that can be asked is just how effective integrative and legitimizing strategies pursued by early medieval kings actually were. Further, the focus on legitimation should not make us forget the fact that land grants were also about the transfer of land rights that crucially affected agrarian structure and agrarian relations. Therefore, there is a constant need to look beyond the linkages between kings and donees, at the implications that these transfers had for rural society.

In this brief summary of some of the aspects of the history of ancient and early medieval Orissa as revealed in the inscriptions, and how this data impinges on the larger debate, I would like to mention certain areas that require further investigation. There is sufficient ground to question the validity of the hypothesis of a subcontinental decline in urban centres and trade in the early medieval period.[34] There is consequently a need for a better understanding of the precise nature of settlement patterns, urbanization, and trade in early medieval Orissa. There is also a need for a clearer assessment of the administrative organization of kingdoms. The political changes need to be placed within a broader social context that supplements a focus on class with greater attention to caste and gender relations. Clearly, there are still many under-explored areas. Greater clarity about these would help to contextualize the epigraphic evidence of the kind that has been summarized here.

There is no denying that the debate about the economy, polity, and society of early medieval India has been a rich and fruitful one from many points of view. But it has also been constricting, with researchers often trying to fit their data into one or the other explanatory model, and not trying to move beyond them. The debate has also had its share of casualties. The preoccupation with feudalism has led to a dearth of meaningful studies of the literature, philosophical ideas, religion, art, and architecture of early medieval India and a lack of acknowledgement of the cultural richness and vitality of the period. Viewed through the spectacles of a feudal paradigm, all these tend to be reduced to simple and sorry reflections of a decadent feudal order. The alternative hypothesis that highlights integration and state formation is less constrained by a self-imposed theoretical strait-jacket and suits areas like Orissa well.[35] Nevertheless, some of its insights can be stretched further. Finally, when we are dealing with an area as large as the Indian subcontinent, any explanatory framework for the early medieval period will have to have enough flexibility to accommodate and accept regional and sub-regional diversity.

Notes

1. I refer to the debate on whether early medieval India was feudal or not, not to writings on this period, which obviously go back much further.
2. The literature of this debate is extensive and fairly well-known. Therefore, it does not seem necessary to give a detailed listing of the relevant works. However, a few important references can be cited. An important detailed exposition of the Indian feudalism hypothesis was by R. S. Sharma, *Indian Feudalism: c. 300–1200* (Kolkata: Calcutta University, 1965), which was followed by a number of writings that endorsed, amplified, and sometimes amended the original formulation. The systematic presentation of data to

support the hypothesis of urban decay can be found in Sharma's *Urban Decay in India (c. 300–c. 1000)* (New Delhi: Munshiram Manoharlal, 1987). The feudalism model has been applied to early medieval south India by scholars such as Kesavan Veluthat, *The Political Structure of Early Medieval South India* (New Delhi: Orient Longman, 1993), and R. N. Nandi, *State Formation, Agrarian Growth and Social Change in Feudal South India* (New Delhi: Manohar, 2000). The application of Aidan W. Southall's segmentary state model to early medieval south India is undertaken in Burton Stein's *Peasant State and Society in Medieval South India* (New Delhi: Oxford University Press, 1980). The foremost exponents of the 'integration hypothesis' are Hermann Kulke and B. D. Chattopadhyaya. See especially Hermann Kulke, 'Fragmentation and Segmentation Versus Integration? Reflections on the Concepts of Indian Feudalism and the Segmentary State in Indian History,' *Studies in History* 4 (2) 1982, pp. 237–263 and B. D. Chattopadhyaya, 'Political Processes and Structure of Polity in Early Medieval India', Presidential Address, Ancient India Section, Indian History Congress, 44th session, Burdwan, 1983, reprinted in B. D. Chattopadhyaya, *The Making of Early Medieval India* (New Delhi: Oxford University Press, 1997), pp. 183–222. The questioning of the hypothesis of urban decay can be found in B. D. Chattopadhayaya, 'Trade and Urban Centres in Early Medieval North India', and 'Urban Centres in Early Medieval India: An Overview', in *The Making of Early Medieval India,* pp. 130–154, 155–182. For a refutation of the hypothesis of a decline in the money economy in this period, see John S. Deyell, *Living without Silver: The Monetary History of Early Medieval North India* (New Delhi: Oxford University Press, 1990).

3. A detailed presentation of this data is given in Upinder Singh, *Kings, Brāhmaṇas and Temples in Orissa: An Epigraphic Study,* AD *300–1147* (New Delhi: Munshiram Manoharlal, 1994). A few of the later Sanskrit inscriptions of the period contain Telugu or Oriya elements. There are several Gaṅga inscriptions in Telugu that have been found in various parts of modern Andhra Pradesh. These have not been drawn on for this analysis.
4. I have only considered the feudalism and the 'integration' models in this chapter. The segmentary state model, which has been applied to early medieval south India by Burton Stein is fraught with many difficulties that are fairly well known, and has not been taken up for discussion. In looking at the feudalism and integration hypotheses, the attempt is not to present a comprehensive critique, but to raise new questions.
5. Some of the inscriptions that form part of the discussion here belong to a period a little before what is generally considered to be part of the early medieval period, that is, the 6th to the 12th/13th centuries AD.
6. The dates that have been suggested for the initial year of the Gaṅga era range from the 4th to the 9th century. The dates corresponding to the close of the 5th century seem most plausible. The dates suggested for the initial year of the Bhauma era include 606, 736, 778, and 831. The first of these (which identifies the era used by the Bhauma–Karas with the Harṣa era) seems too early, but those in the middle of the 8th or in the 9th century are more plausible.

7. This was not the first time Magadhan armies had ventured into these parts. The Hathigumpha inscription of Kharavela suggests that the Nandas had already made forays into the area.
8. The relevant references are to Mahendra of Kosala, Vyāghrarāja of Mahākāntara, Mahendragiri of Piṣṭapura, Svāmidatta of Koṭṭura, Damana of Eraṇḍapalla, and Kubera of Devarāṣṭra. The fact that there is no reference to any defeated king who can be located in northern or central Orissa suggests that Samudragupta's armies may have skirted this area. The Gupta era is used in certain late 6th century inscriptions from these areas such as the Sumaṇḍala plates of Dharmarāja and the Kanas plate of Pṛthivīvigraha, but this need not signify effective political domination, especially since by this time the power of the imperial Guptas had crumbled.
9. The *Rājataraṅgiṇī* highlights the bravery of these mercenaries (M. A. Stein, ed., *Kalhaṇa's Rājataraṅgiṇī* (New Delhi: Munshiram Manoharlal, 1960); VIII. 1047, 1082 ff, 1148 ff. Cited in Andre Wink, *Al Hind: The Making of the Indo-Islamic World*, Vol. 1 (New Delhi: Oxford University Press, 1999), p. 239.
10. We do not know enough about the administrative organization of the early kingdoms of this period. On the basis of the Midnapore inscription of Somadatta, in which the king claims that he followed the *Manu-śāstra*, H. Kulke has suggested that the kings of this time organized their rule according to the law books, that is, Dharmaśāstras ('Royal Temple Policy and the Structure of Medieval Hindu Kingdoms', in A. Eschmann, H. Kulke and G. C. Tripathi, eds, *The Cult of Jagannath and the Regional Tradition of Orissa* (New Delhi: Manohar, 1978), p. 127. The extent to which claims of this sort made in inscriptions can be accepted as descriptive of prevailing practices can be questioned.
11. Some of the reasons for this are given later in this book.
12. A further point that merits attention is the simultaneous spread of a pan-Indian brahmanical ideology during this period. See B. P. Sahu, 'Brahmanical Ideology, Regional Identities and the Construction of Early India', *Social Scientist* 29, (7–8) July–August 2001, pp. 3–18. An illuminating description and discussion of the interplay between the process of brahmanization and the formation of a regional tradition is by Kunal Chakrabarti, *Religious Process: The Purāṇas and the Making of a Regional Tradition* (New Delhi: Oxford University Press, 2001). For Orissa, we have the important work edited by Eschmann, Kulke and Tripathi, *The Cult of Jagannath and the Regional Tradition of Orissa*.
13. This seems to refer to the right of enjoying the sound of five instruments—trumpet, tambour, conch-shell, kettledrum, and gong.
14. The problem of definition applies to the term 'tribe' as much as it does to the term 'state'. Ancient Indian historians tend to use both terms in a loose, dichotomous sense.
15. The *praśasti* of the Ādi-Bhañjas explains this reference by telling us that Gaṇadaṇḍa Vīrabhadra, the progenitor of the lineage, burst out of the egg of a peahen in the great hermitage of Koṭyāśrama, where he was reared by

the great *ṛṣi* Vasiṣṭha. The further elaboration of this story introduces us to the 88,000 sons of Vīrabhadra. It says that due to the prayers of these sons, Vīrabhadra was protected by Rāmadeva and was made lord of 88,000 villages.

16. The Śailodbhava origin myth speaks of a man named Pulindasena, famed among the people of Kaliṅga. Although endowed with virtue, strength, and greatness, he did not covet sovereignty, but worshipped the Svayambhū for a man capable of ruling the earth. He obtained this boon, and saw a man emerging from the splintering of a rock. This was the lord Śailodbhava, who became the founder of the illustrious lineage.
17. The Chandeswar plates of Mādhavavarman's grandson Dharmarāja credit Dharmarāja with having taken the purificatory bath on the occasion of the performance of the Aśvamedha and the Vājapeya. While this may represent a second performance or at least a claim to the performance of these sacrifices by a Śailodbhava king, it may also be a reference to or echo of the events of Mādhavavarman's reign. The timing of Mādhavavarman's performance of the sacrifices can be connected to his throwing off allegiance to Śaśāṅka and his assumption of an independent status.
18. F. Kielhorn, 'Buguda Plates of Mādhavavarman', *Epigraphia Indica* 3, 1894–1895, p. 44, v. 11.
19. On Stambheśvarī, see A. Eschmann, 'Hinduization of Tribal Deities in Orissa: The Śākta and Śaiva Typology', in A. Eschmann, H. Kulke and G. C. Tripathi, eds, *The Cult of Jagannath and the Regional Tradition of Orissa*, pp. 79–98.
20. *Gotra* is the patrimonial exogamous clan system of the brāhmaṇas. The *gotras* are divided into *gaṇas*, each of which have their own *pravara*. The *pravara* consists of the name or names (one, two, three, or five) of supposed ancestral *ṛṣis*. The *pravara* of the various members of a particular *gaṇa* have the name of the eponymous *gotra ṛṣi* in common. In course of time, as the boundaries of the *gotra* came to acquire certain elasticity, the *pravara* came to form a more precise basis for defining the exogamous group. *Anupravara* is a term that we do not encounter in the Sūtra literature. In the inscriptions of Orissa, it seems to have had much the same connotations as the *pravara*.
21. The Neulpur plate records a grant made in favour of 200 brāhmaṇas of the four Vedas, including the *Atharva Veda*. The donees are described as *caturvidya* brāhmaṇas belonging to various *gotras* and *caraṇas*, representing more or less equally *caraṇas* schools of the four Vedas (Bahvṛca, Vājasaneya, Chāndīśa, and Atharva). R. D. Banerji, 'Neulpur Plate of Subhakara', *Epigraphia Indica* 15, 1919–1920, pp. 1–8.
22. The inscriptions which associate the donees with ritual expertise are the two grants of Pṛthivi-mahārāja, the Midnapore plate of Śubhakīrti, the Bonda plates of the Pāṇḍuvaṁśī king Tīvara, the Dhenkanal plate of the Śulkī king Raṇastambha, and the Baripada plates of the Nandodbhava king Devānanda.
23. The following inscriptions do make such associations: The Kanas plates of Lokavigraha and Bhānudatta associate Brāhmaṇas of the Maitrāyaṇīya school with the *maṭha* of Maṇināgeśvara. The Indian Museum plates of

the Śvetaka Gaṅga king Indravarman associate certain brāhmaṇas with a temple of Mādhava and Svayambhū. The Visakhapatnam plates of the Kaliṅganagara Gaṅga king Devendravarman describe a brāhmaṇa named Somācārya as the superintendent of a shrine of Dharmeśvara-bhaṭṭāraka. The Terundia plate of the Bhauma–Kara king Śubhākara II records a grant to six brāhmaṇas for the upkeep of the *maṭhas* and *maṇḍapas* established by these brāhmaṇas in their native village. The two sets of the Baudh plates of the Bhauma–Kara queen Tribhuvanamahādevī associate certain brāhmaṇas with a temple of Umā–Maheśvara. The Madras Museum plates of the imperial Gaṅga king Vajrahasta associate the Brāhmaṇa donees with a temple of the god Koṭīśvaradeva. The Murupaka grant of the imperial Gaṅga king Anantavarman Coḍagaṅga entrusted the protection of the temple of the deity Narendreśvaradeva to five brāhmaṇas of the village.

24. *Manu* 4. 218 and *Mahābhārata* 13.35.23 state that the food and gifts of a king take away a brāhmaṇa's lustre. The *Yajñavalkya Smṛti* (1. 213) states that a brāhmaṇa, who though entitled, does not accept a gift, attains the highest world. *Manu* 4. 186 asserts that a brāhmaṇa should not frequently resort to accepting gifts as this leads to the loss of his spiritual power.
25. Two of these instances come from Period I, four from Period II and seven from Period III. In Period I, there are the Bobbili plates of Candavarman and the Ningondi plates of the Māṭhara king Prabhañjanavarman. In Period II, we have the Ganjam grant of the Śvetaka Gaṅga king Pṛthvīvarmadeva, the Kalahandi grant of the Kaliṅganagara Gaṅga king Vajrahasta, the Chicacole grant of the Kaliṅganagara Gaṅga king Anantavarman, and the Angul plate of the Bhauma Kara queen Dharmamāhadevī. In Period III, there are the following records of tax-paying grants: the Jurada plates of Neṭṭabhañja, the Talcher plate of the Śulkī king Kulastambha, the Puri plate of the Śulkī king Kulastambha, the Talcher plate of the Tuṅga king Gayāḍatuṅga, the Asiatic Society plate of the same king, and the two sets of the Patna plates of the Somavaṁśī king Janamejaya Mahābhavagupta.
26. N. Lahiri, *Pre-Ahom Assam: Studies in the Inscriptions of Assam between the Fifth and the Thirteenth Centuries* AD (New Delhi: Munshiram Manoharlal, 1991), p. 137.
27. Cynthia Talbot, *Precolonial India in Practice: Society, Region, and Identity in Medieval Andhra* (New Delhi: Oxford University Press, 2001), p. 44.
28. Veluthat, *The Political Structure of Early Medieval South India*, p. 209.
29. The literary and epigraphic evidence for royal grants goes back many centuries. In the Gupta period, there are few land grants made by the Imperial Guptas and many more made by subordinate rulers. However, the significant proliferation of land grants in different parts of the subcontinent and their becoming an important component of royal policy are features that can be associated with the post-Gupta period.
30. There are two such instances in Period II. The Chicacole plates of the Kaliṅganagara Gaṅga king Devendravarman record an endowment to 300 brāhmaṇas, and the Neulpur plates of the Bhauma-Kara king Śubhākara records a grant to 200 brāhmaṇas (though 202 donees are actually named).

31. Talbot's analysis of the Andhra inscriptions brings out the close connection between strong polities and high levels of epigraphic production (mostly donative records) in a contiguous region (Talbot, *Precolonial India in Practice*).
32. This issue has been addressed by Kulke ('Royal Temple Policy…'). He talks of vertical legitimation through the patronage of autochthonous deities and horizontal legitimation through the building and patronage of imperial temples. He presents the Gaṅga patronage of the Jagannātha temple as a combination of both kinds of legitimation processes.
33. Kulke has directed attention to Max Weber's important contribution to the understanding of such issues ('Max Weber's Contribution to the Study of 'Hinduization' in India and 'Indianization' in Southeast Asia', in H. Kulke, *Kings and Cults: State Formation and Legitimation in India and Southeast Asia* (New Delhi: Nag Publishers, 2001), pp. 240–261.
34. See B. D. Chattopadhyaya, 'Trade and Urban Centres in Early Medieval. North India', and 'Urban Centres in Early Medieval India', pp. 130–154 and 155–182. The evidence from south India too does not fit in with the hypothesis of a decline in trade and urban centres. Further, Wink's insistence (*Al-Hind…*) that we look at the Indian subcontinent as part of a broader world that was becoming increasingly knit together through trade and politics is persuasive. Wink, however, seems to go to the other extreme by inflating the role played by the Indian Ocean trade in the political history of the dynasties of early medieval India.
35. Recent studies suggest that it also suits other areas such as Andhra (Talbot, *Precolonial India in Practice*), Bengal (Chakrabarti, *Religious Process*), and Rajasthan (Nandini Sinha-Kapoor, *State Formation in Rajasthan: Mewar during, the Seventh–Fifteenth Centuries* (New Delhi: Manohar, 2002).

SECTION II

Archaeologists and the Modern Histories of Ancient Sites

5

Archaeologists and Architectural Scholars in 19th Century India

The second half of the 19th century was a momentous time in the history of Indian archaeology. Archaeology emerged as a distinct discipline within the larger sphere of antiquarianism and archaeological investigations were given a firm organizational foundation with the establishment of the Archaeological Survey. Alexander Cunningham (1814–1893) so dominated the field of Indian archaeology between the 1860s and 1880s that these decades are rightly known as the Cunningham era (Figure 5.1).[1]

One of the remarkable aspects of the impressive antiquarian and archaeological scholarship of this period was that it was largely the product of leisure-time pursuit. Cunningham was a military engineer and between 1834 and 1861, he managed to combine his official work with his antiquarian interests, writing on diverse subjects such as numismatics, the temples of Kashmir and the *stūpa*s of central India and Ladakh. He retired from the army with the rank of major general at the age of 47 to take the job of archaeological surveyor, a post he held from 1861 to 1865. During these years, he systematically surveyed and documented over 166 sites in various parts of north India and confirmed through excavation the identification of many ancient cities such as Takṣaśilā, Kauśāmbī, Śrāvastī and Rāmagrāma. The Survey was cut short in 1865 because the government no longer wanted to fund it.

This chapter was previously published in Parul Pandya Dhar (ed.), *Indian Art History: Changing Perspectives* (New Delhi: DK Printworld and National Museum Institute, 2011).

Figure 5.1
Alexander Cunningham

Courtesy: Archaeological Survey of India

But Cunningham came back to India some years later to take over as director general of the Archaeological Survey, a post he held from 1871 to 1885. During these years, he explored a large number of sites, conducting excavations at several important ones such as Mathura, Bhita, Bodh Gaya, Rajgir, Takht-i-Bahi, Shahr-i-Bahlol, Manikyala, Harappa, Bharhut, Besnagar, Sanchi, Sahet-Mahet, Taxila and Khajuraho. The 23 volumes of *Archaeological Survey Reports* (which included some contributions made by his assistants) stand as direct testimony to his work as director general. During these and his post-retirement years, he also wrote 8 major books and about 40 scholarly papers on varied themes.

This chapter has three interrelated aspects. First, I will focus on Cunningham's contribution to the history of Indian sculpture and architecture, looking closely at three of his books. I will go on to discuss the debate about the place of the study of art and architecture in the activities of the Archaeological Survey. The third aspect I will go on to emphasize is the political aspect of the 19th century debate about architectural issues such as the antiquity of the arch. Apart from published material, there is a considerable amount of archival material which reveals several unknown facets of the people and processes that played an important part in the development of archaeological ideas and institutions during this eventful half century.

Cunningham's Writings on Art and Architecture

Alexander Cunningham's most important long-term contribution to scholarship was the fact that he made a strong and convincing case for the exploration of non-textual paths to the Indian past. He repeatedly and successfully made his case before the antiquarian community and the colonial state.[2] Cunningham's writings represent a life-time's commitment to such explorations. The quality of leadership he gave the Survey stemmed from this commitment along with his ability to effectively handle and deal with a wide range of sometimes rather difficult people including government officials, his assistants and various scholars—British and Indian—some of whom were also strong critics and rivals.

Cunningham is best known as a field archaeologist. However, he often used the word 'archaeology' in a sense which included many approaches to the study of the past, not only those dealing with material remains. His instructions to his assistants, published at the beginning of volume 3 of his *Archaeological Survey Reports*, contain an explicit statement about his understanding of what an archaeological survey should involve.[3] The study of sculpture and architecture was an important part of the archaeological enterprise. The memorandum speaks with feeling and enthusiasm about the aesthetic aspects of Indian art and also suggests that it might offer something of value to contemporary architecture. But though sculpture and architecture certainly had a place in archaeological documentation, for Cunningham they were just a small part of a discipline whose scope extended to all remains that helped illustrate the manners and customs of ancient times.

Cunningham's archaeological reports are strewn with descriptions of sculpture and architecture. The report for 1871–1872[4] offered a tentative chronological framework for the classification of Indian architectural style. The primary classification was into two periods—Hindu (1000 BC to 1200 AD) and Muhammadan (1200–1700 AD).[5] His nomenclature of the phases of the Hindu period showed considerable emphasis on foreign influence as well as a general focus on north India. The reports show increasing descriptions of sculpture and architecture, including medieval architecture, over time. Cunningham's first piece of writing on an architectural subject focused on the temples of Kashmir.[6] Here, I want to look closely at his three major works on Buddhist art and architecture—*The Bhilsa Topes* (1854), *The Stûpa of Bharhut* (1879) and *Mahâbodhi* (1892).

Cunningham's life-long fascination for Buddhism is well known and is something he is often criticized for (As if every scholar does not have his or her own special interests and obsessions!). His 'Buddhist bias' was due to a combination of at least three factors. One was the publication of translations of the travellogues of the Chinese pilgrims Faxian and Xuanzang.[7] These sources must have excited the young military engineer who himself led a life on the move with a map in his hand, one who had a keen interest in historical geography and a strongly empirical bent of mind.[8] Cunningham immediately recognized how the Chinese accounts could be used to plot many places of ancient India on a modern map. But if he was going to follow in the footsteps of the Chinese pilgrims (actually he very often strayed from their route), he was bound to end up spending a lot of his time tracking down Buddhist sites.

Second, the decades during which Cunningham's archaeological career was unfolding were the very ones when western scholars were making important strides in discovering, translating and studying Buddhist texts. Therefore, it is not surprising that he himself was interested in the history of Indian Buddhism and sought to make his own unique contribution to the subject. Third, Cunningham's interest in Buddhism was fueled by the fact that for him, the Buddha and Buddhism marked both a pinnacle as well as a dominant force in Indian history. Like many other western scholars of the time, he saw the Buddha as a radical religious and social reformer, one who stood up against a corrupt and arrogant Brahmin priesthood to preach the abolition of caste and the equality of all mankind, introducing to India a code of 'pure and practical morality'.[9] For all these reasons, it is not surprising that Cunningham's footsteps and his pen were drawn towards the Buddhist sites of early historic India. He did document and describe many Hindu temples and was not entirely unappreciative of their aesthetic aspect. But the Hindu temple did not cast its spell over him in the same way as the Buddhist *stūpa* did.

Apart from their Buddhist theme, another similarity between *The Bhilsa Topes*, *Stûpa of Bharhut* and *Mahâbodhi* was that in all three cases, Cunningham had an important part to play in the discovery of the remains he was describing. And yet the three books were separated by many years, and if we examine and compare them, we can see a development and increasing maturity in his understanding of Buddhist sculpture and architecture. This increasing maturity partly reflected the advances in knowledge made by the wider scholarly community vis-à-vis Buddhism. It also constituted Cunningham's own significant contribution to this growing body of knowledge.

The Bhilsa Topes (1854)

The full title of book—*The Bhilsa Topes or Buddhist Monuments of Central India: Comprising a Brief Historical Sketch of the Rise, Progress and Decline of Buddhism; with an account of the opening and examination of the various groups of topes around Bhilsa*—reveals its author's primary interests. A large part of the book is devoted to the history of Buddhism in India. It included a discussion of the life of the Buddha, his doctrines, the social impact of his teachings, the factors that attracted women to the Order, the Buddhist Councils, monastic rules, aspects of chronology, the schisms, Buddhism in Aśoka's time, the subsequent history of the religion and its decline. It discussed the description, classification, and significance and symbolism of *stūpas*; the building of *stūpas* and the ceremonies associated their construction; the location of the eight original relic *stūpas*; and the meaning of Buddhist symbols. Cunningham was aware of the existence of different Buddhist sects, changes in the complexion of the religion, and the theistic and tantric elements that became strong in its later phases. But he says little about all these things.

The 1850s were a time when the mists of confusion and uncertainty surrounding the early history and doctrines of Buddhism were beginning to lift. Cunningham drew heavily on the research and findings of various European scholars.[10] But his perspective was significantly different from theirs. He emphasized the importance of non-textual evidence for historicizing the Buddhism of the texts. Cunningham's *The Bhilsa Topes* was, in fact, the first detailed examination of the history of Indian

Buddhism which incorporated archaeological evidence from Buddhist sites in a substantial manner.

One of its important aspects was the description of the discoveries made by Cunningham and Maisey when they opened over twenty-seven *stūpas* at Sanchi, Sonari, Satdhara, Bhojpur, and Andher during January–February 1851. This makes *The Bhilsa Topes* an important document for the *modern* history of these sites, a history that has many different ingredients—discovery, documentation, destruction, conservation, repair and relocation. Cunningham and Maisey were expert *stūpa* openers. They made careful measurements and opened a vertical shaft down the exact centre of the *stūpa*. Their aim was to find the relics embedded in the *stūpa* core. The entire operation generally took no more than 2–3 hours.

The most sensational discoveries were made at Sanchi. Stūpa No. 1 at Sanchi yielded nothing, but Stupa No. 2 contained the relics of ten monks associated in Buddhist tradition with the missions sent out by Aśoka to the Hemavata country. Stupa No. 3 contained the relics of two monks well known from the texts—Sāriputta and Mahāmoggalāna. Subsequently, relics of these two monks were also discovered by Cunningham and Maisey in Stūpa No. 2 at Satdhara. All this was important evidence of the historicity of monks who were mentioned in the Buddhist texts.

Like many scholars of his time, Cunningham was struck by cross-cultural similarities. He saw connections between the *stūpas* of Buddhist India and the 'Druidical colonnades' of Britain, between the Buddhist veneration of trees and the English reverence for the oak. Of the various sites, Sanchi—which he identified with the Sha-chi of Faxian's account—was discussed in the greatest detail. The descriptions of the site, *stūpas*, structures and sculptures were accompanied by plans and sections drawn to scale and based on careful measurement. There were also several drawings of architectural features, sculptures, sculptural details and motifs.[11] *The Bhilsa Topes* gave a comprehensive cataloguing of the text and translation of the Sanchi inscriptions. For Cunningham, inscriptions were the important key to ascertaining the age of any historical monument.

The discoveries included the shaft of an Aśokan pillar to the south of Stupa No. 1. Its magnificent capital with the four addorsed lions lay nearby (Figure 5.2).[12] To the north of the Great *Stūpa* were the remains of another broken pillar. This one was originally crowned by a capital consisting of a larger than life-size *dhoti*-clad human figure, which Cunningham thought might represent the Maurya emperor Aśoka.[13]

Cunningham described the bas reliefs of Sanchi (he dated them to the early 1st century AD) as 'more original in design and more varied in subject than any other examples of Eastern sculpture which I have seen in

India'.[14] For him, these sculptures were, above all, an entry point into history, especially Buddhist history. Using various kinds of textual evidence as a guide, he gave a detailed description of the reliefs.[15] He identified the main themes of the sculptures as scenes from the life of Śākyamuni, religious processions, the worship of *stūpa*s and trees, and the adoration of the symbols of the Buddhist triad. Some of his interpretations were correct: for instance, the scenes of the conception, Māyā's dream and the Great Departure. But there were places where he was completely wrong. Take, for instance, his interpretation[16] of a boat scene as representing the Buddha's *nirvāṇa* (Figure 5.3).[17] Or his suggestion[18] that a scene depicted on the left pillar of the eastern gateway of *Stūpa* No. 1 showed the supreme Buddha being worshipped as a flame.[19] With the benefit of hindsight, we can identify many of his interpretations as incorrect. But this is not surprising given the fact that this was a preliminary account and that it reflected the still very imperfect understanding of early Buddhism among Western scholars at the time.[20]

Cunningham realized that that at this stage, the vocabulary of Buddhist sculpture consisted of a set of symbols and avoided the representation of the Buddha in anthropomorphic form.[21] He identified a number of symbols that occurred repeatedly—the *cakra*, *triratna* and *śrīvatsa*—as especially important, and saw a kinship among them. Taking matters further, he suggested an affinity between the Buddhist *triratna* and the Jagannatha triad.

He missed the *Jātaka* scenes completely.[22] This is not surprising as European translations of the *Jātaka* stories were not yet available. Cunningham also missed out on the significance of the *yakṣa*s and *yakṣī*s who are regular features of the sculptural programme of Sanchi and other early Buddhist sites. For instance, he describes a female bracket figure on the western gateway as a 'Nachni' or dancing girl[23] and what struck him the most about her was her rather Tibetan looks.[24]

Cunningham took the reliefs seriously as valuable reflections of ancient Indian manners and customs.[25] For instance, the scene on the northern gateway of Stūpa No. 1 showing the perambulation of a *stūpa* suggested to him what people must have done in ancient times when they visited a *stūpa*. Cunningham recognized the fact that many of the scenes and motifs in the Sanchi reliefs had nothing particularly Buddhist about them. They included city-tableaux, ascetic life and 'some little domestic scenes which I would rather attribute to the fancy of the artist than to their particular significance in a Buddhistical story'.[26] Everyday scenes caught his eye, as for instance a kitchen scene on the south pillar of the eastern gateway of Stūpa No. 1.[27] Not surprisingly for a military

Figure 5.2
Line drawing of Sanchi capitals

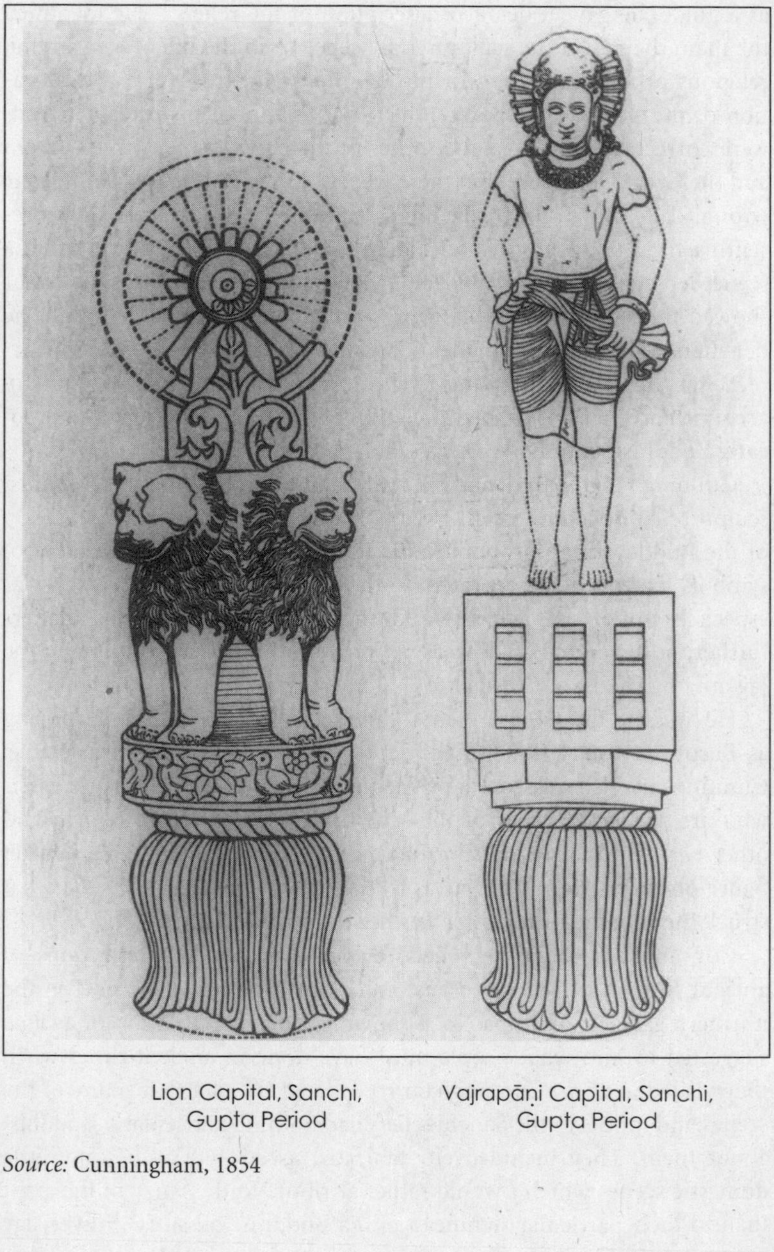

Lion Capital, Sanchi, Gupta Period

Vajrapāṇi Capital, Sanchi, Gupta Period

Source: Cunningham, 1854

Figure 5.3
Sketch of relief on left pillar of Eastern Gateway, Sanchi

Source: Cunningham, 1854

man, he was interested in the way in which the quiver was fastened to a soldier's back in a siege scene and the short, broad swords that soldiers carried.[28] In fact, there is a long digression on the subject of swords and illustrations of the types of weapons depicted on the reliefs (Figure 5.4).

At this stage, Cunningham was indifferent to purely ornamental motifs and there are hardly any illustrations of these: 'The outer faces of the pillars are ornamented with flowers, garlands, and other devices, which need not be detailed.'[29]

The Stûpa of Bharhut (1879)

The Stûpa of Bharhut was published in 1879, over 20 years after *The Bhilsa Topes*. This was a detailed description of the architecture, sculpture and inscriptions of single site—Bharhut—which Cunningham himself had discovered in November 1873. At about this time, photography started becoming part of archaeological documentation and this book included a large number of clear, well-produced photographs.[30] Sometimes there is a combination of photographs and drawings, with the drawings used to fill in the missing bits. These were accompanied by a map of the site, plans and elevations of the *stūpa* and other structures, drawings of the sculptures, and the text of the inscriptions.

Due to the ruined condition of the Bharhut *stūpa*, Cunningham had to reconstruct in his mind how its various parts must have fitted together. He reconstructed the design of various parts of the eastern gateway (Figure 5.5). We also find him using indigenous terminology such as *toraṇa*, *sūci* and *thabho* to describe the various parts of the Bharhut *stūpa*. This book represented the first attempt to interpret the relief sculptures of Bharhut. The understanding of Buddhism among Western scholars, including Cunningham, had grown since the 1850s.[31] But the most important factor that enabled Cunningham to accurately and confidently interpret the sculptures was the fact that the Bharhut sculptors had been very helpful and had labelled many of the scenes.

European scholars had by this time become more aware of the *Jātakas*.[32] Cunningham also tells us[33] that after his discovery of the Bharhut *stūpa*, he was in constant correspondence with the Pali scholar Childers and a Sri Lankan Buddhist priest named Subhuti, especially regarding the *Jātakas*. Cunningham relied heavily on Subhuti for a list of the *Jātaka* stories and their English translation. The book has long summaries of *Jātaka* stories, noting the ones depicted on the *stūpa* sculptures.[34] Cunningham noted the similarities and discrepancies between the *Jātaka* 'titles' in the Bharhut

Figure 5.4
Weapons and other paraphernalia represented in reliefs at Sanchi and Udayagiri

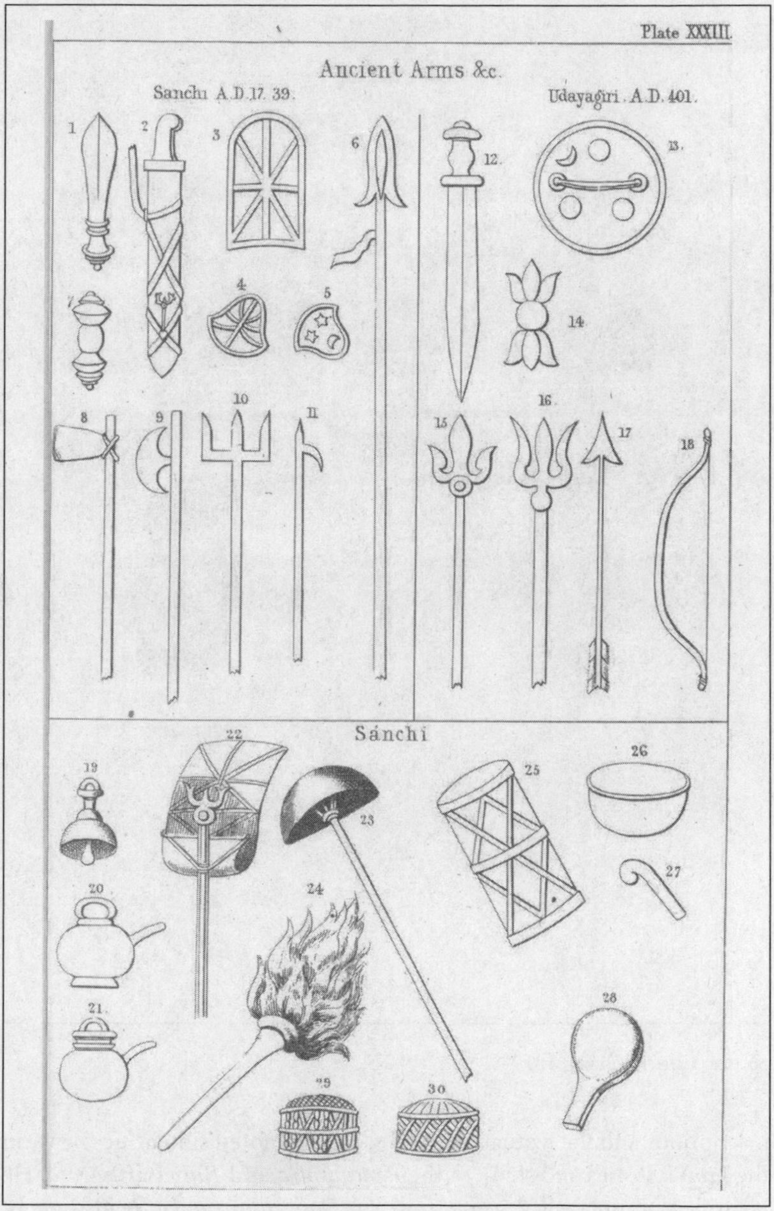

Source: Cunningham, 1954

Figure 5.5
Reconstruction of what the Eastern Gateway of the Bharhut Stūpa may have looked like

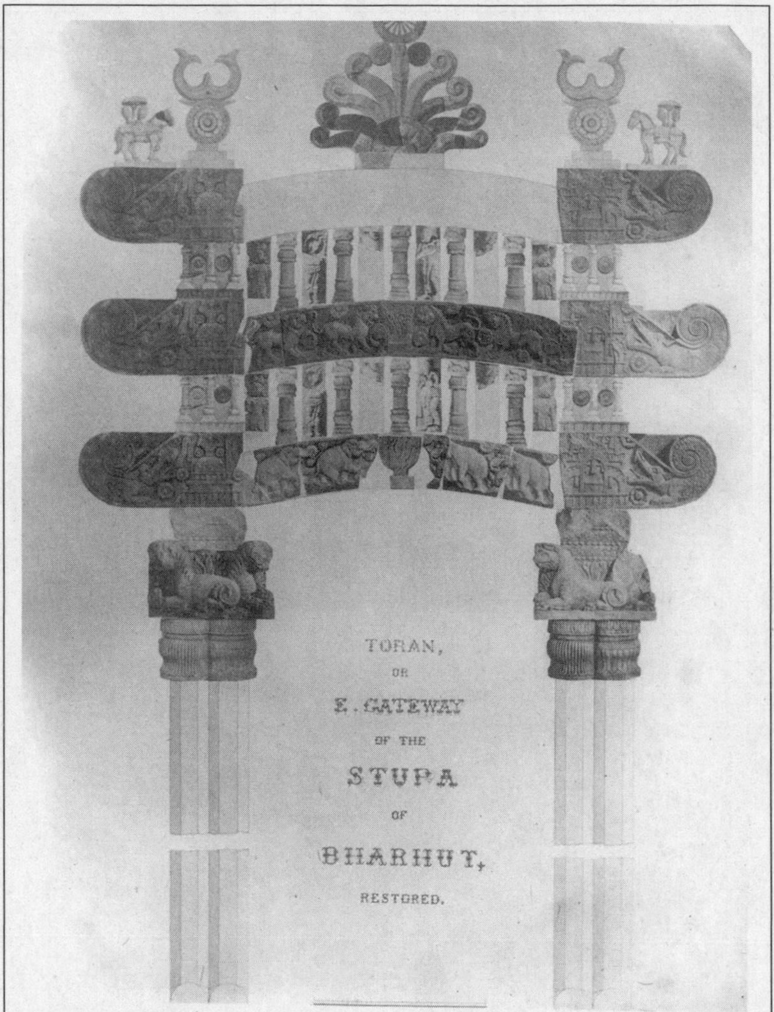

Source: Cunningham, 1879

inscriptions and the textual references. He also noted similarities between the *Jātaka* stories and those of the *Pañcatantra* and *Kathāsaritsāgara*. He identified an unlabelled scene from the *Daśaratha Jātaka*, read some of the Bharhut narrative reliefs as scenes from the story of Rāma in exile, and concluded that the Rāma legend was popular even in early Buddhist times.

As in the case of Sanchi, Cunningham saw the Bharhut reliefs as important sources of information on Indian history. He identified the major scenes from the life of the Buddha.[35] He also noted the representation of 'historical scenes' such as the processions of the kings Ajātaśatru and Prasenajit to visit the Buddha,[36] and Anāthapiṇḍika paving the ground of Jetavana with gold coins. He recognized the main symbols of the Buddha in the sculptures—the *stūpa*, wheel, bodhi tree, Buddhapāda and the *triratna*.[37] As in *The Bhilsa Topes*, he continued to maintain that the trinity of Jagannātha, Subhadrā and Balabhadra worshipped in Orissa must have been derived from the Buddhist *triratna* symbol.[38]

The labels helped Cunningham to identify the over thirty large *yakṣa*s and *yakṣī*s, *nāgarāja*s, *apsarā*s and *devatā* figures who formed an important part of the sculptural programme of Bharhut. (About half were inscribed with their names.) He was now able to hold forth on these subjects[39] and recognized their importance.[40] Then there were the plethora of trees, animals, fruits and flowers. Using the inscriptional labels as a guide, Cunningham discussed the trees that the various Buddhas were associated with. Other sculptures, especially those connected with monkeys were, according to him, scenes of pure humour.[41]

Cunningham was still interested in the military scenes and arms depicted in the relief sculptures. He described clothes and head-dresses and remarked on the richness and profusion of the ornaments worn by men and women,[42] giving many details and illustrations of these (Figure 5.6). He discussed and illustrated different kinds of tattoos[43] visible in the sculptures. He also described the many other things depicted in the Bharhut reliefs—palaces, *vajrāsana* canopies, thrones, pillars, hermitages, houses, vehicles, furniture, utensils and musical instruments.[44]

He had now developed a keen interest in ornamental motifs:

> About one half of the full medallions of the Rail-bars and the whole of the half medallions of the Pillars are filled with flowered ornaments of singular beauty and delicacy of design, of which numerous examples are given in the accompanying plates.[45]

Several plates contain sketches of the medallions with floral and other decorative designs (Figure 5.7).

The Stûpa of Bharhut gave the text and translation of 66 Bharhut inscriptions, occasionally citing Rajendralala Mitra and Childers on certain points of translation. On the basis of the palaeography of the inscriptions and the simplicity of the pillar capitals, Cunningham estimated that the Bharhut *stūpa* must have been built between c. 250–200 BC.[46]

Figure 5.6
Ornaments represented in Bharhut reliefs

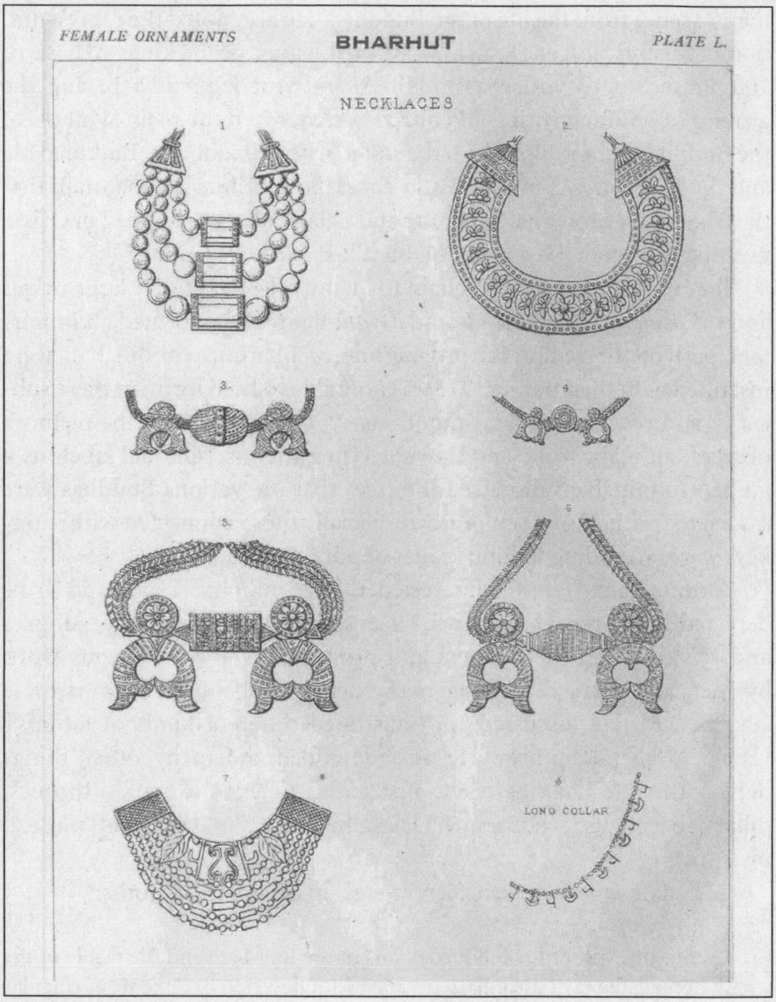

Source: Cunningham, 1879

Mahâbodhi (1892) and the Debate on the Arch

Cunningham's *Mahâbodhi or the Great Buddhist Temple under the Bodhi Tree at Buddha-Gaya* (1892) was a comprehensive account of the Mahābodhi temple at Bodh Gayā. It was published several years after he

Figure 5.7
Bharhut medallions

Source: Cunningham, 1879

retired as director general of the Archaeological Survey of India.[47] An important part of the book is Cunningham's account of the excavations at the site and the discoveries that resulted. In fact, the history of the temple from the 3rd century BC to the 11th century AD were revealed during the process of excavation and repair. The book gave a detailed description of the temple, monasteries, the bodhi tree and sculptures of different ages, accompanied by many illustrations, including photographs. There is a description of the many small *stūpas*, which he referred to as 'votive *stūpas*' that dotted the site and an account of the many interesting terracotta seals. The inscriptions, including the Chinese and Burmese ones, were also described and discussed.

At Bodh Gayā, the accounts of the Chinese pilgrims were crucial for Cunningham. One of the important conclusions he had reached long before was that the temple as seen by Faxian in the 4th century and Xuanzang in the 7th century was more or less similar to what it looked like in the 19th century, in spite of all the repairs and alterations that had taken place in between.[48] But excavations at the site had also revealed vestiges of the oldest stage of the temple. For Cunningham, these were of paramount importance.

> The importance of the Mahâbodhi Temple for the history of Indian art is quite unique, as it gives us the oldest existing remains of both sculpture and architecture. The sculptures of the Bharhut Stûpa date from the flourishing period of the Sunga Dynasty, about BC 150, whereas the Mahâbodhi remains belong to the period of Asoka, just one century earlier.[49]

Cunningham was an expert at reconstructing the shape of disappeared monuments by putting together various clues. He used the position of the original *vajrāsana* throne and a cloistered walk discovered during the excavations and the Bharhut reliefs to reconstruct what the Mahābodhi temple of Aśoka's time must have looked like.[50]

But the Mahābodhi temple presented some peculiar problems and raised a different set of controversial issues. One had to do with arches and the other had to do with the restoration work that was conducted at the temple by J. D. M. Beglar (Figure 5.8) with Cunningham's approval in 1880–1884.

As for many European scholars, for Cunningham too, the story of Indian sculpture was one of decay, from the high point achieved due to Greek contact to 'the wooden inanities and bestial obscenities of the Brahmanical temples'.[51] But while he was convinced that the ancient Indians had learnt the art of *sculpture* from the Greeks, he was equally convinced that the art of stone *architecture* was known to them before the time of Alexander's invasion.[52] He also thought that the Hindus knew the arch in ancient times. In the course of his archaeological reports, Cunningham had drawn attention to the arches in the shrine areas and porch of the Bhitargaon temple near Kanpur, an instance of an arch and vaulted roof at Nongarh (in Lakhisarai district, Bihar), and in the chamber enshrining the Nirvāṇa Buddha at Kushinara.

Figure 5.8
J. D. M. Beglar

Courtesy: Friends of the Kern Institute, Leiden

But it was the arches of the Bodh Gayā temple that became a major issue of discussion and dispute among scholars. Ranged on one side were Rajendralala Mitra and Cunningham, who argued that the arches in the temple represented an early, pre-7th century phase in its construction and that this was proof that the ancient Hindus knew the use of the arch.[53] The most vociferous representative of the other side was James Fergusson, who argued that the Bodh Gayā arches belonged to a later structural phase and that the absence of the arch was one of the chief defects of Hindu architecture.[54]

Mahâbodhi contains Cunningham's last statement on the contentious issue. Here,[55] he reiterates his view that the voussoir arch was known (although sparingly used) by the ancient Indians. He asserts that the arches and vaults of the Mahābodhi temple were not part of the original construction (by which he presumably meant the temple of Aśokan times) but were added later to give support to the older walls. He thought that this must have happened before the 7th century, as he re-iterates that the present temple, in spite of the repeated bricks and additions, was essentially the same structure seen and described by Xuanzang in 637 AD.[56]

The Archaeologists versus Architecturalists

This takes us to the concluding part of my chapter—the bitter dispute between the archaeologists and architectural scholars over the place of architectural study in the Archaeological Survey. This dispute involved issues of academic and methodological concern as well as personal ambitions and rivalries. It was connected with different visions of the path that the Archaeological Survey should take and with the larger political framework of colonial India.

Apart from Cunningham, many other scholars of the time wrote on ancient Indian art and architecture. The reputation of James Fergusson and James Burgess, in fact, far exceeded Cunningham's in this sphere.[57] Cunningham's approach to art and architecture was different from that of the Fergusson–Burgess duo; it was more contextual and historical. Like Cunningham, Burgess and Fergusson also sought to influence public policy. Their vision of the Archaeological Survey saw it as an agency that should concentrate not on field archaeology but on producing high-quality architectural studies. This is, in fact, what the archaeological surveys of western India (established in 1873) and southern India (established in 1881) under Burgess did.[58]

My own entry-point into the debate/dispute between the archaeologists and architecturalists was a copy of James Fergusson's *Archaeology in India with Especial Reference to the Works of Babu Rajendralala Mitra* (1884). This book is a crude, virulent, racist attack against Rajendralala Mitra, written against the background of the sensation created by the Ilbert Bill, which sought to allow native Indian judges to try Europeans at the local level. It is a very angry book; it was anger that led Fergusson to reveal his racist ideas with amazing candour. He states right at the outset that he had written this book to discredit Rajendralala Mitra's scholarly work and to use him as an example to demonstrate the absurdity of the Ilbert Bill.[59] This book provides clear and direct evidence of the political ramifications of architectural debates in 19th century India.

Among the central points of disagreement between Mitra and Fergusson was their assessment of the degree of foreign influence on Indian art and architecture and the question of whether style or inscriptional evidence formed the more reliable gauge of the age of historical monuments. Fergusson had always favoured the former, Mitra (like Cunningham) the latter. Apart from Mitra, the book also had diatribes against Cunningham, his assistants Beglar and Carlleyle, and F. S. Growse.[60] He took Cunningham and Beglar to task for the shoddy restoration work at Bodh Gayā and Growse for the work done in Brindaban.

But the copy in the Central Archaeological Library which fell into my hands happened to be the personal copy of J. D. M. Beglar, an Armenian engineer with the Bengal Public Works Department, who went on to become one of Cunningham's assistants (Figure 5.9).[61] As I said earlier, Fergusson's is an angry book. Beglar's copy of Fergusson's book is heavily annotated with even angrier, in fact, enraged comments scrawled over several pages in pencil, many of them concentrated in the chapter on Bodh Gayā. They give Beglar's take on the book. He writes that Fergusson had tried to discredit the Archaeological Survey of India to make Burgess and his surveys appear in a flattering light. He writes that the aim of the book—to attack Mitra, Cunningham, his assistants, and Growse—was quite clear to those who knew the close relationship between Fergusson and Burgess and the latter's disappointment at not having been appointed director general of the Archaeological Survey in 1871.

Is this just 19th century office gossip, not worthy of being discussed in scholarly analysis? No, because the bitter conflict between the Cunningham team and the Fergusson–Burgess team is borne out by the contents of the book as well as by archival sources. Till now, I had not thought about Beglar's motives in pencilling in those comments. Some of them are the kinds of things a person writes in their books for their own benefit. But it now seems to me that many of the comments were written by a very angry Beglar for the benefit of future readership. We do not know the details of when or how this book found its way into the Archaeological Survey library, but it adds a raw and personal dimension to the history of Indian archaeology and to the story of the conflict between archaeologists and architecturalists in 19th century India.

Figure 5.9
Page from Beglar's copy of Fergusson's Archaeology in India

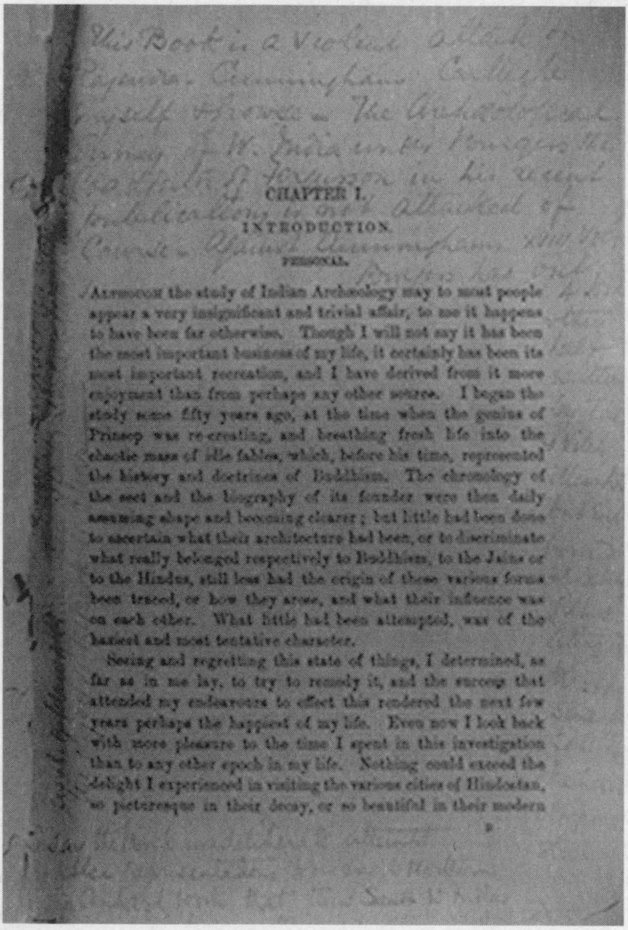

CHAPTER I.

INTRODUCTION.

PERSONAL.

ALTHOUGH the study of Indian Archaeology may to most people appear a very insignificant and trivial affair, to me it happens to have been far otherwise. Though I will not say it has been the most important business of my life, it certainly has been its most important recreation, and I have derived from it more enjoyment than from perhaps any other source. I began the study some fifty years ago, at the time when the genius of Prinsep was re-creating, and breathing fresh life into the chaotic mass of idle fables, which, before his time, represented the history and doctrines of Buddhism. The chronology of the sect and the biography of its founder were then daily assuming shape and becoming clearer; but little had been done to ascertain what their architecture had been, or to discriminate what really belonged respectively to Buddhism, to the Jains or to the Hindus, still less had the origin of these various forms been traced, or how they arose, and what their influence was on each other. What little had been attempted, was of the haziest and most tentative character.

Seeing and regretting this state of things, I determined, as far as in me lay, to try to remedy it, and the success that attended my endeavours to effect this rendered the next few years perhaps the happiest of my life. Even now I look back with more pleasure to the time I spent in this investigation than to any other epoch in my life. Nothing could exceed the delight I experienced in visiting the various cities of Hindostan, so picturesque in their decay, or so beautiful in their modern

B

Courtesy: Aditya Arya

Notes

1. For a detailed analysis of this important phase in the history of Indian archaeology and the ideas and work of Alexander Cunningham, see Upinder Singh, *The Discovery of Ancient India: Early Archaeologists and the Beginnings of Archaeology* (New Delhi: Permanent Black, 2004).
2. This is a fact that should not be forgotten in criticisms of his 'text-aided archaeology'. Critiques of Cunningham's work and method point out many

flaws, mostly with the benefit of hindsight. I think it is more meaningful to judge a scholar by the standards of his own time, taking into account the constraints and limitations of his context and situation.

3. Cunningham, *Report for the Year 1871–72,* Archaeological Survey of India Reports, Kolkata (1873), Introduction, pp. iv–xi.
4. Cunningham, *Report for the Year 1871–72,* p. 2.
5. The Hindu period (1000 BC–1200 AD) was further subdivided into the following sub-phases: Archaic (1000–250 BC), Indo-Grecian (250–257 BC), Indo-Scythian (AD 319–700), Medieval Brahmanic (AD 700–1200). The last of these was followed by the 'Modern Brahmanic' phase (1200–1750) (Alexander Cunningham, *Report for the Year 1871–72,* p. 2).
6. Alexander Cunningham, 'An Essay on the Arian Order of Architecture, as Exhibited in the Temples of Kashmir', *Journal of the Asiatic Society of Bengal* 17 (1848): 241–327.
7. Remusat, Klaproth and Landress's *Foe Koue Ki ou Relation des Royaumes Bouddhiques* was published in 1836. Stanislas Julien's account of the life and travels of Xuanzang was published in 1853 and his complete French translation of the travelogue was published in two volumes in 1857–1858.
8. Mapping was also an important aspect of the knowledge collection project of the colonial state.
9. Alexander Cunningham, *The Bhilsa Topes*, or *Buddhist Monuments of Central India: Comprising a Brief Historical Sketch of the Rise, Progress and Decline of Buddhism—With an Account of the Opening and Examination of the Various Groups of Topes around Bhilsa* (London: Smith, Elder, 1854); 1997, Reprint edition, New Delhi, pp. 51, 53.
10. Turnour, Hodgson, Hardy, Lassen, Burnouf, de Koros, Prinsep and Wilson were among those whose work Cunningham drew on. The publication of Pali texts received a fresh impetus some years later with the founding of the Pali Text Society by T. W. Rhys Davids in 1881.
11. Some of the drawings were made by Major H. M. Durand of the Royal Engineers and the rest, we can assume, were made by Cunningham himself.
12. The boldness of line and the accuracy of the delineation of the feet of the lions of the capital (four large front claws and one small hind claw) convinced Cunningham that the lions had been sculpted by a Greek artist.
13. Later research assigned this pillar to the Gupta period and identified the figure surmounting the pillar as the *bodhisattva* Vajrapāṇi.
14. Cunningham, *The Bhilsa Topes,* pp. viii–ix.
15. Cunningham, *The Bhilsa Topes,* p. 201 ff.
16. Cunningham, *The Bhilsa Topes,* p. 204; Pl. 11.
17. Cunningham suggested that the passenger on the boat was the Buddha. It did not occur to him that this was not possible, as he himself had pointed out that the Sanchi reliefs never depict the Buddha in human form. Foucher suggests that the panel in question perhaps represents the miracles that brought about the conversion of the Kāśyapa brothers. John Marshall and Alfred Foucher, *The Monuments of Sanchi*, Vol. 2, (1940); 1982 Reprint edition, New Delhi: Swati Publications, p. 51.

18. Cunningham, *The Bhilsa Topes*, pp. 207–210.
19. Foucher (Marshall and Foucher 1940 vol. 2, Pl. 52) suggests that this might be an allusion to the miracle of the Buddha creating fire to allow the Brāhmaṇas to warm themselves after bathing.
20. For a detailed account of this, see C. Almond Philip, *The British Discovery of Buddhism* (Cambridge: Cambridge University Press, 1988).
21. Cunningham, *The Bhilsa Topes*, pp. 209–210.
22. Five *Jātaka* stories are depicted at Sanchi (Marshall and Foucher, 1940, vol. 1, pp. 224–225)—the Chaddanta, Mahākapi, Ṛṣyaśṛṅga, Śyāma and Vessantara *Jātaka*s.
23. Cunningham, *The Bhilsa Topes*, pp.189–190; Pl. 14.
24. This particular bracket figure is not listed in the Marshall volumes and must have disappeared or got detached.
25. Cunningham, *The Bhilsa Topes*, p. 191.
26. Cunningham, *The Bhilsa Topes*, p. ix.
27. Cunningham, *The Bhilsa Topes*, pp. 205–207; Foucher interprets it as a lively tableau of Uruvilvā village (see text of Marshall and Foucher, 1940, vol. 2, Pl. 52a1).
28. Cunningham, *The Bhilsa Topes*, p. 216.
29. Cunningham, *The Bhilsa Topes*, p. 201.
30. The first photographs in the Archaeological Survey Reports appear in the Reports for 1873–1874 and 1874–1875, which were published in 1879 and 1880 respectively.
31. *The Stûpa of Bharhut* cites authorities such as Spence Hardy, Burnouf, Julien, Beal, Upham, Bigandet, Foucaux, Fausboll, and de Koros.
32. The early works on the *Jātaka*s were those by V. Fausboll (1877–1897), T. W. Rhys Davids (1880) and E. B. Cowell (1895–1913).
33. Alexander Cunningham, *The Stûpa of Bharhut* (London: W.H. Allen, 1879), p. vi.
34. Cunningham, *The Stûpa of Bharhut*, pp. 48–82. He identified 22 *Jātakas*—the Baka, Miga, Nāga, Yava-Majhakīya, Laṭuva, Chhadantīya, Isi-Siṅgīya, Yambumane Avayesi, Kuruṅga Miga, Haṁsa, Kinnara, Asadrisa, Daśaratha, Isi-Migo, Uda, Seccha, Sujāto Gahuto, Biḍāla or Kukkuṭa, Magha Deva, Bhisa Haranīya, Vitura Punakaya, and one unnamed one. Apart from Subhuti, Cunningham also cited Fausboll, Burnouf, Spence Hardy and Beal as sources of information on the stories.
35. Cunningham, *The Stûpa of Bharhut*, p. 83.
36. Cunningham noted that the former was depicted on an elephant, the latter in a chariot, exactly in the way in which the Buddhist chronicles described.
37. Cunningham, *The Stûpa of Bharhut*, p. 106.
38. Cunningham, *The Stûpa of Bharhut*, pp. 111–112.
39. Cunningham, *The Stûpa of Bharhut*, pp. 19–29.
40. In his discussion of the *yakṣa*s, Cunningham cites the writings of Hardy, Burnouf and Foucaux's translation of the *Lalitavistara*.
41. Cunningham, *The Stûpa of Bharhut*, pp. 104–106.
42. Cunningham, *The Stûpa of Bharhut*, p. 34.
43. Cunningham, *The Stûpa of Bharhut*, pp. 39–40.

44. Cunningham, *The Stûpa of Bharhut*, pp. 124–126.
45. Cunningham, *The Stûpa of Bharhut*, p. 18.
46. Later research has indicated that the construction of the Bharhut *stupa* extended over several stages covering more than a century, from the 3rd century BC to the 1st century BC, and that the inscriptions were inscribed between c. 125–175 BC.
47. The late publication of this book was partly because of the fact that the photographic negatives got lost along with Cunningham's papers and antiquities, when the *Indus* sank off the coast of Sri Lanka. The collotypes for the Bodh Gayā volume had to be prepared from the photographic prints, which were luckily preserved.
48. Alexander Cunningham, *Mahâbodhi or the Great Buddhist Temple under the Bodhi Tree at Buddha-Gaya* (London: Allen, 1892); 1998 Reprint edition, Delhi, p. 18.
49. Cunningham, *Mahâbodhi*, p. iv.
50. According to the *Lalitavistara*, the site on which the temple stood was pointed out by Upagupta to Aśoka, who gave 100,000 pieces of gold for the building, near the small village of Uruvilā/Uruvilvā.
51. Alexander Cunningham, 1873. *Report for the year 1871–72,* p. 100.
52. The 'proof' that he cited for this came from Rajgir. Cunningham's argument for the pre-Mauryan antiquity of stone architecture was based on evidence from the Vaibhara cave (mentioned in Buddhist texts) and the stone structure known as Jarasandha-ki-baithak (which seems to have been a watch tower). The Vaibhara cave was a rough excavation, the lower portion of which was later lined with brick. According to Cunningham, this cave was undoubtedly the quarry from which the stones for Jarasandha-ki-baithak came. Therefore, he argued, the Baithak must be as old as the cave, that is, it must go back to the time of the Buddha or even earlier. Actually, it is very difficult to ascertain the precise age of Jarasandha-ki-Baithak in particular and other early remains (including caves and structures) at Rajgir. Archaeological investigations at this important site have been fairly limited, although they do indicate a Northern Black Polished Ware level and hint at an earlier occupation as well. The Rajgir fortifications went through several stages of construction in mud, brick and stone, and it is difficult to date them precisely. But it is indeed likely that the stone fortifications go back to a pre-Mauryan age, because Rajgir started losing its political importance after the transfer of the Magadhan capital to Pāṭaliputra in the middle of the 5th century BC during the reign of Udayin. If this is so, then Cunningham's arguments are plausible, though not conclusive. Many years later, James Fergusson, in his *Archaeology in India with Especial Reference to the Works of Babu Rajendralala Mitra* (London: Trübner, 1884; 1974 Reprint edition, New Delhi), pp. 12–13, ridiculed Cunningham's claim about the pre-Mauryan origins of Indian monumental stone architecture and asked whether he had ever substantiated his claim with any evidence. Whether the claim stands or not, Cunningham did, in fact, cite evidence for his hypothesis, which Fergusson seems to have been unaware of, or perhaps chose to ignore.

53. According to Rajendralala Mitra, *Buddha Gaya, the Hermitage of Śákya Muni* (Kolkata: Bengal Secretariat Press, 1878), p. 110, the arches and the temple were of roughly the same period; the arches had been inserted some time after the completion of the temple. It was difficult to say when exactly this was done, but the arches were definitely in place long before Xuanzang visited Bodh Gayā in the 7th century.
54. Rajendralala Mitra gave the temple a very early date (about 200 BC) while James Fergusson placed it as late as the 14th century AD. Cunningham's view differed from both. He identified many layers in the construction of the temple, starting from the Mauryan period and extending into the medieval. But like Mitra, he thought that the temple that stood at Bodh Gaya was essentially the same one that Xuanzang saw in the 7th century, and that it had been subsequently repaired but not rebuilt, as Fergusson imagined.
55. Cunningham, *Mahâbodhi*, pp. 85–86.
56. Cunningham, *Mahâbodhi*, p. 18.
57. Burgess was a trained architect who went on to become Principal of the J. J. School of Art in Mumbai. Fergusson was an indigo merchant who had turned to the study of architecture with a vengeance, producing fine, detailed architectural works.
58. Their publications included monographs on the monuments of the Belgaum and Kaladgi districts, Kathiawad and Kutch, the Bidar and Aurangabad districts of the Nizam's dominions, and the Buddhist cave temples in the Deccan.
59. Fergusson (*Archaeology in India*, p. iv) also claimed that he was the victim of a long-term conspiracy. According to him, Mitra's *The Antiquities of Orissa* and *Buddha Gaya* had become 'practically gigantic pamphlets written for the purpose of exposing my iniquities and ignorance', promoted by the Government of Bengal. He tried to point out how Mitra had committed innumerable blunders in his descriptions of the Katak caves, the temples of Bhubaneswar, and Bodh Gayā.
60. Growse served as Collector of Farukhabad and was the author of *Mathura: A District Memoir* (1883).
61. Beglar was assistant in the Archaeological Survey between 1871–1879. Subsequently, the Bengal Government appointed him to supervise the repairs to the Bodh Gayā temple (1880–1884), and he occupied the post of archaeological surveyor in the Bengal province between 1885 and 1890.

6

Amaravati: The Dismembering of the *Mahācaitya* (1797–1886)

Amaravati (in modern Guntur district, Andhra Pradesh) on the banks of the Krishna River was a major Buddhist centre of ancient India. The history of this *stūpa*-monastery complex spans some 17 centuries, from its inception in the 3rd century BC to its demise in the 14th century AD. Once abandoned, nature took its course, and the *stūpa* gradually came to be enveloped in layers of dust and debris which eventually obscured it completely from sight. Then, towards the end of the 18th century, Amaravati was discovered by a local *zamindar*. This discovery was followed by the first documentation of the site by Colonel Colin Mackenzie.

Ironically, the documentation, exploration, and excavation of the *Mahācaitya* of Amaravati was accompanied by its steady disappearance. Equally ironical was the fact that this steady disappearance of the *stūpa* was accompanied by attempts by scholars to reconstruct its lost design. As its stones were carried off to form part of newer buildings or melted down for lime by local inhabitants, dug up by amateur and not-so-amateur archaeologists, and sent off to museums in Madras and London, very little indication of the grandeur of this Buddhist establishment eventually remained at Amaravati itself.

This chapter was previously published in *South Asian Studies* 17 (1), 2001, pp. 19–40.

The Discovery of Amaravati and the First Documentation

Colonel Colin Mackenzie of the Mysore Survey had heard in the course of his travels of some interesting finds unearthed in the town of Amareswaram in the Krishna valley. In February 1797, he had the opportunity to investigate them. Having set up camp at Ibrampattan, Mackenzie despatched his interpreter Cavelli Venkata Boria along with some Brahmins and two *sipahi*s to Amareswaram 'with directions to make some previous inquiries into the history of the place: and to conciliate the inhabitants; particularly the *Bráhmen*s, who are apt to be alarmed on these occasions'.[1] Mackenzie himself left Ibrampattan the next morning by moonlight and reached Amareswaram at daybreak. The temples in the town were new. They had been recently built by the Chintapalli Raja, who had moved his residence here when Lachmipuram, his previous headquarters, had been occupied by English troops.

Mackenzie was the first to document the remains at Amaravati. His account[2] indicates the condition of the site at the end of the 18th century. Mackenzie described a circular trench, about 10 ft. wide and 12 ft. deep. dug into a mass of masonry composed of bricks 16 inches square and 4 inches thick. The central part of the mound was still untouched. In the trench lay a broken white stone slab with some carving on it, of which Mackenzie directed his draftsman Sydenham to make a sketch. Leaning against the outside of the trench stood three or four more slabs, carved on one side and plain on the other. Mackenzie conjectured that the whole mound may once have been faced with such carved stone slabs. He identified the stone as a white marble, locally known as 'pal-rayi' or milk-stone. Mackenzie described eight sculptured slabs which he saw in or around the site. Two were inscribed, but Mackenzie could not read the Brahmi letters,

Mackenzie was intrigued. He learnt that this place was called 'Dipaldina' ('the hill of lamps'). About a year ago, in the course of removing a large stone from the place to a temple being built by the Raja, workmen had hit on the brickwork. This had induced them to dig the trench in search of more building material. Their shovels had turned up several white stones, many of which broke in the process of exhumation. Local tradition connected the sculptures with the Jaina religion, but Mackenzie could find no conclusive proof of this. On the basis of the few specimens he had examined, he could offer no conclusions about the purport or meaning of the sculpted stones.

The Colonel Returns

Mackenzie's 1797 visit to Amaravati had been very brief, as was his account of what he saw there. In March 1816, he came back to Amaravati.[3] As the recently appointed Surveyor General of India, he now had greater resources at his command. He remained at Amaravati till August, and left his draftsmen working there till the end of 1817.[4] Mackenzie left no detailed written account of his operations at Amaravati. He was, however, able to substantially add to his preliminary observations in a paper entitled 'Ruins of Amravutty, Depauldina and Durnacotta,' published posthumously in 1823 in the *Asiatic Journal and Monthly Register.* We can get some sort of idea of Mackenzie's operations at Amaravati from this account and from a comparison of two site plans that are included in the Mackenzie manuscript collection (see Figures 6.1 and 6.2).[5]

By this time, Mackenzie was able to form a clearer idea of the broader context of the remains at Dipal-dina. He realized that the ancient remains found at the contiguous sites of Amaravati, Dipal-dina, and Dharanikota were of great historical importance. As for the precise nature of this historical significance, he cited a local tradition, according to which the ancient name of Dipal-dina was Doop Mogasallah. 'Mogasallah' was a Telugu word for a court for public affairs and the distribution of justice. Local tradition held this to be the place where an ancient king named 'Mookunty-maharaze' had held his *durbar.*

Mackenzie gave an account of the founding of the town of 'Amravutty', an event directly connected both with the discovery and the beginnings of the destruction of its ancient remains. The place was famous for its Śaiva temple of Amareśvara. Towards the close of the 18th century, Raja Vassareddy Venkatadry Naid, Zamindar of Chintapalli, visited the shrine and decided to move his residence to this place. The Raja invited brahmins, *bania*s, and others to come and settle in the new town, offering them financial assistance for building their homes. In the course of executing this plan, he hit on the idea of digging in the mounds around the place for bricks which could be used for his own residence. Many large bricks were found and used. While all this was going on, the Raja learnt that certain Muslims who were setting up house at the south end of the town had dug into the mound of Dipal-dina and had found large bricks and carved stones. Thinking these to be clues to a hidden treasure, the Raja ordered his Muslim subjects to move elsewhere, and embarked on a treasure hunt. The digging along the eastern skirt of the mound revealed a small shrine in which was found an image which the Raja whisked off to

Figure 6.1
Mackenzie's 'Sketch of Deepauldinna at Amrawutty', 1816

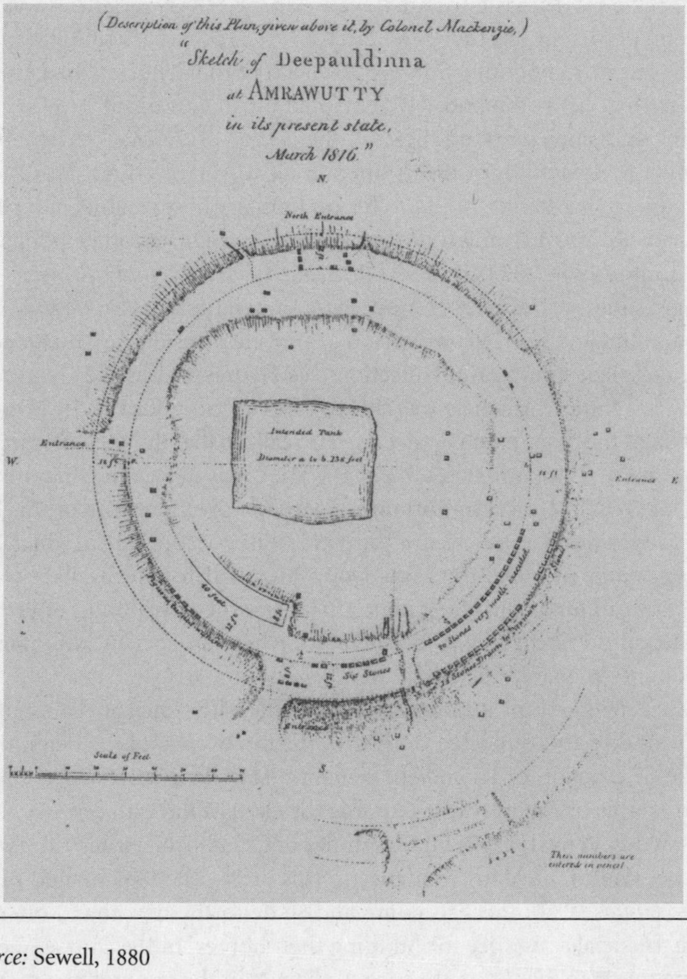

Source: Sewell, 1880

the Amareśvara temple. To the west of the shrine were two pillars, which seemed to be part of the entrance to a small shrine. The western side revealed a small structure with a large 'votive' lamp, evidently made of copper (this was later melted down). On the north side of the mound was a four-pillared brick structure containing a cross-legged headless image.[6]

The Raja decided to build a large reservoir in the middle of Dipaldina. This event seems to have been separated from the founding of the town and the initial digging activities on the mound by several years.

Figure 6.2
Mackenzie's 'Plan and Section of the Tope at Amravati', 1817

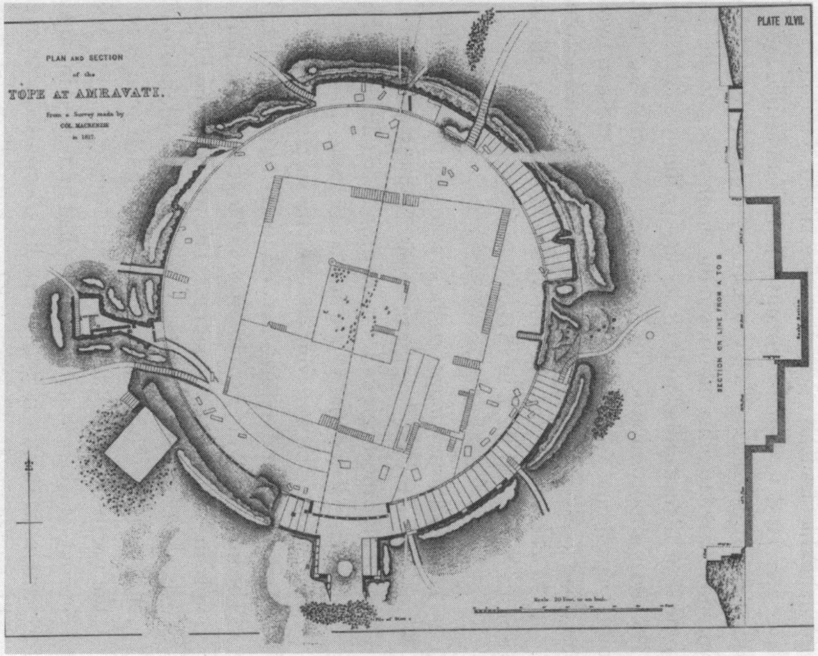

Source: Fergusson, 1868

This is suggested both by the fact that the gaping hole that marked the site of the proposed tank was not there when Mackenzie first visited the site (at that time the mound was relatively undisturbed) and also the detail that he gives us that the construction of the reservoir was brought to a halt in march 1816 due to the inroads of the Pindaris and the subsequent death of the Raja in August of the same year.

Mackenzie gave a detailed description of the modern town of Amaravati, describing the major buildings (including the Amareśvara temple), the chief festivals celebrated there, and local traditions associated with the area. He described the remains of an ancient fortified settlement at Dharanikota, situated some 500 yards from the western end of Amaravati town, and referred to other mounds in the vicinity. He also drew attention to some 17 or 18 megalithic stone circles about a mile west of Dharanikota.

The most important aspect of Mackenzie's account was the description of 'Depauldina' as he saw it in 1816 and 1817, close to two decades after he had first visited the place. Juxtaposing the written account of the site with Mackenzie's Plans, the following points can be made about the state of the Amaravati *stūpa* in 1816–1817:

1. The most drastic change was the large trough opened in the centre of the mound for building the reservoir. This was about 108 ft. square, and for the most part 24 1/4 ft. deep, a few feet deeper in the middle. Mackenzie stated that a large number of stone slabs, many of them broken, could be seen lying about on the surface of the reservoir.
2. Mackenzie identified an inner and outer ring of stones, 13 ft. apart. The inner and outer circuit of stones together were fully exposed only in the southeast quadrant. The whole of the inner ring lay exposed in the other quadrants as well. Some of the stones of this ring in the south-west quadrant and a much smaller number in the north-east quadrant, were still in place; the rest had disappeared. Mackenzie states that they had been used in repairing the temples of the town, and several had been used to make a flight of steps to the Shivaganga tank (another tank in the town). Large sections of the outer ring seem to have been still largely covered with debris. Mackenzie describes some sections of the outer ring that seem to have been *in situ.* (He refers to stones joining each other through projecting rims fitting into grooves.)
3. Mackenzie described the inner ring of slabs (which actually lined the *stūpa*) as 'cemented to each other with strong mortar, and

supported by a wall of masonry rising to a moderate height in the rear…'[7]

4. The stone pavement between the *stūpa* and the railing could be identified. It had been exposed mainly in the north-eastern and south-eastern quadrant.
5. Mackenzie stated quite clearly: 'A great part of the mound remains uncleared; of the exterior row only the south-east quarter, and the entrance in that direction have been opened….'[8]

Mackenzie commented on the very fine and unusual nature of the carving on the stones. He observed that all the stones seemed to have originally been painted red and varnished; over time the colour had faded to a copperish red. He also referred to the discovery of coins and inscriptions at Dipal-dina. But as far as the purport of the main structure on the mound was concerned, he was still mystified.

> In the state that the mound is in at present, it is impossible to form any conjecture whether there was any, and what sort of building formerly standing in the centre, or for what purpose it was intended. But if any opinion may be formed barely from the sculptures that are represented, it would appear to have been *a* place consecrated to religious worship, but by a different sect from the Hindoos of the present day, as there are none of the mythological sculptures to be seen among the numerous sculptures to warrant a supposition in favour of the Brahminical devotion.[9]

The Mackenzie Collection in the British Library includes a bound volume containing 82 drawings—86 sheets in all, including duplicates and loose sheets (*OIOC*, WD 1061). The title inscribed on the volume is: *India Antiqua Illustrata or An Essay to Illustrate the Ancient History, Inscriptions, and Religion of India—by Drawings of Remarkable Sculptures, Inscriptions, Buildings, Coins and Other Existing Remains of Antiquity.* Its contents comprise a map of the site, two plans of the mound (one with a section drawing), a sketch of the stone circles in the neighbourhood, and a large number of beautiful drawings of sculptures and inscriptions. These drawings were made by the artists and draftsmen who were part of Mackenzie's team: T. Anderson, C. Barnett, M. Burke, J. Gould, H. Hamilton, J. Mustie, J. Newman, W. Sydenham, Najibullah, Pyari Lal, and Sheikh Abdullah. The drawings are inscribed with dates, and occasionally with comments, but the position or location of the sculptures they depict are not clear.

The Amaravati drawings, like the rest of the enormous amount of material Mackenzie collected in the course of his extensive travels, were never published by him. Some of his Amaravati plans and drawings later found their way into James Fergusson's *Tree and Serpent Worship*, Robert *Sewell's Report on the Amaravati Tope*, and James Burgess' *The Buddhist Stūpas of Amaravati and Jaggayyapeta.* In 1881, W.A. Franks privately published a *List of Drawings from the Amaravati Tope, Southern India, Made for Colonel* C. *Mackenzie.* Fergusson[10] refers to three copies of the Mackenzie drawings. He states that one was sent to the Asiatic Society in Calcutta, the second deposited in Madras, and the third sent to the Court of Directors. On the other hand, Barrett[11] asserts that there was only one copy, the one preserved in the Library of the Asiatic Society of Bengal. This was borrowed by Walter Elliot in 1846 and submitted to the Governor of Madras in 1854, and was not heard of since.

Mackenzie removed a number of sculpted stones from Amaravati. A fragmentary note written by him, dated 7 April 1817, and pasted onto the volume of drawing, states that 11 stones of Dipal-dina, including an inscription (i.e., an inscribed stone) were given over to the charge of Major Cotgrave at Masulipatam.[12] These eventually found their way to Calcutta. Two were presented by Mackenzie to the Asiatic Society of Bengal, from where they were sent to the Indian Museum in Calcutta. The other nine pieces were sent to the East India Company's Museum on Leadenhall Street, London, probably sometime after Mackenzie's death in 1821.[13]

James Burgess[14] refers to the removal of a larger number of stones. He writes that seven sculptured slabs were sent by Mackenzie to the Museum of the Asiatic Society of Bengal, 4 (including an inscribed one) were transmitted to the India Office via Madras, and at least 16 others reached London. According to Burgess, it is probable that most of the stones cleared by Mackenzie's assistants in order to make drawings were left exposed at Amaravati itself, where they must have been taken off or burnt into lime by local inhabitants. When he visited the site in 1881, he was able to identify only one.

The stones sent by Mackenzie to Masulipatam remained there for many decades. In 1830, one Mr. Robertson, Collector of Masulipatam, brought down some more sculpted slabs from the site. He went on to arrange 33 slabs in the square of a new market-place named after himself. The details of which part of the Amaravati *stūpa* complex these were removed from are not known. In 1835, the spectacular stones in the market place caught the attention of Sir Frederick Adam, Governor of Madras, who ordered them sent to Madras to be placed in the Museum of the Literary Society. This removal eventually took place 20 years after the order was given. During this period, some of the most beautiful pieces ended up adorning the garden of a Mr. Alexander, Master Attendant. The Government succeeded in retrieving these only in 1880, when they were sent by Burgess to Madras.[15]

The 'Elliot Marbles'

Many years elapsed between Mackenzie's second visit to Amaravati and the next series of investigations at the site. In 1845, Walter Elliot, Commissioner of Guntur, visited Amaravati and indulged in some haphazard excavation. Elliot found the mound in much the same condition as Mackenzie had left it in 1816. The impression conveyed by Elliot is that the site had not been significantly disturbed over the last few decades. He states that he saw very few of the marbles recycled in more recent buildings in Amaravati.

Elliot's operations at Amaravati began with his discovery of the western gateway. The sculpted stones he found included two lions that had flanked the entrance, the shaft of a monolithic column and a miniature *stūpa* that had probably surmounted it, portions of other pillars that had formed the entrance, and five slabs on the dome of the *stūpa* opposite the entrance.[16]

Two sketches of sections of the western gateway pencilled by Sir Walter Elliot[17] corroborate the fact that a large proportion of the stones that were uncovered under his supervision in this sector were *in situ*:

> It is probable that the other 3 entrances will be found in a more or less perfect state, and that much of the outer wall or 'rail' will also be discovered to be erect and *in situ*, especially on the west half of the circle; whilst the sculptures of the 'inner rail', or what I should term the base of the dehgope proper, are probably buried deeply under the jahis of the excavated tank. Most of the upright slabs laid open by me had never been disturbed, but, as I explained to Mr Fergusson, a few only had been rearranged to form a small chamber or shrine in the gateway…[18]

From the sculptures he unearthed, Elliot was able to form 'a tolerable idea of the plan and purpose of the edifice'. He surmised that the *stūpa* of Amaravati must have corresponded to the type of *stūpa* repeatedly depicted on the sculpted slabs. Elliot communicated his notes and sketches to James Fergusson. Fergusson thought that the Amaravati *stūpa* must have been fairly small, one of several structures on the Dipal-dina mound. Elliot, on the other hand, was of the opinion that the structure which occupied the site of the mound was huge, probably one of the most magnificent 'dehgopes' (i.e., *stūpa*s) ever built.

Walter Elliot's excavations at Amaravati added next to nothing to the documentation of the site. What it *did* lead to was the largest haul of sculptures from the place. Elliot sent a large number of pieces to Madras, where they lay for many years in the open in front of the College.[19] In 1853, after the Court of Directors made inquiries about them, they were placed at the front entrance of the Central Museum 'more or less exposed to the forenoon sun, but otherwise sheltered'.[20]

In 1856, Edward Balfour, who had recently taken over charge of the Madras Museum, asked Rev. William Taylor to compile and publish a description of the 'Elliot Marbles'. Taylor did the job but his account of the sculptures and the inscriptions was of little value '...for having no idea of what was put into his hands, and discarding the Pali alphabet, which had been recovered by scholars of note, he evolved one of his own, and gave transcriptions that are simply nonsensical, while his account of the sculptures is utterly useless except as a list of the stones and their dimensions'.[21]

Taylor listed 79 pieces of sculpture, of which two were already missing. He added to these 37 pieces which had arrived from Masulipatam in April/May 1856. Seven additional pieces had also surfaced by the time the collection was photographed in Madras by Captain Tripe in 1858 or 1859. Elliot managed to procure 44 more pieces; these included those wrested with some difficulty from Mr. Alexander. By 1859, 121 pieces of the 'Elliot Marbles', as the lot had come to be known, were sent to London.[22] According to Boswell, other pieces were sent to the Central Museum, Madras, some to the Bezwada Museum, and a few remained in the possession of Captain Maiden, Master Attendant in Masulipatam.

The 121 'Elliot Marbles' arrived in London in 1860 and remained at Beale's Wharf in Southwark for a year. This was the period when, in the aftermath of the 1857 Revolt, the rule of the East India Company had made way for that of the British Crown. There was no place for the sculptures to go. In 1861, they were finally moved to the stables of Fife House where the India Museum had been housed. A few of the best pieces were placed along the outer wall of Fife House, while the rest continued to languish in the stables. Here, they lay till, in January 1867, James Fergusson found them.[23]

James Fergusson and the Amaravati Marbles

In the fall of 1866, Henry Cole, one of the leading figures in the movement for the reform of western industrial design, suggested to the architectural scholar James Fergusson that he put together a display on

Indian art and architecture for the Paris Exhibition, scheduled to be held in 1867.[24] Fergusson agreed, and decided to prepare a collection of photographs for the event. He thought that the effect of his display would be enhanced if supplemented with some plaster casts of Indian sculpture or architectural fragments. Fergusson's search for models for casting led him to the India Museum at Fife House, where he decided on four sculptures from Amaravati. Here, he received the startling information that a large collection of sculpted stones from the same site were stored in the coach-house of Fife House. Fergusson investigated and found the stones.

This discovery made Fergusson alter his plans. He decided to abandon the idea of making casts and instead to send four or five actual specimens of the Amaravati sculptures to the Paris Exhibition. More important, he decided to bring out and photograph all the pieces of sculpture to the same scale, in order to effect a photographic restoration of the monument. Dr. Forbes Watson, Director of the India Museum, supported the plan, and provided the services of Griggs, the Museum photographer. The Amaravati marbles were brought out in the open and photographed on a scale of 1/10th their actual size. Using as his guide the frequent depiction of the *stūpa* in the sculptures themselves, Fergusson put together his photographs like the pieces in a jigsaw puzzle, and at the end of the exercise, he was confident that he knew the position of at least 9/10th of the 160 fragments in the India Museum collection.[25]

The Amaravati photographs were exhibited in Paris. Subsequently, in June 1867, Fergusson exhibited them and read a paper on the subject (later published) to the Royal Asiatic Society.[26] Fergusson went on to apply to Sir Stafford Northcote, Secretary of State for India, for financial assistance to enable him to publish the most important photographs with an explanatory text. Having obtained this, he got to work on the project. It is around this time that Fergusson stumbled on the beautiful sketches of Sanchi by Lieutenant-Colonel Maisey and received a set of photographs of the site from Lieutenant Waterhouse. Fergusson decided to enlarge the scope of his work to include Sanchi as well as Amaravati. The result was *Tree and Serpent Worship*, published in 1873.

Tree and Serpent Worship is an important book. It was the first detailed photographic and textual account of the Amaravati *stūpa*. Sanchi had already been dealt with by Alexander Cunningham in his *Bhilsa Topes* (1854). However, Fergusson's work included reproductions of Maisey's drawings and Waterhouse's photographs of Sanchi as also some of Mackenzie's material on Amaravati, making these available for the first time to a wider audience. The series of maps, drawings and photographs were accompanied by an explanatory text. Fergusson placed the Amaravati remains a few centuries later than the Sanchi *stūpa.* According to him, the history of the Amaravati *stūpa* stretched from c. 200 AD to c. 500 AD. He assigned the *stūpa* to the 3rd century and the 'outer rail' to the 4th century (on the basis of architecture and inscriptions). The 'inner rail' he held to be more modern. He did not rule out the possibility of some older structure having been situated at the site. *Tree and Serpent Worship* included an Appendix by Cunningham, giving the text and translation of 20 Amaravati inscriptions.

Fergusson thought that several structures had been situated on the Dipal-dina mound. He estimated that the *stūpa* was not more than 30 ft. to 35 ft. in diameter, and rose to a height of about 50 ft. The rest of the area, he suggested, had been occupied by other structures made of wood, including a nine-storeyed pagoda (based on accounts in Ceylonese tradition to a place called Diamond Sands, which Fergusson identified with Amaravati), a *vihāra,* a *caitya* hall, a *dharmaśālā,* and other buildings[27]).

Fergusson's interpretation of the Sanchi and Amaravati sculptures and remains is indicated in the title he chose to give to his volume. That these were Buddhist monuments was undeniable. He was able to identify several Buddhist scenes and motifs, although the *Jātaka* scenes eluded him. But what struck Fergusson as the most significant aspect of the Sanchi and Amaravati sculptures was the strong substratum of tree and serpent worship that they revealed. Most of Fergusson's long introduction to the volume is an exercise in comparative mythology, emphasizing the ubiquitous presence of tree and serpent worship in almost all parts of the world. His interpretation of the Amaravati sculptures was strongly influenced by this presupposition and preoccupation.

Another point Fergusson emphasized was the strong Bactrian influence on the Amaravati sculptures. This led to a more general pronouncement on the origins of art and architecture in India: 'We can now assert with confidence that all the permanent forms of art arose in India after its inhabitants were brought into contact with western civilization, by the establishment of the Grecian kingdom of Bactria.'[28]

Fergusson's understanding of Indian art and architecture was closely linked to his understanding of Indian history, ethnography, and religion.

He was one of many scholars of the time who were floundering about in these waters. Fergusson identified two original races of India—the Aryan and the Dravidian (whom he saw as a Turanian race, 'Turanian', after the fashion of the time, being used as a catch-all phrase for non-Aryan groups). To these, he was prepared to add a third race—the aboriginal inhabitants of north India. The Aryans, with their belief in the soul's immortality, produced literature but did not deign to build mundane edifices of brick and stone. This was left for the more down-to-earth but intellectually inferior Turanians. The intermixture of blood had important repercussions for the history of Indian architecture. 'The result of this distinction, in so far as the present subject is concerned, is this: so long as the Aryans retained their purity of blood and supremacy of power, no permanent buildings were erected in India…'[29] Fergusson also identified various racial groups depicted in the sculptures of Sanchi and Amaravati. According to him, the principal race represented in the latter were the Nagas.[30]

Given the strong racial underpinnings of Fergusson's understanding of history, it is not surprising that many years later, against the background of the Ilbert Bill controversy, he went on to write what must be one of the most blatantly racist works written by a scholar of stature. Published in 1884, *Indian Archaeology, with especial reference to the works of Babu Rajendralala Mitra* was a virulent and crude attack on the Indian scholar mentioned in its title. The broader agenda, which Fergusson frankly boasts of, was to prove and highlight the inherent inferiority of the intellectual calibre of Indians in general.

Boswell's Report

Displayed and admired in Paris, and now the subject of a book written by a well-known expert on architecture, the Amaravati sculptures continued to stay in the limelight that had found them. This was also the time around when (in 1871) the British Government of India established the Archaeological Survey of India, with Major General Alexander Cunningham as its first Director General.

Archival sources reveal that except at the very end of it all, Cunningham had little role to play in the controversy over what should be done with the Amaravati sculptures. Not only this, on the occasions when he was asked to express an opinion or give advice or direction regarding the Amaravati question, his responses were invariably delayed, and generally began with an apology and explanation of the delay. Cunningham's attitude was in sharp contrast to the note of urgency that comes out regarding the matter on the part of the Secretary of State for India, the Madras Government, or individuals such as Robert Sewell. Part of Cunningham's tardiness in response was no doubt due to the fact that his establishment was very small (he had only himself and his two assistants) and the task of archaeological exploration and documentation enormous. Given the constraints of his situation, Cunningham's own operations and interests were directed towards northern and central India.

In June 1869, the Board of Revenue of the Madras Government had requested J.A.C. Boswell, Officiating Collector of the Kistna district, to prepare a report on the ancient remains worthy of note and preservation in the district. Boswell submitted his report the next year, and large extracts of it were subsequently published in 1871 in *The Indian Antiquary*.[31] The Report detailed a series of archaeological remains, arranged by Boswell in some sort of chronological order. These naturally included the Buddhist remains in and around Amaravati.[32]

Reporting on the state of the Dipal-dina mound, Boswell wrote that there were some 10 or 12 sculpted stones lying on the surface and that a few of the best ones had been buried to protect them from injury. He urged that further research into the site of Amaravati was bound to yield important results. He mentioned another untouched mound in the vicinity of Dipal-dina. After listing a series of important remains in the Kistna district, Boswell recommended that the Government take further steps in the matter in consultation with James Fergusson.

Boswell's Report led to the first serious discussion in official circles on the systematic steps that needed to be taken to excavate and preserve the Amaravati remains. The Report was sent by the Madras Government to the Secretary of State for India in the India Office. In a Despatch dated 12 April 1871, from the India Office to the Government of Fort St. George, the Secretary of State stated that he had consulted Mr. Fergusson, Sir Walter Elliot, and Mr. Rost (the Librarian of the Royal Asiatic Society) about the Amaravati issue and that he was enclosing their responses. 'I will only add', the Secretary of State wrote, 'that I shall be ready to sanction any well-considered plan for preserving these valuable archaeological remains, and making fresh excavations, and that Major-General Cunningham, who has lately been appointed Archaeologist to the Government of India, should be consulted as to the best method of proceeding in the matter.'[33]

Rost confined himself to expressing his appreciation of Boswell's Report and emphasizing the desirability of obtaining accurate copies of the ancient inscriptions. Fergusson and Elliot had more to say on the matter. Fergusson stated that when Boswell's Report had been sent to him, it was accompanied by a personal letter from Lord Napier asking for advice on what should be done since the season was too far advanced to organize a regular expedition. Fergusson had suggested a preliminary step of sending a photographer down to Amaravati. Even a native artist would do, provided he was accompanied by a European and could draw plans or at least take measurements and note down details. Had this been done or not, Fergusson asked? As for an expert who could guide the investigations at Amaravati, Fergusson stated that there was no one in England (he was obviously excluding himself as he was not in a position to take up the job) who had the knowledge or zeal to carry out the task. In India, there was only one man he could confidently recommend as having the requisite knowledge of archaeology and love of the subject. This was James Burgess, who, Fergusson went on to say, was likely to be employed as Archaeological Surveyor to the Bombay Presidency and would hence not be available for work at Amaravati.[34]

Sir Walter Elliot strongly recommended the resumption of the excavation of the Amaravati mound under competent supervision. He went on to detail Mackenzie's and his own operations at the site. The first thing to do was to consult General Cunningham 'whose intimate acquaintance with Buddhist architecture and literature would enable him to give the most useful instructions'. The superintendence of the work should be entrusted to a skilled officer of the Department of Public Works, who should be furnished with a copy of both Colonel Mackenzie's ground plan and of the recent correspondence, and should be instructed to make a detailed study of all foundations and make careful plans, drawings, and measurements. Elliot referred to many other Buddhist remains in the Kistna district that deserved to be explored, commenting on how some of these were in danger of destruction. He gave the example of the demolition by the local Collector in about 1840 of a mound of brick-work at Gudivada, known to locals as Langa-dibba, in which had been found four stone vases, each containing a crystal reliquary. The mound had been destroyed in order to obtain materials for repairing the high road between Bezwada and Bunder.

Elliot also took the opportunity to try to clear himself from charges of negligence towards the Amaravati sculptures he had removed to Madras.

> I trust that I may be allowed to correct an erroneous but often repeated statement that the sculptures 'lay exposed to the sun and rain for fourteen years till they were sent home to England in 1856'. It was not likely that after the trouble and expense I had incurred in securing these relics, I would then have utterly neglected them. In point of fact, they were deposited in the old

> College at Madras immediately on being landed, whence they were carried to the Central Museum on its establishment, and ranged in and around the spacious wall on the left hand of the entrance.[35]

Elliot alleged that the fault lay elsewhere:

> The only neglect they experienced was after their arrival in London, where some of the slabs placed outside the Museum at Fife House were so corroded by the atmosphere as, in a great measure, to obliterate the delicate carving; the rest fortunately were covered by the hay in the stables of the Museum and so escaped a similar fate.[36]

There is a note in the margin of this document signed by Forbes Watson. It was a response to Elliot's allegation that the Amaravati sculptures had suffered damage in the India Museum and Fergusson's that many of the sculptures had been dumped in a pile of rubbish in the coach house:

> The slabs referred to were placed outside under a verandah roof, which protected them from the direct action of the weather. It is the case, however, that they did suffer from the corroding effects of the London atmosphere. The 'hay in the stable' comes under the same category as the 'rubbish' under which Mr. Fergusson found them. An old canvas tent, three or four small bales of seed-cotton, and a skeleton model of an Indian temple, were the only articles under which the marbles deposited in the coach-house at Fife House lay during the time they were in store there.[37]

The whole set of papers—Boswell's Report along with the Enclosures penned by Fergusson, Elliot, and Rost—were sent to Cunningham, the Director General of the recently constituted Archaeological Survey of India. In his response, Cunningham wrote that he thought Boswell was the best person to supervise further excavations at Dipal-dina, and that he had been in communication with him. He stated that he was aware of the fact that Boswell was seriously ill and had proceeded to England on a year's medical leave:

> ...Mr. Boswell now tells me that he does not know of any one competent to undertake charge of the excavations this season. Had he remained he would have been glad to have undertaken the work himself under my instructions; and to him I could have entrusted the operations with full confidence that they would have been carried out with vigour and intelligence.
>
> Under the circumstances, I think it most advisable to postpone any operations until Mr. Boswell's return from sick leave. I have no Assistant whom I could depute to superintend this work, and without Mr. Boswell's immediate supervision, I could not entrust the excavations to an inexperienced person.[38]

Boswell did not survive to return to India to take up further excavations at Amaravati. In the meantime, official agencies were galvanized to some extent into making inquiries about some of the points raised in the above-mentioned official exchange. Thus, the Superintending Engineer of the Second Division reported to the Secretary of the Madras Public Works Department that, contrary to the claim made by Sir Walter Elliot, the mound of Gudivada was untouched and intact. He admitted that bricks from the Bhattiprolu *stūpa* mound, on the other hand, had been used for road material for some years, but that it was not known who was responsible for initiating this activity.[39] The Board of Revenue of the Madras Government also initiated an attempt to secure for the Madras Museum the two Amaravati sculptures which reportedly lay in the compound of the house of Captain Richardson, Master Attendant at Masulipatam. The Government Order concerning the issue mentioned the fact that one of the Members of the Board of Revenue recalled there being twelve stones there when he had been Collector of the district, and that twenty-eight were listed in the account of Major Congreave. An inquiry was ordered into what had happened to all these stones.[40]

Sewell Offers His Services

The Amaravati excavations remained on hold for five years till the matter was reopened by Robert Sewell, Acting Head Assistant Collector of the Kistna district. In March 1875, Sewell formally applied to the Collector of his district for investigating the Amaravati remains:

> I know that the Government desire that the explorations should be carried out by experts, and I am quite aware of my deficiency in that respect. I do not, therefore, ask to be permitted (at any rate for the period) to interfere to any great extent with such relics as the Amravaty sculptures, but I think that the Government will see that there is a great deal that may be done by an amateur like myself in preparing the way for those more skilled.[41]

In view of the considerable attention that had by now been drawn to the neglect and damage suffered by the 'Amaravati marbles' at various hands, Sewell took great pains to emphasize that he would exercise the utmost care and caution in his conduct of the operations. He outlined what he thought he could do. Since it was doubtful whether any of the sculpted rails of Amaravati remained in their original place, he would devote himself to the clearing of the debris in the area. If, in the process, he encountered any portion of the rail still standing, he would leave it in its place and report it at once. If he found any loose stones, he would note their exact position and store them, till such time as the Government wanted to remove them to some museum:

> The great double rail, if it had been left in its original position, would have been one of the finest relics in India; but it is now so injured and demolished that there is now really no object to be gained in leaving the stones where they are.[42]

If money could be spared, any detached stones should be sent to England; if not, to the Madras Museum. In the meantime, any stones found could be sent to the museum at Bezwada, where they could be carefully stored and catalogued. If the Government thought it too 'dangerous' to entrust him with this work, Sewell said he would be content to confine himself to certain other explorations, such as the clearing and documenting of the Undavilly caves and rock-cut temple, and the Bhattiprolu *stūpa*. He requested permission to occasionally open and explore the structure and contents of megalithic burials ('kistvaens and cairns'). He also asked for permission to collect and place in the Bezwada Museum some of the more valuable pieces of sculpture that the workmen of the Public Works Department were wont to unearth during their activities:

> I can assure the Government that my operations will be conducted with the greatest care, for I am far too interested myself in the question to do any injury to any of these remains; whenever I come upon anything of value which unscientific hands ought not to meddle in I will at once cease work and report.[43]

Sewell's request for a grant of Rs. 1000 was approved by the Madras Government. At the same time, the matter was referred to the Government of India. While the Madras Government expressed its willingness to take up Sewell's offer, Sewell himself had confessed that he was no expert. It was, therefore, thought desirable to try to secure the services of Lieutenant Cole of the Royal Engineers, a man who was considered to have the expertise required for the job and who was on the verge of leaving England for India. The Madras Government was keen to have the ancient remains in the Kistna district explored in as exhaustive a fashion as possible. It also asked that the matter be referred to Major General Cunningham, for advice.[44]

Alexander Cunningham gave his opinion on the matter several months after it was referred to him, explaining that he had not responded immediately as he wanted to examine Colonel Mackenzie's manuscript volumes in the library of the Asiatic Society, particularly the map and plan of the site, before formulating a response. Unfortunately, he seems to have forgotten about the whole thing while in Calcutta. He had searched for, but could not locate the notes he had made in London after examining the Mackenzie Manuscripts in the India Office. Therefore, he was constrained to rely on his memory in making the following recommendations:

> As well as I can remember, the whole of the Stûpa itself has been removed, even including its foundations, so as to form a circular tank surrounded by a high mound. This mound I believe to have been formed due to the rubbish and earth thrown out from the excavated Stûpa, and beneath it lies the remains of the double railing which once surrounded the monument. It is therefore very much to be desired that the whole of this circular ring of the mound should be explored; and I would recommend that the work should be begun from the interior of the circle, the whole of the excavated earth and rubbish being thrown into the circular tank.
>
> In making these explorations it is especially desirable that all standing stones, or stone work *in situ*, should be left undisturbed until the exact position of each piece and a general plan of the whole have been made by some competent surveyor. As Mr. Sewell himself seems to be fully alive to the importance of leaving such stones in their original places, the work of exploration might safely be entrusted to him; and I would most strongly recommend that the sum of one thousand Rupees, which he has asked for this purpose, should be granted to him.[45]

Cunningham emphasized that Sewell's proposals for exploring the Undavilly caves, Bhattiprolu *stūpa*, and the Pidugurala mound were also worth pursuing. In the meantime, he urged that a meticulous search be made for carved stones in the town of Amaravati and its neighbourhood, that impressions be taken of all inscriptions, and that if possible, they be photographed as well. He also suggested a search for the rock referred to in Mackenzie's map of the site as the Sāsanam Rock. Cunningham concluded on a note that emphasized the importance of collecting and analyzing inscriptional rather than sculptural evidence from Amaravati, and his continuing disagreement with James Fergusson over the general issue involved:

> In conclusion, I beg to express my opinion that inscriptions should be most diligently sought for as it is to them that we must look for the *history* of the Stûpa. We already possess more than a sufficient number of sculptures to show the style of art which prevailed when the Stûpa was erected. From the sculptures Mr. Fergusson has inferred that it must have been built in the 4th

century AD. From the inscriptions, on the contrary, I infer that it was erected towards the end of the 1st century AD. As the forms of the alphabetic characters afford a much surer criterion than the style of the sculptures for determining the date of any building, I trust that the importance of securing every fragment of inscription may be kept in mind.[46]

Sewell's Operations at Amaravati

In June 1876, the Madras Government gave Robert Sewell the green signal to proceed with explorations at Amaravati. Although Sewell had made his proposal with great enthusiasm, he was so preoccupied with his routine administrative duties that he did not find the time to visit Amaravati till May 1877.[47] He had, however, begun work at the rock temple at Undavilly (Undavalli), clearing the debris to reveal a magnificent four-storeyed temple. In May 1877, he spent a week excavating at Amaravati. In a letter written some three years later, Sewell stated the site 'had not been disturbed to any purpose since Sir Walter Elliot's explorations in 1840...'[48] He was talking about a period of 37 years.

When Sewell first visited Amaravati a hollow cup-like basin was all that remained of the Chintapalli Raja's reservoir.[49] This was surrounded by a mound of earth and stones, sloping more steeply on the inner than on the outer side (Figure 6.3). On the mound, which varied from 150 to 200 ft. across, were smaller undulating mounds, intersected by the courses of water channels. A few 'somewhat damaged and discoloured marbles' were lying about, and 'a fine but terribly mutilated slab', originally unearthed for display for the District Collector, lay fully exposed on the top of the mound on the west. Sewell made 'a slight excavation' in the south of the mound and found two small sculptures embedded near the surface. He then had all the exposed stones covered with earth and left.

When Sewell came back to Amaravati at the end of 1877, he took measurements, made a plan, and fixed the cardinal points as accurately as possible.[50] In the southeast quadrant, he uncovered seven unsculpted stones. Towards the south of the circle, he exposed two stones he had excavated when he was here last. His main excavations were concentrated in the north-west quadrant, where he found a portion of a platform (Figure 6.4). Sewell's excavation resulted in the discovery of about 90 'new and splendidly preserved sculptured marbles, with promise of plenty more as the excavations proceed'.[51] He managed to clear only 100 ft. of the platform. Sewell had the newly discovered Amaravati stones and the Undavilly rock

Figure 6.3
The site in April, 1877

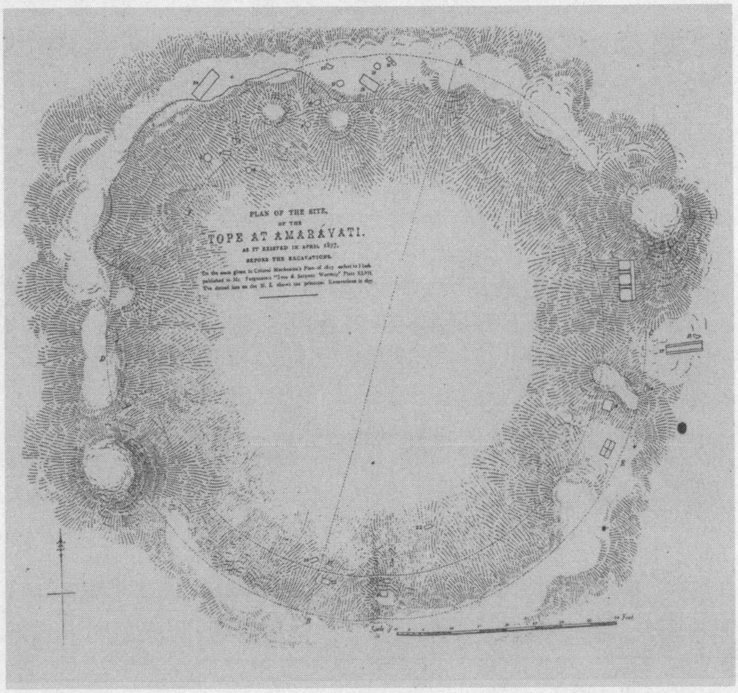

Source: Sewell, 1880

temple photographed, but his funds permitted nothing better than the employment of 'an unskilled Native photographer' for the job, and he was not particularly happy with the results.

Sewell asserted that the Amaravati sculptures ought to be photographed professionally, and prepared for publication by a School of Arts student or engraver. An even better solution, he suggested, was to send the whole lot of stones to England, to join those that had already been shipped there. He spoke of the difficulty of protecting the stones *in situ:*

> The stones left lying exposed on the surface have lately been most seriously mutilated and destroyed. I have left a man in charge, but the small amount of money now at my disposal will not allow me to keep him on for long, unless the Government sanction a permanent establishment for the purpose or remove the stones to England.[52]

Figure 6.4
Sewell's 1877 Excavation in the North-West Quadrant

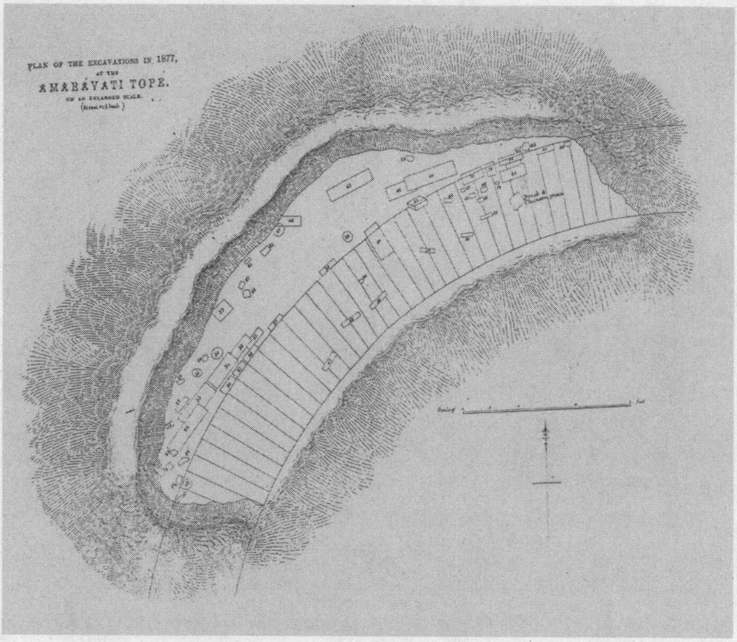

Source: Sewell, 1880

Sewell pointed out that he had used up more than half of the sanctioned grant and that the remainder would not be sufficient to finance the completion of the work. More funds were therefore urgently required. It was equally important, he emphasized, to put someone exclusively on the job:

> The best proof that this is so will, perhaps, be found in the fact that, though extensively interested in the subject, I could not find leisure from my ordinary official duties *for a whole year,* to commence the excavations at Amravati, only 17 miles from my headquarters.[53]

Sewell reported that he had obtained the copies of the inscriptions in Sir Walter Elliot's possession, but had found, on comparing them with the originals, to be quite useless, as they were full of mistakes. He suggested that Dr. Burnell was the best man in the Presidency to handle the work of translating the inscriptions, but since he was a senior official on

Judge's pay, the Government would no doubt be reluctant to release him from his regular official duties. Sewell went on to humbly offer his own services for conducting an archaeological survey of the area. Appealing to the bureaucratic concern for economy, he urged that this would be the most economical expedient. Justifying the sanction of additional funds for the project, Sewell pointed out that in 1868, the Madras Government had been authorized to spend Rs. 13,000 per annum on the archaeology of the Presidency, not a penny of which had been spent to date. This fact, he asserted, had recently been brought to the notice of the Viceroy by the Home Government. Rs. 13,000 was precisely the amount he now sought Government sanction for. The project Sewell outlined included further excavations at Amaravati, but was much larger in its scope:

> If the Government would order me to devote myself to the archaeological survey of the portion of the Madras Presidency about the Kistna and Godavery Rivers, and would allow me the ordinary pay which I should draw if employed in the usual routine work, I think I could promise great results. I should complete the excavations of the marbles at Amravati. I should be enabled to visit and check letter by letter all the original inscriptions with the copies that I have. I could take impressions or rubbings of most of them, and, after translating them, could compile, as I believe, a complete history of the at present very dim periods preceding the Muhammadan conquest, I could also get careful drawings made of all the most important sculptures and localities. And, generally, I would have time, which I have not now, to turn out very valuable work.[54]

The Madras Government passed on Sewell's proposal to the Government of India. Sewell refrained from sending in a full report on his excavations at Amaravati, waiting for a reply to his proposal. In the meantime, the sculptures he had unearthed at Amaravati in May 1877 lay at the site, awaiting a decision as to their fate. Sewell had appointed a peon to guard them, but the monthly salary of Rs. 5 'is steadily eating up the grant allowed for the excavations'. He was still waiting for the sanctioning of a photographer and draftsman. Sewell was anxious to move those sculptures that were out of their original position and estimated the cost of transporting them by punt to Madras as Rs. 150. As for the stones that were *in situ*, he suggested the simple expedient of loosely covering them with a foot or so of earth till more permanent arrangements were made.[55]

The Madras Government ultimately sanctioned the retention of the peon stationed at Amaravati on a salary of Rs. 5 per month, as also the sum of Rs. 150 for the removal of the stones from the site to the Central Museum at Madras. It appealed to the Government of India for an additional grant of Rs. 1,000 for explorations at Amaravati. In April 1979, Sewell packed his bags and went back to England. He had received no response to his proposal. He had, however, reached an important conclusion on the basis of his own excavation and his careful study of Mackenzie's plans and account of the site. He was convinced that Fergusson had been wrong in thinking that the Amaravati mound was the site of a number of structures. To Sewell, it was clear that it was the site of a single structure, a single large *stūpa.*

Horsfall Steps in

In February 1880, the Madras Government suddenly directed J. G. Horsfall, Collector of the Kistna district, to complete the excavation of Amaravati immediately. This hasty decision seems to have been the result of a visit to the site by the Duke of Buckingham, Governor of Madras. The long prevarication over the issue was brought to a sudden end by giving a free hand to a man who had no qualifications for the job, and the result was a hastily-conducted, sloppy excavation, which resulted in the removal of still more sculptures, adding little of value as far as the documentation of the site was concerned.

Horsfall began excavation work at Amaravati on 16 February 1880 and continued to personally supervise it up to 3rd March.[56] It was not until 1st March, when all the work was nearly done, that a draftsman arrived to assist him. Horsfall proudly reported that, unable to get the work taken up on contract, he directly hired the labour for the job at highly economical rates. On 3rd March, Horsfall had to leave Amaravati for the Bapatla taluk. He placed the draftsman in charge of 'the trifling work that remained to be done'. When he came back to the site on 24th March, Sergeant Coney had already photographed much of the *stūpa.* Horsfall was thus not present for the most part when the work of drawing and photography was being conducted.

As for the results of the excavation, Horsfall himself admitted that nothing much had been gained: 'The results obtained from the excavation, may, I fear, prove somewhat disappointing.'[57]

Horsfall had hoped to discover stones of the outer and inner circles in their entirety. Instead, he found evidence of vandalism and destruction everywhere. He put the blame on religious iconoclasts.

> ...in some cases I found that sculptures had been broken up and ground to small pieces to form a bed as it were for some wretched brick hovel, itself

> too small for human habitation, and which could apparently have been intended merely for the deposit of a light or of pious offerings. Traces of several such buildings were found, but one only in anything like a state of preservation. Another instance of the fury with which the demolisher worked is afforded in one of the heads above referred to; this was found buried some depth below the pavement concealed in a hole in a stone, as if the destroyer, not satisfied with breaking the statue in pieces and disfiguring the features, had purposely buried the head so effectively as to prevent its discovery in future. The other heads were also buried below the level of the pavement.[58]

He did not give many precise details regarding his operations at Amaravati. He did refer to the discovery of a brick basement running around the inner side of the circle, about 1 ft. below the level of the pavement. He also mentioned having encountered very large quantities of bricks, suggesting that there were once many brick buildings immediately next to the *stūpa*. He ascertained the position of the southern gateway. He also uncovered a number of sculpted stones. He did not specify the number, nor give any detailed description, simply saying that they were similar to those already described by Mr. Fergusson and that they gave plenty of evidence of tree and serpent worship. He himself was quite confused about the significance of the motifs on the sculptures.

Horsfall reported that his draftsman had made a plan of the *stūpa* and that he would shortly submit this, along with descriptive notices of the various stones, to the Government. He also referred to the discovery of a dozen or more inscriptions, 'all but one too short probably to throw any light on the history of the Place'. He suggested that tracings should be taken of these, and suggested that Sewell's Munshi, Somayazulu, could carry out this task. He also mentioned the discovery of coins and pottery. Some of these were sent along with four sculpted stone heads to Masulipatam, from where they were to move on to Madras.

The fallout of Horsfall's operations included the discovery of a relic casket a little to the east of the southern gateway. This contained what seemed to be human relics, a tooth, and some fragments of bones. Although stones continued to be dug up, Horsfall 'considered it not advisable to go on excavating'. For reasons unspecified, he told the draftsman to cease work and wound up the operations.

The Madras Government sent Horsfall's brief report for comments to Sewell, who had finally been recalled to India in January 1881 as Officer on Special Duty in connection with the archaeological survey of the Madras Presidency.[59] Sewell wrote back, confining himself to the connection between his own 1877 excavation and that conducted by Horsfall:

> ...With this in view I avoid all criticism beyond the expression of my opinion: (1) that the paper of details and copies of inscriptions are of little scientific value, not being sufficiently accurate or explicit; (2) that the plan seems to have been carefully executed, but is difficult to work from as sections are wanting, or descriptions showing the levels at which the marbles were found, these levels often being of the greatest importance...[60]

Sewell added that while the plan drawn by the Public Works Department officers was more accurate than his own (which he had drawn from rough notes and measurements), it was unfortunate that they had given new numbers to all the stones. This double numbering made the task of correlating the two plans difficult. Nevertheless, he suggested the plan be lithographed and circulated to all those to whom it might be of interest. As for the photographs taken by Sergeant Coney, they were good, but not good enough for a reconstruction of what the *stūpa* looked like in its original condition. Sewell expressed regret that the 'wretched hovels' mentioned by Horsfall could not have been preserved or at least drawn. And what were they—Buddhist shrines? Votive *stūpas*? How old were they? Horsfall's report suggested no answers to these important questions.

Sewell went on to recommend further excavation, but a scientific one (which Horsfall's excavation certainly had not been):

> ...And I would strongly urge on Government the advisability of incurring whatever expenditure is required without stint, providing that a competent scientific surveyor be the person in charge of the work. This monument has no equal probably in the world, and it would be deplorable if when once properly undertaken, its complete examination should be hindered by want of funds...[61]

Horsfall's clumsy doings at Amaravati had set off a series of alarm bells in England as well, and with good reason. The India Office sent a despatch on the matter to the Governor of Madras, and a copy of this to the Viceroy.[62] In this Despatch, Hartington noted that the Madras Government had instructed the Collector of Kistna district to excavate Amaravati. The India Office wanted to know to what extent the instructions given to Horsfall had been carried out, and whether requisite precautions had been observed by him. Hartington observed that the instructions should have included the making of accurate plans and sections showing the situation and relative height of every stone uncovered in the course of the work. Further:

> Nothing is said in the Proceedings referred to of the Collector of Kistna's special qualifications as an archaeologist for undertaking these excavations.

> It is obvious that even inconspicuous fragments of sculptured stones which would seem of little consequence to any one not especially acquainted with the traditions and art of Buddhism in India might be really of the utmost importance to an expert observer as affording indications of the history and meaning of this deeply interesting monument of antiquity which is unequalled for the delicacy of its details by any of the remains of Indian architectural art…
>
> I am therefore under some anxiety to hear further from Your Excellency as to the steps taken for the proper excavation and conservation of the Amravati Tope. If these operations are not already completed, it should be borne in mind that the work of the examination and survey of an ancient monument of such unique value should be entrusted only to some competent archaeologist and scholar with such engineering assistance as you can most conveniently place at his disposal. When an accurate record had been furnished of the results of the excavations you have ordered, it will then be necessary to determine what further steps should be taken for the preservation of these sculptures which have excited a keen interest in Europe.[63]

A copy of Hartington's Despatch was sent by the Home, Revenue and Agricultural Department to Alexander Cunningham for comments. Cunningham remained silent for almost two years, in the course of which several reminders were issued to him.[64] By the time he found time to reply, the Archaeological Survey of Southern India had come into being, under the charge of James Burgess, and Amaravati fell within his jurisdiction.

Burgess versus Cole

James Burgess was an architect and a close associate of James Fergusson. In 1873, he was given charge of the Archaeological Survey of Western India, and in November 1881 his duties were extended to include the Archaeological Survey of Southern India as well. Burgess had a special and keen interest in ancient Indian architecture and sculpture, and an approach to Indian archaeology that was significantly different from that of Cunningham.

Burgess's appointment coincided with another one. In the same year, Captain H. H. Cole was appointed Curator of Ancient Monuments. Both Burgess and Cole had very definite ideas about their role in the documentation and preservation of Indian antiquities and archaeological sites. Amaravati became a trial of strength between them, and led to a full-blown discussion and debate, often very acrimonious, over the broader question of conservation policy.

At the time when Burgess and Cole took up their respective appointments, a batch of Amaravati sculptures was lying exposed at the site since Horsfall's excavation. When Burgess visited the site during December 1881 to January 1882, he reported that the stone slabs had been

> ...pounded to pieces in the most regardless way during the 'rough and ready' excavations in February 1880. No arrangements were made to register the condition of the mound during the progress of the excavations, and consequently all the information that might have been then secured has been entirely lost.[65]

The site had the appearance of a large, roughly circular pit, about 75 yards in diameter, with extensions at the cardinal points (Figure 6.5). Burgess counted 255 slabs (these included those uncovered and then buried for safety by Sewell) laid around the circle, 44 stored by Sewell in a shed, and 29 in the Bezwada Library (a total of 329). He discovered about 90 more in the course of his own excavations.

Burgess's detailed account of the Amaravati *stūpa*[66] identified several structural phases belonging to different periods. His description and interpretation of the sculptures was integrated with the inscriptional evidence and was accompanied by the text and translation of a large number of inscriptions and a series of photo-lithographs of the same. Burgess estimated the diameter of the Amaravati *stūpa* as about 138 ft. at the base, narrowing to over 90 ft. near the summit, and placed its height at between 80 ft. and 100 ft. He thought that this huge *stūpa* had been faced with sculpted slabs and surrounded by a double rail, carved on both sides.[67]

Many of the exposed stones Burgess found were not *in situ* and he thought that the best of the lot (he identified over 170) should be immediately removed to Madras where they could be placed in the Central Museum. This had to be done at once as the water levels in the Krishna were fast receding, and it would soon be impossible to move them down the river. Burgess asked for the immediate despatch of the necessary equipment and an experienced officer to the site.[68]

In January 1882, a large number of selected Amaravati stones lay packed at the site, ready for shipment down the river. The heavier stones were wrapped in straw ropes and some of the smaller ones were given the additional protection of wooden cases. However, the arrival of a telegram from the Madras Government froze all operations. The Curator of Ancient Monuments had been in communication both with the Madras Government and the Viceroy regarding the Amaravati sculptures. The Government of India had intervened and decreed that Captain Cole

Figure 6.5
The Amaravati Stūpa in 1881

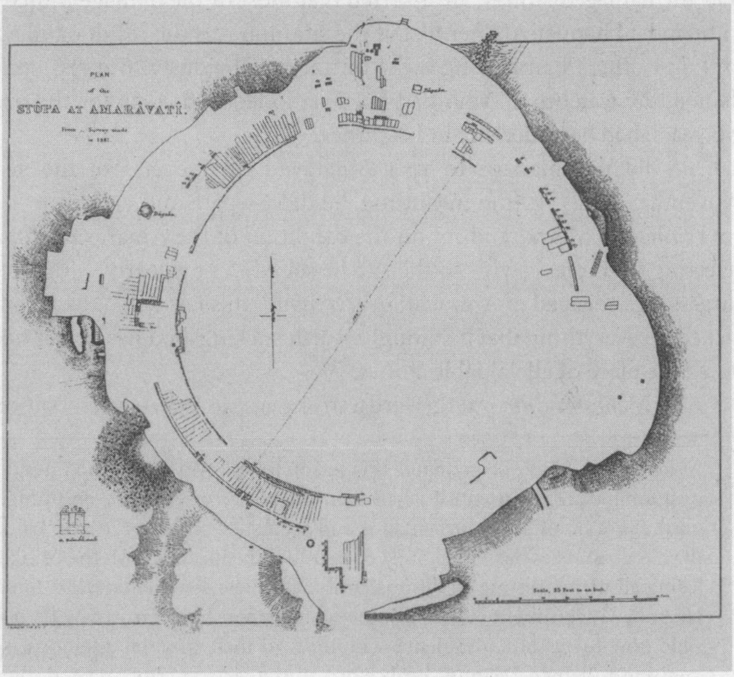

Source: Burgess, 1881

should be allowed to visit the site and give his opinion on the matter before any further action was taken.[69]

Opinions had been sought from Sewell and Cunningham. Sewell had reported that some of the Amaravati stones were so out of place that there was no harm in removing them, while others could be preserved *in situ.* Cunningham had reported that it was utterly impossible to restore any portion of the *stūpa in situ* as most of the stones had either been used up in buildings in the neighbourhood or had been shipped to England. It was best to remove the remaining ones to Madras, so as to ensure their protection.[70] Nevertheless, the Viceroy decreed that Captain Cole ought to be given the opportunity to visit the site and give *his* opinion. While Burgess fretted and fumed at the delay, the waters in the canals of the Krishna receded. Clearly, it would not be possible to whisk the Amaravati sculptures away for many months now.

While Burgess had been busy packing up the Amaravati sculptures, Horsfall had paid a visit to the site and absolved himself of all blame vis-à-vis the damaged stones. He asserted that most of the damage inflicted on them had happened after he left the site, and was the result of village boys and others hammering away on them. Obviously, Burgess complained, the watchman, who had been stationed at the site for the past two years, had been derelict in his duties.[71]

Cole did not manage to visit Amaravati till the end of the year (November 1882). In the meantime, he did prepare and submit to the Government a Memorandum on the condition of the Amaravati *stūpa.* Referring to Burgess's visit to the site he stated; 'I now learn ... that Dr. Burgess was engaged at Amravati *over a month* this last cold season, and packed up everything that he thought worth packing, and has in fact *ransacked* the place of all valuable stones.'[72]

Cole's *Memorandum* put forward a strong case for *in situ* preservation:

> As explained, I have been unable this season to visit Amravati, and intended postponing my report until I had seen the place, surveyed it, and judged on the spot of all the arguments for and against *preservation in situ.* Under the circumstances described, it is evident that the locality is on the brink of losing all its interesting traditions, and that unless some *energetic action* is taken by Government it will lose them altogether. How far it may be possible now to restore any of the sculptures to their original positions is a question to which I cannot reply until all the facts are investigated; but I have no hesitation in counselling the preservation of the marbles (now at the Madras Museum and those lying packed) in a suitable manner on the site *at Amravati.* Even should it prove impossible to replace them as they stood, I recommended the erection of a small building where these carvings would be properly displayed and absolutely safe, and the railing-in of the site of the great Buddhist Tope, securing, as far as possible, all the existing masonry of the building.[73]

Cole strongly expressed the view that valuable ancient antiquities should not be removed from India to England. He spoke of the Sanchi *stūpa* having escaped two great dangers—one when in 1853, General Cunningham had advised the removal of the fallen gateways to the British Museum, and the second in 1868, when the Eastern Gateway was nearly carried away to Paris (at the last minute it was decided to display a cast rather than the original at the Exhibition). Cole suggested that the needs of the British Museum in London and the Central Museum in Madras (which already housed several valuable sculptures from Amaravati) could be met by displaying plaster casts, and that there was no need to send any more stones to these places:

> If all beautiful and valuable remains are to be ruthlessly torn from their ancient sites, the outlying districts of this country will be rapidly robbed of all their interesting records. I believe, moreover, that the policy of preserving ancient monuments *for India is* a sounder one than carting them away to European Museums.[74]

One of the several arguments made by Burgess for the removal of the Amaravati sculptures from the site was the inaccessibility of the place. Cole pointed out that India was being rapidly opened up by communication networks of many kinds. Travellers and scholars from many countries were visiting her ancient cities and temples 'and it seems to me a *suicidal and indefensible policy to allow the country to be looted of original works of ancient art when there exist the means of making facsimiles scarcely distinguishable from the original!*'[75]

Cole also countered Burgess's argument that there was no point in leaving the sculpted pieces where they were because the ignorant natives were unaware of their significance. He cited an Order of the Governor in Council (No. 985 of 20 January 1881) which expressed satisfaction at the 'cordial interest' displayed by 'natives of various classes' in Sewell's operations at Amaravati.

Cole ended by quoting Burgess's own remarks on the desirability of preserving *in situ* the materials of certain old buildings in Ahmedabad. Why, Cole asked, should not the same principle be applied to Amaravati? Besides, since the Amaravati case was a matter concerning the conservation of an ancient monument, and not of archaeological research, it came within his own jurisdiction and not that of the Archaeological Survey.[76]

Throughout the whole controversy, Burgess maintained that the stones that remained at Amaravati were too scattered to permit the restoration of even a small part of the Amaravati *stūpa.*

> Amaravati has not been an 'Architectural Monument' for centuries. No two complete stones are together *in situ,* nor can three be found entire that were originally in juxtaposition.
>
> If Captain Cole only condescended to ask me what was the character and extent of the remains at Amaravati, I would have most readily given him every information. The Amaravati Stūpa has been so utterly destroyed, and the remaining fragments are so few relatively to its original extent, that the ablest living archaeologists differ in their views of its original form; and as the villagers destroy and carry off the slabs to burn into lime, any attempt at conservation on the spot would be futile. No one, who had informed himself as to the amount and condition of the materials, and recognised the difficulty of the problem, would suggest such an attempt.[77]

Burgess alleged that Cole's stand on the matter was motivated by something other than a commitment to the principle of *in situ* preservation. His real aim, he asserted, was to wrest South Indian architecture out of Burgess's hands and to prepare an illustrated work on the subject at Government expense. If Cole were allowed to have his way, this 'would cut my department off from all connection with architecture—the branch which of all others I am best fitted to deal with'.[78]

Cole's Recommendations

Cole visited Amaravati in November 1882 and submitted his Report in December of that year.[79] He had inspected the 175 fine stones packed and stored in a fenced enclosure about half-a-mile north of Amaravati by Burgess. They seemed to be in good condition. They had been taken out of their cases and cocoon of straw; the flood waters had cleaned them and had not harmed them in any perceptible way.

Cole gave the following list of the sculpted stones that still lay at Amaravati:

Sculptures of Dr. Burgess's selection on the river-bank		175
Sculptures at Tope—	In a shed to the North, in boxes	8
	loose	43
	In situ	195
		246
Total		421

According to Cole, a large number of stones were obviously in their original place, and it was possible on the basis of these to trace the position of the railing and of the structure that must have stood in the centre of the mound. The stones listed as deposited in the shed to the north of the mound were those placed there by Sewell in 1877. In the western part of the circumference of the structure, a part of the stone terrace, although much damaged, was still in its original place. Elsewhere, portions of the railing were in position. The southern entrance could be traced. The position of the stones indicated part of the outline of the original structure. Apart from these, there were various smaller fragments and masonry slabs in position to complete the demarcation of the railing and the plinth of the *stūpa* itself.

Cole's Report exonerated the Hindu natives of Amaravati of responsibility for the shattered condition of the masonry and the sculptures.

It was true, he wrote, that many years ago, the grandfather of the present *zamindar* had removed bricks and stones from the mound for his buildings, but he would have been concerned with simple removal of the material, not with smashing and destroying the sculptures. Cole insisted that any damage suffered by the sculptures must represent the handiwork of the iconoclast Aurangzeb, when he conquered the area and established himself in the forts of Kondapilli and Kondavid nearby: 'The place is now easily accessible to any idle boy who wishes to pass away his time in hammering off carved surfaces, but it is really surprising to me how little evidence there is of damage of this kind.'[80]

Cole's specific recommendations were as follows:

1. The masonry terrace-rails and fragments that were still standing in their original position should be rendered secure. The existing portions of the terrace should be re-laid on concrete and in cement. The rails should be supported in their places by a solid foundation of concrete and by using iron bars to prop the uprights and hold them in position.
2. All the fragmentary sculptures should be collected and placed under a permanent shed in the centre of the circular enclosure.
3. The embankment of earth formed around the *stūpa* by the demolition of the mound in past years should be gently sloped off so as to prevent the falling in of earth, which had happened during the last rainy season.
4. A seven-feet high masonry wall should be built around the ruins and the entrance gate placed under lock and key.
5. A small house for a custodian should be built near this gate.[81]

Cole vetoed in strong terms the idea of moving the 175 stones selected by Burgess to the Madras Museum, saying that there was no room there indoors for them and that an open-air display would expose them to the destructive atmospheric conditions of the town. The Madras Museum (or any other Museum that was interested) could display plaster casts. The Amaravati stones should be left at Amaravati:

> *This course I strongly recommend to Government. The conservation of the structure will not be promoted by still further scattering its component parts,* and I do not see what special benefit will be secured by removing the originals to the Madras Museum as proposed.[82]

Cole was advocating *in situ* conservation, not restoration. Considering the fact that it was not possible to identify the precise original position of the removed stones, any attempt at restoration was neither possible nor desirable. What he did suggest was, that since it was certainly possible to identify which part of the *stūpa* complex the stones belonged to, they could be placed on the ground in these positions, where they could be easily examined and appreciated. Cole also advocated complete photographic documentation of all the best sculptural pieces, and suggested that a professional photographer be engaged for the job. A special officer should be appointed to carry out all these recommendations. He estimated the cost of preparing casts and photographs to be about Rs. 5,000.

Cole's recommendations were sent to Burgess for comments, and the slanging match between the two men continued. Burgess opposed Cole's recommendation of relaying the slabs of the old terrace on concrete and cement as it would alter what remained of the original structure.[83] He even opposed Cole's suggestion that a masonry wall be built around the site, on the grounds that this would only amount to a temptation to Telugu boys, natives of a hilly country, to jump over it. On the other hand, he found the suggestion of building a shed to protect the stones remaining at the site, as also the appointing of a custodian, acceptable. If there was not enough room in the Madras Museum to house the sculptures, some of them could be displayed in the Government School of Arts. There was no harm in having casts of some of the pieces made, provided the funds could be obtained. The casts could be made under the supervision of the Superintendent of the Madras School of Arts. Burgess added that it would be cheaper to have the casts made at Madras rather than at Amaravati.

According to Burgess, the fact that Cole himself admitted that the restoration of any part of the Amaravati *stūpa* was impracticable amounted to an admission that there was no structure worth the name left to conserve. This clearly indicated that the remains at Amaravati fell within the domain of archaeology and not within that of conservation. He argued that the disposal of the Amaravati sculptures fell squarely within the jurisdiction of the Archaeological Survey of the Madras Presidency. If General Cunningham was permitted to do as he pleased at Bharhut, with no reference to Cole, why should he, Burgess, be subjected to undue interference at the hands of the meddlesome Curator of Ancient Monuments? Burgess argued that he did not stand alone in his point of view on the matter of the 'Amaravati marbles'. His opinion was shared by all those who had been connected with the site over the years—the Collector Mr. Horsfall, the Sub-Collector Mr. G. Mackenzie, the engineer Mr. Grant, and the former First Assistant Collector Mr. R. Sewell. If the Government required further advice, it could consult General Cunningham.

Meanwhile, Sewell continued to urge the Madras Government to do *something* about the Amaravati sculptures. He pointed out that apart from the stones that lay exposed at the site after Horsfall's excavations, those that he himself had excavated in 1877 had been lying exposed for the last six years. The stones that Burgess had packed and removed to the river bank had lain there waiting for Cole's inspection, and in that period had been exposed to great danger due to the flooding of the river. While this had not caused any appreciable damage, their continued exposure to sun, wind and rain could not but harm them:

> As each year passes by and nothing is done to save them, the process of destruction is steadily going on, and if this treatment is continued, all the rare beauty of the lately-excavated marbles will be lost by their becoming weatherworn like all the rest previously excavated. I would, therefore, earnestly entreat Government to take some immediate steps to save them.[84]

Cunningham's Verdict

The Madras Government took up Burgess's suggestion that the Director General of the Archaeological Survey of India be asked for his opinion on the matter. This time, Cunningham obliged with a fairly swift response, requiring only one reminder. This is what he stated:

> There is so little now remaining on the side of the Amarávati Stupa that I do not think it is worth while to attempt any kind of restoration. I am a strong advocate for the conservation of all ancient buildings that actually exist, and also for the restoration of such as can be restored. When I suggested in 1853 that the gateways of the Sânchi Stupa might, with advantage, be removed to the British Museum, my sole object was their preservation, as I was but too well aware of the danger to which they were exposed if left much longer neglected. But since Major Cole obtained his present appointment, I have been a staunch advocate for the complete restoration of the Sânchi Stupa.[85]

Cunningham's solution to the impasse fell more or less in line with Burgess's views on the matter. Since so many of the sculpted stones had already been removed from Amaravati, he thought that the best course of action was to remove the selected stones to the Madras Museum. There they would be safe as well as accessible and could be displayed in such a manner as would give a fair idea of their original arrangement. As for the rest of the stones lying scattered at the site, they could, as suggested by Cole, be placed under a shed in the centre of the circle of the ruins, under the care of a *chawkidar*. The best specimens of sculpture should be photographed, and if casts were to be made, Burgess was correct in stating that it would be cheaper to have this work done in Madras rather than at Amaravati.

Presented with Cunnntngham's verdict on the matter, the Madras Government decided to settle the matter and to accept Burgess's plan of action. Orders were issued to that effect. Cole was not, however, a man to give up easily. He still had one more card (not an ace, but a card nevertheless) up his sleeve. He wrote to the Viceroy directly, referring to the recent Government of India Resolution of 8 June 1883 concerning the preservation of archaeological remains *in situ* or in museums.[86] He argued that the said Resolution could not have been before the Madras Government when the orders on the Amaravati case had been passed. The Resolution and the orders must have crossed each other on the way. The Resolution, which laid down principles to guide Local Governments, endorsed the principle of *in situ* preservation. It clearly stated that only isolated remains, the original site of which was unknown, were to be removed to museums. Cole stated that he had met the Governor of Madras on 2 December 1882, and that the latter had supported his proposals. After going over Burgess's and Cunningham's letters on the matter, Cole said that he saw in them no argument that would induce him to alter his recommendation of *in situ* preservation of the Amaravati sculptures. In fact, General Cunningham's suggestion of setting up slabs and pillars to give an idea of their original arrangement could be done at Amaravati, rather than in the Madras Museum. Attacking the archaeologists, Cole made the following sharp remark:

> I submit that the province of the Archaeological Surveys is to write ancient History and not to go about the country pilfering tons of sculptures from well-known monuments.[87]

Cole urged the Madras Government to reconsider its decision of removing the Amaravati sculptures to the Madras Museum, and to implement the directives embodied in the 1883 Resolution.

The Removal of the Amaravati Sculptures to the Madras Museum

Cole's last shot proved to be in vain. He had all along been a lone voice as far as the whole matter was concerned. The Government of India declined to reopen an issue that had dragged on inconclusively for so long and in which the majority opinion was clearly ranged against Cole.

Burgess's recommendations were implemented, and the stones that had been patiently waiting near the bank of the Krishna were removed from Amaravati to the Madras Museum. But Burgess did not have the last laugh in the matter. He had had his way as far as the removal of the choice sculptures from Amaravati to Madras was concerned, but he was far from happy about what happened to them once they reached Madras.

In March 1886, on Cunningham's retirement, Burgess was promoted to the position of Director General of the Archaeological Survey. Burgess had all along maintained that he should supervise the unpacking and arrangement of the Amaravati sculptures on their arrival in Madras. This did not happen. For some reason, the job of arranging the stones that reached the Madras Museum was entrusted to the Acting Surgeon General with the Government of Madras, a man named Bidie. Bidie arranged the Amaravati stones in the Madras Museum as he thought fit, and had many of them embedded in cement for display.

Burgess was furious about the whole thing, and minced no words in expressing his displeasure. He shot off a letter to the Madras Government stating that he had heard from those who had visited the Museum and seen the display that it left much to be desired, and that his own visit there had confirmed his worst fears—the Madras Government had caused irreparable damage to one of the most valuable collections of sculpture in India:

> I have seen many museums, but never one in which a valuable collection was arranged with so little knowledge and care, nor so needlessly injured by casing in a cement that can never be removed.[88]

Both the arrangement of the sculptures and their being embedded deep in masses of Portland cement, out of which they could never be extracted, was disastrous. 'Anything more barbarously stupid is hard to conceive.' Burgess went on to list the 'barbarisms' that had been perpetrated in the hotch-potch arrangement of the priceless sculptures, in flagrant violation of their original architectural placing or their differences in style and age. He further alleged that certain sculptures still lay about, uncared for, in the Museum:

> Few museums have received so important a collection of sculptures; none has shewed itself so unworthy by such wanton and ignorant abuses of such a trust.[89]

The Madras Government directed Bidie to respond to the charges made by the Director General of the Archaeological Survey. Bidie defended himself by asserting that he had consulted all literature available on the sculptures, examined the stones carefully, and solicited the advice of Colonel Morant, an architect, 'whose respect for these valuable antiquities was just as great as my own', before commencing his task. He complained of the various difficulties he had faced in arranging such a heterogenous collection. He also reported that many 'scientific visitors' from various parts of the world had visited the Museum and expressed their approval of his display.[90]

The Madras Government was satisfied with Bidie's response. At the same time, it expressed regret at the 'extraordinary attack' on the Madras Museum by the Director General of the Archaeological Survey, and on his incorporation of items of gossip in his official communication. It referred to the infrequent visits paid by Burgess to the Madras Presidency and observed that his interest in the province had been chiefly manifested in fault-finding.[91] Burgess was also officially ticked off by the Government of India. He was informed that the Governor General in Council

> ...has perused your letter in question with much regret. His Excellency in Council cannot refrain from expressing his opinion that the remarks made in your letter ... are altogether wanting in the moderation and judgement which should characterize official documents; while they are equally open to objection as failing to show that respect which the Government of Madras has a right to expect in communications made to it more particularly when such communications relate to the proceedings of officers serving under its order.
>
> The Government of India earnestly trusts that such proceedings will not recur, and that in your future correspondence you will be careful to avoid giving any ground of offence to Local Governments, on whose co-operation the success of the Archaeological Survey must largely depend.[92]

Conclusion

Subsequent to the events described above, several excavations were carried out at Amaravati. Alexander Rea excavated the site in 1888–1889, 1905–1906 and 1908–1909. In 1958–1959, further excavations were carried out by the Archaeological Survey of India under the superintendence of R. Subrahmanyam and K. Krishna Murthy. In 1973–1974, I. K. Sharma conducted excavations at a site close to the *mahācaitya.* In 1974–1975, A. Ghosh's excavations provided a clearer chronological framework for the cultural sequence of the site.

Some of the sculptural pieces which were unearthed in the course of these various excavations were assembled and displayed in a Museum at the site. But most of the most beautiful stones had been slowly but steadily removed from the site during the course of the 19th century. During that period, every subsequent plea for removal of stones had sought justification in prior removals. Only once in the history of the 'Amaravati marbles' did the stones have a strong spokesman arguing for their *in situ* preservation. But eloquent and determined as he might have been, Cole's arguments came too late, and moreover, he had all the other authorities on the subject ranged against him. This, in spite of all the strongly worded Resolutions on *in situ* preservation passed and circulated by the colonial government.

Today, those interested in getting a glimpse of the former magnificence of the Amaravati *stūpa* can venture into the portals of the Madras Museum, the British Museum in London, or the small site museum at Amaravati itself. They can leaf through catalogues and publications on the subject produced by these museums. However, the result of a century and three-quarters of explorations and excavations at Amaravati is that today, the site of one of the greatest *mahācaitya*s of ancient India is marked by a nondescript mound ringed by a few forlorn stones.

Acknowledgements

I am grateful to the Ancient India and Iran Trust, Cambridge for the grant of a Charles Wallace visiting fellowship over the summer of 1999 which enabled me to examine relevant archival material in the British Library.

Notes

1. Colin Mackenzie, 'Account of Extracts of a Journal', *Asiatic Researches* 9, 1807, pp. 272–278.
2. Mackenzie, 'Account of Extracts of a Journal'.
3. James Fergusson, *Tree and Serpent Worship: Or Illustrations of Mythology and Art in India in the First and Fourth Centuries after Christ. From the Sculptures of the Buddhist Topes at Sanchi and Amravati* (London: W. H. Allen, 1873), p. 149, cites the following remark made by H. H. Wilson (*Ariana Antiqua*, p. 32), a man who had a long and intimate connection with the Mackenzie Collection: 'I have not found any description of it (i.e., the Tope at Amravati) among his papers but from a few brief memoranda it appears to have been visited by him repeatedly, and in 1816 to have been measured and surveyed.' This suggests that Mackenzie visited Amaravati several times between 1797 and 1816.

4. Robert Sewell, *Report on the Amaravati Tope, and Excavations on its Site in 1877* (London, 1880), p. 13. According to Mildred Archer, *British Drawings in the India Office Library*, 2 vols. (London, 1969), p. 530, Mackenzie's draftsmen continued to work at the site till August 1819 and the fair-copying continued till 1820.
5. The first of these was printed in Sewell, *Report on the Amaravati Tope, and Excavations on its Site in 1877*, Plate I, facing p. 22. Its title reads: 'Sketch of Deepauldinna at Amrawutty in its present state, March 1816.' The second plan was printed in James Fergusson's *Tree and Serpent Worship*, as Plate XLII. The original title of the second plan read: 'Plan Descriptive of the Present State of the Mound of Depaldenna at Amravutty shewing what has been cleared out and what still remains to be removed. Laid down from actual Measurements. June 1817.'
6. The Raja also discovered a new stone relic casket in the course of his digging. Inside was a crystal box containing a small pearl, some gold leaf, and 'other things of no value'. These he kept in his *tosha khana* till, in 1863, they were secured by Walter Elliot and deposited in the Madras Museum. This information is contained in a letter from Sir Walter Elliot (dated 12 June 1867) cited by Fergusson (*Tree and Serpent Worship*, p. 164n). Some of these details are also mentioned by Boswell, 'On the Ancient Remains in the Krishna District'.
7. Colin Mackenzie, 'Ruins of Amravutty, Depauldina and Durnacotta', *Asiatic Journal and Monthly Register* 1823, p. 438.
8. Mackenzie, 'Ruins of Amravutty, Depauldina and Durnacotta', p. 469.
9. Mackenzie, 'Ruins of Amravutty, Depauldina and Durnacotta', p. 469. In a footnote on the same page, Mackenzie suggested that the structure at Dipaldina may have been connected with the Druid religion.
10. Fergusson, *Tree and Serpent Worship*, p. 150.
11. Douglas Barrett, *Sculptures from Amaravati in the British Museum* (London: Trustees of the British Museum, 1954), p. 22.
12. Barrett, *Sculptures from Amaravati in the British Museum*, p. 23, refers to a letter dated 6 September 1819, from Mackenzie to Cotgrave preserved in the British Museum, which also mentions this.
13. Barrett, *Sculptures from Amaravati in the British Museum*, p. 23
14. J. A. S. Burgess, *The Buddhist Stupas at Amaravati and Jaggayapeta* (Vol. 6 of the *Archaeological Survey of Southern India* series) (London: Trübner, 1887; 1996, Reprint edition, New Delhi), p. 17.
15. Burgess, *The Buddhist Stupas at Amaravati and Jaggayapeta*, p. 17.
16. Elliot's notes and papers were lost in passage to England, and we only have bits of information about his activities at Amaravati his correspondence. The most detailed of these accounts is contained in a letter dated 18 February 1871, written by him to the Under Secretary of State for India, Enclosure No. 2. Home Proceedings, Public, 19 August 1871, No. 76, *Oriental and India Office Collection (British Library) Home Proceedings: Proceedings of the Home Department (OIOC)*.

17. These are reproduced by Robert Knox, *Amaravati Buddhist Sculpture from the Great Stupa* (London: British Museum Press, 1992), p. 17, Figure 5 and p. 227, Figure a).
18. Letter dated 18 February 1871, from Elliot to the Under Secretary of State for India.
19. For Elliot's denial of this point, see supra, p. 162.
20. Burgess, *The Buddhist Stupas at Amaravati and Jaggayapeta*, p. 18.
21. Burgess, *The Buddhist Stupas at Amaravati and Jaggayapeta*, p. 18.
22. According to Sewell (*Report on the Amaravati Tope, and Excavations on its Site in 1877*, p. 20), the sculptures sent by Mackenzie, Robertson, and Elliot were by this time hopelessly mixed up.
23. For details of how the Amaravati marbles moved from Fife House to the British Museum, and the acquisition by the latter of a few additional pieces, see Knox, *Amaravati Buddhist Sculpture from the Great Stupa*, pp. 18 ff.
24. These details are given by Fergusson in the Preface to his *Tree and Serpent Worship*, pp. iii ff.
25. Fergusson, *Tree and Serpent Worship*, p. 151.
26. James Fergusson, 'Description of the Amravati Tope in Guntur', *Journal of the Royal Asiatic Society* 3, 1867, pp. 132–166.
27. Fergusson, *Tree and Serpent Worship*, pp. 164, 213–214.
28. Fergusson, *Tree and Serpent Worship*, p. 221.
29. Fergusson, *Tree and Serpent Worship*, p. 78.
30. Fergusson used a number of terms as racial categories. Apart from the Aryans and Dravidians, he referred to the Hindus (originally pure Aryans, corrupted through the intermixture of blood), and Dasyus (bearded non-Aryan aboriginals, essentially snake-worshippers). He associated the Nagas with the Dasyus and the Yavanas (Fergusson, *Tree and Serpent Worship*, pp. 92, 157).
31. J. A. C. Boswell, 'On the Ancient Remains in the Krishna District', *Indian Antiquary* 1 (1872): 149–155.
32. Letter No. 1301, dated 31 March 1870, from Boswell to the Acting Secretary to the Board of Revenue; Home Proceedings, Public, 27 May 1871, No. 1. *OIOC.*
33. Letter no. 9, dated India Office, London, 12 April 1871, from the Secretary of State for India to the Government of Fort St. George. Home Proceedings, Public, 27 May 1871, No. 1. *OIOC.*
34. Letter dated 20, Longham Place, 8 February 1871, from Fergusson to the Under Secretary of State for India. Home Proceedings, Public, 19 August, 1871, No. 76, Enclosure No. 1. *OIOC.*
35. Letter dated Wolfebe, Hawick N.B., 18 February 1871, from Sir Walter Elliot to the Under Secretary of State for India. Home Proceedings, Public, 27 May 1871, No, 1. Enclosure no. 2. *OIOC.*
36. Letter dated Wolfebe, Hawick N.B., 18 February 1871, from Sir Walter Elliot to the Under Secretary of State for India. (Sewell, *Report on the Amaravati Tope, and Excavations on its Site in 1877* also referred to the 'real damage that was visible on the Amaravati sculptures that found their way to England'.)

37. Letter dated Wolfebe, Hawick N.B., 18 February 1871, from Sir Walter Elliot to the Under Secretary of State for India.
38. Letter No. 101, dated Simla, 9 August 1871, from Alexander Cunningham to E.C. Bailey, Secretary to the Government of India. In Home Proceedings, Public, 27 May 1871, No. 1. *OIOC.*
39. Letter dated 10 August 1871. Home Proceedings, Public, 21 October 1871, No. 47. *OIOC.*
40. Proceedings of the Board of Revenue, dated 16 November 1872, No. 2218. Cited in Home Proceedings, Public, February 1873, No. 356. *OIOC.*
41. Letter No. 96, dated Mangalagherry, 19 March 1875, from Sewell to the Collector of the Kistna district. Home Proceedings, Public, May 1876, No. 61. *OIOC.*
42. Letter No. 96, dated Mangalagherry, 19 March 1875, from Sewell to the Collector of the Kistna district.
43. Letter No. 96, dated Mangalagherry, 19 March 1875, from Sewell to the Collector of the Kistna district.
44. Letter No. 1564, dated Fort St. George, 3 November 1875, from the Under-Secretary to the Government of Madras to the Officiating Secretary to the Government of India. Home Proceedings, Public, May 1876, No. 60. *OIOC.*
45. Letter No. 295, dated Agra, 6 March 1876, from Major General Alexander Cunningham to the Officiating Secretary to the Government of India. Home Proceedings, Public, May 1876, No. 62. *OIOC.*
46. Letter No. 295, dated Agra, 6 March 1876, from Major General Alexander Cunningham to the Officiating Secretary to the Government of India.
47. This and most of the following information is contained in a letter dated Charing Cross, 18 August, 1877, from Robert Sewell to Col. Yule, Home Proceedings, Public, November 1877, No. 88. *OIOC.*
48. Letter from Sewell to the Under Secretary of State for India, dated Isle of Wight, 5 April 1880. Home Proceedings, Surveys, July 1880, No. 25, Part B, *National Archives of India (NAI).*
49. Sewell, *Report on the Amaravati Tope, and Excavations on its Site in 1877* was published in 1880. When he heard that the Governor of Madras had initiated fresh excavations at the site, Sewell decided there was no point in holding on to the information he had gathered, and went on to publish his Report.
50. Sewell, *Report on the Amaravati Tope, and Excavations on its Site in 1877.*
51. Letter dated Charing Cross, 18 August 1877, from Robert Sewell to Col. Yule. Home Proceedings, Public, November 1877, No. 88. *OIOC.* A later document indicates that Sewell found a total of 89 marbles at Amaravati and 26 at cither places. (Letter dated Creycliffe-Bonchurch, Isle of Wight, 5 April 1880. From Sewell to the Under Secretary of State for India. Home Proceedings, Surveys, July 1880, No. 25. Part B, *NAI*).
52. Letter dated Charing Cross, 18 August 1877, from Robert Sewell to Col. Yule.
53. Letter dated Charing Cross, 18 August 1877, from Robert Sewell to Col. Yule.
54. Letter dated Charing Cross, 18 August 1877, from Robert Sewell to Col. Yule.
55. Letter No. 52, dated Bezwada, 29 January 1879. From Robert Sewell to the Collector of the Kistna district; Home Proceedings, Public, April 1879, No, 107, *OIOC.*

56. Horsfall gave an account of his activities at the site in letter No. 794 to the Chief Secretary to the Government of Madras, dated Masulipatam, 16 April 1880. Home Proceedings, Archaeology, October 1881, No. 17, Part A. *NAI.*
57. Letter No. 794 to the Chief Secretary to the Government of Madras, dated Masulipatam, 16 April 1880.
58. Letter No. 794 to the Chief Secretary to the Government of Madras, dated Masulipatam, 16 April 1880.
59. Sewell's immediate duties were to draw up lists of antiquities in the Presidency and to procure translations of inscriptions. His work was supposed to pave the way for a more detailed survey. He was expected to submit to the Government of India a brief quarterly report of work done and in progress.
60. Letter No. 639, dated Greenwood, Ootacamund, 20 August 1881, from R. Sewell, Madras Civil Service, on Special Duty, to the Chief Secretary to the Government of Madras, Home Proceedings, Surveys, October 1881, No. 17, Part A. *NAI.*
61. Letter No. 639, dated Greenwood, Ootacamund, 20 August 1881, from R. Sewell, Madras Civil Service, on Special Duty, to the Chief Secretary to the Government of Madras.
62. Despatch (Statistics and Commerce) No. 38, from Harlington, India Office to the Governor-in Council, Fort St. George, dated 30 September 1880. Proceedings of the Home. Revenue and Agriculture Department, Surveys/ Archaeology, 1880, No. 56, Part B. *NAI.*
63. Despatch (Statistics and Commerce) No. 38.
64. Proceedings of the Home, Revenue and Agriculture Department, Surveys/ Archaeology, 1880, No. 56, Part B. Notes on file. *NAI.*
65. Letter No. 15, dated Amaravati, 30 December 1881, from Burgess to the Chief Secretary, Government of Madras. Home Proceedings, Archaeology and the Conservation of Ancient Monuments, July 1882, No. 2. *NAI.*
66. Burgess, *The Buddhist Stupas at Amaravati and Jaggayapeta.*
67. Burgess, *The Buddhist Stupas at Amaravati and Jaggayapeta*, pp. 19–22.
68. Letter No. 15, dated Amaravati, 30 December 1881, from Burgess to the Chief Secretary, Government of Madras.
69. Letter No. 9, dated 16 June 1882 from A. Mackenzie, Secretary to the Government of India to the Secretary to the Government of Madras. Home Proceedings, Archaeology, June 1882, No. 9, Part A. *NAI.* Also, Letter No. 413, dated 16 June 1882, from C. G. Master, Chief Secretary to the Government of Madras to the Chief Secretary to the Government of India. Home Proceedings, Archaeology and the Preservation of Ancient Monuments, July 1882, No. I, Part A. *NAI.*
70. Letter No. 9, dated 16 June 1882 from A. Mackenzie, Secretary to the Government of India to the Secretary to the Government of Madras, notes on file.
71. Letter No. 16, dated Amaravati, 27 January 1882, from Burgess to the Chief Secretary to the Government of Madras. Home Proceedings, Archaeology and the Preservation of Ancient Monuments, July 1882, No. 4, Part A. *NAI.*
72. *Memorandum on the present condition of the Amaravati Tope in Madras*, dated Masulipalam, 24 November 1882. Quoted in Letter No. 711, dated

Madras, 2 December 1882, from Captain Cole to the Chief Secretary to the Government of Madras. Home Proceedings, Archaeology, July 1883, No. 9, Part A. *NAI.*

73. *Memorandum on the present condition of the Amaravati Tope in Madras.*
74. *Memorandum on the present condition of the Amaravati Tope in Madras.*
75. *Memorandum on the present condition of the Amaravati Tope in Madras.*
76. *Memorandum on the present condition of the Amaravati Tope in Madras.*
77. Letter dated Edinburgh, 27 July 1882, from Burgess to the Secretary to the Government of India. Home Proceedings, Archaeology and the Conservation of Ancient Monuments, September 1882, No. 12, Part A. *NAI.*
78. Letter dated Edinburgh, 2 August 1882, from Burgess to the Secretary to the Government of India. Home Proceedings, Archaeology and the Conservation of Ancient Monuments, September 1882, No. 11, Part A. *NAI.*
79. *Memorandum on the present condition of the Amaravati Tope.*
80. *Memorandum on the present condition of the Amaravati Tope.*
81. *Memorandum on the present condition of the Amaravati Tope.*
82. *Memorandum on the present condition of the Amaravati Tope.*
83. Letter No. 24, dated Gujarat, 9 March 1883, from Burgess to the Chief Secretary to the Government of Madras. Home Proceedings, Archaeology, July 1883, No. 9, Part A. *NAI.*
84. Letter No. 2, dated Chingleput, 29 April 1883, from Sewell, Acting Sub-collector, Chingleput to the Chief Secretary to the Government of Madras, Home Proceedings, Archaeology, July 1883, No. 9, Part A. *NAI.*
85. Letter No. 24, dated Shimla, 30 May 1883, from Major General Cunningham to the Chief Secretary to the Government of Madras. Home Proceedings, Archaeology, July 1883, No. 9. Part A. *NAI.*
86. Letter No. 138, dated Shimla, 2 July 1883, from Cole to the Government of India. Home Proceedings, Archaeology, July 1883, No. 11, Part A. *NAI.*
87. Letter No. 138, dated Shimla, 2 July 1883, from Cole to the Government of India.
88. Letter No. 240, dated Hospet, 16 April 1886, from Burgess to the Chief Secretary to the Government of Madras. Home Proceedings, Archaeology and the Conservation of Ancient Monuments July 1886, No. 10, Part A. *NAI.*
89. Letter No. 240, dated Hospet, 16 April 1886, from Burgess to the Chief Secretary to the Government of Madras.
90. Letter No. 0-80, dated Ootacamund, 19 May 1886 from C. Bidie to the Chief Secretary to the Government of Madras. Home Proceedings, Archaeology and the Conservation of Ancient Monuments, July 1886, No. 10, Part A. *NAI.*
91. Order passed by the Governor-in Council, Madras. Home Proceedings, Archaeology and the Conservation of Ancient Monuments, July 1886, No. 10, Part A. *NAI.*
92. Letter No. 224, dated Shimla, 20 July 1886, from A.P. MacDonnell, Officiating Secretary to the Government of India to the Director General of the Archaeological Survey of India. Home Proceedings, Archaeology and the Conservation of Ancient Monuments, July 1886, No. 11, Part A. *NAI.*

7

Buddhism, Archaeology, and the Nation: Nagarjunakonda (1926–2006)

One of the intriguing aspects of Indian Buddhism is that its symbolic importance has always been in much greater proportion to the number of practising Buddhists in the subcontinent. The doctrines, followers, and patrons of this religion have consistently enjoyed a privileged position in the historiography of ancient India, both in colonial as well as post-colonial discourse. One of the reasons why Buddhism has consistently attracted more interest than any other Indic religion is the fact that it spread far beyond the subcontinent, and had a major cultural impact on many regions of Asia.[1] In the colonial period, Buddhism came to be considered by many European historians and archaeologists as the best of all non-Christian religions, and there was a romanticization of its rationalism and egalitarian social ethos.[2]

After Indian independence, these factors coalesced with another important one—the importance of non-violence in the Indian freedom struggle. As a result, Buddhism retained an importance not only in interpretations of the Indian past, but also in assuming an iconic position in representations of the Indian nation. Apart from the conversions of the members of the Scheduled Castes to this religion, associated most closely with the leadership of B. R. Ambedkar, Buddhism's ideas and ideals also found strong support among other nationalist leaders such as Jawaharlal Nehru. This explains the adoption of the Aśokan Sarnath capital as the symbol of the Indian nation and the *cakra* as the central symbol of the national flag. Thus, in independent India, there was not merely a retention, but a strengthening of a vision of ancient India that privileged Buddhism (especially at the political level), along with its chief patron Aśoka and the ideal of *ahiṁsā*. This highly influential understanding of the ancient Indian past in which Buddhism was assigned an exalted place had an important impact on archaeological and conservation policies, both in colonial as well as independent India, and that is the focus of this chapter, albeit in the context of a specific important site, namely Nagarjunakonda.

Situated on the banks of the river Krishna and surrounded on three sides by offshoots of the Nallamalai hills, Nagarjunakonda (in Guntur district, Andhra Pradesh, India) was a 15 sq km site rich in remains ranging from the prehistoric to the medieval periods (Figure 7.1). In spite of its long history and variegated religious landscape, the site was especially celebrated for Buddhist remains of the 3rd and 4th centuries, when it was known as Vijayapurī, capital of the Ikṣvāku dynasty (Figures 7.2 and 7.3). Apart from the vast amount of data generated by excavations here, Nagarjunakonda is also important because it offers excellent material for a study of the presuppositions and agendas of archaeological research in pre-colonial and independent India.

The history of the exploration, excavation, documentation and interpretation of the remains at this site reveals several distinct phases. Discovered in 1926 by A. R. Saraswati (Assistant to the Archaeological Superintendent for Epigraphy), it was excavated in early 1927 by Muhammad Hamid Kuraishi and subsequently by A. H. Longhurst.[3] Longhurst's report represents the first stage in the interpretation of Nagarjunakonda, one in which it was seen essentially as a Buddhist site.[4] The second series of excavations were conducted by T. N. Ramachandran in 1938. The results, published many years later in 1953, for the first time drew attention to the many Hindu temples in the early historic city.[5] This report situated Nagarjunakonda within a framework dominated by regional history and the sentiment of regional pride.

In the 1950s, during the hey-day of Nehruvian socialism with its emphasis on heavy industry and big dams, plans for building a massive irrigation dam across the Krishna river were drawn up. A major implication of these plans was that once the dam became functional, the spectacular site of Nagarjunakonda would be permanently drowned in the river waters. This led the Archaeological Survey of India (hereafter ASI) to initiate a massive

Figure 7.1
View of the excavated Buddhist remains at Nagarjunakonda

Courtesy: Archaeological Survey of India

Figure 7.2
Site of the mahācaitya before excavation

Courtesy: Archaeological Survey of India

Figure 7.3
The mahācaitya, reconstructed on Nagarjunakonda hill

Source: Author

project of exploration, excavation and documentation. Before the valley was turned into a gigantic lake, about 136 new structures and structural complexes were unearthed; nine of the most important structures were transplanted and rebuilt on top of the Nagarjunakonda hill and on the banks of the reservoir; smaller-scale replicas of 14 other structures were made. This project is unique in the history of archaeological research and conservation in India. The first part of the report of the 1954–1960 excavations, published in 1975, focused on the site's prehistoric and megalithic remains.[6] The second part, published as recently as 2006, was suffused with the sentiment of national pride, with frequent, rather florid eulogies of the site and of the Ikṣvāku dynasty.[7] The report offers a consolidated view of the early historic remains, artefacts, and inscriptions of the ancient 'city of victory'.

This chapter uses hitherto unexamined archival sources to discuss two important moments in the modern history of Nagarjunakonda. The first comprises the discovery and early interpretations of the site in colonial times, and how these intersected with the issue of the appropriate repository of the Buddhist relics found here. The second moment is located in post-independence times and touches on the place of Buddhism in the nationalist imagination, archaeological policy, and the conflict between the preservation of the ancient historical heritage of India and the development concerns of the new Indian nation.

The Announcement of the Discoveries at Nagarjunakonda

In early February 1927, John Marshall, Director General of the ASI received a short letter from Muhammad Hamid Kuraishi, officiating Superintendent with the Southern Circle of the ASI. It said:

> You will be glad to know that I have discovered at Nagarjunikonda a number of stupas and Monasteries, two Apsidal chaityas and some 20 long Brahmi inscriptions all belonging to the 2nd–3rd century AD. Minor antiquities such as seals and coins or Relics have not been coming forth. But I have found two bricks which bear clear marks or symbols somewhat similar to those discovered by Mr. Yazdani sometime back.[8]

The name of the site clearly did not ring a bell because a week later, Marshall penned the following note on the letter: 'Please let me know

Figure 7.4
Kuraishi's letter announcing his discoveries and John Marshall's note

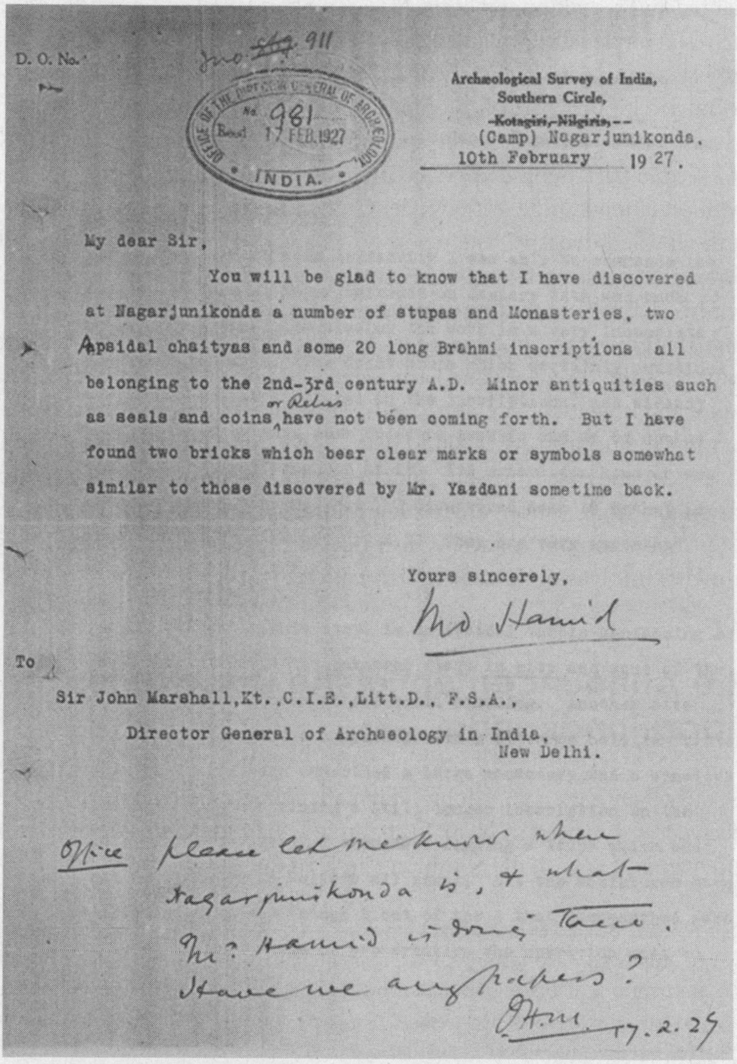

D. O. No. ~~Jno 54~~ 911

OFFICE OF THE DIRECTOR GENERAL OF ARCHAEOLOGY
No. 981
Recd 17 FEB.1927
INDIA.

Archæological Survey of India,
Southern Circle,
~~Kotagiri, Nilgiris,~~
(Camp) Nagarjunikonda,
10th February 1927.

My dear Sir,

You will be glad to know that I have discovered at Nagarjunikonda a number of stupas and Monasteries, two Apsidal chaityas and some 20 long Brahmi inscriptions all belonging to the 2nd-3rd century A.D. Minor antiquities such as seals and coins or Relics have not been coming forth. But I have found two bricks which bear clear marks or symbols somewhat similar to those discovered by Mr. Yazdani sometime back.

Yours sincerely,
Md Hamid

To

Sir John Marshall, Kt., C.I.E., Litt.D., F.S.A.,
Director General of Archaeology in India,
New Delhi.

Office please let me know where Nagarjunikonda is, & what Mr. Hamid is doing there. Have we any papers?
JHM 17.2.27

Courtesy: Archaeological Survey of India

where Nagarjunikonda is and what is Mr. Hamid doing there. Have we any papers?'[9] (See Figure 7.4.)

Before going on leave in 1926, A. H. Longhurst, Superintending Archaeologist of the Southern Circle had directed Kuraishi to carry out some trial excavations at Alluru and Gummadidurru in Kistna district and Nagarjunakonda in Guntur district. Kuraishi had gone to Nagarjunakonda with high hopes. He was accompanied by the epigraphist Hiranand Shastri, who was hopeful (because of certain inscriptional references) that they would be able to locate the *caitya* connected with the corporeal relics of the Buddha.[10] Unfortunately, the owner of the land was uncooperative and withheld permission to dig. The trial excavations eventually took place between 24 January and 12 February 1927 and Kuraishi had to sorrowfully leave the work incomplete. However, as he pointed out, there was enough evidence to show the importance of the place—in fact, he hoped that it might well rival Hampi, the site of the capital of the great Vijayanagara empire.

Marshall swiftly obtained some information about the sites that Kuraishi was busy with and realized their importance. This is clear from the congratulatory telegram he shot off to him soon after:

> Hearty congratulations on your important finds at Nagarjunikonda Alluru and Gummadidurru... Please take measures to protect all sites and antiquities found stop Orders will issue later regarding disposal of latter stop Meanwhile everything should be retained in your charge carefully marked and handed over with full descriptive lists to Mr. Longhurst stop Kindly furnish duplicate of lists to me and report fully as to measures taken and proprietorship of three sites.[11]

The realization of the importance of the site led to a conflict within the Southern Circle of the ASI. Kuraishi sent in a preliminary report on the trial excavations at the sites of Alluru, Gummadidurru and Nagarjunakonda and wanted to publish a more detailed Memoir on the subject. He wrote to Longhurst, requesting the preparation of a site map and photographs that had been taken during the excavations. Longhurst curtly told him that there was no need for him to include Nagarjunakonda in the Memoir, as the excavations at that site were incomplete and that John Marshall had instructed him (Longhurst) to carry out further excavations there and that he (Longhurst) would write the report himself.[12] The turf war reached Marshall's door, and the Director General supported the idea of the publication of Kuraishi's report, provided it was edited and published in the annual report of the

ASI, not as a Memoir (since the excavations were incomplete).[13] In the conflict between an Indian subordinate and a British superior, Marshall unambiguously supported the former.[14] He was very sharp and critical of the piece written by Longhurst for the 1926–1927 report of the ASI, describing it as below standard and telling him that because of this, he was publishing Kuraishi's account instead. Marshall also expressed the hope that in his report for the next year, Longhurst should discuss his own work at the sites (he had subsequently taken up excavations there), and should not poach on Kuraishi's work.[15]

Apart from internal conflicts within the ASI about who should get credit for the Nagarjunakonda finds, two major problems at this stage were how to protect the ancient remains on the 13 acres of land on which the discoveries had been made, and the place of deposit of the antiquities and relics.[16] The land was declared protected under section 5 of the Ancient Monuments Preservation Act of 1904.[17] The owner had been difficult—he had apparently demanded that the antiquities from the site should be kept in a museum connected with Andhra University so that he could have the opportunity of seeing them whenever he felt like. The problem was that there was no museum attached to the University![18] The Southern circle of the ASI was of the view that the artefacts found at the site should be kept at the site itself till the land was acquired, and then perhaps sent off to the Madras Museum. Marshall was keen that the collection be kept together and that the tragedy of dispersal, which had happened at Amaravati, be avoided.[19] The Indian Museum, Calcutta was keen to acquire some of the sculptures and Marshall was sympathetic to their request.[20] Alarm bells were set off when Longhurst reported an attempt to steal some sculptures and inscribed pillars and whisk them off to France, and arrangements were swiftly made for a watchman at the site.[21] Throughout, Marshall expressed keen interest in the finds and sought information about the work at the site and about its antiquities.

The question of where the material unearthed at these sites should be deposited also excited some public interest and stirred up the sentiment of Andhra pride. An article dated 5 April 1928 published in *Swarajya* newspaper, observed, with reference to Marshall's announcement of the discoveries of the Buddhist remains at Gummadidurru, that the ancient treasures of Andhra should be kept in Andhra itself and that it was alarming that the Archaeological Department of Madras was thinking of sending them off to far off Calcutta. These remains should be kept at Bezwada to form the nucleus of an Andhra museum, or failing that, sent to the Madras Museum:

> We are sure the Andhra public will make their voice felt and see that the sentiments of the people are respected in this matter.[22]

One of the most sensitive issues was that of the relics that had been found at Nagarjunakonda in the *stūpa* known as the *mahācaitya*. These had been discovered by Longhurst and are described in his preliminary report. There was a pea-sized bone fragment in a tiny round gold box; this had been placed in a silver *stūpa*-shaped receptacle (which was very corroded when found) with some gold flowers, pearls, and garnets; this in turn had been placed inside a red earthenware pot along with a few white and coloured crystal beads (Figure 7.5).[23] Longhurst was aware of the fact that the relics were 'a matter of some political importance'.[24] In 1928, Marshall relinquished charge to write up his monographs and Harold Hargreaves officiated as Director General between March 1928–1931. When it came to the issue of the announcement of the dramatic discovery of the Nagarjunakonda finds, especially the relics, it was Hargreaves who called the shots. In fact, for a long time, the relics issue was carefully kept under wraps.

Figure 7.5
Reliquary and relics found in the mahācaitya

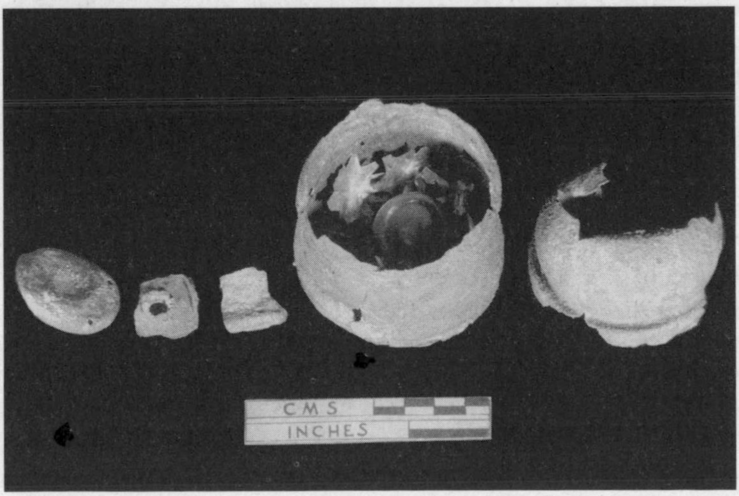

Courtesy: Archaeological Survey of India

There was a major difference of opinion and conflict between Longhurst and Hargreaves about where the announcement of the discoveries should be made and this conflict reflects the changing perspectives within the ASI. Longhurst reported to Hargreaves that he had sent a brief account of 'my discovery' to the *Illustrated London News* and to the noted Dutch Sanskritist and epigraphist J. Ph. Vogel 'so that scholars in Europe may know of the discovery'.[25] The reply was a curt telegram telling him to stop any such publication.[26] In 1924, Marshall had announced the discovery of the Indus civilization in the *Illustrated London News*. But now this route of publicizing a major archaeological discovery in India was vetoed on the grounds that the discovery must first be published in a publication of the ASI, or in an Indian newspaper. According to Hargreaves, doing otherwise went against clear government policy and was bound to arouse objections in the Legislative Assembly.[27] Longhurst, on the other hand, was keen on creating a splash in the European press and initially refused to comply with the instructions communicated to him. Finally, confronted with the threat of disciplinary action, he was obliged to fall in line and instructed the *Illustrated London News* not to publish his piece.[28]

Buddha relics were hot news and the *Illustrated London News* was desperate to carry the story, but their plea for permission to do so elicited a terse reply in the negative from the Archaeological Department.[29] When the editor pressed the issue, asking for reasons for the denial of permission, Hargreaves replied that according to the Government of India orders, officers of the ASI were not allowed to publish the results of their research in any journal other than that of the ASI without government approval.[30] The *Illustrated London News* then sought permission to publish just the story of the Buddha relics, promising to carry an acknowledgment to the Government of India and the Director General of the ASI, but permission for this too was denied.[31]

Ultimately, with Longhurst fretting and fuming at the delay, the story of the discovery of the Nagarjunakonda relics was published in the *Hindustan Times* and the *Anand Bazar Patrika* on 31 January 1930, over a year after they had been discovered.[32] The story was essentially an official communiqué drafted by Hargreaves and moderately edited by Longhurst. In the piece, Nagarjunakjonda was presented as a Buddhist site and the discovery of 'an authentic relic' of the Buddha was highlighted. The relics had completely overshadowed the other remains that had been found at the site. The names of the Indian officers A. R. Saraswati (who had discovered the site) and Muhammad Hamid Kuraishi (who had first excavated there) were not mentioned. Hargreaves and Longhurst got all the credit for the exciting discoveries at Nagarjunakonda.

The bone relic itself was initially kept in Longhurst's office safe and was subsequently transferred to a locker in the Imperial Bank of India in Madras.[33] But it was recognized that what was to be done with the relic was not a matter that could be left to the judgement of archaeologists. Higher-level government agencies and national sentiment were involved.

The Politics of Relics

In the early 1930s, with the bone relic safe in the bank vault in Madras, the Government of India narrowed down its options to three—to keep the Nagarjunakonda relics at the site itself, to send them to a Ceylonese vihāra (monastery) at Kelaniya near Columbo, or to hand them to the Maha Bodhi Society. The latter two had applied for the relics to the Viceroy. The Madras Government and the ASI were of the view that the ancient remains should be kept in a site museum at Nagarjunakonda itself and that the place should be made more accessible to visitors by road.[34] But this did not apply to the relics, which were recognized as antiquities of an entirely different order.

The claims of the Ceylonese vihāra were put forward in early 1930, soon after the announcement and were supported by the Governor of Ceylon, which addressed the Governor of Madras on the subject:

> I have the honour to enclose a copy of a letter... addressed to me by the Venerable Mapitigama Dhammarakkhitta, incumbent of the Buddhist Vihara at Kelaniya, near Colombo. I attach, in original, the documents which accompanied his letter...The writer of the letter asks me to approach the proper authority and to represent the fervent hope of Ceylon Buddhists that it may be possible to obtain from India, for preservation in the Kelaniya Temple, the relic of the Buddha recently discovered at Nagarjunikonda. The letter was handed to me by two very distinguished Buddhist laymen, who may be regarded as exponents of Buddhist opinion among the Low-country Sinhalese and the Kandyans respectively. They assured me that Buddhists throughout the Island would be very grateful for the gift of this relic, and would regard the Kelaniya Temple as eminently suitable for its custody. I understand that there have been precedents of such presentations of relics discovered in India to Buddhist communities outside India, and I venture therefore to submit the request to Your Excellency with an expression of my support.[35]

The Maha Bodhi Society jumped into the fray at a later stage, in mid-1932:

> We have learnt with great pleasure that recently a number of Buddha's relics were discovered at Nagarjunikonda. As a Buddhist society which is interested in the preservation of the sacred body relics of Lord Buddha, we are writing to request you to be so good as to obtain the same for our Society. We have already received a number of valuable relics from the Government of India, namely the Bhattiprolu relic at present safely enshrined at the Calcutta Vihara and the Taxila relics enshrined in the Mulagandhkuti Vihara, Benaras. As you are aware relics of Lord Buddha are highly sacred to the Buddhists and are objects of worship, *it therefore wounds the feelings of the Buddhists to see them exhibited in museums for ordinary visitors* (emphasis added). As our Society has already made arrangements to preserve them in a proper manner, we hope you will be graciously pleased to obtain these relics and present them to Mulagandhakuti Vihara where they will be placed for worship along with other relics presented by the Government of India.[36]

It is interesting to note that although this formal application for the relic from the Maha Bodhi Society came in 1932, the Society's candidature for custody of the relic had been an issue of discussion within the Government of India from 1930 onwards and seems to have been mooted by Hargreaves, officiating Director General of the ASI. In that year, Hargreaves had been asked for his opinion on where the Nagararjunakonda bone relic should be kept. He expressed the view that since the Ceylonese vihāra was a living Buddhist monument, and that since Hindus did not worship the Buddha (although they acknowledged him as an *avatāra* of Viṣṇu), the request of the Ceylonese vihāra was reasonable. Nevertheless, in view of the ideas expressed in the legislative assembly, where the issue had apparently been raised on 17 February 1930, it would not be politic to send relics out of the country. Hargreaves suggested that the vihāra being built at Sarnath by 'Indian Buddhists' was the best option. He also drew attention to the fact that the government had already presented some relics from Taxila to that establishment. He pointed out that the completion of the temple was delayed due to the lack of funds, and that if pious Buddhists were to find out that a relic of the Buddha was going to be re-enshrined in the temple, the supply of funds would increase enormously.[37]

However, it was not only Buddhist sentiment, but also Hindu sentiment and Indian nationalist sentiment that were perceived to be involved. Hargreaves suggested that Hindu opinion on the matter would probably be satisfied by keeping the relics in the country. G. S. Bajpai

(Secretary to the Government of India in the Department of Education, Health and Lands) agreed with Hargreaves' view, pointing out 'that the sending of these relics even to Ceylon would raise a storm in this country'. He added that 'it is not so much a question of religion as a nascent national sentiment that what historically belongs to India should remain in India' and that a Resolution against sending historical remains in India to other countries had been passed in the Assembly in 1928. Bajpai asked the Director General of the ASI if he could suggest names of individuals and institutions in India from whom the government could solicit views on the matter of the relic.[38] The earlier track record of the government was also recapitulated, namely that the relics found at Taxila had been presented by John Marshall to a Buddhist temple in Ceylon in 1916. Well before that, certain other relics had been presented to the King of Siam in 1898, who had distributed them in his own country and to Burma, Ceylon and Japan. The Government of India consulted the Bengal government and through them the Bengal Buddhist Association and Maha Bodhi Society in Calcutta, as well as the Madras Government.

That there was an important distinction between regular antiquities and relics was also underlined by an official named J. H. Page, who suggested that while the antiquities of Nagarjunakonda should be kept in a site museum, which should be made accessible by the building of a motorable road, the bone relic should be handed over to a living Buddhist shrine.[39] Also in question was whether the relic was an authentic corporeal relic of the Buddha; some doubts had been raised on this point by Daya Ram Sahni, who had taken over as Director General of the ASI in July 1931.[40] In fact, the government was also inclined to test the waters of public opinion (this was the suggestion of Fazl Husain, member of the Viceroy's Executive Council in charge of archaeology) by planting the story of the discovery of the relic in certain newspapers and then taking note of the reactions. Sahni did, in fact, prepare such a note, but it was not published.[41] He himself approved of the idea of handing the relic over to the Maha Bodhi Society on the grounds that such a decision would be 'received with acclamation all over the country'. He suggested that a modern silver replica of the original silver casket should also be made and presented. He also pointed out that it was quite customary to make ceremonial presentations of Buddhist relics on behalf of the Viceroy, and that the most appropriate occasion to present the Nagarjunakonda relic to the Mulagandhakuti Vihara would be in December 1932, on the occasion of the celebration of its first anniversary. 'Buddhists from distant countries are expected to attend this anniversary and will carry news of this valuable gift to their brotherhood.'[42]

Two successive Director Generals of the ASI had strongly endorsed the idea of handing the relic over to the Maha Bodhi Society and their arguments coincided with the views of the government.

The final decision was communicated to the Government of Ceylon:

> ... after very careful consideration, the Government of India have decided to present the Buddha relic discovered at Nagarjunakonda in the Madras Presidency to the Mulagandhakuti Vihara at Sarnath, Benares. In view of the immemorial sanctity of Sarnath as one of the four principal places of Buddhist pilgrimage, it was thought that this decision would probably be popular with Buddhists throughout the world.[43]

The ASI also transferred to the Society a park that they had laid out around the Mulagandhakuti Vihara.[44]

This is how the antiquities from the site of Nagarjunakonda remained in a site museum that was built for them, but the bone relic was sent off to the Mulagandhakuti Vihara in Sarnath. The ultimate transfer of the Nagarjunakonda relic to this temple has to be seen against the larger background of the history of relic diplomacy in India and decisions made by the colonial state on what was the most appropriate kind of place to house such finds made by archaeologists. It is also connected with the history of Anagarika Dharmapala and the Maha Bodhi Society, their efforts to establish control over the sacred Buddhist places and to create a monumental repository of relics in the Mulagandhakuti Vihara at Sarnath. It is to this aspect that we now turn.

The Transfer of the Nagarjunakonda Relic to Mulagandhakuti Vihara

The Mulagandhakuṭi Vihara (literally 'the monastery of the principal scented chamber') at Isipatana in Sarnath, the celebrated site of the Buddha's first sermon, was inaugurated on 11 November 1931 (Figure 7.6). *Maha Bodhi*, the journal of the Maha Bodhi Society described that day as 'preeminent in the History of Buddhism—perhaps of the world.'[45] There were repeated references to the revival of Buddhism at this place, 800 years after Muhammad Ghori's armies had swept across India. The ceremonies had a marked cosmopolitan air, with participants, patrons and representatives from various parts of India, Ceylon, Burma, Tibet, China, Japan and Europe. The highlight of the ceremonials was the presentation of a relic from the Dharmarājika *stūpa*

Figure 7.6
Mulagandhakuti Vihara, Sarnath

Source: Author

at Taxila by the Government of India through Daya Ram Sahni, Director General of the ASI.

An ailing Devamitta Dhammapala (the name assumed by Anagarika Dharmapala after he donned the monk's robes) was present. A message of support from the Hindu Mahasabha was read out on the occasion. Jawaharlal Nehru was there, along with this wife and sisters, and he presented the national flag to the Vihara as a goodwill gesture from the Congress Working Committee. The president of the Maha Bodhi Society received the Taxila relic from Sahni, declaring that the merit rising out of the ceremony establishing the Vihara should be transferred to all beings, and expressed a hope for the long life of Dhammapala. Dhammapala had brought three saplings from Anuradhapura to be planted near the temple—one was planted by himself, another by Sahni, and the third by two monks from Ceylon. The Taxila relic was enshrined by Dhammapala in the vault of the temple on 13 November. Dhammapala's speech on the occasion explains the importance of this temple. He talked about how it had been his long-cherished dream to see Holy Isipatana in Buddhist hands and how this dream had now been fulfilled.[46]

The Maha Bodhi Society had a long-term involvement in conserving and developing Buddhist sacred places in India. The Society had an archaeological section, which exhorted the public to supply information about any Buddhist monuments or ruins located in their locality. It was in response to the Society's petition that the Maharaja of Nepal had sanctioned Rs. 20,000 for 'improving' Lumbini. Many pages of the Society's journal were often filled with accounts of the discoveries made in the course of the exploration and excavations at sacred sites, the pathetic conditions there, and the need to do something about this. Conservation was linked to control. An article by Bhikkhu Ottama of Burma, published in *Maha Bodhi* in 1932, thanked Alexander Cunningham and John Marshall for discovering the Buddhist relics at many ancient sites and urged that the chief Buddhist sacred places should be handed over to Buddhists so that they could be restored and developed for devout pilgrims.[47] The most well-known of the Society's attempts to establish control over such places was its attempt to stake its right to control the Maha Bodhi temple.[48] But this was part of the Society's larger agenda of extending its control over *all* the major sacred places of Buddhism in India.

The first anniversary of the opening of the Mulagandhakuti Vihara was scheduled to take place in the winter of 1932. The *Maha Bodhi* journal announced the forthcoming festivities and invited Buddhists from all over the world to come and participate. It was also announced that on the occasion, the Taxila relic, which had been kept enshrined at Taxila for 20 centuries, would be displayed for worship. The festivities were finally held on 27–29 December 1932, and the highlight of the events of the first day was the presentation of a corporeal relic, supposedly of the Buddha, found at Nagarjunakonda. Devamitta Dhammapala was not there because he was ill, but he sent a message.

The stamp of pan-Buddhist internationalism was writ large on the event.[49] The gifts to the temple included a huge brass-gilded bell presented by the United Buddhist Society of Japan and a beautiful drum gifted by a Japanese priest. The bell contained inscriptions in Japanese and Sanskrit, symbolizing the meeting of the cultures of India and Japan. A gold-gilded image of the Buddha was presented by an official from Darjeeling. But the most spectacular gift was the one made by the Government of India—the Nagarjunakonda bone relic. The relic was ceremonially presented to the temple on behalf of the Viceroy of India, the Earl of Willingdon, by Daya Ram Sahni, the Director General of the ASI.[50] The Maha Bodhi Society had initially invited Fazl-i-Husain, member of the Viceroy's Executive Council in charge of archaeology; he could not attend and had deputed Sahni to take his place. In his address to the gathering on 27 December, Sahni gave a brief account of the Nagarjunakonda excavations and the inscriptions found at the site, and described the *mahācaitya* where relic had been found. What was especially important in his address was his certifying before the devout gathering (on the basis of inscriptions found at the site) that the bone relic was an *authentic* corporeal relic of the Buddha.

The relic was handed over by Sahni to a Sinhalese high priest, who carried it on his head in a procession from the Sarnath site museum around the Dhamekh stupa to the temple.[51] After three circumambulations of the temple, it was taken inside to a strong room, where it was displayed for worship in a glass case for three days, and we were told that thousands of people turned up for *darśana*. Devamitta Dhammapala's message was read out by Pandit Sheo Narain (the Collector of Banaras), who added that Sahni's name would go down in history:

> ... the name of Mr Sahni will go down to posterity when the history of the revival of Buddhism is written. Mr. Sahni as an excavator at Sarnath, as a Superintendent of (the) Archaeological circle and now Director General of Archaeology will be remembered by generations to come as a person of learning, scholarship and research, a gentleman who always has been taking keen interest in Buddhistic matters and to whose labours and zeal (the) Maha Bodhi Society is deeply indebted.[52]

Various lectures were delivered, on issues ranging from how the Buddha's *dhamma* would save a decadent world, the tenets of Tibetan Buddhism, and 'the burning question of the day'—Buddhism and untouchability.[53]

The first anniversary celebrations at Mulagandhakuti Vihara and the celebration of the receipt of the Nagarjunakonda relic were overshadowed by the death of Devamitta Dhammapala a few months later on 29 April 1933 (Figure 7.7). The importance of the temple in the agenda of the Maha Bodhi Society is evident from the fact that one portion of his corporeal relics was, according to his wishes, enshrined in this very temple.[54] This temple was visualized as becoming a receptacle of relics from major Buddhist sites and more so, as a major international centre of Buddhism.[55] A strong pan-Buddhist internationalism was evident in the various activities there, including the painting of frescoes on the temple walls by the well-known Japanese artist Kosetsu Nosu.

It may be noted that on the occasion of the second anniversary of the establishment of the Mulagandhakuti Vihara (celebrated between 11–13 November 1933), the Nagarjunakonda relic was once again carried out in an international procession and venerated. Rahul Sankrityayan presided

Figure 7.7
Statue of Anagarika Dharmapala outside Mulagandhakuti Vihara, Sarnath

Source: Author

over the anniversary meeting in the temple hall, and Jawaharlal Nehru, who happened to be at Sarnath at the time, also attended. Further, during the Buddhist conference held on 13 November in the Vihara hall, Dharma Aditya Dharmacharyya, General Secretary of the All-India Buddhist Conference, mooted the idea of an international university at Sarnath. This idea was greeted with great enthusiasm by many other speakers, although one M. M. Barua of Chittagong suggested that in spite of the fact that the Buddhists were poor, if they concerted together, they could easily create a Nalanda University within a few years.[56] In fact, several of those present gave in their donations for the foundation of a Buddhist University. In this airing of the idea of an international university at Sarnath, we see a precursor of the idea of an international university of a different kind recently established at Nalanda.

The Post-1947 Issue: Heritage versus Development

In independent India, Nagarjunakonda became the centre of an entirely different issue with much larger ramifications. The economic agenda of the new India involved an emphasis on heavy industry and big dams such as Bhakra Nangal, Damodar, Hirakud, and Nagarjunasagar. Dams symbolized 'the nation's will to march forward with strength, determination and courage'.[57] The Nagarjunasagar dam was supposed to be built across the river Krishna. What made this project different from others was that the dam would completely destroy what had come to be widely recognized by then as an extremely important and valuable archaeological site. During the time that the issue was under consideration, various options were aired and considered—to build the dam somewhere else, walling in the ruins by building a subsidiary dam, and the relocation of the historical monuments.[58] The larger context of what was essentially a development versus heritage issue included subsidiary issues such as the role of museums in independent India.

Not surprisingly, the ministry of Irrigation and Power had a perspective that was different from that of the Ministry of Education and the ASI. The irrigation project was estimated as having the potential to provide water for vast tracts of parched land.

> Dead monuments are a great heritage and we should not let them get perpetually buried but of greater importance is the feeding of the hungry millions of this area. Are we going to let the dead starve the living?[59]

The ASI pointed out that the Ministry of Irrigation and Power was not being helpful and had not understood the international importance of the site. The then Director General M. S. Vats suggested that a committee, of which he should be a member, should review the whole issue and see whether it was possible to find an alternative location for the dam.[60] The technical committee of engineers set up by the Planning Commission had said no other site was possible. But the Ministry of Education agreed with the ASI that the engineers had not properly appreciated the historical importance of the site and agreed that an expert committee should be set up. In view of the conflict between the Education and Irrigation/Power ministries, the former asked for a review of the whole matter by a committee set up by the Planning Commission.[61] In the meantime, at a meeting of the Central Advisory Board of Archaeology, Hiren Mukherjee made a strong plea for the saving of the Nagarjunakonda site, arguing that the submergence of the site would be a 'disaster of the first magnitude to the cultural heritage of the country'.[62]

In 1954, it was decided to send a joint inspection to the site, including representatives of the Department of Archaeology, Government of Hyderabad, Andhra Planning Commission, and the Ministry of Irrigation and Power. It was also agreed that the views of the governments of Hyderabad and Madras states should be ascertained. Ultimately, the engineers won the battle, with the committee concluding that no other site was possible for the dam.[63]

Prime Minister Nehru took great personal interest in this problem. In his speech while laying the foundation stone of the Nagarjunasagar dam on 10 December 1955, he had described it as one of the greatest temples of modern India. But he was keenly aware of the heavy price that would have to be paid for building this temple. The idea of a massive excavation project before the dam became operational, and that of salvaging the structures, had been in the air for many years and met the Prime Minister's approval, and he gave instructions to this effect immediately after laying the foundation stone of the irrigation project.[64] In fact, so seized of the matter was Nehru that the same evening, he shot off a lengthy confidential note on the subject to Maulana Azad, the Education minister, emphasizing the importance of the site, and the measures that must be taken to save as much as could be saved.

> This morning I performed the ceremony of laying the foundation-stone of the great dam of Nagarjuna Sagar... Afterwards, I went to the site of the excavations of the ancient cities of Sri Parvat and Vijayapuri. Nearly all this vast area is going to be submerged when the dam is built and which will

> be called the Nagarjuna Sagar. This site of excavations is one of the most important and vital in India. The idea that this place, where so much of our ancient history and culture lie hidden under the earth, should be lost forever under the new lake has distressed me greatly. Yet the choice had to be made for the sake of the needs of today and tomorrow.[65]

It should be noted that during the deliberations about the issue of the dam and the site, the latter was usually discussed as one of the most important Buddhist sites in India, associated with Nagarjuna, the founder of the Mādhyamika school. (It is interesting to note that the dam was also named after him.) The sentiments of Buddhists were often also alluded to. This is how Nehru saw it too—he took special note of the fact that a Buddha relic had been found at the site and that the place was an international centre of Buddhism in ancient times.[66]

Once the decision was made to go ahead with the dam and to initiate a massive excavation project before the submergence of the site, there was the problem of convincing the farmers to agree to the excavations, failing which, it would become necessary to acquire the land.[67] Again at Nehru's instance, it was decided to use quick tactful persuasion rather than go in for lengthy legal processes involving land acquisition, and the Prime Minister suggested that emergency provisions should be invoked wherever necessary, given the urgency of the excavation plan.

Three committees were set up to look into various aspects of the ancient site. One was an Expert Committee, set up at the express instructions of Nehru: It was mooted in December 1955 and officially set up on 14 March 1956, to look into the location of the Nagarjunakonda museum and to look at the feasibility of moving some of the monuments to the top of the hill or to another site altogether, where they would be well above the water level.[68] It was to include the Secretary of the Ministry of Education (as chairman), the Chief Architect of the CPWD, an engineer of the Andhra government with a rank not lower than that of Superintending Engineer, the Principal of the J. J. School of Art Bombay, and the Director General of the ASI (A. Ghosh). The Government of Bombay suggested the inclusion of H. D. Sankalia, Director of Deccan College, Poona in place of the Principal of the J. J. School of Art, on the grounds that the need of the hour was a person who had experience of archaeological excavations and a deep interest in history.[69] The government response was that the Director General, ASI, would take care of that aspect, and that the Principal of the School of art was required to give advice on the preparation of models. The committee swung into action and swiftly gave its recommendations. These included the preparation of a scale reproduction on the hill of the entire site, showing the location of the various monuments; the transplantation of selected monuments; and the construction of scale models of some of the most important ones.[70] The recommendations of this expert committee were accepted. Jafar Ali, the chief engineer of the Nagarjunasagar dam was also co-opted into the committee in May, on A. Ghosh's suggestion.

There were two other committees that were supposed to deal with other aspects of the gigantic dual irrigation-cum-conservation project. A Policy Committee was enjoined to ascertain whether the hill to be converted into an island as a result of the irrigation project would be able to withstand the water pressure. Its answer was in the affirmative.[71] There was also a coordination committee set up in 1957—its function was to coordinate the activities of the Nagarjunasagar project and the Nagarjunakonda excavation projects.[72]

The project presented major challenges for the ASI and these had to be dealt with by making special provisions. A special branch of the ASI was established at the site in 1954 and R. Subrahmanyam was place in charge of operations as Superintendent, Department of Archaeology, Nagarjunakonda Excavation Project. It was known that the area would be submerged by early 1960 at the latest, when the dam became functional, and the archaeological investigations, once initiated, went on with extraordinary gusto.[73] It was also clear that there was a need to appoint a senior, experienced archaeologist as a special officer for a period of three years. At the recommendation of A. Ghosh, T. N. Ramachandran (Joint Director General, ASI) was brought in 1958. He was familiar with the site as he had excavated it in 1931, and it was expected that Ramachandran would write up the report of the excavations within the next two years.

It should be noted that as Nagarjunakonda was an isolated site and the work was envisaged as lasting several years, all kinds of provisions had to be made for the staff involved in the dam-building and excavation activities.[74] Schools and medical facilities had to be provided. The hill-top that would house some of the transplanted monuments had to be meticulously landscaped and planned. Funds for the project were to be divided according to the following formula—the cost of the excavations was to be borne by the ASI; funds for housing and other amenities, removal of the monuments, building of the site museum, and so on, were to be provided by the Nagarjunasagar irrigation project (subject to an upper limit of Rs. 600,000).[75] Monthly progress reports of the excavations were submitted by the archaeological team and there was both energy and urgency in the reports of the discoveries that were being made at a rapid rate. There were enormous technical problems related to the transplantation of the selected monuments, and the scale models that were to be built, and these had to be swiftly addressed. And all this went on under the pressure of constant scrutiny and pressure from several quarters. Several Members of Parliament took interest and the prime minister himself constantly urged that no expense should be spared in the excavation and conservation work. The idea of moving the museum and the monuments to the hill-top seems to have been Nehru's, and he personally monitored the progress, down to minute details such as the place of an exit door in the front wall of the museum.[76]

The Final Plea

And yet, as late as in 1957, when work at the site and on the dam had been well underway for many years, the issue became the subject of a lengthy debate in the Rajya Sabha, the Upper House of the Indian parliament. V. K. Dhage, an independent member of the Rajya Sabha, moved a private resolution on the need to take all steps to preserve the site of Nagarjunakonda.[77] The resolution was sent for comments to the Director General, ASI, who gave a resume of all that had transpired, pointed out that no other location was possible for the dam, and also gave a description of the massive scale of the ASI operations at the site and the steps being taken for the preservation of the antiquities. A day before the notice for this resolution was issued, a deputation of the Rajya Sabha members, including V. K. Dhage met the Minister of Education and suggested that a committee of MPs be set up to ascertain whether the government had made the right decision.[78] The bill was taken up for discussion in the Rajya Sabha and the government opposed it. It explained the whole sequence of events, the discussions and deliberations, and argued that that it was trying to protect as much as could be protected. Dhage pointed out that this site was important 'not only from the point of view of Buddhistic history but also from the point of view of Hindu history'. He pointed out that he was not asking for an abandoning of the irrigation project and made an impassioned plea that the site be saved by building a 500 ft. long wall around it *within* the dammed up waters of the Nagarjunasagar. He also pointed out that if preserved, the site would attract Buddhist pilgrims not only from India but also from all over the world. The income that would accrue to the government would more than compensate for the cost of building this wall. He argued that taking a utilitarian view on this matter would strike at the root of the Indian civilization:

> If we destroy this town (of Vijayapurī) I feel that we shall have marked a *kalank* (mark of disrepute) on our face that soon after independence we were so short-sighted that we were not able to save this city at all.

However, Kishen Chand, an MP from Andhra Pradesh, rose to speak soon after and pointed to the great benefits that would be brought to the farmers of Andhra with the building of the dam and that all other alternatives such as shifting the site of the dam or building the wall were impractical. B. K. P. Sinha, an MP from Bihar, observed that there were a huge number of historical monuments in India and one could not go on trying to save them all on sentimental grounds. Indian culture was not so fragile that it would perish with the destruction of this one monument:

> I therefore feel that, if it is necessary in the interests of the people of Andhra that a dam should be built and Nagarjunakonda submerged, let it be submerged. Let us take care of the living, and the dead shall be taken care of.

Nehru also spoke during the lengthy debate, reiterating the government's quandary and final decision, and declaring that the matter was non-negotiable at this stage. Dhage's resolution was rejected, but the Prime Minister suggested that two MPs (one from each House) should be added to the coordination committee. The following amended resolution was also moved, but defeated, after the debate:

> This House is of the opinion that Government should appoint a committee consisting of ten Members of Parliament and two others being persons possessing special knowledge of the subject to inquire into and report on measures to protect and preserve the town of Nagarjunakonda in view of its association with early Buddhist history and the development of various schools of Buddhistic thought.[79]

Nagarjunakonda had again been cast in the by now familiar, but very one-dimensional role, as a site whose importance rested entirely on its Buddhist connections.

During the 1950s and 1960s, there were parliamentary questions about the progress of the excavation and conservation work; details of the various phases of the irrigation project; whether the central government was considering taking over the irrigation project (irrigation was a state, not a central subject); the escalation of costs; the water requirements of neighbouring states; the building of the site museum; the number of times that the committees had met, new discoveries at the site; and the development of the site as a tourist centre.[80] During subsequent years, occasionally questions were asked about the conservation activities at the site and developing it as a tourism destination. More recently, there was also a parliamentary question about the publication of the excavation report.[81] The first volume had been published in 1975; the second volume was finally published in 2006, almost half a century after the excavations.

Conclusions

The modern history of the ancient site of Nagarjunakonda presents us with many unique features. The scale of excavation and conservation work at Nagarjunakonda was unprecedented and has not been equaled since. The amount of political involvement in the events at the site, including the interest of parliamentarians, was also unprecedented and remains unmatched. What is ironical is that the rich archaeological potential of the site came to light as part of the preparations for its death by drowning in the waters of the Nagarjunasagar dam.

The excavations at Nagarjunakonda brought to light a wide range of remains, ranging from the prehistoric to the medieval, revealing it to be a complex, multi-layered and multi-period site. However, the official correspondence emanating from different statesmen, ministries, and agencies, including the ASI, generally emphasized its early historic Buddhist connections as well as its fabled connections with the famous Buddhist scholar Nagarjuna. Nehru himself was acutely aware of the importance of the Buddhist heritage of India and of the Asian ramifications of this heritage, and his vision of India's ancient and modern history left an important imprint on the site.[82] This was not his personal vision alone, but there were other, different visions as well. This is revealed by the parliamentary debate on the national flag, which brought out the different understandings of the symbolism of the colours and the *cakra*. It is interesting to note that while there was a long parliamentary debate on the national flag, there was none on the national emblem—the lion capital of Aśoka's Sarnath pillar, with its strong Buddhist resonance.

Relic diplomacy was something that went on in both colonial and independent India. On 14 January 1949, Jawaharlal Nehru made an impassioned speech while receiving the Sanchi relics which had been sent back to India from the Victoria and Albert Museum, London, before handing them over to the Maha Bodhi Society.[83] He spoke of the Buddha as a messenger of peace and asserted that Buddhism had 'more than anything else laid the foundation of Greater India and established cultural unity of an abiding value between India and many parts of Asia'. In 1955, he presented some of these relics to Ceylon, expressing the hope that the gift would 'further cement the bond of friendship between these two neighbouring countries'.[84] The Indian government was not the only one engaging in relic diplomacy. In 1957, at a ceremony in Nalanda, Nehru received relics of the Chinese pilgrim Xuanzang (apparently a small part of his skull), along with some books about the Chinese pilgrim from the Dalai Lama on behalf of the Chinese government.[85] The full story of relic diplomacy in modern times still remains to be written.

Underlying Indian relic diplomacy was an acute awareness of the international ramifications of India as the homeland of Buddhism. Buddha Jayanti was apparently made a public holiday 'for certain international reasons'.[86] In 1957, Nehru saw a 10-reel film on the Buddha titled *Gotama the Buddha*, produced by the Films Division by Bimal Roy Productions, and suggested that copies of this film be sent to the principal missions abroad, especially to Burma and Ceylon.[87]

The physical landscape of Nagarjunakonda graphically reveals the various processes that have been discussed in this chapter. Over the last few years, the Indian government has been aggressively developing ancient Buddhist sites for international spiritual tourism revenue generation, and Nagarjunakonda has also become part of these circuits.[88] The consistent emphasis on the Buddhist element in the history of the site is writ large all over its landscape.[89] The Indian government is not alone in realizing the benefits to be reaped through such activity, and reference may be made here to recent Chinese attempts to develop Lumbini as a pilgrim-tourist destination, and Nepalese resistance to it. All these developments are important parts of the modern histories of ancient sites.

The issues examined here in the context of Nagarjunakonda continue to be of great relevance even today: Where should ancient artefacts be deposited and viewed? What should be done in the case of artefacts which are associated with special religious significance? Should they be museumized, or should they be deposited in places of active worship, or should they be made objects of worship in museums? The most serious problem concerns the conflict between heavy-investment modernization projects on the one hand and the conservation of sites and monuments on the other, a conflict in which fierce battles to preserve heritage are sometimes fought, and more often than not, lost.

Acknowledgements

I would like to acknowledge a grant I received from the University of Delhi for this research, as well as the valuable help in collecting data rendered by my research assistants Kanika Kishore, Kanika Kalra, and Tarun Kumar.

Notes

1. Of course it was not the only religious tradition to do so. Jainism remained confined to certain regions of the subcontinent, but Hindu influences travelled along with Buddhist traditions to the lands of mainland and island Southeast Asia.
2. See Philip Almond, *The British Discovery of Buddhism* (Cambridge: Cambridge University Press, 1988), pp. 47–49.
3. Nagarjunakonda' literally means Nagarjuna's hill (*koṇḍa* is Telugu for hill). An inscription (J. Ph. Vogel, 'Prakrit Inscriptions from a Buddhist Site at Nagarjunikonda', *Epigraphia Indica* 20, 1929–1930, pp. 1–36) refers to a monastery called Cula-Dhammagiri on Siriparvata on the eastern side of Vijayapurī. This suggests that the early historical city was known as Vijayapurī. A Tibetan tradition refers to the famous Buddhist philosopher Nāgārjuna spending the later part of his life in a monastery at Śrīparvata. This is the basis of the supposed connection of this site with Nāgārjuna. It may be noted that several early writings refer to the site as Nagarjunikonda.
4. A. H. Longhurst, *The Buddhist Antiquities of Nagarjunakonda, Madras Presidency*. Memoirs of the Archaeological Survey of India. No. 54. Reprint edition (New Delhi: Archaeological Survey of India, [1938] 1999).
5. T. N. Ramachandran, *Nagarjunakonda 1938*. Memoirs of the Archaeological Survey of India No. 71. Reprint edition (New Delhi: Archaeological Survey of India, [1953], 1999).
6. R. Subrahmanyam et al., *Nagarjunakonda (1954–60): Volume I*. Memoirs of the Archaeological Survey of India No. 75 (New Delhi: Archaeological Survey of India, 1975).
7. K. V. Soundararajan, ed. *Nagarjunakonda (1954–60): Volume II (The Historical Period)*. Memoirs of the Archaeological Survey of India No. 75 (New Delhi: Archaeological Survey of India, 2006).
8. Letter dated 10 February 1927, file no. 911 of the Archaeological Department, 1926–1930, Subject: Excavations at Nagarjunakonda, in the archives of the ASI, p. 126. The rest of the material in this section is also based on this file.
9. Marshall's hand-written note dated 17 February 1927, on the letter cited above.
10. File no. 911, p. 122, ASI.
11. Telegram dated 22 February 1927, file no. 911, p. 129, ASI.
12. File no. 911, p. 20, ASI.

13. File no. 911, p. 38, ASI.
14. There is also a personal angle—Longhurst happened to be Marshall's brother-in-law.
15. File no. 911, p. 172, ASI.
16. File no. 911, p. 49 ff, ASI.
17. File no. 911, pp. 82, 192 ff, ASI.
18. File no. 911, p. 58, ASI.
19. File no. 911, p. 87, ASI.
20. File no. 911, pp. 30, 32, ASI.
21. File no. 911, pp. 150, 160, ASI.
22. File no. 911, p. 165, ASI.
23. File no. 911, pp. 185–186, ASI.
24. File no. 911, p. 181, ASI.
25. File no. 911, p. 204, ASI.
26. File no. 911, p. 209, ASI.
27. File no. 911, p. 210, ASI.
28. File no. 911, p. 213, ASI.
29. File no. 911, pp. 220–221, ASI.
30. File no. 911, pp. 227–229, ASI.
31. File no. 911, p. 226, ASI.
32. File no. 911, pp. 228, 229, ASI.
33. File no. 911, pp. 246, 249, ASI.
34. Letter from the Deputy Secretary to the Government of Madras, Finance Department, No. 28890-E.T.-2, dated fort St. George, 18 November 1930, file no. 317-1/32-F, Notes, Forests, No. 3, Department of Education, Health and Lands. National Archives of India (hereafter NAI).
35. Letter from the Governor of Ceylon to the Viceroy, dated 27 February 1930, file No. 317-1/32F., No. 1, Department of Education, Health and Lands, NAI.
36. Letter from the Secretary, Maha Bodhi Society, dated the 7 July 1932, Department of Education, Health and Lands, Forest Section, 1932, F.317-1/32.F, No. 4, p. 9, NAI. It is not clear who in the Government this letter was addressed to.
37. Hargreaves' note dated 5.5.30, Department of Education, Health and Lands, Forest Section, 1932, F.317-1/32.F, No. 1, p. 1, NAI.
38. Note dated 9 August 1930 by G. S. Bajpai, Department of Education, Health and Lands, Forest Section, F.317-1/32.F, No. 1, p. 2; NAI.
39. Note dated 1 April 1931, Department of Education, Health and Lands, Forest Section, F.317-1/32.F, No. 1, p. 3, NAI.
40. Note dated 2 August 1932, Department of Education, Health and Lands, Forest Section, F.317-1/32.F, No. 1, p. 4, NAI.
41. Note dated 2 August 1932, Department of Education, Health and Lands, Forest Section.
42. D. R. Sahni's Note dated 8 December 1932, Department of Education, Health and Lands, Forest Section, F.317-1/32.F, No. 2, pp. 5–6, NAI.
43. Letter to the Colonial Secretary, Ceylon, No. F.-317-1/32-F., dated New Delhi, 20 December 1932, Department of Education, Health and Lands, Forest Section, No. 6, p. 10, NAI.

44. File no. 115/2/33/F., Notes, Nos. 1-5, Dept. of Education, Health and Lands, Forest Section, NAI.
45. *The Maha Bodhi*, Journal of the Maha Bodhi Society, 1931, p. 520.
46. *Maha Bodhi*, 1932, pp. 232–233.
47. *Maha Bodhi*, 1930, pp. 234–235.
48. See Nayanjot Lahiri, 'Bodh-Gaya: An Ancient Buddhist Shrine and its Modern History (1891–1904)', in Timothy Insoll, ed., *Case Studies in Archaeology and World Religion* (Oxford: BAR International Series, 1999), pp. 33–44; Alan Trevithick, 'British Archaeologists, Hindu Abbots, and Burmese Buddhists: The Mahabodhi Temple at Bodh Gaya, 1811–1877', *Modern Asian Studies* 33 (3), 1999, pp. 635–656.
49. See *Maha Bodhi,* 1933, pp. 38–41.
50. *Maha Bodhi*, 1933, pp. 1–4.
51. The Sarnath museum, established in 1910, is the oldest site museum set up by the ASI.
52. *Maha Bodhi*, 1933, p. 39.
53. *Maha Bodhi*, 1933, pp. 39–41.
54. For a description of this ceremony, see *Maha Bodhi*, 1933, pp. 285–287. The other portions (p. 289) were enshrined in the Maligakande temple in Columbo.
55. Note the comment made in *Maha Bodhi,* 1933, pp. 39 in the account of the anniversary celebrations: 'We have every reason to expect that some day we shall have larger collections of relics in Sarnath, which is growing into an international Buddhist centre.'
56. *Maha Bodhi*, 1933, pp. 513–520.
57. From Nehru's speech while inaugurating the Bhakra Nangal canal system at Nangal on 8 July 1954, Nehru, (*Selected Works*, Second Series, Vol. 26, gen. ed. S. Gopal, Delhi: Jawaharlal Nehru Memorial Fund, 2000), p. 132.
58. Extract from the notes of Ministry of Education, file no. F.3-30/52-A2, NAI.
59. Note of A. N. Khosla dated 6 September 1952, extract from the notes in the Ministry of Education file no. F.3-30/52-A2, NAI.
60. Extract from the notes the Ministry of Education file no. F.3-30/52-A2, note of M. S. Vats, Director General, dated 13.7.52, NAI.
61. Extract from the notes the Ministry of Education file no. F.3-30/52-A2, note of E. Kolet, dated 23.4.53, NAI.
62. As reported in *The Hindu* newspaper dated 17 August 1953. Hiren Mukherjee was a member of the Communist Party of India–Marxist, with a strong interest in history and culture.
63. Ministry of Education, C.I, 1957, file no. 4-6/57.C.I, p. 2, NAI.
64. Ministry of Education, C.I, 1955, file no. 3-125/55 C.I, NAI.
65. Note from Nehru to the Minister for Education, dated 10 December 1955, Guntur, Ministry of Education, C.I, 1955, file no. 3-125/55 C.I, pp. 19–20, NAI.
66. Note from Nehru to the Minister for Education, dated 10 December 1955, Guntur; Ministry of Education, C.I, 1955, file no. 3-125/55 C.I, pp. 21–22, NAI.
67. Letter dated 3 January 1956 from T. S. Krishnamurti, Under Secretary to the Government of India to the Secretary, Public Works Department; letter dated 21 December 1955 from V. V. Subramaniam, Secretary to the

Government, Public Works and Transport Dept., Govt. of Andhra Pradesh, to N. Bhagwandas, Collector of Guntur; Ministry of Education, C.I, 1955, file no. 3-125/55 C.I, pp. 25–26, NAI.

68. Letter from D. Chakravarti, Under Secretary to the Government of India (GOI) to the Director General of Archaeology, Ministry of Education, C.I, 1955, file no. 3-125/55 C.I, pp. 38–39, NAI.
69. Letter dated 14 January 1956 from the Under Secretary to the Government of Bombay, Education Department to the Secretary to the GOI, Ministry of Education, C.I, 1955, file no. 3-125/55 C.I, p. 31.
70. Minutes of the meeting of the Expert Committee held on April 18 and 19, 1956; Ministry of Education, C.I, 1955, file no. 3-125/55 C.I, pp. 42–49.
71. The members of this committee included K. K. Dutta of the Geological Survey of India and R. Subrahmanyam, superintendent of the Nagarjunakonda excavation project, apart from the administrator of the Nagarjunasagar project or his nominee, and a nominee of the Central Water and Power Commission. Ministry of Education, C.I, 1957, file no. 4-6/57, C.I, p. 27.
72. This committee consisted of the Governor of Andhra Pradesh in the chair; the chief Minister of Andhra Pradesh; the Administrator, Nagarjunasagar; the Joint Secretary, Ministry of Education; the Director General, ASI; and the Chief Engineer, Nagarjunasagar Dam. Ministry of Education, C.I, 1957, file no. 4-6/57, C.I, pp. 27–28. Details of the deliberations of the three committees are also available in file no. F3-51/58, C.I (1958), ASI archives.
73. Letter dated 19 Oct. 1957 from A. Ghosh, DG, ASI to Dr Lakhani, Ministry of Education, C.I, 1957, file no. F3 147/57, C.I, p. 30, NAI.
74. Details of all these activities and deliberations behind them are contained in File no. F3-51/58 C.I, 1958 (ASI Archives).
75. Self-contained note on Nagarjunakonda excavations; Ministry of Education, C.I, 1957, file no. 4-6/57 C.I, pp. 25–32.
76. File no. F3-51/58, C.I, 1958 (ASI Archives), pp. 160, 165. Jawaharlal Nehru, Second Series, H. Y. Sharada Prasad and A. K. Damodaran, eds *Selected Works*, Vol. 31 (New Delhi: Jawaharlal Nehru Memorial Fund, 2002), pp. 103–106, 108–109; Vol. 32, pp. 95–96.
77. The Notice for the Resolution was issued on 11 March 1957. See Ministry of Education, C.I, 1957, file no. 4-6/57, C.I, NAI.
78. Ministry of Education, C.I, 1957, file no. 4-6/57, C.I, p. 6, NAI.
79. Notice of Amendment to be moved in Rajya Sabha on 22 March 1957, Ministry of Education, C.I, 1957, file no. 4-6/57, C.I, p. 35. Details of the debate can be read in the Proceedings of the Rajya Sabha on 22 March 1957, pp. 386–412. K. Dhage and N. G. Ranga joined the coordination committee. The MPs were invited to visit the site and two members were co-opted into the coordination committee.
80. V. K. Dhage himself raised several of these questions on different occasions.
81. Parliamentary Question No. 2343 raised by M. P. Charan Das Mahant; date of reply: 14 December 1999.
82. What the Buddha and Aśoka meant to him emerges from his many writings, including *The Discovery of India*.

83. Jawaharlal Nehru, 'Selected Works of Jawaharlal Nehru', Vol. 9, in S. Gopal, ed., *Second Series* (New Delhi: Jawaharlal Nehru Memorial Fund, 1990), pp. 101–103. The relics were supposed to be those of the famous monks Sāriputta and Mahāmoggalāna, but, as pointed out by Debala Mitra, were actually from the nearby site of Satdhara. The role of the Bhopal durbar in ensuring that the relics came back to Sanchi and were housed there has been discussed in Nayanjot Lahiri, 'Buddhist Revival and the Restoration of Sanchi', in Nayanjot Lahiri and Upinder Singh (eds), *Buddhism in Asia: Revival and Reinvention* (New Delhi: Manohar, 2016), pp. 81–114.
84. *Maha Bodhi*, 1955, p. 331.
85. Nehru, *Selected Works Second Series*, Vol. 36, pp. 185–188.
86. Nehru, *Selected Works Second Series*, Vol. 36, p. 224.
87. Nehru, *Selected Works Second Series*, Vol. 36, pp. 194–195.
88. Upinder Singh, 'Exile and Return: The Reinvention of Buddhism and Buddhist Sites in Modern India', *South Asian Studies* 26 (2), 2010 pp. 193–217.
89. See Singh, 'Exile and Return' for details of this aspect.

8

Exile and Return: The Reinvention of Buddhism and Buddhist Sites in Modern India

A great deal of scholarly attention has been bestowed on the early history of Buddhism in the Indian subcontinent, but the understanding of its longer-term trajectories is very inadequate. The general view is that Buddhism declined drastically during the early medieval period (c. 600–1200 CE). However, there are grounds for arguing that the hypothesis of a virtual extinction of Buddhism during that period is at least in part the result of a lack of investigation and the non-acknowledgement of textual, epigraphic, and archaeological evidence that suggests otherwise.[1]

Eastern India is often seen as the last Buddhist bastion, where monasteries such as those of Nālandā, Odantapura, Vikramaśilā, and Somapurī flourished under the patronage of the Pāla kings.[2] But there is evidence from other regions as well. In Orissa, remains of early medieval *stūpas*, monasteries, and sculptures are known from Lalitagiri and Ratnagiri. Many Buddhist *vihāras* were built during this period in Nepal. The *Chachnāmā*, an early 13th century Persian translation of an old Arabic

This chapter was previously published in *South Asian Studies* 26 (2), 2010, pp. 193–217.

history of Muhammad bin Qasim's conquest of Sind in the early 8th century, suggests that Buddhism was an important part of the religious landscape of this north-western region. In Kashmir, the Ratnagupta and Ratnaraśmī monasteries at Anupamapura flourished in the 11th and 12th centuries. Several major ancient Buddhist monastic centres—for instance those at Sanchi (in modern Madhya Pradesh), Amaravati (in Andhra Pradesh), and Nalanda (in Bihar)—continued to flourish until the 12th to 13th centuries. Even after the 13th century, the monastic tradition was alive in the western Himalayas in Ladakh, Lahaul, and Spiti, which had close connections with the monasteries of Tibet. In fact, some of these monasteries have a more or less continuous history from the early medieval period right down to the present. It is clear that Buddhism never really disappeared from India, though it did decline, and was relegated to the geographical, political, and cultural margins.

Just as problematic as the assessments of the extent of Buddhism's decline are the explanations for this decline. While the Turks have been blamed for the sack of Nālandā at the close of the 12th century, they were certainly not responsible for the demise of monasteries in other parts of the country. Apart from the Turks, the most frequently cited reasons for the religion's decline include its being swallowed up by Hinduism due to its lack of distinctiveness, the 'open frontier' between Buddhism and local cults, 'corruption' by Tāntric influences, a decline in political patronage, and the *saṅgha*'s loss of material support due to economic dislocation caused by frequent wars.[3]

There is a view that Buddhism's eclipse was never complete, and that there was a connection between its lingering, simmering ancient residue and the Buddhist resurgence in modern India. For instance, Benoy Gopal Ray has argued that a handful of Buddhists survived in Bengal after the religion had virtually disappeared in other parts of the subcontinent, and that this spark was re-ignited by Buddhist revivalist movements in the late 19th century.[4] Similarly, there is a hypothesis that in Orissa the religion did not disappear but went underground and survived in the form of a 'crypto-Buddhism' (a combination of Tāntric, Buddhist, and Vaiṣṇava elements), its echoes surfacing several centuries later in the Mahima Dharma movement of the 19th century.[5] Notwithstanding such assertions, there is no doubt about the ultimately relatively diminutive dimensions of an identifiably Buddhist *saṅgha* and laity in medieval times. Buddhism survived on the margins and may have left a strong latent impression on Indian soil, but its revival, or rather reinvention, in the 19th and 20th centuries seems to be largely a result of completely new factors and forces.

According to the 2001 Census of Religions carried out by the Government of India, Buddhists constitute about 0.8% of the total Indian population, a mere 7,955,207 out of a total population of 1,028,610,328. They are sprinkled all over the country, with larger concentrations in the north-east and in Maharashtra: Sikkim (28.1% of the state's population), Arunachal Pradesh (13%), Mizoram (7.9%), Tripura (3.1%), Jammu and Kashmir (1.1%), Himachal Pradesh (1.2%), and Maharashtra (6%).[6] A comparison of the data for 1961, 1971, 1981, and 2001 suggests that the numbers of Buddhists in India have more than doubled between 1961 and 2001, from approximately 3,256,000 in 1961 to 7,955,207 in 2001. Of course, this is within an overall phenomenon of population growth, in which the numbers of adherents of other religions have increased as well.

But it is not just a matter of numbers. Apart from the 'official' Buddhists, i.e., those who declare themselves as Buddhists in the census operations, Buddhism has a larger constituency and acceptability, especially among the Indian intelligentsia. Trevor Ling talks of two types of Buddhism in modern India—one is a comprehensive religious and cultural package, the other is personal and has a strong philosophical and meditational element.[7] It is the appeal of the latter that explains the otherwise perplexing fact that in spite of the negligible presence of Buddhists in India at the time of Indian independence, the *cakra* (wheel) and the addorsed lions of the Sarnath capital of the Maurya emperor Aśoka, symbols with strong Buddhist resonance, were incorporated by the newly born Indian state into its national flag and national emblem.[8]

The idealized view of Buddhism as an ancient faith marked by rationality, non-violence, and an egalitarian message was one of several competing 20th century imaginings of the ancient Indian past, but it was one that was and continues to be very influential. In this construction of ancient India, the Buddha—the charismatic founder of the faith—and Aśoka—its most famous royal patron—are valorized for the virtues they are seen to have embodied and propagated. This idealization of Buddhism had its roots in the West's discovery and understanding of Buddhism,[9] but it also seems to have been connected with the centrality of non-violence in Gandhian nationalism. It is also significant that this valorization of Buddhism has not—at least until now—been seen as particularly threatening or problematic by adherents of India's other religious communities and their leaders.

What is most directly significant from the point of view of this chapter is that within the national and international community of Buddhists, India's status as the homeland of Buddhism (we know how important homelands are!), never really forgotten, is becoming increasingly important. And although it never completely left India, Buddhism has returned, although in different forms.[10] The extent of this revival should not be exaggerated: in actual demographic terms it is of modest proportions, but its global visibility and impact are greater than what the demographic statistics would lead us to expect. The most important source of this revival is the conversion of people belonging to Scheduled Castes and Tribes to Buddhism. Another important factor is the exile and internationalization of Tibetan Buddhism. These two factors have connected with an increasing state interest in promoting 'spiritual tourism' in an increasingly globalized world. Simultaneously, fueled by improving bilateral ties and pan-Buddhist sentiment, there has been increased Japanese investment in the conservation of ancient Buddhist sites in India. The main argument of this chapter is that the conjunction of all these factors has led to a distinct and sustained revitalization of Buddhist pilgrim-cum-tourist circuits, increased activity at many ancient Buddhist sites, and a dramatic resurrection, or rather reinvention, of many extinct ones.

The reinvention of Buddhism in modern India may not have happened were it not for the fact that in spite of Buddhism's earlier decline and peripheralization, and in spite of the vandalism inflicted by time and archaeologists, the material remains of ancient Buddhism were, and still are, very visible all over the subcontinent. These continue to provide important anchors for the Buddhist revival, and the revitalized ancient remains have in turn become potent symbols as well as catalysts of this revival, ones that are likely to multiply in number and increase in importance and visibility in the coming decades.

Certain aspects of this phenomenon have been noted and discussed by some scholars. For instance, Toni Huber has described the Tibetan diaspora's very deliberate use of ancient Buddhist sites in India as a resource to further its own concerns.[11] Catherine Becker has detailed how the Tibetan Buddhists' Kālacakra celebrations in 2006 altered the landscape of Amaravati in Guntur district, Andhra Pradesh.[12] However, there is need for a broader historical perspective, one which takes into account many other features of the revitalization of ancient Buddhist sites within the larger context of the 20th century Buddhist revival in India. Apart from the activities of the Tibetan exiles, there are several other important aspects of this larger context including Dalit conversions, global flows of tourists and pilgrims, government investment in sites associated with spiritual tourism, and international cultural diplomacy in the form of the funding of conservation projects. This chapter discusses how all these factors have coalesced to generate a reinvention of Buddhism and Buddhist sites in modern India.

Ambedkar, the Neo-Buddhists, and Ancient Buddhism

The most important source of the resurgence of Buddhism in modern India has been an internal socio-political one, and consists of the conversion of sections of the Scheduled Castes or Dalits, the modern representatives of communities which suffered centuries of oppression and marginalization in caste society as 'Untouchables'. This process is inextricably linked with Bhimrao Ramji Ambedkar (1891–1956) and the dramatic event that took place in Nagpur in the state of Maharashtra in western India on 14 October 1956, the year when the 2,500th anniversary of the Buddha's *parinibbāna* was celebrated in various parts of South and Southeast Asia. On that day, in a large open field—later known as the Diksha Bhumi—Ambedkar took Buddhist vows, along with 400,000 of his 'Untouchable' followers, publicly declaring their conversion to a new faith.

Although Buddhist conversions are generally associated with Ambedkar, it is important to note that the Buddhist revivalist movement in India had a background and precursors.[13] The Maha Bodhi Society, founded by the Ceylonese Anagarika Dharmapala in 1891, was an institution which contributed greatly towards generating an international interest in Buddhism within and outside India. But there were other institutions and individuals as well. For instance, in 1891 Kripasharan set up the Bauddha Dharmankur Sabha, which was very active in Bengal.[14] In South India Pandit Iyothee Thass (1845–1914) established the Sakya Buddhist Society (also known as the South Indian Buddhist Association), and spearheaded a social protest movement among Paraiya labourers which spread through the labour diaspora to South Africa and Burma.[15]

Ambedkar had declared in 1935 that although he had been born a Hindu, he would not die one. But he took a long time to reach the decision to lead his community into the Buddhist fold, and it was a decision that was simultaneously personal and political. Ambedkar's personal interest in Buddhism is said to have been sparked off by a book on the life of Gautama Buddha given to him by one of his teachers in Bombay in 1908. But as a political leader of India's 'Untouchables', Buddhism was neither his first nor his only choice, and he carefully weighed it against other options such as Sikhism, Christianity, and Islam. A combination of several factors gave Buddhism an edge for being chosen as the religion of salvation for India's oppressed and marginalized millions—the fact that the Buddha's teaching could easily be mined for messages of egalitarianism, rationality, and ethics; its international presence; its deep roots in Indian soil (this was very important for Ambedkar); and the fact that in the mid-20th century, there were actually very few Buddhists in India. The field was more or less clear—the new converts would not have to contend with any strong, entrenched ecclesiastical elite.[16] His opponents called the mass conversion at Nagpur a political stunt; most of his own political advisors and colleagues were against the idea, but Ambedkar's stature was such that that they all fell in line.

From the point of view of this chapter, several things seem especially significant about the Nagpur conversion ceremony. A replica of the Sanchi *stūpa* was prominently displayed on the dais, a reminder of Buddhism's long, grand heritage in ancient India. The sentiment of pan-Buddhist internationalism was palpable. The dignitaries seated on the dais included D. Valisinha, the General Secretary of the Maha Bodhi Society.[17] Ambedkar took his vows from a Burmese *bhikkhu* named U. Chandramani, apparently the oldest Buddhist monk in India at the time. After the event, messages of congratulations flowed in from prominent individuals from other Buddhist countries, such as the Prime Minister of Burma.[18] Ambedkar had appropriated ancient Indian Buddhism, linked it with modern, internationalized Buddhism, and transformed it into something new, something he himself called *Navayāna* ('the new vehicle'). The strong element of anti-Hindu sentiment and protest that accompanied the ceremony was very evident from the vows taken by Ambedkar and the other converts.[19] Early Buddhism had to a large extent adjusted itself to existing social hierarchies and created in the *saṅgha* an island of equality in the midst of a very unequal world; it had also co-existed with the Hindu cults without undue acrimony. In the 20th century, in Ambedkar's hands, Buddhism blended with strident social protest and political assertion, and took on a sharp anti-Hindu stance.

True religion, in Ambedkar's view, was an important aspect of society, one that was necessary to maintain the moral basis of both individual and community. In his opinion, the Buddha, like Marx, put forward a doctrine aimed at radically transforming society. But Ambedkar went on to argue that while both Marx and the Buddha put forward a call for social equality, Buddhism was superior to Marxism because of the peaceful, democratic means it advocated to achieve this end.[20] Ambedkar's book, *The Buddha and his Dhamma,* was completed just before he died, and was published posthumously in 1957. Written in pithy, lively point-form, this book presented his final and most detailed understanding of the Buddha's life and ideas. He asserted that there was a fundamental difference between the western notion of religion and the idea of *dhamma* in Buddhism; the latter was preeminently social and moral, and its purpose was to reconstruct the world. True *dhamma* (*saddhamma*) is that which breaks down barriers between man and man, which maintains that worth and not birth is the measure of man, and which promotes social equality. Ambedkar described the confusion about what constituted the core of the Buddha's teaching as in large part a result of the misreporting of his ideas by monks. He asserted that the touchstone of ascertaining whether a particular interpretation of the Buddha's teaching was correct or not was whether that interpretation was logical and rational. He denied that the four noble truths made Buddhism a pessimistic doctrine. He scoffed at the hagiographical explanation of the Buddha's disenchantment with worldly life as a result of witnessing the 'four sights' in Kapilavastu. As for the role of the *saṅgha,* he asserted that the *bhikkhus* should be servants of society.[21]

Ambedkar clearly saw himself as an agent for the revival of a once-great Indian religion and wanted his book to inspire and ignite the reader to change his destiny. The *Buddha and his Dhamma* ends with prayers for the return of the Buddha to his native land and for the spread of his *dhamma.* Not everyone was impressed. A review of the book in *Mahabodhi,* the journal of the Maha Bodhi Society in Calcutta, described it as a dangerous book, and remarked that it should have been titled *Ambedkar and his Dhamma.*[22]

Ambedkar used the term 'neo-Buddhists' to refer to the Scheduled Caste converts. The prefix 'neo' was apt for two reasons—they were new converts to the religion, and the religion they embraced was in fact a new interpretation of Buddhism, one with a strong element of social and political protest. Indian neo-Buddhism differed from Buddhisms in other parts of the world in many fundamental ways, including in its religious ideas and social orientation. It was essentially a lay Buddhism, one in which lay leaders predominated and monks played a very insignificant role. During the 1950s and 1960s the majority of the converts came from two groups among whom Ambedkar enjoyed an especially strong following—the Mahars of Maharashtra (who had traditionally been service providers in villages—watchmen, removers of cattle carcasses, wall-repairers, etc.) and the Jatavs of Agra (largely employed in shoe-making) in Uttar Pradesh. Ambedkar also invented a new myth of origin for the neo-Buddhists, one which connected them directly with ancient India and ancient Buddhism. His hypothesis (put forward in his essay, *The Untouchables*, published in 1948) was that the 20th century 'Untouchables' were the descendants of the Buddhists of ancient India, 'broken men' who stuck to their religion and to beef-eating, and who were reduced to their pathetic position due to the machinations of the Brahmins.

The mass conversion of Dalits to Buddhism does not, however, seem to have had a massive or sustained legacy after Ambedkar, and today the vast majority of the Scheduled Castes in India are in fact not Buddhist. There have been a few episodes of conversions of members of Scheduled Caste and Tribe groups, including some well-publicized ones, in recent times. For instance, on 27 October 2002, a small number of Dalits publicly converted to Islam, Buddhism, and Christianity at a ceremony held in Gurgaon, near Delhi. The organizers were the All-India Confederation of Scheduled Castes and Scheduled Tribes Organisations and the Lord Buddha Club.[23]

On 4 November 2004 a Diksha (conversion) ceremony was organized in Delhi by the All India Confederation of Scheduled Castes/Scheduled Tribes Organizations and the Lord Buddha Club. The number of conversions that took place on that day is debated. It seems that about 20,000 people eventually took their vows, but the organizers allege that the police had prevented as many as 50,000 people from entering the city. In fact, the rally was originally supposed to be held in the centrally located Ram Lila grounds and the venue had to be shifted to the more out-of-the-way Ambedkar Bhavan due to police insistence that it would create a law and order problem.[24]

One of the biggest post-Ambedkar conversion rallies took place on 28 May 2007 when it was reported that about 50,000 (100,000 according to some sources) Dalits and tribals converted to Buddhism at Mahalaxmi Race Course in Mumbai, on the fiftieth anniversary of B. R. Ambedkar's death and the Nagpur Diksha. The ceremony was organized by an organization called the Babasaheb Ambedkar Pratishthan, and was apparently also supposed to be a show of strength by a Dalit leader of Maharashtra named Ramdas Athawale (alias Udit Raj), who sought to establish his credentials as the true torch-bearer of Ambedkar's legacy.[25] A Dalit writer named Laxman Mane, who had organized a smaller conversion of some 140 tribals at Nagpur in 2006, was also involved. Monks from several countries were present on the occasion. The Dalai Lama was scheduled to attend, but for some reason did not make an appearance.

On the whole, it is evident that mass conversions of Dalits and tribals to various religions (mainly Buddhism, Christianity, and Islam) are not as frequent or substantial as certain Hindu groups who have spear-headed moves towards the passing of strict anti-conversion laws in some states maintain. This is in spite of the fact that according to law, Scheduled Caste converts to Buddhism and Sikhism do not lose their special privileges after conversion, whereas converts to Christianity and Islam do.

Various reasons have been cited for the sparseness of Buddhist conversions in the post-Ambedkar era. Although Adele Fiske's study was based on data collected in 1966–1967, its conclusions are still relevant. There is the very loose structure of Buddhist organizations, the lack of co-operation and coordination among them, political in-fighting, a weak financial and personnel base, and the absence of a charismatic leadership transcending local, regional, and caste boundaries. Connected to the last point is the fact that neo-Buddhism is basically a lay religion, one in which the *saṅgha* has little presence or importance (Ambedkar's attitude towards the *saṅgha* was one of suspicion and distrust). There is a lack of interest among young neo-Buddhists to don monastic robes, and the training facilities for monks or *baudhacharya*s (laypersons who can officiate at life-cycle rituals) are weak.[26]

Instead of looking towards religious conversion, Scheduled Castes today seek more direct gains through political positioning both within parties with a wide social base or through association with political parties that explicitly have a Dalit base. The electoral successes of the Bahujan Samaj Party in Uttar Pradesh are illustrative of the latter trend. Although the fortunes of this party were significantly diminished in the 2009 national elections, there is no doubt that today, in their quest for social justice and advancement, groups low in the caste hierarchy seek salvation through politics rather than through religion. Political parties, for their part, can no longer ignore the Dalits.

Tibetan Buddhism in India and Its Links with Ladakh, Lahaul, and Spiti

The second major facet of the increased visibility of Buddhism in 20th and 21st century India has its source in political processes in India's neighbourhood. In ancient times Tibet was home to the Bon religion.

According to tradition, Buddhist influences started making their impact there from the reign of King Songsten Gampo in the 7th century. Tibetan Buddhism was strongly influenced both by Indian Buddhism and by the autochthonous Bon traditions. Buddhism was transmitted to Tibet by many Buddhist monks, the best known among whom were the Indian monks Śāntarakṣita, Padmasambhava, and Atisa. The various Tibetan sects identified themselves as belonging to the Mahāyāna stream with respect to their philosophy and religious practice, and were strongly influenced by Buddhist *tantra* (known as Vajrayāna or Mantrayāna). The 'dark period' of the 9th and 10th centuries was followed by a revival in the 11th to 15th centuries, during which time the major Tibetan sects such as the Nyingmapa, Kagyu, Sakya, and Geluk took shape.[27]

The exile of Tibetan Buddhism from Tibet and its refuge in India was a 20th century phenomenon, and was a direct outcome of the Chinese invasion of Tibet in 1949 and the subsequent Chinese crack-down on Buddhist monastic institutions. In 1959, ten years after the invasion, Tenzin Gyatso, the fourteenth Dalai Lama and the chief spiritual leader of the Tibetan Buddhists, fled to India along with about 85,000 followers. Subsequent to that event, a Central Tibetan Administration, functioning as a government in exile, was established. It continues to function, with headquarters at McLeodganj in Dharamsala in Himachal Pradesh. The internationalization of Tibetan Buddhism was thus a result of its forced exile from its homeland.

With the help of the Indian government, the United Nations High Commission for refugees, and various foreign donors, the Tibetan refugees were ultimately settled in fifty-two settlements spread across ten Indian states (apart from thirty-five settlements in Nepal and seven in Bhutan). The largest numbers of refugees were located in five settlements set up between 1960 and 1974 in the southern state of Karnataka. The new settlers mainly devoted themselves to agriculture (they also took to agro-based industries and handicrafts) and established monasteries and schools. The biggest settlement of Tibetan refugees is the Lungsung-Samdupling settlement in Bylakuppe, Karnataka. Starting off with a population of 3,000, this now consists of seven villages or camps, with an average of 30 families in each camp.

Over 8,000 Tibetans live in Dharamsala, which is also the official residence of the Dalai Lama. The Tibetan government in exile has set up a library and archives of Tibetan works, and has made efforts to promote the study of Buddhist philosophy and Tibetan language and culture, including the study of traditional Tibetan medicine, astrology, and handicrafts. Several monasteries and nunneries are located in the town.

Although physically concentrated in India, the Tibetan diaspora has an international spread. The Department of Information and International Relations of the Government in exile places the Tibetan diaspora at about 111,170. Of these, 85,000 live in India, 14,000 in Nepal, 1,600 in Bhutan, and 1,540 in Switzerland. About 640 Tibetans are scattered across other countries of Europe, 110 in Scandinavia, 7,000 in the USA and Canada, 1,000 in Taiwan, 220 in Australia and New Zealand, and 60 in Japan. Thus, in contrast to the neo-Buddhist movement, which has an essentially Indian perspective, Tibetan Buddhism has acquired a strong international flavour. This has led to a greater international visibility of the Tibetan Buddhists in India, a highlighting of the ancient Indian Buddhist heritage, and of the fact that India is the original homeland of Buddhism. A corollary to the substantial international exposure that Tibetan Buddhism has received and the interest it has attracted is that the second half of the 20th century has seen the creation of a Buddhist following beyond Asia in Europe and America, one that is notable not so much for its numbers as for the high-profile celebrity status of some of its members.

The international awareness and sympathy that the Tibetan cause enjoys today has much to do with the current Dalai Lama. He has travelled to over sixty-two countries, meeting many dignitaries and heads of state (most recently President Obama of the United States), and has received numerous international awards including the 1989 Nobel Peace Prize for leading a non-violent struggle for the liberation of Tibet. He was awarded the Congressional Gold Medal—the highest civilian honour in the United States of America—in 2006. Although he has visited Japan, Cambodia, Indonesia, Malaysia, Mongolia, and Taiwan, the maximum number of foreign visits made by the Dalai Lama have been to the United States and Germany. Devotees from various countries come to seek his blessings and guidance in Dharamsala. Through his discourses, visits, and various kinds of initiation ceremonies held in different parts of the world, the Dalai Lama has personally played an important role in highlighting the plight of the Tibetan refugees and strengthening the international profile of Tibetan Buddhism.

While the scale of international, especially western, attention that Tibet has received in recent years may appear novel and unprecedented, it is important to remember that this attention is part of a longer-term engagement. Donald S. Lopez Jr has pointed out that Tibet and Tibetan

Buddhism have long been a focus of European desire and fantasy. In the 18th and 19th centuries, western scholars considered 'Lamaism' (the term they used for Tibetan Tāntric Buddhism) as a corrupt version of the original pristine faith. The mid-20th century Tibetan diaspora led to a significant shift in attitude and perspective. Buddhism started claiming American and European converts and became internationalized. Now, because of Tibet's seclusion, Tibetan Buddhism came to be considered as *more* authentic than that of any other land, and became an object of academic inquiry in western universities. This academic inquiry had an urgency about it, as its practitioners saw themselves as engaged in a rescue operation to save a culture that stood on the brink of extinction.[28] Lopez has also elaborated on the creation of a new sort of myth about Tibet as a perfect, ethereal, idyllic world before the Chinese invasion. In this new mythologizing, Tibet is seen as a spiritual panacea for a materialistic western world.[29]

But coming back to India, it should be noted that the persecution and exile of Tibetan Buddhism has in fact contributed towards revitalizing Buddhism here, especially in the northern mountainous areas of Lahaul and Spiti (in the state of Himachal Pradesh) and in Ladakh (in the state of Jammu and Kashmir), regions where the Buddhist tradition has ancient roots. In Lahaul-Spiti, the evidence of the Buddhist impact dates from the 8th century, and this impact became especially marked between the late 10th to 12th centuries under the patronage of the Guge kings, although the situation in the neighbouring areas of central and southern Himachal was different.[30] Although it looks like a remote area, Laxman S. Thakur points out that Lahaul-Spiti and specific sites within the region, Kinnaur in particular, occupied a strategic position between two major international trade routes—the silk route which linked China, India, central Asia, and Europe; and the Great Northern Trade route of the subcontinent, which swept from the eastern Indian port of Tāmraliptī across the Gangetic plain to Taxila in the north-west. The brisk trans-Himalayan Indo-Tibetan trade was in fact an important sustaining feature of the economy of Lahaul-Spiti from early times. The area was also a cultural melting-pot—people of diverse origins traversed the high mountain terrain, bringing in new ideas and technologies and enriching its cultural mosaic.[31]

This cultural mosaic is visible, for instance, in the paintings at Tabo (in the Spiti valley), one of the most important ancient and still-active monasteries. Its history goes back to the late 10th century and its walls bear exquisite murals. When the monk Geshe Sonam Wangdu came from

Tibet to Tabo in 1976, there were only two monks living there; today it houses 45 monks.[32] The Dalai Lama has visited Tabo several times; he conferred the initiation into the practice of Kālacakra *tantra* there in 1983, and sat on the throne of the main temple in 1996 to celebrate the thousand-year anniversary of the monastery. In 2004 he visited the monastery to teach and bestow the Vajradhātu initiation. He was supposed to visit the monastery again in 2009 to consecrate the Kālacakra *stūpa* being built there, but the visit did not take place. It was during the time of Geshe Sonam Wangdu that the new Kālacakra temple (in which the initiation was held) was built. The Tabo monastery has for many years now been running a school for training young monks as well as making arrangements to send some of them to monastic universities elsewhere.[33]

Close interaction with Tibet is also a centuries old phenomenon in Ladakh in Jammu and Kashmir, where Buddhists are concentrated in the north and east, while Muslims predominate in the south and west. The Buddhist parts of the region are marked by ubiquitous lamas (monks), *chorten*s (the term used for *stūpa*s in this region), *gompa*s (monasteries), colourful prayer flags, and *mani* walls with prayer stones bearing prayers and invocations in the Tibetan script. Buddhism made its impact on Ladakh from much earlier times, but the major Ladakh monasteries date from the 11th to 19th centuries, when royal patronage became available, and many of them are living institutions with a rich but highly endangered artistic heritage. A prominent example is Alchi monastery, noted for its exquisite murals, which was founded in the 11th century by a Tibetan noble who extended his political control over Ladakh.[34]

From a long-term point of view, it is important to note that in the western Himalayas, the connections through patronage and interaction between Buddhist monasteries and the villages in which they are situated have been increasing in strength. Although most of the senior monks in these monasteries are Tibetan, a few young monks are drawn from nearby villages. Many monasteries are involving themselves in secular education, thereby consolidating their links with the aspirations of the laity. Lamas play an important part in the daily life of the people, especially in the performance of life-cycle rituals, and also function as astrologers and exorcists. There is a close interdependence between monasteries and villages. In Ladakh (as also in Lahaul and Spiti), families frequently give over a son to the monkhood, farm the monastery's land in return for a share of the produce, make donations to monasteries, and extend financial help to monks on various occasions.[35]

Clearly, then, the monastic tradition is thriving in Ladakh, Lahaul, and Spiti, and the long-standing religious and cultural links with Tibet have strengthened since the 1960s. In fact, there has been an interesting reversal—in ancient times, Tibetan monks imbibed learning from the Buddhist homeland. Now, exiled from its own home, Tibetan Buddhism is playing a key role in consolidating and deepening the Buddhist tradition in Ladakh, Lahaul, and Spiti.[36]

Dalit Buddhism and Tibetan Buddhism: An Unbridgeable Chasm?

There does not seem to be any significant interaction between the two faces of the Buddhist revival in modern India—the Dalit and Tibetan movements. Dalit Buddhists do not figure prominently among the supporters of the Tibetan cause. The Dalai Lama, for his part, has only occasionally spoken about issues of social inequality and the Dalits. For instance, when a million Dalits were expected to convert to Buddhism on 14 October 2001, under the aegis of the All India Confederation of Scheduled Caste/Scheduled Tribe Organizations, the Dalai Lama reportedly made a supportive statement.[37] Similarly, as mentioned earlier, he was supposed to be present at the mass conversion rally of Dalits and tribals in Mumbai in May 2007, but eventually did not participate, for unknown reasons.

The Dalai Lama emphasizes that formal conversion to Buddhism is not sufficient in itself; it is essential that converts (Dalit or otherwise) deeply imbibe the religious doctrines.[38] There is also a major divergence in the orientation of the two movements. The Dalai Lama's Middle Path, emphasizing love and compassion, even towards one's adversary, has in recent years been questioned even within the Tibetan community.[39] It has never struck a chord with Dalit Buddhists, for whom Buddhism constitutes a way out of the harsh and sometimes brutal realities of caste oppression and conflict. It has also been suggested that the Tibetan Buddhists have little to gain from integrating with a group that has a low social and economic status,[40] but the chasm between Tibetan and Dalit Buddhists runs much deeper than this.

Apart from enormous differences in religious belief and practice, there is also the radical difference in the place of the monastic tradition.

As mentioned earlier, monasticism is of little importance among Dalit Buddhists, among whom full-time monks are few and unimportant, and several Buddhist organizations offer short-term crash courses for monks and lay *Baudhacharya*s. This is a far cry from the rigorous and long-term training required for becoming a monk in the Tibetan tradition. The enormous cultural divide, including that of language, between neo-Buddhists and monks from other lands has been a major reason why the few attempts made by the former to connect themselves with monastic communities in various parts of the world have not been very successful. Dalit converts do not feel comfortable with monks from other countries and prefer interfacing with monks or laypersons from their own community:

> Buddhist monks from other countries have played a minor role in the mass conversion movement [of the Scheduled Castes] of the past decade. Differences in rite, custom, and language have hampered the efforts of monks from Japan, Tibet, Burma, Cambodia, and Ceylon. Several laymen said, 'We are Indians, we do not want to adopt Japanese or Ceylonese ways'. Others indicated that monks should be recruited from Scheduled Caste communities so they would know the language and mentality of the people.[41]

Furthermore, the Tibetan Buddhists in India have very self-consciously and deliberately maintained their distance, not only from Dalit Buddhists but also from the rest of India and Indians. The scattered Tibetan communities in India are 'intentionally nonassimilative' and the overall level of acculturation among exiles in is rather low.[42] I noticed in the course of my travels in Ladakh, Lahaul, and Spiti that senior Tibetan monks, including those who had lived in India for decades, did not know how to speak any Indian language. Huber has argued that the exiles have no real interest in India, except for their own settlements and the sacred places associated with Buddhism, with which they identify strongly. Further, he asserts that although official statements made by the Dalai Lama and the Tibetan government in exile allude to India being the birthplace of the Buddha and Buddhism and therefore a Holy Land, for a variety of reasons, most Tibetans living in India have an ambivalent, even negative, attitude towards their adopted country.[43]

Given all this, it is hardly surprising that on the occasions when neo-Buddhists and Tibetan Buddhists do interface, nothing much happens:

> I met two Tibetan monks living in the guest room of a very simple vihara in a very small poor Buddhist community outside Pune in Maharashtra. They

> had been there several weeks and had learned enough Pali to chant some formula familiar to the Maharashtrian Buddhists, and were making plaster Buddha images from molds they had brought with them to repay the hospitality they were given. No other communication was possible, and I expect the connection did not last long.[44]

The deep cultural divide between the Buddhisms of the Dalits and the Tibetans constitutes a huge obstacle to the prospect of the emergence of a pan-Buddhist unity in India. These two Buddhisms are embedded not only in very different cultural matrices but also in very different political contexts and orientations. For Ambedkar, Buddhism was a way of raising the position of the Scheduled Castes to a new level vis-à-vis the upper castes, linked to a strident rejection of Hinduism and all that it stood for. For the Tibetan Buddhist elite, on the other hand, it is part of a way of life that is threatened, one that has to be zealously protected in exile. While Dalit Buddhist organizations and Tibetan Buddhists share a history of persecution and may on some occasions share a platform, the political, social, ideological, and cultural differences between the two are too great to allow any genuine dialogue. While Tibetan Buddhism has embraced, in fact thrives on, internationalism and international support, the neo-Buddhist movement has an inward orientation. Nevertheless, there is at least one important spatial meeting ground between Dalit Buddhists, Tibetan Buddhists, and Buddhists from other parts of the world. This meeting ground is created by pilgrimage.

Pilgrimage as a Meeting Ground

The importance of pilgrimage in religious practice cuts across religious, cultural, and chronological divides. The history of the spread of Buddhism within and beyond the subcontinent is one of peripatetic monks and pilgrims, and the travel and transformation of ideas and practices over vast geographical distances. In the context of this chapter, it is important to recognize the significance and impact of pilgrimage not only as part of Buddhist religious practice, but also as an important event in the lives of the individuals who launched Buddhist revivalist movements, such as Anagarika Dharmapala and B. R. Ambedkar. All revivalist movements have connected themselves with the ancient places made sacred through association with the Buddha. Some of these are multi-religious sites, which have seen struggles for control between different religious communities. The best known example is Anagarika Dharmapala's staking claim to Bodh Gaya, which was in the 19th century a pilgrimage site for Buddhists and Hindus alike, igniting a dispute which still lingers.[45]

Reflecting on the nature and potential of pilgrimage, Victor Turner points out that pilgrimages are liminal phenomena, in some ways similar to rites of passage. In the course of pilgrimage, the structures of everyday social life are altered by *communitas. Communitas* is different from the sense of community which arises from a geographical area of common living—the bonds of *communitas* transcend this. Where pilgrims come from is as important as where they go, and the nature and intensity of the bonds created by pilgrimage also depend on the journey itself. Furthermore, society and culture impinge on the process, and there are limits to the *communitas* that is generated—inherent social divisions are attenuated, not completely eliminated.[46]

For Indian Dalit Buddhists, visiting the ancient Buddhist sites is a way in which they can connect themselves with a great heritage to which they can lay claim, a compensation for the marginalization and low social status they experienced over many centuries. The neo-Buddhists of Maharashtra frequent Ajanta, Ellora, and Karle, and many of the guides at the Ajanta and Ellora caves are Dalit Buddhists.[47] Festivals such as Buddha Jayanti are often celebrated at the caves at Aurangabad, Nasik, and Junnar. Ancient Buddhist sites provide neo-Buddhists with a rich store of emblems for their buildings and their homes, and Dalit Buddhist homes are often decorated with photographs of Sanchi, Sarnath, and Bodh Gaya.[48]

Elleanor Zelliot argues that the neo-Buddhist movement does not ultimately have a physical centre located at a particular *place.* It is B. R. Ambedkar, considered a *bodhisattva* by many of his followers, who constitutes the centre. Therefore, the site where he was cremated in Mumbai is an important place of pilgrimage, as is the Diksha Bhumi in Nagpur (Figure 8.1).[49] Actually, a better way of describing the situation is to acknowledge that for Dalit Buddhists, there are *two* kinds of pilgrimage destinations—those connected with Ambedkar and those connected with ancient Buddhism. But while the former are few, the latter are many, and have the potential to increase enormously in number.

As for the Tibetan Buddhists, it should be recalled that pilgrimage was for centuries an essential part of Tibetan life, connected not only with Buddhism, but rooted in an older autochthonous view of the mountains, valleys, rivers, lakes, caves, and other features of the physical landscape as pulsating with the presence of spirits, demons, and deities. The Tibetan word for pilgrimage is *gnas skor*—literally, 'circling around an abode'—an allusion to the act of circumambulation that was generally carried out at such places.[50] Pilgrimage welded together diverse and distant parts

Figure 8.1
Modern stūpa marking the site of the Diksha Bhumi

Source: Author.

of Tibet and contributed in a significant way towards creating cultural unity.[51] Major places in this pilgrimage network included Lhasa and Mount Kailash, but the many available pilgrim guide books describe a plethora of major and minor/local pilgrimage destinations.

India was known to Tibetan monks and lay Buddhists from ancient times as a land of many sacred places associated with the founder of the faith. After the Chinese invasion of Tibet in 1949, the Chinese government clamped down on outside travel for two decades, and pilgrimage to India became virtually impossible. Pilgrimage within Tibet itself was declared a punishable offence, on the ostensible grounds that it represented feudal superstition.[52] Chinese policy has varied since then, but travel of Tibetans to India has always been subject to government surveillance and regulation, especially since many of those who traveled to the sacred sites in India ostensibly as pilgrims often stayed on to seek political asylum.

After 1959, with the movement between Tibet and India having become problematic, the Tibetan exiles had to focus on the already-known pilgrimage spots within India, notable among which were the ancient sites and still-functioning old monasteries. Huber has perceptively drawn attention to how the Tibetan exile elite has been engaged in an 'intensive and strategic ritual use of the landscape of the Buddha in India' and that it has been trying actively to colonize these ancient sites in a way that is very similar to what the Maha Bodhi Society tried to do in the early 20th century.[53] However, what is equally important to note is that this activity intersects with other group interests in these sites, including those of Indian neo-Buddhists, domestic and international tourists, pilgrims and pilgrim-tourists, the Indian government, and the governments of East Asian Buddhist countries, especially Japan.

Pilgrimage in Its Modern Forms

Anthropological studies have established that although pilgrimage is an important religious activity cutting across cultural, religious, and chronological divides, it has several extra-religious dimensions as well. For pilgrims themselves, this culturally accepted expression of religious piety has always been entangled to varying degrees with other motivations—the desire to take a break from the tedium of everyday life, 'get away from it all', see new places, and seek adventure. From the larger historical perspective, the connections between pilgrimage, commerce, and politics are very well-known and are illustrated by the age-old congruence of trade and pilgrim routes. Victor Turner, in fact, identifies solemnity, festivity, and trade as three foci of pilgrimage throughout history. He talks about the 'field' generated by a pilgrimage centre and speculates about the historical role of pilgrimage in the development of cities, markets, and roads.[54]

In our own time, the terminology connected with the flourishing tourism industry includes what is often referred to as 'spiritual tourism'. The question that is directly relevant to this chapter is this: does this fall within the category of religious activity, tourist travel, or both? Spiritual tourism is a broad term that includes travellers with many different backgrounds, motivations, and interests, travelling to destinations that have some sort of religious import. What is central to the argument of this chapter is that a segment of these travellers can in fact be described as pilgrims or pilgrim-tourists.

Destination, intent, and self-perception define the pilgrim, and apart from the religious associations of the places visited, the only way of actually ascertaining the extent to which visitors to Buddhist sites can be described as pilgrims is through visitors' surveys. The magnificent site of Ellora in Maharashtra includes twelve Buddhist, seventeen Hindu, and five Jaina caves. The site, which was given the status of a World Heritage Site by UNESCO in 1983, was and is still located at the intersection of several local, regional, and subcontinental trade and pilgrimage routes. It is interesting to note that in a recent 2009 survey of 'off-season' visitors to Ellora,[55] 51% of the Indian visitors characterized themselves as pilgrims and were travelling on well-established pilgrimage routes.[56] In spite of the fact that the Archaeological Survey of India officially discourages active worship at the site, this does not deter pious visitors (Hindus, Buddhists, Jainas, others) from expressing their religiosity in various ways, something which is especially visible at the Kailāśanātha temple. As for foreign visitors to Ellora, the survey showed that most of them came from Europe (46%) and North America (26%), while Asians followed with a lower 21%. However, these statistics do not give an accurate picture, as a large number of travellers from Japan and Southeast Asia regularly visit the Buddhist caves, but not during the hot summer months, which was the time when the survey was conducted. Many East Asian and Sri Lankan visitors who were interviewed described themselves as pilgrims; some of them tried to meditate in the Buddhist caves, in spite of being disturbed by the noisy ambience. It is evident that although spiritual tourism appears to be a new phenomenon, and while the level of the overt religious/ritualistic activity conducted at the destinations may not be on par with what is seen at popular living shrines, some of what is included under the umbrella term of spiritual tourism can, in fact, be seen as a new form of an old practice, i.e., pilgrimage, transformed in the context of an increasingly globalized world.

The promotion of spiritual tourism, especially in sites on the Buddhist circuit, is now a very self-conscious aim of the Indian state. The tourism industry has been growing rapidly and is recognized as an exceptionally fast-growing sector of the Indian economy, with a very high revenue-capital ratio and employment generation potential. The numbers of foreign tourists arriving in India were estimated at about 2.73 million in 2003 and 3.92 million in 2005, reflecting a growth of 43.6% over the two-year period. Foreign exchange earnings from tourism similarly showed an increase of 35% in 2004 and 20% in 2005 over the previous year, taking these earnings from a total of US$ 3.5 billion in 2003 to US$ 5.7 billion in 2005.

Those involved in formulating tourism policy in India are acutely aware of the revenue potential of tourists and pilgrim-tourists, and the development of Buddhist tourism circuits, along with other thrust areas such as rural tourism and eco-tourism, are major areas of interest for the Indian government. The fact that until recently, culture (which includes historical sites and structures) and tourism were handled by the same ministry reflects the fact that the Government of India has tended to see these two arenas as closely related. (The departments of culture and tourism were separated recently.) The Tourism Department gave central financial assistance to the tune of approximately Rs 935 million between the eighth and tenth five year plans to develop Buddhist circuits. During the past few years, twenty-two Buddhist sites in the country have been singled out for special attention, and fourteen projects amounting to about Rs 572 million were sanctioned for infrastructural development at twelve sites. Recent reports of Parliamentary Standing Committees have identified various key tourist circuits that need to be developed, including the Buddhist circuits of Andhra Pradesh (with a special focus on Nagarjunakonda and Amaravati), Bihar and Uttar Pradesh (Bodhgaya, Rajgir, Nalanda, and Varanasi), central India (Sanchi), and Jammu and Kashmir (Leh).[57] The Parliamentary Standing Committee's report for the year 2007–2008 was especially strong in its emphasis on the need to promote tourism, encourage public–private partnership, increase fund allocation for the Archaeological Survey of India, and enhance investments in the conservation of historical monuments.[58] A major campaign entitled 'Come to India—Walk with the Buddha' was recently launched and was directed especially towards the Southeast Asian and domestic markets. Government tie-ups are being planned for a common promotional campaign for Buddhist sites in India, Bangladesh, Bhutan, Nepal, and Sri Lanka.

The various states of the Indian union are currently vying with each other to promote their ancient Buddhist sites as exciting tourist destinations. While Bihar is exceptionally well-endowed with such sites, the ubiquitous presence of ancient Buddhist remains means that other states need not feel left out. In Orissa, infrastructure at the Buddhist circuit sites of Ratnagiri, Lalitagiri, Udayagiri, and Langudi is being improved, and a Peace Park is being planned at Dhauli. In February 2007, the Ministry of Culture and Tourism tried to improve Buddhist tourism in this state by organizing the first Buddha Mahotsav on top of the Dhauli hills, in conjunction with the Maha Bodhi Society of India and the Kolkata-based Nirvan Buddhist travel organization. The festival coincided with the world-wide celebration of the 2550th anniversary of the Buddha's *parinibbāna.* Other states, including Uttar Pradesh, Himachal Pradesh, Jammu and Kashmir, and Andhra Pradesh, are similarly trying to develop and promote Buddhist pilgrim-cum-tourist sites.

The government of the state of Andhra Pradesh has recently begun to realize that it houses an exceptionally large number of ancient Buddhist sites. It is interesting to note that apart from the older well-known sites of Amaravati and Nagarjunakonda, even recently excavated sites such as Bavikonda (excavated in 1982–1987) and Thotlakonda (excavated in 1988–1993) are quickly being developed for tourist traffic, and a Rs 500 million project has already been drawn up for the purpose. The Thotlakonda Tourism Project includes, among other things, plans to develop food courts, gardens, a Buddhist archaeological museum, a circular train, and a sound-and-light show. In tune with the times, the State Museum of Archaeology in Hyderabad has opened a Holy Relics Gallery, where relics from Andhra Buddhist sites are on display. In an interesting departure from orthodox museum practice, visitors/devotees are encouraged to use the room to meditate (Figure 8.2). The aim is to attract visitors by linking the display with current religious and spiritual concerns.

A recent study conducted by the Federation of Indian Chambers of Commerce estimated that about 200,000 Buddhist tourists visit India every year and that these numbers could increase by 400% (generating over US$ 1 billion of revenue) if the Buddhist circuits were developed properly. The Buddhist circuit attracts East Asian tourists in particular. Japan is among India's foremost tourism-generating markets—Japanese tourists have been coming to these destinations for a long time and many an intrepid tour guide has learnt to speak their language. It is estimated that in 2005, about 102,000 Japanese tourists arrived in India, and the

Figure 8.2
People meditating in the Holy Relics Gallery, State Museum of Archaeology, Hyderabad

Courtesy: Sonali Dhingra

numbers of visitors from other East Asian countries are also growing. The major destinations of the pilgrim-tourists on the Buddhist circuit are Sarnath, Kusinagara, Bodhgaya, Nalanda, Rajgir, Vaishali, Sanchi, Amaravati, and Nagarjunakonda. Thc government plans to link the major Buddhist sites by a world class rail network, beginning by connecting Bodhgaya, Rajgir, Nalanda, and Vaishali. Dharamsala too is a destination for Indian and international pilgrims and tourists.

On 17 and 18 February 2004, the Ministry of Culture and Tourism organized an International Conclave on Buddhism and Spiritual Tourism in New Delhi. It was inaugurated by the then President, A. P. J. Abdul Kalam. The conclave brought together 400 devotees and dignitaries from over twenty-five nations, including Cambodia,

Singapore, and Mongolia, the Dalai Lama delivering the keynote address. On 19 February, the conclave shifted to Bodh Gaya for the official ceremony, where the Mahabodhi temple was declared a World Heritage Site. This event highlights the connections between the revenue interests of the Indian state, the desire of pious Buddhists from all over the world to travel to sites associated with the Buddha's life, and the significance of the presence of Tibetan Buddhists in India.

East Asian Investment in the Conservation of Ancient Buddhist Sites in India

The expansion of Buddhist spiritual tourism can also be seen as part of a larger range of interactions between India and East Asia, particularly Japan, especially with regard to the conservation and promotion of India's Buddhist heritage. But it is equally important to recognize that this is a more recent representation of much older networks of Asian interactions. For instance, the Mahabodhi temple at Bodh Gaya attracted international Buddhist pilgrims and patrons throughout ancient and early medieval times. Until at least the 7th century, pilgrims from Sri Lanka, Nepal, Burma, China, Korea, and Central Asia were visiting the shrine. The evidence of these interactions comes from Chinese accounts as well as Nepalese coins and Burmese, Nepalese, and Chinese inscriptions found at the site. But from the point of view of this chapter, it is also significant that apart from the visits of devout monks and lay people, there were also several attempts to 'repair' the shrine. Two Burmese missions had effected 'repairs' to the temple in the 12th and 13th centuries. Much more is known about the 19th century mission: in 1874–75 the Government of India received a request from king Mindon's foreign minister that they be allowed to repair the Mahabodhi temple.[59] Three 'Burmese gentlemen' arrived in Bodh Gaya in January 1877, obtained permission from the chief mahant of the temple, and spent about six months in the area. During this time, they cleared away a large area around the Mahabodhi temple, and engaged not only in repair, but also in fresh construction. When the activities of the Burmese came to the notice of archaeologists, the Government of Bengal asked them to leave, and took on the task of repairing the Mahabodhi temple itself. The conservation work carried out here became the focus of a heated debate concerning restoration and conservation among archaeologists and architectural scholars in India, but that is another story.[60] What is most significant from the point of view of the arguments being made here is that in the late 19th century, the status of the Mahabodhi temple was recognized by a Burmese ruler who sought to enhance his prestige by repairing a Buddhist shrine located in the homeland of Buddhism, well beyond the political borders of his own domain.

In recent years, the international involvement in conservation work at Buddhist sites in India has increased significantly. The Indian government has accepted foreign aid for several projects related to conservation and tourism, several of them connected with Buddhist sites, and many of them involving investments by a country in which Buddhism has a strong presence, namely Japan. For several years now, the Japan Bank of International Cooperation (JBIC) has been offering loans for infrastructural development at Ajanta and Ellora. The total expenditure on the first phase of this project was Rs 1,275 million. For the second phase, Japanese loan assistance to the tune of Rs 2,992 million (7,331 million yen) was expected (the total projected cost of the second phase is Rs 3,600 million).[61] The project involves the conservation and protection of the sites, improvement of airport facilities, and upgrading of tourism-related infrastructure. The implementation of the project lies with the Ministry of Tourism of the Indian government, with the active involvement of the Archaeological Survey of India. It is interesting to note that the JBIC loan covers a micro-credit programme to help fund the training and marketing activities of artisans living in and around Ajanta and Ellora (apparently, not enough is being done in this regard). The Government of India has also entered into an agreement with the JBIC for loan assistance of about Rs 3,956 million for infrastructure development at Buddhist sites in Uttar Pradesh and Bihar, specifically at Sarnath, Kusinagara, Kapilavastu, Sravasti, and Sankisa (the total project cost is Rs 6,800 million). The JBIC, for its part, is also apparently interested in improving infrastructure at Buddhist sites in Sikkim, Ladakh, and Madhya Pradesh.

Furthermore, the Japanese interest in Indian Buddhist sites is part of a larger phenomenon of improving bilateral ties between India and Japan and the latter's forwarding of a series of loans through Official Development Assistance.[62] These loans have helped finance development projects of various kinds, apart from the conservation of India's cultural heritage. Currently, Japan is the only country giving assistance for the conservation of historical sites in India. The 2007 joint statement towards the Japan–India Strategic and Global Partnership included specific mention of Japanese assistance in developing tourism-related infrastructure in India, including the Buddhist pilgrimage circuit.

It is also worth noting that Japan is the largest contributor to the World Heritage Fund and that the UNESCO/Japan Trust Fund for the Preservation of World Cultural Heritage has funded the restoration of many important historical sites in other parts of the world, such as those at Angkor (Cambodia), Jiaohe City and the Hanyuan Hall of Daming Palace (China), monuments in Hue City (Vietnam), Wat Phu (Laos), and Bagan (Myanmar). The fund financed conservation work at Mohenjo Daro and at various Buddhist monuments in the Gandhara region in Pakistan. In India, this Fund was responsible for financing the restoration of the main *stūpa* and some other structures at Sanchi and Satdhara in Madhya Pradesh.

The promotion of tourism along Buddhist circuits is also part of ongoing processes of co-operation among the larger community of South Asian and East Asian countries. For instance, the promotion of this circuit and eco-tourism are the two key target areas identified by the South Asia Subregional Economic Cooperation (SASEC) countries, which comprise Bangladesh, Bhutan, India, Nepal, and Sri Lanka. SASEC's 10-year Tourism Development Plan, with a special focus on integrating nature and culture, is receiving Japanese funding through the Asian Development Bank.

It should also be noted that Japanese archaeologists have been involved in the excavations of two key Buddhist sites in South Asia. In 1992–1995, the Japanese Buddhist Federation sent a team headed by Satoru Uesaka to excavate Lumbini in Nepal. The Federation also helped fund conservation work at the site, especially the repair of the Māyādevī temple. Archaeologists from Kansai University, Japan, working in collaboration with the Archaeological Survey of India, were involved in several seasons' excavation at Shravasti in Uttar Pradesh in 1958–1959, 1986–1988, and 1993–1994.

Modern temples built by East Asian communities are a common sight at Buddhist pilgrimage sites such as Kusinagara, Bodhgaya, Rajgir, and Sarnath. Sarnath has several modern Buddhist temples built and maintained by monks from Tibet, China, Japan, and Myanmar. The most important monastery-shrine complex at Sarnath is the Mulagandhakuti Vihara, built by the Maha Bodhi Society of India, which enshrines relics found at Taxila and Nagarjunakonda. The walls of this temple have paintings by the Japanese artist Kosetsu Nosu, and the original 'World Peace

Bell' of this temple (which had to be replaced in 2005 due to damage) was donated by the Japanese Buddhist community.

The transformation of ancient Buddhist sites due to increasing international involvement and investment and the demands of the tourist industry is visible in many places, but has not been adequately documented, in part no doubt because this kind of investigation is not considered a serious scholarly endeavour. There are, however, a few exceptions. For instance, David Geary's study of the Mahabodhi temple directs attention to the ways in which the site has been transformed due to commercial factors linked directly to the booming tourism industry.[63] The international presence at the site increased steadily from 1956 onwards, and today, the environs of the temple are dotted with many temples, *vihāras*, and guest-houses built by groups from several countries including Sri Lanka, Nepal, Bhutan, Myanmar, Thailand, Japan, Vietnam, and Mongolia. Geary discusses the ways in which the local community living in and around this relatively poor part of the state of Bihar have participated and benefited economically from the increased tourist traffic, for instance, through the making and selling of Buddhist souvenirs, and how the increasing stakes have simultaneously led to friction and conflict among local shop-keepers and hoteliers. The international flavour of Bodh Gaya is reflected in its international temples, the occasional marriages between Japanese women and Indian tour guides (who speak fluent Japanese), and the wide range of cuisines on offer in restaurants. The government of Bihar is well aware of the great revenue generation potential of the Mahabodhi temple and has been busy trying to improve infrastructure, for instance, through a plan to make an eighteen-hole golf course. The completion of the Gaya international airport in 2002 made the site much more accessible to visitors. This was also the year in which Bodh Gaya was declared a World Heritage Site by UNESCO, making it the first 'living' Buddhist site to be given this coveted status. Bodh Gaya is an ancient Buddhist site which continued to see varying volumes of pilgrim traffic over the centuries, and is today a flourishing pilgrim and tourist destination. But thanks to tourists, pilgrims, and pilgrim-tourists, many a 'dead' Buddhist site is also coming to life again.

The Reinvention of Extinct Buddhist Sites

One of the most interesting features of the contemporary Buddhist revival in India is the resurrection, or rather reinvention, of several extinct ancient Buddhist sites as a result of a conjunction of the factors outlined in earlier sections. One of the important recent developments in this context is the concerted appropriation of ancient Buddhist sites by Tibetan Buddhists through large-scale ceremonials which have religious and political import, and which bring together and unite the scattered Tibetan diaspora and its sympathizers.[64] The most important of these ceremonials is the Dukhor Wangchen or Kālacakra initiation. This initiation into the practice of Kālacakra *tantra* is an important part of Tibetan Buddhism, and the fourteenth Dalai Lama has conducted more Kālacakra initiations than any of his predecessors. The first two conducted by him were held in Lhasa in Tibet (in 1954 and 1956). Thereafter, they have been held in various parts of the world, including in Los Angeles (1989), New York (1991), Barcelona (1994), Ulan Bator (1995), Sydney (1996), and Toronto (2004). Within India, the initiations have been held in various places, including Dharamsala (1970), Bylakuppe (in Karnataka, 1971), Bodh Gaya (1974, 1985, 2003), Leh (in Ladakh, 1976), Tabo (1983, 1996), Kyi (in Spiti, 2000), and Sarnath (1990).

In 2006, the thirtieth Kālacakra was held at Amaravati in the Guntur district of Andhra Pradesh. Until then, this place was, at a popular level, known more for its Śaiva Amareśvara temple than for the ruins of a Buddhist complex that dates from the 3rd century BCE to the 13th century CE. The *mahācaitya* at Amaravati was gradually destroyed and dismantled after the 13th century, irrevocably so during the 19th century (Figure 8.3).[65] But between the 5th and 16th of January 2006, the Kālacakra brought it to life again (Figure 8.4). The idea of organizing the event at this place was apparently that of one of its sponsors—the Busshokai Centre of Kanazawa, a small group in Japan devoted to the study of Tibetan Buddhism. The result was that the winter of 2006 saw thousands of devout Buddhists from all over the world converge at Amaravati.

The main organizer of this event was the Norbulingka Institute based in Dharamsala, and substantial funds and resources were provided by the Government of India, the state government, and the Central Tibetan Administration. The Andhra Pradesh government spent some Rs 500 million on infrastructure including road improvement, sanitation, electrification, medical facilities, drinking water, and a helipad for VIPs. Houses, schools, and colleges were converted into hotels, and hundreds of tents were set up to house visitors. The valedictory function was conducted by the Dalai Lama, and several state ministers and high-ranking officials attended. The audience included as many as 80,000 to 100,000 people from different parts of the world including India, China, Mongolia, Tibet, the Netherlands, Australia, Ireland, Japan, Iceland, Southeast Asia, and South America. The presence of American film actor

Figure 8.3
The Amaravati mahācaitya today

Courtesy: Sonali Dhingra

Figure 8.4
Kālacakra celebrations at Amaravati, January 2006

Courtesy: Tenzing Sonam

Richard Gere contributed the important glamour quotient. The Andhra Pradesh government clearly saw this event as an opportunity to place Amaravati firmly on the world spiritual tourism map.

Becker has described in detail how the landscape of Amaravati was dramatically altered by the Kālacakra. The Archaeological Survey of India raised the level of the drum of the ruined *stūpa* mound, propped up sculpted limestone slabs against it, and added a new metal railing. Devotees added prayer flags, garlands, and ceremonial paraphernalia. A colossal 125 foot image of the seated Buddha (funded by devotees and government agencies) was installed, together with a much smaller gilded image of *ācārya* Nāgārjuna, right across the street from the already-standing statue of Ambedkar. Becker states that on the occasion of the Kālacakra, the remains of the ancient Amaravati *stūpa* were infused with 'a new sacred authority . . . a relic-like quality', the result of a combination of re-used ancient elements and much new imagery.[66]

A few days before performing the ceremonials at Amaravati, the Dalai Lama inaugurated the Holy Relics Gallery in the Andhra Pradesh Museum in Hyderabad, where, as mentioned earlier, ancient remains mix with current spiritual interests within the precincts of a museum. He also visited the site of Nagarjunakonda, no doubt because of the strong visibility of the 3rd to 4th century Buddhist remains of the ancient Ikṣvāku capital of Vijayapurī, which was once located in this place.

The Dalai Lama's footprints are as visible in the western Himalayas as in South India. Reference was made earlier to the two Kālacakras held at Tabo. In August 2007 the Dalai Lama delivered teachings on 'The Thirty-Seven Practices of a Bodhisattva' and Kamalaśīla's 'Middle Stages of Meditation' at Nako, a small, picturesque village in the Spiti Valley in Himachal Pradesh. On this occasion, he also conducted an Avalokiteśvara initiation and a Dechok initiation. When I visited Nako in the summer of 2007, it was humming with development activity and anticipation of the forthcoming event. It is interesting to note that this major ceremonial event also coincided with the holding of an academic one—an international seminar on the culture of the north-western Himalayas.

The Iconography of Convergence: Nagarjunakonda

The reinvention of Buddhism in India and India's increasing stature as Buddhism's original homeland are perhaps not surprising when seen as part of the long-term history of Buddhism in the subcontinent. This chapter has emphasized that the convergence of various processes that have contributed to this resurgence can be seen especially clearly at Buddhist pilgrimage sites which attract Dalit Buddhists as well as East Asian and other international pilgrim-tourists. This convergence is vividly represented in the varied iconography that marks the landscape of these sites. While Becker has described some aspects of this at Amaravati, it can be seen even more graphically at Nagarjunakonda.

Situated on the banks of the river Krishna and surrounded on three sides by offshoots of the Nallamalai hills, Nagarjunakonda (in Guntur district, Andhra Pradesh) was once a 15 square kilometre valley, rich in remains from the prehistoric to medieval periods. Tragically, most of these remains were permanently drowned in the waters of the Krishna River when a major multi-purpose dam project was initiated at this place in 1955. In the heady optimism of post-Independence socialism, big dams represented the new India's hopes for a prosperous future, and if it was necessary to sacrifice an ancient site in the interests of development and modernization, that would have to be done.

The explorations and excavations at Nagarjunakonda have a very long history. Discovered in 1926 by A. R. Saraswati, the site was excavated by Muhammad Hamid Kuraishi and subsequently by A. H. Longhurst. Longhurst's report (published in 1938) represents the first stage in the interpretation of the site, one in which it was seen essentially as a Buddhist site (Figure 8.5).[67] The report on the second series of excavations by T. N. Ramachandran (published in 1953) drew attention to the many Hindu temples in the early historic city.[68] During the 1950s, as plans for building the dam across the Krishna were drawn up, Nagarjunakonda's impending submergence led the Archaeological Survey of India to undertake a massive project of exploration, excavation, and documentation. About 136 new structures and structural complexes were unearthed, and before the valley was turned into a gigantic lake, nine of the most important structures were transplanted and rebuilt on top of the Nagarjunakonda hill, which became an island in the midst of the lake created by the dam. Smaller-scale replicas of fourteen other structures were fabricated and set up on the banks of the reservoir. The first part of the report of the 1954–1960 excavations (published in 1975), by R. Subrahmanyam and others, focused on the site's prehistoric and megalithic remains, while the second part, edited by K. V. Soundararajan (published as recently as 2006), offers a consolidated view of the early historic remains, artifacts, and inscriptions.[69]

In spite of the abundant evidence of its varied, changing, and multireligious character, there has always been a strong tendency for both

Figure 8.5
Ruins of the early historical mahācaitya, *Nagarjunakonda*

Source: Author

scholars and the Indian government to privilege one particular aspect of Nagarjunakonda—its early historic Buddhist remains. The reasons for this privileging include the Buddhist bias of early archaeologists in colonial India. There is also the strong resilience of a tradition of uncertain historicity which connects this place with the renowned Buddhist scholar-monk Nāgārjuna. To this can be added the Indian government's deliberate privileging of the Buddhist connections of the site to promote its own perspective and its revenue interests, and it is these connections which are advertised abundantly in and around the place.

Today, the most imposing edifice at Nagarjunakonda is a modern construction—the gigantic Nagarjunasagar dam, the largest masonry dam in the world, the centrepiece of a massive project which took place between the 1950s and the 1970s (Figure 8.6). While laying its foundation stone on 12 December 1955, Prime Minister Jawaharlal Nehru declared that he was founding one of the many new temples of humanity that were being built all over India. This excerpt from his speech is displayed prominently on the outer walls of the lift tower of the dam, both in English and in Telugu translation. However, the ancient Buddhist links of Nagarjunakonda can be seen everywhere, even at the dam site. A

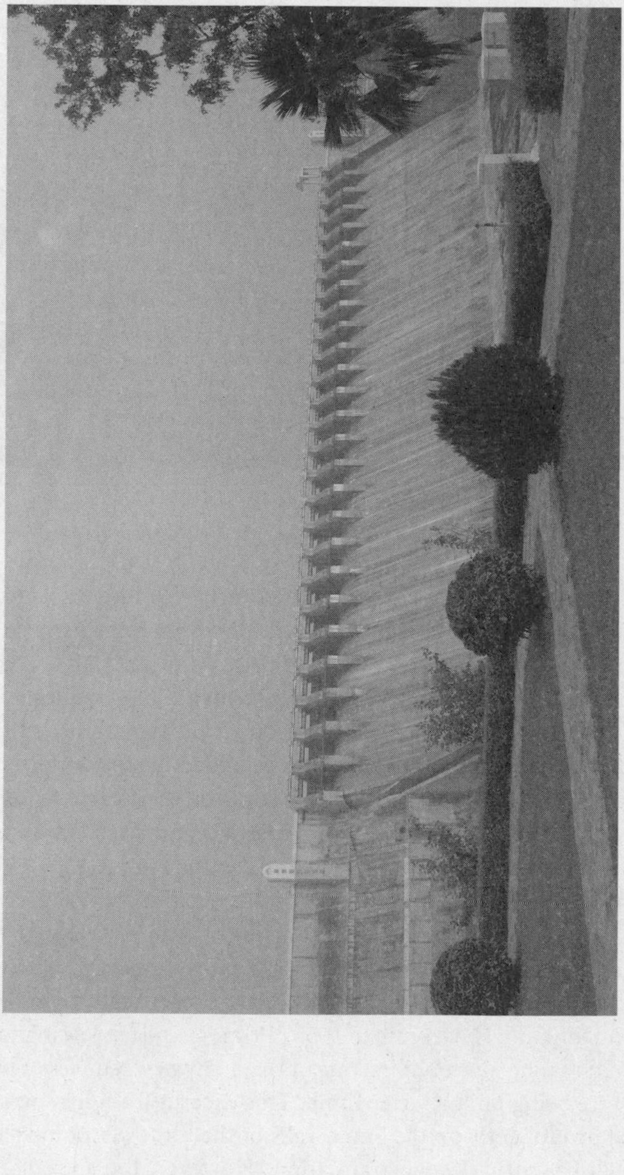

Figure 8.6
The Nagarjunasagar dam

Source: Author

Figure 8.7
Nāgārjuna portrait in the dam gallery

Source: Author

modern artist's painted portraits of Nāgārjuna hang in the dam gallery (Figure 8.7), while a gilded concrete image of the monk stands prominently at the gallery exit (Figure 8.8). Even the dam railing is a crude modern copy of a typical ancient Buddhist railing (Figure 8.9).

On Nagarjunakonda island, where some of the ancient structures were rebuilt, is the guest house where Nehru stayed in the winter of 1955 when he came to lay the dam's foundation stone. There is also a museum where a selection of the archaeological material discovered in the course of excavations over the years is displayed. In a play on the name 'Nagarjunakonda', a serpent motif is woven continuously into the small stone screens that are interspersed along the outer walls of the museum building. Inside, to some extent because the Buddhist reliefs and images outnumber the stone sculptural remains associated with Hindu temples, the display has an overpoweringly strong Buddhist emphasis.

Domestic tourists, pilgrims, and pilgrim-tourists, and those from other countries including Japan, Tibet, and Sri Lanka, visit the site. There is no flood of Buddhist pilgrims—yet. But that the process is underway is evident from clues strewn amidst the *kikar* trees and landscaped gardens crossed by oleander-lined paths on Nagarjunakonda island. Many of these clues date from the time when the Kālacakra was held at nearby Amaravati. Heaps of piled-up stones are reminiscent of the votive

Figure 8.8
Gilded Nāgārjuna image near dam gallery exit

Source: Author

offerings seen all over the barren mountainous terrain of the western Himalayas. Colourful prayer flags flutter incongruously over a megalithic burial site reconstructed by the Archaeological Survey of India (Figure 8.10). Small sign-boards identify the *pipal* saplings planted by the Dalai Lama during his brief visit (Figure 8.11).

Figure 8.9
Railing of the Nagarjunasagar dam

Source: Author

Figure 8.10
Prayer flags fluttering over reconstructed megalithic burial

Source: Author

Figure 8.11
Pipal *sapling planted by the Dalai Lama on Nagarjunakonda island*

Source: Author

The modern town, which consists of two parts—Vijayapuri North and Vijayapuri South—has a large number of gilded statues, most of them installed in 2005, during the dam's Golden Jubilee celebrations. There are statues of former Prime Minister, Indira Gandhi; former president, Neelam Sanjiva Reddy; former Minister for Irrigation, K. L. Rao; former chief minister, Brahmananda Reddy; the first chief engineer of the dam, Mir Jaffer Ali; and also the more recent chairman of a local cement factory. Strongly reminiscent of the stones raised in the early historical city of Vijayapurī (the ancient name of Nagarjunakonda) in memory of heroes who died in battle many centuries ago, there is a modern 'Martyrs' Memorial' which names the engineers and workers who lost their lives during the dam's construction (Figure 8.12). As at the dam site, here too, mingling with the images and ideas of modern times, are iconic representations of more ancient, imagined, connections. In front of the recreation club in Vijayapuri South is a statue of the Buddha (Figure 8.13). A Nāgārjuna image stands at the entrance to the right earth dam, the entrance to the power station is ornamented with a gigantic plaster *stūpa* façade (Figure 8.14), and there is a large image of Nāgārjuna over the side entrance. The ancient Buddhist connections of Nagarjunakonda were evidently in the forefront of the consciousness of those who designed the landscape of the modern dam-city, and these connections were deliberately and repeatedly emphasized by them.

The Dalit connection is also represented iconically at Nagarjunakonda. In the main fenced-in *chowk* of Vijayapuri South is a large concrete canopy supported on four pillars which bear quadruple lions (part of the emblem of the ancient Maurya emperor Aśoka as well as of the modern Indian nation state), a *cakra* (wheel), and an elephant (Figure 8.15). One of the many connotations of the elephant is its symbolic association with the Bahujan Samaj Party, a political party which ostensibly represents the interests of India's Dalits. Under the canopy, high on a three-tier pedestal, stands B. R. Ambedkar, in his familiar dress and pose—bespectacled, blue-suited, his right arm raised up, the index finger of his hand pointing in a firm, didactic gesture. The iconography of Ambedkar (which usually also includes a fountain pen and a book, representing the Constitution of India, in the drafting of which he played a leading role) deliberately emphasizes a westernized, educated man.[70] On top of the canopy is a smaller seated gilded figure of the Buddha, seated in the *vitarka mudrā* of giving instruction. In this *chowk,* what we have is a remarkable ensemble of images that graphically illustrates many of the processes that

Figure 8.12
The 'Martyrs' Memorial'

Source: Author

Figure 8.13
Buddha bust outside Recreation Club

Source: Author

Figure 8.14
Façade of Nagarjunasagar Power Station

Source: Author

Figure 8.15
Chowk of Vijayapuri South

Source: Author

have been discussed in this chapter. The East Asian connection is likely to strengthen as Nagarjunakonda becomes more firmly placed on the Buddhist pilgrim-tourist circuit.

The images of the Buddha and Nāgārjuna, commemorations of the Dalai Lama's visit, the statue of Ambedkar at the cross-roads, and the visits of Indian and international tourists and pilgrim-tourists—all these aspects converge and blend into the landscape of Nagarjunakonda. As is the case at other Buddhist sites, these are not the symbols of the revival of an old religion, once dominant, and subsequently relegated to the cultural margins. Although anchored in ancient Buddhism and its sacred places, in reality, they represent an entirely new conjunction of factors and forces, internal as well as international, religious as well as utterly mundane.

Conclusions

Asian Buddhism's interest in and interaction with ancient sites in India goes back to very early times. From the mid-20th century onwards, this interest and interaction became more intense due to the factors outlined in this chapter. In fact, new Buddhist sects and organizations are currently actively marking their presence on Indian soil in many ways, including through the construction of new kinds of *stūpas*.[71] Unlike popular religious sites which are bustling centres of active worship, extinct sites offer a large number of wide open spaces with great potential for appropriation by Buddhist groups who are seeking to expand their presence and visibility. These places have the additional advantage that there is little competition from entrenched rival religious groups, although the history of Bodh Gaya shows that there will always be latent potential for future competition, contestation, and conflict at those sites that have a multi-denominational profile and history. This would, in fact, apply to a large number of sites, since most ancient Indian 'Buddhist' sites have connections with the Hindu and Jaina traditions as well.

The reinvention and increased visibility of ancient Buddhist sites in India can be traced to a variety of sources, including the neo-Buddhist and Tibetan Buddhist movements, state recognition of the enormous tourist potential of these sites, and the increasing East Asian and, indeed, international interest in them. It has been argued in this chapter that a significant segment of the people who travel to the sites on the spiritual tourism circuits can be described as pilgrims or pilgrim-tourists. Some of these sites may seem rather out of the way and difficult to access. This is thc case with Nagarjunakonda, for instance, which is not only difficult to reach but is also located in an area where Naxalite (left-wing extremists) are very active. On 30 April 2006 a tourist boat headed for the island was blown up by Naxalites, thankfully after its occupants had been made to disembark. But for the intrepid and adventurous pilgrim-tourist, the arduousness and dangers of the journey can be a challenge rather than discouragement.

We are currently witnessing the steady expansion of the circuits of spiritual tourism, and given the large number of ancient Buddhist sites, the possibilities are virtually endless. It remains to be seen whether and to what extent these sites can actually foster a sense of *communitas* among those who visit them, specifically among the Dalit Buddhists, Tibetan Buddhists (and their non-Tibetan adherents and supporters), and East Asian Buddhists. Given the enormous differences between the cultural matrices in which all these Buddhisms are embedded, the potential for this seems fairly limited at present.

The reinvention of Buddhism and Buddhist sites in modern India can be seen as a new phase in the history of Buddhism in India, one which is fueled by many processes operating in an increasingly globalized world. The long-term prospects of this reinvention can only be a matter of speculation. The vitality and survival of Buddhist monasteries and communities have always been dependant on their relationship and level of integration with their hinterland. It should be noted that due to globalization, the hinterland of Buddhist communities has expanded enormously and that it is, more than ever before, not governed by spatial proximity.

Finally, it should be mentioned that the increased activity at ancient Buddhist sites presents opportunities for many, but also presents dangers to the sites themselves. As these sites become more visible, as they are appropriated by religious groups, and as the money flows in to swiftly develop them as heritage sites and destinations for spiritual tourism, crucial decisions have to be made. The reinforcement of the drum of the Amaravati *stūpa* represents a modest modification of an ancient structure. But there are instances *of stūpa*s having been reconstructed in their entirety, sometimes not very tastefully, as at Satdhara in central India. The reinvention of Buddhism and Buddhist sites, therefore, brings to the fore many important and complex policy issues related to the conservation and restoration of ancient monuments.

Acknowledgements

This is a revised version of a paper I presented at a conference organized by Ryukoku University, Kyoto, and the Indian Council for Cultural Relations in Kyoto, Japan on 5 October 2007. I would like to acknowledge the help given by Tenzing Sonam, Ritu Sarin, Arjun Mahey, and Yaaminey Mubayi in the course of my research for this paper. I would also like to acknowledge the valuable comments and suggestions made by the anonymous referee of an earlier version of the paper. Thanks are also due to the India International Centre library and to Prof. K. T. S. Sarao and Neha Sarao for locating crucial readings.

Notes

1. For instance, J. Leoshko has underlined such a lack of investigation of 'later material' from the site of Bodh Gaya. J. Leoshko, *Sacred Traces: British Explorations of Buddhism in South Asia* (Aldershot: Ashgate, 2003), pp. 3–4.
2. Nālandā is located in the Nalanda district of Bihar; Odantapura is near Nalanda; Vikramaśilā is identified with Antichak in Bhagalpur district, Bihar; Somapurī is identified with Paharpur in Rajshahi district, Bangladesh.
3. T. Ling, *Buddhist Revival in India: Aspects of the Sociology of Buddhism* (London and Basingstoke: Macmillan, 1980), pp. 11–46.
4. B. G. Ray, *Religious Movements in Modern Bengal* (Santiniketan: Visva-Bharati, 1965).
5. N. N. Basu, 'Modern Buddhism and Its Followers in Orissa', *Archaeological Survey of Mayurbhanj*, 1, 1982, p. 12. Founded by Mahima Gosavi, this movement combined social protest with *bhakti* and had certain Buddhist elements in its ideas and organization. For details, see also G. Omvedt, *Buddhism in India: Challenging Brahmanism and Caste* (New Delhi: SAGE Publications, 2003), pp. 225–227.
6. Several Buddhist groups claim that these figures were deliberately understated, and that many Buddhists, especially new converts, were counted as Hindus during the census.
7. Ling (*Buddhist Revival in India*, p. 134) describes it as a quickening of interest with potential for further growth rather than a revival.
8. This is something for which B. R. Ambedkar apparently took credit, but was evidently supported by other leaders as well.
9. P. C. Almond, *The British Discovery of Buddhism* (Cambridge: Cambridge University Press, 1988).
10. Ling, *Buddhist Revival in India,* p. 134, describes it as a quickening of interest with potential for further growth rather than a revival.
11. T. Huber, *The Holy Land Reborn: Pilgrimage and the Tibetan Reinvention of Buddhist India* (Chicago: University of Chicago Press, 2008).
12. C. Becker, 'Remembering the Amaravati Stūpa: The Revival of a Ruin', in J. Hawkes and A. Shimada, ed., *Buddhist Stupas in South Asia: Recent Archaeological, Art-Historical, and Historical Perspectives* (New Delhi: Oxford University Press, 2009), pp. 268–287.
13. A. Fiske, 'Scheduled Caste Buddhist Organization', in *The Untouchables in Contemporary India*, ed. J. M. Mahar (Tucson: University of Arizona Press, 1972), pp. 113–118.
14. Ray, *Religious Movements in Modern Bengal,* pp. 165–168.
15. Omvedt, *Buddhism in India,* pp. 236–240.
16. The conversion of lower castes to Buddhism (as also to Islam and Christianity) was known in earlier periods in Indian history. But there were many important differences between these earlier events and what happened at the Diksha Bhumi in Nagpur in 1959. In this case, the conversion was that of a large section of an entire caste (the Mahar caste of Maharashtra, to which Ambedkar belonged); the converts built their own religious organization

and held on to many aspects of their social customs, leadership, and caste loyalties; and the conversion was that of a group of people who were already connected to a political party that represented their interests. See E. Zelliot, *From Untouchable to Dalit: Essays on the Ambedkar Movement* (New Delhi: Manohar, 1992), pp. 126–127, 191–192. Ambedkar had founded the Independent Labour Party in 1936. The name of this party changed to the Scheduled Castes Federation in 1942 and to the Republican Party in 1957.

17. According to Omvedt, the members of the Maha Bodhi Society were actually alarmed by Ambedkar's plan. Note the telegram sent to him by the secretary of the Maha Bodhi Society in Calcutta: 'Shocked very much to read your decision to renounce Hindu religion… Please reconsider your decision'. (Cited in Omvedt, *Buddhism in India*, pp. 258–259). Later, the Society argued that if the Dalits must convert, it should be to Buddhism. Omvedt argues that the reason was obvious: in India the Maha Bodhi Society was dominated by Bengali Brahmins and they were not particularly happy about a Dalit influx into the Buddhist fold.
18. D. Keer, *Dr. Ambedkar: Life and Mission* (Mumbai: Popular Prakashan, [1954] 1962), pp. 494, 489.
19. After the standard declaration of taking refuge in the Buddha, the Dhamma, and the *saṅgha* was made, Ambedkar himself administered to his followers 22 additional vows, which included an emphatic repudiation of the worship of the Hindu gods and also a rejection of the idea that the Buddha was an *avatāra* (incarnation) of Viṣṇu.
20. See Ambedkar in V. Rodrigues, ed., *The Essential Writings of B. R. Ambedkar* (New Delhi: Oxford University Press, 2002), pp. 172–189.
21. B. R. Ambedkar, *The Buddha and his Dhamma* (Mumbai: Siddharth College, 1957), pp. x, xi, 301–309, 316–336, 350–351, 511–512.
22. Cited in Ling, *Buddhist Revival in India*, p. 91.
23. Posted in *The Tribune*, 28 October 2002. The function was organized to condole the killing of five Dalits in Dulina village in Jhajjar district on 28 October. It is reported that at least 12 Dalits took the vows of Buddhist monks, 12 among those present declared themselves as converts to Islam, and one married couple converted to Christianity. Apart from Udit Raj, chairman of the All-India Confederation of Scheduled Castes and Scheduled Tribes Organizations, the well-known film director Mahesh Bhatt was also present. The first convert to Islam was converted by the President of the All-India Muslim Morcha, and leaders of the Jamiat Ulama-i-Hind were also present. The couple was converted to Christianity by the President of the All-India Christian Council.
24. Posted in *The Hindustan Times*, 4 November 2004.
25. 'Thousands of Dalits Embrace Buddhism', see http://www.international-reporter.com/News-2143/thousands-of-dalits-embrace-buddhism.html (accessed 27 July 2010).
26. Fiske, 'Scheduled Caste Buddhist Organization', pp. 113–142.
27. D. S. Lopez, Jr, ed., *Religions of Tibet in Practice* (New Delhi: Munshiram Manoharlal, 1998), p. 24.

28. D. S. Lopez, Jr, 'Foreigner at the Lama's Feet', in D. S. Lopez, Jr, ed., *Curators of the Buddha: The Study of Buddhism under Colonialism* (Chicago and London: University of Chicago Press, 1995), pp. 251–295.
29. If all this sounds cold and unsympathetic towards the Tibetan cause, Lopez is quick to add that 'to allow Tibet to circulate in a system of fantastic opposites . . . is to deny Tibet its history, to exclude it from a real world of which it has always been a part, and to deny Tibetans their agency in the creation of a contested quotidian reality. During the past three decades fantasies of Tibet garnered much support for the cause of Tibetan independence. But those fantasies are ultimately a threat to the realization of that goal.' D. S. Lopez, Jr, *Prisoners of Shangri-La: Tibetan Buddhism and the West* (Chicago and London: University of Chicago Press, 1999), p. 11.
30. L. S. Thakur, *Buddhism in the Western Himalayas: A Study of the Tabo Monastery* (New Delhi: Oxford University Press, 2001), p. 35.
31. Thakur, *Buddhism in the Western Himalayas*, p. 5.
32. T. Sonam, 'The Geshe of Tabo', *Tibetan Bulletin* (1990).
33. See http://www.tabomonastery.org/ (accessed 27 July 2010).
34. Nawang Tsering, *Alchi: The Living Heritage of Ladakh: 1000 Years of Buddhist Art* (Leh: Central Institute of Buddhist Studies, 2009).
35. J. Rizvi, *Ladakh: Crossroads of High Asia* (New Delhi: Oxford University Press, 1983; 1998 Reprint), pp. 208, 220.
36. I must add that the 'revitalization' of these monasteries also has its limits. The remote monasteries of Ladakh, Lahaul and Spiti are desperately in need of funding and attention from the Indian government to help preserve their unique historical and artistic heritage.
37. 'I am always expressing, telling and sharing with new Buddhists, particularly those who come from the so-called lower castes, that taking to Buddhism should not result in resentment among other religions or caste systems. . .' . 'If some people from this country [India] follow the dharma, it is good. After all, I describe Buddhism and Hinduism as twin brothers and sisters.' *The Times of India*, 10 April 2001. The Dalai Lama here seems to have been trying to downplay the element of conflict associated with Dalit conversions.
38. I am grateful to Tenzin Geyche Tethong, the personal secretary of the Dalai Lama, for bringing this to my attention.
39. This emerges graphically in *The Sun Behind the Clouds: Tibet's Struggle for Freedom*, a recent film by Ritu Sarin and Tenzing Sonam (White Crane Films, 2009).
40. Zelliot, *From Untouchable to Dalit,* pp. 235–236.
41. Fiske, 'Scheduled Caste Buddhist Organization', pp. 135–136.
42. Huber, *The Holy Land Reborn,* p. 346.
43. Huber, *The Holy Land Reborn,* pp. 348, 350–358.
44. Zelliot, *From Untouchable to Dalit,* pp. 235–236.
45. A. Trevithick, 'British Archaeologists, Hindu Abbots, and Burmese Buddhists: The Mahabodhi Temple at Bodh Gaya, 1811–1877', *Modern Asian Studies*, 33 (3), 1999, pp. 635–656. Also, Nayanjot Lahiri, 'Bodh Gaya: An Ancient

Buddhist Shrine and its Modern History (1891-1904', in Timothy Insoll, ed., *Case Studies in Archaeology and Religion* (Oxford: Archaeopress, 1999), pp. 33–44.

46. V. Turner, *Dramas, Fields, and Metaphors: Symbolic Action in Human Society* (Ithica and London: Cornell University Press, 1974). Turner takes the term *communitas* from Paul Goodman but gives it a new meaning.
47. Zelliot, *From Untouchable to Dalit,* pp. 230–233.
48. G. M. Tartakov, 'Art and Identity: The Rise of a New Buddhist Imagery', *Art Journal*, 49 (4), 1990, p. 410.
49. Zelliot, *From Untouchable to Dalit,* p. 245.
50. Huber, *The Holy Land Reborn,* p. 121.
51. M. Kapstein, 'The Guide to the Crystal Peak', in D. S. Lopez, Jr., ed., *Religions of Tibet in Practice* (New Delhi: Munshiram Manoharlal, 1998), pp. 103–04.
52. Huber, *The Holy Land Reborn,* pp. 338–346.
53. Huber, *The Holy Land Reborn,* pp. 338, 372. Huber provides an excellent discussion of the interactions between Tibet and India across the centuries.
54. Turner, *Dramas, Fields, and Metaphors,* pp. 221, 226.
55. Yaaminey Mubayi, personal communication.
56. These people additionally described their interest in Ellora as fueled by awareness of its historical importance and the beauty of its sculpture, something they had come to learn of from their school text-books (Yaaminey Mubayi, personal communication).
57. See the Report of the Department-related Parliamentary Standing Committee on Transport, Tourism, and Culture, 79th report on demands for grants (2004–05, demand no. 93) of the Ministry of Tourism (Parliament of India, Rajya Sabha, available online).
58. See the Report of the Department-related Parliamentary Standing Committee on Transport, Tourism, and Culture's 120th report on demands for grants (2007–08) (Parliament of India, Rajya Sabha, available online).
59. Trevithick, 'British Archaeologists, Hindu Abbots, and Burmese Buddhists', pp. 648–651; Upinder Singh, *The Discovery of Ancient India: Early Archaeologists and the Beginnings of Archaeology* (New Delhi: Permanent Black, 2004), pp. 218–221.
60. Singh, *The Discovery of Ancient India*, pp. 218–230.
61. The balance is supposed to be obtained from various government agencies such as the Archaeological Survey of India, the Airport Authority of India, and five State Government agencies.
62. Many of these details are from the data provided on the Internet by the Ministry of Foreign Affairs of Japan. New Japanese loans were frozen following the nuclear test conducted by India in May 1998; the freeze was lifted on 26 October 2001.
63. D. Geary, 'Destination Enlightenment: Branding Buddhism and Spiritual Tourism in Bodhgaya, Bihar', *Anthropology Today,* 24(3), 2008, pp. 10–14.
64. Huber, *The Holy Land Reborn,* pp. 358–373.
65. Singh, *The Discovery of Ancient India,* pp. 249–290 and Chapter 6 of this book.

66. Becker, 'Remembering the Amaravati Stūpa, p. 268.
67. A. H. Longhurst, *The Buddhist Antiquities of Nagarjunakonda, Madras Presidency,* Memoirs of the Archaeological Survey of India, no. 54 (New Delhi: Archaeological Survey of India, 1938); 1999, Reprint.
68. T. N. Ramachandran, *Nagarjunakonda 1938*, Memoirs of the Archaeological Survey of India, no. 71 (New Delhi: Archaeological Survey of India, 1953); 1999, Reprint.
69. R. Subrahmanyam and others, *Nagarjunakonda (1954–60): Volume I,* Memoirs of the Archaeological Survey of India, no. 75 (New Delhi: Archaeological Survey of India, 1975); K. V Soundararajan, ed., *Nagarjunakonda (1954–60): Volume II (The Historical Period),* Memoirs of the Archaeological Survey of India, no. 75 (New Delhi: Archaeological Survey of India, 2006).
70. 'The personality which Ambedkar presented with that elitist image was arrogant, caustic, aggressive, never violent but rarely polite. To realize the impact of this figure, one must place it alongside the stereotype of the Mahar (the "Untouchable" caste that Ambedkar belonged to)'. Zelliot, *From Untouchable to Dalit,* p. 59. Tartakov argues that such images express the history and aspirations of neo-Buddhists, and that the portraits and statues of Ambedkar are genuine revolutionary art, art as an instrument for social change (Tartakov, 'Art and Identity', pp. 411–416).
71. J. Kim, 'What Makes a Stūpa? Quotations, Fragments, and the Reinvention of Buddhist Stūpas in Contemporary India', in Hawkes and Shimada, *Buddhist Stupas in South Asia*, pp. 289–309.

SECTION III

The Intersection of Political Ideas and Practice

9

Governing the State and the Self: Political Philosophy and Practice in the Edicts of Aśoka

The Maurya empire (c. 324/321–187 BCE) was the first virtually all-India empire, and the inscriptions of Aśoka (c. 268–232 BCE), the third king of the Maurya dynasty, are the first self-representations of imperial power in the subcontinent. These inscriptions constitute a corpus of inscribed texts exceptionally rich in political ideas, which have not been analyzed closely enough because of historians' obsession with connecting them with various religious and textual traditions, Buddhist or otherwise, or reducing them to a legitimizing strategy. This essay attempts a fresh interpretation of Aśoka's political philosophy as expressed in his inscriptions, with a special focus on identifying their interconnected ideas and arguments regarding the relationship between political power, goodness, and violence. The larger argument is that ideas related to political power and violence in ancient India (and indeed in other cultural contexts as well) need to be analyzed through a close and nuanced reading of texts and inscriptions. The latter in particular offer valuable insights into the ways in which early Indian states perceived

This chapter was previously published in *South Asian Studies* 28 (2), 2012, pp. 131–145.

and represented themselves, and an analysis of such self-representations should complement the historian's usual approach towards ancient political systems, which consists of describing and analyzing them using the conceptual categories of history or anthropology.

Aśoka has been the special focus of much adulation as well as dispassionate debate, especially with regard to his renunciation of war, ardent espousal of Buddhism, and vigorous propagation of a set of ethics.[1] The three major foci of debate regarding Maurya rule are the nature of the Maurya empire; the extent and impact of Aśoka's pacifism; and something that Aśoka's inscriptions refer to as *dhamma* (the Prakrit equivalent of the Sanskrit *dharma*, a word difficult to translate into English, carrying with it connotations of goodness, virtue, and duty). The hypothesis of a highly centralized polity has made way for a more realistic and textured view of the Maurya empire.[2] While some historians have argued that Aśoka's pacifism seriously undermined the military backbone of the Maurya empire, others have suggested that the extent and impact of his pacifism have been grossly exaggerated.[3] The *dhamma* of Aśoka's edicts has been variously understood as a Buddhist lay ethic, a set of politico-moral ideas, a sort of universal religion, or an Aśokan innovation.[4] It has also been interpreted as essentially a political ideology which sought to knit together a vast and diverse empire.[5] The comparative exercises and the tendency to reduce Aśoka's ideas to legitimization strategy have prevented a careful, detailed analysis of the internal logic and the implications of those ideas, and the focus on ascertaining the element of centralization or decentralization in the Maurya empire has prevented the asking of a range of other important questions about the nature of that empire.

Aśoka's fame is itself an obstacle to any fresh assessment, as are the underlying presuppositions of most historical analyses that have been attempted so far. These presuppositions include the ideas that there existed in 3rd century BCE India a discrete and well-defined 'religious' domain with which Aśoka's *dhamma* intersected and negotiated; that this 'religious' domain comprised a set of 'religions' consisting of defined and discrete sets of doctrines, ethics, and practices; that the essentials of these 'religions' can be grasped through a study of one or another set of texts; that the 'religious' domain can be distinguished from a discrete 'political' domain; that the ideas of an individual (in this case, an emperor) can be best understood by comparing and trying to equate them with some known package of ideas contained in a particular text or corpus of texts; that in the context of ancient states, a distinction can be made between the personal and the political; and that royal/imperial proclamations and actions should be primarily interpreted as legitimizing strategies. All these presuppositions are reflected, for instance, in analyses of Aśoka's *dhamma,* which have compared it with the ethics embodied in various textual traditions, without recognizing that these traditions were very fluid at the time, and that the categories and identities which existed in later times or in modern state systems simply did not exist in the Indian subcontinent in the 3rd century BCE.

The principal sources for the history of the Mauryas are Aśoka's inscriptions, the *Arthaśāstra* of Kauṭilya, and Megasthenes' *Indica.* To these can be added evidence from Purāṇic and Buddhist sources and numismatic and archaeological evidence, as well as a handful of non-Aśokan inscriptions. The apparent wealth of the primary source material is offset by the peculiar problems presented by the three principal sources. The *Arthaśāstra* is a normative text which describes a potential, not a historical, state, and its dates remain a subject of debate. Megasthenes' *Indica* is lost and its contents can only be ascertained through epitomes (paraphrases) in later writings such as those of Diodorus, Arrian, and Strabo. Aśoka's inscriptions are obsessive and eloquent about *dhamma,* but seem frustratingly opaque regarding other aspects of Maurya state and society. Added to these problems is the fact that historians have tended to read one source through another,[6] with the aim of correlating their testimony, an enterprise which is not illegitimate in itself, but which is often conducted without adequate acknowledgement of the qualitatively different nature of these sources, due to which, notwithstanding the occasional congruence, there are bound to be many contradictions in their testimony.

In contrast with earlier studies, there is now increasing awareness among scholars that inscriptions are inscribed texts and have to be as meticulously analysed as texts, and that epigraphic production has to be considered as a process, one which includes the composition, inscribing, propagation, and reception of the inscriptions.[7] It is also essential to situate epigraphic texts in their larger material and archaeological contexts, and to bear in mind that the sculptural motifs associated with Aśoka's inscriptions were as integral to the nature and the reception of the *dhamma* message as the inscribed words.[8] This essay goes further and emphasizes that the *ideas* expressed in inscriptions deserve much more serious attention than they have often received. The specific focus is on carefully analysing the expressed and implied political ideas of Aśoka's edicts, especially their imperial vision, and on making inferences about how that imperial vision grappled with the political realities and problems of a virtually subcontinental, and culturally and economically highly variegated, 3rd century BCE Indian empire.

The Emperor's Wish and Command

Aśoka's inscriptions represent the earliest corpus of royal inscriptions in the Indian subcontinent, and in this respect mark an important innovation in royal practice.[9] Historians have classified them into minor rock edicts, major rock edicts, separate rock edicts, major pillar edicts, minor pillar edicts, and cave inscriptions. Internal chronological references indicate that the minor rock edicts were the earliest, followed by the major rock edicts and then the major pillar edicts; the cave inscriptions and minor pillar edicts were inscribed at various points in time. The majority of the inscriptions are written in the Brahmi script and in dialects of Prakrit, which was to remain the language of political power in the subcontinent for several centuries before being replaced by Sanskrit. Mansehra and Shahbazgarhi in the north-west have sets of rock edicts in the Prakrit language and Kharoshthi script. The northwestern part of the empire (which included areas of modern Pakistan and Afghanistan) also yielded one Greek, four Aramaic, one Greek-Aramaic and one Aramaic-Prakrit inscription.[10] It should be noted that the Prakrit section of the Aramaic-Prakrit inscription from Kandahar is transliterated in the Aramaic script, and the Aramaic Pul-i-Darunta inscription contains Aramaic transliterations of some Prakrit words. Aśoka's inscriptions are unique in terms of the occurrence of sets of inscriptions (for instance, the rock edicts usually occur in sets of fourteen edicts, except at Dhauli and Jaugada, where RE 13 is replaced by SRE 1 and 2, which are also found on a stone slab at Sannati; the pillar edicts usually occur in sets of six, except for the Delhi-Topra pillar, which has seven edicts), and in the repetition of the content of individual or sets of inscriptions in several places. The message embodied in them was evidently not considered specific to a single place and was sought to be propagated in written form at multiple key points in the empire, at places which were to have a long-term importance on trade routes and in the religious and/or political landscape. The major rock edicts are mostly distributed along or near the margins of the empire; the pillar edicts are concentrated in north

India; the minor rock edicts have the widest distribution, with a notable clustering in the Andhra–Karnataka area in the south.

Judging from the frequent use of the first person in the Prakrit inscriptions and their strong personal tone, it can be inferred that Aśoka had an important role in determining their content.[11] The frequent use of the optative, imperative, and gerundive indicates that they do not merely contain the emperor's ideas and words, but his desires and his commands, tempered occasionally by a self-reflectiveness that mitigates their authoritarian tone. The absence of the use of the first person and the considerable variations in the content of the Aramaic and Greek inscriptions indicate that in the northwestern part of the empire local officials exercised considerable freedom in determining the content of the edicts.

The Prakrit dialects could not have represented the dialects spoken over most of the Indian subcontinent, and the variations in the language of the inscriptions cannot therefore be understood as a reflection of the linguistic map of the subcontinent. The explanation of the linguistic pattern lies in the main audience of the edicts, which consisted not of the general populace but of high-ranking administrative officials. This is confirmed by Aśoka's statement (SRE 1 and 2) that instructing his officials was his chief means of attaining his objective (i.e., the propagation of *dhamma*). The pattern of the languages and scripts of the edicts suggests that the official cadres in most parts of the subcontinent were familiar with both the Prakrit language and Brahmi script, while those men who were posted in the northwest were not. This further suggests the recruitment of officials from among the local communities and the existence of a multi-lingual administration in those areas. A later inscription from Gujarat—the Girnar inscription of Rudradāman (c. 150 CE)—refers to a Yavana (Greek or westerner) named Tuṣāspha who completed the construction of a water reservoir called Sudarśana during the time of Aśoka; this suggests that during Aśoka's time, Greek or Persian officials were appointed even in areas other than the northwest.

Writing proclamations on stone was a novelty in 3rd century BCE India and endowed the king's word with an endurance and impact that transcended time, one that was not contingent on the inscriptions actually being read or even readable. This can be inferred from the presumably low literacy levels at the time as well as from the fact that the inscriptions were often inscribed on surfaces or levels where they could not be read—for instance on the horizontal surface of rocky outcrops, or high up on pillars, far beyond eye level. What was more important was that the ideas they embodied should be heard, orally disseminated, and discussed widely. The epigraphic form of Aśoka's *dhamma* message co-existed simultaneously with the oral and documentary forms maintained in certain administrative offices, and the king himself moved around the countryside incessantly instructing people in *dhamma.* The last point is evident from the statement (MRE 1) that he had spent 256 nights (or days) on tour, no doubt busy spreading *dhamma.* The many references in the inscriptions to speaking and hearing the *dhamma* message indicate a striking mix between writing and orality. The need to have the edicts inscribed was to provide multiple permanent, indelible reference points, mainly for the propagation of *dhamma* by Aśoka's officials, as well as for the king's successors.

The main audience of the edicts can be divided into three segments—the direct audience (the officials); the indirect audience (the mass of the emperor's subjects), who were expected to receive their king's message via various intermediaries, largely in oral form; and the future audience (posterity). Several of Aśoka's inscriptions explicitly state that they were written so that they would last long, in fact forever, so that his successors would devote themselves to the promotion of *dhamma* and so that the people followed its tenets. Even if most of his subjects could not read them, the king's inscribed words had important and enduring symbolic value. From a political perspective, the major rock edicts can be understood as frontier markers, where the written commands of the king announced to the traveller that he was crossing over a liminal threshold into a new kind of space, a new kind of imperial domain. What kind of imperial domain this was can only be understood through a careful analysis of the political ideas expressed in the edicts.

Aśoka's Idea of Empire

Aśoka principally saw himself not as an inheritor but as an innovator, as a king who had inaugurated a new kind of kingship, one that would be a model for his successors. This may be why his inscriptions do not contain any genealogy or specific reference to his predecessors. The reference to the king as *lājā Magadhe* ('king of Magadha', in the Bairat-Calcutta MRE) indicates an element of territoriality, but one that focuses on the nuclear area of the empire rather than its supposed vast expanse. As we shall see later, the edicts talk of two kinds of empire—a political and a moral one. It should be noted that 'Asoka' (the Prakrit equivalent of Sanskrit Aśoka), which occurs in only four inscriptions,[12] is usually understood as the king's personal name. It literally means 'without sorrow', and since in the Buddhist tradition, one who is free from sorrow is an enlightened being, this may well have been a name taken by the king after he came under the influence of the Buddha's doctrine. Similarly, there is nothing unassuming about his more frequently occurring titles *devānaṁpiya,* which means 'dear to the gods',[13] and *piyadasi,* which can be variously translated as 'he who looks upon at that which is beloved/dear/auspicious', 'he who looks affectionately/amiably', or, given the unstandardized usage of the time, 'one who is dear to look at'. Although the word *piya,* which occurs in both titles, has a wide range of meanings and nuances, it seems that the element of affection is emphasized both in the context of the relationship between the king and the gods and the king and his people. As we shall see further on, the edicts emphasize the affective element in other ways as well.

Aśoka had a strong sense of history, but his sense of history was one that was epic in scale, scope, and expectations. On occasion (for instance in certain versions of MRE 1), he invokes age-old tradition (*poraṇā pakitī*); but he more often presents himself as initiating new measures, such as an increased accessibility to officials and the creation of a special cadre of officials to propagate *dhamma.* He remarks on the desire of past kings to make men progress by promoting *dhamma* (PE 7) and their lack of success in this enterprise, contrasting this with his own success. He sees himself (or at least presents himself as such) as intervening in and reversing a course of long-standing human moral decline, describes his reversal of this decline as dramatic and efficacious, and confidently asserts that his successors will continue to promote *dhamma* until the end of the aeon (*kalpa*) (RE 4, RE 5, PE 7).

The specific references in the edicts indicate that the geopolitical world with which Aśoka was familiar extended from the subcontinent to northern Africa and the Mediterranean. The word used frequently to refer to his own political dominion is *vijita* (literally, 'that over which victory has been achieved'), and in one place he asserts that his dominions are extensive (*mahālake hi vijite*) (RE 14). There is a single reference to him as king of Magadha (Bairat-Calcutta MRE) and also to his capital city Pāṭaliputra (RE 5), which is contrasted with the outlying areas (*bāhira*); here the term *bāhira* seems to refer to all the areas outside the political centre. Other terms used for political units are *janapada,* which refers to the king's territory and the people who inhabit it. The word *visaya* also occurs (RE 13, Girnar) in the sense of the king's dominion. The reference to the legendary epic-Purāṇic unit of Jambudvīpa (in certain versions of MRE 1) could refer to the whole earth or to a land-mass of which the subcontinent was a part. Here, we are told, men and gods now mingle due to the king's zealous propagation of *dhamma*.

Ancient Indian kingdoms were known by their political centres rather than by their borders, which in any case were fluid and shifting. Aśoka's edicts refer to three kinds of borderers: those living or ruling beyond his political domain; those living within but at the edge of this domain; and those who notionally lived within the king's domain and had been defeated but not subdued. The first two categories are discussed here; the third one will be discussed further on. The king's own political realm is distinguished (RE 2) from that of bordering (*pacanta*) kingdoms. In the south, these were the principalities of the Cōḷas, Pāṇḍyas, Sātiyaputras, Keralaputras, and Tāmraparṇī (Sri Lanka). In the northwest, there was the Yona (Greek) king Antiyoka and his neighbouring kings. In another inscription (RE 13), Aśoka claims to have won *dhamma-vijaya* (victory through *dhamma*) among all his borderers (*saveṣu ca aṁteṣu*) up to the domain of the Yona king Antiyoka, and beyond that in the land ruled over by Turamaya, Antikini, Maka, and Alikasudara; and in the south, where the Cōḷas and Pāṇḍyas were ruling, as far as Tāmraparṇī.[14] It is noteworthy that nowhere in Aśoka's edicts is there mention of bordering kingdoms in the north or northeast, no doubt because state polities had not emerged in those areas at the time.

However, the awareness that there were Greeks and other ethnic groups within this obviously multi-ethnic empire is evident from the reference to the *dhamma-mahāmātas* (officers in charge of spreading *dhamma*) propagating *dhamma* among the Yavanas, Kāmbojas, Gandhāras, Riṣṭikas, Pitiṇikas, and other western borderers (*aparātā*) (RE 5). It is also clear from the fact that Aśoka (RE 13) talks of having achieved victory through *dhamma* even in his own territory (*evameva hida raja-viṣavaspi*), among the Yonas, Kāmbojas, Nābhakas, Nābhapaṅktis, Bhojas, Pitinikas, Āndhras, and Pulindas.[15] Rock edict 2 reflects a recognition of certain geopolitical units and boundaries, but indicates that Aśoka's welfare measures (specifically the provision of medical treatment, the planting of herbs, trees, and roots for men and animals, and the digging of wells along roads) extended beyond such boundaries. This indicates that Aśoka understood his moral jurisdiction as extending well beyond his political domain.

Aśoka's notion of his constituency extended to all living beings (*pāṇas*, *jīvas*, *bhūtas*); this is why the king announces measures undertaken for the welfare of both humans (*manusa*) and animals (*pasu*) (RE 2). He states explicitly that his concern for people extends beyond his concern for his personal kin, to people near and far (PE 6). Apart from the already cited references to various ethnic groups and inhabitants of different geopolitical units, he frequently distinguishes between sections of his people on the basis of social standing, referring, for instance, to the high (*usaṭa*) and low (*chuda*) (RE 10). Other categories among his subjects that are singled out for specific mention include Brāhmaṇas, *samaṇas* (renunciants), householders, women, those who were devoted to the practice of *dhamma*, and those who were not. The *dhamma* officers are especially enjoined (RE 5) to occupy themselves with all sects, servants and masters, Brāhmaṇas and *ibhyas*,[16] the destitute, aged, and prisoners. The king also distinguishes between members of different sects who reside in his kingdom, specifically mentioning the *saṅgha* (Buddhist monastic order), Nirgranthas (Jainas), and Ājīvikas (PE 7). The reference to the distinction between one's own sect (*ātma-pāsaṇḍa*) and another's sect (*para-pāsaṇḍa*) and the exhortation to people not to denounce the sects of others (RE 12) presume the existence of sectarian identities and tensions, if not conflict. However, while making such distinctions, the overall emphasis of the edicts is on inclusiveness—the king is at pains to emphasize that his attention is directed to *all* sects and sections (*nikāyas*) of his populace (PE 6).[17]

Aśoka's edicts declare that his most important duty is to help his subjects attain happiness in this life and, more importantly, happiness and heaven in the next through instruction in *dhamma*, which is (RE 4) the best work. The Dhauli version of rock edict 5 states that the *dhamma* officers were occupied everywhere, over the whole earth. This confirms that while concerned with issues of governance related to his political realm, Aśoka also had in mind a higher, moral imperium which transcended the bounds of political dominion.

The Good, the Self, and the State

The central element in this moral empire is a king who is the premier source of ideas and injunctions regarding what is good, and who embodies in himself a model of exemplary behaviour. In this mimetic moral empire, officials and subjects emulate the king in his practice of *dhamma*, and even in its propagation, although of course to a significantly lesser degree. *Dhamma* includes what is good (*sādhu*); the imperative to practice the good additionally endows it with the sense of duty. This imperative does not lie in an idea of goodness for the sake of itself but in an understanding of an individual's long-term self-interest—through the operation of the law of *kamma/karma* (not specifically mentioned, but definitely implied), goodness yields *puiña/puṁña* (*puṇya*, i.e., merit) and beneficial fruits (*phala*) in the next life, and forms a stairway to heaven (*svaga*). Contrary to what Romila Thapar suggests,[18] heaven is not a superficial add-on in Aśoka's *dhamma*. In fact, it stands at the core of the king's political philosophy: individuals desire to achieve heaven and the king has an obligation to help his subjects (actually all humankind) achieve this goal, an obligation expressed in the form of the idea of a debt (*anana*) he owes to them (RE 6, SRE 2). This transforms goodness into a central political issue, and this is why the king is obliged to explain and inculcate goodness among his subjects and to create a state apparatus for this purpose in his political realm and even beyond.

In this political philosophy, there is a close connection between being good and doing good; between the cultivation of inner virtues and the elimination of negative emotions and propensities; between the individual and society. The virtues that are emphasized include self-control (*sayama*), purity of thought (*bhāva-sudhitā*), liberality (*dāna*), gratitude (*kataṁñatā*), firm devotion (*daḍha-bhatitā*), truthfulness (*saca*), and purity (*soca*). In terms of outward conduct, the emphasis is on behaviour appropriate to various key social relationships within and beyond the household—obedience to the mother and father; respect for elders; courtesy and liberality towards Brāhmaṇas and renunciants; courtesy to slaves and servants; liberality towards friends, acquaintances, and relatives; moderation in expenditure and possessions; and guarding one's speech. The appropriate conduct towards all living beings includes an emphasis on compassion (*dayā*); gentleness (*sayama*); and abstention from injuring (*avihiṁsā*) and from killing (*anālambhā*).[19]

The good is defined not only in absolute terms but also in terms of what it is not; in terms of what falsely appears to be good and what is truly good; in relative terms of what is good and what is better; and in terms not of short-term objectives but the longer-term goal of achieving endless merit or heaven. The converse of doing and being good and attaining merit and heaven is falling prey to danger (*parisrava*), sins (*pāpa, āsinavas*),[20] and earning demerit (*apuṁñya*). What is not stated but implied is that truly virtuous actions arise from virtuous inner dispositions. Aśoka takes delight in playing with ideas and in pouring new meaning into old words, emphasizing the elements of re-definition, substitution, and innovation. For instance, in rock edict 9, he expresses disapproval of the usual *maṅgala*s (auspicious ceremonies, including rites of passage) practised by people, especially women, asserting that these are of a lower order (*chuda*) and pointless (*nirartha*) because they may not yield the desired results, and that the fruits that they may yield are intermittent and inferior to those arising from the *dhamma maṅgala*s (the ceremonials, i.e., practice, of *dhamma*), namely the attainment of desired objects in this life as well as the next. *Dāna* (making ritual gifts, liberality) too is discussed and redefined: although liberality is part of the good, if a person makes abundant gifts but is lacking in certain qualities (self-control, purity of mind, gratitude, and firm devotion), he is a low person (RE 7). True liberality, *dhamma-dāna,* consists in propagating to others the appropriate behaviour towards slaves and servants, parents, friends, acquaintances, and relatives, and abstention from killing living beings. This too leads to happiness in this world and endless merit in the next. In this scheme of things, the king's subjects become active participants in the creation and maintenance of the moral empire.

The edicts emphasize exertion and effort (*parākrama, utsāha, utthāna, uyāma*), admitting the difficulty of being and doing good, and project the king as the premier source of *dhamma.* The connection between the *dhamma* of the edicts and that of Buddhist doctrine is an issue that has been much debated. Even if we discount the collective testimony of the later Buddhist textual tradition, Aśoka's inscriptions unequivocally indicate his affiliation with Buddhism. The king declares himself to be a lay follower of the Buddha's teaching (*upāsaka,* Sākya, Budha-Sākya, MRE 1) and indicates that his *dhamma* tours began after his pilgrimage to Bodh Gayā (RE 8). The Bairat-Calcutta minor rock edict announces his faith in the Buddha, *dhamma,* and *saṅgha,* states that what has been said by the Buddha has been well-said, and describes the Buddha's teachings as the true *dhamma.* It also lists six sermons on *dhamma,* presumably from Buddhist texts. Further, there is an overlap between the tenets of Aśoka's *dhamma* and the *dhamma* prescribed for the laity in the Buddha's teachings.[21] Aśoka's allegiance to Buddhism is also displayed by the minor pillar edicts at Lumbini and Nigali Sagar, while the 'schism edict' indicates the position of authority he exercised vis-à-vis the Buddhist monastic order. A Buddhist imprint can also be seen in the reference to the white elephant bringing happiness to the whole world on the Girnar rock; the figure of an elephant and the word *gajatame* ('the best elephant') inscribed at Kalsi; and the elephant and the word *seto* ('the white one', i.e., the white elephant) at Dhauli.[22] But while the Buddhist inspiration cannot be denied, it is also clear that the range of Aśoka's *dhamma* injunctions is not identical in number or in content to that prescribed for the laity in Buddhist texts, nor is it exclusive to the Buddhist tradition. This is also evident from the sculptural motifs associated with the Aśokan pillars, which should be considered as being in consonance with and an important part of the communication of, the *dhamma* message—all of them have a Buddhist significance, but all of them also have a much wider symbolic resonance in the Indian religious and cultural traditions.[23] Aśoka evidently considered *dhamma* to be embodied in the teachings of other sects as well, stating that the various sects have in common an emphasis on self-control and purity of mind (RE 7). This idea is most strongly expressed in rock edict 12, where the king expresses his desire that there should be a growth of the essentials (*sāra-vaḍhī*) of all sects (*pāsaṇḍas*) and that an atmosphere of concord (*samavāya*) should prevail.

Although *dhamma/dharma* is a widely pervasive idea in Indian thought, what is significant are the ways in which this idea is integrated into Aśoka's political philosophy through the positing of a close connection between the individual's pursuit of *dhamma* and the goals of the state. The cultivation and control of the emotions and dispositions have a central place in this understanding of politics and governance. Effective governance of the self and the pursuit of goodness directed towards the goal of happiness in the next life and the attainment of heaven is the aim of the subjects. Ensuring the benefit/welfare (*hita*) and happiness (*sukha*) of all beings in this world and the next and/or their attainment of heaven are the aims of their ruler. The inscriptions thus talk of two kinds of interconnected governance—of the self and of the state. Also relevant in this regard is the paternalistic idea of kingship (*sava munise pajā mamā*, 'all men are my children') (SRE 1 and 2), which combines affection and authority. Taken together, we are presented with an idea of moral sovereignty resting on a belief in the obligation, and hence duty, that the king has towards all beings, a duty which, as has already been mentioned, extends within and beyond his political domain.

The Argument Against War

The fact that Aśoka saw the welfare of all beings as his goal obliged him to engage with the issue of the violence of humans towards each other and towards animals, and to take steps to mitigate the suffering caused by such violence. As mentioned at the outset, the debate about Aśoka's non-violence has generally focused on the extent and impact of his pacifism, and its contribution to the decline of the Maurya empire. There are two diametrically opposite views on this—that this pacifism irrevocably weakened the military basis of the empire (Raychaudhuri), and that Aśoka's pacifism has been greatly exaggerated and that it was tempered with a strong element of pragmatism (Thapar). However, in this debate, the ideas related to violence and war expressed in the inscriptions have not been examined closely enough. Aśoka's abjuration of war should not be summarily dismissed as a pragmatic stance taken by the inheritor of a vast, virtually subcontinental empire, the consolidation of which was complete.[24] It has to be situated within a larger web of ideas and should be understood as a strong and reasoned moral response to the problem of violence in the political sphere.

The most famous of Aśoka's expressions on the subject of state violence in the form of war is found in rock edict 13, which talks of the disastrous results of a specific war—a war against Kaliṅga in eastern India—and on that basis generalizes about the consequences and hence undesirability of all wars. Some of these ideas are anticipated in the frequent insistence in many other edicts on non-injury to all living beings. They are also anticipated in an inscription (RE 4) where Aśoka says that due to *his* practice of *dhamma*, the call of *dhamma* (*dhamma-ghosa*) has replaced the sound of the war drum (*bheri-ghosa*) and that he has shown the people aerial chariots, elephants, masses of fire, and other divine figures. In their reversal of key images associated with the battlefield, these statements figuratively but dramatically express the king's abjuring of warfare.

Rock edict 13 goes further. It is not merely a declaration of Aśoka's renunciation of war but a reflection on the consequences and implications of war, containing a redefinition of the injury caused by war, and a redefinition of the idea of righteous victory, which is a key element in Aśoka political philosophy. The Kaliṅga war, which the edict dates eight years after the king's consecration (*abhiṣeka*),[25] was clearly a transformative event in Aśoka's life, or at least he presents it as such. The statement that when Kaliṅga was subdued (*vijita*) 150,000 people were carried away as captives, 100,000 were killed in action, and many times that number perished directs attention to the magnitude of this war by pointing to its heavy casualties. Although the edict suggests that this was Aśoka's first and last war as king, he could not have been a stranger to war—he must have been exposed to it as a prince. The nature of the description of the war, with its citation of rhetorically high figures designed to overawe, may in fact point to changes in the nature of warfare in 3rd century BCE India towards a kind of conflict which involved much higher levels of military deployment than before, higher casualties, and mass deportation of captives, perhaps even of non-combatant citizenry.

Aśoka talks of his own pain and the pain of others, of his remorse (*anuṣaye/anusocana*), and of his ardent espousal and propagation of *dhamma* after the event. We do not know whether the king was an active participant in the combat, but the edict suggests two ideas—that as head of the state, the king assumes responsibility for the *totality* of the consequences of the war, not just for violence or injury caused by him personally; and that true repentance can mitigate, possibly even cancel, the karmic consequences arising from such responsibility. However, the king does not put his pain and remorse on display in Kaliṅga itself (RE 13 is replaced by SREs 1 and 2 at Dhauli and Jaugada), either out of sensitivity, shame, pragmatism, or a combination of all these things. It should also be noted that the king expresses his remorse for the war, but does not ask for forgiveness from those on whom it was inflicted.

There is no word for war (or for peace) in rock edict 13; instead, the references are to the killing, death, and deportation that accompany war and the nature of the injury and pain it causes. Although high casualty figures are cited in the inscription, Aśoka asserts that military campaigns are deplorable even if the number of casualties is small. Further, he extends the scope of injury (*upaghāta*) caused by war beyond those who suffer physical injury, death, or capture. He asserts that the injuries arising from war also include the (emotional) injury that is caused to all those who are loved by or are attached to the direct sufferers, namely to their friends, acquaintances, companions, and relatives. He especially singles out the injury caused in this manner to Brāhmaṇas, renunciants, members of various sects, and householders who are devoted to the practice of the good, asserting that he considers this kind of injury even more deplorable than that of those who suffer directly. The implication is that the suffering arising from war extends far beyond that of individuals who suffer physical pain or death. This suffering is shared by a larger community of people, and the emotional suffering experienced by the good is more painful to the king than the inevitable physical casualties of war.

These ideas are accompanied by the deployment of the metaphor of victory for a new dhammic purpose. It is a dramatic redeployment, because Aśoka takes words and ideas usually associated with military victory, redesigns their content, and uses his new formulations to make a powerful indictment of war. *Dhamma vijaya* ('victory through *dhamma*') is not a *conquest* but a *victory* consisting of effectively propagating *dhamma* everywhere, a victory that Aśoka claims to have won up to and even beyond the frontiers of his kingdom, not once but repeatedly, suggesting that the inculcation of *dhamma* is not a one-time event but a constant 'battle', requiring continuous exhortation and effort. Dhammic victory is declared to be the best victory, not because it gives the king satisfaction (*piti*), which is of little consequence in itself, but because it leads to fruits in this world and, even more importantly, in the next. Aśoka urges his sons and grandsons to aim at this kind of victory rather than military victory, and to take pleasure in exertion. Recognizing that they may be disinclined to abjure war completely, he urges them to be merciful and moderate in their punishment if they do take pleasure in it.

Although rock edict 13 focuses on the abjuring of fresh military campaigns, it does not abjure the use of force to suppress recalcitrant forest people and/or forest chieftains (*aṭavi*), who, in fact, posed a serious impediment and challenge to the expansion of all pre-modern Indian empires.[26] The tone of rock edict 13 changes when the king exhorts these people to follow *dhamma*, announces that he can forgive that which can be forgiven, and reminds them of the power he possesses in spite of his repentance, so that they may not be shamed and killed. For, he explains, the king desires towards all beings abstention from causing injury, restraint in dealing with them, and impartiality in the face of violence/crimes committed by them.[27] The implied message to the forest people is that they should not provoke him.

The rejection of conventional military victory is accompanied by a rejection of the conventional basis of a king's fame. Aśoka states that he did not set much store by fame (*yasa, kīti*) except for that arising from his success in inducing people to follow *dhamma*, now and in the future (RE 10). This stands in contradistinction to the general basis of a king's fame in the ancient world, which rested to a considerable extent on his martial achievements. In Aśoka's political philosophy, war and military victory are not essential parts of politics or empire. In fact, they are seen as undesirable and reprehensible; they have no place in Aśoka's idea of a moral empire.

Empire and Ecology

As mentioned earlier, Aśoka included all living beings in his moral constituency; therefore when he talks of non-violence, he means non-violence towards all living beings (*jīvas, prāṇas*), which include humans (*manusa*) and animals (*pasu*). The importance attached to animals in the discussion of *dhamma* in the edicts can be correlated with the striking prominence of the representation of animals (especially the lion, bull, and elephant) on the capitals of the Aśokan pillars.

In his various injunctions, Aśoka has both wild and domesticated animals in mind, and his focus is on abjuring the injury as well as killing of animals. The non-killing of living beings is part of the good (RE 11), as is controlled behaviour/gentleness towards them (RE 9), and such practice leads to the accumulation of merit and the attainment of heaven. Rock edict 4 refers to the increase in various vices in times past, including the injury and killing of living beings, and asserts that the promotion of *dhamma* by the king has led to an unprecedented promotion of the non-injury and non-killing of living beings (*anāraṁbho prāṇānaṁ avihīsā bhūtānaṁ*) and other virtues.

Rock edict 1 talks of the king's attempts to curb violence towards animals in three contexts—the killing of animals in sacrifices; in certain popular festive gatherings (*samājas*); and in the royal kitchen.[28] (The second and third contexts also implicitly refer to hunting animals for food). His confession in this edict that three peacocks and a deer were still being killed daily for food in the royal kitchen suggests a resistance to the imposition of vegetarianism among the members of the royal household, in spite of the wishes of the king. Rock edict 8 suggests an elimination of the violence inherent in the king's pursuit of pleasure, that is through the royal hunt: Aśoka announces that royal pleasure tours (*vihāra-yātās*), which must have included hunting, have been replaced by *dhamma* tours, which included visiting Brāhmaṇas and ascetics and giving them gifts, meeting the aged and giving them gold, meeting people of the kingdom or the countryside (*jānapada*), instructing them in *dhamma*, and discussing *dhamma* with them. It is interesting that the edicts do not refer to the other standard royal vices (*vyasanas*) that are mentioned in the Indian political tradition, namely addiction to alcohol, women, and gambling. That the abjuration of hunting applies not only to the king but also to the people in pursuit of their livelihoods is implied in the general exhortations not to kill any living beings, and in the claims (in one of the Laghman Aramaic inscriptions and the Shar-i-Kuna Greek-Aramaic inscription) that hunters have stopped hunting and fishermen have stopped fishing due to the king's propagation of *dhamma*. Even if this was a gross exaggeration of the success of his policy, as pointed out by Aloka Parasher-Sen,[29] the king's injunctions in this respect may have seriously affected the livelihoods of communities of hunter-gatherers.

The Aśokan edicts do not contain any elaborate discussion of *why* violence against all beings is to be avoided, but they do imply three reasons—that such violence injures life; that it has harmful effects for the person who commits it, in the sense that he incurs sin (*pāpa*) and demerit (*apuṁñya*); and that the avoidance of such violence is meritorious. Pillar edict 3 categorically associates fierceness, cruelty, and anger—the very propensities which are associated with violence—with sin and demerit. These ideas may well have been rooted in the Buddha's teachings, in which Aśoka explicitly declares his personal faith in certain inscriptions. However, it should be noted that non-injury was an important element in other contemporary sects as well—for instance in Jainism, and probably also among the Ājīvikas[30]—although there was considerable variation in its philosophical basis and the extent to which it was practised. The full import of Aśoka's ideas and measures in relation to animals can, in fact, only be understood against the background of the larger Indian understanding of human–animal relations, especially in view of the inevitable interconnectedness of humans and animals in the karmic universe, which was a widely prevalent idea that cut across religious and sectarian divides.[31] It should also be noted that Aśoka's exhortations against injuring and killing animals and humans are accompanied by announcements of positive welfare measures undertaken by the king for them (RE 2), specifically the provision of medical treatment; the planting of herbs, root plants, and fruit trees; and the digging of wells and planting of trees along roads. This is an attitude which extends far beyond a concern that animals (and humans) should not be harmed; it attaches great positive value to ensuring their welfare and presents this as an important duty of the king.

If the most powerful statement against the violence of war occurs in rock edict 13, the most detailed statement about the protection of animals occurs in pillar edict 5. If we compare the ideas expressed in the first rock edict with those of pillar edict 5, we see a consistency in the commitment to non-violence towards animals, but also a difference. The hesitant statement of imperfect implementation of vegetarianism within the royal household has made way for a wide range of sweeping and very specific injunctions against causing various kinds of injury to specific types of animals and also to their habitat. These injunctions were issued 26 years after the king's consecration (i.e., in the twenty-seventh year after that event), and therefore refer to events that took place relatively late in his reign.

The first part of the order is a declaration that certain species of animals are *avadhiya*, that is, not to be killed. These include certain kinds of birds, fish, insects, and mammals,[32] not all of which can be identified with certainty, but all of which are wild. That they were mostly animals which were not usually killed by humans for food or for any other purpose is suggested by the statement that this ban is also to apply to all four-footed animals that are useless (i.e., from the point of view of human use) and are not eaten. The exception is the rhinoceros, which must have been hunted for its horn, bones, skin, and possibly also meat.[33] Other than the rhinoceros, the species declared inviolable seem to have been ones that would not be killed in large numbers in ordinary circumstances anyway, that is, they were not especially endangered. The blanket ban against killing is also applied to females of certain domesticated species, namely female goats, ewes, and sows who are pregnant or lactating, as well as to young animals less than six months old. These injunctions suggest a special concern for potential and nascent life. Thirdly, the edict declares a prohibition against killing animals that were hunted in the elephant-forests (*nāga-vana*s) and fish in the fishermen's preserves (the prohibition is both against killing and selling). It can be noted that elephants were an extremely important economic and military resource for the state at the time, and the 'elephant-forests' were home to many other types of fauna as well.[34] However, this ban applies to certain specific days,[35] which, according to one calculation, would work out to 24 days in a year, in addition to the *uposatha* (fast days), the number of which is not certain and which may have been twice or four times a month.

There are three other general prohibitions: husk containing living animals (*tuse sajīve*) must not be burnt, and forests (*dāve*) should not be burnt needlessly or in order to kill living beings. This indicates that the natural habitat of animals should not be destroyed through burning, presumably either while clearing land for agriculture or while driving out animals during hunting. Further, the king declares that living beings must not be fed with living beings. The term used here is *jīva*, which has generic connotations of all living things, but the context suggests that it refers specifically to animals not being fed with other animals. This imposition of vegetarianism on domesticated animals may sound radical, but seems more to have been a confirmation of prevailing practice.

The edict not only talks of curbing the killing of animals, but also seeks to regulate certain other kinds of injury caused by humans to domesticated animals, specifically castration and branding. Thus, it is declared that cocks are not to be castrated, presumably at any time. Bulls, goats, rams, and boars are not be castrated on certain specific days,[36] amounting to some 72 days in a year, apart from all auspicious days (*sudivasāye*).

The branding of horses and bulls is banned on certain specific days, adding up to 47 days in a year.[37]

Pillar edict 5, which for the most part deals with measures concerning animals, ends with a statement that the king had ordered the release of prisoners every year until the twenty-sixth year after his consecration. The implication is that imprisonment and its attendant curtailment of freedom was associated with cruelty to human beings, and that this type of cruelty could be mitigated by ordering a periodic release of prisoners. Such periodic releases, in fact, seem to have been a part of the model of benevolent kingship in ancient India.[38]

A question that arises is: given the repeated emphasis on non-injury as part of *dhamma,* what was the need for the level of detail reflected in pillar edict 5? On the one hand, this edict elaborates on the forms of violence towards animals that are to be avoided, if not effectively banned; specifies the species that are given protection; and extends protection to the natural habitat of animals. However, although because of all this, pillar edict 5 *appears* to carry the injunctions against violence towards animals further, it in fact takes a pragmatic stance in acknowledging, permitting, and regulating such violence, taking human need into account. This is in stark contrast to the blanket, and no doubt unimplementable, exhortations of non-violence that we see in the earlier edicts. What is also evident in this edict is the ritualization of non-violence towards animals to coincide with specific days in the lunar calendar which were considered auspicious, especially the full moon days of the Cāturmāsī months (Āṣāḍha, Kārttika, and Phālguna) and of the constellations of Tiṣya and Punarvasu. Furthermore, while the ban on killing animals in the elephant-forests on certain days would have benefited elephants and other animals that shared their habitat, it should be noted that lions and bulls (which in certain areas may well have shared the elephants' habitat),[39] which occur as imperial emblems on the capitals of Aśoka's pillars, are not mentioned specifically in the list of protected animals. In fact, the rhinoceros is the only large mammal included in the list of animals that are not supposed to be killed at any time. The general impression conveyed by several edicts is that the king had voluntarily abjured hunting and believed (or claimed) that hunters and fishermen in his domain had given up their traditional vocations. On the other hand, pillar edict 5, in fact, reflects an attempt to effect a mitigation and calendric regulation of violence against animals, not a complete elimination of such violence. Of course, in spite of Aśoka's tall claims of success, the ability of the state to implement such measures effectively was severely limited.

Justice and Violence

Apart from the violence inherent in war, hunting, and domesticating animals, Aśoka's inscriptions also dwell on the violence inherent in the administration of justice. Separate rock edict 1, addressed to officers known as the *nagalaviyohālakas*, raises the problem of people suffering as a result of unfair imprisonment and harsh treatment, and exhorts officials to deal with all such cases with fairness and impartiality. Justice is discussed in greater detail in pillar edict 4, which discusses the duties of officers known as the *rājūkas*. The main point emphasized in this edict is that the *rājūkas* should discharge their duties vis-à-vis the handing out of rewards and punishment fairly and fearlessly, and that there should be impartiality (*samatā*) in judicial proceedings and punishment.[40] The assertion that the king has entrusted the people *directly* to their care may be an allusion to certain intermediary officials having been removed. Aśoka exhorts the *rājūkas* to understand what causes the people pleasure and pain and instructs them to be just in meting out punishment, telling them that he expects them to do their job fearlessly, confidently, and well. This could either imply that the *rājūkas* were subject to pressures of various kinds, or that there was a problem because of the conflict between non-injury (a tenet of *dhamma*) and the fact that they were on occasion required to inflict violence in the administration of justice. Apart from exhorting them, the king also takes the precaution of telling them to obey other officials known as the *pulisāni*, who were evidently keeping an eye on them. The analogy used for the *rājūkas* in this edict is that of an experienced wet-nurse (*dhāti*), one associated with affectionate feminine care and nourishing, which can be seen as complementary to the paternalistic sentiment associated with the king in other inscriptions. The aim of the *rājūkas* is, in fact, the same as that of the king—to ensure the welfare and happiness of the people entrusted to their care in this world and the next.

For a king obsessed with non-injury, the most extreme kind of punishment—the death sentence—was naturally an issue of concern, and pillar edict 4 announced a three-day respite to prisoners condemned to death, explaining that this was to give their relatives (*ñātikās*) time to persuade the *rājūkas* to grant them life; or, if this failed, to give the prisoners time to distribute gifts or undertake fasts (*upavāsa*) to attain happiness in the other world. This three-day respite has been often cited by historians as an indication that Aśoka did not abolish the death penalty and that there were, therefore, serious limits to his commitment to non-violence. Etienne Lamotte suggests that it reflects a belief in the significance of a person's thoughts at the time of death.[41] Apart from enabling the convict to undertake last-minute measures to try to attain happiness in the next world, the edict suggests a context in which execution swiftly followed sentencing, and in which even a three-day reprieve was a significant concession. In effect, Aśoka sought to temper the violence inherent in capital punishment in three ways: by exhorting the judicial officers to be fair; by ensuring that there should be time and opportunity for a last appeal before the execution of the sentence; and by granting the condemned man an opportunity to prepare for his next life if this appeal failed.

The *nature* of the laws does not form part of this discussion of justice; the focus is on fairness and moderation in the application and execution of the law. There is a recognition of flaws in the justice delivery system and the announcement of the introduction of certain ameliorative measures. Further, the king projects himself as a maintainer of justice and simultaneously distances himself from the inevitable instances of actual injustice, for which the responsibility is placed squarely on his officials.

Problems of Consolidation and Governance

This should make it evident that for all their obsessive interest in *dhamma*, the edicts also grapple with certain practical problems of governing a vast and variegated empire. Reference has already been made to the fact that rock edict 13, which refers to the Kaliṅga war which happened when eight years had elapsed since Aśoka's consecration, was not inscribed in Kaliṅga itself, probably because it may have touched a raw nerve among the inhabitants of that region. But going by the latest chronological reference in them (in RE 5), the entire set of rock edicts could only have been inscribed after 13 years had elapsed since Aśoka's consecration, that is, several years after the war. This means that even five years after the war, that event was considered a sensitive issue in Kaliṅga. Furthermore, it is noteworthy that the separate rock edicts which were inscribed there—at Dhauli and Jaugada—reflect the king's concern with the practical problems of governing a province that was not particularly far from Pāṭaliputra, the capital of the empire. These edicts were also inscribed at Sannati in Karnataka. Both these edicts are about *nīti* (politics, governance) and we have in them the clearest statement of Aśoka's view of the chief problems that lay in the way of good governance, and also of the solutions to these problems. As will be apparent from the details below, the king talks of various means he had adopted to achieve his objective of inculcating *dhamma,* and asserts that instruction to the specified officers is his principal means, although he also recognizes the gap between instruction and implementation. These two edicts further indicate that Aśoka dealt with the practical problems of governance through exhortation as well as surveillance. They also effectively bring out the connections between *dhamma, kamma/karma,* and governance, and between the interests of the individual and the fulfilment of the goals of the state.

As mentioned earlier, separate rock edict 1, addressed to officers known as the *nagalaviyohālaka*s, talks of the problems of injustice, unfair imprisonment, and harsh treatment of prisoners. The fact that an entire edict is devoted to these issues highlights the importance of justice as a key element in Aśoka's idea of good governance. The concern expressed here is one that is emphasized in various ancient Indian political treatises and texts—that the king's punishment must be both fair and moderate. The edict also points to the reasons why officials may not, in fact, behave with fairness, namely because of their negative dispositions (envy, anger, cruelty, hastiness, lack of perseverance, laziness, and fatigue), and exhorts them not to let these predispositions (especially anger and hastiness) arise. These arguments are given weight by pointing to the benefits of obeying Aśoka's exhortations to be fair and compassionate in meting out justice: it will please the king, to whom the officials owe a debt; it will yield great merit; and it will help the concerned officials attain heaven. These positive assertions are accompanied by a warning that the non-observance of these instructions will yield great evil (*mahā-pāpa*). But it is clear that Aśoka adopted a dual policy; the exhortations and warnings for self-regulation are accompanied by a pragmatic deterrent—an announcement that quinquennial and triennial surveillance tours would be launched by the king and by the provincial governors to ensure that the officials concerned were behaving in the prescribed manner.

Apart from the problems involved in the administration of justice, Aśoka also refers to the problem of incomplete pacification and consolidation. Separate rock edict 2 begins in a similar way to the above inscription, and mentions Aśoka's paternalistic concerns. The main theme of this edict, addressed to officers known as the *mahāmāta*s, concerns the policy that was to be followed vis-à-vis the unsubdued borderers (*antānaṁ avijitānam*). While Kaliṅga could certainly be considered a bordering province/region on the eastern edge of Aśoka's empire, the implication that its inhabitants (or at least a significant section among them) were *avijita* (unsubdued) is noteworthy. The key to the explanation is provided by the rest of the inscription, which focuses on the need for officials to create confidence (*asvāsana*) among the borderers.[42] It seems that even several years after the war, Kaliṅga still presented problems and challenges of consolidation and governance. Clearly, Aśoka was alluding to the problem of incomplete pacification and consolidation, which had extended many years after the military victory over Kaliṅga, and which must have applied to other regions as well.

The solution to this problem offered by Aśoka is that his officials should convince the unsubdued borderers of his paternalistic benevolence, and also of the following: that the king loves them like himself; that they should not fear him; that they should have confidence in him; that they may expect happiness and not misery from him; that they should practise *dhamma;* and that by doing so they could attain happiness in this world and the next. Reassurance is tempered with firmness in the mention of the king's will and his unshakeable resolution and vow, and in the statement that the borderers should also be told that the king will forgive that which can be forgiven (similar to his warning to the forest people in RE 13). Although there was clearly a special reason for having the separate rock edicts inscribed at Dhauli, Jaugada and Sannati, the content of the second one clearly indicates that the issues that this inscription talks about—the need to inspire confidence in the people—applied to *all* parts of the empire. It is evident from the ideas expressed in the two separate rock edicts that Aśoka saw the essence of the problem of political consolidation and its solution primarily in psychological terms, but at the same time, pragmatically put in place a surveillance machinery to ensure compliance.

The Theory and Practice of Governance

Attempts to ascertain whether Aśoka's *dhamma* was personal or ideological, religious or secular, social or political are doomed to failure, because they presume the existence of dichotomous distinctions that did not exist in this 3rd century BCE empire. Viewing *dhamma* purely as legitimation ideology fails to consider the internal logic of the ideas expressed in the edicts; indeed, even if it is considered as legitimation ideology, its ideas deserve close scrutiny.

Aśoka's inscriptions provide a unique first-hand account of the theory and practice of governance by an ancient Indian emperor. The king defines a political sphere, connects it with a moral sphere, indicates his engagement with a political constituency beyond his kin, and identifies the different tiers in the concerns and apparatus of governance. Aśoka's definition of the political sphere includes himself, the royal household, officials (at the central, provincial, and district levels), and his people (subjects). This is a state that was involved in activities related to taxation, the administration of justice, and the mitigation of violence. But the edicts simultaneously identify a second kind of empire, a moral one, the geographical extent of which was much greater than the king's political realm, and in which the goal was the inculcation of happiness among all beings, including humans and animals. The political and moral empires overlap and the edicts deal with issues related to both.

Politics, ethics, and metaphysics are closely interlinked in ancient Indian political discourse in general, and are fused together in Aśoka's edicts. The importance of the moral aspects of kingship appears in many early Indian texts, including the *Arthaśāstra,* but what is striking in the edicts is not so much the occurrence of this element as the overwhelming emphasis and importance it is given in Aśoka's political philosophy. The edicts emphasize the mimetic nature of the practice of *dhamma*—officials and subjects must follow the exemplary dhammic behavior of the king. And yet, while emphasizing the moral aspects of kingship, the edicts simultaneously grapple with important issues connected with governance and the exercise of political power, especially those related to justice, violence, and war.

Due to the overwhelming importance given to the state's avowed interest in the moral sphere, the edicts' engagement with *nīti*—issues of governance—has sometimes been underestimated or missed.[43] It is notable that even in the moral sphere, exhortation of the officials and subjects was backed by practical measures to ensure that the exhortations did not go unheeded. There is no doubt that the inscriptions reflect the existence of a multi-tiered administrative hierarchy in the capital and the provincial centres (Taxila, Ujjayinī, Tosali, and Suvarṇagiri seem to have been such centres), the involvement of the state in revenue matters, and the administration of justice, as well as the inculcation of *dhamma.* A unique aspect of the system of governance reflected in Aśoka's edicts is its peripatetic quality, with the king, his officials, and inspection teams constantly on the move in the discharge of their duties. In between the political centres and cities were vast tracts of unpacified and partially pacified forests which constituted a rich and vital economic resource, but the forest people and chieftains posed a serious challenge to the power of the imperial state. Aśoka's edicts recognize this fact and make a concerted attempt to extend and assert the king's political and moral authority over all these areas and even beyond them.

Standing alone with the presuppositions of the entire ancient Indian political tradition ranged against it, Aśoka's political philosophy does not consider war as a natural or desirable element of statecraft, political expansion, or empire. Instead, it is seen as a reprehensible source of pervasive suffering, for which the king as initiator and possible beneficiary bears full responsibility, and which must, therefore, be avoided as far as possible. War is not an arena for the ostentatious display of heroic action in Aśoka's edicts. Victory and fame are retained but redefined; they are firmly removed from the martial sphere, and repositioned in the dhammic sphere. What is more, war and its consequences are seen as the subject of serious reflection and ethical inquiry, to be considered along with other forms of violence prevalent in state and society. Clearly, Aśoka's abjuration of war should not be understood merely as a pragmatic political strategy, but rather as a radical political stance rooted in ethical and metaphysical concerns.

His inscriptions suggest that Aśoka saw himself—or at least deliberately presented himself—as presiding over a moral empire that included all beings. The long-term well-being of the realm and society is seen as being dependent on their members imbibing certain ethical imperatives which were embedded in the various religious sects of the time, including, but not limited to, Buddhist sects. The edicts indicate the existence of sectarian identities and suggest sectarian rivalries, tensions, or conflicts, but they also point to a shared substratum of ethics that cut across the sectarian divide. The dhammic sphere is distinguished from the sectarian sphere, but there is an overlap in their ethics. In this description of the relationship between *dhamma* and *pāsaṇḍa,* Aśoka in fact accurately describes an important long-term aspect of the relationship between different Indic 'religions', that is, the existence of distinct doctrines with a shared and overlapping ethical substratum. The ideal relationship between sects visualized by Aśoka is one of mutual respect, understanding, and concord (*samavāya*), and the creation of conditions which allow the promotion of the essence of all sects (*sāra-vaḍhi*) (RE 12). This attitude has far greater positive and dialogic value than what is conveyed by its usual and very inaccurate description as an attitude of 'tolerance'.

However, even if the source of *dhamma* is to be found in the ethical teachings of various sects, the edicts leave no doubt that it is the king who is the prime effective announcer and propagator of *dhamma.* And even if they overlap, the messianic words of the king are projected as much more powerful and efficacious than the teachings of the sects. This is implied in the fact that the world is described as having experienced a severe moral decline (in spite of the existence of these sects) and that this decline is said to have been reversed only as a result of the king's initiatives and exertions. The elements of self-righteousness and arrogance are not absent in Aśoka's early inscriptions, but they do become stronger in the pillar edicts. For instance, in pillar edict 2, the king talks of the benefits, including that of life, that have been bestowed by him on bipeds and quadrupeds, birds, and aquatic animals, and also claims to have bestowed on all the gift of eyesight (*cakhu-dāna*)—that is, insight into the truth.

Therefore, although Aśoka emphasizes ethics and the moral aspect of kingship and empire, there is no doubt that the message conveyed by the edicts is ultimately also political. Psychology, dispositions, and emotions have an important place in this political philosophy. While the importance of the governance of the self is emphasized in many early Indian philosophies and traditions, Aśoka makes the governance of the self—of the ruler and the ruled—the cornerstone of his political philosophy. In this theory of governance, there is no clear distinction between the administrative and dhammic domain. The officers concern themselves with propogating *dhamma* because the king's and their own goals extend to ensuring the people's happiness in this life and the next, their accumulation of merit, and their attainment of heaven; their activities in this regard spill out beyond the king's political domain. Aśoka's ideas about war and peace (discussed, for instance, by Richard Salomon),[44] or indeed any other aspect of his *dhamma*, cannot be understood unless they are correlated with all these inter-related elements.

Aśoka's edicts deal with certain perennial problems of power and authority; they represent a bold attempt to assert and emphasize the moral foundations of royal authority and empire, the nature of the good, and the close connection between the governance of the state and the self. They also seriously engage with the problem of violence and conflict in the political and social spheres. The problems of violence against both humans and animals are addressed; that against the latter is sought to be mitigated, not eliminated. The king's abjuration of war is based on a reasoned critique of it, is related to the larger problem of violence, and is connected with ethical and metaphysical concerns. King, officials, and subjects are united in their shared quest for moral perfection and in a vigorous campaign of moral engineering, premised on an optimistic belief in the cultivation and perfectibility of human character, sentiment, and behaviour, all grounded in culturally-embedded ideas related to *karma* and merit. Yet, singular as Aśoka's vision of empire is in several respects, it should be noted that his political philosophy addresses issues that were central to the larger discourse of politics in the texts and inscriptions of ancient India, especially issues connected with the relationship between politics, violence, and war.[45] Furthermore, while a comparison between the various sources reveals certain differences in ideas and emphasis, there are also many points of congruence. For instance, political treatises such as the *Arthaśāstra* and *Nītisāra* also emphasize victory rather than conquest (although of a different kind) and urge that the king must govern himself in order to govern his kingdom well.

The ultimate declared aim of Aśoka's political theory and practice was neither the expansion of territorial power nor the maintenance of social order. Instead, it was an extremely radical and intrusive aim: the moulding and transformation of the mental and emotional dispositions, attitudes, and behaviour of all humankind.[46] As we have seen, the means for achieving these ends included orders, injunctions, instruction, argument, and persuasion—through oral and written media as well as through personal example. The obedience of the subjects was an important prerequisite for these strategies to bear fruit. Making citizens virtuous is an aim that is also found in the political thought of Plato and Aristotle, but Aśoka is the only known historical king to actually have created and used state machinery to try to achieve such a goal.

Acknowledgements

I would like to acknowledge the useful discussions I had with Vijay Tankha and Mahesh Rangarajan in the course of writing this chapter.

Notes

1. For an overview and discussion of the sources and debates concerning Aśoka and the Maurya period, see Upinder Singh, *A History of Ancient and Early Medieval India* (New Delhi: Pearson Longman, [2008] 2009), Chapter 7.
2. See Gerard Fussman, 'Central and Provincial Administration in Ancient India: The Problem of the Mauryan Empire', *Indian Historical Review* 14 (1–2), 1987–1999, pp. 43–72; Romila Thapar, *The Mauryas Revisited* (Kolkata: K.P. Bagchi, 1984).
3. For these two views, see H. C. Raychaudhuri, *Political History of Ancient India from the Accession of Parikshit to the Extinction of the Gupta Dynasty*, with a Commentary by B.N. Mukherjee (New Delhi: Oxford University Press, 1996), pp. 309, 324; Romila Thapar, *Aśoka and the Decline of the Mauryas* (Delhi: Oxford University Press, [1963] 1997), pp. 201–203.
4. See B. M. Barua, *Aśoka and his Inscriptions* (Kolkata: New Age Publications, [1946] 1955), pp. 225–271; D. Devahuti, 'Aśoka's Dissent from the Hindu and the Buddhist Goals and Methods of Chakravarti, the Great Conqueror', in S. C. Malik, ed., *Dissent, Protest and Reform in Indian Civilization* (Shimla: Institute of Advanced Studies, 1977).

5. See Thapar, *Aśoka and the Decline of the Mauryas*; Thapar, *The Mauryas Revisited.*
6. See, for instance, John S. Strong, *The Legend of King Aśoka: A Study and Translation of the Aśokāvadāna* (Princeton: Princeton University Press, 1983), pp. 8–12 for a critique of the tendency of scholars to interpret the Buddhist legends about Aśoka in the light of the edicts and vice versa, and also of the failure of historians to take into account the literary form and religious intent of the legends.
7. For recent perspectives on these and other aspects of Aśoka's inscriptions, see Patrick Olivelle, Janice Leoshko and Himanshu Prabha Ray, eds., *Reimagining Aśoka: Memory and History* (New Delhi: Oxford University Press, 2012).
8. Upinder Singh, 'Texts on Stone: Understanding Aśoka's Epigraph-Monuments and their Changing Contexts', *Indian Historical Review* 24, 1998, pp. 1–19.
9. There are a few inscriptions (the Piprahwa casket, Sohgaura and Mahasthan inscriptions) which may be pre-Aśokan, but their dates are debated. For a list of Aśokan edicts, see F. R. Allchin and K. R. Norman, 'Guide to the Aśokan Inscriptions', *South Asian Studies* 1, 1985, pp. 43–50; and K.R. Norman, 'The Languages of the Composition and Transmission of the Aśokan Inscriptions', in Olivelle, Leoshko and Ray eds., *Reimagining Aśoka,* pp. 38–62. The citations from the edicts in this paper have standardized the orthographic variations and are principally based on the following sources: E. Hultzsch, *Corpus Inscriptionum Indicarum, I: Inscriptions of Aśoka* (New Delhi: Archaeological Survey of India, [1924] 1991); D. C. Sircar, *Aśokan Studies* (Kolkata: Indian Museum, [1979] 2000); B. N. Mukherjee, *Studies in Aramaic Edicts of Aśoka* (Kolkata: Indian Museum, 2000). In some places in this essay, the more familiar Sanskrit forms of certain words have been used. In citations, the following abbreviations have been used for the inscriptions: RE for rock edict, PE for pillar edict, and SRE for separate rock edict.
10. See Mukherjee, *Studies in Aramaic Edicts of Aśoka*; Harry Falk, *Aśokan Sites and Artefacts* (Mainz am Rhein: Verlag Philipp von Zabern, 2006). Harry Falk, 'The Diverse Degrees of Authenticity of Aśokan Texts', in Patrick Olivelle, ed., *Aśoka in History and Historical Memory* (New Delhi: Motilal Banarsidass, 2009), pp. 5–18 has argued that the Aramaic Taxila and Laghman inscriptions were not issued by Aśoka.
11. Margaret Cool Root, *The King and Kingship in Achaemenid Art: Essays on the Creation of an Iconography of Empire* (Leiden: E. J. Brill, 1979) has emphasized the important personal interest and involvement of kings in key imperial projects in the near-contemporary Achaemenid empire.
12. The name 'Asoka' occurs in the MRE 1 at Maski, Udegolam, Nittur, and Gujjara.
13. For a detailed discussion of this epithet and its absence in Buddhist legends of Aśoka, see Madhav M. Deshpande, 'Interpreting the Aśokan Epithet Devānaṃpiya', in Patrick Olivelle, ed., *Aśoka in History and Historical Memory* (New Delhi: Motilal Banarsidass, 2009), pp. 19–45.

14. Antiyoka is identified with Antiochus II Theos of Syria; Turamaya with Ptolemy II Philadelphus of Egypt; Antikini with Antigonus Gonatas of Macedonia; Maka with Magas of Cyrene in north Africa; and Alikasudara with Alexander of Epirus or Alexander of Corinth.
15. The identification of some of these terms is problematic. However, the Yavanas, Kāmbojas, and Gandhāras can definitely be placed in the north-west; the Bhojas, Riṣṭikas, Āndhras, and Pulindas can be located in trans-Vindhyan India.
16. *Ibhya* could either mean rich people or low people.
17. In rock edict 13, *nikāya* refers to Brāhmaṇas and *samaṇas*.
18. Thapar, *Aśoka and the Decline of the Mauryas,* p. 149.
19. References to these constituent elements of *dhamma* are mentioned in many edicts. It is interesting to note virtues that are *not* mentioned specifically—for instance, chastity, temperance, and honesty. Of course, these could theoretically have come within the purview of self-control.
20. Pillar edict 3 enumerates the following *āsinavas* (sins): fierceness (*caṁḍiye*), cruelty (*niṭhuliye*), anger (*kodhe*), pride (*māne*), and envy (*isyā*). Rock edict 10 talks of the need to avoid the danger (*parisava*) of demerit (*apuṁñya*).
21. There is debate about the identification of the six texts. But there is no doubt about the close resemblance between the code of conduct prescribed in the edicts and that prescribed for the laity in Buddhist texts such as the *Sigālavāda Sutta.*
22. According to Buddhist tradition, the Bodhisattva entered the womb of his mother Māyā in the form of a white elephant. However, it should be noted that the white elephant also has an importance in Jainism, and appears (along with a white bull and a lion) as a portent in the list of fourteen (sixteen, according to Digambara tradition) dreams that Triśalā, mother of the future Mahāvīra, had at the time when he was conceived in her womb.
23. See Singh, 'Texts on Stone', pp. 6–13.
24. Thapar, *Aśoka and the Decline of the Mauryas,* p. 168.
25. All dates in the edicts are to be understood as expired years.
26. *Aṭavi* means forest, but here it is used in the sense of *āṭavikāḥ*, which, in the *Arthaśāstra,* refers to forest people and forest chieftains.
27. There is a striking similarity between this sentiment and the statement with reference to the unconquered borderers in separate rock edict 2, where the king states that he will forgive what can be forgiven.
28. There is debate about the meaning of the word *hida* ('here') which precedes these announcements. Rather than referring only to the places where the edicts were inscribed, this word should probably be understood as meaning 'here, in my dominion'.
29. Aloka Parasher-Sen, 'Of Tribes, Hunters and Barbarians: Forest Dwellers in the Mauryan Period', *Studies in History* 14 (2), 1998, pp. 187.
30. A.L. Basham, *History and Doctrines of the Ājīvikas: A Vanished Indian Religion* (London: Luzac, 1951), pp. 122–123.
31. For early Buddhist perspectives on the relationship between animals and humans, see James P. McDermott, 'Animals and Humans in Early Buddhism', *Indo-Iranian Journal* 32, 1989, pp. 269–280.

32. The animals and their tentative identifications (after Hultzsch and Sircar, as per note 8) are: *suka* (parrot), *sālika* (maina birds), *aluna* (a reddish-brown bird), *cakavāka* (goose), *haṁsa* (bar-headed goose), *nandi-mukha* (a type of water bird), *gelāṭa* (?), *jatūka* (bat), *ambākapīlika* (queen ants or mango-tree ants), *daḷī* (terrapin turtle), *anaṭhikamacha* (boneless fish), *vedaveyaka* (some kind of fish), *gaṅgāpupuṭaka* (an aquatic animal living in the Gaṅgā river, possibly the Gangetic dolphin), *saṅkujamacha* (skate fish), *kaphaṭa* (tortoise), *sayaka* (porcupine), *paṅnasasa* (leaf hare), *simala* (antler stag), *saṇḍaka* (wild bull), *okapiṇḍa* (?), *palasata* (rhinoceros), *setakapota* (white dove/pigeon), and *gāmakapota* (village pigeon).
33. Shibani Bose (personal communication) points out that the Indian rhinoceros, while a very adaptable animal, prefers habitats which provide ample wallows and swampy feeding grounds. In spite of the absence of rhinoceros bones at excavated sites, the depictions in terracotta and soapstone seals and discs cited by Joachim Bautze, 'The Problem of the Khaḍga (*Rhinoceros unicornis*) in the Light of Archaeological Finds and Art', in J. Schotsman, J. Taddei, and M. Taddei, ed., *South Asian Archaeology* (Naples: Instituto Universitario Orientale, 1983), pp. 405–433 suggest that in Aśoka's time these animals were around at least in the middle and lower Gangetic valley. In fact, Bautze points out that as late as the 18th century, there were so many rhinoceroses in North Bengal and Assam that a French map of India describes that area as 'Contrée de Rhinoceros'.
34. On the military importance of the elephant and 'elephant-forests' in the Maurya period, see Thomas R. Trautmann, 'Elephants and the Mauryas', in Mahesh Rangarajan and K. Sivaramakrishnan, ed., *India's Environmental History,* I: *From Ancient Times to the Colonial Period* (Ranikhet: Permanent Black, 2012), pp. 152–181.
35. These are the three Cāturmāsīs (the full moon days of the three months of Āṣāḍha, Kārttika, and Phālguna) and the Tiṣya full moon (i.e., the full moon day of the Tiṣya constellation, in the month of Pauṣa), for three days in each case—the fourteenth and fifteenth day of one lunar fortnight (*pakṣa*) and the first of the next. G. Bühler, 'The Pillar Edicts of Aśoka', *Epigraphia Indica,* 2, 1894 pp. 264 sees this prohibition as applicable to the other months as well, and states that they added up to 56 days in all. On the meaning of Cāturmāsī, see D. C. Sircar, *Inscriptions of Aśoka* (New Delhi: Publications Division, Ministry of Information and Broadcasting, Government of India, [1957] 1967), p. 23; Bühler, 'The Pillar Edicts of Aśoka'.
36. These were the eighth, fourteenth, and fifteenth days of every lunar fortnight, as well as the (full moon days of) Tiṣya, Punarvasu, and the three Cāturmāsīs.
37. These were the (full moon days of) Tiṣya, Punarvasu, and the fortnights (*pakṣas*) of the Cāturmāsīs.
38. It should be noted that the concern for the welfare of prisoners is also expressed in RE 5, which talks of the *dhamma* officers distributing money to prisoners who have children and releasing those who are aged or have committed crimes due to being misled.
39. Mahesh Rangarajan, personal communication.

40. Scholars have discussed other possible meanings of *samatā,* but this seems the most appropriate one.
41. Etienne Lamotte, *History of Indian Buddhism: From the Origins to the Śaka Era,* trans. Sara Webb-Boin under the supervision of Jean Dantinne (Louvain-la-Neuve: Institut Orientaliste, 1988), p. 232.
42. It should be noted that the creation of confidence among the constituent elements of the state is also emphasized in the political treatises.
43. See for instance Andre Wink, 'Sovereignty and Universal Dominion in South Asia', in Jos J. L. Gommans and Dirk H. A. Kolff, ed., *Warfare and Weaponry in South Asia 1000–1800* (New Delhi: Oxford University Press, 2001), p. 110.
44. Richard Salomon, 'Ancient India: Peace Within and War Without', in Kurt A. Rafflaub, ed., *War and Peace in the Ancient World* (Oxford: Blackwell, 2007), pp. 53–65.
45. For a discussion of how these issues are treated in two important ancient political treatises, the *Arthaśāstra* and the *Nītisāra,* see Upinder Singh, 'Politics, Violence, and War in Kāmandaka's *Nītisāra*', *The Indian Economic and Social History Review* 47 (1), 2010, pp. 29–62. For a discussion of how these issues are treated in a highly influential *kāvya,* see Upinder Singh, 'The Power of a Poet: Kingship, Empire and War in Kālidāsa's *Raghuvaṁśa*', *The Indian Historical Review* 38 (2), 2012, pp. 177–198. These constitute Chapters 11 and 12 of this book.
46. To some extent, Aśoka seems to have recognized the gap between his ideals and his actual achievements, although towards the end of his reign, he seems to have been convinced that he had succeeded in effectively closing this gap.

10

Inscribing Power on the Realm: Royal Ideology and Religious Policy in India (c. 200 BCE–300 CE)

In the history of the Indian subcontinent, the five centuries between c. 200 BCE and 300 CE were marked by agrarian expansion, urban efflorescence and momentous developments in the religious and cultural spheres. The proliferation of states and a series of invasions from the northwest were accompanied by new forms of expression of political power and authority. Political ideology was expressed through coinage and kings increasingly marked their power on their realm through inscribed words, images and monuments. The ancient Indian epigraphic world was dynamic and interactive.[1] The epigraphic process included conceptualization, execution, reception, and reaction. Information about the form and content of inscriptions flowed across dynasties and regions, resulting in epigraphic continuities and innovations, and the emergence of pan-Indian patterns of discourse which allowed for regional variations. Inscriptions were often in conversation with each other and, as in

---

This chapter was previously published as the 28th J. Gonda lecture in 2022 by the J. Gonda Fund Foundation of the Royal Netherlands Academy of Arts and Science (KNAW), Amsterdam.

all conversations, it is not only what is said but what is left unsaid, that is important.

The Maurya emperor Aśoka (*c.* 268–232 BCE) initiated the practice of inscribing power on the realm in the form of words and visual symbols. His inscriptions include autobiographical elements and self-eulogy and can be collectively seen as a royal chronicle in multiple instalments and iterations. But the epigraphic *praśasti* (panegyric) which appeared at the turn of the millennium was significantly different in style and content; its relationship with power and its intertexuality with *kāvya* has been perceptively highlighted by Sheldon Pollock.[2] The *praśasti* was a highly condensed and carefully crafted political artefact, rooted in the literary culture of its time; it presented an idealized description of the king and his rule and came to be considered essential for the transformation of power into legitimate authority. It endowed the political claims of a king with dynastic depth by embedding him within a lineage and within a larger political and cultural tradition. It created a political map, locating him in relation to his contemporaries, by defining the *raja-maṇḍala* (circle of kings) of which he was a part. The *praśasti* can also be understood not only through what it expressed but through what it sought to conceal, invisibilize and transform into something else—namely political violence.[3]

In the early history of political poetry, the Junagadh/Girnar inscription of Rudradāman (c. 150 CE) and the Allahabad inscription of Samudragupta (composed towards the end of his c. 350–70 CE reign) are usually singled out for special mention.[4] The former offers the earliest use of fine Sanskrit prose to herald political power in a novel way, presenting a model of a warrior-king possessing many benevolent, pacific virtues. The latter uses verse and prose to combine claims to political paramountcy with territorial specificity and an even more elaborate, impressive and expressive advertisement of martial prowess balanced with benevolent and peace-time accomplishments. However, if these are identified as elements of a new 'classical' vision of Indian kingship, the earliest inscriptions to embody them are older. They are the Hathigumpha inscription of Khāravela, king of Kaliṅga, and the inscriptions of the Sātavāhana and western Kṣatrapa rulers of the Deccan; and they were not in Sanskrit but in Middle Indic. This point has been convincingly made by Andrew Ollett,[5] but I would like to take the argument further. I am going to focus not so much on the issues of language and script (which are no doubt important), but on the dialogic and circulatory aspects of epigraphic content and political practice.[6]

My basic argument is that the fundamental template of ancient Indian political ideology and religious policy was established during the period c. 200 BCE–300 CE through a continuous dialogic process.[7] While Aśoka remains an important reference point, I focus on three themes:

I. Religion, ideology and historical memory in the Hathigumpha inscription of Khāravela (1st century BCE)
II. The foundation of a new Purāṇic Brahmanical kingship in Sātavāhana and Western Kṣatrapa/Kṣaharāta inscriptions at Naneghat and Nashik (1st century BCE to the 1st century CE)
III. Royal religious policy and persecution in early historic India

I argue that the ways in which kings inscribed their power in words and proclaimed it visually and monumentally were important parts of the cut and thrust of political interactions, and that there is a need to look afresh at the issue of epigraphic influence across dynasties and centuries.

Religion, Ideology, and Historical Memory in the Hathigumpha Inscription of Khāravela

The nuclear area of the earliest post-Maurya state in Odisha was situated in the lower Mahanadi valley and delta; its chief monumental markers were located in the Udayagiri and Khandagiri hills (in Khordha district). There are over 30 excavated caves in the sandstone hillsides, and Cave 14 on Udayagiri hill, known as the Hathigumpha (Figure 10.1), contains a 17-line royal inscription in fine Middle Indic literary prose (Figure 10.2). It is an epigraph of *mahārāja* Khāravela of the Mahāmeghavāhana family and Ceti (Cedi) lineage, a Kaliṅgādhipati (lord of Kaliṅga) who ruled in the 1st century BCE.[8] The composer of the text displays masterful powers of compression. After an invocation to the *arhat*s and *siddha*s, and an introduction to the lineage and greatness of the king, one single line (l. 2) describes his childhood, education and training as a prince, and his nine-year stint as *yuvarāja* leading up to his royal consecration at the age of 25. Then follows a succinct but vigorous annual report of his achievements over 13 years of his reign.[9] The text focuses on three main themes: the king's military accomplishments, his benevolent activities, and his being an ardent follower and patron of Jainism.

Figure 10.1
The Hathigumpha (Cave 14), Udayagiri hill

Source: Author

Figure 10.2
The Hathigumpha inscription

Source: Author

The Hathigumpha inscription combines a strong sense of territoriality with an imperial ideal.[10] The account of Khāravela's military victories begins with his second year when, disregarding Sātakarṇi (*acitayitā Sātakaṁnim*), he despatched his army to the western regions. A Yavana king,[11] a Pāṇḍya king, as well as the Musikas (or Asikas), Raṭhikas, Bhojakas, and an Ava king of Pīthuṁḍa are those over whom Khāravela claims to have scored military victories.[12] There are references to his two attacks against Magadha (lines 7–8 and 12), a victorious expedition against Bharadhavasa (i.e. Bhāratavarṣa, which here seems to be used as a generic term for north India), his breaking up a confederacy of the Tramira (Dramira) country, and terrifying the kings of Uttarāpatha. The narrative of victories is accompanied by an advertisement of the enormous riches—jewels, horses, elephants and pearls—that they yielded. The action-packed narrative suggests Khāravela's extensive dominion in the north, south, east and west and creates an impression, an illusion, of a king who had impressed his might over virtually the entire subcontinent.

The inscription also highlights the king's benevolence towards his subjects in its description of his furthering their material prosperity by spending a large sum of money (35,000 of an unspecified currency)[13] on various activities in the capital Kaliṅganagarī—repairing gates, walls and structures which had been damaged by a storm; building the embankments of a lake, tanks and cisterns; and restoring gardens. The reference to Khāravela entertaining his people (*pakatiyo ca raṁjayati*; l.4) and bestowing favours (*anugaha*) amounting to hundreds of thousands (of an unspecified currency) on the people of the town and countryside (l.7) is suggestive of the conceptual vocabulary of the political treatises.[14]

The activities of year 13 (ll. 14–16), when Khāravela engaged in a number of activities connected with the Jaina *saṅgha*, are presented as the climax of his reign.[15] This was when he convened a huge conclave (*saṁghayana*) on the Kumārī hill (Udayagiri), which attracted wise monks (*samanas*) and ascetics (*tapasins*) from a hundred quarters; built a lavish structure (which cost 75,00,000 of an unspecified currency) associated with the *saṅgha*, and had the seven-fold Aṅgas swiftly compiled. Khāravela describes himself as a layman devoted to worship (line 14: *pūjānurata-uvās[aga]*, i.e. *upāsaka*), and as one who had realized the nature of *jīva* and *deha*. The description suggests an especially ardent follower of the Jaina doctrine and a great benefactor of the *saṅgha*.

The last two lines of the inscription sum up the king's greatness by describing him as the king of peace (*khemarājā*), king of prosperity (*vaḍharājā*), king of monks (*bhikhurājā*),[16] king of dharma (*dhamarājā*), accomplished in extraordinary virtues, one who respected all sects (*sava-pāsaṁḍa-pūjako*), a repairer of all temples (*sava-de[vāya]tana-saṁkhāra kārako*), one whose chariot and army were irresistible, wielder of the wheel (*cakadharo*), one whose wheel/power was protected and irresistible (*gutacako pavatacako*), descended from the royal sage (*rājasi*) Vasu, a great victor (*mahāvijayo*), *rājā siri* Khāravela.[17] Although the modest term *janapada* is used for his realm (in line 11), the description of Khāravela's far-flung military victories and the repeated references to the wheel leave no doubt that he was claiming the imperial status of a *cakravartin*.[18]

Apart from creating a linear chronicle of Khāravela's achievements, the Hathigumpha inscription invokes the historical memory of a long and bitter conflict between Kaliṅga and Magadha. The reference (line 6) to Khāravela in his fifth year, extending into his capital a canal that had been excavated 300 years previously by king Nanda[19] is an allusion to a Magadhan invasion of Kaliṅga long before his time. Khāravela's first attack against Magadha was when in his eighth regnal year (lines 7–8), he sacked Goradhagiri, before moving on to torment Rājagaha, i.e. Rājagṛha (*Goradhagiriṁ ghātāpayitā Rājagahaṁ upapīḍāpayati*). The second attack took place in his twelfth year (line 12), when he caused great terror (*vipulaṁ bhayaṁ*) among the people of Magadha, made king Bahasatimita (Bṛhaspatimitra) bow at his feet, brought back the riches of Aṅga and Magadha, and retrieved and installed an image of a Kaliṅga *jina* which had long ago been taken away by king Nanda.[20]

But the most interesting thing about the Hathigumpha inscription is not who it mentions but who it skips over—the Mauryas. In Rock Edict 13, Aśoka described his war against the Kaliṅgas as a terrible, cataclysmic event that turned him away from the violence of war towards the propogation of peace and *dhamma*. The Maurya victory over Kaliṅga was indelibly marked on its landscape by Aśoka's major rock edicts inscribed at Jaugada and Dhauli, which deliberately omitted Rock Edict 13. (Figures 10.3 and 10.4) The Hathigumpha inscription ignored the Maurya invasion, a humiliating defeat that still rankled.

The silence about a defeat is not in itself surprising in a *praśasti*, but I would like to argue that the composer of the Hathigumpha inscription had read Aśoka's edicts, probably those at Dhauli and Jaugada, and that Khāravela's inscription is in direct dialogue with Aśoka's edicts, whose script could still have been read.[21] There are several marked differences between the contents of Khāravela and Aśoka's inscriptions, especially in their attitude towards war, but there are several interesting connections.

Figure 10.3
The Dhauli rock

Source: Author

Figure 10.4
Close-up of Aśoka's inscriptions at Dhauli

Source: Author

Aśoka is a *rājā*, Khāravela is a *mahārāja*. Both mention the *abhiṣeka* as an important event.[22] Both emphasize the kings' personal virtues.[23] Both use hyperbole—Aśoka for the casualties in the Kaliṅga war and for the number of years that *dhamma* had been declining before he came along; Khāravela for the huge sums of money he had spent on various benevolent activites. Both mention subduing the Raṭhikas and Bhojas. Aśoka hits out at popular festivals known as *samājas*; Khāravela entertains the capital city with *samājas* and *utsavas* (he himself is said to be a master of music).[24] Aśoka boasts of spreading *dhamma* among the Yavanas, Khāravela of defeating them. Aśoka talks of his many benefactions to his people, especially through teaching them about *dhamma* and helping them attain happiness and heaven. Khāravela shows a more materialistic bent of mind, making gifts of money and promoting their material prosperity.[25] Aśoka projected himself as an emperor and a prophet of piety, possessing vast political power and a universal moral authority. Khāravela's power and authority were based on military victories, benevolence towards his subjects, and religious patronage. Both kings made their personal religious leanings (Buddhist/Jaina) clear but extended their benevolence towards Brāhmaṇas and declared their respect for all religious sects (*pāsaṇḍas*).[26] Aśoka hyphenated Brāhmaṇas and śramaṇas, by frequently invoking them together. Khāravela de-hyphenated them, extending patronage to Brāhmaṇas, but singling out Jaina ascetics (*samana* here refers to Jaina ascetics, not ascetics or renunciants in general) for special patronage. Aśoka announced a general reduction of taxes at Lumbini.[27] Khāravela bestowed *parihāras* (presumably tax exemptions) on Brāhmaṇas (line 9) (and on masons in l. 13). The frequent occurrence of the all-embracing *sava* (all) in the expression of the universalistic nature of Khāravela's power can be seen as an echo of the frequent occurrence of the word in Aśoka's inscriptions. The references to *dhamma* and peace in the Hathigumpha inscription can be traced to a Jaina influence but could just as well have been an echo of Aśoka's obsession. Aśoka set up pillars inscribed with his *dhamma* message; Khāravela refers to setting up pillars inlaid with beryl for some grand structure.[28] Aśoka's words and actions breathe austerity and restraint, Khāravela's breathe wealth and opulence. But the anonymous composer of the Hathigumpha inscription clearly used the edicts as a reference point and sought to establish Khāravela's reputation and superiority in relation to Aśoka.

The Jaina centre at Udayagiri–Khandagiri may have been aimed at surpassing anything created by Aśoka. Writing almost a century ago,

Jayaswal and Banerji reported traces of polish in the Hathigumpha, which suggest a failed attempt to imitate the polished granite finish of the Maurya-period caves in the Barabar–Nagarjuni hills (in present-day Jehanabad district, Bihar), which were the combined result of conceptual innovation, engineering skill and enormous effort and expenditure.[29] But even though unsuccessful in recreating the dazzling Maurya polish, the Udayagiri–Khandagiri complex surpassed the Barabar–Nagarjuni complex in a different way, via sculptural embellishment, especially in the Ranigumpha (Figures 10.5 and 10.6) and Manchapuri caves (Figure 10.7), which seem to include scenes from Khāravela's life, executed in a fine, distinctive artistic style.[30]

I hope I have made a convincing case that the Hathigumpha inscription was an epigraphic chronicle with a long historical memory that not only included Khāravela's contemporaries (including the Sātavāhana Sātakarṇi) but also his predecessors, specifically the Nandas and Mauryas of Magadha. Khāravela sought to eclipse the latter by inscribing his power at Udayagiri in a novel, distinctive way. The attempt was not especially successful. Aśoka strode like a colossus into Asian Buddhist legend and the history books. Khāravela, on the other hand, does not seem to

Figure 10.5
Ranigumpha, Udayagiri

Source: Author

Figure 10.6
Reliefs in Ranigumpha, Udayagiri

Source: Author

Figure 10.7
Relief in Manchapuri cave, possibly representing Khāravela's retrieval of the Kaliṅga jina

Source: Author

be remembered even in Jaina tradition (perhaps because of his boasts of violence) and is usually treated by historians as a provincial ruler.[31] However, in its balancing and advertising of the many facets of royal power in a royally sponsored religious establishment, the Hathigumpha inscription has great importance in the history of ancient Indian political ideology. It also contains the earliest epigraphic reference to the term *parihāra*, lists of which were to later become an important feature of royal land grants.[32] Knowledge of Khāravela's inscription and the magnificent Jaina centre in which it was located must have travelled beyond his realm to the domain of his contemporaries.

The Emergence of Purāṇic Brahmanical Kingship: Sātavāhana and Western Kṣatrapa/Kṣaharāta Inscriptions at Naneghat and Nashik

The Sātavāhana empire straddled the eastern and western parts of the Deccan from about the late 2nd century BCE up to the mid-3rd century CE.[33] The profusion of monumental and epigraphic material here far exceeds that produced under the Mahāmeghavāhanas and is quite distinctive in style and content.[34] Of course, not all of it was the result of royal patronage. The historical context was a strong urban commercial base that was rooted in agrarian expansion, an increased monetization of the economy and expanding trade networks. Writing on stone became increasingly used to express religious munificence, piety and aspirations, not only by kings, but also by wealthy landowners, craftsmen, merchants and guilds.[35]

The Mahāmeghavāhanas and Sātavāhanas were contemporaries and must have been aware of each other's monumental and epigraphic practice. Apart from the reference to Sātakarṇi in the Hathigumpha inscription, certain similarities between the inscriptions have been noted.[36] Who influenced who depends on their chronology, which is marked by uncertainty. The Sātavāhanas would also have been aware of the Aśokan inscriptions at Sopara, Sannati, Erragudi and the cluster of minor rock edicts on the Andhra–Karnataka border. The Śaka Kṣatrapas of the Kṣaharāta line, whose domain lay to the north of the Sātāvāhanas (and included areas of modern-day Gujarat and Rajasthan), would have been aware of the Aśokan rock edicts at Girnar. The script of these inscriptions would still have been readable. So, the material markers of Aśoka's power would have been known to both the Sātavāhanas and the Kṣatrapas.

In the second half of the 1st century BCE, the Sātavāhanas marked their territory in an innovative and dramatic way through word and image at Naneghat (in Pune district, Maharashtra), one of the important passes connecting the western coastal strip with the Deccan plateau.[37] (Figure 10.8) The plateau dips sharply between two hills into a steep descent (Figure 10.9) consisting of uneven basalt slabs revealing a

Figure 10.8
Naneghat

Source: Author

Figure 10.9
The Naneghat descent

Source: Author

Figure 10.10
Cave 11, Naneghat

Source: Author

Figure 10.11
Cave 11 interior

Source: Author

breathtaking view on a clear day. There are three groups of excavated caves at Naneghat.[38] Unlike other cave sites of the time, these were not monastic habitations. Cave 11 is the most important. (Figure 10.10) Architecturally

Figure 10.12
Cave 11: Feet of figures

Source: Author

unremarkable but conceptually unique, practically every aspect of it is a puzzle and has been debated. On the back wall of a 2.7 m high and 8.7 m square hall, the undulating rock surface and traces of feet are the ghostly remnants of what was once an imposing Sātavāhana group portrait consisting of eight life-size figures standing in relief. (Figures 10.11 and 10.12) Label inscriptions over the heads give their names (Figure 10.13).[39]

Figure 10.13
Artist Vibha Oke's imagining of the Sātavāhana group portrait in Cave 11

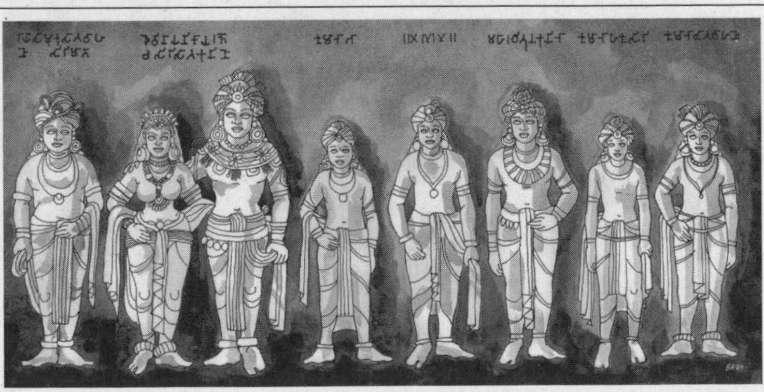

Source: Author

This group portrait is flanked by a 20-line inscription, the first ten lines of which are engraved on the left side wall and lines 11–20 on the right wall (Figure 10.14).[40] This long Middle Indic inscription is that of a Sātavāhana queen, whose name has not survived, but can be inferred to be Nāyanikā (usually redacted to Nāganikā) of the label inscription, wife of Sātakarṇi I (third king in the line, deceased by the time the inscription was engraved) and mother of king Vediśrī ('Vedisiri' survives in the inscription).[41] The inscription is badly damaged, so several details are obscure. The invocation at the beginning is to *dharma* (I am using the more familiar Sanskrit equivalents), [Prajāpati], Indra, Saṁkarṣaṇa, Vāsudeva, Candra, Sūrya, the lokapālas—Yama, Varuṇa, Kubera and Vāsava (Indra)—and Kumāra (Kārttikeya). There is a damaged section where various individuals are eulogized, including the queen's son Vediśrī (the reigning king); a Dakhināpaṭhapati, i.e. Dakṣiṇāpathapati (perhaps Simuka, father-in-law of Nāganikā); and a *mahāraṭhi*.[42] This is followed by a eulogy of the queen who is described as leading a life befitting a pious royal widow ascetic. This makes way for a very long list of sacrifices, some which seem to have been performed by the queen's husband along with her; and others performed by her on her own.[43] The former include the *rājasūya* and two *aśvamedhas*. Apart from the long

Figure 10.14
The long Naneghat inscription

Source: Author

list of sacrifices, what is striking is the specification of the lavish *dakhinā* (*dakṣiṇā*, sacrificial fee) given on these occasions, including huge sums of money (silver *kahāpanas*, i.e. *kārṣāpaṇas*), cows, horses, chariots and villages. The dominant emphasis is on the performance of *yajña*s, but some *smārta* elements are also present—the references to the gods, the queen performing *vrata*s, and king Vediśrī performing *pūrta* activities,[44] bestowing wealth and boons on supplicants, and fulfilling their desires.

Apart from its vigorous language and style, other notable features of the Naneghat inscription are its universal, imperial vocabulary—the obeisance to *dharma*, the description of the king (perhaps Simuka) as *apratihatacaka* (*apratihatacakra*, a universal monarch, the wheels of whose chariot roll on unimpeded)—combined with a claim to overlordship over a supra-regional geographical space in the epithet Dakṣiṇāpathapati.[45] In these respects, it matches the inscription of the Kaliṅgādhipati Khāravela. But the similarity ends here. While the Hathigumpha inscription contains a balanced, diachronic presentation of great achievements, accompanied by an advertisement of the king as a great patron of the Jaina *saṅgha*, the Naneghat inscription has an exceptionally strong Brahmanical stamp. I would like to suggest that through the ostentatious boast of so many sacrificial performances (perhaps one of the longest lists found in an ancient Indian inscription), some of which involved animal sacrifice, the Sātavāhana queen Nāganikā (who appears along with her husband on coins, and who continued to wield authority during her son's reign) was proclaiming the establishment of a new kind of kingship, one that was significantly different from that of both Aśoka and Khāravela. This strong assertion must also have been a strident reaction to the political threat posed by the Śaka Kṣatrapas. The Śakas were not just political rivals who had established their domain to the north of the Sātavāhana realm. They were Scythians, nomadic warriors from the Eurasian steppes, cultural aliens, *mleccha*s (barbarians).[46] The concept of *mleccha*, which originated in earlier times, gained traction during the centuries when wave after wave of warriors—Bactrian Greeks, Scythians, Parthians and Kuṣāṇas—crossed the Hindu Kush and established their political control over various parts of northwestern, northern and western India.

The labelled royal reliefs and the long inscription at Naneghat must have been conceived as inter-related elements of a powerful assertion of Sātavāhana power. Perhaps the Sātavāhanas were responsible for opening up the route via Naneghat or promoting trade along it. Outside the cave, there are rows of cisterns to the left and right.[47] Trade caravans and enemy armies that took this route (or at least the latters' scouts) would have stopped and marvelled at this impressive marker of the power of the Sātavāhana kings.

While Naneghat marks the arrival of a new, aggressive sacrificial Brahmanical royal ideology in Dakṣiṇāpatha (tempered with some *smārta* elements), over a century later at Nashik (in Nashik district, Maharasashtra), we see its transformation into a Purāṇic Brahmanical ideology. The Pandulena caves (about 8 km southwest of the city) on a hill that used to be known centuries ago as the Tiraṇhu (Triraśmi) hill, herald a new kind of relationship between religious patronage and political conflict.[48] War provided the background and the context. In about the third quarter of the 1st century CE, the army of Nahapāna, the Śaka Kṣatrapa ruler of the Kṣaharāta line, under the command of his son-in-law Uṣavadāta (his name is often redacted to Ṛṣabhadatta), moved southwards, engaged the Sātavāhana army in fierce combat, and established control over the coastal and inland regions of western India. Uṣavadāta's expeditions were not mere plundering raids; they were attempts to establish control over the economically important ports of western India and their access to the cities of the hinterland.[49] When Uṣavadāta arrived at Nashik during the course of his military campaign, a Buddhist establishment already existed in the caves, one which had attracted lay patronage from political elites and members of the urban community.[50] Uṣavadāta had Kṣatrapa power boldly inscribed here by commissioning the construction of the large, elaborately ornamented Cave 10 (Figures 10.15, 10.16 and 10.17). The verandah of this cave has three inscriptions of Uṣavadāta (Senart No. 10, 12, 14a; the last of these is fragmentary) and two of his wife Dakhamitrā (Senart 11, 13). The Kṣatrapa inscriptions display interesting experimentation with Middle Indic and Sanskrit.[51]

Let us look closely at two of Uṣavadāta's inscriptions (Senart's No. 10, 12), inscribed in the verandah.[52] In the first of these, emblazoned in big, bold Brahmi letters across the verandah's back wall (Figure 10.18), Uṣavadāta is introduced as the son-in-law of the king (*rājan*), the Kṣaharāta Kṣatrapa Nahapāna and the son of Dīnīka.[53] The main purport of the inscription is to record Uṣavadāta's excavation of the cave (*leṇa*) and cisterns (*poḍhi*), and the purchase and gift of a field (bought from a Brāhmaṇa Aśvibhūti at the price of 4000 *kahāpaṇa*s) to provide food for monks of the *saṅgha* of the four quarters (*cātudīsa bhikhusagha*) living in his cave (*mama leṇe*). However, the better part of the inscription is devoted to a eulogy of Uṣavadāta as an extraordinarily generous patron of Brāhmaṇas—he had given 16 villages to the gods and Brāhmaṇas; caused 100,000 Brāhmaṇas to be fed the whole year round

Figure 10.15
Nashik: Cave 10

Source: Author

Figure 10.16
Nashik: Cave 10 interior

Source: Author

Figure 10.17
Nashik: Cave 10, close-up of interior panel (this seems to be a later reworking of the original panel, which probably represented a stūpa flanked by devotees)

Source: Author

Figure 10.18
Uṣavadāta's inscription (Senart No. 10) over doorway in Cave 10 verandah

Source: Author

and had given eight wives to Brāhmaṇas at the *tīrtha* of Prabhāsa. He had performed various charitable acts such as building rest houses, wells, tanks, gardens and ferries.[54] He had also donated 32,000 coconut trees in Nānaṅgola village to groups of Carakas (this is probably a reference to Caraka Brāhmaṇas) at certain specified places. The inscription states that Uṣavadāta had rescued his Uttamabhadra ally from the Mālayas, after which he had bathed in the Puṣkara tank and given 3000 cows and a village (presumably to Brāhmaṇas). Clearly, no contradiction was seen in the fact that an inscription recording gifts to the Buddhist *saṅgha* mainly advertised Uṣavadāta as an extraordinary patron of Brāhmaṇas and as a performer of various charitable works for the populace.

Uṣavadāta's other inscription in Cave 10 (Senart No. 12) (Figure 10.19) announces further benefactions for the monks while advertising his munificence towards Brāhmaṇas. It states that in year 42 (these refer to Nahapāna's regnal years), Uṣavadāta gave this cave to the *saṅgha* of the four quarters, and made an *akhaya-nīvi* (*akṣaya-nīvi*) gift of 3000 *kāhāpaṇas* invested in two weavers' guilds (*kolika-nikāya*) at Govadhana (Govardhana), the specified interest of which was to pay for the cloth money and other needs of the monks (*civarika kuśaṇamūle*).[55] In its various forms, the technical term akhaya/akṣaya-nīvi refers to a grant made

Figure 10.19
Uṣavadāta's inscription (Senart No. 12) on left wall of Cave 10 verandah

Source: Author

in perpetuity, which does not however permit the alienation or destruction of the principal.[56] Uṣavadāta also gave 8000 stems of coconut trees in Cikkhalapadra village for the monks. The addendum to the inscription states that in addition to the previous donation, in year 45, a sum of 70,000 *kahāpaṇa*s was settled on the venerable gods and Brāhmaṇas.

I would like to argue that Uṣavadāta's inscriptions at Nashik are in direct conversation with the Naneghat inscription of Nāganikā. Uṣavadāta may have actually been to Naneghat during the course of his military campaigns in Sātavāhana territory; at the very least, he must have known of it through his military or epigraphic intelligence. I wonder whether the images of Sātavāhana royalty at Naneghat were naturally eroded or deliberately defaced; if the latter, Uṣavadāta's army or agents would be the obvious culprits. The cave that Uṣavadāta commissioned at Nashik could not match the strategic location of Naneghat, but it was architecturally and sculpturally much more impressive. Although it lacked royal portaits, it marked Kṣatrapa power in impressive and forceful inscribed words. Uśavadāta laid his claim to upholding *dharma* (l. 3 describes him as *dharmātman*). In striking contrast to Nāganikā's epigraph, his inscriptions do not mention sacrifices or *dakṣiṇā*. No matter how politically powerful they were, no matter how hard they sought to assimilate themselves into the Indian cultural fabric, the yājñic (sacrificial) form of legitimation was closed to these *mleccha* kings.[57] Instead, Uśavadāta's inscriptions ostentatiously advertise his munificence towards Brāhmaṇas in other ways and highlight elements of the Purāṇic *pūrta* dharma such *tīrtha* (pilgrimage), *dāna* (ritual giving) and charitable acts.[58] In these ways, the Śaka Kṣatrapas made a significant impact on the evolution of ancient Indian political ideology.

It is difficult to estimate exactly how long the Śaka interregnum lasted.[59] But it was an exceptionally intense conflict involving a reestablishment of Sātavāhana control over the area by king Gotamiputa Siri-Sadakaṇi/Śātakaṇi, i.e. Gautamīputra Sātakarṇi. When this happened, the inscriptions in 'Nahapāna's cave' (Cave 10) were not touched. Instead, Gautamīputra commissioned the excavation of a more magnificent cave (Cave 3) nearby, no doubt in order to eclipse the cave endowed by his enemy. (Figures 10.20, 10.21 and 10.22) The left wall of the verandah has two inscriptions dated in his 18th and 24th regnal years (Senart nos. 4, 5).[60] (Figure 10.23)

The two inscriptions do not dwell on royal eulogy; they get right down to business. The first (consisting of six lines) records an order issued by the king in his 18th year from the royal camp of victory of the

Figure 10.20
Cave 3

Source: Author

Figure 10.21
Cave 3, interior

Source: Author

Figure 10.22
Cave 3, close-up of interior panel

Source: Author

Figure 10.23
Cave 3: Gautamīputra Sātakarṇi's inscriptions (Senart Nos 4, 5) on left wall of verandah

Source: Author

Vejayanti army at Govadhana (on the right bank of the Godavari, about 7 miles west of Nashik) (Senart, No. 4). That the Kṣatrapas had been ousted from the Nashik area but that Sātavāhanas had not fully regained their erstwhile position of power is indicated by the fact that the only epithet Gautamīputra is given in this inscription is Benākaṭakasvāmin, lord of Benākaṭaka.[61] The inscription records the gift of 200 *nivartana*s of land (referred to as *amha-kheta*, 'our field') in Aparakakhaḍi (Western Kakhaḍi) village that previously fell within the jurisdiction of Uṣavadāta.[62] The beneficiaries were the Tekirasi (i.e. Triraśmi) monks. The inscription does not refer to the technical term *akhaya-nivi*, nor does it mention gifts of monetary investments, but it contains an important addition to the technical vocabulary of land grant charters, in the earliest lists of *parihāra*s, specific exemptions and privileges associated with land grants. The gifted land was not to be entered (by agents or soldiers of the king) (*apavesa*); not to be interfered with (*anomasa*); not to be dug for salt (*aloṇakhādaka*); not to be interfered with by the district officers (*araṭhasavīnayika*); and was to enjoy all kinds of immunities (*savajātapārihārika*).[63] These *parihāra*s are also listed in Gautamīputra's second inscription in this cave (Senart No. 5).[64]

If Gautamīputra Sātakarṇi's inscriptions in Cave 3 at Nashik mark an important stage in the evolution of the technical vocabulary of royal religious grants, the most significant Sātavāhana intervention in expressions of royal ideology was made in the same cave in the early 2nd century CE. It is an 11-line inscription of Gautamīputra's mother, Gotami Balasiri, i.e. Gautamī Balaśrī (Senart, No. 2), dated in the 19th regnal year of Gautamīputra's successor, Vāsiṭhīputa Siri Puḷumāyi, i.e. Vāsiṣṭhīputra Pulumāvi (reigned c. 84–119 CE).[65] Inscribed in bold letters on the verandah's back left wall (Figure 10.24), it was clearly meant to be the most important donative record in the cave. It states that Gautamīputra had had this cave made and the queen mother had given it to the monks of the Bhadāvanīya *nikāya*; and that Gautamī Balaśrī's grandson, king Vāsiṣṭhīputra Pulumāvi, had gifted nearby Piśācīpadra village for the cave's embellishment.[66] In terms of political ideology, the Nashik inscription of Gautamī Balaśrī reflects a major development when compared with the inscriptions discussed so far, namely, the inscriptions of Aśoka, the Hathigumpha inscription of Khāravela, the Naneghat inscription of Nāganikā, and the Nashik inscriptions of Uṣavadāta and Gautamīputra Sātakarṇi.[67]

In fact, it is not in its description of the reigning king Vāsiṣṭhīputra but of the deceased king Gautamīputra that we get the first full expression of what can be described as the classical Indian model of a great king and a great emperor. The most important of Gautamīputra's achievements (l. 6)

Figure 10.24
Gautamī Balaśrī's inscription on the back wall of Cave 3 verandah

Source: Author

are contained in his epithets as one who was an exterminator of the Kṣaharāta lineage (*Khakharātavasa-niravasesakara*) and restorer of the glory of the Sātavāhana family (*Sātavāhanakulayasa-patithāpanakara*). His political domain is described with great specificity as consisting of many lands across central and southern India.[68] He had succeeded in destroying his enemies: the Śakas, Yavanas and Pahlavas (*Saka-Yavana-Pahlava-nisūdana*). His extensive dominion and political paramountcy are alluded to in the statements that his horses had drunk the waters of the three oceans, that his commands were obeyed and feet worshipped by all the princes of the circle of kings. These martial achievements are punctuated by references to other attributes including his physical beauty; his obedience to his mother (not his father!); his pursuit of the three goals of human existence; his being the abode of the sacred texts (āgamas) and the refuge of royal fortune (Śrī). His commitment to non-violence is reflected in the statement that he was averse to hurting even an enemy who had done him offence.[69] The king's relationship with his people is highlighted in the statements that he shared in their joys and sorrows, levied and used taxes fairly, and organized festivals (*samājas*).[70] There is also a powerful assertion of Brāhmaṇa identity. Gautamīputra is described as a destroyer of the arrogance of the Kṣatriyas (*khatiya-dapa-māna-madana[damana]*) and a peerless Brāhmaṇa (*eka-bamhaṇa*). Simultaneously, the fact that he embodied all the necessary Kṣatriya qualities for a great king is proclaimed through his prowess and lustre being compared with that of several Kṣatriya heroes.[71] Apart from extending his benevolence to Brāhmaṇas, he is said to have prevented the mixture of *varṇas* (*vinivatita-cātuvaṇa-sakara*). This is the earliest occurrence of this idea in inscriptions. Gautamīputra's eulogy is thoroughly permeated with epic Purāṇic elements.

In stark contrast to the sacrifice-centred image of kingship in Nāganikā's Naneghat inscription, here there is no reference to the king as sacrificer. Further, the description of Gautamīputra in Gautamī Balaśrī's inscription far surpasses Uṣavadāta's epigraphs in literary style and the range of royal attributes and achievements. This epigraph takes forward the idea of the inscription as dynastic chronicle. It tempers the king's martial qualities with irenic and benevolent virtues, something already visible in Khāravela's Hathigumpha inscription. Uṣavadāta's generous benefactions to Brāhmaṇas are replaced by a strong assertion of the Brāhmaṇa identity of the king himself. The inscription announces the arrival of a full-blown Purāṇic Brahmanical kingship, heralded in an inscription recording a grant to Buddhist monks. It is not an accident that this powerful construct of power which included a strong assertion of Brāhmaṇa identity came in the wake of a traumatic Sātavāhana political recovery, after beating back the Śaka *mlecchas*.[72] An exceptionally talented composer must have been given the commission—perhaps by the Queen mother herself—to compose this important political inscription. Through an anonymous poet's composition, the bitter conflict with the Śakas and Gautamīputra's successful comeback became indelibly inscribed into Sātavāhana political memory and into history.

The impact of innovations in epigraphic expression and practice in the western Deccan was directly related to the nature, extent and longevity of the Sātavāhana dynasty's political power and prestige, which were of an order capable of arousing a desire for emulation among contemporaries and successors.[73] The epigraphic—archaeological imprint of the Sātavāhanas—not necessarily in the form of their direct donative activity but in the broad sense of references to their rule in word and/or image—is visible at places as far apart as Sanchi in central India and Amaravati and Nagarjunakonda in Andhra Pradesh.[74]

The most striking testimony to the celebrity status attained by the Sātavāhanas comes from the Adhālaka mahācetiya (*mahācaitya*) that stood at Kanaganahalli (in Gulbarga district, Karnataka). Although there are no Sātavāhana donative inscriptions here, kings of this dynasty are mentioned in 56 inscriptions.[75] Even more striking is a series of exceptionally fine reliefs depicting several Sātavāhana kings.[76] (Figures 10.25 and 10.26) Their full importance emerges from Monika Zin's reconstruction of their original arrangement on the dome near the northern āyaka, adjacent to scenes from the life of the Buddha and representations of Aśoka.[77] It is very likely that the set of slabs was commissioned either by Pulumāvi or by a high-ranking Sātavāhana noble or official on his behalf. The Sātavāhanas displayed an acute sense of history by having themselves inserted into the sculptural programme of the Adhālaka mahācaitya not as mere donors but as important historical actors, along and on par with Aśoka. Unlike Khāravela, the Sātavāhana kings' pitch for a place in later historical memory was successful.[78]

Royal Religious Policy and Persecution

A religious policy that was eclectic in its distribution of royal patronage reduced but did not completely eliminate religious conflict and violence. Aśoka's Rock Edict 12, which expresses a fervent desire for a growth of

Figure 10.25

Kanaganahalli relief; the accompanying inscription reads: rāyā sātakaṇ[i mahāce](t)[i]yasa r(u)pāmayāni payumāni oṇ(o)yeti *('King Sātakarṇi donates silver lotus flowers to the mahācetiya').*

Image courtesy Robert Arlt

Figure 10.26
Kanaganahalli relief; the accompanying inscription reads: 'rāya puḷumāvi ajayatasa ujeni deti' *('King Pulumāvi gives Ujeni to Ajayata').*

Image courtesy Robert Arlt

the essentials (*sāra-vaḍhī*) of all sects (*pāsaṇḍa*s) and for an atmosphere of genuine mutual respect, dialogue and concord, in fact, suggests the existence of the opposite. Aśoka's schism edict suggests a high level of discord within the Buddhist *saṅgha*, so much so that the emperor felt constrainted to intervene. Buddhist tradition provides the earliest references to active religious persecution and violence in the Indian context in legends associated with Puśyamitra Śuṅga.[79] Although the stories of Puśyamitra's persecution are clearly exaggerated for dramatic effect, they must have some historical basis.[80]

As discussed earlier, Khāravela's Hathigumpha inscription alludes to a Jaina icon that was embroiled in the political conflict between the Nandas and Mahāmeghavāhanas. Although the inscription announces the king's respect for all religious groups, Khāravela has been accused by some historians of having engaged in religious persecution not in Kaliṅga but in Magadha.[81] The Barabar and Nagarjuni hills in Bihar contain Maurya period inscriptions recording gifts to the Ājīvikas, one of which (B4) gives the name of the hill as *Khalatika pavvata*.[82] The only sculptural embellishments at Barabar are over the door of the incomplete Lomaśa Ṛṣi cave (Figure 10.27), which includes a frieze depicting elephants approaching some oblong spindle-like elements (Figure 10.28).[83] There is no reason to interpret the latter as *stūpa*s and hence nothing to indicate that the cave was intended for Buddhist monks.[84]

Figure 10.27
Lomaś ṛṣi cave, Barabar hills

Source: Author

Figure 10.28
Frieze over doorway of Lomaś ṛṣi cave

Source: Author

But something significant did happen in the Barabar–Nagarjuni hills in post-Maurya times. The word ājīvikehi in several Maurya period inscriptions in the caves was deliberatedly chiselled out, leaving the names of the royal donors intact.[85] As mentioned earlier, the Hathigumpha inscription refers to Khāravela sacking or destroying Goradhagiri, which has usually been identified with the Barabar hills on the basis of two one-word inscriptions reading 'Gorathagiri' (apparently in letters matching the Maurya period inscriptions) found at Barabar.[86] On this basis, it has been suggested that Khāravela was responsible for the expulsion of the Ājīvika ascetics and the erasure of their name in these hills.[87] But was the selective defacement of a single word in four inscriptions the kind of activity that an army in the heat of battle would engage in? The strong language in the Hathigumpha inscription (*Goradhagiriṁ ghātāpayitā*) does not make sense if this place was merely a settlement of Ājīvika ascetics, even if relations between the Ājīvikas and Jainas were marked by tension or conflict.[88] There is no solid archaeological evidence for Barabar being a military stronghold.[89] In my view, the two single-word inscriptions mentioning Gorathagiri at Barabar do not conclusively establish that this was the place mentioned in Khāravela's inscription. The Barabar hills lie about 83 km west of Rajgir. It is much more likely that the Goradhagiri of the Hathigumpha inscription was a hill to the south of Rajgir. The Kaliṅga army must have approached

Figure 10.29
Fortifications of Rājagṛha

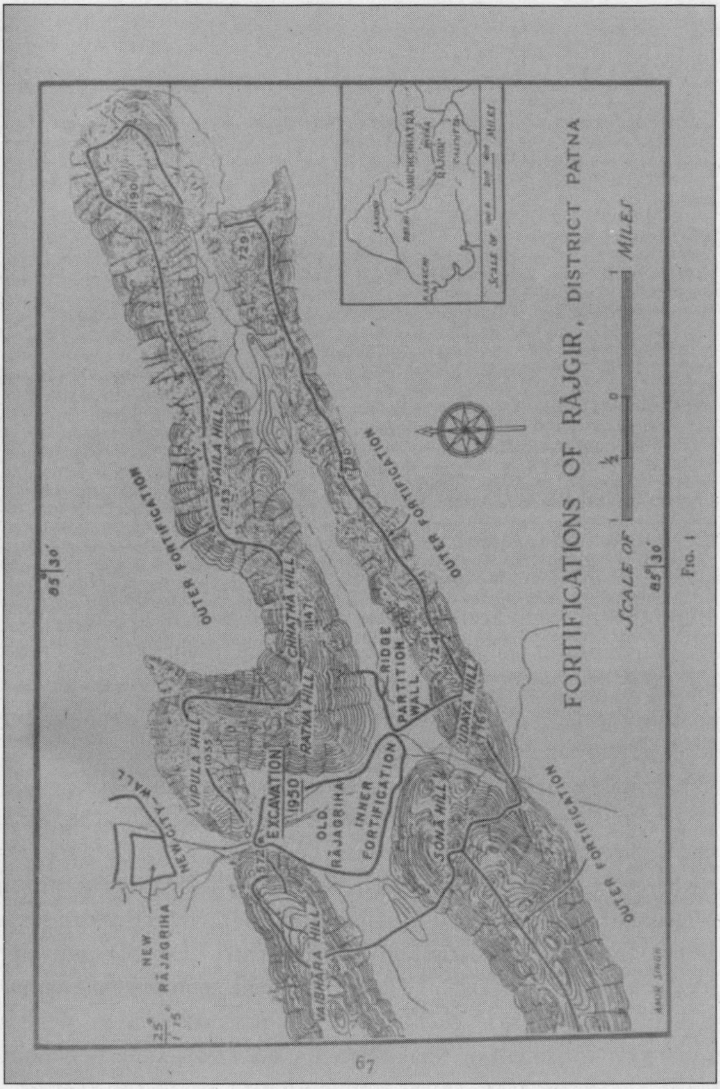

Source: A. Ghosh, 'Rajgir 1950,' *Ancient India* No. 7.

the city from the south, from the gap between the Sona and Udaya hills (Figure 10.29) and breached the outer fortifications. The inner fortification wall of Rājagṛha, and the city itself, would have been right in front of them.[90] Khāravela stands exonerated of religious vandalism.

However, there are several layers to the connection between political and religious competition and conflict. This is clear from the context of war that is visible in certain religious grants, as at Nashik in the case of the Kṣatrapas and Sātavāhanas. It is also clear from the imprecatory verses that swiftly became a standard part of land grant charters, warning later kings against rescinding the grant that had been made. I see these dire warnings as more than routinely repeated formulae —as an indication that the rescinding of royal land grants was far more frequent than might be imagined and as an acknowledgement that religious grants were implicated in political conflicts.

Conclusions

Against the background of an increasing complexity of state structures with a developing bureaucratic and fiscal apparatus, and widening political networks that included subordinates and allies, inscriptions took on the role of dynastic and inter-dynastic chronicles, reflecting a centuries' long historical memory, responding to the material markers of prececes-sors, rivals and enemies, employing sophisticated techniques of literary expression, subtle rejoinders, deliberate omission and attempted erasure. A focus on both what was said and left unsaid indicates much more about epigraphic response and influence that initially meets the eye.

Although Aśoka's inscriptions are unique and highly idiosyncratic, the ways in which he marked his power on his realm were recognized by later ambitious kings and had a strong impact on their political and epigraphic practice.[91] The inscriptions of Aśoka, Khāravela, the Western Kṣatrapas and Sātavāhanas were part of a wide, interactive circulation of epigraphic information and played important roles in the evolution of royal ideology and religious policy. A crucial factor in the evolution of political ideology during c. 200 BCE and 300 CE was the '*mleccha* effect'—the invasions of a series of 'outsiders' from Central Asia and Afghanistan—which created an upheaval in the subcontinental political firmament. The '*mleccha* shock', or more specifically, the 'Śaka shock', is clearly expressed in Gautamī Balaśrī's elaborate description of her son Gautamīputra's restoration of the glory of the lineage after a long and bitter struggle.

Aśoka introduced the association of tax concessions for religious reasons (at Lumbini); the idea of the perpetuity of a religious gift was introduced during the reign of his successor Daśaratha (at Barabar). Khāravela bestowed gifts and favours on his subjects and Jaina monks, and *parihāra*s on Brāhmaṇas. But the new idea of the pious gift that emerged in western India involved a formal process of documentation and the transfer of several specific exemptions and privileges which had to be specified through the use of a technical, legal vocabulary and process.[92]

Western India was the nuclear area for the creation of the basic template of royal land grant charters. But the interventions made by the Kṣatrapas and Sātavāhanas were not only significant in crafting the basic epigraphic template of royal ideology. They were also important in creating a template for royal religious policy. The central ideas of a royal land grant, including its political underpinnings, eternal nature, fiscal and other privileges, and legal status, were now in place. The world of money and property coalesced with the world of pious gifts and merit in a new way.[93] All the basic elements of the land grant charter, starting with the auspicious symbols and invocation, are present in inscriptions of the Sātavāhanas, except for the imprecatory verses at the end. This was an addition made by their Ikṣvāku and Vākāṭaka successors. A major change in post-Sātavahāna times was that copper plates swiftly replaced stone as the favoured surface for recording royal land grants.[94] Another important change was that in the Kṣatrapa–Sātavāhana period, apart from kings, private individuals too appear as donors of land (for instance at Junnar and Kanheri), but in later times, land grants became almost entirely a royal monopoly. Over time, the number of *parihāra*s in land grants increased, as did the stipulations of the boundaries of the gifted land.

Although from the point of view of religious history, the most striking feature of the period c. 200 BCE–300 CE is the expansion of Buddhist establishments across the subcontinent, it can be inferred from the content of inscriptions that this period also witnessed an increasing Brahmanization of royal courts. It is not a coincidence that the emergence of a strong Brahmanical foundation of royal ideology and religious policy occurred during the very time when dynasties claiming to be Brāhmaṇas (Śuṅgas, Kāṇvas, Mitras, Sātavāhanas) came to the fore in different parts of the subcontinent.[95] Between c. 200 BCE and 300 CE, Brāhmaṇas took on the role of composers of royal epigraphic documents and became recipients of royal land grants. This was in addition to the many other roles they played in royal courts—as ritual experts, political advisors, administrative officers, military commanders, poets, writers and intellectuals. The combination proved unbeatable. Bureaux of epigraphic composition and transcription must have been important parts of the administrative apparatus of kingdoms and would have been manned by literary-minded politically oriented Brāhmaṇas who travelled, transcribed and studied inscriptions of contemporary rulers, and gathered epigraphic intelligence so that they could present their own patron in an appropriate, comparable or superior light.[96] This is the only possible explanation for the striking similarities and continuities in epigraphic conventions across the regions of the subcontinent, as well as the dialogic nature of inscriptions. Instead of trying to draw direct lines of influence, it may be more useful to think of information about monumental and epigraphic practice circulating across kingdoms, leading to a variety of borrowings, adaptations, and reactions.[97]

The model of royal religious policy that emerged during c. 200 BCE–300 CE was one where political patronage did not mirror the personal religious persuasions of a ruler but had a strong, continuing emphasis on the patronage of Brāhmaṇas. This was not the result of a supposed innate Indian attitude of 'tolerance', a word which is not useful in contexts marked by religious plurality and the absence of what may be described as a state religion. It was certainly not what Aśoka had in mind when he made a passionate plea for genuine inter-religious dialogue, respect and concord. In the times of later kings, the policy of inclusiveness in religious patronage was a pragmatic political response to an extremely variegated religious landscape in which there were multiple foci of worship within and beyond the dominant religious traditions. This policy of political elites mitigated but did not eliminate religious tension and violence, as is evident from accounts of conflict and persecution, which increased during later centuries.[98] But the basic ancient Indian model—if we would like to speak of one—consisted of a highly pragmatic and stable alliance between kings and Brāhmaṇas, one that was especially adept at making negotiations with a variety of religious, regional and tribal traditions.

Acknowledgements

I am grateful to the Board of the J. Gonda Fund Foundation of the Royal Netherlands Academy of Arts and Sciences for the honour of inviting me to deliver the twenty-eighth Gonda lecture (10 June 2022) in memory of Jan Gonda, a great scholar whose work I greatly admire. I would like to thank Professor Dr Wout von Bekkum, Chair of the J. Gonda Fund

Foundation for the invitation and Professor Dr Peter Bisschop for chairing the lecture. I owe special thanks to Ms Linda Groen for all her effort towards helping me arrive in the Netherlands and making the event happen after two years of the Covid-19 pandemic.

Notes

1 In recent years, the processual and intertextual nature of epigraphic discourse has been increasingly recognized. See, for instance, Daud Ali, 'Royal Eulogy as World History: Rethinking Copper-Plate Inscriptions in Cōḻa India', in Ronald Inden, Jonathan Walters and Daud Ali, *Querying the Medieval: Texts and Practices in South Asia* (New Delhi: Oxford University Press, 2000), pp. 165–229; Whitney Cox, 'Scribe and Script in the Cālukya West Deccan', *Indian Economic and Social History Review* 47, 1 (2010), pp. 1–28; Andrew Ollett, *Language of the Snakes: Prakrit, Sanskrit, and the Language Order of Premodern India* (California: University of California Press, 2017); Elizabeth A. Cecil and Peter C. Bisschop, 'Columns in Context: Venerable Monuments and Landscapes of Memory in Early India', *History of Religions*, 58, 4 (March 2019), pp. 355–403; Mekhola Gomes, Digvijay Kumar Singh and Meera Visvanathan, eds, *Social Worlds of Premodern Transactions: Perspectives from Indian Epigraphy and History* (Delhi: Primus Books, 2021).

2 Sheldon Pollock (*The Language of the Gods in the World of Men: Sanskrit, Culture, and Power in Premodern India*, Berkeley, University of California Press, 2006) has described the epigraphic *praśasti* as political and public poetry. While the political aspect of the *praśasti* is not in doubt, the extent to which it was public can be questioned on the grounds of access and literacy.

3 Genealogies suggested smooth transfers of power and concealed violent intra-dynastic power struggles. The descriptions of wars against other states advertised victories but concealed defeats or alluded to them obliquely. The king's violence against his own subjects was concealed by pious allusions to his maintenance of social order (Upinder Singh, *Political Violence in Ancient India*, Cambridge MA, Harvard University Press, 2017, p. 154).

4 It is interesting to note that these are located respectively on a rock and pillar that bear Aśoka's inscriptions. The Junagadh rock has, in addition, a 5th-century inscription of the Gupta king Skandagupta.

5 Ollett, *Language of the Snakes*, especially Chap. 2; and Andrew Ollett, 'Sātavāhana and Nāgārjuna: Religion and the Sātavāhana State', *Journal of the International Association of Buddhist Studies*, 41 (2018), pp. 421–472. Also see Meera Visvanathan, 'The First Land Grants: The Emergence of an Epigraphic Tradition in the Early Deccan', in Gomes et. al., eds., *Social Worlds of Premodern Transactions*, pp. 1–24.

6 I am not going into the issues about the structure of polities here. The Maurya empire was evidently not a centralized empire; little is known about the details of the kingdom of Kaliṅga under Khāravela; the Sātavāhana and

Kṣatrapa inscriptions suggest multi-tiered polities with increasingly elaborate bureaucratic and fiscal structures.

7 For the purpose of the analysis, I define the political domain in broad terms to include kings, members of the royal household, subordinate rulers, and political, administrative and military elites. I use the term 'religion' too in a very broad sense to include not only institutionalized religions such as Jainism and Buddhism but also Brāhmaṇas, who were major players at the political level and important mediators of social values and religious practice.

8 The dates suggested for Khāravela range from the 2nd century BCE to 1st century CE. I am placing him in the mid-1st century BCE. The Hathigumpha inscription is fragmentary in parts and there are divergent readings and interpretations of various segments. See K.P. Jayaswal and R.D. Banerji, 'The Hathigumpha Inscription of Kharavela', *Epigraphia Indica*, 20 (1929–30), pp. 71–89. Also see D.C. Sircar's reading, which differs in several significant respects (*Select Inscriptions bearing on Indian History and Civilization*, Vol. 1: *From the Sixth Century B.C. to the Sixth Century A.D.*, Calcutta, University of Calcutta, 1942, pp. 213–221). The language is Middle Indic of a western variety. According to Jayaswal and Banerji ('The Hathigumpha inscription of Kharavela', pp. 72–73), although the inscription seems to have been carefully inscribed, the forms of the characters differ in places and the writing seems to have been done by three different hands. An interesting system of spacing has been followed: there is a space before almost every proper name and a longer space for a full stop. The first few lines of the inscription are inscribed on the brow of the cave and continue on a surface that forms part of the roof. Jayaswal and Banerji reported great difficulty in reading the last eight to nine lines on the sloping roof surface; they had to partially lie down to read them. All this is curious, given the amount of effort, skill and money that must have been invested in having the inscription inscribed. It could not have been due to a miscalculation about the space that would be required for the record, because the letters would presumably have been written on the rock before they were engraved. In any case, like many other ancient inscriptions, the Hathigumpha inscription was not primarily meant to be read. As in the case of Aśoka's inscriptions, we can infer periodic ceremonial readings. Regarding Khāravela's name, S.K. Chatterji suggests that it was derived from the the Dravidian 'kar' (which means black) and vel (lance)—one who has a black or terrible lance. Sircar points out that the name Kāḷavela occurs in the *Mahāvaṁsa*. He suggests that it may also be the equivalent of Sanskrit Kṣāravela—'having salt on the shore', that is, the ocean (Sircar, *Select Inscriptions*, vol. 1, pp. 213–214, fn 1). In this essay, I will be oscillating between the Middle Indic and Sanskrit forms of words, often using the more familiar Sanskrit forms, but retaining the former in quotes from the inscriptions.

9 One of the many interesting features of the inscription is the fact that from line 3 onwards, it moves from the past to the present tense, giving it a unique, vigorous flavour.

10 This is reflected in five references to Kaliṅga in the inscription—Khāravela being the lord of Kaliṅga (l. 1), born in the Kaliṅga-rājavaṁśa (l. 3); the city of Kaliṅganagarī (l. 3); a structure built by earlier kings of Kaliṅga (l. 5); and the Kaliṅga *jina* (l. 12).

11 According to Sircar, *Select Inscriptions* 1, p. 216, fn 5, Jayaswal and Banerji's reading of 'Dimita' (Demetrios) in line 8 is doubtful.

12 For a discussion of the identifications of the rulers and place names in the inscription, see Jayaswal and Banerji, 'The Hathigumpha Inscription of Kharavela', pp. 80–86.

13 These were probably silver *kārṣāpaṇas*.

14 So is the reference in line 10 to his three-fold policy of *daṇḍa* (force), *saṁdhi* (treaty, peace) and *sāma* (conciliation). In the *Arthaśāstra*, there are several references to the king's *anugraha* (favour) and *parihāras* (exemptions).

15 The readings of this section of the inscription are significantly different. In Jayaswal and Banerji's reading, the king gives royal maintenance (*raja-bhitini*), silken clothes (*cina-vatāni*) and white clothes (*vāsā-sitāni*) to monks associated with a *kāya-nisidīya*. The last term is interpreted by them as a relic memorial, and *arahata-nisīdiyā* in l. 15 as the relic depository of the *arhat* on the hill. The terms *nisidīya/nisīdiyā* in ll. 14 and 15 bear similarity with *nisidhi* or *niśidhi*, which in later times referred to Jaina memorial stones set up in memory of those who had performed ritual death. There is, however, no evidence that the worship of bodily relics existed at this time among the Jainas. Sircar's reading does not contain any reference to silk or white clothes, and he sees in *kāya-nisidīya* a reference to a place to spend the monsoon retreat. See Piotr Balcerowicz, *Early Asceticism in India* (London and New York: Routledge, 2016, pp. 254–267) for a detailed discussion and on the word being derived from *ni+sad*, not *ni+ṣidh*.

16 Going by references in Aśoka's inscriptions and those of the Sātavāhanas and Western Kṣatrapas, this seems to refer to Buddhist monks. B.M. Barua, however, reads Iṁdarāja ('who was like Indra, king of the gods') in place of *bhikhurāja* (B.M. Barua, *Old Brāhmī Inscriptions in the Udayagiri and Khaṇḍagiri Caves: Edited with New Readings and Ciritical notes*, Calcutta: University of Calcutta, 1929, p. 29, p. 46).

17 In the Purāṇas, Vasu Uparicara is king of the ancient Cedi dynasty.

18 An inscription of Khāravela's chief queen (*agamahisi*) in Cave 9 at Udayagiri seems to describe him as the *Kaliṅga-cakavati* (i.e. *cakravartin* of Kalinga); this portion of the inscription is, however, rather damaged and difficult to read with any certainty.

19 *Nandarāja-tivasasata-oghāṭitaṁ*. Rather than a reference to a Nanda era, which we do not have any evidence of, this probably refers to the number of years that had elapsed between the building of the canal by the Nanda king and its extension by Khāravela. *Tivasasata* has been read as 103 or as 300; the latter suits the gap between the Nandas and Khāravela better. Jayaswal and Banerji's reading of a reference to the Maurya era (*Muriya-kāla-vochinaṁ*) in line 16 is a misreading (See Sircar, *Select Inscriptions*, p. 218, and n. 13).

Shashi Kant (*The Hāthīgumphā Inscription of Khāravela and the Bhabru Edict of Aśoka*, New Delhi: D.K. Printworld, [1971], 2000, p. 35) reads this as year 103, and as a reference to the Mahāvīra era of 527 BCE.

20 The identity of the Kaliṅga *jina* is uncertain. Jayaswal and Banerji ('The Hathigumpha inscription of Kharavela', p. 85) suggest this could be a reference to Śītalanātha, who is said to have been born at Bhadalapura, possibly a place in the old Godavari district of the erstwhile Madras Presidency. They also read in line 12 a reference to Khāravela driving his elephants into the Sugaṁgīya palace (*hathī Sugaṁgīya[m] pāyayati*) which is mentioned in the *Mudrārākṣasa* as the name of Candragupta Maurya's palace. However, Sircar reads the relevant phrase as *hathasaṁ Gaṅgāya pāyayati*, which gives an interesting reference to Khāravela having made his elephants and horses drink the water of the Gaṅgā.

21 Aśoka was clearly directly involved in the composition of his edicts and in the way in which he was projected through them. It is difficult to ascertain whether and to what extent Khāravela was involved in the composition of his inscriptions. For a description of the Aśokan edicts at Dhauli and Jaugada, see Falk, *Aśokan Sites and Artefacts: A Source-Book with Bibliography* (Mainz Am Rhein, Verlag Philipp von Zabern, 2006, pp. 258–269). The Udayagiri-–Khandagiri complex is located just over 16 km from Dhauli and a little over 10 km from Sisupalgarh. Dhauli could represent Tosali, while Jaugada could represent Samāpā, mentioned in the edicts as Maurya administrative centres. Alternatively, Sisupalgarh could represent Tosali or Khāravela's capital Kaliṅganagarī. Excavations here revealed remains of a large, 1 sq. km large, planned city enclosed by a rampart, gateways and moat; a monumental, pillared structure and stone-lined ponds in the centre; and several residential buildings (R.K. Mohanty and Monica Smith, 'Excavations at Sisupalgarh, 2008', *Man and Environment*, 34, 1 (2009), pp. 47–56. Another identification suggested for Tosali is Radhanagar (see R.K. Mohanty and B. Tripathy, 'The Prehistoric and Early Historic Cultures of Orissa', *Pragdhara* 9, 1997–98, pp. 88–89).

22 The reference to *rājasūya* in line 6 read by Jayaswal and Banerji was dismissed by Sircar, who reads *rājaseya*. Jayaswal and Banerji read *agiṇathiyā* in line 9; they suggested that it could be derived from Sanskrit *agnīṣṭi* and may refer to a Vedic sacrifice. Sircar finds this part of the line illegible.

23 Khāravela is said to have been endowed with auspicious marks (*lakhana*s) and possessing virtues (*guṇa*s) whose fame had reached the four quarters (l. 1). The former reminds us of the idea of the physical marks of the *mahāpuruṣa*, an idea which is present in Buddhist and Jaina traditions.

24 On the political aspects of *samāja*s and *utsava*s, see B.D. Chattopadhyaya, 'Festivals as Ritual: An Exploration into the Convergence of Rituals and the State in Early India', in B.D. Chattopadhyaya, *The Concept of Bharatavarsha and Other Essays* (Ranikhet, Permanent Black and Ashoka University), pp. 138–162.

25 Of course, rock edict 8 does state that Aśoka's *dhamma* tours included giving gifts to Brāhmaṇas and śramaṇas, meeting the aged and giving them gold.

So the materialistic aspect is not absent, but is overpowered by emphasis on dhammic teaching.

26 In the discussion of the duties of the *dhamma-mahāmātas* Aśoka's pillar edict 7, there is reference to their being occupied with the various *pāsaṇḍas*; the Nirgranthas, Ājīvikas, Brāhmaṇas and members of the (Buddhist) *saṅgha* are mentioned specifically. There is a debate on the meaning and relationship between the various categories used in the inscriptions. Patrick Olivelle (Patrick Olivelle, 'Gṛhastha in Aśoka's Classification of Religious People', in Patrick Olivelle, ed., *Gṛhastha: The Householder in Ancient Indian Religious Culture*, New Delhi: Oxford University Press, p. 46, p. 52) suggests that the *pāsaṇḍas* were religious communities that included *pravrajitas* and *gṛhasthas*.

27 This is generally understood as removing the *bali* and reducing the *bhāga* to one-eighth (from one-sixth). For an alternative reading of *aṭhabhāgīya* as referring to Aśoka's installing a portion of the Buddha's bodily relics at Lumbini, enclosed by a stone railing, a portion of which was later transferred to Sarnath, see Harry Falk, 'The Fate of Aśoka's Donations at Lumbini', in Patrick Olivelle, Janice Leoshko and Himanshu Prabha Ray, eds., *Reimagining Aśoka: Memory and History* (New Delhi: Oxford University Press, 2012), pp. 204–216.

28 Jayaswal and Banerji read *caturo ca veḍūriya-gabhe thaṁbhe* (l. 16).

29 Jayaswal and Banerji ('The Hathigumpha inscription of Kharavela', p. 72) state that below the inscription, the walls of the cave have been chiselled straight 'and at places are as beautifully polished as those of the Barābar caves'. They also refer to a dressed and polished section of the side wall of the cave. I could not identify these during my recent visit, but I have no doubt about the accuracy of the observation made by Jayaswal and Banerji almost a hundred years ago. According to Vidya Dehejia, the technique of polishing stone architectural surfaces was restricted in ancient Indian architecture to the Barabar and Nagarjuni hills (see Vidya Dehejia and Peter Rockwell, *The Unfinished: Stone Carvers at Work on the Indian Subcontinent*, New Delhi: Roli Books, 2016, p. 24, p. 26). The Udayagiri–Nagarjuni hills are made of coarse-grained sandstone, while the caves in the Barabar–Nagarjuni hills were carved out of granite outcrops. While polished granite is amenable to a metallic finish, the Maurya craftsmen were also able to produce a highly polished finish on sandstone pillars.

30 The most magnificent reliefs are carved on the façade of the upper story of Cave 1 (currently known as the Ranigumpha) in which some of the figures can be recognized as royalty from their attire, umbrella and entourage. It is possible that the relief carvings in the Ranigumpha and Manchapuri caves tell the story that the Hathigumpha inscription narrates in words. (See Sushil Chandra De, 'Khāravela in sculpture', *Orissa Historical Research Journal* 11, 1, 1962, pp. 36–40.) On the sculptures at the site, see Debala Mitra, *Udayagiri and Khandagiri* (New Delhi: Archaeological Survey of India, [1960] 1992, pp. 20–31); Janice Leoshko, 'Artfully Carved: Udayagiri/Khandagiri in Orissa', *Artibus Asiae*, 70, 1, 'To My Mind:': Studies in South

Asian Art History in Honour of Joanna Gottfried Williams, Part 2 (2010), pp. 7–24. The Hathigumpha seems to have been connected with an apsidal temple made of laterite slabs on top of the Udayagiri hill, located directly above it. There are other royal inscriptions at Udayagiri (see R.D. Banerji, 'Inscriptions in the Udayagiri and Khandagiri Caves', *Epigraphia Indica* 13, 1915–16, pp. 158–60). Three inscriptions are inscribed in Cave 9 (the lower storey is known as Manchapuri and the upper story as Swargapuri). In the Swargapuri, an inscription in the raised space between the second and third doorways begins with an invocation to the *arhat*s and records the excavation of the cave (*lena*) for the *samana*s of Kalinga. The donor is the unnamed chief queen (*agamahisi*) of Khāravela, who gives details of her own lineage. The fourth line of the inscription (which is damaged and difficult to read) seems to describe Kharavela as the *Kaliṅga-cakavati* (i.e. *cakravartin* of Kalinga). If this reading is correct, it is the earliest epigraphic use of the epithet *cakravartin*. Two inscriptions in the lower story (Manchapuri) also record the benefactions of royalty. One of them describes the cave as the *lena* of the Aira *mahārāja* Kaliṅgādhipati, whose name has been read as Kuḍepasiri or Vakradeva. It is not clear whether these were predecessors or successors of Khāravela. Another inscription (on the right wall of the veranda of the same in the cave) describes it as the *leṇa* of *kumāra* Vaḍukha. On the back wall of the veranda, there is a relief that may represent the retrival of the Kaliṅga *jina*. Other donors are mentioned in the Udayagiri—Khandagiri inscriptions, some whose background cannot be ascertained. The donor of the Bagh cave was Sabhūti, a *nagara-akhadaṁsa* (town-judge?) (Banerji, 'Inscriptions in the Udayagiri and Khandagiri Caves', p. 163).

31 In fact, in Jaina tradition, it is not Khāravela but the Maurya king Candragupta who is remembered.

32 The Hathigumpha inscription seems like a bit of a dead end in Kaliṅga itself because after Khāravela, state formation in this region went through a long lean period, taking off again only in the 4th century CE. See Upinder Singh, *Kings, Brāhmaṇas and Temples in Orissa: An Epigraphic Study, AD 300–1147* (New Delhi: Munshiram Manoharlal, 1994); and Bhairabi P. Sahu, *The Making of Regions in Indian History* (New Delhi: Primus, 2020), Chapters 2–4. Although the amount of archaeological data on early historical sites in Odisha has been steadily increasing, it does not suggest the existence of states with a well-developed administrative infrastructure or fiscal outreach, or an economy marked by urbanism, extensive trade and a high degree of monetization.

33 Although the term 'empire' has varying connotations, in my view, the geographical extent of Sātavāhana political influence/control across the eastern and western Deccan eminently qualifies it to be described as an empire. There is continuing debate about Sātavāhana chronology. There is a long chronology consisting of thirty kings who ruled for about 460 years, and a short chronology which consists of nineteen kings ruling for about 260 years. I am going by the hypothesis that Sātavāhana rule began in the 2nd century BCE. Vidya Dehejia, *Early Buddhist Rock Temples* (London, Thames

and Hudson, 1972), pp. 19–21, suggests 120/110 BCE for the beginning of Sātavāhana rule; Shailendra Bhandare (*Historical Analysis of the Sātavāhana Era: A Study of Coins*, PhD thesis, Bombay University, 1999) suggests c. 150 BCE; Ollett (*The Language of the Snakes*, p. 189) suggests c. 120–96 BCE.

34 For a description of the caves of western India, see Dehejia, *Early Buddhist Rock Temples*; S. Nagaraju, *Buddhist Architecture of Western India (c. 250 B.C. – c. A.D. 300)* (Delhi: Agam Kala Prakashan, 1981); Pia Brancaccio, ed., *Living Rock: Buddhist, Hindu and Jain Caves in the Western Deccan* (Mumbai: Marg, 2013). For an argument that there was more form than substance in the Sātavāhana polity, see Carla M. Sinopoli, 'On the Edge of Empire: Form and Substance in the Satavahana Dynasty', in Susan E. Alcock, Terence N.D'Altroy, Kathleen D. Morrison and Carla Sinopoli, eds, *Empires: Perspectives from Archaeology and History* (Cambridge: Cambridge University Press, 2001), pp. 155–178.

35 Non-royal patronage is visible at Udayagiri–Khandagiri, but not on the same scale. It is very prominent at other early Buddhist sites such as Sanchi, Bharhut and Amaravati. All this marks a major change from the Maurya period, when writing on stone was basically used to record the ideas and activities of the emperor.

36 Jayaswal and Banerji ('The Hathigumpha inscription of Kharavela', p. 73) suggest that the language of the Hathigumpha inscription indicates that the composer was 'a man from Western India who wrote in a literary dialect'. Ollett (*Language of the Snakes*, p. 27) credits the Sātavāhanas with radical innovations in epigraphic discourse and the invention of Prakrit literature. He also suggests the impact of the language, literary style and phraseology of the long Naneghat inscription on the Hathigumpha inscription. In the Naneghat inscription, Sātakarṇī is *apratihatacaka*; Khāravela is *apatihata-caka-vāhana-balo*. The Hathigumpha inscription refers in line 2 to Khāravela having launched an expedition against the western regions 'disregarding Sātakarṇi' in his second regnal year. That inscription was inscribed after Khāravela's 13th regnal year. Khāravela's rule is placed roughly in the mid-1st century BCE. The long Naneghat inscription seems to have been inscribed after Sātakarṇi's death. So it is possible, but not certain, that the Hathigumpha inscription is a bit earlier than that inscription.

37 Naneghat is located 24 km west of the town of Junnar and 45 km east of the important port of Kalyan. It is possible but not certain that Junnar may represent one of the early Sātavāhana capitals; its location on an important trade route that went on to Paithan and Ter made it commercially extremely important.

38 For a description, see Nagaraju, *Buddhist Architecture of Western India*, pp. 256–258, p. 432.

39 The label inscriptions read (left to right) as follows: Rāyā Simuka Sātavāhano sirimāto; Devi Nāyanikāya raño ca Siri-Sātakanino; Kumāro Bhāya[lo*]; (the next inscription is broken and hence illegible); Mahārathi Tranakayiro; Kumāro Hakusiri; Kumāro Sātavāhano (Vasudev Vishnu Mirashi, *The History and Inscriptions of the Sātavāhanas and the Western Kshatrapas*,

Bombay, Maharashtra State Board for Literature and Culture, 1981, p. 20). The images convey dynastic depth and indicate the importance of the queen's natal ties as the Mahāraṭhi may have been her father. For some of the views on the royal portrait gallery, especially on whether the individuals depicted in the reliefs were alive or dead at the time when the carvings were made, See A. M. Shastri, *The Sātavāhanas and the Western Kshatrapas: A Historical Framework* (Nagpur: Dattsons, 1998), pp. 102–112.

40 There are debates over whether the various relief sculptures were made in instalments or at the same time, and on the chronological relationship between the label inscriptions and the long one.

41 For the text, see Mirashi, *The History and Inscriptions of the Sātavāhanas and the Western Kshatrapas*, pp. 5–16. Apart from the use of matronyms by Sātavāhana kings, inscriptions point to the position of authority enjoyed by women of the royal household, possibly reflecting a cognatic kinship system. Sociological studies give unequilocal evidence in the context of contemporary South and Southeast Asia that women have greater agency and authority in cognatic societies compared with patrilineal ones. On the kinship system of the Sātavāhanas, and the evidence of cross-cousin marriage among them, see Thomas Trautmann, *Dravidian Kinship* (Cambridge: Cambridge University Press, 1981, pp. 363–374). The Sātavāhana queen's name has been variously redacted as Nāganikā and Nāyaṇṇikā. It should be noted that on coins, the queen's name occurs as Nāganikā (along with that of her husband Siri-Sātakaṇi).

42 The *mahāraṭhi*s were one of several categories whose position could vary from that of a subordinate to an independent ruler.

43 These are: *agnyādheya*, *anvārambhaṇīya*, *aṅgārika*; *rājasūya*; a second *aśvamedha*; *saptadaśātirātra*; *bhagaladaśarātra*; *gargatirātra*; *gavāmayana*, *aptoryāma*, *aṅgirasāmayana*, *śatātirātra*, *āṅgirasatriātra*, *chandomapavamānatrirātra*, *āṅgirasatriātra* (this is mentioned twice); *aṅgirasāmayana* (of six years' duration), *trayodaśātirātra*, *daśarātra*. There has been a long-standing debate on whether these sacrifices were performed by Nāganikā, her husband, by the latter with her participation, or by her son Vediśrī. See Alice Collett, 'Reimagining the Sātavāhana Queen Nāgaṇṇikā', *Journal of the International Association of Buddhist Studies*, 41 (2018): 329–358.

44 Line 4 has *putadasa*, Skt. *pūrtadasya*. Bühler read the word as *putradasa* and understood it as the Middle Indic form of *putradasya*, referring to the king as giver of sons.

45 Ollett (*Language of the Snakes*, pp. 30–35) points out that although written in a western variety of Middle Indic, which is continuous with the language of Aśoka's inscription in western India, the Naneghat inscription anticipates later traditions of Sanskrit *praśasti*. He argues that in view of its unprecedented literary quality, especially its quality of *ojas* (power), this inscription marks the emergence of the idea of a language of power which was defined by stylistic and aesthetic qualities. Of course, if the Hathigumpha inscription is a bit older than the Naneghat one, then it is Khāravela's inscription

that should get this credit. But Ollett's larger point about the Naneghat inscription is convincing—namely that it articulated a new vision of political power, one in which *dharma* and *dakṣiṇā* were key, 'a fusion of authority, one enacted through ritual and another disseminated through the instruments of exchange' (Ollett, *Language of the Snakes*, p. 31).

46 On the concept of the *mleccha*, see Aloka Parasher, *Mlecchas in Early India: A Study in Attitudes towards Outsiders upto AD 600* (New Delhi: Munshiram Manoharlal, 1997).

47 One of the cisterns has the inscription: 'Sopārayakasa Goviṁdadāsasa deyadhama poḍhi' (Nagaraju, *Buddhist Architecture of Western India*, p. 342).

48 For a description of the caves and summary of the inscriptions, see Nagaraju, *Buddhist Architecture of Western India*, pp. 258–281, 343–345. For the text of the inscriptions, see E. Senart, 'The Inscriptions in the Caves at Nasik', *Epigraphia Indica*, 8 (1905–1906): 59–96.

49 This conflict is also alluded to in classical accounts. See Lionel Casson, 'Sakas versus Andhras in the Periplus Maris Erythraei', *Journal of the Economic and Social History of the Orient* 26, 2 (1983): 164–177 for an argument that it was the Sātavāhanas and not the Śakas who created the trade disruption.

50 There are donations by other members of the political elite in the Nashik caves—of a royal official, a *mahāmāta* of king Kṛṣṇa, the wife of a royal treasurer (*bhaṁḍākārika*) and the wife of a *senāpati*. These mingle with gifts made by a female ascetic, householder, *lekhaka*, *yavana*, and three collective gifts—by a *gahapati-negama*, a *negama* and the people of Nāsika. The last of these, gift of the Dhaṁbika village by the Nāsikas, that is the people of Nasik, is significant because it is a non-royal land grant. The term 'collective patronage', is often used to refer to non-royal gifts made during this period. This is a misnomer. It should properly be used for gifts that record donations made collectively by groups of people.

51 Uṣavadāta's inscriptions at Nashik mark an important stage in the gradual transition from Middle Indic to Sanskrit as a language of power (see Ollett, *Language of the Snakes*, especially Chap. 2). Ollett (pp. 39–40) talks about the Kṣaharāta experimentation and two paths in language use. The Karle path, reflected in Uṣavadāta's inscription at Karle, used Middle Indic for all epigraphic purposes and was a continuation of earlier language practices. The Nasik path used Sanskrit for politically expressive purposes and Middle Indic for documentary purposes. This division of labour can be seen in one of Uṣavadāta's Nashik inscriptions (Senart No. 10), although it is not seen in his inscriptions No. 12 and 14a in the same cave.

52 See Senart, 'The Inscriptions in the Caves at Nasik', pp. 59–96. Uṣavadāta's inscription no. 10 (5 lines) is inscribed on the back wall of the verandah, under the ceiling; Dakhamitrā's No. 11 (2 lines) is in the verandah, over the doorway of the left cell; Uṣavadāta's No. 12 (6 lines) is immediately below No. 11; Dakhamitrā's No. 13 (3 lines) is over the doorway of the right cell; Uṣavadāta's no. 14a (3 lines) is on the right wall of the court beyond the verandah. Fragmentary No. 14b is below No. 14a. The later inscription of the Ābhīra ruler Īśvarasena (No. 15) is on the left wall of the court.

53 The fragmentary inscription 14a additionally describes Uṣavadāta as a Śaka.

54 There is striking use of the first person, inserted in the manner of a quote in ll. 3–4.

55 Out of the 3000 *kārṣāpaṇas* (monthly), 2000 were invested in a weaver's guild at one *paḍika* (*pratika*) (monthly) per cent; 1000 *kārṣāpaṇas* were invested in another weavers' guild with an interest of three-fourth of a *paḍika* (monthly) per cent. The meaning of *akhaya-nivi* is clear from the stipulation that the *kārṣāpaṇas* were not to be repaid; only their interest was to be enjoyed.

56 The idea of the permanence of a religious gift actually occurs earlier, in the three inscriptions of the Maurya ruler Daśaratha in the Nagarjuni hills, which use the phrase ā-caṁdama-sūliyaṁ (to last as long as the moon and the sun). In later land grant inscriptions, this became ā-candrārkam. Grants given under the *nivi-dharma* or *akṣayanivi dharma* do not fully correspond to the modern idea of private property which includes the right to buy, sell, bequeath, inherit or mortgage. Apart from occurring in Uṣavadāta's inscription (No. 12) at Nashik in connection with a monetary investment, the term also occurs in inscriptions No. 15 and 17 at Nashik. Meera Visvanathan argues that textual and epigraphic evidence indicate that *akhayanivi* began as a monetary endowment and then moved to land. See Meera Visvanathan, 'Usavadāta's Akhayanivi: the eternal endowment in the eary historic Deccan', *Journal of the International Association of Buddhist Studies* 41 (2018): 510–533.

57 In the Purāṇas, the Śakas are invariably included in lists of *mlecchas*, a category that included foreigners and tribal groups. As pointed out by D. C. Sircar (*The Successors of the Sātavāhanas in Lower Deccan*, Calcutta: University of Calcutta, 1939, p. 154), kings belonging to foreign dynasties or tribes are not known to have performed the *aśvamedha* sacrifice, even after they had been Hinduized.

58 The fact that two inscriptions in Cave 10 at Nashik mention Uṣavadāta's wife Dakhamitrā could be an echo of the importance of queen Nāganikā in the Naneghat inscription or a reflection of the importance of women of the royal household among Kṣaharātas as well.

59 That it lasted several years is indicated in Uṣavadāta's Nashik inscriptions which refer to activities in this place ranging from years 42 to 45 (these dates are understood as referring to Nahapāna's regnal years). Given the uncertainty of specific dates, I am placing both Gautamīputra and Uṣavadāta in the 1st century CE. Bhandare ('Historical Analysis of the Sātavāhana Era') places Gautamīputra's accession in 60 CE.

60 No. 4 is inscribed on the left wall of the verandah, under the ceiling; No. 5 is in inscribed in continuation with No. 4, separated from it by a *svastika*. See Senart, 'The Inscriptions in the Caves at Nasik', pp. 71–75. Dehejia (*Early Buddhist Rock Temples*, pp. 159–160) suggests that Cave 3 seems to have been modelled on Cave 10. That may be, but it also sought to surpass Cave 10, as it is more elaborately ornamented and, there are also several differences between the two (see Nagaraju, *Buddhist Architecture of Western India*, pp. 267–268).

61 This refers to the territory around the Benā or Vainganga river (in the Bhandara district in the northeastern part of Maharashtra, east of Nagpur).

62 We see a similar process of regranting of land at Karle.

63 Similar terms occur in Inscription No. 5 as well as in the later No. 3, dated in year 19 of Vāsiṣṭhīputra Pulumāvi.

64 The previous grant seems to have been made in haste after a major military victory, without doing due diligence. Gautamīputra's second inscription in the same Cave 3 (Senart No. 5) (lines 6–12) records a grant made in the name of the king and his mother, six years later, in the king's 24th regnal year. Because the previously gifted field in the village of Kakhaḍī was untilled and the village uninhabited, the king was substituting that earlier gift (of 200 *nivartanas*) by 100 *nivartanas* of land in a royal village (*rājakaṁ kheta*; the name of the village is not specified) on the outskirts of the town. The *parihāras* are then listed, as in the earlier inscription.

65 As pointed out by Ollett (*Language of the Snakes*, pp. 35–38), the language is usually described as Prakrit or Middle Indic, but its use of figures of speech and long compounds suggest that it is neither Sanskrit nor Prakrit (of the kind found in the *Gāthāsattasai*). It is *kāvya*, political poetry that reflects a new kind of cultural practice. Ollett also suggests that the Sātavāhanas went through a brief phase of experimenting with 'political Sanskrit' during and after their conflict with Nahapāna. Inscription No. 3 (4 lines), dated in year 22 of Pulumāvi's reign, is engraved in continuation with No. 2, separated by a *svastika*; it records the exchange of village Sudisaṇa (gifted in the king's 19th regnal year) with another one, Sāmalipada. The cave is referred to as the Devi-leṇa (Queen's Cave) and the beneficiaries are monks of the Bhadāyaniya school.

66 The purpose of the last act was the king's desire to honour his grandmother and as a *dhama-setu* ('bridge of dharma', suggesting a transfer of merit) for his father. At the end of the inscription, there is the phrase *savajātabhoganiraṭhi*, which can be understood as a general *parihāra*, declaring that the king had given up his rights of enjoyment over the land.

67 The inscription opens with a eulogy of *mahādevī* Gautamī Balaśrī, described as mother of the king of kings (*rājarāño*) Gautamīputra Śrī Sātakarṇi; as following the way of life of the wife of a royal sage (*rājarisi-vadu*); as one who is devoted to truth, charity, forgiveness and nonviolence; and always engaged in penance, self-control, restraint and fasting (ll. 9–10). The description of the queen mother can be read as a combination of the conduct of a royal widow-ascetic with with virtues that are common to Buddhist ethics and Brahmanical *sāmānya dharma*. It reminds us of the picture of Nāganikā in the Naneghat inscription. Vāsiṣṭhīputra is described very briefly at the end of the inscription as the lord of Dakṣiṇāpatha (*Dakhiṇāpathesara*) and as devoted to his grandmother.

68 He was king of Asika (Ṛṣika), Asaka (Aśmaka), Mu aka (Mūlaka), Suraṭha (Surāṣṭra), Kukura, Aparanta (Aparānta), Anupa (Anūpa), Vidabha (Vidarbha), and Akarāvantī; he was also lord of the Vindhya, Chavata (Ṛkṣavat), Pāricāta (Pāriyātra), Sahya, Kaṇhagiri (Kṛṣṇagiri), Maca

(Mañca), Siriṭana (Śrīstana), Malaya, Mahendra (in Kaliṅga), Seṭagiri (Śvetagiri) and Cakora mountains. The emphasis on mountains in this inscription is striking—Gautamīputra's great strength is also compared with the Himavat, Meru and Mandāra mountains. For identifications, see Senart, 'The Inscriptions in the Caves at Nasik', p. 62; Mirashi, *The History and Inscriptions of the Sātavāhanas and the Western Kṣatrapas*, Part II, pp. 43–44.

69 References to nonviolence occur frequently in Aśoka's inscriptions but are absent in Khāravela's Hathigumpha inscription.

70 This is similar to Khāravela. Aśoka had mixed feelings about *samājas*.

71 His prowess (*pratāpa*) is said to be on par with that of Rāma, Keśava, Arjuna and Bhīmasena; his lustre (*tejas*) is compared with to that of Nābhāga, Nahuśa, Janamejaya, Sagara, Yayāti, Rāma and Ambarīṣa.

72 The term *mleccha* does not occur in the inscription, but I think it is implied in the fact that the Śakas, Yavanas and Pahlavas are treated as a group in l. 5 and in the reference (l. 6) to Gautamīputra having prevented the mixture of *varṇas*.

73 For several examples of later imitations, see Sircar, *The Successors of the Sātavāhanas in Lower Deccan*. For a more general discussion of the issue, see Sheldon Pollock, 'Empire and Imitation', in Craig Calhoun, Frederick Cooper and Kevin W. Moore, eds., *Lessons of Empire: Imperial Histories and American Power* (New York, London: The New Press, 2006), pp. 175–188.

74 On the latter, see Akira Shimada, *Early Buddhist Architecture in Context: The Great Stūpa at Amarāvatī (ca. 300 BCE-300 CE)* (Leiden" Boston, Brill, 2013).

75 Maiko Nakanishi and Oskar von Hinüber, *Kanaganahalli Inscriptions*. Annual Report of the International Research Institute of Advanced Buddhology at Soka University for the Academic Year 2013, vol. 17 (2014), Supplement, p. 21.

76 These were probably executed during the reign of Vāsiṣṭhīputra Pulumāvi in the 2nd century CE. The kings mentioned in the label inscriptions are Matalaka, Sundara, Sātakarṇi and Pulumāvi. On the inscriptions, see Oskar von Hinuber, 'Buddhist Texts and Buddhist Images: New Evidence from Kanaganahalli (Karnataka/India)', *ARIRIAB* 19 (March 2016): 7–20. For the sculptures, see Monika Zin, 'Kanaganahalli in Sātavāhana art and Buddhism' and Monika Zin, *The Kanaganahalli Stūpa: An Analysis of the 60 Massive Slabs Covering the Dome* (New Delhi: Aryan Books, 2018). For the site report, see K. P. Poonacha, *Excavations at Kanaganahalli (Sannati, Dist. Gulbarga, Karnataka)* (New Delhi: Archaeological Survey of India, 2011). A slab showing a king making a gift by pouring water from spouted vessel has the inscription: *rāyā sātakaṇ [i mahāce](t)[i]yasa r(u)pāmayāni payumāni oṇ(o)yeti* ('King Sātakarṇi donates silver lotus flowers to the mahācetiya') (Nakanishi and von Hinüber, 2014, pp. 30–31, I. 7). This seems to represent Gautamīputra Sātakarṇi. Another, more unusual relief foregrounds a king pouring water into the right palm of another king, with the accompanying inscription '*rāya pu umāvi ajayatasa ujeni deti*' ('King Pulumāvi gives Ujeni to Ajayata') (Nakanishi and von Hinüber, 2014, pp. 33–34, I. 9). As

suggested by von Hinüber ('Buddhist Texts and Buddhist Images'), this seems to be seems to be a visual record of a political event—Vāsiṣṭhīputra Pulumāvi handing over the city of Ujjayinī to his Kṣatrapa rival Caṣṭana, a political setback being presented as an act of magnanimity. Both reliefs depict Sātavāhana kings in attitudes of extraordinary generosity.

77 Representations of Aśoka are flanked on both sides by scenes from the Buddha's life or places connected with his life; and the latter are flanked by the depictions of the Sātavāhana kings. Monika Zin has suggested that the images of Sātavāhana kings at Kanaganahalli could reflect the association of kings with prosperity. She rightly observes: 'Placing the kings around 'Aśoka,' and the Buddhist symbols at his side, accords the Sātavāhanas not only the prestige of being depicted with Aśoka in a prominent position of the *stūpa*, but also implicity represents them, like Aśoka himself, as Buddhist rulers' (Zin, 'Kanaganahalli in Sātavāhana art and Buddhism: King Aśoka in front of the *Bodhi* tree', p. 550).

78 They are mentioned, for instance, in the *Gāthāsattasai*, Jaina texts such as the *Tiloyapaṇṇatti*, Nāgārjuna's *Precious Garland*, Xuanzang's *Xiyuji*, Bāṇa Bhaṭṭa's *Harṣacarita*, the *Līlāvaī*, Rājaśekhara's *Kāvyamīmāṁsā*, and in various various legends about king Sālivāhana. This is apart from the references to the 'Āndhra' kings in the Purāṇas.

79 Early versions of the story are given in the *Divyāvadāna* and the *Aśokāvadāna* and are echoed in several later texts. See John Strong, *The Legend of King Aśoka: A Study and Translation of the Aśokāvadāna*. Princeton, NJ: Princeton University Press, 1983). For details of these and other accounts of persecution, See K. T. S. Sarao, *The Decline of Buddhism in India: A Fresh Perspective* (New Delhi: Munshiram Manoharlal, 2012), Chap. 5. For a larger argument about the violence involved in the decline of Buddhism in India, see Giovanni Verardi, *The Gods and the Heretics: Crisis and Ruin of Indian Buddhism* (New Delhi, Aditya Prakashan, 2018). According to John Marshall, the Aśokan brick core of the great stupa at Sanchi revealed evidence of 'wantonly inflicted' damage which he saw as corroboration of the stories of persecution in the Buddhist texts (John Marshall and Afred Foucher, *The Monuments of Sāñchī* vol. 1, Calcutta: Government of India Press, 1940, p. 23). Puśyamitra has also sometimes been held responsible for the destruction of the Ghoṣita monastery at Kaushambi and the Deorkothar stūpa in central India.

80 Possible evidence of religious conflict also comes from sites further south. A Nagarjunakonda inscription, dated in year 30 of the Ābhīra ruler Vasuṣeṇa, seems to tell the story of a war and the consequent re-installation of a wooden image of the Aṣṭabhujasvāmin. See Richard Salomon, 'Aṣṭabhujasvāmin: A Reinterpretation of the Ābhīra Inscription from Nagarjunakonda', *Indo-Iranian Journal* 2013: 397–417; *Early Inscriptions of Āndhradeśa (EIAD)* École française d'Extrême-Orient (Paris, France) in collaboration with the HiSoMA Research Centre (Lyon, France) and TGIR Huma-Num (France), Inscription no. 65. However, readings of the inscription vary considerably. An inscription from Phanigiri in Andhra Pradesh praises the superiority

of the Buddha over Śiva and Kṛṣṇa, revealing competition, if not conflict, between their worshippers. See Peter Skilling and Oskar von Hinüber, 'An Epigraphic Poem from Phanigiri (Andhrapradesh) from the Time of Rudrapuruṣadatta', *Annual Report of the International Research Institute of Advanced Buddhology at Soka University* (March 2010): 14, 7–14. According to Peter Skilling ('New Discoveries from South India: The life of the Buddha at Phanigiri, Andhra Pradesh', *Arts Asiatique* 63 (2008): 96–118), broken images at Phanigiri suggest a violent end to this Buddhist complex.

81 See, for instance, Balcerowicz, *Early Asceticism in India*, pp. 250–251, 254.

82 The fact that Khalatika is mentioned in the works of the grammarians Kātyāyana and Patañjali suggests that the place was well-known (Falk, *Aśokan Sites and Artefacts*, p. 269; Balcerowicz, *Early Asceticism in India*, pp. 242–243). Falk takes *khalatika* as referring mainly to the slippery entrance boulder located to the left of the Patal Ganga stream, from which it was erroneously applied to the entire group of hills (*Aśokan Sites and Artefacts*, p. 258). For a description of the Barabar-Nagarjuni caves and their inscriptions, see Falk, *Aśokan Sites and Artefacts*, pp. 255–279; Falk "Barabar Reconsidered," *South Asian Archaeology* 1999, ed. Ellen M. Raven (Groningen, Egbert Forsten, 2008), pp. 245–251; and Balcerowicz, *Early Asceticism in India*, pp. 242–273. For a detailed discussion of the Lomaśa Rishi cave, and the date and details of its architrave, see John C. Huntington, 'The Lomās Ṛṣi: Another Look', *Archives of Asian Art*, 28 (1974/75): 34–56. It is likely that Barabar was a centre of Ājīvika ascetics well before Aśoka's time and that the emperor chose to upgrade it with the addition of some spectacular architectural innovations, rendering wooden form into stone and adding the remarkable polish. This gave the caves a sonic quality that magnified even the smallest sound or movement, a feature well-suited to the ascetic practice of the Ājīvikas, which involved extreme stillness. Balcerowicz, *Early Asceticism in India*, p. 245, pp. 268–269.

83 The interior roof, walls and floor of the Lomaśa Ṛṣi cave, and the hut carved inside it, are unfinished. The reason for this could be the death of the patron Aśoka or a fissure in the ceiling created by the excavation (See Huntington, 'The Lomās Ṛṣi: Another Look', pp. 44–45).

84 I disagree with Nayanjot Lahiri (*Ashoka in ancient India*, Ranikhet: Permanent Black in Association with Ashoka University, 2015, pp. 228–235), who argues that the Barabar caves may have simultaneously housed Ājīvikas, Buddhist monks and other ascetics, putting in practice Aśoka's belief in inter-religious dialogue. In far away Kanaganahalli, *Khalatiko pavato* is inscribed beneath two panels carved in an early style (c. 1st century BCE) that depict a mountain along with a *bhadrāsana*, connecting the mountain with the Buddha or the worship of the Buddha. For a description, see Monika Zin, *The Kanaganahalli Stūpa*, pp. 82–84; Pl. 14. For the inscription, see Nakanishi and von Hinüber, *Kanaganahalli Inscriptions*, IV.5, Pl. 36, p. 105. This composition could reflect a confusion—between Khalatika and some other hilly place in Magadha, for instance Rājagṛha. It could also represent a post-Daśaratha situation when Buddhist monks replaced the

Ājīvika ascetics in the Barabar–Nagarjuni hills. But given the absence of strong evidence of a Buddhist occupation at the site, the most likely explanation is that at distant Kanaganahalli, a famous Ājīvika centre in Magadha was misunderstood as a Buddhist one, due to its Aśokan connection.

85 The attempts to delete the reference to the Ājīvikas (ājīvikehi) is visible in three of the Barabar inscripitions (B1, B2, B3) and one of the Nagarjuni inscriptions (N 3). In B1 it is almost completed removed and in the others partly effaced (Balcerowicz, *Early Asceticism in India*, pp. 249-50).

86 V. H. Jackson, ed. *Journal of Francis Buchanan kept during the survey of the districts of Patna and Gaya in 1811-1812* ([1925], New Delhi, Madras, Asian Educational Services, 1989, Appendix 2, pp. 197–209). As Jackson points out, Gorathagiri is mentioned in the *Mahabhārata*. When Kṛṣṇa, Arjuna, and Bhīma head eastwards from the land of the Kurus towards Magadha to kill Jarāsandha, they cross the Gaṅgā and Śoṇa rivers and reached the Magadhan country. 'Upon reaching Mount Goratha, always teeming with wealth of cattle, rich in water, and beautifully wooded, they set eyes on the city of Magadha (*Magadhaṁ puram*)'. (*Mahābhārata* 2. 18. 30, transl. J. A. B. van Buitenen. *The Mahābhārata 2. The Book of the Assembly Hall and 3. The Book of the Forest*, Chicago and London, University of Chicago Press, 1975, p. 68.) This suggests that Gorathagiri was located close by the west of Rājagṛha (Rajgir). Although the Barabar hills are located to the west of Rajgir, they are quite far—about 83 km away—and they rise to a maximum of 1023 ft, which would not have afforded a view of Rājagṛha,

87 A. L. Basham (*History and Doctrines of the Ājīvikas: A Vanished Indian Religion.* London, Luzac, 1951, pp. 158–159) cites A. Banerji-Sastri on this point. On the debate, see Balcerowicz, *Early Asceticism in India*, pp. 249–251.

88 On the fluidity of categories such as Nirgrantha and Ājīvika, see Johannes Bronkhorst, 'The Riddle of the Jainas and Ājīvikas in Early Buddhist Literature', *Journal of Indian Philosophy*, 28, 5/6 (December 2000): 511–529.

89 Alexander Cunningham (*Four Reports made during the years 1862-63-64-65*, New Delhi: Archaeological Survey of India, 1871, p.p. 43–44) commented on the Barabar basin being a strong, naturally defensive position and mentioned traces of walls on the surrounding hill ('it seems certain that the place must once have been used as a stronghold'). However, the dates of the walls are uncertain. Shashi Kant (*The Hāthīgumphā Inscription of Khāravela and the Bhabru Edict of Aśoka*, p. 54) understands Gorathagiri as a hill fortress, serving Rājagṛha, and states that it was located in the Barabar hills. But it seems very unlikely that Barabar was simultaneously an abode of ascetics and a military stronghold. For the different views on this point see Harry Falk, 'Barabar Reconsidered', p. 247; Balcerowicz, *Early Asceticism in India*, pp. 267–268.

90 In later centuries, the profile of the hills evidently did change. On the doorway of the Karna Chaupar cave Barabar are two short inscriptions in Gupta-period Brahmi, reading 'Bodhimūla' and 'Kleśa-kāntāra,' which suggested to Basham a Buddhist occupation, but could just be visitors' graffiti. A clearer change in the complexion of the site is indicated after the 5th

century. An inscription in the semi-circular space above the entrance to the Lomaśa Ṛṣi cave records the Maukhari prince Anantavarman, son of Śārdūla, installing an image of Kṛṣṇa in the cave (referred to as Pravaragiri). In the Nagarjuni hills, the Gopika cave (which has an inscription recording an endowment to the Ājīvikas by the Maurya ruler Daśaratha) has an inscription of Anantavarman, which records that the prince placed an image of Kātyāyinī in the cave and gave a village for the support of the goddess Bhavānī. The Vadathika cave on the Nagarjuni hill has an inscription of the same Maukhari prince recording the setting up of an image of Bhūtapati and Devī. When Cunningham visited the site (Cunningham, *Four Reports*, p. 42), there was a Śaiva temple with a *liṅga* called Siddheśvara on the highest hills, which seemed to go back to the 6th or 7th century. In still later times, the site was occupied by Muslim fakirs.

91 For a different view, see Richard Salomon, 'Aśoka and the "Epigraphic Habit" in India', in Patrick Olivelle, ed. *Aśoka in History and Historical Memory* (Delhi: Motilal Banarsidass, 2009), pp. 45–52. Salomon acknowledges that Aśoka established the 'epigraphic habit,' but asserts that his edicts had little influence on later royal epigraphs. He describes Aśoka's inscriptions as experimental probes, representing a false start.

92 These inscriptions also mention various participants and elements in the land grant process—writer, executor the officer who wrote down the verbal order, the deed and registration. The idea of a gift as an investment, not only a transfer of material items (money, land or both), but also in terms of the possibility of the transfer of the resulting *puñya*, is quite different from ideas of *dāna* in early Buddhist texts. Ideas of property and transfer of merit are reflected in the Mūlasarvāstivāda Vinaya and in inscriptions, which Gregory Schopen has written so eloquently about. See for instance, his essays in *Bones, Stones and Buddhist Monks: Collected Papers on the Archaeology, Epigraphy and Texts of Monastic Buddhism in India* (Honolulu: University of Hawai'i Press, 1997). There is a possible connection between the idea of the transfer of property/usufructory rights on the one hand and the transfer of merit on the other. On the larger issue of textual and epigraphic expressions of the ideas and practices related to property, see Timothy Lubin, 'The Theory and Practice of Property in Premodern South Asia: Disparities and Convergences', *Journal of the Economic and Social History of the Orient*, 61, 5/6 (2018): 803–850.

93 However, the Sātavāhana penchant for visual self-representation does not seem to have acquired traction.

94 The oldest known copper plate grant in India belongs to the Ikṣvāku period. This is the Patagandigudam grant. See Harry Falk, 'The Pātagaṇḍigūḍem copper-plate grant of the Ikṣvāku king Ehavala Cāntamūla', *Silk Road Art and Archaeology* 6 (1999–2000), 275–283; and *Early Inscriptions of Āndhradeśa*, Inscription No. 55.

95 Brāhmaṇa migrations and intermarriages with local women and into families of political elites have to be factored into the social and political history of ancient India. Despite the fact that Brāhmaṇas were never a homogeneous

group, texts and inscriptions suggest the existence of a strong sense of Brāhmaṇa social identity.

96 In fact, it is entirely possible that the inscriptions of Uṣavadāta and the Sātavāhanas were both the products of the same bureau that must have continued to exist even when territories changed hand on account of wars.

97 Of course, the evolution of epigraphic discourse was mediated by regional and local cultural specificities. For instance, in Orissa, the portrayal of king as sacrificer was never a significant feature of royal ideology, and the tribal element surfaced in various ways. See Singh, *Kings, Brāhmaṇas and Temples in Orissa*, Chap. 2.

98 See Singh, *Political Violence in Ancient India*, pp. 240–242; 467–468. Also see Upinder Singh, *Ancient India: Culture of Contradictions* (New Delhi: Aleph Books, 2021), Chap. 5.

11

Politics, Violence, and War in Kāmandaka's *Nītisāra*

The historiography of early medieval India (c. 600–1300 CE) has been dominated by the question of whether this period should be understood within the frameworks of the integrative, feudal or segmentary state models.[1] Initially enlightening, the half century or so of this debate has reached an impasse, and the debate itself has become an obstacle to fresh thinking. Clearly, it is time to frame new questions and re-think the ways in which we can think about the early medieval.

A comprehensive, historically grounded intellectual history of this age does not exist, a fact that is especially surprising considering that these centuries were marked by exceptional intellectual vitality. One of the many issues that have received inadequate scholarly attention is the reciprocal relationship between early medieval political processes and the intellectual engagement with these processes in texts of the time. The most important intervention against this indifference has been made by Sheldon Pollock, who has emphasised the fact that the cognitive production of political orders is a significant and integral constituent of these orders and that it is, therefore, essential to explore the 'political imagination', which includes ideas and aspirations of rule.[2] Ronald Inden has analysed the representations of the concepts of mastery, lordship and

This chapter was previously published in *The Indian Economic and Social History Review* 47 (1), 2010, pp. 29–62.

political hierarchy in early medieval India in literary and epigraphic sources.[3] And Daud Ali has offered a very thought-provoking, though homogenised, analysis of the representations of courtly culture in texts, inscriptions and art of the first millennium.[4]

While drawing on the insights of these scholars, my own perspective differs in several respects. While I am interested in analysing the political discourse (I prefer this term to Pollock's 'political imagination') represented in texts, I think it is important that such an analysis must be very carefully calibrated with respect to chronology and spatial context and should not end up presenting an over-homogenised picture of either the discourse or the politics of the time. Further, while identifying shared ideas, and those with an exceptional longevity, it must be equally sensitive to differences in perspective, emphasis and argument within texts of a particular genre and across texts belonging to different genres produced at different points of time.

The focus of this chapter—a close analysis of the *Nītisāra* ('The Essence of Politics') of Kāmandaka—is part of a larger study of political ideas. Comparisons with the *Arthaśāstra* provide a useful basis for identifying this text's perspective. Apart from the *Nītisāra*'s representation of the morphology of monarchical power, I also examine how the text engaged with an important political problem, namely the interface between kingship and violence, with special reference to punishment, hunting and war. The issue of violence in Indian intellectual traditions and history has many facets, and there are some illuminating works on the subject.[5] Violence and non-violence have especially been discussed in the context of sacrifice, religion (Vedic religion, Hinduism, Buddhism and Jainism), asceticism, vegetarianism, and Buddhist and Jaina environmental ethics. War has often been discussed by scholars in the context of the Buddhist tradition and works such as the *Bhagavad Gītā* and *Mahābhārata*. More off the beaten track is Daud Ali's analysis of the social meanings of violence, gastronomy and war in the *Kaliṅkattupparaṇi*, a riveting 12th century text composed in the Cōḻa court.[6] There is, nevertheless, a need for a more comprehensive, diachronic study of the ways in which the issue of violence was dealt with in ancient and early medieval India. The focus of such a study must not only be on understanding representations of violence, but also on arguments and attitudes towards its various forms.

Historicising normative texts raises a fundamental question about the relationship between theory and practice. Pollock has pointed out that in the Indian intellectual tradition, *śāstra* ('theory') is generally held to precede and govern *prayoga* ('practical activity'), and suggests that the ideas that came to be associated with the nature of *śāstra* may be connected with the belief in the transcendent character of the Vedas.[7] However, he himself points to the fact that there were exceptions to this position, significantly enough, in works on politics and medicine. A further necessary caveat to this argument is that śāstric self-representation should not be conflated with the way in which śāstric knowledge was actually produced in early India. The discipline of history assumes that the creation of a textual tradition involved an interface with its historical context, and it can be demonstrated that historical reality intruded into many a 'normative' text. However, the biggest challenge in historicising ancient and early medieval political treatises is to meaningfully anchor their political discourses (the plural is deliberately used to underline their diversity in type and perspective) in the peculiarities and demands of their genre, and in their evolving and changing political contexts, without slipping into the error of presenting these discourses as either insulated from or direct reflections of those contexts.

Kāmandaka's *Nītisāra* and Kauṭilya's *Arthaśāstra*

Kāmandaka's *Nītisāra* is a treatise on politics written in Sanskrit verse, consisting of 20 *sarga*s (cantos) subdivided into 36 *prakaraṇa*s (sections).[8] It discusses the principles according to which a king should rule his kingdom and how he could attain political paramountcy and prosperity for himself and his subjects. As is the case with many early Indian texts, it is difficult to ascertain when and where the *Nītisāra* was written. Estimates of its age generally range between the 1st and 7th centuries CE.[9] The evidence recently cited to suggest the contemporaneity of the *Nītisarā* with the Gupta emperor Candragupta II (c. 375–415 CE) is not convincing.[10] A more cautious approach, placing the text between c. 500–700 CE is better, and the *Nītisāra* can thus be situated at the threshold or the advent of the early medieval.

Among the ancient Indian political treatises, it is Kauṭilya's *Arthaśāstra* that has naturally attracted the maximum attention of scholars, being the first surviving text on the subject and also because of its masterly coverage of an enormous range of issues related to statecraft. The *Arthaśāstra* has often been treated simplistically by historians as a direct description of the Maurya state and administration. Such a treatment is problematic because it is a theoretical treatise, not a descriptive work, and although its origins could date to the Maurya period, its compositional history extends into the early centuries CE.[11]

As for the *Nītisāra*, historians have cited stray references from the text to illustrate aspects of Gupta or post-Gupta polity, administration and revenue systems, but the text as a whole has not received the attention it deserves. This, in spite of the fact that it acquired an authoritative reputation, being cited in many later Indian works and also travelling to Southeast Asia.[12] The scholarly neglect of the work may have been in part because of problems of dating, but the most important reason why it has not been taken seriously enough is that Kāmandaka has been viewed as a derivative, unoriginal thinker who tried to simply parrot Kauṭilya's ideas, sometimes incorrectly.[13] This essay seeks to prove that a close reading of the *Nītisāra* does not support such an assessment. It is also emphasised that political treatises of this kind have to be recognised as important sources for and, in fact, as important constituent elements of, ancient and early medieval polities.

Because of its śāstric nature, the *Nītisāra* should certainly not be read as a direct description of how states were actually governed or royal policies formulated during the time of the Gupta and Vākāṭaka empires and their immediate aftermath. And yet, it offers a perceptive, graphic morphology—often abstract rather than literal—of the structure and relationships of monarchical power politics of its time. This morphology was rooted in various things: the genre and scholarly tradition within which the text situated itself, the specific historical and political context in which it was produced, and the ideas and perspective of the author, including his philosophical moorings.

Beyond the question of what such texts can tell us about the times in which they were written, it is also necessary to recognise their great influence. The authors of such treatises were learned Brāhmaṇas, at least some of whom were closely associated with royal courts. The presumed audience—and also, in large part, the subject—of these works was the 'political class': people associated with the exercise of political power in various ways. This included kings (more specifically the *vijigīṣu*—the king desirous of extensive conquest), royal officials, counselors, courtiers,[14] military commanders, ambassadors and others. Texts like the *Nītisāra* are, therefore, not only representative of a political discourse rooted in the political realities of their time, but also made an impact on those realities. It should also be noted that the ideas of the political theorists were known, absorbed and expressed in poetry, drama, didactic stories and sayings, and reached wider audiences through written, oral and performative traditions.

Tradition, Authority and Debate

Before entering into an analysis of the political discourse of the *Nītisāra*, it is necessary to look carefully at certain general issues related to the production of knowledge in ancient and early medieval India. Ancient śāstric discourse on politics was part of an intellectual milieu marked by continuous and wide-ranging debate, a fact often masked by the constant invoking of tradition. Texts that came to be considered authoritative often claimed to be abridged (*saṁkṣipta*) versions of earlier works.[15] New scholarship presented itself as part of a venerable tradition of long standing, absorbing the latter's weight and authority through association, even if it disagreed with that tradition in radical ways. In fact, it can be argued—and this point is borne out by the *Arthaśāstra*—that in spite of the great premium placed on tradition, disagreement with earlier authorities ultimately contributed to a scholar's reputation.[16]

Citations were an important way of positioning a new text and author in relation to older scholarly traditions. In the *Nītisāra*, there are references to the collective wisdom of the *vṛddha* (elderly), *vidyāvṛddha* (those mature in wisdom), *vidu* (learned ones) and those described as *maṇḍalajña* (experts in the science of the *maṇḍalas*), *arthajña* (experts in *artha*), *śāstrārthacintaka* (those who think about the meaning of the *śāstras*) and *pūrva munis* (sages of the olden days). The text also refers in two places to popular wisdom embodied in *laukika* verses.[17] Kāmandaka cites various specific schools and authorities—the Mānavas, Indra, Maya, Bṛhaspati, Uśanas, Viṣṇugupta, Puloma, Śukra, Viśālākṣa, Parāśara and Bharadvāja—expressing his agreement or disagreement with them.[18] These are cited frequently in other ancient texts (including, for instance, the *Arthaśāstra* and the *Mahābhārata)* as authorities on the science of politics and on *dharma*. The fact that the maximum number of differing views are cited in the section on *maṇḍalayoni* ('the nave of the circle of kings', *Nītisāra [NS]* 8.12) suggests that the conduct of inter-state relations was a topic of especially heated debate. This is being emphasised here because the authors of ancient Indian texts have often been considered as amorphous 'types', completely smothered by tradition and the convention of their genre, with little scope for expressing their distinctive points of view.

While Bṛhaspati is the most frequently cited authority in the *Nītisāra*, it is Viṣṇugupta, alias Kauṭilya, the author of the *Arthaśāstra*—referred to on two occasions as 'our guru'[19]—who holds the preeminent position for Kāmandaka. The text opens with a salutation to the god Gaṇeśa, the king,[20] and Viṣṇugupta, in that order. The eulogy of Viṣṇugupta (*NS* 1.2–6) describes him as one who was born in a great lineage with descendants famous all over the world for their *ṛṣi*-like conduct in not accepting gifts of any kind; who was as effulgent as the sacrificial fire; who was so well-versed in the Vedas that he had mastered through his intellect all four of them as though they were one; who through his powers, as irresistible as furious thunder, had uprooted the great and powerful Nandas; who, like the god Śaktidhara (Kārttikeya), through the exercise of his *mantraśakti* (power of counsel) had single-handedly secured the world for Candragupta, the moon among men; the learned one, who had produced the nectar of *nītiśāstra* out of the mighty ocean of *arthaśāstra.* The precise identity and background of the author or authors of many ancient Indian texts is often elusive. But this description of Viṣṇugupta can be read as a portrait of the political Brāhmaṇa—the kind of advisor considered by Kāmandaka to be most suited (and most likely) to deliver the teaching on politics. This may well have been a self-portrait of Kāmandaka himself. The connection with Viṣṇugupta was also important for establishing the bona fides and boundaries of the discipline that the *Nītisāra* dealt with, and that is probably why Kāmandaka ascribes the invention of *nītiśāstra* to his famous predecessor.

The *Nītisāra* describes its subject of inquiry as *nīti* (explained as derived from *nayana*, leading or administering) (*NS* 2.15),[21] *daṇḍanīti* and *rājavidyā*. The *Arthaśāstra* and *Nītisāra* have major overlaps in content and concerns and share a common political vocabulary, including the key ideas and theories of the *saptāṅga rājya* (the seven-limbed state), *rājamaṇḍala* (the circle of kings) and *ṣāḍguṇya* (the six measures in the context of inter-state relations). But there is also much that is different, not only in style—the *Arthaśāstra* is in the aphoristic *sūtra* style interspersed with a few verses, while the *Nītisāra* is entirely in verse—but also in specific details and over-all tenor. For instance, a detailed discussion of internal administration and civil and criminal law are missing in the *Nītisāra,* as is the advocacy of strict state control over various aspects of the economy, often considered the hall-mark of the *Arthaśāstra.* This reflects the narrower scope of *nītiśāstra* as compared with *arthaśāstra,* as well as differences in views about the potential state held by Kauṭilya and Kāmandaka. Both were concerned with political expansion and consolidation, but the *Nītisāra* does not share the *Arthaśāstra*'s grandiose and overwhelming vision of state power. Neither does its author share Kauṭilya's faith in the efficacy of black magic as a political and military tool, a detailed discussion of which is absent in the text. And, as we shall see later, Kāmandaka also disagreed with Kauṭilya on various specific issues related to the interface between kingship and violence. It is necessary to emphasise this point, because as mentioned above, many scholars have mistakenly described the *Nītisāra* as an unoriginal derivative text which repeats, often poorly, the ideas of the *Arthaśāstra*.

In the many-faceted and vibrant intellectual milieu of ancient and early medieval India, disciplinary boundaries were understood and the political treatises selfconsciously situate themselves within a larger knowledge universe. But knowledge and ideas also readily flowed across disciplinary boundaries. The texts on polity share with the Dharmaśāstra and philosophical texts ideas related to *karma* (the consequences of action), rebirth, *caturvarga/trivarga* (the four or three goals of human life) and *varṇāśrama dharma* (*dharma* based on *varṇa* and *āśrama*). In fact, V.P. Varma points out that the metaphysical foundations of ancient Indian political thought had important implications for the kinds of questions that the latter asked and did not ask.[22] The texts on polity and Dharmaśāstra share a concern about ethics, and the political theorists in fact constructed a sub-specie of *dharma*, one that was geared towards the realisation of the political goals of the king.

The four *vidyā*s (branches of knowledge) described by Kāmandaka as essential for the preservation of the world, are *anvīkṣikī* (philosophy), *trayī* (the three Vedas), *vārtā* (economics) and *daṇḍanīti* (the science of politics). The *Nītisāra* is unequivocal in asserting the preeminence of *daṇḍanīti* among all the branches of knowledge, on the grounds that the latter are useless in its absence (*NS* 2.9).[23] Nevertheless, as we shall see, its ideas about politics are imbued with philosophical, ethical and metaphysical presuppositions.

The inter-disciplinary dialogue of which the political treatises were a part extended to other realms of specialised scholarship as well. In fact, the organic theory of the *saptāṅga rājya* may have more connections with medical knowledge than hitherto suspected. It seems to be more than a coincidence that *āyurveda* talks of seven elements of the body and the political treatises talk of the seven elements or limbs of the state.[24] The discussion of the *vyasana*s (calamities) and concerns for purification (*śuddhi*) of the various elements of the body politic (for instance, of the *maṇḍala*s) in texts such as the *Nītisāra* also resonate with issues of health, disease and cure with which the medical treatises grappled, albeit in the context of the body politic rather than the human body.[25]

The political and medical treatises also share a great concern with poison—the different types, their symptoms, antidotes and how to identify a poisoner. In this particular sphere, the scholars of *arthaśāstra* and *nītiśāstra* must have benefitted from the knowledge and experience of the medical experts. It is also interesting to note that in two places in the *Nītisārā*, there are specific surgical analogies. *Nītisārā* 5.8 states that the king punishes corrupt royal officers who accumulate wealth in the same way as a swollen abscess is operated on and bled out (*āsrāvayed upacitān*) (by a surgeon). And in *Nītisārā* 6.13, the king is told to act like a surgeon (*śalya*) in eliminating those who trouble the people.

The Vijigīṣu's Quest for Power

The prime subject as well as audience for the *Nītisāra* was the king (*rājan*), whose various epithets announce him as lord of the earth, of all men, and of the *maṇḍala*s (*mahipati, pārthiva, pṛthvīpati, mahibhuja, bhūpati, kṣitibhuja, nṛpa, narapati, nareśvara, maṇḍalādhipa*). Monarchy (*rājya*) is the only kind of state mentioned by Kāmandaka, as his work post-dates the annihilation of the major oligarchies (*gaṇa*s and *saṁgha*s) by the Gupta emperor Samudragupta (c. 350–70). This is in contrast to the *Arthaśāstra*, which discusses oligarchies, although it too considers monarchy as the norm and addresses its teaching to the king.

The king is not defined by what he is but what he aspires to become. The kind of monarch that the *Nītisāra* (and the *Arthaśāstra*) has in mind is one who is ambitious and upwardly-mobile, a *vijigīṣu*—a king desirous of attaining political paramountcy, one who seeks dominion over the whole earth washed by the ocean (*samudraprakṣālitā dhāritrī*) (*NS* 16.35). The graphic image—one which endures in texts and inscriptions over several centuries—of the paramount king is that of one who plants his foot on the heads of enemies adorned with excellent helmets and bejeweled crowns (*NS* 14.12).

While the *Nītisāra* has a strong sense of the past, the past it invokes is not one that modern historians would regard as 'historical'. In fact, the deliberate avoidance or erasure of the latter is because the text's discourse (like that of other *śāstra*s) speaks of universals, not particulars.[26] It is not surprising that a work that claimed to lay down the principles of polity for all time to come ignored the inconsequential kings of mundane petty power politics and drew its illustrations from the gods, demons and men of the epic-Purāṇic tradition, whose fame or notoriety transcended time and space. Apart from analogies between the king and the elements of nature,[27] the *Nītisāra* frequently compares him with the gods, especially Indra, Yama and Prajāpati. The text abounds in references to Paraśurāma, Ambarīṣa, Yudhiṣṭhira, Bhīma, Nala, Janamejaya and Rāma, leaving no doubt that the *Mahābhārata* and *Rāmāyaṇa* were pivotal to Kāmandaka's political discourse, in fact, more so than to that of the *Arthaśāstra.*[28]

The *Nītisāra,* like many texts of ancient and early medieval India, talks of the intimate connection between kingship—*rājatā* (*NS* 20.16)—and the prosperity of the king, his realm and his subjects. Śrī and Lakṣmī represent fortune and prosperity as well as goddesses personifying these things, and many of the references to them are clustered in the *Utsāhapraśaṁsā* ('in praise of energy') *prakaraṇa* (in *NS* 14). The feminine deification of fortune lent itself well to the use of gendered imagery, one that is overtly sexual, even violent; this is found frequently not only in the political treatises but also in Sanskrit *kāvya.* Śrī and Lakṣmī are fickle, but cling to the righteous king like his shadow.[29] A ruler who is intelligent but inactive due to his addiction to *vyasana*s (vices), loses the favours of Śrī, just as an impotent man is discarded by women (*stribhiḥ ṣaṇḍa iva*; *NS* 14.8). A ruler desirous of enjoying Śrī should not behave like an impotent man; he must always strive to control her with his manly powers, just as a husband controls his wicked wife (*NS* 14.10). An ever energetic ruler gains possession of Śrī by adopting the conduct of the lion (*siṁhavṛtti*), just as a man deals with his wicked wife by dragging her by the hair (*NS* 14.11). The reference to Lakṣmīs (in the plural) entering the king endowed with various virtues, like streams enter the ocean (*NS* 14.7) and the occasional mention of Śrī, too, in the plural, has a distinct polygynist tinge.

The Morphology of Monarchical Power

The emphasis on the power and ambitions of the *vijigīṣu* should not obscure the fact that the polity of ancient Indian political treatises such as the *Arthaśāstra* and *Nītisāra* is an organic one, where the king is embedded in a web of complex, reciprocal relationships with the other *prakṛtis* (elements of the state), listed by Kāmandaka as *svāmin* (lord, king), *amātya* (counselor), *rāṣṭra* (domain), *durga* (fort), *koṣa* (treasury), *bala* (military might) and *suhṛt* (ally).[30] This interconnectedness should not be lost sight of in discussions of the structure of the polities of early medieval India. Ali has rightly pointed out that historians have tended to focus on the figure of the king, ignoring those around him, including the royal household and other members of the courtly elite.[31] This is in spite of the fact that the ancient and early medieval texts have plenty to say about the importance of these groups.

The *Nītisāra* underlines the fragility of power and the inherent instability of all political and personal relationships and offers a graphic morphology of the political world of its time. In its basic respects, this morphology is similar to that offered by several other texts, and one that has been described by Ali.[32] However, this morphology is being spelt out here for three reasons. First, it is an essential part of the *Nītisāra*'s mapping of politics. Second, Ali's analysis conflates features of texts of different kinds (including *kāvya* and treatises on *kāma*, polity and architecture) and centuries (ranging from c. 300–1200 CE), and while these shared a substratum of common ideas, there were also differences of perspective, emphasis and detail. Therefore, it becomes necessary to identify and isolate the *Nītisāra*'s specific perspective. And third, the focus in the discussion here is not only on courtly culture but on something larger than that, a sphere that can be called the political. For it must be noted that the king and his court were the epicentre of a complex and far-reaching web of political relationships, manouevres and intrigues, one which extended far beyond the court into the domains and courts of neighbouring and distant kings and chieftains, as well as into the forest.

The fundamental premise that underlies Kāmandaka's entire discussion of politics is the view that human nature is essentially selfish and that all people are *arthārthin,* that is, seek to further their personal interest. The challenge for the *vijigīṣu* was to harness other people's desire to further their self-interest to ensure the satisfaction of his own ambition and desire for political aggrandisement.

From the point of view of the king, the world was a treacherous but challenging place. Fate was definitely a factor (*NS* 12.20) to be reckoned with, but political success required many inherent and cultivated positive qualities (*guṇa*s) and a great deal of deliberate effort. Kāmandaka's long list of *guṇa*s that the king should possess (there are similarities with the *Arthaśāstra* in this discussion) reveals an important aim of the political theorists—to temper brute power with virtue.[33] According to the *Nītisāra*, the many *guṇa*s necessary to become a successful *vijigīṣu* included nobility of ancestry, intelligence, truthfulness and powers of endurance. The most important quality, however, was *pratāpa* (prowess). Energy (*utsāha*) and constant vigilance were also required to safeguard and extend political power. The maintenance and extension of this power did not only involve coercive power and conquest. It was essential to skillfully use force (*daṇḍa*) along with the other political expedients (*upāyas*), namely *sāma* (pacification), *dāna* (giving gifts) and *bheda* (creating dissension), in order to generate and maintain confidence (*viśvāsa*) in the various *prakṛtis*. Confidence, in turn, was an essential prerequisite for eliciting loyalty and love (*anurāga*) from subjects, soldiers and allies—the kind of loyalty and love that would extend over many generations. There is no separate word for loyalty in the text, but it is subsumed in other terms such as *sevā* (service) and *bhakti* (devotion), and is emphasised by assertions that the king should not be forsaken by his courtiers.

The political importance of the royal household in the politics of the monarchical states of the time is amply evident in the *Nītisāra*'s detailed discussion of princes and the harem in Book 7. Members of the harem (*antaḥpura, avarodhana*) were the *abhyantara jana* (inner people) and included the king's mother, his wives, courtesans (*rūpajīvās*) and the many attendants who waited on all these women. The harem was a place of pleasure and sensual indulgence. It was also the locus of the serious business of producing heirs—an issue that the *Nītisāra* does not see as a problem, the virility of the king perhaps never being in doubt. And yet, as for Kauṭilya, it was also a place of danger and intrigue, one where the king was strongly advised never to completely lose his head in the pursuit of sexual pleasure or emotional engagement.

In *the Nītisāra* (16.28), there are seven types of people associated with the king—his own men, those of his allies, those who have taken refuge with him, those related to him, those associated with him for some specific purpose or action, his servants, and those won over by various services and gifts. The category of the king's own men (*nija*) included his courtiers (*anujīvīs*), to whom he was tied with complex ties of reciprocity. An entire *sarga* (*NS* 5) is devoted to the relationship between the *svāmin* and his *anujīvīs*. The latter are mentioned in the same breath as the *bandhu* (kinsmen) and *mitra* (friends), and the summary of their duties includes giving the king good counsel, dissuading him from inappropriate acts and implementing his desires (*NS* 5.50).[34] High-ranking royal officials such as *amātyas*, *mantrīs*, *sacivas*, *adhyakṣas*, *dūtas*, *mahāmātras*, the *purohita*, the *senāpati* and astrologers appear to be included in the category of courtiers. There is a long list of the ideal qualities of an *anujīvin,* but it is interesting to note that the synopsis of the most essential qualities include high birth and proficiency in the Vedas (*NS* 5.12–15). The discussion of the relationship between the king and his courtiers was, no doubt, rooted in the contemporary political context—specifically in the need for the king to create around him a group of capable and loyal courtiers, and the latter's desire and ambition to move up in the courtly hierarchy. The relative status of an individual in this hierarchy was determined by the level of proximity, physical as well as affective, to the king.

The king was advised to show his courtiers respect, to pay them in accordance with services rendered, never to discontinue payments they had been enjoying, to offer suitable gifts and rewards, to promote them and to maintain their internal hierarchies. The goal was to have obedient (*anugata*), loyal and satisfied courtiers. From the point of view of the courtiers, a king is described as worthy of being served by virtue of his possession of good qualities of character, devotion to duty, prosperity and generosity. The last of these was important, for what could not be attained by a courtier who was favoured by a prosperous and generous king? On the other hand, a king who could not provide materially for his people (including his courtiers) would be forsaken by all, like a dried-up tree is forsaken by birds and a milk-less cow is forsaken by its calf.[35]

The most evocative and most entertaining part of Kāmandaka's treatment of the king's relationship with his courtiers is his lengthy and very specific discussion of the protocol and decorum of the *rājasabhā* or *saṁsad* (court) (*NS* 5.17–34). The challenge for the courtier was to be counted among those who were cultured (*sabhya, ārya*). He was advised to meticulously tailor his deportment and behaviour to prevailing court protocol and propriety in accordance with his rank and position. And yet, he had to simultaneously strive to rise above others in the court milieu by making a strong, distinctive impression, especially on the king.

Kāmandaka's discussion of court protocol, broadly similar to that offered by Kāuṭilya (*Arthaśāstra [AS]* 5.4), is general enough to be considered as fairly close to the basics of protocols actually existing in various royal courts of the subcontinent during the time. The intelligent (*medhāvin*) courtier had to be formally admitted into the royal assembly hall. He was advised to be properly attired, to take his allotted seat and to wait patiently for his turn to pay respect to the king with due humility. According to Kāmandaka, the *anujīvin* should be conversant with what was appropriate to place and time (*deśakālajña*) and should be an expert in interpreting the king's gestures, appearance and movements (*iṅgitākāratattvavid*). He should be very careful about where and how he looked and how he spoke, and was advised to gaze intently at the king's face in order to observe his reactions and to listen very attentively to whatever the lord said.

Just as important as creating the right impression was avoiding creating an adverse one. There were many things that the *anujīvin* was advised not to do under any circumstances (*NS* 5.23–33). He should never display any arrogance, never imitate the king's attire or manner of speech, and never occupy someone else's place or seat. Unseemly behaviour liable to attract adverse attention and, therefore, to be strictly avoided in the presence of the king, included talking or laughing loudly, coughing, spitting, sitting in an ungainly posture, yawning, stretching limbs and making sounds by twisting the fingers. In times of emergency, the *anujīvin* could be daring and take the initiative in addressing the king, but even then, only with due politeness.

While attempting to move closer to the king and up the ladder of success (these two things were synonymous), the ambitious courtier had to reckon with those who shared these ambitions and those who had already achieved them. Apart from being deferential towards the king, he was advised to be respectful towards superiors and the king's sons, friends, companions and favourites (*vallabha*s). Such people, it is pointed out, could pierce the heart of the courtier in the *saṁsad* by their ridicule (*NS* 5.19–20). The courtier was also advised to avoid meeting or interacting with women (presumably of the harem) and their supervisors, habitual sinners, messengers from hostile chiefs, and those who had been dismissed by the master (*NS* 5.32).

In its description of the overlap between the personal and the political, the *Nītisāra* offers an important insight into the polities of mid-first millennium India. Some insights can also be gleaned by noting what the text does *not* mention or highlight. The political elites of the time must have been internally divided into factions, and the inter-relationships among these factions must have had many complex strands, including alliance, competition, rivalry and hostility. The *Nītisāra* is intriguingly reticent on this important issue and this reticence may have been deliberate.[36] Kāmandaka's aim may have been to deliberately mask elements of factionalism and conflict within the political elite and to emphasise and thereby try to inculcate within that elite a certain cohesion that did not exist in actuality. This may be why the text describes the courtiers as united in their service to the king, repeatedly emphasising the personal benefits that could be reaped through such service. The composers of *kāvyas* and gnomic literature may well have brooded over the fact that a loss of autonomy was the corollary of the courtier's dependence,[37] but political thinkers such as Kāmandaka did not waste their time reflecting on this issue.

Emotions were an important part of Kāmandaka's political discourse, and political success was considered to be considerably dependent on the ability to create in oneself and in others certain desirable emotional states and dispositions.[38] In his interactions with his courtiers, the king's aim was to secure their devotion (*bhakti*), loyalty and affection. For courtiers, a crucial objective was to obtain royal affection (*anurāga*), and to regain it if it was lost for some reason or another. There was also the more pragmatic aim of acquiring permanence (*sthāne sthairya*) of position (*NS* 5.5), something no doubt difficult in a polity where everything was always in a state of flux.

In terms broadly similar to those of the *Arthaśāstra* (*AS* 5.5), but in greater detail, the *Nītisāra* explains how the *anujīvin* could gauge the success or failure of his attempts to worm his way into his master's affections. Kāmandaka lists the visible signs of a king who was attached (*anurakta*) and one who was indifferent or hostile (*virakta*) (*NS* 5.35–38). A king who regarded a courtier with favour would express delight on meeting him, accept his views with appreciation, offer him a seat close to his own and make solicitous enquiries about his welfare. He would not hesitate to meet the courtier alone in an inner chamber and would entrust confidential tasks to him. On hearing other people praise the *anujīvin*'s work, the king would applaud and congratulate him. He would mention the courtier's name and praise his qualities in the course of his discussions with others. Otherwise unpalatable words would be tolerated from a favoured courtier, and the king would act on his advice.

The description of the signs of a king displeased with his *anujīvin* are more graphic and are also dilated upon (*NS* 5.39–46). While the courtier was still talking about an undertaking and its results, the king might suddenly break out in laughter, and moving towards him with a frowning face, suddenly walk out of the room. However appropriate the observations made by such an employee might be, the king would pay no heed to them and, stopping him in the midst of his speech by expressing dissatisfaction, he would instead accept a contrary opinion. Feigning was also a strategy of expressing disfavor. If the king was lying in bed and was entreated for a favour by the courtier, he would pretend he was still asleep. If the courtier tried to wake him up, he would pretend to continue to be asleep. The good qualities of an out-of-favour courtier would never be recognised and he would be the object of frequent cutting remarks, censure (*parivāda*) and derision. His services would be dispensed with for imaginary faults. Promised rewards would be withheld and other people would receive the credit for his meritorious actions. The king would be indifferent to such an *anujīvin*'s fortune or ruin and would incite his rivals (*vipakṣa*) against him.[39] These, according to Kāmandaka, are the signs of a master who is *virakta*. Kauṭilya gives a similar, but more concise account, but adds that a king's disfavour could also be understood through intimations in the form of a change in behaviour of animals and birds, for instance, in the barking of a dog or a heron flying towards the left (*AS* 5.5.10).

The *Nītisāra* (like the *Arthaśāstra*) indicates the great importance of the king's kinsfolk in the world of political power. Apart from their place within the royal household, allies included those related by blood (*aurasa*) (*NS* 4.74). But in a situation where feigning and double-dealing were intrinsic parts of political culture, the king could never rely on their loyalty or allegiance, and the danger of betrayal was not a possibility, it was a very likely probability. A king supported by his brothers was invincible (*NS* 9.46), but a king could not trust even his father for seeking shelter (*NS* 11.35), let alone his sons and wives. The latter were, in fact, among the greatest sources of danger to him.

Personal friendship too had a place in political discourse and in the political world.[40] Kings had to win over friends through kindness (*NS* 3.33) and they were the king's companions during his leisure-time pursuits (*NS* 7.34). The killing of friends was one of the various possible causes of war (*NS* 10.4), along with other causes including dishonor, the killing of kin and the abduction of women. The king's friends seem to be distinct from the *vallabha*s or favourites, although one can imagine that there must have been some overlap between the two categories. The *vallabha*s seem to have been considered especially problematic characters by Kāmandaka. In fact, they are the only group singled out for specific mention in the *kaṇṭakaśodhana* ('removal of thorns') section (*NS* 6.9) and are also mentioned as one of several sources of fear to the subjects (*NS* 5.82). It may be noted that the phrase *vallabha-durlabha* ('not to be entered by royal favourites') in numerous land grant inscriptions of the early medieval period suggests that the *vallabha*s were identified as potential trouble-makers for the donees, villagers, or both.

The terms denoting friendship and cordiality had many different nuances, and the vocabulary of kinship and friendship extended to many political relationships. The familial term *parivāra* is used synonymously for *saciva*s (counselors) (*NS* 4.10). The ally is referred to as *mitra* or *suhṛt*. Cordiality had to be cultivated with the *maṇḍalika*s (governors) of distant regions and with governors of forts. Attachment, estrangement, love, loyalty, confidence and friendship are sentiments that are invoked to describe relations between king, courtiers, subjects and other rulers. Disposition and sentiment were clearly important ingredients in the *Nītisāra*'s political discourse and, presumably, in the monarchical power politics of its time. Of course, revealing as the basic morphology of monarchical power and courtly life that is represented in the *Nītisāra* is, it is essential to keep in mind that it is an idealised and aestheticised morphology.[41]

Dangers to King and Kingdom

Like his counterpart of the *Arthaśāstra*, the king of the *Nītisāra* too inhabits a very dangerous world, and his foremost challenge (and indeed duty) is to protect himself. The detailed description of the king as a figure assailed at all times and from all sides by the threat of assassination, especially through poison, may have been realistic. And even if it is exaggerated, it suggests that this was considered a very real threat and a source of anxiety for kings and political theorists alike. It was because of the ever-present danger to his person that the king was advised to be well protected, ever-vigilant, and to sleep lightly like a *yogin* (*NS* 16.44).

Going by the lengthiness of the discussion, the most dangerous place for the king was the harem (*NS* 7.41–50). This was a space where there was much coming and going, and all these movements required careful regulation. Members of the *antaḥpura* were to be watched over by officers known as *antaḥpurāmātya*s. Spies in various disguises were also to keep a strict watch over everyone.[42] There is something rather bizarre about the scene painted by Kāmandaka—he suggests that the king move about the *antaḥpura* escorted by daring, mailed and turbaned hunchbacks (*kubja*s), hunters (*kirāta*s) and dwarfs (*vāmana*s). Within the harem, the king should always be protected by armed palace guards (*antaravaṁśika sainya*). Men of (over?) 80 years and women of 50 years and eunuchs should be appointed as attendants to members of the harem. Even when going to meet his mother, the king should first ensure the purification of undesirable elements from the harem. While entering his mother's apartment, he should be escorted by trustworthy armed followers and should not linger in narrow passages or deep alleys, lest he be attacked by murderous assailants.

The *antaḥpura* was a place of pleasure where the king engaged in sexual activity with wives and courtesans (*rūpajīvā*s), but Kāmandaka seems to recommend that the king should not sleep there, as no matter how beloved she might be, too much confidence must never be placed in a woman. To hammer home the point, numerous examples are given of treacherous queens who had killed their husbands. Sons, too, were a source of serious trouble, and had to be both protected and protected from (Kauṭilya too warns of these problems). The first verse of the *Rājaputrarakṣaṇa prakaraṇa* (in Book 7) suggests that this section is concerned with the protection *of* princes. But the subsequent discussion makes it abundantly clear that it is really about protection of the king *from* princes. Whether descriptive or exaggerated, the entire discussion indicates that these issues were considered central to the safety and survival of the king.

Political success did not only involve the king keeping his own house in order, it also required effective management and manipulation of many other relationships. Beyond his own household and court, the king interacted with those of other kings. Allies, neutral parties and enemies could be identified according to certain principles and could be dealt with effectively in various ways. The enemy (*ari*) was a potent source of danger to the king and to his sovereignty. What complicated matters was the fact that in the circle of kings, relationships were ever-changing—at one stroke, allies could become enemies and vice versa (*NS* 8.72–73).

Potential trouble-makers included those only partially integrated into the circle of kings—*sāmanta*s (bordering chiefs or rulers) and *āṭavika*s (forest dwellers), frequently mentioned in the same breath (*NS* 14.29; 15.22). In the *Nītisāra,* as in the *Arthaśāstra,* the term *sāmanta* does not yet have the connotations of a subordinate feudatory, which it acquired in later times.[43] The category of subordinate rulers, in fact, seems to be represented in the discussion of types of alliances rather than of the *sāmanta*s. For instance, there is a discussion of the various kinds of treaties or agreements that could be concluded with a weaker or defeated power. Among these, the *puruṣāntara sandhi* carried the express obligation that the army chiefs (*yodhamukhya*s) of the ally would serve the *vijigīṣu*'s interests (*NS* 9.13). But there is no detailed description of the elaborate protocols that involved an ostentatious display of the hierarchy of power between paramount and subordinate kings, of the sort that are found in texts of later centuries.

Ancient Indian political theorists were tuned in to the dangers of political crisis and collapse. In several places, Kauṭilya alludes to the danger of an insurrection by disaffected subjects (*prakṛtikopa*) (e.g., *AS* 1.19.28). Kāmandaka classifies disturbances that could assail the kingdom into two categories—internal (*antaḥprakopa*) and external (*bāhyaprakopa*) (*NS* 16.19–21). The former, described as potentially more harmful, included disaffection among the royal *purohita*, *amātya*s, princes, members of the royal family, commanders and chiefs of army contingents. *Bāhyaprakopa* included disaffection among provincial governors, frontier guards, forest people and those compelled to surrender.[44]

But the king's most dangerous enemy was the king himself. The *Nītisāra* talks at great length about the problems that a kingdom faces due to the king's own character and dispositions. These include *vyasana*s emanating out of vanity (*mada*), anger (*krodha*) and attachment to sensual pleasures (*kāma*) (*NS* 15.23). A kingdom in which the king is afflicted by *vyasana*s is in deep trouble, even if the other *prakṛti*s are functioning well. The king was also implicated in a number of problems arising out of the fact that the exercise of power invariably involved violence of various kinds, and it is to this that we now turn.

The Problem of Political Violence

There are many problems in correlating the connotations of the value-loaded term English word 'violence' with what is often taken as its closest Indian counterpart—the Sanskrit word *hiṁsā*. Although violence has been a perennial feature of human history, its definition, the difference between legitimate and illegitimate infliction of injury or use of force, and the grounds of justification for or condemnation of these are very culture-specific.[45] War forms a central event in the two great Sanskrit epics and the dilemmas and problems associated with large-scale military conflict are more graphically revealed in the *Mahābhārata* rather than the *Rāmāyaṇa*.[46] But it also looms large or lurks on the fringes of many an ancient and early medieval text. In the political treatises, it is centre stage.

Without going into the intricacies of semantic issues related to violence, the focus here is on certain specific activities associated with kingship that, according to our contemporary notions of violence, inevitably involved a measure of violence towards humans or animals—the punishment of criminals, war and hunting. The *Nītisāra*, like the Indian tradition in general, distinguishes between legitimate and illegitimate force. It is evident that the political theorists were concerned with theorising the limits of force and violence perpetrated by the state in these spheres. The fact that *daṇḍa* means both force and justice directs our attention to the insistence that the use of force must never be impulsive or random but must always be tempered by reflection and calculation, involving a judicious compromise between the demands of political expediency and justice.

As for Kauṭilya, for Kāmandaka too, the goals of kingship were the attainment of enduring political paramountcy and the prosperity of the king and his subjects. Attaining these goals often involved using violent and what would ordinarily be considered deceitful means, and the political theorists were not squeamish about such matters. *Daṇḍa* involves suppression (*damo daṇḍa iti khyāta, NS* 2.15) and as mentioned above, it means both coercive power as well as justice. The opening verse of the *Nītisāra* refers to the king as the wielder of *daṇḍa* (*daṇḍadhara, NS* 1.1). He maintains *varṇāśrama dharma* through *daṇḍaśakti* (the power *of daṇḍa*) (*NS* 2.34). *Daṇḍa* must be exercised to ensure the protection and promotion of the prosperity of the *prajā* (subjects), and there was a reciprocal relationship between the prosperity of the *prajā* and the *rājan* (*NS* 1.14).

Kāmandaka offers various justifications for violence, referred to in one place as *siṁhavṛtti* ('the policy of a lion') (*NS* 12.25). The most important of these is the attainment of desired ends, specifically the expansion and consolidation of political power. Violence is also justified on the grounds of what would result from its absence. In this world, according to Kāmandaka (*NS* 2.40), people move about in different directions, trying to pursue their own interests by devouring others, as though out of greed for the latters' flesh. *Daṇḍa* is necessary, otherwise *mastyanyāya* ('the law of the fish', i.e., the big fish eating the smaller fish), the much favoured, enduring trope for disorder par excellence in many ancient Indian texts, prevails.

The discussion of *upāṁśudaṇḍa* (secret killing) includes advice on the *modus operandi* to kill adversaries, and the section on *māyā* describes various sly tactics to defeat enemies (*NS* 6.10–13). Enemies can be legitimately killed by the secret administration of poison or by enlisting the services of estranged court physicians (*NS* 9.70). Harshness or violence may also be necessary to deal with dishonest and impious people (*NS* 6.5), those who obstruct the course *of dharma*, or *rājavallabhas* who create trouble, individually or collectively (*NS* 6.10). Kāmandaka recommends that royal favourites (*nṛpavallabhas*) should be killed through *upāṁśudaṇḍa* if they cause loss of lives and become a source of anxiety to the people (*NS* 18.11).

Justice is another important justification for violence. However, the king must be careful to blend the use of coercive power (*daṇḍa*) with *naya* (legal procedure) in order to be praised as a *yuktadaṇḍa* (*NS* 15.12). He is urged to use *daṇḍa* as firmly as Daṇḍin (i.e., Yama), but blended with the impartiality of the nature of the earth and compassion similar to that shown by the creator Prajāpati towards his own created beings (*NS* 3.1). Coercion must be tempered with justice and a sense of proportion, for excessively harsh punishment terrifies the people, just as leniency makes the king worthy of contempt (*NS* 6.15). So far, all this is in conformity with the attitude of many ancient Indian texts.

A difference in perspective emerges when Kāmandaka speaks of three types of *daṇḍa*—capital punishment, fines and rigorous punishment causing bodily and mental suffering. There are two types of execution: open (*prakāśadaṇḍa*) and secret (*upāṁśudaṇḍa*). An intelligent ruler desirous of religious merit should not inflict capital punishment on Brāhmaṇas and men of *dhārmika* disposition or on *antyajas* ('outsiders' or outcastes); the reason for excluding the latter is not made explicit (*NS* 18.13). In fact, according to the *Nītisāra,* capital punishment (*prāṇāntika daṇḍa*) should be avoided even for the gravest offence, with the exception of the most serious one, namely *rajyāpahāra* (usurpation) (*NS* 15.16). Kāmandaka's disapproval of capital punishment is in sharp contrast to Kauṭilya, who recommends the death penalty for several offences apart from those that are treasonable, from robbing the treasury to stealing or killing or inciting someone to steal or kill an animal belonging to the royal herd.[47]

Embedded in a political discourse that is peppered with disquisitions on violence, there is also mention of the virtue of *ahiṁsā* (non-injury). *Ahiṁsā,* refined speech (*sunṛtā vāṇī*), truthfulness (*satya*), purity (*śauca*), pity (*dayā*) and forgiveness (*kṣamā*) constitute the *sāmānya-dharma,* the *dharma* which is applicable to all people, irrespective of *varṇa* and gender (*NS* 2.32). The code of conduct of the *vijigīṣu* includes avoiding the company of dishonest and unrighteous folk, offering support to honest people and observing *ahiṁsā* towards all beings (*NS* 14.51). This is in tune with the *Arthaśāstra,* which expresses similar views (1.3.13; 1.7.2). But Kāmandaka's distinctive stance on violence, already hinted at in his position on capital punishment, is reflected more clearly in discussions of specific issues such as the royal hunt and war.

The King, the Forest and the Hunt

In many cultures, in many chronological contexts, the royal hunt has been seen as a natural activity for kings, and in fact as an important expression of the king's sovereignty. The importance of the royal hunt has been recognised by scholars in the context of the Mughal emperors,[48] but not so in the context of earlier rulers of the subcontinent. The hunting expeditions of the Mughals are described in the Persian chronicles and represented in miniature paintings, and the authors of these chronicles did not consider hunting a problematic activity from either a pragmatic or an ethical point of view.[49] The ancient Indian political theorists, on the other hand, had much to say on the matter. And one of the most significant aspects of the *Nītisāra* is its opposition to the royal hunt, an activity that was considered by Kauṭilya as integral to the king's way of life.

The forest and forest people loom large in the writings of political theorists. For Kāmandaka (as for Kauṭilya and the Sanskrit poets), the forest was a place associated with renunciants and ascetics. But more importantly, the political theorists recognised it as a place exceptionally rich in economic and military resources—especially elephants, which were greatly prized for their role in war—and where kings built forts (*vanadurga*). Elephant enclosures (i.e., forests) and regular forests were two of the eight sources of income (*aṣṭavarga*) of the state (*NS* 5.78–79). Forest dwellers (*āṭavikas*) were by nature *adhārmika* (impious), *lubdha* (greedy), *anārya* (uncultured) and *satyabhedin* (untrustworthy) (*NS* 19.8). Forest troops (*āraṇyaka/āṭavika bala*) had to be used by the king in his military campaigns, but they were even more unreliable than troops alienated from the enemy camp (*NS* 19.9–10). From the king's point of view, the forest was, at the end of the day, a lucrative, but problematic space.

The forest was also a place where the king hunted, but Kāmandaka had strong reservations about this activity. The dangers of the *yānavyasana* (the calamity of the march), described in the *Nītisāra* just before those of *mṛgayāvyasana* (the calamity of the hunt), appear to apply to both (*NS* 15.19–22).[50] These include the physical strain resulting from prolonged riding, accidental fall or injury, and the loss of horses or chariots. Further, there is the suffering caused by hunger, thirst, exhaustion, severe cold, storm, heat, and wastage of resources. Travelling through areas that are very hot, sandy or thorny, or dense forests infested with prickly creepers and shrubs, or hilly areas prone to falling boulders, or tracks that are uneven due to stones, earthen mounds and ant hills—all this causes much distress. Enemies may be lurking among rocks, rivers, or forests, and there is the possibility of sudden capture or death at the hands of *sāmanta*s, *āṭavika*s and others. The other dangers specifically arising out of the *mṛgayāvyasana* include the possibility of the king being attacked by his own followers or kinsmen, captured by enemies, or mauled by bears, pythons, wild elephants, lions or tigers. He may lose his way in the forest, with the path obscured due to smoke arising from forest fires, and may be reduced to wandering around helplessly (*NS* 15.23–24).

According to Kāmandaka, these potential dangers could to some extent be neutralised by ensuring that the king rides on the back of a swift but easily controllable animal, by having the outskirts of the forest carefully examined and protected against all dangers, and ensuring that their interiors are well lit and rendered free of ferocious animals (*NS* 2.36). But this does not fully settle matters. For Kāmandaka, as for Kauṭilya, hunting, along with women, drinking and gambling, is a royal vice. But while Kāmandaka is willing to accept moderate levels of indulgence in women and drink, gambling and hunting are to be shunned as far as is possible.

Apart from the physical dangers it entails for the king, Kāmandaka's objection to hunting is also based on the fact that this activity could lead to the king wasting his time, and also that any kind of addiction weakens character. But his most important argument is that hunting is a great *vyasana* (*mahat vyasana*) because of the inherent evils of taking life (*doṣāḥ prāṇaharāḥ*) (*NS* 15.26).

To make sure that he has covered all the ground concerning this issue, Kāmandaka lists the various supposed benefits of hunting (*NS* 15.25). He cites the view that hunting provides the king with physical exercise which, in turn, results in his developing endurance, immunity from indigestion, heaviness and susceptibility to catching cold. Another argument proferred by some in favour of hunting is that it develops skill and excellence in hitting stationary or moving targets with arrows. These are, in fact, precisely the arguments made by Kauṭilya in the *Arthaśāstra* (8.3.46). But Kāmandaka firmly refutes them by asserting that all these benefits can be obtained through other means. For instance, maladies such as indigestion can be remedied through regular physical exercise, and marksmanship in archery by practising with artificial targets (*NS* 15.27). This is in sharp contrast to Kauṭilya, who considers hunting as the least harmful of the *vyasana*s (*AS* 8.3).

Kāmandaka also suggests another interesting alternative (*NS* 15.28–40) to the regular royal hunt. Kauṭilya too refers to this option, though very briefly. For a king who is unable to give up hunting, an artificial, sanitised game forest should be created (*mṛgāraṇya*), where he could hunt for sport (*krīḍā*) alone.[51] The features of this game forest are then specified: It should be located just outside the town (presumably the capital city), should be over half a *yojanā* in length and breadth, and should be surrounded by a ditch and ramparts so that the animals cannot escape. It should be situated at the foot of a hill or next to a river, and should have plentiful supplies of water and grass. It should not have thorny creepers, shrubs, or poisonous plants. Any crevices in the ground should be filled up with earth and gravel, and the surface should be leveled by removing stumps of trees, mounds of earth and rocks. It should be made attractive with well-known flower-bearing and fruit-bearing trees providing pleasing, thick and cool shade. The pools in this park should be shallow, abounding in flowers and birds of different species, and cleared of ferocious aquatic animals. The park should have beautiful creepers laden with flowers and leaves inside and on the sides of the surrounding ditch. It should be provided with animals such as she-elephants and their young ones, tigers and other big game with their teeth and nails removed, and horned animals whose horns have been broken. A space outside the park should be cleared of trees and pillars, and the ground should be leveled, so that it is inaccessible to enemy forces and enhances the feeling of comfort for the king. The park should be guarded by trustworthy forest people who are resolute, hardy, painstaking, and conversant with the moods of wild animals. The king's own men, of boundless energy and experienced in hunting, should introduce various wild animals into the park. The king may then enter it for sport, accompanied by a select group of trusted attendants, without detriment to his other duties. As he enters, fully armed soldiers should carefully stand guard outside, vigilant for signs of danger to their royal master.

In his detailed description of an artificial, sanitised game forest for the royal hunt, Kāmandaka offers a compromise between the royal predilection for hunting and the dangers and problems that this activity entailed.[52] In spite of describing this option, it is noteworthy that Kāmandaka disapproves of hunting not only on pragmatic grounds, that is, the physical danger to the king and the possibility of it entailing a neglect of royal duties. He also objects to it on two moral grounds—that is, it harms the king by weakening his character, and it involves violence against animals. The second argument indicates that it is not *excessive* hunting alone that is considered a problem; hunting itself is problematic because of the fact that it does violence to animals. This stand against an activity conventionally associated with kingship can be further connected with Kāmandaka's stand on the most violent of all political activities—war.

The Problem of War

In ancient and early medieval India, battles were fought (as they are now as well), for a variety of reasons including the control of land and resources and as an assertion of political hegemony, and given the endemic nature of war, it is not surprising that disquisitions on the subject abound in texts. In the context of ancient India, the Maurya emperor Aśoka is considered the foremost exemplar and proponent of the principle of non-violence at the political as well as personal level. His thirteenth rock edict is, in fact, a remarkable document, giving a strong, reasoned critique of war, raising the discourse of kingship and conquest to a completely new level. However, although the political theorists recognised war as a necessary instrument of state policy, they also recognised its dangers and problematic nature. Moreover, attitudes towards war could and did differ.

Ali briefly refers to the complex and ambivalent connection between courtly manners and violence, arguing that while military prowess and ritualised and honourable violence were important parts of courtly culture, they came to be tempered by irenic values and an emphasis on compassion, kindness and gentility.[53] My own perspective on the issue of violence is different. The focus here is not the relationship between violence and courtly manners and culture, but on violence as a politico-ethical problem, and the ways in which the political theorists addressed this problem.

General disquisitions on war (*vigraha, yuddha*) can be distinguished from the strategies to be adopted in military expeditions (*yāna*), and Kāmandaka, like Kauṭilya, discusses both. As mentioned earlier, the key player whose interests are central to the *Nītisāra* is the *vijigīṣu*, and there are detailed discussions of military strategies and formations. In fact, the text culminates in a description of a successful military campaign. However, within all this, it also makes a strong case for the exercise of extreme caution in waging war, and the case it makes is not simply one of expediency. Thus, while there is much that is in common between the *Arthaśāstra*'s and *Nītisāra*'s discussion of the conduct of inter-state relations, for instance in the idea of twelve elements in the *rājamaṇḍala* (circle of kings) and the six strategies (*guṇa*s), there is also much that is significantly different.[54]

Various aspects of war are discussed in the *Vigrahavikalpa prakaraṇa* (in Book 10) and in other sections as well. The typology of war in the *Nītisāra* includes the basic distinction between *kūṭayuddha* (secret war) and *prakāśayuddha* (open war) (*NS* 19.54). *Kūṭayuddha* includes duping and enticing the enemy, nocturnal raids and setting up camouflaged encampments. Kāmandaka asserts that the king does not transgress *dharma* by killing the enemy through the tactics of *kūṭayuddha.* The example given is that of Aśvatthāman killing the sons of the Pāṇḍavas while they were asleep. Kāmandaka also gives a detailed listing of the causes of war (*NS* 10.3–5) such as the usurpation of the kingdom, the abduction of women, the luring away of learned men and soldiers, the killing of friends and political rivalry. He also mentions a third kind of war—*mantrayuddha* (diplomatic warfare) (*NS* 19.15–17). [55] It may be noted that Kāmandaka does not use Kauṭilya's well-known typology of the types of conquerors—the *dharmavijayin* (who conquers for the sake of glory and is satisfied with the mere submission of the defeated king), *lobhavijayin* (who conquers out of greed and wants to obtain land, money, or both) and *asuravijayin* (who makes conquests like a demon, seizing the land, money, sons and wives of the conquered king and kills him) (*AS* 12.1.10). In the *Nītisāra*, war is no longer graded according to a hierarchy of honour and propriety. The only relevant issues are its cost and chances of success.

What is most significant from the point of view of political theory, especially when seen in the context of the endemic warfare of the time, is the fact that the *Nītisāra* contains many different kinds of very specific arguments against war. Objections to war on pragmatic grounds are to be expected in the political treatises. The basic point on which the experts on politics agreed was that it was essential for the *vijigīṣu* to carefully assess the likely costs and consequences of war. The potential gains of war are territory (this is the most important), allies and wealth, and the king should embark on war only if there was a clear prospect of attaining these (*NS* 10.31). The *Nītisāra* also recommends a long-term perspective on pragmatism, pointing out that political success does not hinge on a single victory. Like Paraśurāma, the king who commands respect from all through his prowess is the one who has to his credit many victories on different battlefields (*NS* 9.51).

Kāmandaka lists 16 types of war (*vigraha*) that should not be fought (*NS* 10.19–23). Although there were those who thought otherwise, for Kāmandaka, there was no point in embarking on war if the enemy was much more powerful and the chances of victory bleak.[56] There was no justification for fighting a more powerful enemy, for clouds can never move in a direction opposite to that of the wind. Even if the enemy equalled the *vijigīṣu* in terms of resources, war could lead to death and destruction, sometimes of both parties. Both would perish like two unbaked pitchers striking against each other, like the demons Suṇḍa and Upasuṇḍa destroyed each other. Other wars that should not be fought included those for the sake of others or for the sake of women, those against venerable Brāhmaṇas, those that promised to be long drawn out, and those undertaken in times when troop movement was difficult.

The risks of war were enhanced by the uncertainties it entailed, and there was no point risking what could be seen for unseen gains (*NS* 16.14). This is why a prudent king should avoid war, even when it was thrust on him. 'As victory in war is always uncertain, it should not be launched without careful deliberation' (*NS* 10.24). The policy of reeds (*vaitasī vṛtti*) rather than that of snakes (*bhaujaṅgī vṛtti*) should be followed, that is, it was better to be flexible rather than attack at the slightest provocation (*NS* 10.35–36).

Kauṭilya too briefly refers to the fact that war entails losses, expenses, marches away from home, and hindrances (*AS* 7.2.2), but Kāmandaka dwells on this issue in greater detail. Apart from the arguments against war based on expediency and the uncertainty of gains, the *Nītisāra* has many verses dilating on the inevitably disastrous results of war, especially one launched hastily without due consideration and consultation. If a ruler acts in a way contrary to the *śāstra* and suddenly falls on an enemy, it is unlikely that he will be able to get out of this situation without feeling the impact of the enemy's sword (*NS* 12.6). In the course of war, the king could, in a single instant, suffer the loss of wives, friends, allies, wealth, kingdom, fame, and even his own life (*NS* 9.75). In view of the fact that war necessarily entails loss of men and resources, various difficulties and the death of principal officers, an intelligent ruler should not continue war, even if he has to willingly accept hardship, for war has inherently disastrous consequences (*doṣas*) (*NS* 9.73). Considering the constant anxiety and mental suffering resulting from war, the intelligent ruler should not indulge in frequent warfare (*NS* 9.74). Thus, Kāmandaka argues persuasively, recourse to war, especially frequent war, must be avoided.

Kāmandaka also points to the fact that wars often served the selfish interests of members of the political class other than the king. For instance, *mantrī*s (ministers) may desire a prolongation of war due to their self-interest, and a ruler who acts on their counsel may simply play into their hands (*NS* 12.41). The idea of setting his house in order before launching on fresh military campaigns is also emphasised when Kāmandaka states that the *vyasana*s of state should be remedied before a ruler launches an attack against the enemy (*NS* 14.18).

The text further points out that war was neither the only nor the best expedient (*upāya*) that could be used by the *vijigīṣu* to achieve his ends. *Sāma* (conciliation), *dāna* (gifts), *daṇḍa* (force) and *bheda* (sowing dissension) were the well-known list of political expedients mentioned by Kauṭilya. Kāmandaka expands this list by adding three more—*māyā* (deceitful tactics), *upekṣā* (indifference) and *indrajāla* (conjuring tricks) (*NS* 18.3). He argues that conciliatory measures should always be adopted to prevent war.

The ancient political treatises refer to three types of power at the command of the king. Of these, Kāmandaka describes *mantraśakti* (the power of counsel) as superior to *prabhuśakti* (the power of lordship, that is, military might) and *utsāhaśakti* (the power of energy) (*NS* 12.7). In this, he is of the same opinion as Kauṭilya.[57] Only by the possession of *mantrabala* does a ruler, following the track of *naya*, become capable of subjugating the powerful enemies who are like vicious serpents (*NS* 12.58). Implicit here is the idea that brute force is not the best option for maximising political gain. Kauṭilya too drives home the point when he asserts that if the *vijigīṣu* uses excessive force, the circle of kings may rise against him and he may be destroyed, or that force (*daṇḍa*) cannot be used against a multitude of people. The political theorists were obviously keenly aware of the limits of the efficacy of force.

The final, culminating *prakaraṇa* (in Book 20) of the *Nītisāra* deals with *prakāśayuddha* (the conduct of open war), and everything in the text seems to be leading up to the crisp description of a successful military charge against the enemy. But before getting to this point, Kāmandaka has offered his audience abundant and diverse arguments to make his point that war must always be a last resort.

Controlling the Controller

While the goal of the *Nītisāra*'s teaching is political success, an awareness of the possibilities of political malfunction through excess, imbalance and tyranny is ever-present. In certain situations, for instance if the king is excessively attached to *dharma* or *artha*, of if he is mentally ill, the functions of the *vijigīṣu* should be discharged by *mantrī*s possessing the requisite qualities (*NS* 14.60). The ability of the king to achieve his political ambitions hinged on his ability to effectively control the various *prakṛti*s of the state. The *Nītisāra,* like many other texts, recommends that the king cultivate discipline, self-control and equanimity in himself, in princes, and among his subjects.[58]

The very first *prakaraṇa* of the *Nītisāra*, the *Indriyajaya prakaraṇa*, deals with the topic of the control of the senses.[59] The *Arthaśāstra* too emphasises the importance of discipline and control of the senses (*AS* 1.6.3). Restraint of the passions and self-control are among the important qualities (*ātmasampad*) of the king (*NS* 4.15–19); in fact, these are his pre-eminent qualities, his *ātmasaṁskāra* (*NS* 4.4). These qualities were connected with a character trait that was greatly valorised by political theorists—*vinaya*, which was a cocktail of several things: discipline, good breeding, propriety, humility, modesty, mildness and good behaviour. *Vinaya* is a quality that a king should possess, one that should be inculcated in princes, and a crucial factor in defeat or victory (*NS* 1.66–71).

Ali argues that that for members of the political class, control of the senses was considered a precondition for the enjoyment of sensual and worldly pleasures and self-mastery and equanimity as essential for success in the courtly circle.[60] Even if, as he suggests, the emphasis on *vinaya* in the court context functioned as a powerful worldly idea, a kind of internalised self-regulating mechanism that helped people succeed in getting ahead and also helped maintain the courtly hierarchy, its origins still require explanation. The source for the emphasis on self-control seems to be two-fold. First, as mentioned earlier, the discourse of political theorists was embedded in a larger philosophical discourse. The emphasis on self-control and equanimity in the *Nītisāra* seems to have, in part, sprung from the philosophical underpinnings of the political discourse, the desirability of the control of the senses being a fairly widespread idea in ancient Indian philosophical systems.[61] Early in the text, Kāmandaka defines *anvīkṣikī* as that which develops the self-knowledge (*ātmavidyā*) that looks through happiness and sorrow, and asserts that it is by realising the true nature of joy and sorrow that the king renounces them both (*NS* 2.11). Numerous examples are given to prove the transience of life and its pleasures, and great emphasis is placed on the control of the sense organs (*NS* 3.9). Striking in its Upaniṣadic ring is the assertion (*NS* 4.78) that just as the *antarātman*, residing in the midst of *prakṛti* (nature), permeates (*samaśnute*) the world consisting of moving and unmoving elements, similarly does the king, in the midst of the *prakṛtis* (elements of the state), permeate the world consisting of moving and unmoving elements.

As important as the text's dārśanic underpinnings for understanding the emphasis on royal self-control was its politico-historical context. In an age of political aggrandisement, political theorists must have not only been concerned with the question of how the power of the king could be increased but also with how it could be contained. Emphasising the importance of *mantraśakti* (the power of counsel) could only go so far. Ultimately, in ancient monarchical states, the only agent of effective control on the ambitions and transgressions of the king was the king himself. This may have been the second important element explaining Kāmandaka's (and Kauṭilya's) emphasis on the king controlling himself and his passions. The contradiction that the *Nītisāra* offers—what may in fact be described as an important element in the classical Indian ideal of kingship—is that of a king who aspires to become a world conqueror but who is not moved by the lust for power, or for anything else, for that matter. Renunciation was built into the ideal prototype of the king, and this is reflected in the ideal of the *rajarṣi*, an ideal which is pervasive in the cultural traditions of ancient and early medieval India.[62]

Historicising the *Nītisāra*

Historicising the *Nītisāra* involves contextualising it within the genre of ancient and early medieval Indian political treatises and within the realities of monarchical power politics at the advent of the early medieval. The perspective represented in this text is that of a Brāhmaṇa political theorist who was probably closely involved in contemporary politics, addressing members of the political class, including the king. While the text is broadly speaking 'normative' in nature, within this normative discourse, we can view a morphology of monarchical power politics and we can also see the author grappling with pressing issues of his time, including those related to unbridled and unsatiated royal ambitions and endemic war and violence.

The leading political theorists of ancient and early medieval India had a similar socio-political background and shared similar concerns and conceptual vocabulary, ones which extended beyond their circle to other members of the intelligentsia, including the poets. They participated in the creation of a basic common stock of ideas and metaphors that became part of a relatively stable classical Indian model of kingship which, with regional and chronological variations, spread beyond the confines of the subcontinent into Southeast Asia as well.[63]

Yet, within the parameters of this model, these thinkers had their distinct and distinctive positions and points of view as well. In fact, a close reading of the *Nītisāra* reveals that the usual description of this text as an unoriginal versified summary of the teaching of the *Arthaśāstra* is incorrect. Kāmandaka certainly drew on Kauṭilya's ideas (and those of others as well), but he had his own point of view on several matters. His concerns and opinions can be gauged through a careful analysis of the issues he discusses, his arguments and emphases. Just as interesting as his assertions are his silences. There is only a hint of cleavages within the political elite, and it may be noted that apart from a brief reference to the crime of usurpation, Kāmandaka does not directly discuss issues which must have been of pressing practical import such as disputed succession, coups and dynastic changes.

The morphology of the state, royal court and household in the *Nītisāra* corresponds broadly to that of the *Arthaśāstra*. And yet, in spite of shared rhetoric and imagery, Kāmandaka lacks Kauṭilya's confident, even audacious, vision of political power and empire. This must have been at least in part due to the fact that the core of the *Arthaśāstra*, was composed at least half a millennium, if not more, earlier, during a period of aggressive empire-building, while the *Nītisāra* was composed in a very different political scenario, against the backdrop of imperial decline (of the Guptas and Vākāṭakas). The political battles were now among monarchical states and the oligarchies no longer figured as contenders among the circle of kings. Compared with still later texts, although the ideal of political paramountcy is very important, in the *Nītisāra*, the *sāmanta*s still seem to be bordering chiefs, and the discussion of the protocol between paramount and subordinate rulers is not as detailed or elaborate.

The *Nītisāra*'s ostensible aim was to reveal how the *vijigīṣu* could achieve his goal of political paramountcy and the text often has the ring of idealisation and universalisation, especially when it talks of the ideal virtues of the king. But there seems to be something more than banal idealisation or pious platitude here. Although many of the virtues that are described as desirable in a king are presented as inborn, they are actually cultivable, and the idea that is implicit is that there is a difference between a king who becomes king and one who is worthy of being one. The entire discussion can be seen as an attempt of a political theorist to emphasise the ethical dimension of political discourse.[64]

A similar concern for building bridges between ethics and political realities can be seen in Kāmandaka's discussion of various forms of violence associated with kingship—punishment, hunting and war. While he does justify violent means in order to justify certain ends (justice, the desire for exciting sport, and the goal of territorial expansion respectively), a careful reading of the text suggests a more complex and nuanced perspective. Along with advice, there is a great deal of admonition and warning of the calamities that will afflict the kingdom if a king lacks the necessary virtues or abilities, or if the balance of virtue that is necessary for the other human agents in the *saptāṅga rājya* is disturbed.

The long deliberative sections on war, advocating extreme caution, suggest the despondency of a political thinker who disapproved of the frequent destructive warfare that marked his time. That this disapproval was part of Kāmandaka's larger convictions related to violence and non-violence is evident from his view on capital punishment. It is also evident in his diatribe against the royal hunt, which, contrary to Kauṭilya's view on the matter, is viewed as the worst of the royal vices, and is disapproved of not only on the grounds of expediency but also on the grounds that it involves moral weakening of the king and death to the hunted animals. These radical points of view have, strangely enough, hitherto gone unnoticed in works on ancient Indian political thought, which have incorrectly presented the *Nītisāra* as a feeble versified echo of the *Arthaśāstra*.

Further, embedded in a text which seems to be a celebration of royal and political ambitions, is a strong insistence that the king exercise control over his senses. This insistence may have been a reaction to the disastrous results of the wanton, licentious lifestyle of many contemporary kings and/or as a reflection of the most basic form of self-control that was advocated by many dārṣanic schools of the time. The Upaniṣadic ring of *Nītisāra* 4.78, mentioned earlier in this essay, seems to betray a more specific philosophical orientation. But apart from the philosophical inspiration, the emphasis on self-control can also be seen as an attempt of the political theorists to deal with a very central problem: How was the power of the king to be controlled and checked in a polity which lacked any institutional checks? Virtue, caution and power of counsel were emphasised again and again. But theorists such as Kāmandaka recognised that ultimately, no external controls could be counted on, and the only real control on the king's power was the one that he had to be persuaded to exercise over himself.

Incorporating Perspectives on Violence into Political History

In spite of problems in dating their work precisely, it is essential to incorporate the ideas of the political theorists into historical writings on political processes in ancient and early medieval India. Such an exercise involves situating these texts within their historical context, a careful reading of their opinions and arguments on various issues, and a comparison between texts (and inscriptions) belonging to different periods of time. Comparison reveals much continuity in terms of concepts and vocabulary, but also indicates differences in perspective, and shifts in emphasis and nuance. We have seen that a comparison of the *Arthaśāstra* and *Nītisāra* reflects a refashioning of the political model. While the *Arthaśāstra* can be seen as a brilliant exposition of the dizzy heights of power to which a king could aspire, inspired by the vision of an omniscient, omnipotent and omnipresent state, the *Nītisāra*'s tone is more cautious and restrained. Kāmandaka is certainly concerned with how a king could increase his power and dominion, but he is equally, if not more, concerned with how royal power, war and violence could be contained and controlled. The *Arthaśāstra* reflects an earlier model of an arrogant, absolutist state; the *Nītisāra* represents a later, less exultant reflection on political power, one in which non-violence has significantly tempered the discussion of violence, especially with regard to punishment, the royal hunt and war.

In the contexts of perspectives on war and hunting in ancient and early medieval times, it does not help to necessarily look for evidence of wholesale approval or disapproval of these activities.[65] In fact, the assertion that the issue of *ahiṁsā* was never raised in connection with the king's exercising his own functions in ancient India is inaccurate.[66] These were not questions which involved an either/or choice between the extremes of violence and non-violence (both in general or in their specific manifestations). There was a constant tension between these two poles, and a number of possibilities between them, and the implications of these possibilities were explored in various ways. It is this range of attitudes related to *hiṁsā* and *ahiṁsā* that require careful and extensive investigation.[67]

Apart from the *Arthaśāstra* and *Nītisāra,* there are several other less-known texts on polity, most of them known through fleeting references in secondary literature.[68] We have seen how the subject of *nīti* emerged from within the larger of discipline of *Arthaśāstra.* But issues related to rulership and polity were simultaneously being also taken over and discussed in other kinds of works, principally the Dharmaśāstra texts and the epics, and they were also explored and expressed in poetry, drama, didactic tales and sayings, not only in Sanskrit but in other languages as well.

The question of how political violence was conceptualised, defined, justified, delimited, criticised or condemned in texts belonging to different genres, languages and periods needs to be analysed, and the results of such an analysis should be part of the historian's discourse on political processes in ancient and early medieval India. The sheer pervasiveness of political violence in human history, and the problem it presents in our own time, make an engagement with this issue especially pertinent.

Acknowledgements

I would like to thank the anonymous referee for many extremely valuable suggestions which have been incorporated into the final version of this chapter. I would also like to thank Vijay Tankha, Dilip Simeon, Nayanjot Lahiri, Suryanarayana Nanda, and Seema Alavi for various kinds of help rendered.

Notes

1. The literature on these frameworks is well known and enormous, and it is therefore neither possible nor necessary to give exhaustive references. A good sample of the various views is on display in Hermann Kulke, ed., *The State in India 1000–1700,* Oxford in India Readings, Themes in Indian History Series (New Delhi: Oxford University Press, 1997).
2. Sheldon Pollock, *The Language of the Gods in the World of Men: Sanskrit, Culture and Power in Premodern India* (Berkeley: University of California Press, 2006).
3. Ronald Inden, *Text and Practice: Essays on South Asian History* (New Delhi: Oxford University Press, 2006), pp. 129–178.
4. Daud Ali, *Courtly Culture and Political Life in Early Medieval India* (New Delhi: Foundation Books, 2006).
5. See for instance, Jan E. M. Houben and Karel R. van Kooij, eds., *Violence Denied: Violence, Non-Violence and the Rationalization of Violence in South Asian Cultural History* (Leiden: Brill, 1999).
6. Daud Ali, 'Violence, Gastronomy and the Meanings of War in Medieval South India', *The Medieval History Journal* 3 (2), 2000, pp. 261–289.
7. Sheldon Pollock, 'The Theory of Practice and the Practice of Theory in Indian Intellectual History', *Journal of the American Oriental Society* 105 (3), Indological Studies Dedicated to Daniel H. H. Ingalls 1985, pp. 499–519. He adds that this stance is diametrically opposite to that found in the West, and that adherence to this postulate had profound implications for the production of knowledge in Indian civilisation.
8. The author's name has been read as Kāmandaki by some scholars. The text used for this chapter is Sisir Kumar Mitra's revised edition and translation, which is based on Rajendralala Mitra, ed., *The Nītisāra, or The Elements of Polity by Kāmandaki*, Revised with English Translation by Sisir Kumar Mitra (Kolkata, 1982), which was published between 1849 and 1884. This uses an anonymous commentary called the *Upādhyāyanirapekṣā.* Although I have drawn on this edition, I have relied on my own translation of the text. In references hereafter, *Nītisāra* has been abbreviated to *NS.* The textual citations refer to the *sarga* and verse number.
9. Bhasker Anand Saletore, *Ancient Indian Political Thought and Institutions* (New York, 1963), p. 9.

10. Michael Willis, *The Archaeology of Hindu Ritual: Temples and the Establishment of the Gods* (New Delhi: Cambridge University Press, 2009), pp. 62–63. Willis' hypothesis that the 'Deva' mentioned in the first verse of the *Nītisāra* is none other than Candragupta II, on the grounds that the latter is referred to as 'Deva' or 'Devagupta' in inscriptions, seems weak. So, does his assertion that since Kāmandaka describes himself as a disciple of Viṣṇugupta, alias Kauṭilya, a generation, or 30–40 years, must separate the two political theorists.
11. The date of the *Arthaśāstra* is an issue of continuing debate. Many Indian historians accept R. P. Kangle's argument that the core of the text was composed in the early Maurya period during the last quarter of the 4th century BCE (R. P. Kangle, *The Kauṭilīya Arthaśāstra,* Part III [Mumbai: University of Bombay, 1965], pp. 59–115); of course additions, interpolations and recasting may have extended into the early centuries CE. Western scholars, on the other hand, are persuaded by the results of Thomas R. Trautmann's statistical analysis of word frequencies in the *Arthaśāstra* (R. Thomas Trautmann, *Kauṭilya and the Arthaśāstra: A Statistical Investigation of the Authorship and Evolution of the Text* [Leiden: E. J. Brill, 1971], on the basis of which he has made a case for several different authors. He suggests that Book 2 (which deals with internal administration) may have been completed by c. 150 CE, and the final compilation of the entire text by c. 250 CE. References to the *Arthaśāstra* (abbreviated to *AS*) in this essay are to Kangle's critical edition (R. P. Kangle, *The Kauṭilīya Arthaśāstra, Part I: A Critical Edition with a Glossary* [Mumbai: University of Bombay], 1970). Patrick Olivelle (*King, Governance and Law in Ancient India: Kautilya's Arthasastra: A New Annotated Translation*, New Delhi: Oxford University Press, 2013, Introduction) dates the composition of the text between c. 50 and 300 CE.
12. U. N. Ghoshal, *A History of Indian Political Ideas: The Ancient Period and the Period of Transition to the Middle Ages,* Reprint edition (Oxford: Oxford University Press, [1959], 1966), p. 395, n. 1.
13. See, for instance, Saletore, *Ancient India Political Thought and Institutions,* pp. 54, 289, 340; Ghoshal, *A History of Indian Political Ideas,* p. 383; K.V.R. Aiyangar, *Some Aspects of Ancient Indian Polity,* 2nd edition, (Patna: Eastern Book House, [1935] 1988), pp. 24–25.
14. While the term *anujīvin* literally carries the connotations of dependence and has, therefore, been often translated as 'dependant', in the context of the court, it is better to translate it as 'courtier'.
15, Apart from the *Nītisāra,* this also applies, for instance, to the *Arthaśāstra* and the *Kāmasūtra.* For a detailed discussion of this point, see Pollock, 'The Theory of Practice and the Practice of Theory in Indian Intellectual History', pp. 512–513.
16. Ali (*Courtly Culture and Political Life in Early Medieval India,* p. 276) argument that the *Arthaśāstra* marks a significant shift in the language of lordship, from agonistic to irenic kingship is thought-provoking. However, the shift does not seem to have been a complete one.
17. *NS* 11.32a refers to a *laukika gāthā*, according to which, a living man is likely to secure happiness even after the lapse of a hundred years (this

refers to the cyclical nature of fortune/happiness and misfortune/sorrow). *NS* 14.33 refers to a popular saying (*sārvalaukika pravāda*) that the treasury (*kośa*) is the root (*mūla*) of the king.

18. While some of the schools and thinkers cited were clearly historical, the god Indra and the demon Maya fall within the category of fictive authorities.
19. *NS* 2.6 and *NS* 11.42.
20. According to some scholars, the reference is to the god Viṣṇu, but the verse seems to refer to a generic king.
21. The word '*nīti*' comes from the root 'nī', which means to take away, guide, conduct, lead, and so on. In its broadest sense, it can refer to policy, rules, or precepts governing any aspect of life. But in the context of the text and branch of knowledge being discussed here, *nīti* has a more specific sense related to polity, statecraft and governance.
22. Vishwanath Prasad Varma, *Studies in Hindu Political Thought and its Metaphysical Foundations,* 3rd revised and enlarged edition (New Delhi: Motilal Banarsidass, 1974), pp. 215–217. He argues that the metaphysics of *karma* and *dharma* ruled out the raising of problems such as the individual versus the state, politics versus ethics, and the political accountability of the king to the people.
23. Contrast this with the *Arthaśāstra*'s (1.2.12) description of *anvīkṣikī*—consisting of *sāṁkhya, yoga* and *lokāyata*—as the lamp of all sciences (*pradīpaḥ sarvavidyānām*).
24. The seven elements are chyle, blood, flesh, fat, bone, marrow and semen. The term *doṣa* also occurs in *āyurveda*, but has a different meaning than that in the political treatises. The three *doṣa*s or humours are substances which circulate within the body—*vāta* (wind), *pitta* (choler) and *kapha* or *sleṣman* (phlegm). Disease arises when a humour collects in the wrong area of the body and becomes inflamed (Dominik Wujastyk, *The Roots of Ayurveda: Selections from Sanskrit Medical Writings* [New Delhi: National Mission for Manuscripts and Dev Publishers, 2001], pp. 4, 31). The terms *guṇa* and *doṣa* as indicative of positive qualities and faults occur in many different kinds of discourse, including as features of language in Indian literary theory.
25. For an interesting discussion of the connections between medicine and poetry, see Francis Zimmermann, 'Ṛtusātmya: The Seasonal Cycle and the Principle of Appropriateness', *Social Science and Medicine* 14B (2), 1980, pp. 99–106.
26. Sheldon Pollock ('Mīmāṃsā and the Problem of History in Traditional India', *Journal of the American Oriental Society* 109 [4] 1989 pp. 603–610) has expressed this eloquently in a broader context, arguing that in Sanskritic India, history was not unknown but denied. His hypothesis, which merits careful consideration, is that this was because the authority of the Veda was considered by Mīmāṁsā as based on its timelessness, and that this became a model for all forms of knowledge.
27. He is compared with the sun, moon, Vindhyas, rain-bearing clouds, earth, blazing fire, lion, elephant and snake. He is also compared with the *kalpavṛkṣa* (the wish-granting tree).

28. The Sanskrit epics were pivotal to many other discourses on politics and kingship in ancient and early medieval India. The full extent of this importance—reflected in texts, inscriptions and sculpture from many parts of the subcontinent and beyond—is something which has not yet been fully gauged.
29. *NS* 5.91 A (this *śloka* is marked *kroḍa*, i.e. supplementary in the commentary) and *NS* 14.6.
30. The seven elements of the state in the *Arthaśāstra* are *svāmin, amātya, janapada, durga, koṣa, daṇḍa* and *mitra*. The *Nītisāra* (*NS* 4.1) makes a slight modification in terminology, replacing *janapada* with *rāṣṭra, daṇḍa* with *bala,* and *mitra* with *suhṛt*. It is interesting to note that Bṛhaspati rather than Kauṭilya, is cited as the authority on the seven elements of the kingdom (*NS* 8.5).
31. Ali, *Courtly Culture and Political Life in Early Medieval India,* p. 5.
32. Ali, *Courtly Culture and Political Life in Early Medieval India,* pp. 103–140.
33. In the context in which the word *guṇa* occurs here, it does not (as suggested by Ali, *Courtly Culture and Political Life in Early Medieval India,* pp. 90–91) have any connection with *sattva, rajas* and *tamas.*
34. The text makes a distinction between servants (denoted by *bhṛtya* and *sevaka*) and dependants/courtiers of a higher socio-political standing (denoted by *anujīvin*).
35. *NS* 5.59; 5.63.
36. There is passing reference to hierarchies within the court circle, for instance, in the mention of the honorific paraphernalia such as umbrella, fly-whisk, coachman, and grooms that the *mahāmātras* and certain other high-ranking officials enjoyed (*NS* 13.44). The dependent is advised to observe decorum in deference to other courtiers' rank, and there is mention of his rivals (*vipakṣa*; *NS* 5.40). But there is no direct or detailed discussion of court factions and rivalries.
37. Ali, *Courtly Culture and Political Life in Early Medieval India,* pp. 246–247.
38. Ali has very effectively demonstrated (*Courtly Culture and Political Life in Early Medieval India* p. 183) the coincidence of the terminology of emotions and political dispositions in a variety of courtly literature of the first millennium.
39. As mentioned, earlier, this is one of the few hints about fractures and factions within the courtly circle.
40. Since the terms *suhṛt* and *mitra* are used in the text to refer to personal friends as well as political allies, in some cases, it is not clear which of these meanings is intended.
41. One of the problems in Ali's discussion is that he occasionally slips from his stance of viewing the various discourses on courtly culture as representations to one where these representations are presented as descriptions of courtly life. He does, however, point out that the texts themselves mention the breach of court protocol.
42. *NS* 13.42–43 suggests that spies pretending to be idiots, dumb, blind and deaf persons, eunuchs, *kirātas* (hunters), dwarfs and hunchbacks, petty craftsmen, monks/mendicants, minstrels, slave women, garland-makers, and artists should keep a watch on the members of the harem.

43. See Lallanji Gopal, 'Sāmanta—Its Varying Significance in Ancient India', *Journal of the Royal Asiatic Society* 5 (1–2), 1963, pp. 21–37, for a discussion of changes in the connotations of the term *sāmanta.*
44. *AS* 9.5 has a more general discussion of troubles emanating from the interior and the outer regions.
45. See, for instance, Houben and van Kooij eds, *Violence Denied*, pp. 1–3.
46. Much has been written on this theme. For instance, Danielle Feller Jatavallabhula, 'Raṇayajña: The Mahābhārata War as a Sacrifice', in Jan E. M. Houben and Karel R. van Kooij, ed., *Violence Denied: Violence, Non-Violence and the Rationalization of Violence in South Asian Cultural History* (Leiden: Brill, 1999), pp. 69–103 examines the idea of war as sacrifice in the *Mahābhārata*, while Biardeau (Madeleine Biardeau, 'Ancient Brahmanism, or Impossible Violence', in Denis Vidal, Gilles Tarabout and Eric Meyer, eds, *Violence/Non-violence: Some Hindu Perspectives* (New Delhi: Manohar and Centre de Sciences Humaines, 2003), pp. 85–104) looks at issues related to violence in the *Manu Smṛti* and the *Mahābhārata,* especially at Arjuna's assertion of the impossibility of avoiding violence.
47. *AS* 4.11.11–12; 2.5.17; 2.5.20; 2.29.16.
48. See, for instance, Ebba Koch, *Mughal Art and Imperial Ideology: Collected Essays* (New Delhi: Oxford University Press, 2001).
49. Divyabhanusinh Chavda, personal communication.
50. *Vyasana* can mean vice, calamity or affliction.
51. References to such a sanitised forest occur in *AS* 1.21.23; 2.20.3. *AS* 2.20.4 suggests that the king should, in addition, establish another kind of animal park where animals are welcomed as guests, presumably a sanctuary where they are given protection. Elsewhere (*AS* 2.26.1), Kauṭilya talks of fines that should be imposed on those who kill animals whose killing has been prohibited or those that inhabit the king's reserved park.
52. That this idea was well known is evident in Kālidāsa's *Raghuvaṁśa* (9.53) where Daśaratha is described as going to hunt in a sanitised forest (described in much less detail). It is no coincidence that calamity befalls him there, when he inadvertently kills the son of a blind ascetic, resulting in the curse that leads to the subsequent tragic events. For what could be more graphic than this as an illustration of the calamities that would befall kings who fell prey to the vice of excessive hunting?
53. Ali, *Courtly Culture and Political Life in Early Medieval India*, pp. 99–102.
54. The six *guṇa*s are *sandhi* (alliance), *vigraha* (war), *yāna* (marching on an expedition), *āsana* (staying in one place), *saṁśraya* (seeking shelter), and *dvaidhībhāva* (a double policy of *sandhi* with one king and *vigraha* with another).
55. Kauṭilya too uses the categories of *prakāśayuddha, kūṭayuddha* and *mantrayuddha,* but he adds a fourth one—*tūṣṇīmyuddha* (silent war), which involves the use of secret practices and instigation through secret agents (*AS* 7.6.41).
56. Others differed on this point. For instance, Kāmandaka cites Bharadvāja as stating that a king should fight against the enemy with all his might, like a

lion, and that it was possible for a weaker king to outmanouvre a stronger one through sheer courage (*NS* 9.56).

57. The *Arthaśāstra* too gives primacy to *mantraśakti* (*AS* 9.1.29).
58. The king, through *daṇḍa*, has to restrain his subjects running after vices (*viṣayas*) (*NS* 2.43).
59. It should be noted that a very basic level of self-control is being advocated here. For instance, higher than control over the senses is *ātmajaya* (control over the self).
60. Ali, *Courtly Culture and Political Life in Early Medieval India*, pp. 138, 241, 245.
61. It features, for instance, in *sāṁkhya, yoga,* Upaniṣadic, Buddhist, and Jaina thought.
62. *AS* 1.7.3 in fact describes the life of such a *rājarṣi.*
63. The continuities and variations in the classical model of kingship can be seen clearly in studies of the imaging of kingship in inscriptions belonging to different centuries and to different regions and sub-regions. For an analysis of the details and patterns revealed in the inscriptions of ancient and early medieval Orissa, see Upinder Singh, *Kings, Brāhmaṇas and Temples in Orissa: An Epigraphic Study,* AD *300–1147* (New Delhi: Munshiram Manoharlal, 1994), pp. 82–122.
64. I disagree completely with scholars who argue (e.g., Ghoshal, *A History of Indian Political Ideas,* p. 385) that the politics of texts such as the *Arthaśāstra* and *Nītisāra* is devoid of ethics. In fact, ethics is acknowledged in ancient Indian discourse on politics.
65. Reading between the lines also helps. Doing this, Charles Malamoud ('Remarks on Dissuasion in Ancient India', in Denis Vidal, Gilles Tarabout and Eric Meyer, eds, *Violence/Non-violence: Some Hindu Perspectives*, pp. 209–218) identifies elements of what we call dissuasion in the *Arthaśāstra.*
66. Denis Vidal, Gilles Tarabout, and Eric Meyer, eds., *Violence/Non-violence: Some Hindu Perspectives*, p. 17.
67. This is the focus of my larger study. For a discussion of different views within the Brahmanical tradition towards the specific issue of violence in sacrifice, within and across various periods of history, see Houben ('To kill or not to kill the sacrificial animal (*yajña-paśu*)?'). For an extremely interesting discussion of representations of war in the *Kaliṅkattupparaṇi*, a 12th century Tamil text, see Ali, 'Violence, Gastronomy and the Meanings of War in Medieval South India'.
68. For instance, Kane mentions several texts on *nīti* such as the *Nītinirṇīti* of Yogghama, *Nītiprakāśa* of Janamejaya, *Nītivākyāmṛta* and *the Śukranītisāra.* Sections of the last mentioned of these may be as late as the 19th century (P.V. Kane, *History of Dharmaśāstra [Ancient and Mediaeval Religious and Civil Law in India]*, Vol. 1, Part I; 1990, Revised and enlarged second reprint edition, Poona, pp. 155, 265, 277, 288).

12

The Power of a Poet: Kingship, Empire, and War in Kālidāsa's *Raghuvaṁśa*

The main methodological emphasis of this article is that ideas related to political power in ancient India need to be analysed through a close and nuanced reading of texts in their entirety, in a manner that is sensitive to their genre as well as to the demands of historical inquiry. These ideas are located in texts such as the epics, political treatises, *kāvya,* Dharmaśāstra, architectural treatises and story literature, as well as in inscriptions, art and monumental remains. All these sources situate kingship within a consciously and carefully constructed larger cultural matrix, but how the culturally configured political constructs emerged and developed are processes that need detailed investigation. In fact, a study of kingdoms and empires which looks at their conceptual universe 'from within' should complement the historian's general approach towards ancient political systems, which is to view them from the 'outside', using the categories and conceptual vocabulary of history, anthropology and sociology.

Politics intruded into ancient texts in varying degrees and forms, and while their political discourse had certain shared elements, there were also differences, depending on genre, temporal and historical context,

---

This chapter was previously published in *Indian Historical Review* 38 (2), 2011, pp. 177–198.

and authorial perspective. Political theorists dealt with political issues directly, while litterateurs dealt with them within the aesthetic conventions and idiom of *kāvya.* Therefore, a historical analysis of *kāvya* has to take the aesthetic and representational dimension into account.[1] Poetry and drama were meant to entertain and enthrall, and *kāvya* was often distinguished from *śāstra,* but the didactic potential of *kāvya* was also recognised in certain works on poetics. In fact, the aesthetic and narrative elements of *kāvya* would have made it a very powerful medium for the dissemination of ideas and ideals related to political power among the participants and consumers of literary culture. The specific aim of this article is to explore the political discourse of an extremely influential *mahākāvya,* Kālidāsa's *Raghuvaṁśa,*[2] and to investigate the manner in which it dealt with important contemporary political issues related to kingship, empire and war in ways that were to some extent similar and to some extent very different from political treatises such as Kauṭilya's *Arthaśāstra* and Kāmandaka's *Nītisāra.*[3]

The *Raghuvaṁśa* can be read in many ways. It is an exceptionally fine piece of Sanskrit poetry, a brilliant poetic narrative of the kings of a famous royal lineage, with a vast and varied cast of characters and many dramatic events. But the importance of the work does not only lie in its literary qualities. Along with the *Rāmāyaṇa, Mahābhārata,* Bhāsa's plays and the early inscriptional *praśasti*s, the *Raghuvaṁśa* was among the earliest literary works that dealt directly with political issues. In fact, it provided one of the earliest holistic, authoritative and aesthetically refined delineations of what may be described as the mid-first millennium classical Indian ideal of kingship (this 'classical' model did subsequently undergo some changes over time and space) expressed in the form of high literature. This *mahākāvya* was, hence, an important part of the political processes of the time, namely the creation and consolidation of mature monarchical structures and empires.

Issues related to the exercise and perpetuation of power are central to the *Raghuvaṁśa* and it is political poetry of the highest order.[4] As a political manifesto, the power and influence of this text surpassed Kālidāsa's other works,[5] and extended far beyond the Indian subcontinent. There are references to the *Raghuvaṁśa* in Cambodian inscriptions ranging from the 7th to the 10th century, and an allusion to the work has been traced in an 8th century Javanese inscription.[6] Unravelling the rich political discourse of this poetic work is an important key to understanding its cultural significance and influence; the ideas, locales, characters, events and imagery of the *mahākāvya,* therefore, deserve careful analysis.

The Poet, His Subject and His Sources

A brilliant exponent of the Vaidarbha (western Indian) style of writing, noted for its clarity and mellifulous flow, Kālidāsa had acquired a reputation as one of the literary masters by the 7th century CE.[7] As is the case with most *kavis*, there is more legendary material than biographic detail about him. When exactly he lived and wrote is the subject of much debate; however, a 4th/5th century date seems acceptable and a connection with the city of Ujjayinī is likely.[8] The implied audience of the *Raghuvaṁśa* (as is the case with all *kāvya*) included members of the political elite and those sections of urban society, including poets, courtesans and others, who had a familiarity with the language and its literature.

The theme of the *Raghuvaṁśa* is a royal lineage, one descended from Manu, the legendary progenitor of all earthly kings, but its special focus is on a sequence of kings from Dilīpa to Agnivarṇa. The text consists of 19 *sargas* (cantos). There is a theory that the last two *sargas* are spurious, principally on the ground that going by the conventions of Sanskrit *kāvya*, Kālidāsa could not possibly have intended his work to end on such a pessimistic note. However, poets did sometimes transgress conventions and, as will be argued further in this chapter, the ending of the work has a certain logic.

Various scholars have suggested that Raghu's *digvijaya* (conquest of the quarters), an episode described in great detail in the *Raghuvaṁśa*, was based on the military campaigns and career of one of the kings of the Gupta dynasty—Samudragupta, Candragupta II or Kumāragupta.[9] The possible connections between the Allahabad *praśasti* of Samudragupta (c. 350–70 CE) and the *Raghuvaṁśa* are of special interest. Historians have generally focused their attention on identifying the rulers and places mentioned in lines 13–20 of the *praśasti* in order to reconstruct the contours of Samudragupta's empire. But the inscription has far greater importance than this. Sheldon Pollock perceptively observes that it reflects a new conception of imperial sovereignty, one that was quasi-universal within a bounded geopolitical space; the *praśasti* came to have enormous influence within the subcontinent as well as in Southeast Asia, via Kālidāsa's account of Raghu's *digvijaya,* which, he argues, was modeled on the inscription.[10]

The *digvijaya* of Raghu in the *Raghuvaṁśa* is, in fact, a much more clearly enunciated and detailed *parikramā* (circumambulation) of the subcontinent than is the description of the campaigns of Samudragupta in the Allahabad *praśasti,* and even if indeed Kālidāsa had the inscription before him as a model, it must have been in a general rather than a specific sense. Given the larger scope for the expression and elaboration of political ideas and the stronger narrative component in *kāvya* as opposed to epigraphic *praśasti,* the *Raghuvaṁśa* offers a more detailed, developed and complex model of the conquest of the quarters, and indeed of kingship and sovereignty, than the inscription does. Further, Kālidāsa's work offers a fine, detailed literary exposition of not only ideal kingship, but also of the intersection between these ideals and the realities and problems of monarchical power politics.

The Vālmīki *Rāmāyaṇa* was clearly a major direct source for Kālidāsa's account of Rāma's story in the *Raghuvaṁśa.*[11] In both works, Vālmīki appears as an important character in the events. He is the *muni* who gives Sītā refuge and solace in his *āśrama* and helps her rear her sons Kuśa and Lava. Kālidāsa refers to Vālmīki as the *ādi kavi* (*Raghuvaṁśa [RV]* 15.41).[12] In a clear allusion to the *Rāmāyaṇa's* reference to the birth of the *śloka* metre in the Bālakāṇḍa, he is described as the *kavi* whose grief on beholding a bird killed by a hunter burst out in heroic verse (*RV* 14.70). In both works, it is Vālmīki who teaches Kuśa and Lava to sing his first poetic composition (*RV* 15.33). There is also a direct reference (*RV* 15.63) to Rāma's sons wandering around, and on their teacher's instructions, singing his composition, the *Rāmāyaṇa,* in various places.

And yet, there are many differences between the narrative of the two texts. The principal difference is that the *Rāmāyaṇa's* focus is on Rāma, whereas in the *Raghuvaṁśa,* although Rāma plays an important role (he is the subject of 5 out of the 19 *sargas,* namely *Sargas* 11–15), Kālidāsa tells the story not of a single king but of a *vaṁśa* (as in many other ancient texts, this word is used both in the sense of clan as well as lineage), the sun-born Ikṣvāku clan. The origins of this clan are traced to the mythical Manu, but Kālidāsa's focus is on eight kings—Dilīpa, Raghu, Aja, Daśaratha, Rāma, Kuśa, Atithi and Agnivarṇa—and his narrative ends with an unnamed queen, the pregnant widow of Agnivarṇa. It should also be noted that the genealogies of the *Raghuvaṁśa* and the *Rāmāyaṇa* are different in many respects.[13] Kālidāsa was in fact the first Sanskrit *kavi* to produce a work that focused on a long lineage of kings. (This emphasis on lineage can be correlated with royal inscriptions, which, from the 4th century CE onwards, tend to specify and elaborate on the reigning king's genealogy.) Since the *Raghuvaṁśa* does not deal with one king but a *vaṁśa,* it has a completely different flavour and emphasis compared to the *Rāmāyaṇa.*

Kālidasa's telling of the Rāma story is also different from Vālmlki's for reasons that are in part stylistic and genre specific. Kālidāsa's lengthy descriptions of the seasons and the dalliance of lovers are, more than anything else, part of the stock in trade of the *kavi.* Further, because his work had a much larger canvas, he had to compress Rāma's story considerably; entire incidents are often encapsulated in a single verse. In typical epic style, the *Rāmāyaṇa* contains many stories within stories and much repetition. In the genre of more developed lyric poetry, the *Raghuvaṁśa,* on the other hand, has a more linear narrative, with less use of the 'flash back' technique. This results in a considerable condensing and flattening out of the narrative, as well to some extent of the rich emotional texture of the story, and an occasional repositioning of events.[14]

The religious context within which he was embedded and his own perspective on the Rāma story no doubt also influenced the way in which Kālidāsa moulded its characters and events. Unlike in the *Rāmāyaṇa,* where references to Rāma's divinity are concentrated in the beginning and end of the story, the hero's divinity is constantly emphasised and reiterated throughout the *Raghuvaṁśa's* narrative.[15] But the larger point that must be acknowledged is that like all *kavis,* Kālidāsa used poetic licence; he used it not only in his rendering of Rāma's story but even more so, in his account of the predecessors and successors of Rāma, where he was not dealing with narratives that were as well known. It is these sections that, in fact, gave him the greatest freedom to express his views on kingship.

The Intersection between Poetic and Political Discourse

The political discourse of *kāvyas* and political treatises was embedded in a wider cultural matrix which included frequent appeals to fate and *dharma,* along with the closely allied concepts of the *puruṣārthas, varṇa* and *āśrama.* In the *Raghuvaṁśa,* it is *āśrama* rather than *varṇa* that is repeatedly emphasised. The idealised *āśrama* model of the four life stages applicable to *dvija* males is repeatedly invoked in connection with kingship and is implicit in the description of the lives of many kings, including Dilīpa and Raghu. *Gṛhastha* (the householder's stage) is described as the *āśrama* that enables one to serve all (*RV* 5.10). But the point that is emphasised above all is that the Sūryavaṁśī kings did not cling to the householder stage (*RV* 7.71).[16] Although he does not use the word *saṁnyāsa* (he does use the words *yati* and *muni*), Kālidāsa valorises the idea that the king should renounce the world in the twilight of his life.

Further, the *Raghuvaṁśa* blends philosophical as well as devotional elements into its discussion of the problems associated with political power. Dārśanic elements, specifically an emphasis on equanimity, detachment and self-control (important in many ancient philosophical schools), occur in the political treatises, but are emphasised much more frequently and strongly in the *kāvya.* The *Raghuvaṁśa* also sketches with much greater clarity than the political treatises the very complex relationship between kingship and the gods; the latter appear as interceders, facilitators, competitors as well as objects of devotion (especially in the case of Viṣṇu). The religious landscape of the *kāvya* also includes a strong belief in the efficacy of the performance of sacrifices, pilgrimage and *vrata*s.

The conceptual vocabulary of the political treatises surfaces frequently in different contexts in the *mahākāvya. Sarga* 17 of the *Raghuvaṁśa* is of special interest as it contains the maximum number of references to the principles of *nīti* (which relates to politics, statecraft, governance). This *sarga* is ostensibly devoted to the reign of Atithi, son of Kuśa, and describes him as an exemplary king who meticulously follows the dictates of *nīti* in order to create peace and prosperity throughout his kingdom. Atithi is, in fact, the only king in the *kāvya* who we see actually engaged in the nitty-gritty of administration with any degree of specificity. Raghu is described as being instructed in *sat* (fair/righteous) and *asat* (unfair/deceitful) policies by the *nayavid* (those learned in statecraft, *RV* 4.10). The etymology of the word *rājan*, derived from the king's pleasing his subjects (*prakṛti rañjanāt*), is given by Kālidāsa (*RV* 4.12), and there are several references to the seven elements of the state. For instance, when Dilīpa arrives at Vasiṣṭha's *āśrama,* he assures the *muni* that all is well with the seven *aṅga*s of his kingdom (*RV* 1.60). There is agreement between the political theorists and Kālidāsa on the need for the king to maintain secrecy; for instance, Dilīpa's *mantra* (counsel) is described as hidden, his gestures and form inscrutable (*RV* 1.20). There are several references to the *upāya*s (expedients) of statecraft and to the *śakti*s of royal power.[17] Another important idea that is common to the political treatises and the *Raghuvaṁśa* is that the king's punishment must be fair and measured. Raghu wins the minds of all his people by being *yuktadaṇḍa* (fair and measured in his punishment), like the southern wind, which neither chills nor burns (*RV* 4.8). The *Raghuvaṁśa* also contains several references to the political theorists' conceptual vocabulary of inter-state relations. Raghu seizes the *arimaṇḍala* (domains of his enemies; *RV* 4.4), Daśaratha stands as the *maṇḍalanābhi* (centre of the circle [of kings], *RV* 9.15), and there is also reference to kings following the *vaitasī vṛtti* (policy of canes/reeds, *RV* 4.35), that is, a flexible policy.

The political theorists had much to say on the *vyasanas* (calamities or vices) that could afflict the various elements of the state, including the four vices to which kings were especially susceptible, namely hunting, gambling, drinking and excessive indulgence in women. The *Raghuvaṁśa* talks of these *vyasanas*, dwelling on the problems posed by the royal addiction to hunting and indulgence in women, but not on gambling or drinking. Although Daśaratha is described as not being addicted to the love of hunting, gambling, wine or women (*RV* 9.7), it turns out he does, in fact, have an inordinate love of the hunt and of women. When this king desires to hunt, Kālidāsa writes that his *sacivas* approved because of the benefits of hunting—namely that this activity imparts skills of marksmanship and the ability to hit moving targets, acquaints one with the outward signs of animals' fear and rage, and improves physical stamina (*RV* 9.53). These are the very benefits of hunting listed in the *Arthaśāstra* and *Nītisāra*. Even more interesting is the fact that Kālidāsa describes Daśaratha as hunting in a sanitised forest, as recommended by Kauṭilya and Kāmandaka.[18]

The *Arthaśāstra* and *Nītisāra* dwell considerably on the dangers that confront the king at all times and on the need for him to exercise constant and supreme vigilance. Although Dilīpa is described in one place as guarding his life, but not out of fear (*RV* 1.21), and Kālidāsa does touch on dangers faced by the king while hunting, the king of this *mahākāvya* does not live a life tormented by a perpetual fear of assassination, especially at the hands of his queens and his sons. In fact, in contrast to his counterpart in the political treatises, the king of the *Raghuvaṁśa* does not fear but embraces familial relationships.

The Emotional Landscape of Kingship

The political treatises and *kāvyas* recognise the importance of the royal household, especially princes and women of the *antaḥpura* (harem) in the personal and political lives of kings. Both also attach importance to the relationship between politics and the emotions, but poetic works such as the *Raghuvaṁśa* have a more detailed and rather different kind of treatment of the affective landscape of the royal domain, which included emotions like love, friendship, jealousy, pity and kindness.[19]

The emphasis of the poets is on positive emotions; hatred and anger are presented as negative emotions to which heroes rarely succumb. Several scholars have pointed to Kālidāsa's skill in describing the tension between *kāma* and *dharma*, especially in the context of kingship; however, it should be noted that in both ancient Indian poetic and political discourse, these elements were not necessarily or always in conflict with each other.

Given the fact that the emotions were central to its art and reception, *kāvya* was especially well equipped to dwell on the affective dimension of politics and to illustrate how political fortunes had to constantly interface with human emotions. In the *Raghuvaṁśa*, the dangers of this interface are revealed mainly in the Rāma episode, when intrigue and rivalry within the *antaḥpura* hurtles the royal family towards disaster. Similarly, Aja's excessive love for his queen Indumatī leads him to neglect his royal duties after her death. Nevertheless, as a general rule, in stark contrast to the political treatises, which are replete with frequent dire warnings of the dangers posed by wives and sons, attachment to close kin is not presented as something to be avoided in *kāvya*. Another difference (and this applies to certain other texts, including the epics) is that in many *kāvya*s, great store is set on the king keeping his promise. The word has to be redeemed at any cost, even at the cost of a kingdom. Although there is no direct discussion of this issue in the political treatises, such an attitude is in contrast to the attitude of political pragmatism espoused by the political theorists.

Love is prominent in the affective landscape of kingship in the *Raghuvaṁśa*. The text abounds in descriptions and allusions to love of various kinds. The foremost is the conjugal love between certain kings of Raghu's lineage and their queens. The only type of marriage described in the *Raghuvaṁśa* is the *svayaṁvara* (Aja–Indumatī, Rāma–Sītā), a type well-suited to the theme of romantic and sexual love. Marriage as a means of forging political alliances is also recognised. The queen is repeatedly likened to the earth, and the king is said to enjoy them both (*RV* 8.1, 8.7, 8.28). Although Kālidāsa demurely cloaks conjugal love with duty, asserting that members of Raghu's *vaṁśa* only married for the sake of offspring (*RV* 1.7), the instances of the intensity of this love suggest that power and passion were not considered incompatible. At the same time, the *kāvya* does make a distinction between proper and improper love.

Of the royal couples, three that stand out by virtue of their detailed treatment are Dilīpa and Sudakṣiṇā, Aja and Indumatī, and Rāma and Sītā. The love between Dilīpa and Sudakṣiṇā, a Magadha princess, consists of a mixture of sensual love, tenderness and a mutual commitment to their larger duty towards the *vaṁśa*. Dilīpa has many wives in his harem, but Sudakṣiṇā is his *mahiṣī* (chief queen), the one he loves most, the one he wants a son from. When the royal couple travels to Vasiṣṭha's *āśrama,* Dilīpa is courteous to a fault towards his queen. Sudakṣiṇā, for her part, is the ideal wife, performing her role in the *vrata* perfectly and without complaint. The *dampati* (couple) share a tender, loving relationship and some of the most beautiful verses in the *Raghuvaṁśa* are those that describe Dilīpa's tenderness towards Sudakṣiṇā as they move towards the forest, or as he lovingly ministers to her pregnant cravings. In many ways, theirs is a perfect love, not marred by any enduring calamity. There is a crisis—sonlessness—but that is overcome through joint performance of a *vrata;* the marriage reaches fruition with the birth of Raghu, and the couple's mutual love (*prema*) grows even more intense thereafter (*RV* 3.24).

Although ultimately sacrificed at the altar of kingly duty, the Rāma–Sītā relationship emerges out of a *svayaṁvara* and the sensual nature of this love, specifically Rāma's love for Sītā (and not vice versa) is described by Kālidāsa in several verses.[20] Rāma's desire and love for his wife are eloquently described in *Sarga* 13, as the couple head homewards on the aerial car *puṣpaka,* where Kālidāsa brilliantly weaves Rāma's description of the terrain they traverse with allusions to how he had longed for her in her absence (*RV* 13.26–32).

In contrast, the Aja–Indumatī relationship is based on excessive sexual love. This is clear from the first time they set eyes on each other, during Indumatī's *svayaṁvara,* which is described in great detail by Kālidāsa in *Sarga* 6. All the suitors are bowled over by Indumatī's beauty, and Kālidāsa makes it clear that Indumatī too is looking for perfect physical beauty, which she instantly finds in Aja. It is most definitely intense mutual attraction at first sight. The excessively strong sexual and emotional bonds between Aja and Indumatī are reflected in the fact that Aja wants to kill himself when she dies. Another sharper instance of improper love is Agnivarṇa's love, or rather lust. Excessively, incessantly and indiscriminately bestowed on queens, courtesans and dancing girls, it clearly transcends the limits of perceived propriety.

The *Raghuvaṁśa* reveals a tension between the reality of the polygynous royal household and the monogamous ideal. The former is alluded to in the account of Dilīpa's reign but its implications for creating conflict within the royal household and the larger political structure emerge vividly in the events during Daśaratha's reign. The monogamous ideal is best represented by Rāma, who spurns Sūrpaṇakhā's advances by telling her that he already has a wife, and more poignantly, in the fact that he does not remarry after repudiating Sītā and uses her golden effigy to take her place in the sacrifices he performs. Although most kings of Raghu's lineage are polygynous, there is no doubt that it is the ideal of the loving, dutiful monogamous couple that Kālidāsa presents as the ideal model.

The love between father and son is also an important part of the affective landscape of kingship in the *Raghuvaṁśa.* Dilīpa's love for his son Raghu is described in tender detail, as is the reciprocal love between Raghu and his son Aja. Of course, Rāma's love and sense of duty towards Daśaratha is the most eloquent example of filial love. Fraternal love, too, is valorised and is best represented in Bharata's love for Rāma, which overrides his desire to be king. In fact, the brotherly love (*saubhrātra*) between Kuśa and his brothers is described as hereditary (*RV* 16.1).

The emotional landscape of kingship includes the mutual love between the king and his *prajā* (subjects). Raghu arouses *prīti* (love, attachment) in his subjects (*RV* 4.61). Kuśa is called *paurasakha* (friend of the city-dwellers, *RV* 16.37). But the most graphic illustration of the *prajā's* extreme attachment to their ruler is their following Rāma into the Sarayū river out of love (*vātsalya*) for their beloved king (*RV* 15.100–101).

Friendship mingles with love and permeates several relationships in the *Raghuvaṁśa.* When faced with the lion who threatens to kill the cow under his protection, Dilīpa argues that since they have become friends (*RV* 2.35), the lion surely cannot refuse his request to take his life instead. Friendship is also invoked in the relationship between husband and wife—Aja calls Indumatī his *sakhī* (*RV* 8.67). The account of Rāma's story is especially rich in references to friendship. There is friendship (*sakhya*) between Rāma and Sugrīva; Vibhīṣaṇa is Rāma's *priyasuhṛd* (beloved friend). Rāma is a treasure-house of friendship to his friends, distributing houses, gifts and other things to them (*RV* 14.15). Vālmīki is a friend of Daśaratha and Janaka (*RV* 15.31), and performs the rites for Sītā's sons out of affection for his friends (*RV* 15.31).

In its elaboration of the emotional terrain of kingship, the *Raghuvaṁśa* (along with other *kāvya*s and the epics) points to a notion of royal deportment and propriety that is alien to that of the political treatises. Political expediency and the single-minded pursuit of power are not the prime factors or focus in the king's life. The ethics and aesthetics of politics are subject to emotional pulls of various kinds of relationships, principally, but not exclusively, those based on kinship. And yet, paradoxically, as we shall see further on, the delineation of this rich emotional landscape, ultimately provides the background for a valorisation of detachment and renunciation.

The Qualities of the Ideal King

The epithets, attributes and actions of the Ikṣvāku kings in Kālidāsa's *Raghuvaṁśa* became a powerful embodiment and expression of the ideals of mid-first millennium Indian kingship.[21] The work combined many different aspects of kingship, especially the martial, ritual and benevolent. The centrality of the royal lineage is constantly emphasised and there are four kings who stand out for detailed description of their exemplary qualities and conduct—Dilīpa, Raghu, Rāma and Atithi. It can be argued that Raghu, after whom the *kāvya* and the lineage are known, is the real hero, as he corresponds most closely and directly to the ideals laid out at the beginning of the *kāvya.* Of course, Rāma too is very important, but unlike Raghu, he is a god-king, who can be only partially emulated by his human counterparts.

Much has been written without adequate reflection on the idea of divine kingship in ancient India. As mentioned earlier, the *Raghuvaṁśa* reflects a very complex understanding of the relationship between kingship and the gods. The possibilities of tension, even conflict, between the heavenly and kingly realms are reflected most dramatically in Indra's determination to prevent the performance of Dilīpa's hundredth *aśvamedha* by carrying away the sacrificial horse, and *yuvarāja* Raghu's fierce battle with that god in the third *sarga.* A distinction should be made between kings who are compared with gods, those who embody divine elements, and those who are full-fledged gods. Comparisons with the gods are very frequent in the *Raghuvaṁśa,* very often with Indra, but also with other deities such as Kāma, Kubera, Kārttikeya, Viṣṇu, Varuṇa and the Āśvins. Even Agnivarṇa, a king who is uttterly devoid of virtues, is described as excelling Indra and Kubera (*RV* 19.15). Such analogies are obviously to be understood with reference to exalting the station of the king, not to his individual traits or capacities.

Kings are also described as having elements of godliness in them. So, for instance, we are told that the guardians of the four quarters entered the embryo of Raghu (*RV* 2.75) and that Dilīpa was a portion of the three-eyed god Śiva (*RV* 3.66).[22] But there is a difference between these kings and Rāma, who is a full-fledged god (Viṣṇu) in human form and whose actions are determined and, therefore, justified by his godliness. There is never any ambiguity about Rāma's divinity in the *Raghuvaṁśa.* In the tenth *sarga,* which is suffused with the sentiment of Viṣṇu *bhakti,* Viṣṇu declares his intention to be born as the son of Daśaratha in order to destroy Rāvaṇa (*RV* 10.44). (The other three brothers too are described as portions of the great god.) Rāma's extraordinary prowess is revealed in the eleventh *sarga* and the climax of these events is his triumph over the demon Rāvaṇa. Once his work on earth is complete, Rāma plunges into the Sarayū river and ascends to heaven; Viṣṇu enters his own body, the refuge of all the worlds (*RV* 15.100–103).

Kālidāsa weaves into his poem an astounding range of titles, epithets and attributes signifying the various aspects of kingship. These include *rājan, rājendu, goptṛ, bhartṛ* and *mahārāja.* But what is distinctive about the kings of Raghu's *vaṁśa* is that their political paramountcy is recognised by a congeries of lesser kings. This paramountcy is indicated by titles such as *samrāṭ* (emperor), *gurunṛpa* (lord of kings), *sāmrājyadīkṣita* (installed in imperium), *jagadekanātha* (the sole lord of the world) and *rājñāih rājā* (king of kings).[23] Royal power is personified as Śrī or Lakṣmī, the king's fickle, metaphorical divine spouse.

The most important elements in Kālidāsa's construct of ideal kingship are laid forth in five verses right at the beginning of the *kāvya,* where the traits of the members of Raghu's *vaṁśa* are enumerated (*RV* 1.5–1.9). These include qualities of purity, valour, perseverance, generosity, justice, watchfulness and measured speech. Kings of this *vaṁśa* rule over the entire earth up to the ocean; their chariot reaches high up to heaven; they perform sacrifices in the prescribed manner; they acquire wealth in order to renounce it; they seek victory only for the sake of fame; they marry only for the sake of progeny. It is not individual virtues, but a balance of many virtues and accomplishments that is emphasised.

The specific *dharma* of the king is *kṣatra dharma,* in which protection of the subjects is a prime ingredient. The Kṣatriya is renowned in all the worlds as one who saves (others) from destruction (*RV* 2.53). The king is a *rakṣitṛ, śaraṇya* (one who gives refuge), *āryagṛhya* (supporter of the good/cultured people). Raghu is described in one place as lord of the *varṇa*s and *āśrama*s (*varṇāśramāṇāṁ guru*) (*RV* 5.19). There are several references to the close relationship between Kṣatriya kings and Brāhmaṇa *ṛṣi*s, although the Paraśurāma episode highlights the tension and conflict between the Kṣatriya and Brāhmaṇa *varṇa*s. But the king as maintainer of the order of *varṇa*s and *āśrama*s is not an aspect of kingship that is especially emphasised by Kālidāsa till he comes to Rāma. Rāma is described as having the duty of maintaining the *varṇa*s and *āśrama*s and as being alert in watching over the conduct of their members (*RV* 14.67,85). He is also the only king of Raghu's *vaṁśa* who is described as specifically punishing someone for transgressing the *varṇa dharma*—the Śūdra who had dared to perform austerities had to pay a very heavy price.

Apart from his divinity, another aspect that stands out is the fact that, more than any other king of Raghu's lineage, Rāma is a people's king. Other members of Raghu's *vaṁśa* too are protectors and nurturers of their subjects, but the *prajā* assumes a larger than life role in the Rāma story. They follow Rāma around, they share a mutual relationship of love with him, their opinion leads him to banish a beloved queen, and a query from one of them makes the king launch a hunt for the cause of the transgression of *dharma* in his kingdom. The fear of scandal (*apavāda*) or public censure is mentioned in connection with Raghu, Aja and Rāma. Raghu cannot bear the thought that people might say that a supplicant had gone away empty-handed. The grief-stricken Aja wants to ascend his wife's funeral pyre but desists out of fear of public censure. In the case of Rāma, the matter is more grave: he knows Sītā is innocent and pregnant, and yet he cannot bear the whiff of scandal, and banishes his beloved queen. In all these cases, we see duty overriding emotion.

The ideal king is *nayacakṣu*—one who sees with the eyes of *naya* (wise, prudent governance, *RV* 1.55)—and his wisdom and prudence is reflected in many specific aspects of his rule. Like the political treatises, the *Raghuvaṁśa* too emphasises that the ideal king's punishment must be measured and not excessively harsh. Dilīpa punishes the guilty only for the sake of the maintenance of order (*sthiti*) (*RV* 1.25); as a dispenser of justice to his people, he is *yuktadaṇḍa* (one whose punishments are fair and measured). He is also a generous donor, a *mānitārthin* (one who honours supplicants). Kingship has a paternalistic aspect: by virtue of his educating his subjects in *vinaya* and protecting and nurturing them, Dilīpa is like a father to them, their natural parents merely give them birth (*RV* 1.24). Although the king is a great giver of gifts, on occasion he is reduced to asking for boons, as Dilīpa does before the cow Nandinī. The *kāvya* repeatedly emphasises that the king constitutes a role model for his subjects with respect to proper behaviour. So, for instance, Dilīpa is described as educating his subjects in *vinaya* (*RV* 14.67), an important term in the political vocabulary, which was a cocktail of several things—discipline, good breeding, propriety, humility, modesty, mildness and good behaviour. The benevolence of the king is a general trait and is also expressed ceremonially on certain special occasions. For instance, after his *abhiṣeka,* Atithi orders that prisoners be freed and the death sentence of those awarded capital punishment be commutated. The king's benevolence extends to the animals of his realm as well—it is declared that full-grown bulls are not to be yoked, cows are not be milked, and pet birds such as parrots and others that are confined in cages are to be freed (*RV* 17.19–20).[24]

The *Raghuvaṁśa*'s description of the king's relationship with his *guru* (family preceptor) and Brāhmaṇa *ṛṣis* clearly places them on a pedestal of great respect. The relationship between king and Brahmaṇa *ṛṣi* is presented as one of reciprocity and mutual respect rather than hierarchy. Kings are frequently called on to protect the sacrifices in the *āśrama*s *of ṛṣis;* and it is emphasised that the sacrifices, *mantra*s, blessings and advice of the *ṛṣi*s in turn help maintain the well-being of the kingdom. *Yajña* looms large in the *Raghuvaṁśa* as a pre-eminent aspect of kingship. Dilīpa is *ajasradīkṣāprayata* (constantly engaged in *dīkṣā*s, i.e., for sacrifices). The *Raghuvaṁśa* justifies taxation with reference to *yajña:* Dilīpa milks the earth (a euphemism for realising taxes) for the sake of performing *yajña*s, just as Indra milks the heavens (i.e., creates rain) for the sake of the growth of grain (*RV* 1.26). There are also references to specific sacrifices. The fruits of the conquest of the quarters are surrendered immediately afterwards by Raghu in the performance of a grand *viśvajit* sacrifice. Among the grand sacrifices, the *aśvamedha* is given the greatest prominence—three kings (Dilīpa, Rāma and Atithi) are described as having performed it. Dilīpa performs 99 *aśvamedha*s*;* his hundredth one is interrupted by the god Indra, who is jealous of the fame that this would give the king.

The ideal king is described not only in terms of his actions but also with reference to his inner qualities. That he is capable of detachment is an idea expressed in many places in the *kāvya,* and this is an idea that has both philosophical as well as pragmatic moorings. The kings of the *Raghuvaṁśa* are routinely described as self-controlled, even if their actions indicate them to be otherwise. The king collects wealth, but not out of greed, remains detached while enjoying pleasures, is not attached to vices (*viṣaya*s) (*RV* 1.21, 23); he is *saṁyat,* that is, self-controlled (*RV* 3.20). Raghu does not crave victory, even while on his *digvijaya,* and in fact gives away everything he has in the *viśvajit* sacrifice immediately afterwards. Aja is foremost among the self-controlled (*vaśināmuttama*) (*RV* 8.90). The political treatises such as the *Arthaśāstra* and the *Nītisāra* too emphasise the need for the king to be detached and to control his senses, and they too valorise the *rājarṣi;* but they do not advocate the abdiction of power. The *Raghuvaṁśa* takes the elements of detachment and equanimity to an extreme, advocating complete renunciation of power and the performance of austerities of various kinds towards the end of the king's life, which is quite different from what the political treatises have in mind.

Dilīpa was foremost among kings (*ekapārthiva*) and ruled unrivalled over the entire earth (*ananyaśāsanāmurvī*) as though it was a single town (*RV* 1.30). But that is not the most important aspect of his imperium in the *Raghuvaṁśa.* What is more important is the fact that he is willing to give up the sovereignty of the earth marked by a single umbrella (*ekātapatraṁ jagataḥ prabhutvaṁ, RV* 1.47) for the sake of a cow he has vowed to protect. In this construct of kingship, the true greatness of a king does not lie in his achievement of paramount status (which in itself is not unimportant); it lies in his readiness to spontaneously give it up in the line of pious duty.

It should be noted that many kings of Raghu's line do not die natural deaths. We are told at the beginning of the *kāvya* that the Raghus, at the end of their lives, abandon their bodies through *yoga* (*RV* 1.8). Later, we are told that it was the *kulavrata* of the Ikṣvāku kings to hand over power to their successor in their old age and retire to the forest (*RV* 3.70). This practice had the practical advantage of creating a smooth political transition, but it was essentially rooted in a philosophical matrix and also found a place in the idealised *āśrama* scheme of life stages. Dilīpa drifts off to the forest, and presumably dies a natural death there. Raghu enters life's last *āśrama* and becomes a *yati,* practices *yoga* and meditation, and realizes the ultimate reality. Aja starves himself to death at the confluence of the Gaṅgā and Sarayū. On the completion of his earthly mission, Rāma plunges into the Sarayū along with all his subjects. Nala and Puṣya go off to the forest and attain freedom from rebirth (the latter practices *yoga*). All these details direct attention to the philosophical underpinnings of Kālidāsa's political poetry. In a striking series of verses, the poet describes the parallel paths of king Aja and the renunciant Raghu (*RV* 8.16–25). There is no doubt that Kālidāsa emphasises and valorises renunciation as customary among Raghu's lineage and as a desirable end to a king's life.[25]

Empire and War

The action of the *Raghuvaṁśa* incessantly moves between military marches, the capital city, forest and *tapovana.* These four locales are integral to the conceptualisation of the essential features of kingship and sovereignty that Kālidāsa seeks to convey in his *mahākāvya.* Historians have often dwelt on the dichotomy between *grāma* and *araṇya* in Sanskrit literature.[26] Nevertheless, it must be emphasised that one of the things that must have lent the *Raghuvaṁśa* its enormous normative power and influence was the fact that Kālidāsa knit this and many other very real dichotomies into a harmonious, aesthetically edifying, unified, whole.

One of the important aspects of the *Raghuvaṁśa* as a political manifesto is its very specific and detailed mapping of the subcontinent as a political domain. This mapping takes place three times in the *kāvya*. The first occurs in *Sarga* 4, in the description of Raghu's *digvijaya*, which is the most detailed in terms of its description of the land, its rulers, people and produce. The second occurs in *Sarga* 6, which gives a description of Indumatī's suitors during her *svayaṁvara*. The third occurs in *Sarga* 13, which describes the lands that Rāma and Sītā traverse when they fly back from Laṅkā to Ayodhyā on the *puṣpaka*.

The heroic element is central to the *Raghuvaṁśa's* conception of kingship.[27] War is a natural corollary to kingship, and the reign of a great king must be marked by dazzling military victories. According to *Nāṭyaśāstra* conventions, battle scenes were not to be shown in drama, but they could be described in detail in poetry. Many epithets allude to the king as a great victor, and yet, military power is tempered with righteousness and restraint. Raghu is described as *dharmavijayī* (righteous conqueror, *RV* 4.16), and as one who seeks victory (*vijigīṣu*) but does not crave it (*RV* 1.46). There is also an awareness of devious kinds of war—Atithi is described as seeking alliances with those of medium strength and only attacks an enemy after determining the strength and weakness of his six expedients; although he knows *kūṭayuddha* (deceitful methods of war), he always fights in a righteous manner (*RV* 17.69).

Although the *Raghuvaṁśa* acknowledges that there can be many kings at a given point of time, it also highlights the issue of political paramountcy. There are two references to the term *sāmanta* in the *Raghuvaṁśa* which clearly refer to subordinate rulers, not just neighbouring rulers.[28] The important thing to note is that Raghu's *digvijaya* and the notions of empire and sovereignty that it reflects, do not involve conquest; they involve the demonstration of military superiority by the victor and the acceptance of this by defeated kings. The claim to political paramountcy is also publicly enacted and expressed in the performance of the *aśvamedha*, which is performed by Dilīpa, Rāma and Atithi.

Raghu's *digvijaya* gives a detailed and very specific mapping of the *cakravartikṣetra* (though this word does not occur in the *kāvya*). According to Pollock,[29] Raghu conquers the same territory as Samudragupta, though he moves in the opposite direction. Actually, the Allahabad *praśasti* does not give us a clear idea of the precise directions and sequence of Samudragupta's military campaigns, whereas Kālidāsa's description of Raghu's *digvijaya* (*RV* 4.24–87) is a carefully constructed clockwise circumambulation of the subcontinent. He starts by moving eastward, towards the Eastern Ocean, uprooting kings including those of Suhma, Vaṅga, Utkala and Kaliṅga and the lord of Mahendra mountain on the way. Then he moves southwards along the eastern coast, across the Kāverī, Pāṇḍya country, and the Malaya and Dardura mountains. From here his armies sweep across to the Kerala country and up the western coast to the northwest, where they battle with the Pārasīkas and the Yavanas. Thence, Raghu moves to the north, reaching the Sindhu country, defeating the Hūṇas and Kāmbojas. Then he ascends the Himalayas and fights with the mountain tribes and the Utsavasaṁketas. The last lot of kings who face his wrath are the rulers of Prāgjyotiṣa and Kamarupa. What we have is a mapping of the *cakravartikṣetra* consisting of the entire subcontinent. It is also significant that this mapping is accompanied by reference to the landscape and the produce of these regions, for instance, the betelnut and coconuts of Kaliṅga; the pepper, cardamom and sandalwood trees on the fringes of the Malaya mountain; the pearls of Pāṇḍya country; and the saffron of the Sindhu region. There is the occasional gory description, such as the one of his encounter with the westerners, where he strews the earth with the severed bearded heads of his adversaries (*RV* 4.63). But by and large, graphic descriptions of the violence of war are avoided in favour of abstract aestheticised descriptions of adversaries who are overwhelmed and submit to Raghu; those who are uprooted; others who are uprooted and reinstated; and still others who offer tribute and prostration. There is also reference to Raghu erecting *jayastambha*s (victory pillars) in the spaces between the streams of the Gaṅgā in Vaṅga country (*RV* 4.36).

The perpetual, endemic nature of war in the *Raghuvaṁśa* stands out, as does the constant need to reassert power. Every time a king goes forth on a *digvijaya* or performs an *aśvamedha,* his successor seems to have to do it all over again. The justifications for war include the desire for *digvijaya,* or as corollaries to specific events—for instance, war is inevitable when the jealous suitors attack Aja and his bride Indumatī as they return home. The war between Rāma and Rāvaṇa may seem on the surface to be the result of the abduction of a woman, but it is presented as part of a larger, divine plan. And yet, notwithstanding the importance of victories in battle, Kālidāsa makes it amply clear that kings of Raghu's line seek military success and political paramountcy not for the sake of land or riches (they do not value these things in themselves), but for the sake of *yaśa* (fame).

Thus, the *Raghuvaṁśa* articulates certain important ideas related to war and empire that were to become widely pervasive in the Indian cultural tradition—that empire involved military victories but not necessarily conquests; that the great king won many battles but did not crave victory or its fruits; that having attained victory, he thought nothing of giving up his kingdom and renouncing the world. It is the act of victory and eliciting the acknowledgement of victory, not the actual possession of conquered territories, that is valorised. That is why, having achieved many great victories, a great king could give up his kingdom and walk away, his lustre not only undiminished but actually enhanced.

Flawed Kingship

In spite of his strong idealisation of kingship, Kālidāsa also presents a less than perfect picture of kingship and politics, giving insights into some of the problems associated with monarchical power in mid-first millennium north India. Behind the idealised perfection of the various kings of Raghu's line lurk imperfections, excesses, errors of judgement and addiction to vices. Many of the epithets that are given to kings seem to be routinely bestowed on them without regard to their real character. But there is no doubt that there are good kings and bad kings in the *kāvya;* this is implied in Kālidāsa's statement that the fickleness of Śrī is due to the fault of the person with whom she resides (*RV* 6.41).

As mentioned earlier, the political treatises list four *vyasanas* (vices) that can afflict a king—excessive addiction to alcohol, women, hunting and gambling. Of these, the *Raghuvaṁśa* does not mention gambling, and does not present drinking as a problem. The main focus is on excessive indulgence in women, followed by hunting. The strong warnings about royal vices that are present in the texts on statecraft are absent in the *kāvya,* but the message embedded in the narrative cannot be missed.

Conjugal love and loyalty are prominent in the emotional landscape of the *Raghuvaṁśa.* Three queens are deeply loved by the kings of Raghu's line—Sudakṣiṇā, Indumatī and Sītā. The first two are loved and indulged, the third is loved and abandoned. But the *kāvya* does indicate that excessive love for women is a problem. The best illustration of the unfortunate political fallout of a king's excessive attachment to a queen is reflected in Daśaratha's succumbing to Kaikeyī's scheming, which is an inherent part of the Rāma story. But it also figures in Kālidāsa's description of the reigns of three other kings—Dilīpa, Aja and Agnivarṇa—where the narrative does not necessarily demand it. The curse that almost leads to the extinction of the lineage is triggered off because Dilīpa is eager to unite with his queen, who had just bathed after her menstruation, ostensibly for the production of a son. The potential calamity that this brings on the lineage is averted due to Vasiṣṭha's timely intervention and the arduous *vrata* Dilīpa performs by serving the celestial cow Surabhī's daughter Nandinī for twenty-one days.

Aja's attachment to his queen Indumatī is more excessive than Dilīpa's to Sudakṣiṇā, and has more unmitigated and problematic results. Although Kālidāsa bestows many of the stock epithets of self-restraint on Aja, he also hints at his sensual nature (*RV* 5.65, 5.63). As events unfold, it becomes abundantly clear that this king's character was marked by an excess of emotion, specifically filial and sensual love. Aja begs his father Raghu not to retire to the forest, according to the custom of the kings of his lineage, when he desires to do so. He is also excessively attached to his wife Indumatī, who, unknown to him is actually an *apsarā* named Hariṇī who has been cursed to an earthly existence by the *ṛṣi* Tṛṇabindu. What identifies Aja's love as excessive is the fact that when she dies, he is inclined to ascend his dead wife's funeral pyre, and refrains from doing so only because of his fear of the *prajā's* reproach (*RV* 8.72). He is inconsolable, grieves for his dead wife ceaselessly, and lives on for eight long years only out of duty, waiting for his son Daśaratha to attain maturity. When Aja falls ill, he sees it as a boon, and handing over the throne to his son, he starves himself to death at the confluence of the Gaṅgā and Sarayū. He is finally united with his wife and dallies happily with her in the groves of Nandana.

Aja's flaw was passed on to his son Daśaratha, who overlooked the rights of his eldest son Rāma by succumbing to the ambitions of a beloved wife Kaikeyī. The vice of hunting is also prominent in the *Raghuvaṁśa's* narrative here. Daśaratha dies of grief due to the curse that had been placed on him as a result of a wrong-doing committed by him while hunting, and Dhruvasaṁdhi (one of the later kings of the line) is killed by a lion while engaged in this pursuit.

The second last ruler, Agnivarṇa, whose character and activities are described in great detail in *Sarga* 19, is a debauch, addicted to pleasures and completely indifferent to performing his kingly duties. His harem is in constant tumult due to his excessive sensual indulgence. He dallies with his servant girls, lusts after *nartakī*s (dancing girls) and constantly searches for newer objects of satisfaction. His wives deny him sex due to jealousy. He is a night bird, who enjoys the pleasure of touch; he enjoys music, dance and wine; and he is a skilled dancer, adept in the three modes of dance. He swings on swings with women and paints their feet. The state of his bed, marked with the powder of flowers, a wilted garland, snapped waist-bands and vermillion dye reveals his incessant indulgence in the pleasures of love-making. Ironically, in spite of having many wives and being addicted to sensual pleasure, Agnivarṇa does not have any sons. He falls prey to a terrible sickness due to his over-indulgence and still continues to indulge.[30] The result is a political crisis. Agnivarṇa's ministers have to cover up for his dissolute ways and for his sickness. He ultimately dies of disease, and his *mantrī*s, in consultation with his *purodhas* (*purohita*), swiftly and furtively throw him onto a funeral pyre in the palace garden. It makes perfect sense that this masterly poetic discourse on kingship should describe both the heights of perfection that a king should aspire to as well as the depths of depravity to which he could sink

Problems of Political Power

In the course of a narrative covering the reigns of many kings, apart from the *vyasana*s that can afflict monarchs, Kālidāsa also touches on several other problems related to kingship. As is the case in the epics, the central problem is that of succession, especially the anxiety about the production of heirs. In fact, the work begins with a desire for an heir and ends with the expectation of one. Other issues related to succession include the principle of primogeniture, harem intrigues, periods of regency during the reign of minor kings, and women rulers.

The *kāvya* emphasises the patrilineage and shows a preference for the principle of primogeniture as the most appropriate means for a smooth perpetuation of the lineage and political power. Of course, the principle of primogeniture is central to the narrative of the Rāma story, and not only to Kālidāsa's rendering of it, and the fact that the principle is transgressed in the story suggests that such transgressions did occur, but that there was a strong view which upheld the rights of the eldest son. But such a view was not universal, or at least not universally emphasised. This is clear from the fact that while the political treatises distinguish between good sons and bad sons and talk of how to deal with the latter, they do not emphasise the inalienable rights of the eldest son to succeed to the throne. The *Arthaśāstra* (1.17.52–53) briefly mentions that except in case of a calamity, sovereignty passing on to the eldest son is praiseworthy, and goes on to say that otherwise, the kingdom should belong to the royal *kula*, for a *kula-saṅgha* is difficult to conquer. The *Nītisāra*, for its part, does not discuss the principle that should govern succession.

The *Raghuvaṁśa* offers instances of smooth as well as problematic successions. The ideal norm that is prescribed and emphasised repeatedly is for the king to retire to the forest after handing over the reigns of power to his son and successor. This is what great kings such as Dilīpa and Raghu do. But there are more problematic situations, when the kingdom becomes especially vulnerable. This includes the accession of minor heirs: Sudarśana is just six years old when he becomes king, and Kālidāsa evocatively tells us how subordinate kings bowed before him in spite of the fact that his feet dangled above his golden foot-stool (*RV* 18.41). Ministers play an important role in problematic situations, as they did at the end of Agnivarṇa's reign, when they covered up his illness, reassured the subjects, and ultimately, secretly cremated him. Further, it should be noted that the narrative recognises that when male heirs are unavailable, women rulers can take over—the *Raghuvaṁśa* ends with a pregnant widow on the throne of Kosala.

Like other poets and thinkers, Kālidāsa underlines the inherent instability of conquest and power in frequent remarks about the fickleness of Śrī, the feminine divine personification of royal power. Challenges to the king's power can take the form of jealous rival kings, best illustrated in the narrative of events following the *svayaṁvara* of Indumatī, when the rival suitors (of whom there are many) get together and waylay the marriage party as it moves towards Ayodhyā, and a gory battle ensues. Similarly, when Rāma is exiled and Daśaratha dies, we are told that the kingdom of Kosala became the bait for foes who eagerly watched for its flaws.

Many political problems are glossed over, perhaps in order to offer a normative model for relationships within the royal household. The relationship between kingship and kinship is a central issue. Unlike the political treatises which frankly warn of the dangers posed to the king by the princes, in the *Raghuvaṁśa*, we see in the Rāma story an edifying picture of exceptional filial piety and intense fraternal love. The relationships between kings, wives and sons range from cordiality to intense love. However, the story of Rāma reveals the political complexities and importance of harem intrigues, and valorises the smothering of affective elements due to the dictates of public political propriety.

Conclusions

Notwithstanding strands of commonality, ancient Indian 'normative' discourse on kingship was multi-layered and variegated, depending on genre, period and authorial perspective. *Kāvya* (along with the epics) introduced a narrative and aesthetic element into political discourse, offering normative perspectives on the ideals of kingship but also revealing how these norms were transgressed, as well as offering insights into the problems involved in the exercise of power. Within this genre of texts, the *Raghuvaṁśa* has great importance because of the comprehensiveness and elegance with which it painted the portrait of the ideal king, weaving together his essential attributes among which military victories, the performance of *yajña*s, devotion to *dharma*, a complex relationship with the gods, veneration of the *ṛṣi*s, benevolence towards the subjects, detachment and self-control stand out. Kālidāsa's representation of the kingdom seamlessly knits together city, palace, forest and *tapovana* into an interacting and interdependent whole. These locales are also imbued with enormous politico-cultural significance, and the ways in which they are represented may reflect not only an acknowledgement of their importance but an attempt to transform dangerous or problematic spaces into benign ones. It is the creation of such an all-encompassing imperial universe couched in brilliant Sanskrit poetry that gave the *Raghuvaṁśa* its great importance in India and in Southeast Asia.

Many aspects of this model of ideal kingship are out of place in the world of the political treatises such as the *Arthaśāstra* and the *Nītisāra*—for instance, the immutability of the promise, filial obedience and the value that is placed on the *prajā's* opinion. The *Raghuvaṁśa* took greater and more positive cognisance of kinship relationships (especially within the royal household) and the emotions these were tied up with. *Kāvya* moulded politics to conform to the aesthetic conventions and aims of the genre, but it did not do so in a contextual vacuum, nor was its impact confined to the literary domain. By bringing out the constant intersection of the personal and the political, it in fact draws attention to an important aspect of monarchical power politics in ancient times—the importance of the royal household—one which has surprisingly not been adequately noted by most historians who have studied ancient Indian states.[31]

If the *Raghuvaṁśa* directs attention to the problems of kingship, it also points to solutions. These include following the dictates of *Kṣatriya dharma;* performing *vrata*s; devotion to the *ṛṣi*s; the cultivation of virtues, especially of self-control; the avoidance of *vyasana*s; and most important, the voluntary renunciation of power. The military ambit of the exemplary king is a *digvijaya* of the subcontinent, but the notion of empire (*sāmrājya*) that we encounter in the *Raghuvaṁśa* is one that involves victory but not necessarily conquest. The ideology of the historical empires of ancient and early medieval India needs to be reconsidered in the light of this fact. Further, while victorious wars are a necessary aspect of the rule of a great king, the greatest kings follow up their martial victories by renouncing the fruits of those victories. Renunciation—towards the end of life—is a central aspect of the model of ideal kingship in the *Raghuvaṁśa.*[32]

Many features of the *Raghuvaṁśa's* representation of 'classical' Indian kingship endured for centuries; but influential and enduring as this vision was, it was not the only one. Echoes of these ideas can be seen in many texts and inscriptions of succeeding centuries, but the idea of the king as renouncer does not seem to have been an important part of the ideology of kingship in the long term. Further, we know from a variety of sources that in early medieval India, revenue-free grants of land to Brāhmaṇas and the patronage of temples—not part of the *Raghuvaṁśa's* template of kingship—became important aspects of the ideology and practice of kingship. A close and careful reading of different types of sources, in a manner that is sensitive to the features of their genre, seeking to identify elements of similarity and difference and continuity and change, will reveal how the theory and practice of ancient Indian kingship developed historically over time and across regions.

Acknowledgements

I would like to thank Vijay Tankha for his useful suggestions and comments on this chapter.

Notes

1. Among recent important works that deal sensitively with *kāvya* as a source of history are Daud Ali, *Courtly Culture and Political Life in Early Medieval India* (New Delhi: Foundation Books, 2006); and Shonaleeka Kaul, *Imagining the Urban: Sanskrit and the City in Early India* (New Delhi: Permanent Black, 2010). My own approach differs principally in its insistence that texts, especially those written over a thousand years or so, cannot be treated as a homogeneous unit for historical analysis; each text needs to be looked at carefully

and closely, in order to identify not only commonalities but also differences in perspectives, ideas and contexts.

2. The published sources of the text used for this study are the *Raghuvaṁśa-mahākāvya* with Mallinātha's commentary, and *vyākhyā* and Hindi translation by Acharya Dharadatta Mishra (New Delhi: Motilal Banarsidass, [1974] 2004); and C. R. Devadhar, ed. and trans., *Raghuvaṁśa of Kālidāsa* (New Delhi: Motilal Banarsidass, [1985] 2005). While I have consulted the translations in both these works, this article is essentially based on my own reading and translation. In this article, the terms *kāvya* and *mahākāvya* have both been used for the *Raghuvaṁśa*.
3. Many historians accept R. P. Kangle's argument that the core of the *Arthaśāstra* was composed in the early Maurya period during the last quarter of the 4th century BCE (R. P. Kangle, *The Kauṭilīya Arthaśāstra*, Part III (Mumbai: University of Bombay, 1965), pp. 59–115), but interpolations and recasting may have extended into the early centuries CE. Others are persuaded by Thomas R. Trautmann's statistical analysis of word frequencies in the *Arthaśāstra* (Thomas R. Trautmann, *Kauṭilīya and the Arthaśāstra: A Statistical Investigation of the Authorship and Evolution of the Text* (Leiden: E. J. Brill, 1971), which suggests multiple authors. Trautmann suggests that Book 2 may have been completed by c. 150 CE, and the final compilation of the entire text by c. 250 CE. More recently, Patrick Olivelle (*King, Governance and Law in ancient India*: Delhi, Oxford University Press, 2013) has suggested that while the prehistory of the work may go back to the mid-1st century BCE, the first major redaction (which he calls the Kauṭilya redaction) was composed between c. 50–125 CE, and the second one (which he calls the Śhastric Redaction) to c. 175–300 CE. The date of Kāmandaka's *Nītisāra* is also debated; a date sometime between c. 500–700 CE seems reasonable.
4. Sheldon Pollock has rightly emphasised the importance of exploring the 'political imagination' and has underlined the close connection between *kāvya, praśasti,* and *rājya* (*The Language of the Gods in the World of Men*). He talks of the 'poetry of polity' and has described the royal *praśasti* as 'public poetry' (Pollock, *The Language of the Gods in the World of Men*, pp. 135, 14). The extent to which the *praśasti* was 'public' can, however, be questioned.
5. The fact that there are about 40 known commentaries on the *Raghuvaṁśa,* in contrast to the 20 or so on the *Kumārasambhava,* is significant (Siegfried Lienhard, *A History of Classical Poetry: Sanskrit—Pali—Prakrit* [Wiesbaden: Otto Harrassowitz, 1984], p. 177).
6. Sheldon Pollock, ed., *Literary Cultures in History: Reconstructions from South Asia* (California: University of California Press, 2003), p. 75, fn. 82.
7. This is evident from the fact that the 634 CE Aihole inscription of the Cālukya king Pulakeśin mentions Kālidāsa, Subandhu, Bhāravi, Pravarasena and Hāla as famous poets.
8. See Daniel H. H. Ingalls 'Kālidāsa and the Attitudes of the Golden Age', *Journal of the American Oriental Society* 96 (1), January–March 1976, pp. 15–26.

9. See Manmohan Chakravarti, 'Letter', *Journal of the Royal Asiatic Society of Great Britain and Ireland,* January 1903, pp. 185–186; Ingalls, 'Kālidāsa and the Attitudes of the Golden Age', p. 16; Barbara Stoller Miller. ed., *Theater of Memory: The Plays of Kālidāsa,* trans. Edwin Gerow, David Gitomer and Barbara Stoller Miller (Delhi: Motilal Banarsidass, [1984] 1999), Introduction, pp. 10–12.
10. Sheldon Pollock, *The Language of the Gods in the World of Men: Sanskrit, Culture, and Power in Premodern India* (New Delhi: Permanent Black, [2006] 2007), pp. 240–244.
11. The Purāṇas, especially the *Viṣṇu Purāṇa,* have also been cited (Devadhar, *Raghuvaṁśa of Kālidāsa,* Introduction, p. viii) as a source for the genealogical material, although the geneology of the *Raghuvaṁśa* does not correspond exactly to Paurāṇic genealogies.
12. From this point onwards, while citing specific references, *Raghuvaṁśa* has been abbreviated to *RV.*
13. Sagara, mentioned frequently as the illustrious ancestor of Rāma in the *Rāmāyaṇa,* is scarcely mentioned in the *Raghuvaṁśa* (he is mentioned in *RV* 3.50). Dilīpa and Raghu, who are so prominent in Kālidāsa's work, are mentioned in passing in Vālmīki's work. There are also differences in dynastic succession. In the *Rāmāyaṇa,* the patrilineal succession moves from Sagara to Anśuman, Dilīpa, Bhagīratha, Kakutstha, Raghu, Pravṛddha, Śankhana, Sudarśana, Agnivarṇa, Maru, Praśuśruka, Nahuṣa, Yayāti, Nabhaga, Aja, Daśaratha and Rāma. The *Raghuvaṁśa* geneology, on the other hand, moves from Dilīpa to Raghu, Aja, Daśaratha, and Rāma, and goes on to enumerate a larger number of successor kings, culminating in the unnamed pregnant wife of Agnivarṇa.
14. For instance, in the *Rāmāyaṇa,* Daśaratha's fateful hunting expedition, narrated by him to Kausalyā as a 'flash back', is said to have taken place while he was a prince. But in the *Raghuvaṁśa,* it takes place after he becomes the king. For a further discussion of Purāṇic and epic sources of the *Raghuvaṁśa* material, and the consonance as well as dissonance among them, see M. R. Kale, ed. and trans., *The Raghuvaṁśa of Kālidāsa, Cantos I–X* (Bombay: P.S. Rege, 1922), Introduction, pp. xxiv–xxvii.
15. There is a difference of opinion among scholars on the point of whether Rāma was conceived of as divine towards the end or throughout the process of the evolution of the great epic. For two contrasting views, see J. L. Brockington, *Righteous Rāma: The Evolution of an Epic* (Delhi: Oxford University Press, 1984); and Sheldon Pollock, *The Rāmāyaṇa of Vālmīki,* Vol. 3, *Araṇyakāṇḍa* (Princeton: Princeton University Press [1984] 1991), p. 52.
16. This point is discussed further in this chapter.
17. The four standard *upāyas* are *sāma* (pacification), *dāna* (giving gifts), *bheda* (creating dissension) and *daṇḍa* (force), but certain texts mention some additional ones. The three *śaktis* are *mantraśakti* (the power of counsel), *prabhuśakti* (the power of lordship, i.e., military might) and *utsāhaśakti* (the power of energy). See Upinder Singh, 'Politics, Violence, and War in Kāmandaka's *Nītisāra*', *The Indian Economic and Social History Review*

47 (1), 2010 pp. 29–62 (Chapter 11 of this book). It should be noted that Kālidāsa refers to the number *of upāyas* as four as well as six (*RV* 18.15, 8.21).

18. On the difference in approach towards hunting in these two texts and on the sanitised forest, see Singh, 'Politics, Violence and War in Kāmandaka's *Nītisāra*', pp. 49–52.
19. For a discussion of the royal household and the relationship between politics and emotions in the *Nītisāra* and *Arthaśāstra*, see Singh, 'Politics, Violence and War in Kāmandaka's *Nītisāra*', pp. 44–46.
20. Ingalls' assertion ('Kālidāsa and the Attitudes of the Golden Age', p. 22) that Kālidāsa did not dwell on Rāma's love for Sītā because he did not believe that he loved her can be questioned.
21. For a highly idealised view of Kālidāsa's ideas on kingship, see Rudrakanta Mishra, 'A Critical Evaluation of the Theory and Practice of Kingship as Revealed in the Raghuvaṁśa', *The Journal of the Ganganatha Jha Research Institute* 23, March 1967, pp. 113–146.
22. There are many other references in the *Raghuvaṁśa* to the godliness of the king. These include both comparisons with specific gods as well as general statements that they have godly elements in them.
23. *RV* 2.68, 4.5, 5.23, 17.77. It may be noted that the titles that became the standard markers of sovereignty in inscriptions from the Gupta period onwards—*mahārājādhirāja, paramabhaṭṭāraka* and *parameśvara*—do not occur in the *Raghuvaṁśa.*
24. Although this sort of activity is reminiscent of Aśoka (who also evidently attached special significance to the anniversaries of his consecration), *kāvya* suggests that these were customary ways of celebrating important events such as the royal consecration.
25. It may be noted that the heroes of the *Rāmāyaṇa* and *Mahābhārata* also give up the kingdom after having gone through many arduous trials to obtain it.
26. For instance, Romila Thapar, *Śakuntalā: Texts, Readings, Histories* (New York: Columbia University Press, 2011), Introduction, points to the dichotomies between *grāma* and *araṇya,* nature and culture, *raja* and *ṛṣi, kāma* and *dharma* in the *Abhijñāna Śākuntalam.* Ingalls (Kālidāsa and the Attitudes of the Golden Age, pp. 22–23) refers to the dichotomy between the royal court and the *āśrama,* but perceptively describes the latter as the antidote to the court. However, his suggestion that the *āśrama* of Kālidāsa's works has shades of the *agrahāras* of Gupta and post- Gupta India, is not fully convincing, given what we now know about these *agrahāras.*
27. According to Daniel H. H. Ingalls, *An Anthology of Sanskrit Court Poetry: Vidyākara's Subhāśitaratnakośa* (Cambridge: Harvard University Press, 1965, Introduction, p. 39), Sanskrit literature was more concerned with love than with war, because of its Brāhmaṇa connections and because love was in greater consonance with the religious ideal of unity that most Sanskrit writers espoused. This hypothesis needs to be examined carefully.
28. In one place (*RV* 5.28), Raghu is described as desiring to conquer by force the lord of Kailāśa (Kubera) as though he was a *sāmanta.* In another (*RV* 6.33) the crest-jewels of the *sāmantas* of the king of Avanti are described

as obscured by the dust raised by his horses. On the changing meaning of the word *sāmanta* over time, see Lallanji Gopal, Sāmanta: Its Varying Significance in Ancient India', *Journal of the Royal Asiatic Society* 5, 1963, pp. 21–37.

29. Pollock, *The Language of the Gods in the World of Men,* p. 241.
30. The disease—*rāja-yakṣma,* generally understood as consumption—is described as having been caused by his excessive addiction to the pleasures of love (*RV* 19.48).
31. There are some exceptions. For an analysis of the representation of the king's household in texts such as *the Arthaśāstra* and *Kāmasūtra,* see Kumkum Roy, 'The King's Household: Structure and Space in the Śāstric Tradition', in Kumkum Roy, ed., *The Power of Gender and the Gender of Power* (New Delhi: SAGE Publications, 2010), pp. 271–289. For a recent work highlighting the historical importance and variety of households, see Kumkum Roy, ed. *Essays in Honour of Nandita Prasad Sahai: Looking Within, Looking Without—Exploring Households in the Subcontinent through Time* (New Delhi: Primus, 2015). For a discussion of the importance of the royal household in the *Nītisāra,* see Singh, 'Politics, Violence and War in Kāmandaka's *Nītisāra*', pp. 40, 45–46.
32. According to Ingalls (Kālidāsa and the Attitudes of the Golden Age, pp. 22–23), Kālidāsa offers two solutions to the larger problem of how a person could face the harsh realities of life while maintaining a vision of permanent goodness and beauty—one was the contemplative life of the *āśrama,* the other was personal devotion to a god, in the poet's case, the god Śiva.

13

The State, Violence, and Resistance (c. 600 BCE–600 CE)

Throughout history, the state has functioned as a controller and perpetrator of violence. Recognizing this fact has important implications for an understanding of the state. In my book, *Political Violence in Ancient India*, I examined the theory and practice of political violence in India between c. 600 BCE and 600 CE, with a special reference to the state's punitive role, war and interactions with the forest.[1] I divided this long period up into three overlapping phases—c. 600 BCE–200 BCE, 200 BCE–300 CE and 300–600 CE—representing respectively the foundation, transition and maturity of monarchical states and monarchical ideology in north India. I argued for a connection between the growth and systemization of state violence and increasingly sophisticated attempts to mask, invisibilize, justify and aestheticize this violence. I also argued that all traditions, including the religions of nonviolence such as Jainism and Buddhism, acknowledged that a certain amount of violence was necessary for kings. In fact, political theorists, poets and religious thinkers played important roles in crafting and disseminating ideologies that transformed political violence into something acceptable, positive and necessary for the well-being of subjects and maintenance of the social order. At the same time, ancient Indian political discourse distinguished force that was necessary, proportionate and legitimate from that

---

This chapter was previously published in Hermann Kulke and Bhairabi Prasad Sahu, eds, *The Routledge Handbook of the State in Premodern India* (London and New York: Routledge, 2022).

which was unnecessary, excessive and illegitimate, thereby leaving open a window for questioning the state's coercive power. In this chapter, I take my exploration of ancient Indian political thought and practice further by discussing three issues: the specific ways in which violence was inherent in the early Indian state; the relationship between kingship and gendered/sexual violence; and resistance and rebellion against the state. The sources used are varied in terms of genre, perspective and time-frame and include (especially for the second and third themes) the *Mahābhārata* and the *Rāmāyaṇa* epics, whose composition can be placed roughly between c. 400 BCE and 400 CE; Kauṭilya's *Arthaśāstra*, a political treatise now considered as belonging to the early centuries CE); and Vātsyāyana's *Kāmasūtra*, a treatise on sensual pleasure composed in about the 4th century CE. The focus of this chapter is on the period c. 600 BCE–600 CE, but in some cases, I have carried the analysis forward into later centuries.

Although it is necessary for analytical purposes to recognize the distinction between political processes and ideas, it is just as important to recognize that the two are intertwined. The influence of the 'normative' varied a great deal, but it potentially formed a model or at least a reference point for praxis. Second, if read against the grain, general discussions in normative texts may offer better insights into political realities and processes than the 'factual details' of political history, which were censored, sanitized and worked into a smooth narrative in consonance with the perspectives of the text-composers and their audience. In this respect, all our sources for ancient India are in fact normative; there is no disinterested, value-neutral political narrative.

Locating the intertwined theory and practice of political violence involves identifying the ways in which violence was folded into the structures of state and society, and the multiple, changing discourses around its forms and manifestations. The challenge is to uncover political violence in sources whose function it was to conceal and mask it, to transform it into something else, in fact into many different things. A focus on the structures, ideologies and impact of political violence not only provides insights into the intersection of political thought and practice, but it also allows us to think about political continuities, transitions and disjunctures in a different way.

Violence Is Inherent in the State

Although violence has been a feature of all human societies, including pre-state and non-state societies, the advent of the state ushered in significant changes in the institutional structures for both its control and perpetration. There is the vexed problem of defining the state in a manner that is applicable to different chronological and cultural contexts, and of identifying its diagnostic features, especially in the case of early states.[2] In Indian protohistory, the long-standing idea of peaceful Harappans has hampered a recognition of the rôle of conflict, war and violence in this civilization.[3] On the other hand, the role of warfare in the emergence and interactions of early historic states in north India from c. 600 BCE is abundantly evident in Brahmanical, Buddhist and Jaina sources. In south India, the emergence of states can be tracked from c. 300 BCE onwards on the basis of Sangam texts and Tamil-Brahmi inscriptions, and this history too is replete with the violence of warfare.

The emergence of early historic states was accompanied and followed by increasingly sophisticated theorizing about the institution of kingship which connected the state's use of force with the maintenance of the social status quo. The musings on the relationship between *brahma* and *kṣatra* in Vedic texts were precursors to the later, more systematic and elaborate theorizing. The detailed discussions of the origins of kingship and the duties of the king in texts such as the *Mahābhārata*, *Mānava Dharmaśāstra* and various Buddhist and Jaina works indicate how heavily these textual traditions were invested in politics. All textual traditions visualized taxation in return for protection, the king's punishment as necessary for the maintenance of order, and military power as a corollary of rulership and imperium.

It is not a coincidence that the time when states emerged in the Ganga valley was also the time when *ahiṁsā*-oriented religions came to the fore. These represented powerful responses to certain perennial problems of the human condition, as well as to certain specific aspects of the historical moment in which they were located. The specific contexts of violence in which the emphasis on non-violence emerged included the killing of animals in *yajña*s and the killing of men in wars. War was not invented by the state. Ṛgvedic hymns breathe warfare and the desire for victory. The importance of Indra, the god whose weapon was the thunderbolt, had a great deal to do with his association with war. The elaborate symbolism of rituals such as the *aśvamedha*, *vājapeya* and *rājasūya* indicates the many ways in which the successful management of internal and external conflicts was built into the institution of kingship. The references to violent conflicts between the āryas, *dāsa*s and *dasyu*s (in addition to conflicts among the āryas) illustrate the connection between war and the idea of the Other. In later times, this became even more apparent in the idea of the *mleccha* or barbarian, a category that included 'foreigners' and 'tribals'.[4] Conflict and violence were built into such sociocultural classifications.

From the early historic period onwards, warfare was based on larger and more efficient levels of military organization and deployment than in pre-state or tribal societies; it was dependent at least to some extent on a recruited and salaried class of soldiers who supplemented the hereditary warrior elites, allied troops and mercenaries. Military power was essential for defence against the aggression of others as well as for empire-building. War or the threat of war, supplemented by political and matrimonial alliances, were key factors in the relationships among historical states. Political treatises such as the *Arthaśāstra* considered war as a natural, essential and important part of politics and dealt extensively with its typology, military strategy and the conduct of military operations. Moral dilemmas related to war were addressed in greatest detail in the *Mahābhārata*.

As the stakes of political power rose, the potential for political violence, its incidence and intensity rose too. The history of the rise of kingdoms like Magadha in eastern India is not only one of wars and alliances with other states but also one of violent internal succession conflicts. The story in Buddhist texts of Aśoka killing 99 brothers to become king suggests a prolonged and bloody succession contest. The *Arthaśāstra* recognizes kin as a source of support for the king, but even more so as a danger, and elaborates on the measures required to protect the king from his wives and sons. One of the functions of epigraphic *praśasti*s, which appeared at the turn of the millennium (the 1st century BCE/1st century CE Hathigumpha inscription of Khāravela and the mid-2nd century CE Junagadh inscription of Rudradāman are the important early ones) was to conceal intra-dynastic conflicts, to give the impression of smooth and seamless political transitions, to situate the king within a longer lineage, and to temper the celebration of the king's martial qualities and achievements with a host of pacific and benevolent attributes. In early mediaeval India, the theatres of war increased substantially, and political relations came to be based on more elaborate hierarchies, networks and protocols between 'paramount kings' and their subordinates. All states were dependent on the systematic and sustained appropriation and deployment of economic and human resources. The continued generation and appropriation of the agricultural surplus—essential prerequisites for cities and states—involved coercion and the threat and/or use of force. Theories of the origins of kingship deliberately concealed the coercive element in the appropriation of these resources by introducing the fiction of a voluntary social contract.

The relationship between the king and his *prajā* (subjects) is central to all ancient Indian theories on the origin of kingship. These theories present taxes as the king's wages for his performance of certain duties, especially the maintenance of social order and the prevention of crime, social violence and disorder. For instance, the Aggañña Sutta of the *Dīgha Nikāya* and the Śānti Parva of the *Mahābhārata* recognize the king's grain share as his recompense for performing such duties and present the people as giving a portion of their grain to him of their own accord. The texts often describe one-sixth of the produce as the king's share and advise him to be fair and moderate while imposing taxes. A more detailed enumeration of taxes is contained in texts such as the *Arthaśāstra* and in land grant inscriptions.

While the texts conceal the coercive force involved in taxation, they assert the necessity of this force in discussions of the king's *daṇḍa* (punishment). The king's coercive power and punishment are said to prevent a descent into *matsya-nyāya* (the law of the fish), a violent anarchy in which the mighty devour the weak. In projecting the state as the prime wielder of coercive power, these theories foreshadow modern theories of the state that define it in terms of having a monopoly or near monopoly over force.

Violence and the threat of violence are inherent in all hierarchical and exploitative social institutions and structures based on inequality, subordination and oppression—in the context of ancient India, these comprise the patriarchal family, *varṇa* (hereditary class), caste (*jāti*), slavery and untouchability.[5] The origins of patriarchy, *varṇa* and slavery can be traced to Vedic texts, while caste and untouchability made their appearance in north India during the early historic period. The vocabulary of servitude in the Pali *Tipiṭaka* includes *dāsa*s, *kammakara*s and *dāsa-kammakara*s. The state also extracted *viṣṭi* or forced labour. Various forms of exploitation were involved, both in spheres of state activity as well as private enterprise. The harnessing of labour for state projects required the use or threat of force. Inscriptions mention different kinds of labour used in agrarian operations, some of which must have involved coercion. War was an important source not so much of territory as of resources, including labour resources.

In increasingly complex societies organized along multiple axes of identity and status, political ideology played an important role in inculcating social acquiescence and compliance among subordinated groups.

The four-fold *varṇa* order was generally used as a metonym for the normative social hierarchy, even during times when class and caste (*jāti*) were important bases of social identity. Brahmanical texts and royal inscriptions frequently refer to the king's social role as the maintainer of the order of *varṇa*s and *āśrama*s (the theoretical model of the four life stages, namely *brahmacarya*, *gṛhastha*, *vānaprastha* and *sannyāsa*) and implicate the institution of kingship in a powerful way in the perpetuation of the status quo and existing social hierarchies. Actions against subjects could be justified on the grounds of the need to maintain the social order, which, it could be argued, was ultimately in the interests of the people themselves. The best-known example of this occurs in the Uttarakāṇḍa of the *Rāmāyaṇa*, where Rāma kills the śūdra Śambūka. The moral justification is that the latter had transgressed the *varṇa* order by performing austerities and that this had led to the premature death of an innocent Brāhmaṇa child.

The mechanisms for the settlement of civil and criminal disputes in ancient times were diverse and complex, but the development of a judicial system, even if rudimentary, gave the state the self-asserted right to adjudicate civil and criminal disputes, to pronounce and impose punishments, including the right to take life. Even if the state's actual outreach was limited, its claims to be the highest adjudicator in disputes and to possess the right to punish and inflict pain and death on subjects were backed by its coercive power. Theories of the origins of kingship recognized punishing subjects as an important function of the state. According to the *Mahābhārata* (composed roughly between c. 500 BCE and 500 CE), the king should have compassion for his subjects, prevent the strong from preying on the weak, and prevent social violence and chaos. *Daṇḍa* inspires fear in people and this fear prevents them from killing one other. The king's punishment is described as essential to prevent extreme social violence, but it is repeatedly emphasized that this punishment must be measured, in accordance with proper judicial principles and proportionate to the crime.[6]

The relationship between the coercive power of the state and society is expressed most clearly in Kautilya's *Arthaśāstra*. This theoretical treatise on statecraft contains the first detailed law code in India.[7] Of course, it is a normative work and there is little evidence suggesting that these laws were applied in civil or criminal cases; nevertheless, the text is of great importance in histories of political and legal ideas. The *Arthaśāstra* asserts the state's right to impose retribution, pain and torture on subjects in the administration of justice. It mentions punishments such as fines, confiscation of property, exile, corporal punishment, mutilation, branding, torture, forced labour and death. Kauṭilya accepts and seeks to regulate torture as punishment and as a means of acquiring information during interrogation. Types of torture include striking, whipping, caning, suspension from a rope and inserting needles under the nails. The *Arthaśāstra* also asserts the state's right to take life on the grounds of justice, distinguishing between simple death (*śuddha-vadha*) and death by torture (*citra-vadha*).[8] The latter refers to especially painful deaths which may have also involved public spectacle. The varieties of death by torture include burning on a pyre, drowning in water, cooking in a big jar, impaling on a stake, setting fire to different parts of the body and tearing apart by bullocks.

Kauṭilya, however, was not an advocate of wanton violence. He warns that the ruler who imposes wrongful punishment cannot escape punishment himself. If he were to use the rod of punishment unjustly, through passion, anger or contempt, the rod would become dangerous for him. The king's force and punishment must be rooted in discipline (*vinaya*); only then would it bring prosperity to all living beings.[9] In a polity devoid of institutional checks, knowing the political impulses and appetite for violence, the political theorists were concerned with how these could be controlled. They realized that the only real control on the king's propensity to abuse his power and exercise brute violence was the one that he had to be persuaded to exercise over himself.

Another respect in which violence was inherent in early Indian states is in their interactions with the forest. Here, I am using the word 'forest' as a shorthand for a variety of ecological zones including mountainous, littoral and pastoral tracts, in fact, all those areas inhabited by what can be loosely described as stateless people, whose political and economic modes of being were different from those associated with agrarian states. The conflict between the state and the forest is one of the most important and most underestimated aspects of the political history of ancient and early medieval India. The expansion of agriculture, cities and states involved the steady clearance of forests, but the massive forest clearance in the subcontinent took place in the middle of the 19th century as a cumulative result of population increase, commercial farming and the expansion of the railways.[10] Till then, states were always cheek by jowl with the forest tribes. With the expansion of agriculture, cities and states and the emergence and growth of empires, the forest became an important object of the exploitation and violence *of* the state; but it was also a constant source of violent challenge *to* the state. Exploiting, extracting and controlling valuable economic and military resources such as wood, ivory and elephants involved a steady encroachment on forest habitats and constant conflicts with forest people. The sources are reticent about the details, but Aśoka's stern warning to the forest tribes and Samudragupta's boast of having defeated all the kings of the forest acknowledged that they were important features of the political landscape.[11]

The idea of the *mleccha*, with its pejorative view of tribals and foreigners, sought to distinguish the civilized from the barbarian, presenting the latter as a source of violence against the civilized. The use of violence against *mleccha*s was hence justified. It was Kauṭilya who had the most astute, pragmatic understanding of the close and complex relationship between the state and the forest and forest people. The *Arthaśāstra* has a detailed discussion of different types of forests, classifying them into three main types: *mṛga-vana*s (deer forests), *hasti-vana*s (elephant forests) and *dravya-vana*s (material forests). It recognizes the forest both as an important resource and a threat; it advocates suppressing the forest people as well as using them by incorporating them into the army and the spy system.

In the specific ways discussed above, despite variations in nature, organization and structure, violence is indeed inherent in all states, regardless of their chronological, cultural and historical contexts. There is, of course, also the role of the state in controlling and curbing violence by maintaining order, protecting subjects from external aggression, dispensing justice, punishing civil and criminal crimes, etc. In fact, this second aspect—the idea of the state as a protector against violence—has been traditionally used as a justification of the violence of the state.

When political violence is foregrounded, the old historical debates look different. For instance, with regard to the early mediaeval period in Indian history (roughly c. 600–1200 CE), the feudalism model as well as the so-called 'integrative paradigm' may look more similar than different.[12] The integrative paradigm talks of the acculturation of tribes, transformation of tribes into castes, and cult appropriation and assimilation.[13] All these processes involved the widespread use or threat of violence to bring about the political and social subordination and subjugation of tribal groups. The feudalism model shows greater awareness of conflicts in the political, social and economic spheres, although it misunderstands the raison d'être of land grants. But neither model in fact focuses on the extent to which interstate and intra-state violence were major features of the political processes of these centuries. Violence is embedded in copper-plate grants, which are an important source for the history of early mediaeval India from any perspective. As I have discussed elsewhere, land grants were sometime made in the context of military campaigns and victories.[14] The stern warnings to the cultivators to obey the donees also smack of violent threat. The violent tone of the imprecatory verses at the end of land grant inscriptions warning kings against the rescinding of grants had more than cosmetic value and suggest that land grants were the focal point of various sorts of conflicts, some of which involved the state.[15]

Kingship and Sexual Violence

In ancient Indian political discourse, the idea of the king as the maintainer of the social order (directly or through mediators) extended beyond *varṇa* and āśrama to relationships within the household. In this sense, the king was visualized—at least in theory—as the custodian of the patriarchal norms and the sexual mores within the multitude of households in his realm. Although the importance of the household in political processes has been recognized over the last few decades by a handful of historians,[16] the role of sexual violence in ancient Indian political processes has been scarcely discussed. A close examination of political discourse indicates the manner in which sexuality and gendered violence were woven into the normative ideas of kingship. Like other forms of political violence, the sexual violence of the king too was masked in various ways in the sources and has to be prised out with some difficulty.

Sanskrit *kāvya* (literature) celebrates the king as paradigmatic lover, and in doing so, sanitizes the royal harem (*antaḥpura*) of its sexual exploitation, competition and violence. It presents an idyllic picture of polygynous royal households and harems, thronging with queens, mistresses, slaves and servants, where women of varying rank and standing were available to kings for their sexual indulgence and the production of heirs. Rival women are presented as living in almost perfect harmony with each other, graciously adjusting themselves to the king's shifting fancies; the king maintained the delicate balance among them through an attitude and behaviour of gallantry and courtesy.[17] However, when the veneer is peeled off, the image of the happy harem dissolves into something ugly. Dharmaśāstra, the Sanskrit epics, the *Arthaśāstra* and *Kāmasūtra* provide useful entry points to this alternative view.

Out of the eight types of marriage listed in Dharmaśāstra, two—the Rākṣasa (demonic) and Paiśāca (ghoulish)—involve violence. The

Rākṣasa type of marriage is defined in the *Mānava Dharmaśāstra* as when a man violently abducts a girl from her house, causing death, mayhem and destruction, while she is shrieking and weeping. The Paiśāca marriage is when someone secretly rapes a woman who is sleeping, drunk or deranged in mind. While Paiśāca is considered the most evil (*pāpiṣṭha*) of marriages, the Rākṣasa marriage is considered lawful (*dharmya*) for kṣatriya warriors.[18] Minoru Hara has argued that the latter, with its acceptance and justification of violence, can be seen as an extension of Kṣatriya dharma.[19] Gandharva, a marriage based on sexual union (*mithuna*) and desire (*kāma*), is also a type that is described as appropriate for Kṣatriyas. So, the Kṣatriya is singled out for love as well as violence in marriage. Sometimes the two are connected; e.g. in the *Mahābhārata*, Arjuna abducts Subhadrā by force because he has fallen in love with her; he does so on her brother Kṛṣṇa's advice and with Yudhiṣṭhira's acquiescence.

The reference to sexual indulgence in women (*strī-vyasana*) in the standard list of the vices of kings in Sanskrit political discourse indicates a recognition of the latter's predilection towards carnal excess. Sexual indulgence was acceptable in moderate doses but was considered a problem when it became excessive or obsessive. In the texts, the discussion of this vice is always with regard to its implications for the king and his rule, not for the women who were the object of the king's desire.

Specific episodes of violence against women make their most explicit appearance in the *Mahābhārata* and the *Rāmāyaṇa*. In fact, it is this violence that propels the epic narratives forward. In the *Mahābhārata*, Draupadī, wife of the Pāṇḍava heroes, is often the target. The most famous incident involving physical assault on a woman for political reasons occurs in the Sabhā Parva, when in an episode that unfolds slowly and is narrated in considerable detail, Duhśāsana violently drags Draupadī by the hair into the assembly hall and attempts to disrobe her in front of the assembled Kuru nobles, including her husbands.[20] Dragging a woman by the hair is an act laden with real and symbolic violence.[21] Draupadī does not take this humiliation without protest; she berates her husbands and the Kuru elders for being silent onlookers; she insists that they give their view on the propriety of what has transpired (only Vidura and Vikarṇa speak up); and she seethes with a desire for revenge. Later, in the Virāṭa Parva, while living in disguise along with her husbands in the Matsya court, Draupadī is once again the victim of a violent sexual assault by Kīcaka, a powerful general and brother-in-law of King Virāṭa. In spite of her spurning his advances, Kīcaka persists in pursuing her, kicking her and dragging her by the hair into the assembly.[22] In the incident in the Kuru court, we see assault against a woman being used as a political tool, the woman being treated as proxy for the enemy's honour. In the events in the Matsya court, we see a member of the royal family attempting to rape a woman he thinks is a servant. In both cases, the princely perpetrators of the violence against Draupadī ultimately pay for their transgressions with their life.

Gendered violence is also inherent in the *Rāmāyaṇa*, most prominently in the abduction of Rāvaṇa by Sītā, again an event which is narrated slowly, with considerable detail, drawing attention to Rāvaṇa's brutal violence towards the frail, helpless and terrified Sītā. Rāvaṇa seizes and drags Sītā by the hair and carries her off on his aerial car to Laṅkā. The epic contrasts Rāma and Sītā's monogamous marital relationship based on love and consideration, with the libidinous sex life of Rāvaṇa. The *Rāmāyaṇa* gives two sorts of impressions about Rāvaṇa. In the Sundara Kāṇḍa, Rāvaṇa's women are described as having come to him of their own volition. Although Rāvaṇa abducts Sītā forcefully, he does not force himself on her, because he is in love with her and wants her to come to him willingly. A very different picture of Rāvaṇa's sexuality is presented in the Uttara Kāṇḍa (considered a later interpolation by scholars, but part of the epic nonetheless), where there are many more details about Rāvaṇa's violent past and personality.[23] Here, the reason why Rāvaṇa did not violate Sītā is explained as a curse: In an earlier birth, Rāvaṇa had assaulted a virtuous Brāhmaṇa ascetic woman named Vedāvatī (who was actually Sītā in an earlier birth), seizing her by the hair. She had immolated herself to preserve her chastity, and while doing so, had vowed that she would be born in the future as the daughter of a virtuous man, although not from a human womb, to destroy him. In the Uttara Kāṇḍa, Rāvaṇa is also described as having raped the *apasarā* Rumbhā, who was on her way to a rendezvous with her lover Nalakūbara (son of Kubera, Rāvaṇa's half-brother). When Nalakūbara was told about the incident, he cursed Rāvaṇa that if he ever again tried to force himself on a woman against her will, his head would break into seven pieces. The curse had a dampening effect on Rāvaṇa's predilection for sexual violence.[24] Rāvaṇa's proclivity for sexual violence against women was no doubt due to the fact that he was a demon and a king, and it ultimately led to his downfall and death.

In the epics, assault against women by royal men invites dire retribution, so it is evident that the epic composers did not approve of such behaviour. But the fact that these incidents are described in graphic detail and form extremely important parts of the epic narratives suggests that sexual excess and violence were recognized as salient features of the behaviour of powerful men, who did not always follow the dictates of propriety.[25]

There are several other epic instances of the violence of royal men against women, not all of which are recounted in the same way. In the *Rāmāyaṇa*, Rāma and Lakṣmaṇa's treatment of the *rākṣasī* Śūrpaṇakhā and the cutting off of her nose are presented in a very different vein compared with the narration of the humiliation and violence suffered by Sītā. Śūrpaṇakhā's mutilation is not intended to elicit outrage; in fact, in contemporary performances of the Ram-līlā, it is often presented as a comic episode. However, the mutilation and humiliation of the demoness does directly lead to the abduction of Sītā and the war. In the *Mahābhārata*, an important incident where the cruel treatment and humiliation of a woman invites dire retribution is that of Ambā and her birth as Śikhaṇḍin—neither man nor woman—in order to destroy Bhīṣma.

Vātsyāyana's *Kāmasūtra* (3rd/4th century) provides another important perspective on sexual violence, this one from the point of view of experts on *kāma*, or pleasure.[26] Vātsyāyana describes love as a battle, but the aim of this battle is mutual pleasure. He urges men to be gentle in their lovemaking in order to win a virgin's trust and obtain her consent. He recommends tricks to seduce women but warns that if a man used force with a woman, she would become a man-hater.[27] Techniques of scratching, biting and striking are described as ways to enhance the erotic experience during lovemaking, but these are distinguished from sadistic sexual violence which can result in injury and even death to the woman. While discussing four forms of slapping, Vātsyāyana mentions the 'wedge', a type of slap on the woman's chest, which he describes as prevalent in the South. He criticizes this on the ground that it causes pain to the woman and is dangerous.[28] Interestingly, all the specific instances he cites of the fatal use of slapping techniques during sex have to do with kings: the king of the Cōḻas killed a courtesan named Citrasena by using the 'wedge'; the Kuntala king Sātakarṇi Śātavāhana killed his queen Malayavatī by using the 'scissor' (a slap on the head); Naradeva with the deformed hand blinded a dancing girl in one eye by clumsy use of the 'drill', a slap on the cheeks.[29]

The *Kāmasūtra* has an entire section on the sex life of powerful men.[30] Vātsyāyana begins with two verses stating that kings and high-ranking officers (*mahāmātras*) should not enter other men's homes because their activities are observed by others and set a bad example. But he goes on to recommend certain stratagems if they cannot help doing so. The category of 'men of power' (īśvara) has two levels: higher and lower. The latter includes village headmen (*gramādhipati*), king's officers (*āyuktakas*) and city police chiefs, but most of the discussion focuses on the higher level, especially the king. If a king covets the wife of a man who has lost all his money or is frightened, Vātsyāyana recommends that a beggar woman should convince the woman to come meet a woman of the harem in order to reverse the husband's bad fortune. He also prescribes various ways of taking advantage of women's insecurities and vulnerabilities, using go-betweens to allay their fears and lull them into complacency so that the king could seduce them.

Vātsyāyana also recommends certain 'secret methods' (*pracchanna-yogāḥ*) involving subterfuge as well as violence, which he says are generally used by princes (*rājaputras*). For instance, if the desired woman is already having an affair with another man, she can be seized (the verb used is *saṁgrah*), made into a servant or slave (*dāsī*), and introduced into the harem gradually. Or a spy can falsely accuse her husband of being an enemy of the king, after which she can be seized and inducted into the harem.[31] These references to forcibly seizing a woman in the *Kāmasūtra* contrast with the idyllic picture of the harem presented in *kāvya* texts. Vātsyāyana also refers to the king's cronies (*rāja-vallabha*) as cruel (*niṣṭhura*) and warns courtesans to avoid them, enlarging the circle of politically powerful sexual predators.[32]

Interestingly, immediately after advising kings about strategies for seduction, Vātsyāyana warns that he should not enter another man's home, because it can prove fatal for him. He cites the examples of Ābhira, the Koṭa king, who was killed by a washerman employed by the king's brother when the king went to another man's home, presumably to have sex with his wife; and Jayasena, the king of Vārāṇasī who was killed by the superintendent of horses, presumably, while engaged in a similar activity.[33]

Vātsyāyana approvingly discusses the conduct of open sexual affairs according to the custom of the region. In the course of this discussion, he mentions certain practices which, by the standards of our time, would be considered sexual exploitation.[34] Relying on hearsay, he refers to a practice in vogue among the people of Āndhra—that the virgins of the countryside entered the king's harem on the tenth day after being given in marriage (to their husband), were enjoyed by the king, and then dismissed. Again, citing hearsay, Vātsyāyana says that it is said that among the people of Vatsagulma, women in the harems of men in power under ministers (*mahāmātras*) went to the king at night to give him pleasure. In Surāṣṭra, he tells us, women of the city (*nagara-striyaḥ*) and countryside (*janapada-striyaḥ*) went in groups or individually to the royal court (*rājakula*) for the king's erotic games (*raja-krīḍārtha*). Although Vātsyāyana ends the section by piously stating that a king devoted to the welfare of his people should not use these devices, he does not really seem to disapprove, and asserts that these and other devices for seducing the wives of other men were put into circulation by kings and were used in region after region (*deśe-deśe*).

In addition to discussing acts of the king's sexual use and abuse of women, Vātsyāyana warns male subjects of the dire consequences of having sexual relations with the king's women. He warns the *nāgaraka* (the man-about-town) never to enter the royal harem, even if he can do so easily, because it usually ends in disaster. But if he has considered the matter carefully and still wants to venture into it, the *Kāmasūtra* tells him how to go about doing so.[35] For both Vātsyāyana and Kauṭilya, the king's women are off bounds and having sexual relations with them is fraught with danger and can be fatal. But there is a radical difference in perspective. For Kauṭilya, adultery with the queen is a double crime—it is an extreme violation of patriarchal and political norms. For Vātsyāyana, seducing the queen is to be avoided because it exposes the seducer to danger and death; it is not an act that threatens the social or moral order.

While such references show that sexual excess and violence were associated with kingship in texts belonging to a variety of genres, it is difficult to ascertain the extent of its actual incidence. Unlike other forms of political violence such as war, there is no recorded documentation or detail. Like other forms of violence, there is an attempt to mask it in the idealized presentation of the harem, especially in *kāvya*. Vātsyāyana is an exception, and he discusses the king's sexual violence in a matter-of-fact way without a moralizing gloss. The obfuscation by the sources makes it even more necessary to recognize sexual and gendered violence as part of the theory and practice of kingship.

Rebellion and Resistance

While the inherent violent proclivities *of* the state are integral parts of political discourse and political history, another question that arises concerns violence *against* the state. Since the producers of most of our sources were privileged upper-class males, direct critiques of the politically and socially powerful are rare. The voices of ordinary people, women, lower castes and classes, and the victims of state violence are scarcely audible. There are no statistics, only impressions which emerge through a careful reading of the texts. Indirect evidence of questioning, critique and rebellion can be located in the anxieties of the normative texts, which suggest an acute awareness of the fragility of political power. In this context, James Scott's ideas about weapons of the weak, public and hidden transcripts, and everyday forms of resistance are especially pertinent and useful.[36]

Regicide is built into one of the accounts of the origins of kingship in the Śānti Parva of the *Mahābhārata*. Bhīṣma tells Yudhiṣṭhira that in the Kṛta age, kingship and punishment (*daṇḍa*) did not exist because they were not required.[37] However, men fell prey to error, confusion and greed and the gods approached Brahmā and Viṣṇu to intervene. Viṣṇu produced a mind-born son Virajas, who was followed by his son and grandson Kīrtiman and Kardama. But all these men were inclined towards renunciation and did not want to rule. Anaṅga, next in line, ruled well, protecting his subjects and delivering justice. He was followed by his son Atibala, who learnt the art of governance but did not have control over his senses. The next ruler was Vena, who was dominated by passion and hate, and was unlawful (*vidharma*) in his behaviour towards his subjects. The *ṛṣis* (sages) decided to get rid of this evil king and stabbed him to death with blades of *kuśa* grass. They churned his right thigh and out of it emerged an ugly man named Niṣāda (a forest tribal), who was told to go away as he was unfit to be king. Then they churned Vena's right hand and therefrom emerged Pṛthu, a man with a refined mind and an understanding of the Vedas, the auxiliary texts, *dharma*, *artha*, the military arts and politics. Pṛthu was consecrated king by the gods and sages, and he proved to be a good, exemplary ruler. In this story, there is an acknowledgement of the possibility that kings may have serious flaws, that those who inherit kingship may not want it, that there is something inherently problematic about the institution, and that it may sometimes be necessary to kill kings.

The *Mahābhārata* dilates at length on the king's duties and provides a post-script about what can happen if kings are remiss in performing them. It connects the king's administration of justice with his afterlife—a just king goes to heaven; an unjust one goes to hell. Further, it warns that the excessive cruelty and violence of the king and his neglect of his duties can lead to justified violence *against* him.[38] A cruel king, who does not protect his people, who robs them in the name of levying taxes, is evil incarnate and should be killed by his subjects. A king who, after promising to protect his subjects does not do so, should be killed by them, as though he were a mad dog.[39] So if the king does not perform his duties and is cruel to his people, the *Mahābhārata* sanctions regicide.

There are also several stories in ancient texts of evil kings being justifiably killed, Duryodhana and Rāvaṇa being the best-known examples.[40] However, the overall political discourse of the *Mahābhārata* upholds the king's position and punitive powers. Further, in the case of Duryodhana and Vena, it is not the people who kill kings, but their Kṣatriya rivals in the first instance and Brāhmaṇa *ṛṣi*s in the second. Although some elements of the theories of kingship in texts are echoed in inscriptions of historical kings,[41] there is no direct evidence suggesting that the latent sanction of regicide in the *Mahābhārata* was ever invoked to sanction a historically attested rebellion against the state. This could be because our sources are for the most part 'statist', representing the perspectives and interests of the state, rather than of rebels.

The most comprehensive discussion of possible violence against the state occurs in the *Arthaśāstra*. Kauṭilya is extremely concerned about the threat of assassination, especially through poison, and advises elaborate arrangements for the king's protection. The sources of violence against the king are many, and queens and princes head the list. The violence of queens is singled out for special attention and Kauṭilya gives several specific instances of kings being killed by their women.[42] In sharp contrast to the picture we get from *kāvya*, the harem is an extremely dangerous place for kings. One of the important implications of this is that Kauṭilya considered women as politically relevant figures.

Apart from close kin, other potential sources of violence against the ruler recognized by Kauṭilya are enemy kings; neighbouring kings (*sāmanta*s); disaffected, angry subjects; forest tribes; robbers; *mleccha*s; and mutinous troops. He also talks about the dangers posed by conspiracies, traitors and enemies.[43] He discusses revolts in the interior and exterior (*antaraḥ kopa*, *bāhya-kopa*), and describes the former as more dangerous.[44] He explains how internal and external enemies can be killed, many of the strategies involving secret agents in disguise.[45] In the case of those who cannot be killed openly, such as treasonous high-ranking officers, he advocates silent punishment (*upāṁśu-daṇḍa*), that is, secret killing.[46] Silent punishment can also be used against hostile subjects.[47]

Kauṭilya recognized violence against the king as a serious political problem that had to be dealt with ruthlessly and effectively. The punishment for one who reviles or spreads evil news about the king or reveals secret counsel is the tearing out of his tongue.[48] More severe crimes against the king and kingdom invite more severe punishments. Death by setting fire to the hands and head (*śiro-hasta-pradīpikṁ ghātayet*) is the punishment for one who covets the kingdom (*rājya-kāmuka*), who attacks the king's palace, who incites forest people or enemies (*aṭavy-amitr-otsāhasaka*) or who causes rebellion in the fortified city, countryside or army (*durga-rāṣṭra-daṇḍa-kopaka*).[49] Brāhmaṇas who commit treason should be made to enter darkness (probably blinded). The seriousness of the coalescing of political and sexual transgressions can be seen in Kauṭilya's recommendation that the punishment for one having sex with the king's wife was death by being cooked in a jar.[50] In several cases (including crimes which invite mutilation), Kautilya refers to the possibility of commuting punishments to fines. But unless there was some crucial mitigating circumstance, no commutation was considered possible where the crime merited the death penalty, especially in cases of treason or loss to the state.

Kauṭilya's emphasis on stringent and frequent tests of loyalty for officials indicates an awareness that loyalty could not be taken for granted. The king lived in a world of danger, deceit and subterfuge, constantly fearing betrayal and assassination; he had to ensure constant surveillance to keep track of non-compliance, rebellion and treason; he had to pacify, conciliate or outwit malcontents and crush them through 'silent punishment' when other strategies failed. There were internal and external enmities, including those posed by *mleccha*s and forest people. The many references to popular disaffection and *prakṛti-kopa* (the anger or uprising of the people) are especially significant.[51] Although actual historical incidents of popular revolts are not known in ancient India, these statements can be seen as an expression of the awareness of the *possibility* of and anxiety about widespread and rampant rebellion. In fact, although the *Arthaśāstra* is often read as an endorsement for a totalitarian state, its entire discussion is premised on a recognition of the fragility of the king's power and the violent threats to his life and position from multiple quarters. Kauṭilya advocates ruthless, carefully calculated and effective use of preemptive and post-facto violence *by* the state in order to prevent and respond to violence *against* the state.

Kauṭilya's obsession with spies shows that he realized the importance of information as the basis for effective rule. He also knew about the political importance of hidden transcripts long before James Scott talked about them. What people were saying offstage about the king had to be cunningly prised out through provocative talk and was to be followed up by destroying the speaker. We see such an awareness in the *Arthaśāstra*'s recommendation that spies in disguise should fan out to all parts of the kingdom and listen to what people were saying in private about the king, so that swift action could be taken to stamp out disaffection and revolt.

However, as mentioned earlier, the recorded instances of actual violent rebellions against the state involving individuals or groups beyond the circle of elite groups, political rivals or subordinate rulers are non-existent in ancient India. The reasons include one or all of the following factors—the effective concealment of such incidents by our statist/centrist sources; the effectiveness of the state's coercive machinery; the effectiveness of the legitimizing, hegemonic discourse in suppressing such resistance; and the lack of resources and collective consciousness that would enable the individual victims of state oppression or violence to make common cause and effectively raise the banner of revolt. Social conflicts were often dealt with and diffused (though not entirely resolved) at the religious level, as they simmered but before they boiled over; examples of this are Jainism and Buddhism in the early period, and *bhakti* in later centuries.[52]

Incidents of violent rebellion are known in the early mediaeval period, but none of them were 'popular' rebellions. For instance, the Kaivarta/Kaivartta rebellion in eastern India in the late 11th century was not a 'popular revolt' nor a 'peasant revolt' (using that problematic homogenizing term) as was once suggested. The fact that the Kaivartas were fishermen and boatmen who had turned landowners suggests a social dimension, but the event was basically a revolt of *sāmantas*.[53] The Ḍāmara rebellion in early mediaeval Kashmir involved powerful landlords, not ordinary folk. On the other hand, there are epigraphic references to agrarian conflicts, in some cases involving the state. For instance, a 13th-century inscription from Karnataka refers to the cultivators of a village protesting at their village being converted into a *brahmadeya* (a village gifted by a king to Brāhmaṇas) and a royal army being sent to punish them.[54]

Conclusions

This essay has discussed the ways in which violence was inherent in the state, the connections between political violence and social hierarchies, the place of sexual violence in political discourse, and the state as a target of the violence of others. All political ideologies justify the state's use of violence by referring to its protection of subjects, ensuring their well-being and prosperity, dispensing justice, and maintenance of the security of life, property and social order. An important function of these ideologies is to present the state's violence as a necessary force. In ancient times, the state's coercive power (which could frequently and quickly veer into violence) was presented as necessary to uphold the kingdom; today it is presented as necessary to uphold the nation. Ancient Indian thinkers offer a significant range of responses to the problem of political violence, expressing the tension between the positive principle of non-violence and the need for the state to use coercive force. But they recognized the line between legitimate force and illegitimate violence, the fact that the state had certain fundamental duties, and the fact that these duties were not always discharged.

Investigating the close relationship between the state and violence turns the spotlight on an issue that has been part of political and social life across centuries and cultures, a problem that deserves intensive historical analysis. Such an investigation raises new questions and has important implications for understanding political processes. The factors that define violence and the normalizing processes that justify some measure and kinds of harming or killing by the state or against the state are deeply embedded in social and political structures, institutions and ideologies, as well as in moral and religious values. Without essentializing cultures as inherently more or less violent, and without falling into the traps of cultural chauvinism, there is a possibility of a comparative history of political violence, which identifies similarities and differences in the forms, structures and ideologies of this violence in the ancient world.

Notes

1 Upinder Singh, *Political Violence in Ancient India* (Cambridge, MA: Harvard University Press, 2017).

2 For a recent synthesis of the material on this, see James C. Scott, *Against the Grain: A Deep History of the Earliest States* (New Haven and London: Yale University Press, 2017). For diagnostic features of 'stateness', Scott (*Against the Grain*, p. 118) suggests: walls, tax collection and officials, which point to territoriality and a specialized state apparatus. In the context of ancient India, historians have usually focused on a standing army and tax collection.

3 The idea of the peaceful Harappans and the weakness of the mechanism of force in the Harappan civilization can be questioned. See, for instance, Shereen Ratnagar, *Harappan Archaeology: Early State Perspectives* (New Delhi: Primus, 2016), pp. 161–69.

4 Both these terms are problematic but are used here for the sake of convenience. On the idea of *mleccha*, see Aloka Parasher, *Mlecchas in Early India: A Study in Attitudes towards Outsiders up to AD 600* (Delhi: Munshiram

Manoharlal, 1991). On the concept of tribe, see Sumit Guha, *Tribe and State in Asia through Twenty-Five Centuries* (Association for Asian Studies: Ann Arbor, 2021, Asia Shorts, No. 10).

5 On the connections between caste, gender and violence in the context of ancient India, see Uma Chakravarti, *Gendering Caste: Through a Feminist Lens* (New Delhi: Sage, 2018).

6 See, for instance, *Mbh.* 12.70, 12.121, 12.122.40–41. The editions and translations used here are V.S. Sukthankar, S.K. Belvalkar and P.L. Vaidya, gen. eds., *The Mahābhārata, for the First Time Critically Edited*, 19 vols. (Poona: Bhandarkar Oriental Research Institute, 1933–66); and John D. Smith, *The Mahābhārata: An Abridged Translation*, (New Delhi: Penguin, 2009); and James L. Fitzgerald, *Mahabhārata*, Vol. 7 (11: The Book of the Women; 12: The Book of Peace, Part One) (Chicago: University of Chicago Press, 2004). In references, *Mahābhārata* has been abbreviated to *Mbh.*

7 See Patrick Olivelle and Mark McClish, 'The Four Feet of Legal Procedure and the Origins of Jurisprudence in Ancient India', *Journal of the American Oriental Society* 135 (1), 2015, pp. 33–47.

8 *AS* 4. 11. The Patrick Olivelle edition (*King, Governance and Law in Ancient India.* New Delhi: Oxford University Press, 2013) is being cited here. The *Arthaśāstra* has been abbreviated to *AS* in references.

9 *AS* 1.4.5–16; 1.5.2; 1.19.33.

10 See Michael Williams, *Deforesting the Earth: From Prehistory to Global Crisis* (Chicago and London: University of Chicago Press, 2003), pp. 355–56.

11 For a detailed discussion of the many different ways in which the forest was understood in ancient India, see Singh, *Political Violence in Ancient India*, Chapter 5.

12 For a discussion of the idea of the early mediaeval, see Upinder Singh, *Rethinking Early Medieval India: A Reader* (New Delhi: Oxford University Press, 2011), Introduction.

13 See B.D. Chattopadhyaya, 'Political Process and Structure of Polity in Early Medieval India', in B.D. Chattopadhyaya, *The Making of Early Medieval India* (New Delhi: Oxford University Press, [1983]1997).

14 Singh, *Political Violence in Ancient India*, pp. 334–39. Sometimes there is an interesting twist: The 5th-century Chammak copper plate suggests that there was danger of violence *to* the state from the Brahmana donees.

15 For the changing phraseology of the imprecations, see Naboru Karashima, 'The Past as known from Tamil Inscriptions: Village Community and Challenge to the Caste System.' Keynote Address, Tamil Studies Conference, Toronto, 11 May 2012.

16 See Devika Rangachari, *Invisible Women, Visible Histories* (New Delhi: Manohar, 2009); Kumkum Roy, ed., *Looking Within Looking Without: Exploring Households in the Subcontinent through Time: Essays in Memory of Nandita Prasad Sahai* (New Delhi: Primus, 2015); and Daud Ali, *Courtly Culture and Political Life in Early Medieval India* (Cambridge: Cambridge University Press, 2004).

17 Ali (*Courtly Culture and Political Life in Early Medieval India*) makes a strong and convincing argument about the parallel between the hierarchical relations in the *sabhā* and the harem.

18 *Mānava Dharmaśāstra* 3.33-34. The edition cited here is Patrick Olivelle, *Manu's Code of Law: A Critical Edition and Translation of the Mānava-Dharmaśāstra* (New Delhi: Oxford University Press, 2006).

19 Minoru Hara, 'A Note on the Rākṣasa Form of Marriage', *Journal of the American Oriental Society*, 94, 1974, pp. 296–306.

20 *Mbh.* 2.58–64.

21 See Minoru Hara, 'The Holding of the Hair (Keśa-grahaṇa)', *Acta Orientalia*, 47, 1986, pp. 67–92.

22 *Mbh.* 4. 13–15.

23 For the *Rāmāyaṇa*, see G.H. Bhat and U.P. Shah gen., eds. *The Vālmīki Rāmāyaṇa: Critical Edition*, 7 volumes (Baroda: Oriental Institute, 1960–75); and the translations edited by Robert P. Goldman and others, including Robert P. Goldman and Sally J. Goldman's translation of the Uttara Kāṇḍa (*The Rāmāyaṇa of Vālmīki: An Epic of Ancient India*, vol. 7: *Uttarakāṇḍa*, Princeton: Princeton University Press). *Rāmāyaṇa* has been abbreviated to *Ram.* in references.

24 Rāvaṇa's father Viśravas, who is interrupted by Kaikasī when he is about to perform the *agnihotra* sacrifice, also prophesies that she will bear fierce and cruel sons; he later modifies this by saying the youngest will be righteous.) (*Ram.* 7.9.12–18).

25 There are two other direct accounts of rape in the Uttara Kāṇḍa of the *Rāmāyaṇa*. One is that of Ahalyā, wife of the sage Gautama, who is described in the Uttara Kāṇḍa as having been raped by the god Indra (in other versions of the story, she was tricked into having sex with him) (*Ram.* 7.30.26–27). Gautama cursed Indra that he would lose his permanent position as king of the gods and that half the guilt of all future rapes would be borne by him. The second incident is that of king Daṇḍa raping Arajā, daughter of his chaplain Uśanas Kāvya (Sargas 71 and 72). Uśanas pronounced a curse that this act would lead to the destruction of Daṇḍa and all his men, as well as of his kingdom.

26 The texts used here are Damodar Lal Goswami, ed., *Kāmasūtra by Śrī Vātsyāyana, with a commentary of Jayamaṅgala* (Varanasi: Chowkhamba, 1912), along with the translation by Wendy Doniger and Sudhir Kakar (*Kamasutra*, Oxford: Oxford University Press, 2002). *Kāmasūtra* has been abbreviated to *KS* in references. 2002).

27 *KS* 3.2.4–6.

28 *KS* 2.7.2431.

29 *KS* 2.7.28–30.

30 *KS* 5.5. This is the Īśvara-kāmita-prakaraṇa.

31 *KS* 5.5.26–27.

32 *KS* 6.5.37.

33 *KS* 5.5.28–29.

34 *KS* 5.5.31–36.

35 *KS* 5.6.10–28.

36 For everyday forms of resistance, see James Scott, *Weapons of the Weak: Everyday Forms of Peasant Resistance* (New Haven: Yale University Press, 1985), where he identifies defiance, disobedience, theft, agency, bad behaviour and deviance as modes of resistance in a 20th-century Malay village. On public and hidden transcripts, see Scott (1990). Scott uses the term 'public transcript' to refer to the open interaction between subordinates and those who dominate; and 'hidden transcript' to refer to off-stage discourse of the subordinated social groups, that takes place beyond the observation of those who wield power, and which is 'a condition of practical resistance rather than a substitute for it' (James Scott, *Domination and the Arts of Resistance: Hidden Transcripts* [New Haven and London: Yale University Press, 1990], p. 2, p. 4, p. 191). Also useful is Scott's related concept of infrapolitics, which refers to 'an unobtrusive realm of political struggle', which appears almost invisible, until we look for it (Scott, *Domination and the Arts of Resistance*, p. 183).

37 *Mbh.* 12.59.1–140.

38 *Mbh.* 12.70; 12.121; 12.122.40–41.

39 *Mbh.* 13.60.19–20.

40 For references to the killing of kings in ancient Indian texts, see Walter Ruben, 'Fighting against Despots in Old Indian Literature', *Annals of the Bhandarkar Oriental Research Institute* 48/49, 1968, pp. 111–18.

41 The idea of the king as protector of his subjects and of the social order of the *varṇas* and āśramas are frequently mentioned in rulers' epigraphic *praśastis* (eulogies). There are also occasional references in texts and inscriptions to the subjects intervening in matters related to succession. According to the Purāṇas, the Haryaṅka dynasty came to an end when Śiśunāga was elected by the people. The Khalimpur and Murshidabad plates of Dharmapāla (who ruled eastern India in the late 8th–early 9th century) state that the first Pāla king Gopāla I was made to take the hand of Lakṣmī (that is, was made king) by the people (*prakṛti*) in order to put an end to *matsya-nyāya*, a state of anarchy where the strong oppress and devour the weak. The normative theories of kingship are also invoked obliquely in Sandhyākara Nandī's *Rāmacarita*, while describing King Rāmapāla and the rebels Bhīma and Divya.

42 *AS* 1.20.15–16. Bhadrasena, king of Kaliṅga, was killed by his brother by lying concealed in the queen's chamber; the king of Kārūṣa was killed by his son because he was planning to appoint another son as his heir; the king of Kāśī Mahāsena was killed by his queen Suprabhā over a succession issue. Some of these incidents are mentioned in Bāṇa's *Harṣacarita* and Varāhamihira's *Bṛhatsaṁhitā*. They were clearly famous (Olivelle, *King, Governance and Law in Ancient India*, p. 491, and n.).

43 *AS* 9.5.

44 *AS* 8.2.2–4.

45 *AS* 12.5.

46 *AS* 5.1.4, 7.2.15.

47 *AS* 7.15.27.
48 *AS* 4.11.21.
49 *AS* 4.11.11.
50 *AS*, 4.13.33.
51 *AS* 7.5.19–33; 1.18.1, 1.19.28, 8.3.7.
52 This does not mean that these religious movements should be reduced to the level of a direct expression of social and economic issues; the situation was much more complex.
53 Ryosuke Furui (2014): 95 suggests that the 'popular uprising' element was part of the last phase of the rebellion, which he discusses on the basis of the *Rāmacarita*. For a more comprehensive view of the evidence and historiography of the Kaivarta revolt, see Kunal Chakrabarti, 'Brahmanical Hegemony and the Oppressed Social Groups: Rethinking the Kaivartta Revolt', in Osmund Bopearachchi and Suchandra Ghosh, eds, *Early Indian History and Beyond: Essays in Honour of Professor B.D. Chattopadhyaya* (New Delhi: Primus, 2019); and Sayantani Pal, 'Revisiting the Kaivartta Revolt: Locating the Emergence of a Caste', in Bopearachchi and Ghosh, eds, *Early Indian History and Beyond*. (2019).
54 See R.N. Nandi, *State Formation, Agrarian Growth and Social Change in Feudal South India c. AD 600–1200* (New Delhi: Manohar), pp. 125–27.

SECTION IV

Looking beyond India to Asia

14

Gifts from Other Lands: Southeast Asian Religious Endowments in India

The starting point of this essay is a dissatisfaction with the insularity of most histories of the Indian subcontinent, an insularity which is astonishing considering the enormous historical importance from very early times of the interactions across the various regions of what we now call 'Asia' and 'Europe'. From the perspective of the historiography of early South–Southeast Asia interactions in Indian scholarship, the demise of the problematic 'Greater India' frame was followed by many decades of a virtual neglect of this important historical issue. Although trade links consistently received attention, the manifestations, mechanisms and complexities of the larger range of cultural interactions are still very inadequately explored and understood.

The political dimension is an important part of the historical context of Asian interactions, and changes in perspectives on ancient and medieval polities therefore have a direct bearing on the subject. In the Indian context, the understanding of ancient and medieval empires has swung from one extreme (powerful, highly centralized states) to the other (weak, fragmented, highly decentralized polities). Unfortunately,

---

This chapter was previously published in Upinder Singh and Parul Pandya Dhar, eds, *Asian Encounters: Exploring Connected Histories* (New Delhi: Oxford University Press, 2014).

the critique of 'statist histories' has meant that an overestimation of the power of early Indian states has been replaced by a serious underestimation of their capacities and impact. In the Southeast Asian context too, questions have been raised about the nature of early political systems, and there has been a greater sensitivity than in the Indian context to the need to carefully examine the conceptual vocabulary and apparatus that is used when describing early states and empires.[1]

Recent scholarship has been more attentive to the self-representations of premodern political structures in literary, epigraphic and monumental sources. Such an approach can be extended towards a better understanding of the nature of political interactions between ancient states across the regions of Asia. Examining the web of these political interactions requires adopting multiple perspectives rooted in different aspects of the histories of the various South and Southeast Asian geo-political units involved. Further, although we should be aware of the constraints involved in travel and communication in ancient times, we should not underestimate the level of trans-regional awareness and interactions. In fact, the evidence clearly indicates that ancient monarchs were much more clued into what was happening in distant regions than we might expect them to be.

This chapter takes up one theme in a much larger, very complex story—religious endowments made by Southeast Asian rulers in India.[2] The basic 'facts' about these trans-regional gifts are well known, and historians have generally interpreted them as manifestations of religious diplomacy reflecting commercial and/or political interests.[3] The contention of this chapter is that a close reading of the inscriptions recording such endowments is necessary in order to fully understand the meanings attached to them by those involved in the transactions. The carefully crafted phraseology of the inscriptions, in fact, reveals certain important underlying assumptions about the ideas and relationships that were central to these grants. The questions that are raised in this chapter include: how are the making of such gifts and their significance represented in the idiom of inscriptional discourse, and what do the details of the inscriptional discourse tell us about the act of making such gifts? Is it possible to look at the phenomenon of religious endowments from the intersection of multiple perspectives—from those of Indian and Southeast Asian political histories, commerce and diplomacy, and the history of religions and regions? These questions are addressed here through an analysis of the epigraphic records of gifts made by Southeast Asian rulers at Nālandā, Bodh Gayā and Nāgapaṭṭinam.

The Gift by a Śailendra King at Nālandā

Nālandā fell within the political circuit of the Pāla kings and already seems to have had an Asian renown by the mid-1st millennium CE. Apart from being on the itinerary of Chinese monks such as Xuanzang, a Korean inscription refers to the 13th/14th century Indian monk Tinabotuo being trained and ordained at Nālandā prior to travelling to Beijing.[4] The accounts of Tārānātha and Dharmasvāmin testify to the connections of Tibetan monks with the place. Here, we are particularly concerned with a specific inscription—the Nālandā copper plate of Devapāla.[5] When analyzing this mid-9th century inscription, we should also keep in mind the larger cultural context of interactions between Bengal and Southeast Asia, which included trade and artistic exchange.

The Nālandā copper plate inscription (66 lines of Sanskrit in the Siddhamatrika script) records a grant of five villages by the Pāla king Devapāladeva in his 39th regnal year, at the request of *mahārāja* Bālaputradeva, the Śailendra ruler of Suvarṇadvīpa/Yavabhūmi (both the terms occur) in favour of a monastery built by the latter at Nālandā. The Śailendra dynasty was based in central Java. While several scholars have identified Suvarṇadvīpa/Yavabhūmi with Śrīvijaya, this equation is not free from doubt. Bālaputradeva's request was communicated through an unnamed envoy or envoys. The income from the villages was to provide for the various needs of the *bhikṣu*s living there, for the writing of the *dharma-ratna*s (Buddhist texts), and for the maintenance of the monastery. This inscription can be placed in the 9th century CE.[6]

Although the inscription follows the general pattern of the Pāla land grants, certain aspects are noteworthy in the context of the present discussion. It was a substantial grant—five whole villages in two districts. The importance of the gift is also indicated by the fact that the *dūta* (messenger) was an important person, namely Balavarman, the overlord of Vyāghrataṭī-maṇḍala, who is likened to the right hand of the reigning Pāla king. There are also other unnamed envoys—line 37 refers to a *dūtaka* who orally conveyed Bālaputra's request to Devapāla, while line 63 refers to *dūta*s in the plural.

The inscription contains two separate, sequential *praśasti*s (eulogies) of the two kings involved in the transaction, and there is no direct statement about their relationship in terms of either paramountcy–subordination or of alliance. However, the comparison of the eulogies of Devapāla and Bālaputra leave no doubt that the charter (which must have been composed and inscribed under the direction of the Pāla court) aims at exalting the former and his lineage much more than the latter. The level of detail and specificity in the *praśasti* of the Pāla king is far greater than that of the Śailendra king.[7] The content of the eulogistic verses confirms the inference that can be made on the basis of the number of lines and verses. Bālaputra is praised, and that too using some of the standard imagery associated with the ideal ruler in the Pāla *praśasti*s—there is reference to his martial prowess, and to his fame pervading the universe and being equal to that of the *Mahābhārata* heroes. This ruler of Yavabhūmi or Suvarṇadvīpa is described as an expert in crushing the pride of the rulers of the world. Devapāla, for his part, is said to have ruled from the Himālaya to the ocean, conquered the earth up to the ocean, and subdued the whole world. But beyond this, symmetry makes way for asymmetry in panegyric: there is less specificity about the precise nature of Bālaputra's greatness, and the details of his lineage are rather meagre. The name of his mother Tārā is given, but that of his father is not specified.

The asymmetry becomes even clearer when we compare the royal epithets. Devapāla has the titles of political paramountcy—*parameśvara*, *paramabhaṭṭāraka* and *mahārājādhirāja*. Bālaputra, on the other hand, is a mere *mahārāja*. In the pecking order represented by royal epithets, the ideas conveyed (delicately, but very definitely) by the composer of the *praśasti* are: the king of Suvarṇadvīpa may have been a paramount king in his *own* geo-political sphere (or *maṇḍala*), but was not one in the *maṇḍala* of eastern India. He was not a subordinate of the Pāla king, but an independent, respectable contemporary whose might and glory and level of paramountcy, even in his own *maṇḍala*, were not to be considered equivalent to that of the Pāla king. There is a certain blending of attributes of the two kings, but the descriptions also have a subtle asymmetry. It is the level and extent of hyperbole that is the key to understanding the nature of the relationship that the inscription inscribes. Of course, we are looking at how this relationship was represented by the Pāla court panegyrist. Bālaputra's version, if there had been one, may well have been very different.

Devapāla and Bālaputra do have one important thing in common—they are both described as devotees of the Buddha.[8] The grant fits in with what we know about the strong Buddhist element in the personal religious orientation and patronage policy of the Pālas and Śailendras.[9] The gift is described as a pious, meritorious act (*dharmmādhikāra*, line 51; *sat-kīrtti*; line 65) that would establish virtue over all the world. An important aspect of the inscription is who the merit arising from the gift is supposed to go to. Line 37 states that the villages were granted for the increase in the merit (*puṇya*) and fame (*yaśas*) of Devapāla and his parents. On the other hand, verse 33 may perhaps (there is some ambiguity here) suggest that Bālaputra, having made the request to Devapāla through envoys, made the grant for the welfare (*hitodayāya*) of himself, his parents and the world. If this is the case, the inscription suggests a sharing between the two kings of the merit accruing from the gift. This would then actually be considered a joint donation, both in terms of the donors and the merit-recipients, by two kings who describe themselves as devotees of the Buddha.

It should be noted that the 9th century Nālandā copper plate represents the earliest endowment by a Southeast Asian ruler in the subcontinent. It should be noted that Bālaputra's mind is described as having been attracted by the many excellences of Nālandā (verse 32). This indicates the fame and eminence that this monastic centre had achieved in this part of Southeast Asia by the 9th century.

The Burmese Endowments at Bodh Gayā

We now shift our focus to the long history of Burmese interventions at Bodh Gayā. What is most interesting is that some of the various Burmese 'repairers' of the temple refer to the forgetting and remembering of previous rounds of activity at the site. Further, we are not only looking at activities that affected the physical structure of temple, but which also involved the land that lay in its hinterland, and the worship that was going on in the shrine.

The first piece of evidence comes from Myanmar—an inscription belonging to the reign of Kyanzittha, king of Pagan (c. 1084–1111),[10] found at the Shwesandaw Pagoda in Pyay, Myanmar. This epigraph refers to the temple (it is referred to as the temple of Śrī Bajrās, i.e. the *vajrāsana*) having been destroyed by other kings, and to various activities sponsored there by Kyanzittha. These included sending jewels of various kinds in a ship (this indicates a sea expedition) in order to finance various activities, namely to repair the temple; to buy some land and dig a tank and make dams/embankments/channels for irrigating the surrounding land (presumably this was land under the control of the temple); to make provisions for the burning of perpetual candles in the temple; to present various musical instruments including xylophones; and to arrange for singing and dancing that was finer than ever before.[11] There is no reference to any Indian ruler or monk in this inscription.

Another inscription recording Burmese activities at Bodh Gayā was found at Bodh Gayā itself. It is a late 13th century epigraph, inscribed on a grey basalt slab (20ft × 18ft) that used to be embedded in the east wall of the monastic compound.[12] Its present location is unknown. The language is Burmese of the Arakanese type and the script belongs to the Burmese lapidary variety called Kyouktsa (or stone letters). There are several different published readings and interpretations of this inscription. The epigraph was earlier believed to record a mission sent by a ruler of Arakan (or his overlord, the king of Pagan) to carry out repairs to the temple.[13] According to Ko,[14] the benefactions made to the Bodh Gayā temple may have been made for the spiritual benefit of Alaungsithu (the successor of Kyanzittha), who was the king of Pagan and the overlord of the Arakanese ruler. He further suggests that these benefactions may have been one of the conditions of the restoration of Letyāmengnan to the Arakanese throne due to the intercession of Kyanzittha. On the other hand, Stargardt suggests that the repair project may have been initiated by Kyanzittha and completed by his Arakanese vassal, and points out that it shows the intersection of the religious and commercial interests of Burmese rulers.[15] However, according to Luce,[16] this inscription has been repeatedly misread and misinterpreted. According to his revised reading and translation, which we can accept, the mission was dispatched by the 'Lord of the White Elephant', a king whose identity is unclear. Citing Luce and Ba Shin's reading of the text, Griswold[17] suggests that this might be a reference to king Tarukplyi or more likely his son Klawcwā, or to a crown prince named Klacwā.

On the basis of Luce's translation, the purport of the inscription is as follows: When 218 years of the Buddha's dispensation had elapsed, one of the 84,000 *caityas* built by Siri Dhammasoka (i.e., the Maurya emperor Aśoka), king of Jambudvīpa, at the place where the milk-rice offering had been made (a clear reference to Sujātā's offering of *pāyasa* to Siddhārtha at Bodh Gayā) fell into ruin due to the stress of age and time.[18] A senior *paṅsaku* monk repaired the *caitya*. Thereafter, it fell into ruin again. The 'King of the Law', 'Lord of the White Elephant' sent his *ācārya* Dhammarājaguru to repair it, and the latter took along his pupil Siri Kassapa. When the finances were found to be insufficient, at the request of a Vanavāsi monk, Putasin Maṅ (i.e., Buddhasena, who seems to have been a local ruler) extended a helping hand, which seems to have involved financial assistance. The work was thereafter resumed, and continued from 1296 till 1298 CE. The inscription goes on to give details of the dedication ceremony that was held when the work was completed.

This included offerings of flags and streamers; thousands of offerings of rice alms and lamps; a *kalpavṛkṣa* adorned with gold and silver flowers, cups and garments; and two children styled as the donor's son and daughter. Further, in order to provide for the daily offering of rice at the temple in perpetuity, land, slaves and cattle were bought and dedicated to the shrine. The donor asserts that he had made this meritorious gift so that he could attain *nirvāṇa* and attain sainthood when the Buddha Maitreya arrived.

The inscription shows an awareness of a temple established much earlier at Bodh Gayā by Aśoka and mentions two rounds of disrepair and repair, giving details of the second one. The Burmese activities at Bodh Gayā recorded here seem to have lasted at least two years. It should be noted that Burma has a long tradition of kings 'repairing' shrines. It is unlikely that a distinction was made between repair, embellishment, renovation and adding additional elements or structures to a temple complex. However, Griswold[19] argues that although the two early repair missions made many changes (and he details what these might have consisted of), the Burmese must have respected the basic structure of Mahābodhi. While the inscription refers to the extension of some financial help towards the repair project by a local ruler, it is dominated by an account of the Burmese benefactors and their activities. The audience of the inscription was Burmese, as is evident from the Burmese language and script used in it. This gift had nothing to do with establishing or furthering diplomatic relations with any Indian power. It has to be understood against the background of the nature of the state and kingship in Pagan, where wars of conquest were represented as quests for Buddhist relics and where the relationship between the state and the Buddhist *saṅgha* was a key element in the political system.[20] The kings of Pagan had a close relationship with Sri Lanka, which was the place where monks were periodically sent to be 'purified'. Simultaneously, the monarchy sought to establish connections with India.[21] Apart from the intrinsic importance of Bodh Gayā as the place of Siddhārtha's enlightenment in the Buddhist tradition, the geographical proximity and the long history of trade interactions between Burma and eastern India form the broader context of the choice of this site for the interventions and donative activities of Burmese rulers.

Another issue of interest is the condition at Bodh Gayā at the time when this gift was made. Although there is mention of some financial help being obtained from a local ruler who was evidently not inimical towards Buddhism, there is no reference to any interaction with members of a local *saṅgha*, suggesting that this may have been a relatively 'fallow' period in the institutional control over the shrine and the area. A 12th century inscription at Bodh Gayā refers to the Siṅghala *saṅgha* at Mahābodhi,[22] and suggests the possibility of an inflow of income derived from Sri Lankan pilgrims at around this time. This does not necessarily indicate that the shrine was the focus of heavy pilgrim traffic in the 12th–13th centuries, but simply that it was dominated by a monastic order of Sri Lankan affiliation. Actually, the detailed long-term history of pilgrimage activity at Bodh Gayā remains to be written.[23]

The 13th century Burmese inscription at Bodh Gayā has to be seen in the context of several larger histories—of long-standing India–Burmese commercial interactions,[24] of the intertwining of religious and commercial interests and activities, pilgrimage and donative activities at Bodh Gayā, and especially of the place of royal patronage of Buddhism in Burmese traditions of kingship over many centuries.

A few additional pieces of evidence from the site can be cited here, many of them assembled by B. M. Barua. The Burmese were not the only ones to make their presence felt at Bodh Gayā; there were Sri Lankan and Chinese interventions as well. The earliest recorded set of such activities took place in the 7th or 8th century, and the person responsible was Prakhyātakīrtti, a Sri Lankan monk who had genealogical connections with the island's ruling family. A Sanskrit inscription indicates that his activities involved building a new temple next to the *vajrāsana* (to the west of it and the great temple); provisions for repair; the gift of 100 cows each for two perpetual lamps to be placed before the image of the Buddha in the temple and one in the monastery; and the digging of a water reservoir and laying out of a field for the provision of the monks' needs.[25] Further, five 11th century Chinese inscriptions have also been found at Bodh Gayā, recording gifts by Chinese monks, including those of stone *stūpa*s and a stone slab inscribed with a hymn of praise to the Buddha.[26] One of these inscriptions states that the monk in question had been sent to gift the stone *stūpa* at the command of the Song emperor, indicating that Bodh Gayā was also attracting the patronage of East Asian elites.

Apart from the Burmese inscriptions mentioned above, Burmese elements in certain brick inscriptions and relief carvings are suggestive of the presence and activities of Burmese artisans at the site.[27] The importance of Bodh Gayā for Burmese kings is further indicated by the building of a 16th/17th century 'Mahābodhi temple' at Mrauk U, the ancient capital of Arakan. Htilo Minlo, who ruled from Pagan in the 13th century in fact built a temple in his capital city that was modeled on the celebrated Bodh

Gayā shrine. A 15th century and an early 19th century king are known to have dispatched missions to Bodh Gayā to take plans of the bodhi tree and of the temple, to serve as models for shrines to be built in Burma.[28]

The Burmese engagement with Bodh Gayā seems to have become especially intense in the 19th century. Apart from the activities of the mission mentioned above (sent in 1810 by king Bodawpaya), three inscriptions at Bodh Gayā testify to further Burmese activities at the site. The first was inscribed on what Mitra describes as a bluish bevel-rimmed marble slab mounted on two iron frames in front of the Bāradwāri of the monastery. It is present stored in the precincts of the maṭha. On the obverse of the stone is a long inscription[29]—a bilingual record consisting of 14 lines comprising two 'corrupt Sanskrit' stanzas followed by lines in 'corrupt Pali' and the Nagari script. This is followed by an inscription in 32 lines in the Burmese language (the modern vernacular of Ava) and script; on the reverse is another Burmese inscription consisting of 39 lines. All these inscriptions are interrelated. The first Burmese inscription is supposedly a rendering of the Sanskrit/Pali inscription; the second Burmese inscription deals with the same donation, but there are differences in the level of detail. It is not clear why two inscriptions narrating slightly different versions of the same events were inscribed on the same stone slab. A few interesting aspects of this set of inscriptions can be noted: The main purport is to record that a Burmese king titled Thīti Pavara Suddhama *mahārājādhirāja* sent by land and water, via Arakan, his *purohita* and minister with offerings for the bodhi tree in year 1183 of the Burmese era (of 638; i.e., in 1822)[30] and that before doing so, the king, along with his queen, performed a long-distance dedication ceremony which is described. The expected merit of the gift was that the king might become a Buddha himself, and he shared the merit arising out his good deeds with his parents and ancestors.

Apart from the actual gifts that they record, the inscriptions on the obverse of the slab tell a remarkable story, beginning with Gautama's enlightenment. We are told that the king heard through *yogis* and Brahmins who came from India about a *bodhi* tree near the bank of the Narinzara river at Gayā in the Magadha kingdom; he heard that there was a temple built by Aśoka at the spot where the *Wazira than* (i.e., *vajrāsana*) stood, and that there was also a Burmese inscription there recording the repair of the temple in year 657 (of the Burmese era of 638, i.e., in 1295). The king put two and two together, seeing that the descriptions that he had heard were similar to those given in the books, and surmised that this must be none other than the place of the Buddha's enlightenment. The tree is then described, and we are told that the king did homage to it from a distance, and then dispatched his gifts after performing a dedication ceremony. What we have here is a reference in a 19th century Burmese inscription to the earlier Burmese inscription of the 12th/13th century discussed above! This inscription also suggests that the connections between the Buddha, Aśoka, Bodh Gayā and the earlier Burmese gift had been forgotten and reconstructed. Of course, it is not clear whether the forgetting and remembering are to be taken literally or whether this was a way of emphasizing the dramatic nature of the donor's gifts.

The second Burmese inscription on the reverse of the marble slab gives more details about every aspect—the Buddha and his *dhamma*, the Burmese king, the inquiries he made and who his informants were, his keenness to make offerings to the tree like his royal ancestors Aśoka, Piyatissa and Kaliṅga, and his sending his priest and men to make the gift. The names of the minister composers of the two Burmese inscriptions are different, and another minister is mentioned in the second inscription as having been sent to inscribe the inscription, which, according to its text, was installed on the full moon day in 1183 of the Burmese era, i.e., 1822.

There are two other 19th century Burmese inscriptions at Bodh Gayā.[31] One is a short inscription on a miniature *stūpa* placed as a finial on the balustrade in front of the Bāradwārī. It is a 1823 epigraph, which refers to its having been written by Shime-pu, a resident of Kwan-tshwai. Another inscription is inscribed on the pedestal of an image of Śiva and Pārvatī, which Mitra describes as lying at the foot of the bodhi tree. This 1809 inscription seems to record a gift made by two individuals who came to this place in this connection. Mitra states that these two records are of little interest, except that the second shows how utterly careless the pious travellers were that they did not know that they were having their gift inscribed on the pedestal of a Hindu statue. Actually, both these inscriptions are important from several points of view. They add to the evidence of the Burmese connections of Bodh Gayā. The second one also shows the prominent presence of Śaiva statuary at the place. Why what seems to be a Buddhist donation was inscribed on this sculpture is an intriguing question—was it either due to ignorance, or was the sculpture interpreted differently by the pious Buddhist donors?[32]

Another Burmese attempt to 'repair' the Mahābodhi temple in the 19th century took place in 1874 during the reign of king Mindon and is recorded in Rajendralala Mitra's *Buddha Gaya*.[33] Mitra describes the activities of the 'Burmese gentlemen' who were trying to 'repair' the temple. They were politely asked to leave by the British government.[34]

For the first time, pious inter-regional religious endowments and engagements had stumbled across the barrier of archaeologists and conservationists of a colonial state, who saw such activities as interfering with the 'intrinsic' nature of an ancient historical monument.

The Burmese inscriptions at Bodh Gayā do not necessarily indicate regular or substantial pilgrim traffic at the place. In fact, judging from mid-19th photographs, the temple seems to have been in bad shape at that time.[35] Nor do they indicate a *continuous* political engagement of Burmese elites with the site. But these inscriptions leave no doubt that at certain junctures over a long period of time, the Mahābodhi temple was invoked by Burmese rulers in order to enhance their prestige, and that the temple had an important symbolic significance for Burmese elites.[36] If this is to be understood as religious diplomacy, it was aimed at a home audience, not an Indian one.

The Buddhist Vihāra at Nāgapaṭṭinam

From Bodh Gayā we move southwards to Nāgapaṭṭinam and to two specific inscriptions—the larger and smaller Leiden plates. Much has been written about these inscriptions and even more so about their historical contexts, especially the nature of the Cōḻa state and the nature of Cōḻa interactions with Southeast Asia. The Cōḻas were the only Indian power to extend their arms well beyond the subcontinent. Apart from their frequent military engagements in Sri Lanka, Rājendra's expedition to Śrīvijaya has been the focus of much interest, especially insofar as it is seen as a political act aimed at protecting and enhancing maritime commercial interests.[37]

Here, we are not concerned with the Cōḻa expedition against Śrīvijaya but with certain religious endowments made by Śrīvijaya kings at Nāgapaṭṭinam. The larger Leiden plates[38] record the grant of a village named Āṇaimaṅgalam by Rājarāja I to a Buddhist establishment at Nāgapaṭṭinam known as Cūḷāmaṇivarma-vihāra, constructed by a ruler of Śrīviṣaya and Kaṭāha named Māravijayottuṅgavarman of the Śailendra family, in the name of his father Cūḷāmaṇivarman. The grant was made by Rājarāja in the 21st year of his reign (i.e., in 1006), but the copper plate document (*śāsana*) was issued during the reign of his son Madhurāntaka, i.e., Rājendra I. The smaller Leiden plates of Kullotuṅga[39] (dated in year 20 of the king's reign, i.e., 1090) record a grant of villages to the same Buddhist establishment, described as having been constructed by the Kaḍāram king. Kaḍāram has been identified as being located in the Malay peninsula and was at this time probably under the control of Śrīvijaya, although it is possible that it enjoyed a certain amount of autonomy.[40]

Let us look at the larger and smaller Leiden plates in turn and then juxtapose the evidence of the two sets of inscriptions, especially examining some of the inferences that can be made by reading between the lines. The sheer length of the larger Leiden plates (443 lines inscribed on 21 copper plates) makes it one of the longest Cōḻa inscriptions, and one of the longest inscriptions found so far in the Indian subcontinent. This in itself should point to the importance attached by the Cōḻas to the endowment. Like many Cōḻa inscriptions, this one too consists of two parts—one in Sanskrit, the other in Tamil.[41] The Sanskrit part is in the Grantha script (111 lines covering both sides of five copper plates) and gives the invocation, a detailed Cōḻa genealogy and the purport of the inscription. It tell us that in the 21st year of his reign (i.e., in 1006), Rājarāja Cōḻa gave the village of Āṇaimaṅgalam to a temple of the Buddha in the Cūḷāmaṇivarma-vihāra, which had been built by the ruler of Śrīviṣaya and Kaṭāha named Māravijayottuṅgavarman, who belonged to the Śailendra family, and who was the son of Cūḷāmaṇivarman (the temple was obviously built in his name, i.e., memory). It goes on to tell us that after the death of Rājarāja, his son Rājendra had a permanent edict issued for the village granted by his father.

The Tamil portion of the inscription (this has a few Grantha letters, but is for the most part in the Tamil script) consists of 332 lines covering both sides of 16 copper plates. It repeats the gist of the Sanskrit portion, but gives far greater details of the grant—the details of the land, its boundaries, its income, the many officials associated with the grant, the process of making the gift, the terms of the grant, detailed instructions about water management and the signatures of witnesses. It is interesting to note that the Sanskrit portion of the inscription has the *praśasti*, which the Tamil portion does not have, and the Tamil portion has the details of the grant which are absent in the Sanskrit portion—a division of labour that is known from other Cōḻa records as well.

For the purpose of the subject of this essay, a few noteworthy aspects of this inscription can be singled out. The level and nature of detail about the Cōḻa and the Śailendra king are very disproportionate. The eulogy of the latter is very brief and perfunctory, with no reference whatsoever to his martial qualities or achievements (although he is described as having mastered statecraft). Even more interesting is the fact that the Sanskrit part, which gives the detailed Cōḻa genealogy, was added onto the Tamil portion at a later date (this is clear from the contents). While it is theoretically possible that the Sanskrit portion replaced an earlier Tamil or Sanskrit prelude (in fact many Cōḻa inscriptions have such a division into Sanskrit and Tamil), the length and detail of the *praśasti* may well represent an important and historically significant afterthought—an attempt of the Cōḻas to assert more strongly Cōḻa authority vis-à-vis the grant that had been made, over the Buddhist establishment that it was made in favour of, and also over the Kaḍāram king.

The inscription associates much pomp and show with the grant. It tells us that the ceremony of walking around the boundaries with a female elephant that accompanied the grant involved the participation of assemblies (*sabhās* and *ur*s) of 26 villages. This and the fact that the signatories to the grant included representatives of these and two more villages emphasized the political importance of the grant. The Buddhist establishment seems to have been a very large one, as it apparently took at least nine years to build; its magnificence is indicated in the inscription where it is described as having lowered Kanakagiri, i.e. mount Meru. The relationship between the Śailendra kings, the Cōḻas and this Buddhist establishment extended over several generations, both before and after the Cōḻa invasion of Śrīvijaya. It is likely that a copper plate document was issued during the time of Rājarāja, but that there was some problem, possibly arising out of the hostilities between Rājendra I and the Śrīvijayans in c. 1025–1026 (perhaps the grant was even revoked). Some ten years after the hostilities, some semblance of cordiality seems to have been restored, leading to Rājendra confirming the gift of the village made by his father 29 years earlier.

The smaller Leiden plates are only three in number, but give us an important insight into the later history of this very Buddhist establishment. This inscription is entirely in the Tamil language and script (with a few Grantha letters) and there is no *praśasti*. The inscription gets straight to business. It tells us that messengers (*dūta*s) of the king of Kaḍāram petitioned Rājakesarivarman, (i.e., Kulottuṅga Cōḻa) in the 20th year of his reign (i.e., in 1090) to issue a copper plate in favour of the *saṅgha* of the *paḷḷi* of Cūḍāmaṇivarma-vihāra in Śolakulavallipaṭṭaṇam (i.e., Nāgapaṭṭinam). While this name is mentioned in the inscription, the Cōḻa authority over the establishment is indicated by the reference to the names of two temples that were part of this complex—namely Rājendraśoḷapperumpaḷḷi and Rājarājapperumpaḷḷi, described as having been constructed by the king of Kaḍāram. These may have been two new shrines in the complex. The purpose of the document was to record the details of certain land in several villages assigned to the establishment. The details of the land grant indicate that the land assigned to the *vihāra* as *paḷḷicchanda*s had increased greatly from the time of the earlier inscription.

It may be noted that the endowments recorded in the larger and smaller Leiden plates are also different in several respects from the grant of the Pagan/Arakan king at Mahābodhi. The location of the Buddhist complex at Nāgapaṭṭinam was not dictated by the sacred landscape of Buddhism, but by the fact that this port city had by this time eclipsed Māmallapuram and Kāveripaṭṭinam and had emerged as the premier Cōḻa port.[42] Nāgapaṭṭinam was not known for its Buddhist monasteries, and in fact, the one endowed by the Kaḍāram king may well have been the most magnificent one in the city.

It is also important to note how different this record of Śrīvijaya endowments in another king's domain is from the pattern of the Śrīvijaya inscriptions found in Śrīvijaya itself.[43] Very few Śrīvijaya inscriptions are known (Cœdès in fact talks of the 'architectural poverty and the epigraphic penury' of this kingdom[44]). Most of them are in Malay, with many Sanskrit words, and are written in a variety of the Brahmi script. Even more significant is that notwithstanding certain common religious elements, the ideas of kingship that these inscriptions (although they are older than the Cōḻa ones) reveal, including curse formulae and benedictions connected with *praṇidhāna*s, are completely different in form and ethos from those of the Cōḻa inscriptions. They clearly reflect two very different kinds of discourses on kingship.[45] In terms of language, content and phraseology, the two sets of Leiden plates completely adhere to Cōḻa, not Śrīvijaya conventions.

To all this can be added the evidence of other inscriptions which indicate a different kind of religious endowment from the Kaḍāram end at Nagapaṭṭinam. An inscription in the Śaiva Karonasvāmin temple records a grant made by an agent of the Kidaram (i.e., Kaḍāram) king. Another inscription in the same temple records a grant made by another agent of the Śrīvijaya king in the third regnal year of Rājendra I. A third inscription from the same temple refers to a grant made by an agent of the Kidaram king in the seventh year of Rājendra (1019).[46] These were endowments made before Rājendra's invasion of Śrīvijaya. Taken together, the inscriptions suggest that the activity of Śrīvijaya royal gifting started in Rājarāja's time, with a major Buddhist monastery being established by the Śrīvijaya king at Nāgapaṭṭinam. This was followed by certain gifts made by agents of the Śrīvijaya king at a particular Śaiva temple in the early years of Rājendra's reign. There was a lull in activity thereafter, and for many years after Rājendra's invasion of Śrīvijaya, which must have left some hostile residue. It is some 10 years after that invasion that Rājendra issued an edict confirming the gift made by his father many years earlier. The connections having been restored and confirmed via royal decree, the *vihāra* at Nāgapaṭṭinam received Cōḻa patronage in the form of the grant of land at the request of their Śrīvijaya counterparts 55 years later, during the time of Kulottuṅga I.

There were thus two major foci of donative activity by Śrīvijaya elites in the Cōḻa empire—the Buddhist *vihāra* at Nāgapaṭṭinam (the more important one) and the Karonasvāmin temple.[47] While the commercial interactions between South India and Śrīvijaya preceded Rājendra, his reign marked an important break in terms not only of his launch of naval campaign/s into the latter region but also in the creation of a Buddhist centre sponsored by the Śrīvijayans in a premier Cōḻa port. After this there is a break, and then a resumption much later in the process of endowments during the time of Kulottuṅga.

The major 'foreign' donative activity that we see in the Cōḻa realm was that of the Śrīvijayans. But there was one more player—the king of Kāmboja, who features as donor in two inscriptions. The Karandai copper plate of Rājendra I refers to the present of a chariot by an unnamed Kāmboja king (i.e., a king of Angkor) to Rājendra I, dated in the latter's eighth regnal year, i.e., 1020. This was a unique, magnificent politico-diplomatic gift loaded with symbolic significance. The Chidambaram inscription of Kullottuṅga I, dated in the 44th year of the Kulottuṅga's reign (c. 1114), refers to a gemstone presented by an unnamed Kāmboja king.[48]

The Implications of Trans-regional Endowments

It is noteworthy that the instances of the royal patronage of Buddhist establishments by Southeast Asian kings in India took place at the juncture by when Buddhism had declined in many parts of the subcontinent (eastern India is an exception). These grants point to a qualitatively new stage in the patronage of Buddhist sites and to a new kind of interaction among Asian polities. The Indic and Southeast Asian attitude towards patronage to religious establishments was not one of 'tolerance' (as it is frequently misrepresented as) but of an incorporative kingship within a polytheistic or monolatorous context, and has to be looked at in the context of royal *policy*. Further, I do not think that there are instances of rulers within the subcontinent making religious endowments in the political domain of another subcontinental ruler. Also, as far as I know, there is no epigraphic evidence of the kind of joint donative activity that we have noted here between two South Asian rulers.[49]

If we juxtapose the epigraphic evidence of the various donations discussed above, we can discern the following patterns: The points from where the Southeast Asian royal gifts emanated were Java, Śrīvijaya, Pagan and Angkor. There were two points of the Śrīvijaya and Śailendra interface—Nālandā in eastern India and Nāgapaṭṭinam in South India. Angkor too interfaced with the Cōḻas. The kings of Pagan, on the other hand, had an intense and much longer-term relationship and interaction with Bodh Gayā. In fact, of all the Buddhist sites in India, Bodh Gayā seems to have been of preeminent importance when it came to trans-regional endowments. It should be noted that these and other instances of inter-state patronage discussed here do not fall within the same category. Cōḻa temple construction in Sri Lanka represented yet another type of inter-state religious patronage, signifying an assertion of political power over the island. Further, there is a need to look more closely at how the different types of religious endowments intersected with other kinds of inter-state interactions, including war.

The conceptual framework of *rāja-maṇḍala*s is useful to understand political interactions between the regions of Asia. We should note the fact that we are dealing with several different *sets* of *maṇḍala*s; this is evident in the fact that the rulers in question are not explicitly placed in any direct relationship with each other (cf. for instance, the tributary relations with China, or the pecking order of paramount and subordinate kings that we see in Indian royal inscriptions). The phraseology of the Nālandā inscription suggests an asymmetrical relationship from the perspective of the composers of the inscriptions, but the Śailendra king is not described as a subordinate or vassal of the Pāla king.

Despite the religious and cultural diversity within and between South and Southeast Asia, the fact that religious gifts of this kind could be made suggests certain underlying similarities between these regions—a pluralism in religious context and in royal religious policy. The political context was one in which South Asian ideas of kingship and sovereignty could be extended with ease to include Southeast Asian rulers, although not in a way that was identical to the incorporation of South Asian rulers. Further, notwithstanding their differences and distinctiveness, Buddhism and Hinduism and the idea that religious merit could be transferred and shared, provided a religious context in which such trans-regional gifts could easily be conceptually accommodated. The significance of the transfer of merit as an important feature of Buddhist religious practice in the Buddhist context has been noted, but it should be emphasized that this is by no means only a Buddhist concept and is found in Jaina and Hindu donative inscriptions as well. The belief in the transfer and sharing of merit cut across many religious, cultural and geographical boundaries. This idea, not expounded in detail in religious texts, was evidently a powerful motivating force behind many a pious donation, and its importance cannot be over-emphasized. Further, the political implications of this important idea need to be underlined. Merit was not a fixed quantity, so there was no problem in it being shared by sovereign rulers and feudatories, or even, as we have seen, between rulers who were not in a direct relationship of paramountcy/subordination with each other.

The Ocean in Indian Ideas of Sovereignty

While examining these trans-regional royal gifts, we are dealing with traditions of kingship and sovereignty that had both overlapping as well as distinctive elements, and it is to one aspect of the Indic tradition that we now turn. The term *cakravartin*—the world conqueror, the wheels of whose chariots run unimpeded—itself suggests a land-locked idea of imperial conquest.[50] Of course Indian conquerors refer grandiosely to their victories over the entire earth girded by the oceans. But a question that arises is—what part did the ocean and crossing the ocean have in fantasies of power in ancient India? Was the ocean conceived of as water that connected or separated lands and people? A further question is: how did contemporary, even competing, sovereignties of distant lands intersect with each other?

The Cōḻas were the only Indian kings to send armies across the seas, and it is, therefore, especially pertinent to look at their *praśasti*s and at the place of the ocean in self-representations of Cōḻa imperium. The sea figures in many places in Cōḻa royal eulogy. For instance, the larger Leiden plates refer to Parāntaka protecting the earth girded by the ocean (this image occurs very frequently in royal inscriptions) and to Rājarāja having seen the other shore of the ocean of the collection of the arts. The larger Leiden plates refer to the southern ocean and the smaller plates to the western ocean. More specifically, Rājarāja is described in several inscriptions as 'one who has destroyed the ships at Kāndaḷūr' (*Kāndalūr-Śālai kalam = aṛuttu*). The Tiruvālaṅgāḍu plates state that 'all the waters of the sea were not enough to quench the fire of the Cōḻa king's anger'. The Senur inscription of Rājarāja states that all the kings of the sea (*kaḍal-araiśar*) waited on him. And the Tirukkadaiyur inscription of Rājendra I talks of his having despatched many ships in the midst of the rolling sea and describes his victorious campaign against Kaḍāram.[51]

And yet, we do not find any major art work (sculpture or painting) proclaiming the connection between the Cōḻa kings and the ocean. Neither are there any hero stones depicting sea battles in this region. This is in contrast to the prolific evidence from the domain of the Kadambas of Goa. There are many references in Kadamba *praśasti*s to the ocean. For instance, in a 12th century inscription of the time of Jayakesin II found at Narendra in Dharwar district, Karnataka, apart from the frequent epithet 'lord of the western ocean' and 'lord of the ocean' there are many other references to the ocean.[52] The ruler Chaṭṭayadeva is said to have made a bridge of ships to Sri Lanka; he is described as having sailed over the sea in sport with great pomp from Gove to Surāṣṭra; and there is much oceanic imagery in the inscription. Especially interesting is the reference in verse 19 to king Jayakesin, the lord of the sea, swiftly checking the Cōḻa, who had approached recklessly, as the ocean streams over its boundaries. Further, there are many hero stones showing sea battles found in and around Goa. The inscriptions of the Pālas of eastern India too contain much oceanic imagery of a general kind—there are frequent references to the king as lord of the earth girded by the four (or seven) oceans, to the earth lying between two oceans, and to the king's glory crossing many oceans. A more specific reference is to the southern ocean (*dakṣiṇābdhi*). There are also specific references to bridges, and officers in charge of the fleet (*naukādhyakṣa*, *naubala-vyāpṛtaka*) although these may have been related to riverine rather than maritime activity.[53]

Notions of sovereignty in ancient and medieval India were clearly not oblivious to the sea, but the sea that they had in mind was usually the generic sea which girdled the land. The impetus for seaward political expansion was a rarity. Indic empires saw themselves and *were* generally land-locked ventures, with a few exceptions such as Samudragupta (c. 350–370) who claimed in his Allahabad *praśasti* to have sway over Siṁhala and all the other islands, and the Cōḻas who sailed further afield. But although Indian armies travelled across the Indian Ocean to Southeast Asia only once, religious gifts from other lands arrived on subcontinental soil on several occasions. These trans-regional interactions, whether overland or by sea, tell us something significant not only about the transactions themselves but also about similarities and differences in the nature of the interacting polities and societies.

Notes

1. See O. W. Wolters, *History, Culture, and Region in Southeast Asian Perspectives* (Singapore: Institute of Southeast Asian Studies, 1982), pp. 14–15, 16–21. Wolters' (actually Kauṭilya's) idea of the *maṇḍala* state makes good sense in the Indian context as well.
2. It is not, however, my contention that this was the only or most important element in India–Southeast Asia interactions in premodern times.
3. See, for instance, George W. Spencer, *The Politics of Expansion: The Chola Conquest of Sri Lanka and Sri Vijaya* (Chennai: New Era Publications, 1983), p. 144 and Hermann Kulke, 'The Naval Expeditions of the Cholas in the Context of Asian History', in Hermann Kulke, K. Kesavapany and Vijay Sakhuja, eds, *Nagapattinam to Suvarnadwipa: Reflections on the Chola Naval Expeditions to Southeast Asia* (Singapore: Institute of Southeast Asian Studies, 2009), pp. 1–19. The latter uses the term 'rituo-political donations'.
4. Tansen Sen, *Buddhism, Diplomacy, and Trade: The Realignment of Sino-Indian Relations, 600–1400* (New Delhi: Manohar, [2003] 2004), p. 107.
5. Hiranand Shastri, 'The Nalanda Copper-plate of Devapaladeva', *Epigraphia Indica* 17, 1923–1924, pp. 310–327; N. G. Majumdar, *Nālandā Copper Plate of Devapāladeva* (Rajshahi: Monographs of the Varendra Research Society, 1926), No. 1.
6. Going by the date of 810 generally given for the accession of Devapāla, the inscription and the grant it records (dated in this king's 39th regnal year) can be placed in 849. However, from the standpoint of Javanese history, J. G. de Casparis, *Prasasti Indonesia II: Selected Inscriptions from the Seventh to the Ninth Century A. D.* (Bandung: Masa Baru, 1956) argued that it belongs to c. 860.
7. The *praśasti* of Devapāla and his lineage covers at least 21 lines and 14 verses; that of the Śailendra king and his lineage consists of 10 lines and 8 verses.
8. According to F. Kielhorn, 'The Mungir Copper-Plate Grant of Devapaladeva', *Indian Antiquary* 21, 1892, pp. 253–258, fn. 54, there is double entendre in the invocation, and it praises both the Buddha and Devapāla. This is a debatable point. Although reference to the lord of the earth and benefitting the *prajā* could apply to both, 'Sugata' could not apply to the king. On the other hand, line 17 does give the analogy of the Pāla king inheriting his father's kingdom in the manner in which a *bodhisattva* attains the status of a Sugata, i.e., the Buddha. This is balanced by an analogy between Bālaputra and Siddhārtha, the son of Śuddhodana, in verse 31.

9. These two aspects need to be differentiated, although they did overlap; patronage policy was often much more broad-based than the personal religious inclinations of a ruler.
10. Shwesandaw Pagoda Inscription, *Epigraphia Birmanica* 1, (8), p. 163.
11. Janice Stargardt, 'Burma's Economic and Diplomatic Relations with India and China from Early Medieval Sources', *Journal of the Economic and Social History of the Orient* 14 (1), 1971, pp. 38–62, has pointed out that the material, especially bricks, and the labour would no doubt have been obtained on the spot, and that Indian bricks were much admired and were even imported into and used in Burma.
12. Alexander Cunningham, *Mahâbodhi or The Great Buddhist Temple under the Bodhi Tree at Buddha-Gaya* (London: W. H. Allen, 1892), pp. 76–77; Rajendralala Mitra, *Buddha Gaya: The Great Buddhist Temple—The Hermitage of Sakya Muni* (New Delhi and Varanasi: Indological Book House, [1878] 1972), pp. 206–207; Taw Sein Ko, 'Burmese Inscription at Bodh-Gaya', *Epigraphia Indica* 11, 1911–1912, pp. 118–120; G. H. Luce, 'Sources of Early Burma History', in C. D. Cowan and O. W. Wolters, eds, *Southeast Asian History and Historiography: Essays Presented to G. D. E. Hall* (Ithica and London: Cornell University Press, 1976), pp. 40–42.
13. Ko, 'Burmese Inscription at Bodh-Gaya'. There are different readings of the dates of the activities mentioned in the inscription—657–660, 667–668, 467–468. Ko sees it as an early 13th century inscription, while others suggest an early 12th century date. However, Luce asserts that the correct readings of the dates are 657 and 660, which correspond to 1295 and 1298 CE.
14. Ko, 'Burmese Inscription at Bodh-Gaya', p. 119.
15. Stargardt, 'Burma's Economic and Diplomatic Relations with India and China from Early Medieval Sources', p. 62. Stargardt also points out that the control of Pagan over Arakan was nominal.
16. Luce, G. H. 'Sources of Early Burma History', pp. 40–42.
17. A. B. Griswold, 'The Holy Land Transported: Replicas of the Mahābodhi Shrine in Siam and Elsewhere', *Paranavitana Felicitation Volume* (Columbo: M. D. Gunasena, 1965), pp. 173–221.
18. If 218 refers to the era of 544 BCE, this would correspond to 236 BCE, which would locate the event mentioned here towards the end of Aśoka's reign (c. 268–232 BCE).
19. Griswold, 'The Holy Land Transported', pp. 195–200.
20. For the relationship between kingship, Buddhism, the *saṅgha* and society in Pagan, see Michael Aung Thwin, 'Kingship, the Saṅgha, and Society in Pagan', in Kenneth R. Hall and John K. Whitmore, eds, *Explorations in Early Southeast Asian History: The Origins of Southeast Asian Statecraft* (Ann Arbor: Centre for South and Southeast Asian Studies, The University of Michigan, 1976), pp. 206–256. The claim by Kyanzittha that he had converted a 'Coli king' to the Buddha's doctrine can also be understood in the context of this relationship and was clearly for home consumption (Shwesandaw Pagoda inscription, Prome, *Epigraphica Birmanica* 1(8), p. 165).

21. On various Burmese traditions connecting the kings Anawratha and Kyanzittha with Sri Lanka and India, including the tradition of Kyanzittha having married a princess of Vaiśālī see R. C. Majumdar, *Ancient Indian Colonization in South-East Asia* (Baroda: The Maharaja Sayajirao University of Baroda Press, [1955] 1971), p. 59.
22. See Vinod Vihari Vidyavinoda, 'Two Inscriptions from Bodh Gaya', *Epigraphia Indica* 12, 1913–1914, pp. 27–30. Inscription A.
23. For an important contribution in this direction, see Janice Leoshko, ed., *Bodhgaya: The Site of Enlightenment* (Mumbai: Marg Publications, 1988).
24. See Stargardt, 'Burma's Economic and Diplomatic Relations with India and China from Early Medieval Sources', for a good discussion of these aspects. Burma was also important because the overland route between northeast India and China (often referred to as the southern silk route) passed through here.
25. Benimadhab Barua, *Gayā and Buddha Gayā*. Vol. 2: *Old Shrines at Buddha-Gayā* (Varanasi: Bhartiya Publishing House, [1934] 1975), p. 42.
26. Cunningham, *Mahâbodhi or The Great Buddhist Temple under the Bodhi Tree at Buddha-Gaya*, pp. 67–74.
27. Benimadhab Barua, *Gayā and Buddha—Gayā [Early History of the Holy Land]*, Vol. 1. (Varanasi: Bhartiya Publishing House, [1931] 1975), pp. 206–212.
28. Barua (*Gayā and Buddha Gayā*, Vol. 2, pp. 43–45). Barua does point out, however, that the style of the Mahābodhi temple does not seem to have had a major impact on the architectural style of Burmese temples.
29. Mitra, *Buddha Gaya*, pp. 211–227.
30. There is uncertainty about the precise event that this era marks.
31. Mitra, *Buddha Gaya*, pp. 227–228
32. For a discussion of the 'Hindu mode of encompassment' of the Bodh Gayā remains, see Alan Trevithick, 'British Archaeologists, Hindu Abbots, and Burmese Buddhists: The Mahabodhi Temple at Bodh Gaya, 1811–1877', *Modern Asian Studies* 33 (3), 1999, pp. 635–656. By this time, a mahant had established himself in this place. But this Buddhist inscription is inscribed on an already existing Śaiva image, which amounts to a Buddhist encompassment of a Hindu image. Perhaps both kinds of encompassment were going on simultaneously. On other aspects of the modern history of Bodh Gayā, see Nayanjot Lahiri, 'Bodh-Gaya: An Ancient Buddhist Shrine and its Modern History (1891–1904)', in Timothy Insoll, ed., *Case Studies in Archaeology and Religion* (Oxford: Archaeo Press, 1999), pp. 33–44.
33. Mitra, *Buddha Gaya*, pp. 227–228.
34. Upinder Singh, *The Discovery of Ancient India: Early Archaeologists and the Beginnings of Archaeology* (New Delhi: Permanent Black, 2004), pp. 220–221.
35. The 19th century sketches, on the other hand, show a hint of dilapidation, but a better over-all condition than the photograph does.
36. This is just part of the story. That there is a need to investigate the larger range of religious interactions between Burma and India is suggested by a 13th century Sanskrit–Tamil inscription recording a gift made to a Viṣṇu

temple at Pagan by a person named Kulaśekhara Nambi, evidently a native of Malabar (E. Hultzsch, 'A Vaishnava Inscription at Pagan', *Epigraphia Indica* 7, 1902–1903, pp. 197–198).

37. The Tirukkadaiyur inscription of Rājendra I, inscribed on the base of the central shrine of the Amṛtaghaṭeśvara temple in Thanjavur district, is dated in the 15th regnal year of Rājendra I (i.e., 1027) and describes the expedition of the Cōḻa army against Kaḍāram. There is a reference in the Perumbur inscription of Vīrarājendra to the conquest of Kaḍāram by Vīrarājendra; it is dated in this king's seventh year, i.e., 1070. For these inscriptions, see Noboru Karashima and Y. Subbarayalu, 'Ancient and Medieval Tamil and Sanskrit Inscriptions Related to Southeast Asia and China', in Hermann Kulke, K. Kesavapany and Vijay Sakhuja, eds, *Nagapattinam to Suvarnadwipa: Reflections on the Chola Naval Expeditions to Southeast Asia*, pp. 271–291. For various aspects of the Cōḻa expeditions, see Kulke, 'The Naval Expeditions of the Cholas in the Context of Asian History'.
38. K. V. Subrahmanya Aiyer, 'The Larger Leiden Plates (of Rajaraja I)', *EpigraphiaIndica* 22, 1933–1934, pp. 213–268.
39. K. V. Subrahmanya Aiyer, 'The Smaller Leiden Plates (of Kullotunga I)', *EpigraphiaIndica* 22, 1933–1934, pp. 267–281.
40. On the identity and relationship between Kaḍāram, Śrīvijaya and the Śailendras, see Pierre-Yves Manguin, Tan Sri Dato and Mubin Sheppard, *Sriwijaya: History, Religion & Language of an Early Malay Polity: Collected Studies by Georges Coedès and Louis-Charles Damais* (Kuala Lampur: Monograph of the Malaysian Branch of the Royal Asiatic Society, 1992), pp. 15, 99, 105.
41. It is not, however, the longest. The Karandai plates of Rājendra consist of 2,628 lines inscribed on 57 plates and the Thiruvindalur grant of his son are even longer (Y. Subbarayalu, personal communication).
42. On Nāgapaṭṭinam, see Gokul Seshadri, 'New Perspectives on Nagapattinam: The Medieval Port City in the Context of Political, Religious, and Commercial Exchanges between South India, Southeast Asia and China', in *Nagapattinam to Suvarnadwipa: Reflections on the Chola Naval Expeditions to Southeast Asia*, eds., Hermann Kulke, K. Kesavapany and Vijay Sakhuja, pp. 102–134.
43. See Georges Cœdès in Manguin, Dato and Sheppard *Sriwijaya: History, Religion & Language.*
44. See Cœdès in Manguin, Dato and Sheppard, *Sriwijaya: History, Religion & Language*, p. 43.
45. On Śrīvijayan kingship, see Kenneth Hall, 'State and Statecraft in Early Srivijaya', in Kenneth Hall and John K. Whitmore, eds, *Explorations in Early Southeast Asian History: The Origins of Southeast Asia Statecraft* (Ann Arbor: Centre for South and Southeast Asian Studies, University of Michigan, 1976), pp. 61–106.
46. See Karashima and Subbarayalu, 'Ancient and Medieval Tamil and Sanskrit Inscriptions Related to Southeast Asia and China', pp. 275–278.

47. For the possible identification of this *vihāra* with the 'Chinese pagoda,' see Seshadri, 'New Perspectives on Nagapattinam', pp. 109–118.
48. See Karashima and Subbarayalu, 'Ancient and Medieval Tamil and Sanskrit Inscriptions Related to Southeast Asia and China', pp. 278–279, 283.
49. However, we do see some instances of joint donations of paramount and subordinate rulers.
50. It should be noted, however, that Kālidāsa's *Abhijñānaśākuntala* does refer to a prophecy that Bharata's chariots will roll unimpeded over all the oceans.
51. For the various references, see Aiyer 'The Larger Leiden Plates (of Rajaraja I)', p. 224; and Kulke, 'The Naval Expeditions of the Cholas in the Context of Asian History', pp. 279–280.
52. See Lionel D. Barnett, 'Inscriptions at Narendra', *Epigraphia Indica* 13, 1915–1916, pp. 298–326.
53. See Ramaranjan Mukherji and Sachindra Kumar Maity, *Corpus of Bengal Inscriptions Bearing on History and Civilization of Bengal* (Kolkata: Firma K.L. Mukhopadhyay, 1967), pp. 170, 253, 251, 342–343, 383.

15

Politics, Piety, and Patronage: The Burmese Engagement with Bodhgayā

Trans-regional pilgrimage and patronage have had enduring importance in Asian religious interactions from ancient times till the present. In the context of Buddhism, over the centuries, political elites played an important role in forging links with India, the Buddhist homeland. While kings of Java and Śrīvijaya made religious endowments to monasteries at Nālandā and Nāgapaṭṭinam, Burmese rulers had especially close associations with Bodhgayā.[1] This chapter will survey the evidence of long-term Burmese connections with Bodhgayā and will highlight how certain Buddhapādas ('Buddha footprints') found at the site add significantly to our understanding of these connections. The larger context of this discussion includes the configurations of kingship and the state in Burma in the Pagan and post-Pagan periods and the importance attached to links with India, especially its Buddhist heritage.

These connections were established through a series of interactions, associations, and transpositions. For instance, Tapussa and Bhallika, the two merchants from Utkala, described in the *Vinayapiṭaka* and *Mahāvagga* as the first lay followers of the Buddha, were transformed in 15th century Mon mythology into merchants from Lower Burma who symbolized the ideal lay devotees. The New Pagan Chronicle, the Glass Palace Chronicle, and the Egyin (historical ballads) assert that the kings of Burma were descendants of the solar dynasty of the Sākiyas (i.e., Śākyas).[2] The chronicles tell us that Alaungsithu (1112–1168) visited Mahābodhi; whether he actually did or not, is beside the point. Connections are also claimed with Aśoka—the Mon *saṅgha* was believed to have descended from missionaries sent by this king. Further, several ancient payas (pagodas) in Pagan and elsewhere are ascribed to Aśoka in inscriptions ranging from the 11th to 14th centuries.[3] An inscription of the 15th century king Dhammacetī of Bago describes his desire to imitate the pious kings of ancient times such as Aśokadham marāja.[4] The base of thrones in palaces of Burma's last ruling house, the Konbaung dynasty, was made from earth from several great Indian cities.[5] Apart from the political aspect, monastic and pilgrimage networks also played important roles in knitting together various parts of the Buddhist world.

Mahābodhi Re-creations and Representations

A Kalyani inscription of Dharmmacetī mentions a *mahāthera* named Prānadassi who lived at Sudhammapura and who, through his supernatural powers, transported himself every morning to Uruvela. Here, he swept the courtyard of the Mahābodhi tree and then returned home to beg for alms.[6] For those who did not have such powers, there were other ways of establishing connections with the place of the Buddha's enlightenment.

The importance of the Mahābodhi temple (Figure 15.1) in Burma/Myanmar is reflected in the building of 'replicas', representations of the temple within Paya complexes, temple models, and depictions on seals, sealings, and plaques. A. B. Griswold urges us to think about the nature and function of 'copying' in early Buddhist art, and points out that it actually involved an interpretation of what was essential and the deliberate and selective appropriations of and departures from the 'original'.[7] 'Replicas' should, therefore, be understood as 're-creations' rather than 'copies'.[8] There are two known 'replicas' of the Mahābodhi temple in Myanmar. One is the intact Mahābodhi Paya (built in the first half of the 13th century) in Pagan (Figure 15.2). The second is the Shwegugyi Paya

Figure 15.1
Mahābodhi temple, Bodhgayā

Source: Author

in Bago (c. 1460–1470), built during the reign of Dhammacetī, which today lies in ruins. The chronicles tell us that this king had sent artisans to Bodhgayā to make accurate plans and models of Mahābodhi.[9] Whether or not these two temples were actually based on detailed information obtained from Mahābodhi is a matter of debate. Yet they both show deliberate departures from the original, although the Pagan one is quite faithful to it in basic plan. Both appear to have a symbolic representation of the seven stations, marking events during the seven weeks immediately after the Buddha's enlightenment.[10] However, it is doubtful that the seven stations visible today at the Pagan temple belong to the same time as the foundation of the temple.[11] And although Griswold has correlated the location of the seven stations at Mahābodhi, Chiang Mai, and Shwegugyi, Stadtner has pointed out that some of the features that were identified by Griswold at Shwegugyi as 'stations' are actually newer shrines.[12]

It has been pointed out by Tilman Frasch that apart from the re-creations of the Bodhgayā temple, the square, pyramidal tower of the Mahābodhi type can be seen in various Pagan temples such as Wetkyi in Kubyaukkyi. It can also be seen in temples that chronologically predate and follow the Pagan Mahābodhi, as well in those that are roughly contemporaneous to it.[13] Frasch suggests that the Mahābodhi temple at Pagan was perhaps built because monks fleeing from eastern India to Burma in the wake of the Turkish invasion may have brought with them the distressing news that the Mahābodhi temple at Bodhgayā was under siege and in ruins. The decision to build a new imperial temple on Mahābodhi lines was a statement that Pagan had taken over as the new sacred centre of Buddhism.[14] This suggestion is persuasive. But we can also note the long-standing tradition in Myanmar of building re-creations and models of temples. For instance, in the Kuthodaw Paya in Mandalay, the Mahalokamarazein *stūpa* is modelled on the Shwezigon Paya. There is a model of the Shwedagon Paya *within* the Shwedagon complex in Yangon. In Bago, the Mahazedi Paya contains a 'replica' of the Ānanda Paya of Pagan. And more recently, we have the example of the Uppatasanti pagoda in Nay Pyi Taw, the Myanmar capital, whose towering golden form evokes the Shwedagon in Yangon.[15] We also encounter 'replicas' of relics.[16] 'Replicas' of Payas and relics, and temple models were part of an elaborate network of symbolic association through which shrines connected themselves with others, lending and borrowing eminence and sacrality.

Mention should be made of the Mahābodhi Shwegu in the kingdom of Mrauk U, located near Sittwe in Rakhine province. This is a small

Figure 15.2
Mahābodhi Paya, Pagan

Source: Author

16th/17th century temple on a hilltop; its tunnel-like entrance boring towards the centre is lined on both sides with relief carvings. This Mahābodhi bears no resemblance whatsoever to the one at Bodhgayā. Perhaps it just wears the name as a badge of prestige.

We can also note the presence of modest representations of the Mahābodhi temple in various Payas, most of them fairly recent. For instance, in the Shwedagon in Yangon, huge photographs of Bodhgayā and Sārnāth printed on cloth are mounted on the wall of the Greatest Prosperity Meditation Hall. A 'replica' of the Mahābodhi temple within the Shwedagon complex, built by a printing press owner some time before 1920, has on its *śikhara* various scenes from the life of the Buddha. Such representations of Mahābodhi are found in other Payas as well (for instance, the Shwezigon in Pagan has such structures located in the north, south, and west), and we can note that the spire in these cases generally takes the form of a generic curvilinear Nāgara-style *śikhara* rather than the distinctive straight-lined profile of Mahābodhi.

The ubiquitousness of the *bhūmisparśamudrā* in Buddha images of the Pagan period can also be seen as pointing towards Bodhgayā as the place of the Buddha's enlightenment (Figure 15.3). The influence of the Pāla–Sena school outside India (including in China, Nepal, Tibet, Myanmar, and Java) has been well-recognized, and there are striking similarities between images found in eastern India and Myanmar, leading Susan Huntington to talk of the Burmo-Bengali style of carving.[17] It has also been noted by Huntington that in the Pāla period, Bodhgayā and the *bhūmisparśamudrā* replaced the importance that Sārnāth and the *dharmacakramudrā* had in the Gupta period. The depiction of Māravijaya with the Buddha sitting in *bhūmisparśamudrā* is, in fact, the most popular theme of Pāla art.[18] The strong eastern India–Burma/Myanmar connections help us understand the synchronism in the popularity of this theme in both areas.

The most frequently encountered allusion to Bodhgayā in Myanmar is through the tree—a pipal tree symbolizing the bodhi tree is ubiquitous in Myanmarese Payas. For instance, in the Shwezigon in Yangon, the magnificent bodhi tree in the southeastern corner (no doubt the descendant of many earlier trees) was planted in 1921 and is the object of special worship; its ceremonial watering is an important ritual. There are other, smaller bodhi trees in other parts of the complex as well.

Putting these details together, we get a sense of the great variety and the wide chronological and geographical range of the symbolic allusions

Figure 15.3
Buddha images in bhūmisparśa mudrā, Mahazedi Paya, Bago

Source: Author

to Mahābodhi in Myanmar. These symbolic allusions were accompanied by some very concrete and long-term Burmese interventions at the site.

'Repairing' Mahābodhi

Three long inscriptions talk of the activities of Burmese kings at Mahābodhi, documenting various rounds of 'repair' of the temple.[19] We can note the fact that the longer Burmese inscriptions found at Bodhgayā share many features with royal inscriptions found in Myanmar, many of which record the repair and embellishment of the existing Buddhist temples as well as the endowments of land and other resources. It has been suggested by Frasch that the 'repairers' of Mahābodhi were often usurpers who had a special need for legitimation.[20] The activities of the documented 11th and 13th century Burmese repair missions to Mahābodhi have been reconstructed by Griswold, and those of the 19th century mission are described by Rajendralala Mitra. Although Griswold asserts that the repairers must have respected the basic form of the Mahābodhi temple, he lists fairly numerous and extensive changes, including the possible addition of the radiating arches and vaults, stucco images in the niches, and stucco ornamentation.[21] Mitra too refers to extensive changes made at the site by the Burmese 'repairers'.[22] But these are not the focus of discussion here.

The first epigraph referring to a Burmese 'repair-mission' to Mahābodhi is a long Mon inscription of Kyanzittha (reigned c. 1084–1111) at the Shwesandaw pagoda in Pyay.[23] This refers to the temple of Śrī Bajrās (i.e., the *vajrāsana*) having been destroyed by other kings and Kyanzittha's various acts of benefaction. These included sending an expedition by sea to repair the temple; as well as to buy some land and dig a tank and make embankments for irrigating the land; making provisions for burning candles; presenting various musical instruments; and making arrangements for fine singing and dancing in the temple.

The second inscription is a late 13th century epigraph that was found at Bodhgayā itself (its present location is unknown), of which there are several different published translations. It is inscribed on a grey basalt slab (20 inches × 18 inches) and its language and script are Burmese. The inscription was earlier understood by some scholars as recording a mission sent either by an Arakanese ruler or by his overlord, a king of Pagan.[24] However, according to Gordon H. Luce's revised reading and translation, the mission was dispatched by the 'King of Dharma', 'Lord of the White Elephant'.[25] Griswold suggests that this could be a reference to king Tarukplyi, or more probably, his son Klawcwā, or a crown prince named Klacwā.[26] The inscription tells us that after 218 years from the time of the Buddha's dispensation, one of the 84,000 *caitya*s (temples) built by Siri Dhammasoka, king of Jambudvīpa, at the place where the milk-rice offering had been made (in Bodhgayā) lay in a ruined state.[27] It was repaired by a senior *paṅsaku* monk. Subsequently, it fell into ruin again. The 'King of Dharma', 'Lord of the White Elephant' sent his *ācārya* Dharmarājaguru to repair it, and he took along his pupil Siri Kassapa. But the finances were found to be inadequate, and at the request of a Vanavāsi monk, a local ruler named Putasin Maṅ (i.e., Buddhaṣena) gave some financial assistance. The work was resumed and lasted from 1296 to 1298 CE. The inscription describes the dedication ceremony that followed. Many offerings were made—of flags and streamers; vast quantities of rice alms and lamps; a *kalpavṛkṣa* adorned with gold and silver flowers, cups and garments; and two children styled as the donor's son and daughter. In order to provide for the perpetual daily offering of rice at the temple, land, slaves and cattle were purchased and dedicated to the shrine. The donor made this meritorious gift in order to attain *nirvāṇa* and sainthood when the Buddha Maitreya arrived.

We may take note here of an inscribed copper gilt umbrella found by J. D. M. Beglar 'buried 8 feet under the Burmese ground level'[28] to the immediate west of the Mahābodhi temple, described both by Cunningham and Barua. The umbrella has two short inscriptions—one in Mon or Talaing and the other in Nagari characters with Bengali elements. The one-line Burmese inscription is damaged; Cunningham states that it begins with a date and he could only read the name of one 'Dhama Radza Guru'. The two-line inscription refers, among other things, to the gift of one Dharmarājaguru and also seems to mention the name of a local ruler. Cunningham read the date in this inscription as Samvat 397, which, according to the Burmese era of 638, would correspond to 1035 CE. If this reading is correct, the donation of the bell does not correspond to the dates of either of the two Burmese repair missions, and in fact predates them. Barua, on the other hand, thought that the date on the umbrella was a mistake for 1397 of the Vikrama era (corresponding to 1340 CE) or that it referred to the expired reign of Lakṣmaṇasena (which would correspond to 1567 CE).[29] Whatever may be the correct reading and interpretation of the date, the indication is that high dignitaries from Burma visited Mahābodhi in between the documented repair missions. Cunningham also refers to a short Burmese inscription on one of the bricks of the *āmalaka* of the *śikhara* of the temple,[30] which bears testimony to the Burmese 'repairs'.

The 19th century was a period of the most intense Burmese interactions with Mahābodhi, with important initiatives taken by kings Bagyidaw (reigned 1819–1837) and Mindon (reigned 1853–1878). Judging from mid-19th photographs, the temple was in bad shape at that time. There is a long 19th century Burmese inscription at Bodhgayā.[31] The inscription, which is stored in the precincts of the Mahant's *maṭha*, has two parts—one part is in 'corrupt' Sanskrit and Pali; the other part is in Burmese (Figure 15.4). Its main purpose is to record that a king named Thīti Pavara Suddhama (Bagyidaw) sent though his *purohita* and minister offerings for the bodhi tree in 1822, and that he and his queen performed a long-distance dedication ceremony. The obverse of the slab gives an account beginning with the enlightenment of Gautama, going on to describe how the king heard of this wonderful place, and of a Burmese inscription recording the repair of the temple in 1295 (this seems to be a reference to the 13th century inscription). Among other things, the more detailed Burmese

Figure 15.4
19th century Sanskrit/Pali and Burmese inscription in Mahant's maṭha

Source: Author

inscription on the reverse mentions a minister having been sent to inscribe this inscription.[32]

We can add here certain inscriptions mentioned in Duroiselle's *List of Inscriptions found in Burma.*[33] Inscription No. 1177 (in Burmese and Pali), found near the bodhi tree at Bodhgayā, records the repairing of the shrine in 1821 at Bodhgayā by king Bagyidaw. Inscription No. 1178 (of 1821 CE), also found at Bodhgayā, records the dedication of gold, silver, precious stones and other offerings to the bodhi tree by the same ruler. Unless there is an error in reading their dates, these inscriptions seem to belong to a period before the well-known diplomatic mission of 1830–1833, discussed below.

In 1830, a Burmese diplomatic mission arrived in British India in the aftermath of the first Anglo-Burmese war (1824–1826), during the reign of king Bagyidaw. It stayed in India for three years, trying to meet Governor General William Bentinck in order to engage in certain specific political negotiations, and its activities were described by Colonel Henry Burney, British Resident in Ava. As the political parleys progressed at a snail's pace, the two members of the mission collected dubious intelligence, went sightseeing, and attended an English ball. They took a detour to visit and worship at the bodhi tree at Bodhgayā, in the course of which they discovered the 13th century Burmese inscription. They acquired a 'miraculous' sapling and branches of the tree, and later, in Calcutta, obtained a Buddha image—originally from Bodhgayā—from the Asiatic Society. Although minimal headway had been made in the political negotiations, the members of the mission returned to Burma very satisfied with their religious accomplishments and acquisitions. The Buddha image was received with great ceremonial honour at Ava by none other than king Bagyidaw himself.[34]

The other king of the Konbaung dynasty who was involved in donative and repair activities at Mahābodhi was Mindon. In Duroiselle's list, inscriptions No. 1228 and 1229 record the dedication of precious gems (diamonds, emeralds, rubies, and pearls), umbrellas, banners, and certain other items to the bodhi tree by this king in 1874. One of these inscriptions is in Pali; the other is bilingual, in Burmese and Pali. According to D. C. Ahir, the Pali inscription begins by recounting the accomplishments of Mindon, including the building of the Maha Loka Marazein Paya in Mandalay, the convening of the fifth Buddhist council, and having the three Piṭakas inscribed on stone; the king is compared with Siri Dhammasoka. It goes on to state that the king wanted to propagate the Buddha's *sāsana* in other countries, especially Majjhimadeśa, where the teaching had once flourished but had almost completely died out. Mindon is described as having sent some monks to Majjhimadeśa and to make offerings at Mahābodhi, the most sacred place on earth, where the Buddha had attained enlightenment. In year 1236 of the Burmese era and 2417 of the Buddhist era (i.e., 1874 CE), he sent three high-ranking officials by boat on a pilgrimage to Mahābodhi to make offerings consisting of 511 diamonds, 311 emeralds, 3966 rubies and 623 pearls, along with many ornaments from his royal kinsfolk, ministers, and people. The king expressed the hope that his meritorious deeds would earn him Arhatship and asserted that he shared his merit with all living beings.[35] The present location of this inscription is unclear.

The bilingual inscription is presently located in Bodhgayā in one of the two small Burmese pavilions in the mahant's vegetable garden (Figures 15.5 and 15.6). I have not been able to locate the text and/or translation of this inscription, although it is possible that its contents were roughly similar to those of the Pali inscription discussed above. According to one of the senior *sannyasi*s of the *maṭha*, the other pavilion once housed the 13th century Burmese inscription and that at some

Figure 15.5
The two Burmese pavilions in the Mahant's vegetable garden

Source: Author

Figure 15.6
Bilingual inscription inside one of the Burmese pavilions

Source: Author

point, it was moved into the *maṭha* building for safe-keeping. This suggests that apart from bringing various lavish gifts (which were apparently handed over to the Mahant) and setting up two inscriptions, Mindon's gift-bearing mission also built two small Burmese-style structures in order to house that inscription as well as the older one. A building located next to these structures is believed to represent the rest house or store house built by Mindon's mission. Alternatively, all these structures could have been built during the repair mission that followed soon after the sending of the gifts (discussed later).

For some time after 1874, the Burmese negotiated with the Mahant and the Bengal government about certain 'repairs' that they were interested in carrying out at Mahābodhi, and an agreement was finally reached about what exactly they could and could not be permitted to do at the site.[36] One of the Mahant's stipulations was that the activities of Hindu pilgrims who were visiting the site should not be impeded in any way. In 1876, a 'royal scribe' arrived at the site to draw up plans for the work, and 'repairs' began in 1877. The work seems to have been abandoned due to the death of Mindon in 1878. The activities of this Burmese mission are described in archival records and in Rajendralala Mitra's *Buddha Gaya*.[37] The Bengal government deputed Mitra to visit the site and make a report on what they were doing. Mitra set off alarm bells when he described the extensive clearances and additions the Burmese had made.[38] For the first time after many centuries, a Burmese repair mission had come up against the barrier of archaeologists, who saw such activities as interfering with the 'intrinsic' nature of an ancient monument. This event also highlighted the potential conflict between Hindu and Buddhist claims to Bodhgayā, which reached a flashpoint later, due to the activities of Anagarika Dharmapala.[39]

Mitra mentions two shorter 19th century Burmese inscriptions at Bodhgayā.[40] One was on a miniature *stūpa* placed as a finial on the balustrade in front of the Bāradwārī. It dates back to 1185 (i.e., 1823 CE) and refers to it having been written by Shime-pu, a resident of Kwantshwai. The other one, dated 1171 (i.e., 1809 CE), was on the pedestal of an image of Śiva and Pārvatī lying at the foot of the bodhi tree. This seems to record a gift of two individuals, Nga-pe-tu and Nga Kway, who came to this place. There is also mention of a royal gift in the inscription.

Taken together, all this evidence leaves no doubt that over a long period of time (between the 11th and 19th centuries) at several junctures, Burmese kings belonging to various dynasties connected themselves with

Mahābodhi in order to enhance their prestige, and that the temple had great symbolic significance for Burmese elites. With their long tradition of repairing Buddhist temples at home, Burmese kings extended their activities on several occasions into the lands of Indian rulers in order to 'repair' Mahābodhi, the most internationally renowned of all the Buddhist shrines. It appears that apart from the royal missions documented in the longer inscriptions, there were other royal missions as well, and that non-royal Burmese were also visiting Mahābodhi.

Other Burmese Elements at Bodhgayā

The various rounds of 'repair' of the Mahābodhi temple make it difficult to ascertain what the temple looked like at different points of time and what exactly the results of the Burmese interventions were. But given the fact that there is a long history of these interventions, it is not surprising that several Burmese elements have been noted in the shrine. Some of these must have been the result of pilgrim traffic that may have been unconnected with the repair missions. Cunningham mentions that the granite pavement in the temple and the courtyard was 'covered with rudely carved figures kneeling in adoration after the manner of the Burmese *Siko*' (see Figure 15.7).[41] However, the names in the inscriptions accompanying some of these carvings are not Burmese. Barua refers to granite pillars with lotus medallions with Burmese-looking men and women and *stūpas* of the Burmese type. He adds that the basalt throne of the Buddha image in the Mahābodhi temple also seems to have been the work of the Burmese.[42]

A question that arises is: Were the Burmese 'repairs' conducted by Indian or Burmese artisans and sculptors? The nature and extent of interventions that Griswold talks about and the introduction of Burmese elements into the structure, sculpture, and ornamentation of the temple[43] strongly suggest the involvement of Burmese artisans. In fact, the *Nidāna Ārambhakathā*, which mentions the 15th century mission sent by Dhammacetī to Bodhgayā in order to make detailed plans of the temple, refers to it being accompanied by masons, painters, and builders.[44] The repair missions too may have also been accompanied by such specialists. On the other hand, it has been suggested that the Burmese repair missions must have used Indian artisans who worked under Burmese supervision.[45] Apart from the various 'repairs', were the two small pagoda-like structures made by Indian craftsmen under Burmese supervision? From

Figure 15.7
Burmese figures on pavement slabs

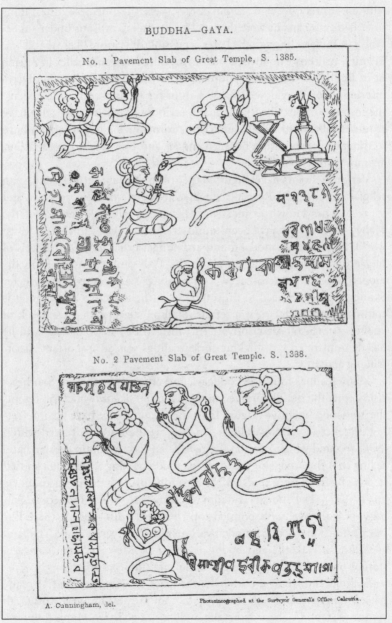

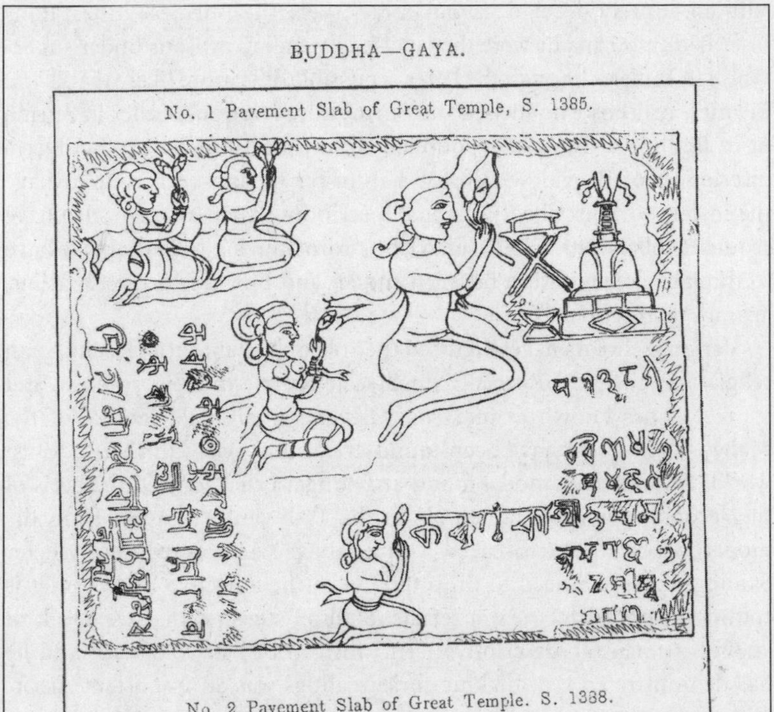

Source: Cunningham, 1871

a practical point of view, it would have been easier for the supervisors to communicate with workers in a language they knew instead of dealing with an entirely 'foreign' labour force. Were the Burmese inscriptions inscribed in Burma or were they incised by Indian artisans under supervision in India? Although the latter is possible, it is more likely that it was Burmese artisans who incised the Burmese inscriptions, either in Burma or in Bodhgayā itself. As mentioned above, the 19th century Bodhgayā inscription of Bagyidaw talks of a minister having been sent to have the inscription inscribed. Bilingual inscriptions such as these may have required collaboration between scribes from both areas. Perhaps we have to think of collaboration between Indian and Burmese artists, masons, artisans, and scribes.

Various scholars have discussed the role of portable artefacts in Asian religious exchanges, especially small-scale temple models, sealings, and stone plaques known as *andagūs*.[46] Several small-scale models of the Mahābodhi temple have been found at various places in the Buddhist world. It was such a model found at Bodhgayā that formed the basis of the reconstruction of the temple in the 19th century. Apart from the models, there are the so-called 'votive tablets'. As pointed out by Peter Skilling, there is a need to drop the use of the adjective 'votive' that is routinely applied to these artefacts. Skilling suggests that we speak of sealings (a neutral, descriptive term) instead of 'votive tablets' and he has demonstrated that making these sealings was an important merit-making activity.[47]

Many sealings found at Bodhgayā and at various places in Southeast Asia depict the Buddha framed under a temple *śikhara* which represents the Mahābodhi temple (Figure 15.8). In Myanmar, we have the interesting evidence of certain sealings which show the Buddha framed within a *śikhara*, and which have on the reverse an inscription in cursive hand saying that this image of the lord was made by king Aniruddha so that he may be freed from *saṁsāra*[48] (Aniruddha or Anawratha ruled during 1044–1077). The Indian Museum, Kolkata has several terracotta sealings—mostly oval with pointed top in shape, with illegible three-line inscriptions; these were found at various sites in Myanmar and Thailand as well as at Nālandā and Bodhgayā in India. Many of them have seal stamps on the back and belong to about the 10th century.[49]

Sealings similar to the Mahābodhi types have been found at many places in Myanmar. Apart from Pagan, they are also found in 16th/17th century Mrauk U. These depict the Buddha seated in *bhūmisparśamudrā*, framed within a *śikhara* that is sometimes very reminiscent of Mahābodhi

Figure 15.8
Mahābodhi sealing

Courtesy: Indian Museum, Kolkata

or sometimes a generic Nāgara spire, with branches of the bodhi tree emerging tendril-like from the temple tower.

It is not necessary that all the sealings or tablets with representations of Mahābodhi were made at Bodhgayā. But what is especially interesting in the context of the present discussion is evidence of Burmese elements in terracotta tablets found at Bodhgayā. Luce describes two Bodhgayā tablets with Mon writing in the Indian Museum.[50] These have the Buddha seated in *bhūmisparśamudrā* under a trefoiled arch surmounted by a spire. There are 40 *stūpa*s on either side of this figure and 28 below. As pointed out by Luce, this adds up to 108, the number of auspicious signs that are supposed to mark the sole of the Buddha. This was one of the favourite themes in Burmese representations of the Buddha, and Luce suggests that these tablets may have been either made in Burma or by Burmese monks or pilgrims who visited Bodhgayā.

Footprint Worship in Burma and Bodhgayā

The veneration of the Buddha's footprints (*settaw* in modern Burmese) has been an important and enduring element in Burmese Buddhism. Writing in the 1930s, U Mya observed that Burmese children were taught to recite a prayer in honour of the Buddha's footprints before going to bed.[51] He also pointed out that one or two Buddha footprints—carved on stone or painted on the roof—are usually found in Buddhist monasteries and temples in every town or village in the country. Mya refers to the different details connected with the Shwesettaw footprints in the *samaing*s (traditional accounts). The legends give a narrative of forgetting and rediscovery. After having been forgotten (for some 2,240 or 127 years, according to the different accounts), the footprints are said to have been rediscovered as a result of a mission, dispatched at the behest of certain monks, by king Thalunmindaya of Ava, in the early 17th century.[52] This story can be seen as an allegorical reference to the revival of footprint worship in Burma.

Although the antiquity of footprint worship in the country may go back a long way, and the footprint at the base of the hill at Shwesettaw, which is devoid of any sculptural embellishment, may belong to the early centuries CE, dateable evidence of footprint worship in Burma begins in the 11th century and comes from Pagan.[53] A stone slab bearing a left footprint is located on the platform of the Lokānanda temple built during the time of Anawratha. Sets of stone footprints are found in two temples built during the time of Kyanzittha, namely in the Shwezigon Paya and in the Ānanda Paya. We can also mention the paintings of Buddha footprints on the roofs of certain Pagan temples, for instance at Wetkyi. U Mya suggests that since the Pagan stone footprints correspond quite closely to the textual prescriptions given in the 8th–11th century *Jinālaṅkāra-ṭīkā* and *Anāgatavaṁsa-aṭṭakathā*, the practice of footprint worship may go back to a few centuries before the 11th century.[54] Footprint worship became increasingly popular during the succeeding centuries in various parts of Burma and is visible at many Payas today.

We can connect the worship of Buddha footprints with the still-continuing Myanmarese tradition of extremely detailed treatment of the soles of the feet in Buddha images. The penchant for representing the Buddha in a reclining pose gave a good view of the soles, which are completely covered with symbols, numbering as many as 108, within small square compartments. The Buddha's foot symbolically contains the whole universe.

The worship of footprints has been and continues to be widespread in India as well, not only within Buddhism, but also in other religious traditions. Buddhapādas were among the aniconic emblems of the Buddha, and we have early evidence of this from sites such as Sanchi, Bharhut, Kesannapalli, Amaravati, and Nagarjunakonda. Buddha footprints continued to be venerated even after the advent of anthropomorphic images. Here, I would like to focus on certain Buddhapādas found at Bodhgayā. Among these, I am especially interested in certain pieces documented by Rajendralala Mitra and housed in the Indian Museum, Kolkata. Some of these Buddhapādas have been discussed by Debjani Paul, but not from the perspective of Burmese connections.[55]

There are differences of opinion about whether the Vaiṣṇavas got the idea of footprint worship from the Buddhists or vice versa, and we need not go into that debate here. However, we cannot ignore the fact that the footprints of Viṣṇu are the central object of worship in the Viṣṇupada temple at Gayā. According to Rajendralala Mitra, the footprint that is the central object of worship in that temple may have originally been a Buddhist emblem, although he admits that there is no proof of this.[56] Debjani Paul has questioned Mitra's hypothesis and has argued that the Gayā Viṣṇupāda tradition could be pre-Buddhist. She also suggests that we can distinguish between Buddha and Viṣṇu footprints on the following bases—from the Gupta period onwards, Viṣṇu's footprints usually occur as a pair, whereas the Buddha's footprints occur as a single print or as a pair; and the *cakra* does not occur on Viṣṇu's footprints.[57] Of course, even if we accept the distinctions suggested by Paul, this does not rule out the possibility that a pair of Viṣṇupādas could have been transformed into Buddhapādas with the simple addition of a *cakra*. On the other hand, B. M. Barua points out that the footprint at Gayā is represented by a single footprint, suggesting and representing the stepping posture of the god (his three strides), and not a sitting or standing posture. He also states that the Viṣṇu footprint in the Viṣṇupada temple and elsewhere is marked by the symbols of the conch (*śaṅkha*), wheel (*cakra*), mace (*gadā*) and lotus (*padma*).[58] Clearly, we need much more careful study of footprint worship in different religious traditions to be able to identify the precise differences in their characteristics.

A question that concerns us here is: When did the worship of Buddhapādas begin in the Mahābodhi temple at Bodhgayā? Barua points out that footprints are not depicted in the early relief sculptures at Bodhgayā.[59] Unfortunately, we do not have any detailed documentation of the Buddhapādas of the Pāla–Sena period. Susan Huntington's discussion of Pāla–Sena sculpture does not deal with these sacred artefacts. However, the accounts of the Chinese pilgrims help us out to some extent. There is no mention of Buddha footprints in Faxian and Xuanzang's descriptions of Mahābodhi. But the 1021 CE Chinese inscription of the monk Yunshu found at the temple site mentions footprints.[60] Yunshu talks of having come from far away to gaze on the land of the Buddha and having seen with his eyes the wondrous footprints in the shrine of the Nirmāṇa-kāya. This suggests that an imposing Buddhapāda was added to the Mahābodhi temple sometime between the time of Xuanzang's visit in the 7th century and Yunshu's visit in the 11th century. This may well have happened just a few decades before the first documented Burmese repair-mission, which took place during Kyanzittha's reign.[61]

Mitra's *Buddha Gaya* mentions and illustrates five Buddhapādas carved on the surface of black hemispherical stones (Plate 43, Figures 1 and 2, 3, 5, 6, 7).[62] The first (Mitra's Figures 1 and 2) is a hemispherical black stone (probably phyllite) bearing a pair of footprints. It was found in front of a pavilion called the Buddhapad (next to the Pancha-Pandava shrine), which was pulled down by the Burmese repairers in 1876 to clear the area in front of the temple, and subsequently rebuilt.[63] It is currently located under a pavilion, which is considered part of the Pancha-Pandava temple, before the Mahābodhi shrine (Figure 15.9A, B). The stone has a diameter of 3ft 6 ¼ in, and its circumference is marked by the etching of three concentric circles with petal ornamentation all along the outer rim. The space within the inner circle is almost completely covered by a pair of footprints. On the upper part of each sole is a three-petalled flower (lotus) with an undulating stem. The remaining part of each foot is covered with various symbols. The central symbol (though it not located in the absolute centre of the sole) is an 8-petalled floral motif within a double-circle (It should be noted that it is not a *cakra*, although it gives the impression of being one). Arranged around it are the following symbols: elephant goad, flag, umbrella, vase with leaves, conch, and fish.

Mitra observed that although the symbols on this Buddhapāda have closer kinship to the repertoire of Hindu symbols, they correspond fully

Figure 15.9A
Pavilion with Buddhapāda, Mahābodhi temple, Bodhgayā

Source: Author

Figure 15.9B
Close-up of Buddhapāda in pavilion

Source: Author

neither to the Vaiṣṇava nor Buddhist symbols as enumerated in texts. According to him, this footprint seems to have been used by Hindus at some point to convert the place to Hindu worship and later came to be interpreted as the Buddha's footprints.[64] On the other hand, Paul asserts that since the feet in question have *cakra*s on the soles, this must be a Buddhapāda. To add to the confusion, on the side of the hemispherical stone, there is a Sanskrit inscription dated in year 1230 of the Śaka era, that is, 1308 CE. It refers to the Aśoka temple (*deul*) of him who is as tender of body as Madana (Kāmadeva) and is all knowing.[65] The inscription does not refer to the Buddhapāda but to the temple, which it seems to attribute to Aśoka. Given its large size (110 cm diameter, 41 cm height, 15½ cm inner circumference) and prominent location, it is very likely that this is the Buddhapāda that Yunshu saw and mentioned in his 1021 CE inscription. In that case, the Buddhapāda is older than the inscription on it.

This raises an interesting possibility. We have seen that while the antiquity of footprint worship in Burma may be quite old, Buddhapādas located in monumental temples become prominent in the early Pagan period. The Burmese repair missions to Mahābodhi also date from this period. Is it possible that this Buddhapāda was added by the Burmese, either by an undocumented early 11th century repair mission or by Burmese pilgrims who started frequenting the site from about this time onwards? This would mean stretching the Pagan–Mahābodhi connection to the beginning of the Pagan period.[66] Although the arrangement of the symbols on this Buddhapāda is not similar to the symbols-in-compartments pattern seen on Burmese footprints, *all* of them occur in the list of 108 symbols collated by U Mya on the basis of textual evidence as well as their occurrence in Burmese Buddha footprints.[67] Further, I do not think that similar Buddhapādas have been found elsewhere in India. Given all this, and its monumental size and placement, we cannot rule out the possibility that this Buddhapāda was some sort of experimental hybrid sacred artefact, reflecting some, but not all features of its Burmese counterparts; and that it was made either by a Burmese artist or by an Indian artist on Burmese directions in the course of an early 11th century Burmese repair mission or at the behest of affluent Burmese pilgrims to Mahābodhi. Alternatively, it is possible that these symbols were added by Burmese visitors to an already established Buddhapāda at Mahābodhi. Interestingly, it was another Burmese mission that demolished the pavilion in which the sacred footprints were located. We do not know why they did so; perhaps it was in order to rebuild the pavilion.

While the attribution of this Buddhapāda or its surface symbols to Burmese intervention may seem speculative, we are on more solid ground when we turn to four other Bodhgayā Buddhapādas on black hemispherical stones (see Mitra's Figures 3, 5, 6, and 7), which have shallow carvings on the flat surface that bears the footprint.[68] Mitra writes that these four stones were recently excavated by the Burmese and had been brought to Calcutta. All the footprints are of one foot and have carvings of conches on the toes.[69] They all have identical *cakra*s consisting of two small concentric circles in the centre from which 16 spokes radiate outwards to meet two concentric circles marking the outer rim of the wheel.

The Buddhapāda drawn in Mitra's Figure 3 (which corresponds to Indian Museum BG-1) has a wheel flanked by a conch on stand on the left, and a spouted vessel on an hour-glass-shaped stand on the right. Above the wheel is a crown, flanked by a *cāmara*-bearing female attendant to the right and a *cāmara*-bearing male attendant to the left. There is a star with curved rays on the heel. Mitra's Figure 5 has a wheel with what looks like a ceremonial seat below it; above the wheel is a female figure whose lower body is that of a bird (*kinnarī*). She faces a lotus bud, and behind her is an object (Mitra describes it as a conch) mounted on a stand. Figure 7 has a wheel, below which is a seat, above which stands a woman in a dancing pose holding a *vīṇā*-like musical instrument, with a lotus to her right.

But we must pay special attention to Mitra's Figure no. 6, which corresponds to the Indian Museum BG 2/A21214 and is the most significant

Figure 15.10
Buddhapāda (BG 2), Indian Museum

Courtesy: Indian Museum, Kolkata

Buddhapāda in the context of the argument being made here (Figure 15.10). This has a *cakra* in the lower part (not in the centre of the sole); above the *cakra* is a human figure playing a flute; to his left is a pitcher supporting a staff with three flags and a pennon; below the wheel are a mountain flanked by two cranes and a peacock sitting on the summit. To the right of the wheel and the figure is a shrine which is clearly Burmese in style.

The various Buddhapādas described by Mitra differ in detail, but are clearly related to this piece and to each other. All of them have conch shells carved within each toe, a feature that is typical of Burmese Buddhapādas. And all the symbols on their soles occur among the 108 symbols found on Burmese Buddha footprints. Given the clear Burmese affiliation of no. 6, I think that all of them point towards a Burmese intervention at Mahābodhi. Certain other aspects of this set of four Buddhapādas are notable (this also applies to the specimens described by Paul). One is the fact that their stone and side carvings are similar to the dome of the Pāla-period miniature *stūpas* ('votive *stūpa*' is the old, misleading nomenclature). This is recognized by Paul, who argues that we have here examples of the *pādacetiya*, the mention of which was noticed by B. C. Law in the *Sāsanavaṁsa*, and which can be understood as a 'votive *stūpa*' enshrining the Buddhapāda as a relic.[70] However, there is a problem with this interpretation. If the footprints were supposed to be placed face-up, as we can assume they must have been, the *caitya* arch or *candraśālā*, which occurs on the rim in the specimens that I have examined, would have been carved upside down, which is inconceivable.[71]

There are other similar Buddhapādas at Bodhgayā. These include two located immediately to the south of the grilled enclosure of the bodhi tree within the Mahābodhi complex (no carvings can be identified on them) (Figure 15.11) and one in the Thakurvadi area of the Mahant's *maṭha* (this just has a wheel in the middle). Two others, however, are especially important in the context of the present discussion. In one of the covered corridors of the Mahant's *maṭha* is a Buddhapāda on a black stone (90 cm diameter, 29 ½ cm in height) with four *candraśālā*s (Figure 15.12). On its surface are carved two feet, with a 16-spoked *cakra* in the centre of each foot, and conches in all the toes. In each foot, to the left of the *cakra* is a flagstaff, to its right a *paṅkhī* (fan), and below it an eight-petalled flower. Beneath the flower is a river with fish swimming in it.

Even more interesting is the evidence in the Mātaṅgeśvara Mahādeva temple, adjacent to the Sujātā mandir at Bodhgayā (Figure 15.13). Here, embedded in a small cell is a Buddhapāda embedded in the ground; only the surface (71 cm in diameter) can be seen. On the circular surface is carved a left foot, with shells in the toes, and double lines marking the folds. In the middle is a 16-spoked *cakra*. Above it is caparisoned bull, with an object on a vase (possibly leaves) to its right. To the left of the wheel is a flag with six pennons, and to its right a fan-like object. Below the wheel is a representation of the legendary Anotatta lake, from which water flows out through rocks in the shape of a lion, elephant, horse and bull. To the left of the lake are trees and a mountain cluster. A bird and tree are carved below the lake.

The form and motifs of two Buddhapādas in the Museum für Indische Kunst in Berlin also suggest that they belong to this group.[72] One of them (MIK I-1154) represents a right foot with a *cakra*, above which is a winged male figure (*kinnara*) holding something in his hands; there is a flower to his left and a brazier to his right. The other one (MIK I-17) represents a left foot, on which are carved a *cakra*, a female figure (who could be a *kinnarī*) playing a musical instrument, with a lotus to her left; there is palanquin on the heel.

It is likely that all these Buddhapādas represent instances of the reuse and transformation of one kind of Buddhist ritual artefact into another.

Figure 15.11
Buddhapādas near the bodhi tree, Mahābodhi temple

Source: Author

Figure 15.12
Buddhapāda in the corridor of the Mahant's maṭha

Source: Author

That is, that at a certain point of time, certain miniature *stūpa*s were decapitated, flipped around, and the footprint carvings added to them. The older miniature *stūpa*s were thereby turned into Buddhapādas. The question that arises is: Why should this have been done? Could it be the result of Vaiṣṇava influence—after all, Viṣṇu's footprints are worshipped in the Viṣṇupada temple nearby? Or is there another possibility?

The fact that there are several similar Bodhgayā Buddhapādas suggests that the conversion of the small *stūpa*s into Buddhapādas represents a process rather than random, desultory acts. This could have been a process initiated either by Burmese pilgrims or one of the early repair missions, perhaps the 11th century one. This would fit in with the rough dates of the Buddhapādas. The mission arrived at the site at a time when the Pāla patronage of Buddhism was waning and found that nothing much was going on there. Apart from 'repairing' the temple, they may have converted some of the miniature *stūpa*s they found there into Buddhapādas, which were an important focus of worship in their own land. Burmese elements were added to the Buddhapādas

Figure 15.13
Buddhapāda at Mātaṅgeśvara Mahādeva temple, Bodhgayā

Source: Author

in the form of carvings, as part of the 'Burmese signature.' This is suggested by the fact that almost all the categories of motifs found on these Bodhgayā Buddhapādas occur among the symbols found on Burmese Buddhapādas,[73] and Burmese affinities can also be seen in the style of representation of shrines, mountain clusters, and human figures.

Now, as mentioned above, Mitra tells us that the Buddhapad pavilion (which had sheltered one of the Buddhapādas) had been pulled down by the Burmese repairers in 1876.[74] He also says that the other four Buddhapādas he describes were excavated by the Burmese gentlemen recently, i.e., in the 1870s![75] It seems that the 19th century Burmese repair mission had stumbled across the interventions of the earlier repair missions that had, among other things, if not introduced, at least promoted footprint worship within the precincts of the Mahābodhi temple. The possibility is tantalizing.

One of the many questions that these Buddhapādas raise is: Who made them? The range of possibilities has been discussed in a more general context above. The making of culturally hybrid artefacts such as the Buddhapādas that I have discussed here may well be the result of Indian artists working under instructions from the Burmese 'repairers' (with the finer details lost in translation), or of a collaboration between Indian and Burmese artisans and artists. The result was a series of Buddhapādas that are different from those found both in India and in Myanmar.[76]

Apart from the Buddhapādas on black stone, which have been discussed above, there is in the Indian Museum another very different Buddhapāda from Bodhgayā; it is much later and seems to belong to the 19th century (Figure 15.14). Mitra describes it as a large flag of white marble (or alabaster) with the figure of a single foot, flanked by two dragons.[77] It is 7 ft 6 in long by 3 ft 6 in broad, and has a left footprint within which are a number of symbols. Mitra states that it was brought from a Burmese temple, where it used to be worshipped as a Buddha footprint. The foot is framed within the sinuous scaly necks of two dragons whose heads face each other at the top of the foot. Each toe of the foot has a conch shell on an hour-glass-shaped stand. The centre of the sole has a circular pattern consisting of concentric circles with several radii, creating 108 compartments, each of which contains a symbol. These include the elephant goad, umbrella, crown, and various kinds of structures, flowers, rivers, mountains, animals, and birds that occur on Burmese Buddha footprints. There are six sets of whorls arranged around the symbols—four above (two large and two small) and two below (both large). A conch is carved on the heel.[78] This is an issue that needs careful examination. There is no doubt whatsoever that this Buddhapāda was made in Myanmar and was brought to Mahābodhi from there. It was not the sort of object an ordinary Burmese pilgrim would have brought along. I think that given its size, weight, and finesse, it must have been brought to Bodhgayā by one of the 19th century royal Burmese missions.

Figure 15.14
19th century Burmese Buddhapāda, Indian Museum

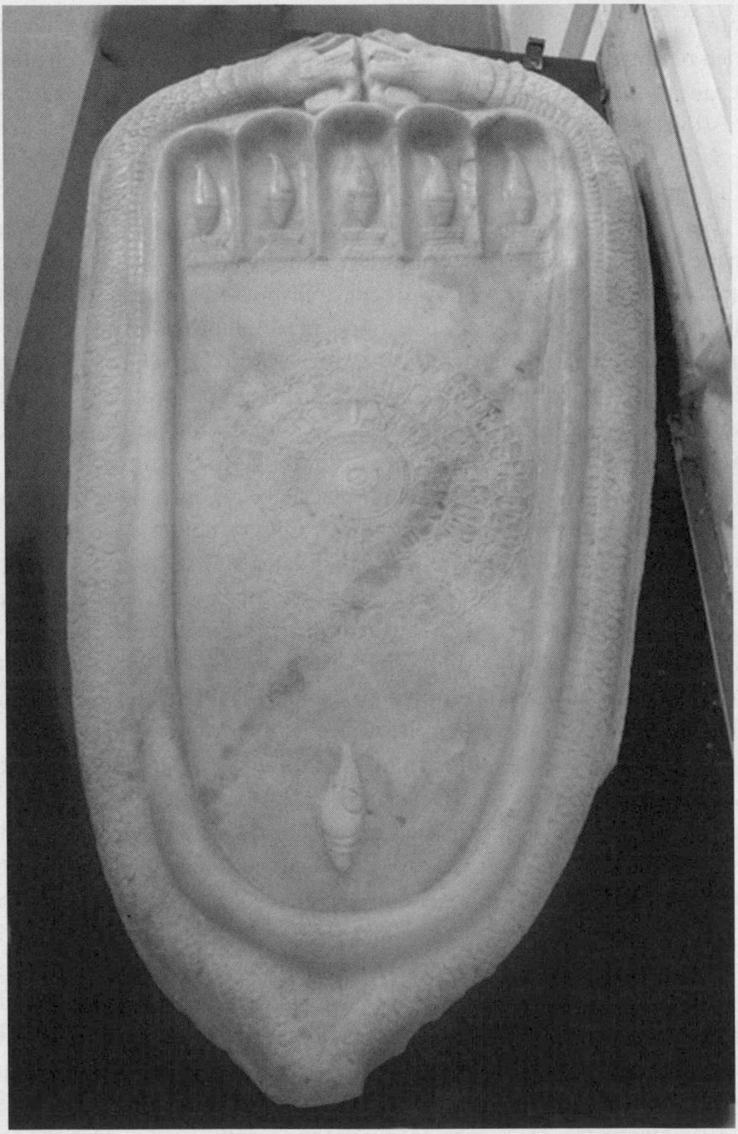

Courtesy: Indian Museum, Kolkata

Conclusions

While the epigraphic evidence of interactions of Burmese kings with Mahābodhi begins from Kyanzittha's reign, it is possible that the beginnings of these interactions go back to before his time. This is not a far-fetched idea, especially given the importance of Anawratha, described in the chronicles as an aggressive conqueror who fought wars in order to acquire Buddha relics, who incorporated lower Burma into the Pagan empire, who brought 30 sets of the Piṭakas from Thaton on 32 white elephants, patronized Buddhism, and laid the foundation of the state-*saṅgha* alliance and the ideology that became the hall-mark of the Pagan polity. Would such an ambitious and successful ruler have ignored Mahābodhi? His inscribed sealings (mentioned above) constitute material evidence suggesting that the kings of Pagan started connecting themselves with Mahābodhi even before the time of the first repair mission was sent by Kyanzittha. Perhaps we can take these connections back even a bit further. As indicated by Michael Aung-Thwin and Maitrii Aung-Thwin, the Pagan period may not mark as great a cultural discontinuity in early Burmese history as is sometimes believed. Further, Anawratha's reign definitely saw an acceleration of processes of expansion and integration, but the Pagan monarchy was in place by the mid-10th century, and the roots of the Pagan ideology of kingship may go back to the time of Anawratha's grandfather Saw Rahan (reigned 956–1001) and father Kyaung Phyu Min (reigned 1001–21).[79] So it is quite possible that Burmese visits to Mahābodhi—those of elites and/or ordinary pilgrims—may go back to the mid-10th or early 11th century.

On the basis of the Buddhapādas found at Bodhgayā, it has been argued here that the early Burmese repair missions and/or pilgrimage activities may well have been responsible, if not for the introduction, at least for the promotion of Buddhapāda worship—a practice that was becoming increasingly popular in Burma precisely at this time—at Mahābodhi. One kind of ritual artefact (the miniature *stūpa*) was transformed into another kind (the Buddhapāda) and resulted in certain interesting specimens of culturally hybrid Buddhapādas. The various 19th century missions continued this process, but in a different way—one of them brought to Mahābodhi a massive, magnificent, white Buddhapāda made in Burma, and added it to the sacred landscape of the temple.

The connections suggested in this chapter have to be understood in their larger historical context, especially those of long-standing commercial traffic and religious affinity between India and Burma. The religious associations were, in turn, connected with the specific nature of the relationship between state and *saṅgha* in Burma over the centuries. The Burmese activities in India were concentrated at Mahābodhi. Why? Geographical proximity was one reason, but not the only one. There were other sacred places associated with the Buddha (such as Lumbini, Sārnāth, and Kusinārā), but the building of a magnificent temple at Bodhgayā created a potent monumental symbol of a momentous event, the Buddha's enlightenment; it was a symbol that fired and continues to fire the imagination of Buddhists all over the world. It was also not a coincidence that this site lay in that part of India where Buddhism enjoyed its last major episode of royal patronage, under the Pālas. After the end of Pāla rule and the decline of Buddhism in India, the international connections, in fact, sustained Mahābodhi.

While assessing the Burma–Bodhgayā links, we should keep a few other things in mind for the sake of perspective. Bodhgayā was located in India but was not only an important *Indian* Buddhist site, but an *Asian* Buddhist site, an important symbolic centre and pilgrimage destination for monks and laity from many lands. Apart from the Burmese, the site also attracted Sri Lankan and Chinese pilgrims and interventions. Further, Mahābodhi was one of the important elements in Burmese kingship at certain points of time, but it was not the only one. Political elites did not look only towards India, they also looked towards Sri Lanka. In fact, the links with Sri Lanka, especially through the policy of periodic 'purification' of the *saṅgha*, which involved the periodic dispatch of Burmese monks to the island, were stronger than those with India. And finally, in spite of the connections with Bodhgayā and Sri Lanka, Burmese Buddhism had a distinct identity of its own, one which derived to a great extent from the interaction of Buddhism with local traditions, especially the very popular *nat* cult, whose imprint is writ large on the landscape even today.

Acknowledgements

This is an enlarged and modified version of a paper titled 'Sacred Footprints—Bodhgaya: The View from Myanmar', presented on 8 March 2014 at a conference organized by the Bihar Heritage Development Society at Bodhgaya. I would like to gratefully acknowledge the very valuable help extended to me by the following while I was working on this paper: Naman P. Ahuja, Christian Lammerts, Sanjukta Datta, Thant Thaw Kaung (Myanmar Book Centre, Yangon), Arlo Griffiths, Parul Pandya Dhar, Dr Venugopal (Director of the Indian Museum, Kolkata),

Satyakam Sen and Anasuya Das (Indian Museum), Amalesh Roy, Su Latt Win, and Saw Htut Sandar.

Notes

1. See Upinder Singh, 'Gifts from Other Lands: Southeast Asian Religious Endowments in India', in Upinder Singh and Parul Pandya Dhar, eds, *Asian Encounters: exploring connected histories* (New Delhi: Oxford University Press, 2014) (Chapter 14 of this book). In this chapter, I will be using both the terms 'Burma' and its current name, 'Myanmar'.
2. Pe Maung Tin and G. H. Luce, trans., *The Glass Palace Chronicle of the Kings of Burma* (Rangoon: Rangoon University Press, [1923] 1960), Introduction, pp. xv, xxi, 1.
3. See, for instance, C. Duroiselle, compiled and ed., *A list of Inscriptions Found in Burma*, Part 1 (Rangoon: Archaeological Survey of Burma, 1921), inscriptions no. 10, 11, 141, 142, 143, 429.
4. *Epigraphia Birmanica*, II, part 2, 1920, p. 19.
5. These included Vārāṇasi, Vesālī and Śrāvasti.
6. Taw Sein Ko, 'The Kalyāṇī Inscriptions Erected by King Dhammacetī at Pegu in 1476 A.D.', (Rangoon: Superintendent, Government Printing, Burma, 1892), p. 50.
7. A. B. Griswold, 'The Holy Land Transported: Replicas of the Mahābodhi Shrine in Siam and Elsewhere', in *Paranavitana Felicitation Volume* (Columbo: M. D. Gunasena, 1965), pp. 206–207, 218.
8. Also see Robert L. Brown, 'Bodhgaya and South-east Asia', in Janice Leoshko, ed., *Bodhgaya: The Site of Enlightenment* (Mumbai: Marg Publications, 1988), p. 102; and Frederick M. Asher, 'Bodh Gaya and the Issue of Originality in Art', in David Geary, Mathew R. Sayers and Abhishek Singh Amar, eds, *Cross-disciplinary Perspectives on a Contested Buddhist Site* (London and New York: Routledge, 2012), pp. 61–76.
9. For details, see Brown, 'Bodhgaya and South-East Asia', p. 108. These are among the various recreations of Mahābodhi in Asia. Two other recreations of the temple are located in Thailand—Wat Chet Yot in Chieng Mai (c. 1455–70) and Chieng Rai (in roughly the same period). Griswold ('The Holy Land Transported') discusses these as well as two temples in China—the Wu-t'a-ssu (1473) and Pi-yun-ssu (1748); and the Mahābodhi temple at Patan in Nepal (16th century).
10. The seven stations are: Bodhipallaṅka (the seat of wisdom, i.e., the *vajrāsana*), Animesacetiya (the place where the Buddha stood gazing at the bodhi tree for seven days without blinking), Caṅkramacetiya (the ambulatory, where he walked back and forth for seven days), Ratanaghara (the 'house of gems' created by the *devas*, where he spent a week thinking about the Abhidhamma), Ajapālanigrodha (the goatherd's banyan tree, where he spent the fifth week and where Māra tried to distract him), the Mucalinda tree (where he was protected by the *nāga* Mucalinda), and the Rājāyatanacetiya (which marked

the place where he received the myrobalan fruit and toothstick from Indra, and later, the food offering from the merchants Tapussa and Bhallika).

11. Griswold ('The Holy Land Transported', p. 217) lists the relative distances of the seven stations at Bago and correlates them with those at Chieng Mai and Bodhgayā. The seven stations are also depicted on Burmese *andagū* plaques (Brown, 'Bodhgaya and South-East Asia', p. 113). A problem with accepting the Pagan temple's seven stations as intrinsic to the original conception of the temple is the fact that the conserved 'fourth station' has a much lower floor level than the temple, and I could not locate a 'fifth week' structure. The seven stations may have been added on later, as an afterthought. For a more recent detailed discussion of the tradition of the seven stations in Burma, see Donald Stadtner, 'A Fifteenth-century Royal Monument in Burma and the Seven Stations in Buddhist Art', *The Art Bulletin* 73 (1) 1991, pp. 39–52.
12. Stadtner, 'A Fifteenth-century Royal Monument in Burma and the Seven Stations in Buddhist Art,' p. 43, fn 12.
13. Tilman Frasch, 'A Remark on the Mahabodhi Temple at Pagan', *Southeast Asian Archaeology,* 1998, p 43–46.
14. Frasch, 'A Remark on the Mahabodhi Temple at Pagan', pp. 46–47.
15. There are, for course, several differences. Apart from the conscious decision to make the Uppatasanti Paya a foot lower in height than its more celebrated counterpart, this modern temple, built between 2006 and 2009 is a hollow pagoda, and its clear, wide circumambulatory path presents a sharp contrast to the numerous subsidiary shrines within the Shwedagon complex.
16. For instance, the Mahamuni Paya in Mandalay displays the replica of a tooth relic given by the Chinese in 2013.
17. Susan L. Huntington, *The 'Pāla–Sena' Schools of Sculpture* (Leiden: E. J. Brill, 1984), pp. 168–169.
18. Huntington, *The 'Pāla–Sena' Schools of Sculpture*, p. 96.
19. For a detailed discussion of these inscriptions see Upinder Singh, 'Gifts from Other Lands' (Chapter 14 of this book).
20. Frasch, 'A Remark on the Mahabodhi Temples at Pagan', p. 42.
21. Griswold, 'The Holy Land Transported', pp. 188–200.
22. Rajendralala Mitra, *Buddha Gaya: The Great Buddhist Temple, the Hermitage of Sakya Muni* (New Delhi and Varanasi: Indological Book House, [1978] 1972), pp. 206–207.
23. 'Shwesandaw Pagoda Inscription', *Epigraphia Birmanica* 1 (8), pp. 147–168.
24. Mitra, *Buddha Gaya*, pp. 65–68.
25. G. H. Luce, 'Sources of Early Burma History', in C. D. Cowan and O. W. Wolters, eds, *Southeast Asian History and Historiography: Essays Presented to G. D. E. Hall*, (Ithica and London: Cornell University Press, 1976), pp. 40–42.
26. Griswold, 'The Holy Land Transported', p. 176, fn. 5 and p. 177.
27. If 218 refers to the era of 544 BCE, this would correspond to 236 BCE, which would locate the event mentioned here towards the end of Aśoka's reign (c. 268–232 BCE).
28. A. Cunningham, *Mahâbodhi: The Great Buddhist Temple under the Bodhi Tree at Buddha-Gaya* (Varanasi: Indological Book House, [1892] 1966), p. 75 and Plate XXIX.

29. B. M. Barua, *Gayā and Buddha-Gayā—Gayā [Early History of the Holy Land*, Vol. 1 (Varanasi: Bhartiya Publishing House, [1931] 1975), p. 210.
30. Cunningham, *Mahâbodhi*, p. 28. Cunningham does not describe this inscription.
31. Mitra, *Buddha Gaya*, pp. 211–227.
32. This suggests that the multi-lingual and bi-script inscriptions were inscribed at Bodhgayā.
33. Duroiselle, *List of Inscriptions found in Burma*, Part 1, Nos. 1177, 1178.
34. For a detailed account of this fascinating mission, see W. S. Desai, 'History of the Burmese Mission to India', *Journal of the Burma Research Society* 26 (2) (August, 1936), pp.71–109.
35. D. C. Ahir, *Buddha Gaya through the Ages* (Delhi: Sri Satguru Publications, 1994), pp. 85–86.
36. For details of the negotiations, see Alan Trevithick, *The Revival of Buddhist Pilgrimage at Bodh Gaya (1811–1949): Anagarika Dharmapala and the Mahabodhi Temple*', (New Delhi: Motilal Banarsidass, 2006).
37. These events and their fallout are discussed in Upinder Singh, *The Discovery of Ancient India: Early Archaeologists and the Beginnings of Archaeology* (New Delhi: Permanent Black, 2004), pp. 220–222, 331.
38. Mitra, *Buddha Gaya*, pp. 65–66.
39. See Nayanjot Lahiri, 'Bodh Gaya: Ancient Buddhist Shrine and its Modern History (1891–1904)', in Timothy Insoll ed., *Case Studies in Archaeology and Religion* (Oxford: Archaeopress, 1999), pp. 33–44; and Trevithick, *The Revival of Buddhist Pilgrimage at Bodh Gaya.*
40. Mitra, *Buddha Gaya*, pp. 227–228, Nos. 16 and 17.
41. Cunningham, *Archaeological Survey Reports*, vol. 1 (Simla: Government Central Press, 1871), p. 9 and Plate VI.
42. Barua, *Gayā and Buddha-Gayā*, vol. 1, pp. 206–212.
43. Griswold, 'The Holy Land Transported', pp. 188–200.
44. Quoted in Griswold, 'The Holy Land Transported', p. 187. However, Donald M. Stadtner ('A Fifteenth-century Royal Monument in Burma and the Seven Stations in Buddhist Art', p. 39) has questioned whether the Bago temple was in fact based on detailed plans obtained from Bodhgayā. This is on the grounds that there is no epigraphic evidence of such a mission and that the condition of the temple in the 15th century, especially that of the seven stations, would have made it difficult to take detailed measurements and plans, even if such a mission had been sent. Stadtner argues that the *Nidāna Kathā* and the descriptions of Southeast Asian pilgrims were the sources of information on the basis of which the Shwegugyi was built.
45. Brown, 'Bodhgaya and South-East Asia', p. 106.
46. Among the many contributions on this subject, see John Guy, 'Offering up a Rare Jewel: Buddhist Merit-making and Votive Tablets in Early Burma', in Alexandra Green and T. Richard Blurton, eds. *Burma: Art and Archaeology* (Chicago: Art Media Resources, 2002), pp. 23–32. On the stone *andagū* plaques, see Claudine Bautze-Picron, 'New Documents of Burmese Sculpture: Unpublished "Andagū" Images', *Indo-Asiatische Zeitschrift* 10, 2006, pp.32–47.

47. Peter Skilling, 'Buddhist Sealings: Reflections on Terminology, Motivation, Donors' Status, School-affiliation, and Print-technology', in Catherine Jarrige and Vincent Lefevre, eds, *South Asian Archaeology* Vol. 2: *Historical Archaeology and Art History* (Paris: Editions Recherches sur les Civilizations, 2001), pp. 677–685.
48. Than Tun, *History of Buddhism in Burma* (unpublished PhD thesis submitted to the Faculty of Arts, University of London in 1956—Revised and Enlarged), pp. 169–170.
49. Anasuya Das, 'Some Interesting Terracotta Plaques from Thailand and Burma in the Collection of the Indian Museum, Kolkata', *Journal of Ancient Indian History* 27, 2010–2011, pp. 167–173.
50. Gordon H. Luce, *Old Burma—Early Pagan*, vol. 1 (New York: J. J. Augustin Publisher, 1969), p. 131. These are described in volume 2, 1970, p. 22, and illustrated in vol. 3 (1970), Plates 30 (a) and (b).
51. U Mya, 'A Note on the Buddha's Foot-prints in Burma', *Annual Report of the Archaeological Survey of India* (1930–31), Part II, pp. 320–321.
52. Mya, 'A Note on the Buddha's Foot-prints in Burma', pp. 321–322. For a detailed discussion of the traditional account of this 'discovery', see Christian Lammerts, 'Taungbhila Sayadaw Tipitakalankara (1578–1650/1) and Buddhist law' (paper presented at the Madison South Asia Conference, 2013).
53. Mya, 'A Note on the Buddha's Foot-prints in Burma', p. 321. The Shwesettaw footprint on the hilltop is encircled by dragons and seems less old than the one at the base of the hill.
54. Mya has illustrated and described the Buddha footprints at Lokānanada and one of the two found at Shwezigon.
55. Debjani Paul, 'Antiquity of the Viṣṇupāda at Gaya: Tradition and Archaeology', *East and West* 35 (1/3) 1985, pp. 103–141. Paul also mentioned two Buddhapādas located at present in the Berlin Museum, Museum für Indische Kunst, Berlin. She points out (p. 117) that one of these has been mis-labelled a 6th century Viṣṇupāda.
56. Mitra, *Buddha Gaya*, p. 125.
57. Debjani Paul, 'Antiquity of the Viṣṇupāda at Gaya, pp. 108, 118, 139–141. Paul points out that although Viṣṇu is associated with the *cakra*, it is a weapon he wields in his hands. On the other hand, wheels on the soles of the feet are among the Buddha's well-known *lakṣaṇas*.
58. B.M. Barua, *Gayā and Buddha-Gayā*, Vol. 2 (Varanasi: Bhartiya Publishing House, [1934] 1975), p. 62.
59. Barua, *Gayā and Buddha-Gayā*, Vol. 2, p. 63.
60. Cunningham, *Mahâbodhi*, p. 69; Geri H. Malandra, 'The Mahabodhi temple', in Leoshko, ed., *Bodhgaya: The site of enlightenment*, (Mumbai: Marg, 1988), pp. 21, 27.
61. Paul ('Antiquity of the Viṣṇupāda at Gaya: Tradition and Archaeology', p. 125) directs attention to the prominent presence of a pair of footprints in front of the main entrance in a 12th century Mahābodhi model in the British Museum. Further, we can note the fact that the 13th century Tibetan monk Dharmasvāmin mentions seeing Buddha footprints at Mahābodhi.

62. Mitra, *Buddha Gaya*, p. 127 has described them and given sketches (Plate 43, Figs. 3, 5, 6, 7).
63. Mitra, *Buddha Gaya*, p. 100–01; Pl. 43, Figs. 1 and 2. Cunningham also gave a drawing of this Buddhapāda in vol. 1 of his *Archaeological Survey Reports* (Plate VII).
64. Mitra, *Buddha Gaya*, pp. 125–27.
65. Mitra, *Buddha Gaya*, p. 201. It has been suggested that Madana could have been used here as an epithet of Viṣṇu.
66. According to Michael Aung-Thwin and Maitrii Aung-Thwin (*A History of Myanmar since Ancient Times: Traditions and Transformations* (London, Reaktion Books [2012] 2013), p. 80, the Pagan monarchy was established by the mid-10th century.
67. Mya, 'A Note on the Buddha's foot-prints in Burma', pp. 324–326.
68. Mitra, *Buddha Gaya*, p. 127.
69. The Buddhapāda discussed above does not have shells on the toes.
70. Paul, 'Antiquity of the Viṣṇupāda at Gaya: Tradition and Archaeology', p. 117–118 and fn 42.
71. I am indebted to my colleague Parul Pandya Dhar for this observation.
72. For a description and illustrations of these Buddhapādas, see Anna Maria Quagliotti, *Buddhapadas: An Essay on the Representations of the Footprints of the Buddha with a Descriptive Catalogue of the Indian Specimens from the 2nd Century* BC *to the 4th Century* AD, Vol. 2 (Kamakura: Institute of the Silk Road Studies, Memoirs, 1998), p. 67.
73. The Anotatta lake seems to be an exception.
74. Mitra, *Buddha Gaya*, p. 101. This reminds us of the 19th century Burmese diplomatic mission discovering the 13th century inscription.
75. Mitra, *Buddha Gaya*, p. 101.
76. The carvings on a Buddhapāda (No. Bihar 4213) in the Indian Museum Kolkata, although on a flat slab and not on a hemispherical stone, have some affinities with the artefacts discussed here. This shows a right foot with a *cakra* on the sole, flanked by birds holding a sash/garland. Over the *cakra* is a multi-armed figure holding a standard; below the *cakra* is a flower, and below that, a river. The two shrines flanking the multi-armed figure appear to be of a Burmese variety.
77. Mitra, *Buddha Gaya*, pp. 125–126.
78. Waldemar C. Sailer, 'A Reading of the 108 Auspicious Illustrations on the Buddha Footprint in the Indian Museum, Calcutta', *Indian Museum Bulletin* 35, 2000, pp. 35–50, suggests that this represents a footprint of Maitreya, not Śākyamuni.
79. Michael Aung-Thwin and Maitrii Aung-Thwin, *A History of Myanmar since Ancient Times: Traditions and Transformations*, pp. 80–81. These scholars point out that Saw Rahan 'purified' the *saṅgha* and Kyaung Phyu Min connected his capital symbolically with the Buddhist universe.

Index*

* f denotes figures and t denotes tables.